SMALL JAVA™

HOW TO PROGRAM

SIXTH EDITION

How To Program Series

Advanced Java™ 2 Platform How to Program

C How to Program, 4/e

C++ How to Program, 4/e

C# How to Program

e-Business and e-Commerce How to Program

Internet and World Wide Web How to Program, 3/e

Java™ How to Program, 6/e

Perl How to Program

Python How to Program

Small Java How to Program, 6/e

Visual C++® .NET How to Program

Visual Basic® 6 How to Program

Visual Basic® .NET How to Program, 2/e

Wireless Internet & Mobile Business How to Program

XML How to Program

Simply Series

Simply C++: An Application-Driven
Tutorial Approach

Simply C#: An Application-Driven
Tutorial Approach

Simply Java™ Programming: An
Application-Driven Tutorial Approach

Simply Visual Basic® .NET: An
Application Driven Tutorial Approach
(Visual Studio .NET 2002 Edition)

Simply Visual Basic® .NET: An
Application Driven Tutorial Approach
(Visual Studio .NET 2003 Edition)

.NET How to Program Series

C# How to Program

Visual Basic® .NET How to Program, 2/E

Visual C++® .NET How to Program

For Managers Series

e-Business and e-Commerce for
Managers

Visual Studio® Series

C# How to Program

Visual Basic® .NET How to Program, 2/E

Getting Started with Microsoft® Visual
C++® 6 with an Introduction to MFC

Visual Basic® 6 How to Program

Also Available

e-books

Premium CourseCompass, WebCT and
Blackboard Multimedia Cyber
Classroom versions

Pearson Choices:
SafariX

ining Courses and Web-Based Training Courses
Prentice Hall

Multimedia Cyber Classroom and Web-Based Training Series

C++ Multimedia Cyber Classroom, 4/E

C# Multimedia Cyber Classroom

e-Business and e-Commerce Multimedia Cyber Classroom

Internet and World Wide Web Multimedia Cyber Classroom, 2/E

Java™ 2 Multimedia Cyber Classroom, 5/E

Perl Multimedia Cyber Classroom

Python Multimedia Cyber Classroom

Visual Basic® 6 Multimedia Cyber Classroom

Visual Basic® .NET Multimedia Cyber Classroom, 2/E

Wireless Internet & Mobile Business Programming Multimedia Cyber Classroom

XML Multimedia Cyber Classroom

The Complete Training Course Series

The Complete C++ Training Course, 4/E

The Complete C# Training Course

The Complete e-Business and e-Commerce Programming Training Course

The Complete Internet and World Wide Web Programming Training Course, 2/E

The Complete Java™ 2 Training Course, 5/E

The Complete Perl Training Course

The Complete Python Training Course

The Complete Visual Basic® 6 Training Course

The Complete Visual Basic® .NET Training Course, 2/E

The Complete Wireless Internet & Mobile Business Programming Training Course

The Complete XML Programming Training Course

To follow the Deitel publishing program, please register at:
www.deitel.com/newsletter/subscribe.html
for the *DEITEL® BUZZ ONLINE* e-mail newsletter.

To communicate with the authors, send e-mail to:
deitel@deitel.com

For information on corporate on-site seminars offered by Deitel & Associates, Inc. worldwide, visit:
www.deitel.com

For continuing updates on Prentice Hall and Deitel publications visit:
www.deitel.com,
www.prenhall.com/deitel or
www.InformIT.com/deitel

Library of Congress Cataloging-in-Publication Data
On file

Vice President and Editorial Director, ECS: *Marcia J. Horton*
Senior Acquisitions Editor: *Kate Hargett*
Associate Editor: *Jennifer Cappello*
Assistant Editor: *Sarah Parker*
Editorial Assistant: *Michael Giacobbe*
Vice President and Director of Production and Manufacturing, ESM: *David W. Riccardi*
Executive Managing Editor: *Vince O'Brien*
Managing Editor: *Tom Manshreck*
Production Editor: *John F. Lovell*
Production Editor, Media: *Bob Engelhardt*
Production Assistant: *Asha Rohra*
Director of Creative Services: *Paul Belfanti*
A/V Production Editor: *Xiaohong Zhu*
Art Studio: *Artworks, York, PA*
Art Director: *Geoffrey Cassar*
Cover Design: *Harvey M. Deitel, Sam Ward, Geoffrey Cassar*
Interior Design: *Harvey M. Deitel, Geoffrey Cassar*
Manufacturing Manager: *Trudy Pisciotti*
Manufacturing Buyer: *Lisa McDowell*
Marketing Manager: *Pamela Hersperger*
Marketing Assistant: *Barrie Reinhold*

© 2005 by Pearson Education, Inc.
Upper Saddle River, New Jersey 07458

10 9 8 7 6 5 4 3 2 1

ISBN 0-13-148660-8

Pearson Education Ltd., *London*
Pearson Education Australia Pty. Ltd., *Sydney*
Pearson Education Singapore, Pte. Ltd.
Pearson Education North Asia Ltd., *Hong Kong*
Pearson Education Canada, Inc., *Toronto*
Pearson Educacion de Mexico, S.A. de C.V.
Pearson Education–Japan, *Tokyo*
Pearson Education Malaysia, Pte. Ltd.
Pearson Education, Inc., *Upper Saddle River, New Jersey*

SMALL JAVA™

HOW TO PROGRAM

SIXTH EDITION

H. M. Deitel
Deitel & Associates, Inc.

P. J. Deitel
Deitel & Associates, Inc.

PEARSON
Prentice
Hall

Upper Saddle River, New Jersey 07458

Trademarks

To my wife, Barbara Deitel, on the occasion
of the 40th anniversary of our first date:

> With love,
> *Harvey*

To my wife, Michelle Deitel, as we
approach our first wedding anniversary:

> I love you.
> *Paul*

Contents

9 Object-Oriented Programming: Inheritance   369

10 Object-Oriented Programming: Polymorphism   413

A Operator Precedence Chart   456

B ASCII Character Set   458

C Keywords and Reserved Words   459

D Primitive Types   460

E Number Systems   461

F Unicode®   474

Preface

"Be faithful in small things because it is in them that your strength lies."
—Mother Teresa

Welcome to Java and *Small Java How to Program, Sixth Edition*! At Deitel & Associates, we write college-level computer science textbooks and professional books. This book, our first Special Edition publication, was a joy to create. Our goal was to design a smaller, lower-priced book for one-semester introductory (CS1) courses based on the major revision of *Java How to Program, Sixth Edition*. *Small Java How to Program, Sixth Edition* (or *6/e* for short) focuses on the core concepts and features of Java covered in Chapters 1–10 of *Java How to Program, 6/e*.

To create *Java How to Program, 6/e*, we put the previous edition of *Java How to Program* under the microscope:

- All of the chapters have been significantly updated and upgraded.

- We changed to an early classes and objects pedagogy. Now students build their first reusable classes starting in Chapter 3.

- All of the GUI in the early chapters has been moved to optional sections.

- We added substantial case studies throughout the book that build on existing classes from earlier chapters.

- We incorporated the new features of Sun Microsystems' latest release of Java— the *Java 2 Platform, Standard Edition version 5.0 (J2SE 5.0)*.

- We updated our object-oriented presentation to the latest version of the *UML (Unified Modeling Language)—UML™ 2.0*.

- We completely revised the design of the book. This new design uses color, fonts and various design elements to enhance a student's learning experience.

All of this has been reviewed meticulously by a team of 28 academic and industry reviewers. To form this Special Edition book, we removed the optional OOD/UML case study that appears in *Java How to Program, 6/e*. The *Tour of the Book* included in this Preface gives instructors, students and professionals a sense of the *Small Java How to Program, 6/e's* coverage of Java and object-oriented programming.

We believe that this book and its support materials have everything instructors and students need for an informative, interesting, challenging and entertaining Java educational experience. In this Preface, we overview the teaching conventions used in the book, such as syntax coloring the code examples, "code washing" and code highlighting. We discuss the software Prentice Hall has bundled with the book as well as the comprehensive suite of educational materials that help instructors maximize their students' learning experience, including the *Instructor's Resource CD*, PowerPoint® Slide lecture notes, lab manuals, companion Web site, course management systems, SafariX (Prentice Hall's WebBook publications) and more.

As you read this book, if you have any questions, please send an e-mail to deitel@deitel.com; we will respond promptly. Please visit our Web site, www.deitel.com, regularly and be sure to sign up for the free *Deitel® Buzz Online* e-mail newsletter at www.deitel.com/newsletter/subscribe.html. We use the Web site and the newsletter to keep our readers and industry clients informed of all the latest news on Deitel publications and services. Please check the Web site occasionally for errata, updates regarding the Java software, downloads and other resources.

Features in *Small Java How to Program, 6/e*

This new edition contains many new and enhanced features including:

Essential Topics for CS1

Small Java How to Program, 6/e focuses on core Java concepts presented in CS1 courses. It is strictly designed for first courses in computing and is appropriate for Computer Science and Information Systems courses.

Updated for the Java 2 Platform Standard Edition 5.0 (J2SE 5.0)

We updated the entire text to reflect the latest release of J2SE 5.0. We have added discussions on the following topics:

- obtaining formatted input with class Scanner
- displaying formatted output with the System.out object's printf method
- using enhanced for statements to process array elements
- declaring methods with variable-length argument lists
- using enum classes that declare sets of constants
- importing the static members of one class for use in another

In addition, we carefully audited the manuscript against the *Java Language Specification* (available at java.sun.com/docs/books/jls/index.html). The programs you create as you study this text will work with any J2SE 5.0 compatible Java platform.

[*Note:* Sun Microsystems recently renamed J2SE from the **Java 2 Platform, Standard Edition 1.5.0** to the **Java 2 Platform, Standard Edition 5.0**. However, Sun decided not to replace all occurrences of 1.5.0 with 5.0 in the online Java documentation (available at java.sun.com/j2se/1.5.0/docs/api/index.html) and in the software installation directory (which is called jdk1.5.0). Sun's Web site accepts URLs that replace 1.5.0 with 5.0. For example, you can use the URL java.sun.com/j2se/**5.0**/docs/api/index.html to access the online documentation.]

New Interior Design

Working with the design team at Prentice Hall, we redesigned the interior styles for our *How to Program Series*. In response to reader requests, we now place the key terms and the index's page reference for each defining occurrence in blue, bold style text for easier reference. We emphasize on-screen components in the bold Helvetica font (for example, **Properties**), and to emphasize program text in the Lucida font (for example, int x = 5).

Syntax Coloring

This book is presented in full color to show programs and their outputs as they typically appear on a computer screen. We syntax color all the Java code, as most Java integrated-development environments and code editors do. This greatly improves code readability—an especially important goal, given that this book contains 4917 lines of code. Our syntax-coloring conventions are as follows:

```
comments appear in green
keywords appear in dark blue
errors appear in red
constants and literal values appear in light blue
all other code appears in black
```

Code Highlighting

Extensive code highlighting makes it easier for readers to spot the featured segments of each program. The highlighting also helps students review the material rapidly when preparing for exams or labs.

"Code Washing"

Code washing is our term for applying comments, using meaningful identifiers, applying uniform indentation conventions and using vertical spacing to separate meaningful program units. This process results in programs that are extraordinarily readable and self-documenting. We have done extensive "code washing" of all the source-code programs in the text and in the book's ancillaries. We have worked hard to make our code exemplary; the code has been scrutinized by distinguished academic and industry reviewers.

Early Classes and Objects Approach

One of the most significant improvements in this new edition: Students are now introduced to the concepts of classes and objects in Chapter 1, and start writing their own customized classes and using objects of these classes in Chapter 3. (Prior editions of this book presented these concepts in Chapter 8.) Moving the discussion of objects and classes to earlier chapters in the book gets students "thinking about objects" from the start and helps students master these concepts more thoroughly. Java is not trivial by any means, but it's fun to program with, and students can see immediate results. Students can get text-based and graphical programs running quickly by using Java's extensive class libraries of reusable components. Students are typically more creative and productive in a one- or two-semester Java course than in introductory C and C++ courses.

Carefully Tuned Treatment of Object-Oriented Programming in Chapters 8–10

We performed a high-precision upgrade of *Java How to Program, 5/e*. The improvements make the material clearer and more accessible to students and professionals, especially those studying object-oriented programming (OOP) for the first time. We have completely rewritten the OOP chapters with an integrated case study on developing an employee payroll hierarchy and we motivate interfaces with a payables hierarchy.

Case Studies

This book is loaded with examples and exercises. Often we build on an existing class introduced earlier in the book to demonstrate programming concepts that enhance an application later in the book. This approach allows students to learn these new concepts in the context of an application that they already know. These case studies include the development of the:

- Time class in Chapter 8
- Employee payroll application in Chapter 9 and Chapter 10
- GradeBook class in Chapters 3, 4, 5 and 7
- polymorphic drawing program in the optional GUI and Graphics case study in Chapters 3–10

Integrated GradeBook Case Study

To reinforce the book's early classes presentation, we have included an integrated case study using classes and objects in Chapters 3–5 and 7. We incrementally build a Grade-Book class that represents an instructor's grade book and performs various calculations based on a set of student grades—finding the average, finding the maximum, and minimum, and printing a bar chart. Our goal here is to familiarize students with the important concepts of objects and classes through a real-world example of a class. We develop this class from the ground up, constructing methods from control statements and carefully developed algorithms, and adding instance variables as needed to enhance the functionality of the class.

GUI and Graphics Case Study (Optional)

The optional GUI and Graphics Case Study in Chapters 3–10 demonstrates techniques for adding visual elements to applications. It is designed for those who want to begin learning Java's powerful capabilities for creating graphical user interfaces (GUIs) and graphics. Each section introduces a few basic concepts and provides visual, graphical examples and complete source code. In the first few sections, we show how to create simple graphical applications. In the following sections, we use the object-oriented programming concepts presented through Chapter 10 to create an application that draws a variety of shapes polymorphically.

Unified Modeling Language (UML)—Introducing UML 2.0

The Unified Modeling Language (UML) has become the preferred graphical modeling language for designing object-oriented systems. All of the UML diagrams in the book comply with the new UML 2.0 specification. We use UML class diagrams to visually represent classes and their inheritance relationships, and to demonstrate the flow of control in each of Java's control statements. The larger *Java How to Program, 6/e* text includes a substantial OOD/UML case study on developing the software for an automated teller machine.

Teaching Approach

Small Java How to Program, 6/e contains a rich collection of examples, exercises and projects drawn from many fields to provide the student with a chance to solve interesting real-world problems. The book concentrates on the principles of good software engineering and stresses program clarity. We avoid arcane terminology and syntax specifications in favor of teaching by example. Our code examples have been tested on popular Java platforms. We are educators who teach leading-edge topics in industry classrooms worldwide. Dr. Harvey M. Deitel has 20 years of college teaching experience and 15 years of industry teaching experience. Paul Deitel has 12 years of industry teaching experience and is one of the world's most experienced Java corporate trainers, having taught about 100 Java courses since 1996 to government, industry, military and academic clients of Deitel & Associates, Inc.

Learning Java via the LIVE-CODE Approach

Small Java How to Program, 6/e, is loaded with LIVE-CODE examples—each new concept is presented in the context of a complete, working Java application that is immediately followed by one or more sample executions showing the program's inputs and outputs. This style exemplifies the way we teach and write about programming. We call this method of teaching and writing the LIVE-CODE Approach. *We use programming languages to teach programming languages.* Reading the examples in the text is much like typing and running them on a computer. We provide all the source code for the book's examples both on the accompanying CD and at www.deitel.com—making it easy for students to run each example as they study it. The book contains 72 complete LIVE-CODE examples consisting of 4917 lines of code.

World Wide Web Access

All of the source-code examples for *Small Java How to Program, 6/e,* (and our other publications) are available on the Internet as downloads from the following Web sites:

```
www.deitel.com
www.prenhall.com/deitel
```

Registration is quick and easy, and the downloads are free. We suggest students download all the examples, then run each program as they read the corresponding text. Making changes to the examples and immediately seeing the effects of those changes is a great way to enhance the Java learning experience.

Objectives

Each chapter begins with a statement of objectives. This tells students what to expect and gives students an opportunity, after reading the chapter, to determine if they have met these objectives. This is a confidence builder and a source of positive reinforcement.

Quotations

The learning objectives are followed by quotations. Some are humorous, some are philosophical and some offer interesting insights. Our students enjoy relating the quotations to the chapter material. Many of the quotations are worth a second look after reading the chapter.

Outline

The chapter outline helps the student approach the material in a top-down fashion. This, too, helps students anticipate what is to come, and set a comfortable and effective learning pace.

4917 Lines of Code in 72 Example Programs (with Program Outputs)

We present Java features in the context of complete, working Java programs. These LIVE-CODE programs range in size from just a few lines of code to substantial examples containing hundreds of lines of code. Each program is followed by a window containing the outputs produced when the program is run, so students can confirm that the programs run as expected. Relating outputs to the program statements that produce them is an excellent way to learn and to reinforce concepts. Our programs exercise the diverse features of Java. The code is syntax colored, with Java keywords, comments and other program text each appearing in different colors. This facilitates reading the code—students especially will appreciate the syntax coloring when they read the larger programs.

302 Illustrations/Figures

An abundance of charts, tables, line drawings, programs and program outputs is included. We model the flow of control in control statements with UML activity diagrams. We use UML class diagrams to model the fields, constructors and methods of classes.

219 Programming Tips

We include programming tips to help students focus on important aspects of program development. We highlight these tips in the form of *Good Programming Practices, Common Programming Errors, Error-Prevention Tips, Performance Tips, Portability Tips* and *Software Engineering Observations*. These tips and practices represent the best we have gleaned from a combined six decades of programming and teaching experience. One of our students— a mathematics major—told us that she feels this approach is like the highlighting of axioms, theorems and corollaries in mathematics books; it provides a basis on which to build good software.

Good Programming Practice

Good Programming Practices *are tips for writing clear programs. These techniques help students produce programs that are more readable, self-documenting and easier to maintain.*

Common Programming Error

Students learning a language—especially in their first programming course—tend to make certain kinds of errors frequently. Focusing on these Common Programming Errors *reduces the likelihood that students will make the same mistakes. It also shortens long lines outside instructors' offices during office hours!*

Error-Prevention Tip

When we first designed this "tip type," we thought we would use it strictly to tell people how to test and debug Java programs. In fact, many of the tips describe aspects of Java that reduce the likelihood of "bugs" and thus simplify the testing and debugging processes.

Performance Tip

In our experience, teaching students to write clear and understandable programs is by far the most important goal for a first programming course. But students want to write the programs that run the fastest, use the least memory, require the smallest number of keystrokes, or dazzle in other nifty ways. Students really care about performance. They want to know what they can do to "turbo charge" their programs. So we highlight opportunities for improving program performance—making programs run faster or minimizing the amount of memory that they occupy.

Portability Tip

One of Java's "claims to fame" is "universal" portability, so some programmers assume that if they implement an application in Java, the application will automatically be "perfectly" portable across all Java platforms. Unfortunately, this is not always the case. We include Portability Tips *to help students write portable code and to provide insights on how Java achieves its high degree of portability.*

Software Engineering Observation

The object-oriented programming paradigm requires a complete rethinking about the way we build software. Java is an effective language for performing good software engineering. The Software Engineering Observations *highlight architectural and design issues that affect the construction of software systems, especially large-scale systems. Much of what the student learns here will be useful in upper-level courses and in industry as the student begins to work with large, complex real-world systems.*

Wrap-Up Section
New in this edition, each chapter ends with a brief "wrap-up" section that recaps what topics were presented and what the student learned in the chapter. We have added this feature to help refresh the student's memory of the material covered and how it relates to the surrounding chapters.

Summary (476 Summary bullets)
Each chapter ends with additional pedagogical devices. We present a thorough, bullet-list-style summary of the chapter. On average, there are 48 summary bullets per chapter. This helps the students review and reinforce key concepts.

Terminology (748 Terms)
We include an alphabetized list of the important terms defined in each chapter—again, for further reinforcement. There is an average of 75 terms per chapter. Each term also appears in the index, and the defining occurrence of each term is highlighted in the index with a blue, bold page number so the student can locate the definitions of terms quickly.

336 Self-Review Exercises and Answers (Count Includes Separate Parts)
Extensive self-review exercises and answers are included for self-study. This gives the student a chance to build confidence with the material and prepare for the regular exercises. We encourage students to do all the self-review exercises and check their answers.

410 Exercises (Count Includes Separate Parts)
Each chapter concludes with a set of exercises, including simple recall of important terminology and concepts; writing individual Java statements; writing small portions of Java methods and classes; writing complete Java methods, classes and applications; and writing major term projects. The large number of exercises across a wide variety of areas enables instructors to tailor their courses to the unique needs of their classes and to vary course assignments each semester. Instructors can use these exercises to form homework assignments, short quizzes and major examinations. The solutions for most of the exercises are included on the *Instructor's Resource CD (IRCD),* which is *available only to instructors* through their Prentice Hall representatives. [**NOTE: Please do not write to us requesting the Instructor's CD. Distribution of this ancillary is limited strictly to college professors teaching from the book. Instructors may obtain the solutions manual only from their Prentice Hall representatives.**] Student readers will have access to approximately half the exercises in the book in the free, Web-based *Cyber Classroom* which will be available in Spring 2005. For more information about the availability of the *Cyber Classroom,* please visit www.deitel.com or sign up for the free *Deitel Buzz Online* e-mail newsletter at www.deitel.com/newsletter/subscribe.html.

Approximately 1900 Index Entries

We have included an extensive index at the back of the book. This helps students find terms or concepts by keyword. The Index is useful to people reading the book for the first time and is especially useful to practicing programmers who use the book as a reference.

"Double Indexing" of Java LIVE-CODE Examples

Small Java How to Program, 6/e has 72 live-code examples and 410 exercises (including parts). We have double indexed each of the live-code examples and most of the more substantial exercises. For every source-code program in the book, we took the figure caption and indexed it both alphabetically and as a subindex item under "Examples." This makes it easier to find examples using particular features. The more substantial exercises are also indexed both alphabetically and as subindex items under "Exercises."

Tour of the Book

Java is one of today's most exciting and rapidly developing computer programming languages. Mastering Java will help programmers develop powerful business and personal computer-applications software. In this section, we take a tour of the many capabilities of Java we explore in *Small Java How to Program, 6/e.*

Chapter 1—**Introduction to Computers, the Internet and the Web**—discusses what computers are, how they work and how they are programmed. The chapter gives a brief history of the development of programming languages from machine languages, to assembly languages, to high-level languages. The origin of the Java programming language is discussed. The chapter includes an introduction to a typical Java programming environment. The chapter allows readers to "test drive" a typical Java application to gain exposure to the type of applications they will learn to create throughout the book. The chapter also introduces object technology and the Unified Modeling Language.

Chapter 2—**Introduction to Java Applications**—provides a lightweight introduction to programming applications in the Java programming language. The chapter introduces nonprogrammers to basic programming concepts and constructs. The programs in this chapter illustrate how to display data on the screen to the user and how to obtain data from the user at the keyboard. This chapter introduces J2SE 5.0's new Scanner class, which greatly simplifies obtaining user input. The chapter also introduces some of J2SE 5.0's new formatted output capabilities with method System.out.printf. Chapter 2 ends with detailed treatments of decision making and arithmetic operations.

Chapter 3—**Introduction to Classes and Objects**—introduces classes, objects, methods and instance variables using five real-world examples. The first four of these examples begin our **case study on developing a grade-book class** that instructors can use to maintain student test scores. The first example presents a GradeBook class with one method that simply displays a welcome message when it is called. We then show how to create an object of that class and call the method so that it displays the welcome message. The second example modifies the first by allowing the method to receive a course name as an argument and by displaying the name as part of the welcome message. The third example shows how to store the course name in a GradeBook object. For this version of the class, we also show how to set the course name and obtain the course name using methods. The fourth example demonstrates how the data in a GradeBook object can be initialized when the object is created—the initialization is performed by the class's constructor. The last example in the chapter introduces floating-point numbers in the context of a bank account class that maintains a customer's balance. The chapter describes how to declare a class and use it to create an object. The chapter then discusses how to declare methods in a class to implement the class's behaviors, how to declare instance variables in a class to implement the class's attributes and how to call an object's method to make that method perform its task. The chapter explains the differences between instance variables of a class and local variables of a method, how to use a constructor to ensure that an object's data is initialized when the object is created, and the differences between primitive and reference types.

Chapter 4—Control Statements: Part 1—focuses on the program-development process. The chapter discusses how to take a problem statement and develop a working Java program from it, including performing intermediate steps in pseudocode. The chapter introduces some primitive types and simple control statements for decision making (`if` and `if...else`) and repetition (`while`). We examine counter-controlled repetition and sentinel-controlled repetition using the **GradeBook class** from Chapter 3, and introduce Java's increment, decrement and assignment operators. The chapter includes **two enhanced versions of the GradeBook class**, each based on the final version presented in Chapter 3. These versions each include a method that uses control statements to calculate the average of a set of student grades. In the first version, the method uses counter-controlled repetition to input 10 student grades from the user, then determines the average grade. In the second version, the method uses sentinel-controlled repetition to input an arbitrary numbers of grades from the user, then calculates the average of the grades that were entered. The chapter uses simple UML activity diagrams to show the flow of control through each of the control statements.

Chapter 5—Control Statements: Part 2—continues the discussions of Java control statements with examples of the `for` repetition statement, the `do...while` repetition statement, the `switch` selection statement, the `break` statement and the `continue` statement. A portion of the chapter is devoted to **enhancing class GradeBook**. We create a version of class `GradeBook` that uses a `switch` statement to count the number of A, B, C, D and F grade equivalents in a set of numeric grades entered by the user. This version uses sentinel-controlled repetition to input the grades. While reading the grades from the user, a method modifies instance variables that keep track of the sum of the grades entered and the number of grades entered, as well as the count of grades in each letter grade category. Other methods of the class then use these instance variables to perform the averaging calculation and display a summary report based on the grades entered. The chapter also discusses logical operators.

Chapter 6—Methods: A Deeper Look—takes a deeper look inside objects and their methods. We discuss class-library methods and examine more closely how students can build their own methods. We present our first example of a method with multiple parameters. A portion of the chapter focuses on developing a game playing application that uses random-number generation to simulate the rolling of dice. This application divides its required work into small, reusable methods. The techniques presented in Chapter 6 are essential to the production of properly organized programs, especially the larger programs that system programmers and application programmers are likely to develop. The topic of method overloading (i.e., allowing multiple methods to have the same name as long as they have different "signatures") is motivated and explained clearly. We introduce the method call stack to explain how Java is able to keep track of which method is currently executing, how local variables of methods are maintained in memory and how a method knows where to return after it completes execution. Additional chapter topics include `static` methods, `static` fields, class `Math`, enumerations and the scope of declarations.

Chapter 7—**Arrays**—explains how to process lists and tables of values. Arrays in Java are objects, further evidence of Java's commitment to almost 100% object orientation. We discuss the structuring of data into arrays of data items of the same type. The chapter presents numerous examples of both one-dimensional arrays and multidimensional arrays. Examples in the chapter investigate common array manipulations, printing bar charts, passing arrays to methods and an introduction to the field of survey data analysis (with simple statistics). The chapter also includes a case study simulating the shuffling and dealing of playing cards in a game-playing application, in addition to the **final two sections of the GradeBook case study**, in which we use arrays to store student grades for the duration of a program's execution. We include two versions of the class. Previous versions of the class process a set of grades entered by the user, but do not maintain the individual grade values in instance variables of the class. Thus, repeat calculations require the user to reenter the same grades. In this chapter, we use arrays to enable an object of the `GradeBook` class to maintain a set of grades in memory, thus eliminating the need to repeatedly input the same set of grades. The first version of the class in this chapter stores the grades in a one-dimensional array and can produce a report containing the average of the grades, the minimum and maximum grades and a bar chart representing the grade distribution. The second version of the class in this chapter (i.e., the final version in the case study) uses a two-dimensional array to store the grades of a number of students on multiple exams in a semester. This version can calculate each student's semester average, as well as the minimum and maximum grades across all grades received for the semester. The class also produces a bar chart displaying the overall grade distribution for the semester. This chapter also introduces J2SE 5.0's new enhanced `for` statement to traverse the elements of an array. Variable-length argument lists (new in J2SE 5.0) are also demonstrated.

Chapter 8—**Objects: A Deeper Look**—begins our deeper discussion of objects and classes. The chapter represents a wonderful opportunity for teaching data abstraction the "right way"—through a language (Java) expressly devoted to implementing new types. Building on the concepts introduced in Chapters 3–7, the chapter focuses on the essence and terminology of classes and objects. In the context of the **Time class case study**, the chapter discusses implementing Java classes, accessing class members, enforcing information hiding with access modifiers, separating interface from implementation, using access methods and utility methods and initializing objects with constructors. The chapter discusses declaring and using constants, composition, the `this` reference, `static` class members and examples of popular abstract data types such as stacks and queues. The chapter introduces the `package` statement and discusses how to create reusable packages. The chapter also presents J2SE 5.0's new `static` import and `enum` capabilities.

Chapter 9—**Object-Oriented Programming: Inheritance**—introduces one of the most fundamental capabilities of object-oriented programming languages, inheritance, which is a form of software reusability in which new classes are developed quickly and easily by absorbing the capabilities of existing classes and adding appropriate new capabilities. In the context an **Employee hierarchy**, this completely revised chapter presents a five-example sequence demonstrating `private` data, `protected` data and software reuse via inheritance. We begin by demonstrating a class with `private` instance variables and `public` methods to manipulate that data. Next, we implement a second class with several additional capabilities. To do this, we duplicate much of the first example's code. In our third example, we begin our discussion of inheritance and software reuse—we use the class from the first example as a superclass and inherit its data and functionality into a new subclass. This example introduces the inheritance mechanism and demonstrates that a subclass cannot access its superclass's private members directly. This motivates our fourth example, in which we introduce protected data in the superclass and demonstrate that the subclass can indeed access the protected data inherited from the superclass. The last example in the sequence demonstrates proper software engineering by defining the superclass's data as private and using the superclass's public methods (that were inherited by the subclass) to manipulate the superclass's private data in the subclass. The chapter discusses the notions of superclasses and subclasses, direct superclasses, indirect superclasses, use of constructors in superclasses and subclasses, and software engineering with inheritance. The chapter also compares inheritance (*is a* relationships) with composition (*has a* relationships).

Chapter 10—Object-Oriented Programming: Polymorphism—deals with another fundamental capability of object-oriented programming, namely polymorphic behavior. The completely revised Chapter 10 builds on the inheritance concepts presented in Chapter 9 and focuses on the relationships among classes in a class hierarchy, and the powerful processing capabilities that these relationships enable. A feature of this chapter is its two polymorphism case studies—a **payroll system using an abstract class Employee** and a **payroll system using an interface Payable**. Both case studies expand on the **Employee hierarchy** introduced in Chapter 9. The first case study processes an array of variables that contain references to Employee objects. All the objects referenced by the array elements have a common abstract superclass Employee containing the set of methods common to every class in the hierarchy. The case study demonstrates that when a method is invoked via a superclass reference, the subclass-specific version of that method is invoked. The case study also shows how a program that processes objects polymorphically can still perform type-specific processing by determining the type of the object currently being processed. This chapter distinguishes between abstract classes and concrete classes, and introduces interfaces—Java's replacement for the feature of C++ called multiple inheritance—in the context of the second payroll case study.

Appendix A—Operator Precedence Chart—lists each of the Java operators and indicates their relative precedence and associativity.

Appendix B—ASCII Character Set—lists the characters of the ASCII (American Standard Code for Information Interchange) character set and indicates the character code value for each. Java uses the Unicode character set with 16-bit characters for representing all of the characters in the world's "commercially significant" languages. Unicode includes ASCII as a subset.

Appendix C—Keywords and Reserved Words—lists all keywords and reserved words defined in the Java Programming Language Specification.

Appendix D—Primitive Types—lists all primitive types defined in the Java Programming Language Specification.

Appendix E—Number Systems—discusses the binary (base 2), decimal (base 10), octal (base 8) and hexadecimal (base 16) number systems.

Appendix F—Unicode—discusses the Unicode character set, which enables Java to display information in many languages. The appendix provides a sample Java program that displays "Welcome to Unicode" in several different languages.

Appendix G—Using the Java API Documentation—introduces the Java API documentation, which provides easy to use and up-to-the-minute information on Java's built-in packages. The appendix discusses what is found in the Java API documentation and how this material is organized. The figures in the appendix demonstrate how to navigate the Java API documentation online, including viewing a package, a class and a method. The appendix also demonstrates how to find a particular package, class or method from the index page.

Appendix H—Creating HTML Documentation with javadoc—introduces the javadoc documentation generation tool. Sun Microsystems uses the javadoc tool to produce the Java API documentation that is presented in Appendix G. The example in this appendix takes the reader through the javadoc documentation process. First, we introduce the comment style and tags that javadoc recognizes and uses to create documentation. Next, we discuss the commands and options used to run the utility. Finally, we examine the source files javadoc uses and the HTML files javadoc creates.

Appendix I—Labeled break and continue Statements—introduces two additional Java statements that allow programmers to alter the flow of control in control statements.

Appendix J—Using the Debugger—demonstrates key features of the JDK 5.0's built-in debugger, which allows a programmer to monitor the execution of applications to locate and remove logic errors. The appendix features a series of step-by-step instructions so students learn how to use the debugger in a hands-on manner.

A Tour of the Optional GUI and Graphics Case Study

In this section, we tour the book's major optional feature—an eight-section case study, on creating graphics and graphical user interfaces (GUIs) in Java. This tour previews the topics covered in each section of the case study. After completing this case study, students will be able to create their own simple graphical applications.

Section 3.9—Using Dialog Boxes—introduces graphical user interfaces and demonstrates handling input and output with dialog boxes. We use predefined JOptionPane dialogs to display information and read text in an application.

Section 4.14—Creating Simple Drawings—introduces Java's graphics capabilities. First, we describe Java's coordinate system, then we cover drawing lines and creating a window that displays drawings.

Section 5.10—Rectangles and Ovals—In addition to drawing lines, Java can also draw rectangles and ovals. In this section, we explain how to call the methods to draw a rectangle or an oval.

Section 6.13—Colors and Filled Shapes—explains how the computer represents colors, how we can use colors in our graphics and how to fill oval or rectangular regions with a solid color.

Section 7.13—Drawing Arcs—describes how Java specifies angles. Then we demonstrate drawing arcs (i.e., sections of an oval) by defining an oval and angular positions along the oval.

Section 8.18—Using Objects with Graphics—describes using objects to represent shapes. We create classes to represent each shape type, store these objects in arrays and retrieve the shapes each time we need to draw them.

Section 9.8—Displaying Text and Images Using Labels—covers creating labels and attaching them to the application window. Applications use labels to display information to the user. Labels in Java can display text, an image or both.

Section 10.8—Drawing with Polymorphism—The individual classes created in Section 8.18 have many similar characteristics. We conclude the case study examining these similarities and redesigning the individual shapes so that they inherit their common functionality from a "base" class and can be processed polymorphically.

Software Included with *Small Java How to Program, 6/e*

A number of for-sale Java development tools are available, but you do not need them to get started with Java. We wrote *Small Java How to Program, 6/e* using only the new *Java 2 Standard Edition Development Kit (JDK), version 5.0.* The current JDK version can be downloaded from Sun's Java Web site java.sun.com/j2se/downloads/index.html. This site also contains the JDK documentation downloads.

The CD that accompanies Small Java How to Program, 6/e, contains several Java editors, including BlueJ Version 1.3.5, JCreator Lite Version 3.10 (Windows Only), jEdit Version 4.1 and jGRASP Version 1.7.0. The CD also contains the NetBeans™ Version 3.6 Integrated Development Environment (IDE). If you have questions about using this software, please read the documentation on the CD, or read our *Dive Into™ Series* publications, which are available with the resources for *Small Java How to Program, 6/e* at www.deitel.com/books/downloads.html. The free Dive-Into™ Series publications help students and instructors familiarize themselves with various Java development tools. These publications include: *Dive Into™ NetBeans, Dive Into™ Eclipse, Dive Into™ JBuilder, Dive Into™ jEdit, Dive Into™ jCreator, Dive Into™ jGRASP* and *Dive Into™ BlueJ*.

The CD also contains the book's examples and an HTML Web page with links to the Deitel & Associates, Inc. Web site and the Prentice Hall Web site. If you have access to the Internet, this Web page can be loaded to your Web browser to give you quick access to all the resources.

Teaching Resources for *Small Java How to Program, 6/e*

Small Java How to Program, 6/e, has extensive resources for instructors. The *Instructor's Resource CD (IRCD)* contains the *Solutions Manual* with solutions to the vast majority of the end-of-chapter exercises, a *Test Item File* of multiple-choice questions (approximately two per book section) and PowerPoint slides containing all the code and figures in the text, plus bulleted items that summarize the key points in the text. Instructors can customize the slides.

Prentice Hall's *Companion Web Site* (www.prenhall.com/deitel) for *Small Java How to Program, 6/e* offers resources for students and instructors. For instructors, the *Companion Web Site* offers a *Syllabus Manager*, which helps instructors plan courses interactively and create online syllabi.

Chapter-specific resources available for students on *Companion Web Site* include:

- Chapter objectives.
- Highlights (e.g., chapter summary).
- Outline.

- Tips (e.g., *Common Programming Errors, Error-Prevention Tips, Good Programming Practices, Portability Tips, Performance Tips* and *Software Engineering Observations*).

- Online Study Guide—contains additional short-answer self-review exercises (e.g., true/false) with answers and provides immediate feedback to the student.

Students can track their results and course performance on quizzes using the *Student Profile* feature, which records and manages all feedback and results from tests taken on the *Companion Web Site*. To access the *Companion Web Site*, visit www.prenhall.com/deitel.

Java in the Lab

Java in the Lab, Lab Manual to Accompany Java How to Program, 6/e (ISBN# 0-13-149497-X) complements *Java How to Program, 6/e* and *Small Java How to Program 6/e* with hands-on lab assignments designed to reinforce students' understanding of lecture material. This lab manual is designed for closed laboratories: regularly scheduled classes supervised by an instructor. Closed laboratories provide an excellent learning environment, because students can use concepts presented in class to solve carefully designed lab problems. Instructors are better able to gauge the students' understanding of the material by monitoring the students' progress in lab. This lab manual also can be used for open laboratories, homework and for self-study. *Small Java How to Program, 6/e*, and the lab manual also are available together in a value pack (ISBN# 0-13-154126-9).

Each chapter in the lab manual is divided into *Prelab Activities, Lab Exercises* and *Postlab Activities*. Each chapter contains objectives that introduce the lab's key topics and an assignment checklist that allows students to mark which exercises the instructor has assigned. The lab manual pages are perforated, so students can submit their answers (if required).

Solutions to the lab manual's *Prelab Activities, Lab Exercises* and *Postlab Activities* are available in electronic form. Instructors can obtain these materials from their regular Prentice Hall representatives; the solutions are not available to students.

Prelab Activities

Prelab Activities are intended to be completed by students after studying each chapter of *Small Java How to Program, 6/e*. *Prelab Activities* test students' understanding of the textbook and prepare students for the programming exercises in the lab session. The exercises focus on important terminology and programming concepts and are effective for self-review. Prelab Activities include *Matching Exercises, Fill-in-the-Blank Exercises, Short-Answer Questions, Programming-Output Exercises* (determine what short code segments do without actually running the program) and *Correct-the-Code Exercises* (identify and correct all errors in short code segments).

Lab Exercises

The most important section in each chapter is the *Lab Exercises*. These teach students how to apply the material learned in *Small Java How to Program, 6/e*, and prepare them for writing Java programs. Each lab contains one or more lab exercises and a debugging problem. The *Lab Exercises* contain the following:

- *Lab Objectives* highlight specific concepts on which the lab exercise focuses.

- *Problem Descriptions* provide the details of the exercise and hints to help students implement the program.

- *Sample Outputs* illustrate the desired program behavior, which further clarifies the problem descriptions and aids the students with writing programs.

- *Program Templates* take complete Java programs and replace key lines of code with comments describing the missing code.

- *Problem-Solving Tips* highlight key issues that students need to consider when solving the lab exercises.

- *Follow-Up Questions and Activities* ask students to modify solutions to lab exercises, write new programs that are similar to their lab-exercise solutions or explain the implementation choices that were made when solving lab exercises.

- *Debugging Problems* consist of blocks of code that contain syntax errors and/or logic errors. These alert students to the types of errors they are likely to encounter while programming.

Postlab Activities

Professors typically assign *Postlab Activities* to reinforce key concepts or to provide students with more programming experience outside the lab. *Postlab Activities* test the students' understanding of the *Prelab* and *Lab Exercise* material, and ask students to apply their knowledge to creating programs from scratch. The section provides two types of programming activities: coding exercises and programming challenges. Coding exercises are short and serve as review after the *Prelab Activities* and *Lab Exercises* have been completed. The coding exercises ask students to write programs or program segments using key concepts from the textbook. *Programming Challenges* allow students to apply their knowledge to substantial programming exercises. Hints, sample outputs and pseudocode are provided to aid students with these problems. Students who successfully complete the *Programming Challenges* for a chapter have mastered the chapter material. Answers to the programming challenges are available at `www.deitel.com/books/downloads.html`.

OneKey, CourseCompass™, WebCT™ and BlackBoard

OneKey is Prentice Hall's exclusive new resource that gives instructors and students access to the best online teaching and learning tools through one convenient Web site. OneKey enables instructors to prepare their courses effectively, present their courses more dramatically and assess students easily. An abundance of searchable presentation material together with practice activities and test questions—all organized by chapter or topic—helps to simplify course preparation.

Selected content from the Deitels' introductory programming language *How to Program* series, including *Small Java How to Program, 6/e*, is available to integrate into various popular course management systems, including CourseCompass, Blackboard and WebCT. Course management systems help faculty create, manage and use sophisticated Web-based educational tools and programs. Instructors can save hours of inputting data by using Deitel course-management-systems content. [*Note:* The e-Book included with OneKey contains the entire text of *Small Java How to Program, 6/e*.]

Blackboard, CourseCompass and WebCT offer:

- **Features to create and customize an online course**, such as areas to post course information (e.g., policies, syllabi, announcements, assignments, grades, performance evaluations and progress tracking), class and student management tools, a gradebook, reporting tools, page tracking, a calendar and assignments.

- **Communication tools** to help create and maintain interpersonal relationships between students and instructors, including chat rooms, whiteboards, document sharing, bulletin boards and private e-mail.

- **Flexible testing tools** that allow an instructor to create online quizzes and tests from questions directly linked to the text, and that grade and track results effectively. All tests can be inputted into the gradebook for efficient course management. WebCT also allows instructors to administer timed online quizzes.

- **Support materials** for instructors are available in print and online formats.

In addition to the types of tools found in Blackboard and WebCT, CourseCompass from Prentice Hall includes:

- **CourseCompass course home page**, which makes the course as easy to navigate as a book. An expandable table of contents allows instructors to view course content at a glance and to link to any section.

- **Hosting on Prentice Hall's centralized servers**, which allows course administrators to avoid separate licensing fees or server-space issues. Access to Prentice Hall technical support is available.

- **"How Do I" online-support sections** are available for users who need help personalizing course sites, including step-by-step instructions for adding PowerPoint slides, video and more.

- **Instructor Quick Start Guide** helps instructors create online courses using a simple, step-by-step process.

To view free online demonstrations and learn more about these Course Management Systems, which support Deitel content, visit the following Web sites:

- Blackboard: `www.blackboard.com` and `www.prenhall.com/blackboard`

- WebCT: `www.webct.com` and `www.prenhall.com/webct`

- CourseCompass: `www.coursecompass.com` and `www.prenhall.com/coursecompass`

Java 2 Multimedia Cyber Classroom, 6/e Through OneKey

Java How to Program, 6/e and *Small Java How to Program, 6/e* will now include a free, Web-based interactive multimedia accompaniment to the book—*The Java 2 Multimedia Cyber Classroom, 6/e*—available in spring 2005 through OneKey. Our Web-based *Cyber Classroom* will include audio walkthroughs of the code examples in the text, solutions to half of the exercises in the book and more. For more information about the new Web-based *Cyber Classroom* and its availability through OneKey, please visit our Web site at www.deitel.com or sign up for the free Deitel® Buzz Online e-mail newsletter at www.deitel.com/newsletter/subscribe.html.

Student users of our *Cyber Classrooms* tell us that they like the interactivity and that the *Cyber Classroom* is a powerful reference tool. Professors tell us that their students enjoy using the *Cyber Classroom* and consequently spend more time on the courses, mastering more of the material than in textbook-only courses. For a complete list of our current CD-ROM-based *Cyber Classrooms*, see the *Deitel® Series* page at the beginning of this book, the product listing and ordering information at the end of this book, or visit www.deitel.com, www.prenhall.com/deitel or www.InformIT.com/deitel.

Pearson Choices

Today's students have increasing demands on their time and money, and they need to be resourceful about how, when and where they study. Our publisher, Prentice Hall, is owned by Pearson Education, which has responded to that need by creating PearsonChoices to allow faculty and students to choose from a variety of textbook formats and prices.

Small Java How to Program, 6/e is our alternative print edition to *Java How to Program, 6/e*. *Small Java How to Program, 6/e* brings the solid and proven pedagogy of our fully updated *Java How to Program, 6/e* to a new, smaller text that is purely focused on first-semester Computer Science (CS1) programming courses and priced lower than our 29-chapter *Java How to Program, 6/e* and other competing texts in the CS1 market.

SafariX WebBooks

SafariX Textbooks Online is a new service for college students looking to save money on required or recommended textbooks for academic courses. This secure WebBooks platform creates a new option in the higher education market; an additional choice for students alongside conventional textbooks and online learning services. By eliminating the costs relating to printing, manufacturing and retail distribution for the physical textbook, Pearson provides students with a WebBooks at 50% of the cost of its conventional print equivalent.

SafariX WebBooks are viewed through a Web browser connected to the Internet. No special plug-ins are required and no applications need to be downloaded. Students simply log in, purchase access and begin studying. With SafariX Textbooks Online students will be able to search the text, make notes online, print out reading assignments that incorporate their professors' lecture notes and bookmark important passages they want to review later. They can navigate easily to a page number, reading assignment, or chapter. The Table of Contents of each WebBook appears in the left hand column alongside the text.

We are pleased to offer students the *Small Java How to Program, 6/e* SafariX WebBook available for Fall 2004. Visit www.pearsonchoices.com for more information. Other Deitel titles available as SafariX WebBooks include *Java How to Program, 6/e* and *Simply C++: An Application-Driven Tutorial Approach*. Visit www.safarix.com/tour.html for more information.

Java How to Program, Sixth Edition

Java How to Program, 6/e is our 29-chapter book that can be used in classes of all levels. It features a new early classes and early objects approach. The book is up-to-date with J2SE 5.0 and includes comprehensive coverage of the fundamentals of object-oriented programming in Java. *Java How to Program, 6/e* features a new optional automated teller machine (ATM) case study that teaches the fundamentals of software engineering and object oriented-design with the UML 2.0 in Chapters 1–8 and 10. Other integrated case studies throughout the text include: GUI and graphics (Chapters 3–12); the Time class (Chapter 8); the Employee class (Chapters 9 and 10) and the GradeBook class in Chapters 3–5 and 7. It also features a new interior design including new colors, fonts, design elements and more. The following is a chapter-level table of contents for the book. [Note: The OOD/UML optional automated teller machine (ATM) case study is not included in *Small Java How to Program, 6/e.*]

Chapters in Both Small Java How to Program, 6/e *and* Java How to Program, 6/e

Chapter 1—Introduction to Computers, the Internet and the Web
Chapter 2—Introduction to Java Applications
Chapter 3—Introduction to Classes and Objects
Chapter 4—Control Statements: Part 1
Chapter 5—Control Statements Part 2
Chapter 6—Methods: A Deeper Look
Chapter 7—Arrays
Chapter 8—Classes and Objects: A Deeper Look
Chapter 9—Object-Oriented Programming: Inheritance
Chapter 10—Object-Oriented Programming: Polymorphism

Chapters Available Only in Java How to Program, 6/e

Chapter 11—GUI Components: Part 1
Chapter 12—Graphics and Java2D
Chapter 13—Exception Handling
Chapter 14—Files and Streams
Chapter 15—Recursion
Chapter 16—Searching and Sorting
Chapter 17—Data Structures
Chapter 18—Generics
Chapter 19—Collections
Chapter 20—Introduction to Java Applets
Chapter 21—Multimedia: Applets and Applications
Chapter 22—GUI Components: Part 2
Chapter 23—Multithreading
Chapter 24—Networking
Chapter 25—Manipulating Databases with JDBC
Chapter 26—Servlets
Chapter 27—Java Server Pages (JSP)
Chapter 28—Formatted Output
Chapter 29—Strings, Characters and Regular Expressions

DEITEL® Buzz Online E-mail Newsletter

Our free e-mail newsletter, the Deitel® Buzz Online, includes commentary on industry trends and developments, links to free articles and resources from our published books and upcoming publications, product-release schedules, errata, challenges, anecdotes, information on our corporate instructor-led training courses and more. To subscribe, visit

```
www.deitel.com/newsletter/subscribe.html
```

Acknowledgments

One of the great pleasures of writing a textbook is acknowledging the efforts of many people whose names may not appear on the cover, but whose hard work, cooperation, friendship and understanding were crucial to the production of the book. Many people at Deitel & Associates, Inc. devoted long hours to this project.

- Barbara Deitel, Chief Financial Officer at Deitel & Associates, Inc. researched the quotes at the beginning of each chapter and applied copy-edits to the book.

- Abbey Deitel, President of Deitel & Associates, Inc., is an Industrial Management graduate of Carnegie Mellon University. She co-authored the Preface. She also suggested the theme and bug names for the cover of the book.

- Andrew B. Goldberg is a recent graduate of Amherst College, where he earned a degree in Computer Science. Andrew is a co-author with us on *Internet and World Wide Web How to Program, 3/e* and contributed to *Operating Systems, Third Edition*. Andrew's contributions to *Small Java How to Program, 6/e* included updating the Chapters 3–10 based on the new early-classes presentation of the book and other content revisions. He also co-authored Appendix J: Using the Debugger.

- Christi Kelsey is a Management Information Systems graduate of Purdue University. She contributed to Chapter 1, the Preface and Appendix J, Using the Debugger. She edited the Index and paged the entire manuscript.

- Su Zhang holds B.Sc and a M.Sc degrees in Computer Science from McGill University. She is co-author with us on *Java Web Services for Experienced Programmers* and *Simply Java Programming*. She has also contributed to other Deitel publications, including *Advanced Java 2 Platform How to Program*, *Python How to Program* and *Operating Systems, Third Edition*. Su contributed to the sections on the new features of J2SE 5.0 in Chapters 7 and 8. She also co-authored Appendix F, Unicode®; Appendix G, Using Java API Documentation; and Appendix H, Creating HTML Documentation with `javadoc`.

- Jing Hu, a participant in the Deitel & Associates, Inc. Summer Internship Program, is a sophomore at Cornell University studying Computer Science. He contributed to the new GUI and Graphics Case Study and the instructor's manual for Chapters 3–8. He also contributed to the sections on video, preconditions/postconditions, assertions and invariants.

We are fortunate to have worked on this project with the talented and dedicated team of publishing professionals at Prentice Hall. We especially appreciate the extraordinary efforts of our Computer Science Editor, Kate Hargett and her boss and our mentor in publishing—Marcia Horton, Editorial Director of Prentice Hall's Engineering and Computer Science Division. Jennifer Cappello managed the review process. Vince O'Brien, Tom Manshreck and John Lovell did a marvelous job managing the production of the book. The talents of Carole Anson, Paul Belfanti and Geoffrey Cassar are evident in the redesign of the book's interior and the new cover art, and Sarah Parker managed the publication of the book's extensive ancillary package.

We sincerely appreciate the efforts of our fifth edition post-publication reviewers and our sixth edition reviewers:

Sun Microsystems Reviewers
Doug Kohlert, Sun Microsystems, Inc.
Brandon Taylor, Sun Microsystems, Inc.

Academic Reviewers
Karen Arlien, Bismarck State College
Walt Bunch, Chapman University
Marita Ellixson, Eglin AFB/University of Arkansas
Bill Freitas, The Lawrenceville School
Joe Kasprzyk, Salem State College
Earl LaBatt, Altaworks Corp./ University of New Hampshire
Brian Larson, Modesto Junior College
Roberto Lopez-Herrejon, University of Texas at Austin
Dean Mellas, Cerritos College
David Messier, Eastern University
Gavin Osborne, Saskatchewan Institute of Applied Science & Technology
Donna Reese, Mississippi State University
Craig Slinkman, University of Texas at Arlington
Mahendran Velauthapillai, Georgetown University
Stephen Weiss, University of North Carolina at Chapel Hill

Other Industry Reviewers
Jonathan Gadzik, Independent Consultant
Anne Horton, AT&T Bell Laboratories
James Huddleston, Independent Consultant
Karen Tegtmeyer, Independent Consultant

Java How to Program 5/e Post-Publication Reviewers
Ben Blake, Cleveland State University
Walt Bunch, Chapman University
Michael Develle, Independent Consultant
Marita Ellixson, Eglin Air Force Base/University of Arkansas
Ephrem Eyob, Virginia State University
Bjorn Foss, Florida Metropolitan University
James Huddleston, Independent Consultant
Brian Larson, Modesto Junior College

David Messier, Eastern University
Andy Novobilski, University of Tennessee, Chattanooga
Bill O'Farrell, IBM
Richard Ord, University of California, San Diego
Gavin Osborne, Saskatchewan Institute of Applied Science & Technology
Donna Reese, Mississippi State University
Craig Slinkman, University of Texas at Arlington
Brandon Taylor, Sun Microsystems, Inc.
Karen Tegtmeyer, Independent Consultant
Sreedhar Thota, Western Iowa Tech Community College
Mahendran Velauthapillai, Georgetown University
Loran Walker, Lawrence Technological University

Under a tight time schedule, they scrutinized every aspect of the text and made countless suggestions for improving the accuracy and completeness of the presentation.

Well, there you have it! Java is a powerful programming language that will help you write programs quickly and effectively. Java scales nicely into the realm of enterprise-systems development to help organizations build their critical information systems. As you read the book, we would sincerely appreciate your comments, criticisms, corrections and suggestions for improving the text. Please address all correspondence to:

deitel@deitel.com

We will respond promptly, and we will post corrections and clarifications on our Web site:

www.deitel.com

We hope you enjoy learning with *Small Java How to Program, Sixth Edition* as much as we enjoyed writing it!

Dr. Harvey M. Deitel
Paul J. Deitel

About the Authors

Dr. Harvey M. Deitel, Chairman and Chief Strategy Officer of Deitel & Associates, Inc., has 43 years experience in the computing field, including extensive industry and academic experience. Dr. Deitel earned B.S. and M.S. degrees from the Massachusetts Institute of Technology and a Ph.D. from Boston University. He worked on the pioneering virtual-memory operating-systems projects at IBM and MIT that developed techniques now widely implemented in systems such as UNIX, Linux and Windows XP. He has 20 years of college teaching experience, including earning tenure and serving as the Chairman of the Computer Science Department at Boston College before founding Deitel & Associates, Inc., with his son, Paul J. Deitel. He and Paul are the co-authors of several dozen books and multimedia packages and they are writing many more. With translations published in Japanese, German, Russian, Spanish, Traditional Chinese, Simplified Chinese, Korean, French, Polish, Italian, Portuguese, Greek, Urdu and Turkish, the Deitels' texts have earned international recognition. Dr. Deitel has delivered hundreds of professional seminars to major corporations, government organizations and the military.

Paul J. Deitel, CEO and Chief Technical Officer of Deitel & Associates, Inc., is a graduate of the MIT's Sloan School of Management, where he studied Information Technology. Through Deitel & Associates, Inc., he has delivered Java, C, C++, Internet and World Wide Web courses to industry clients, including IBM, Sun Microsystems, Dell, Lucent Technologies, Fidelity, NASA at the Kennedy Space Center, the National Severe Storm Laboratory, Compaq, White Sands Missile Range, Rogue Wave Software, Boeing, Stratus, Cambridge Technology Partners, Open Environment Corporation, One Wave, Hyperion Software, Adra Systems, Entergy, CableData Systems and many other organizations. He has also lectured on C++ and Java for the Boston Chapter of the Association for Computing Machinery. He and his father, Dr. Harvey M. Deitel, are the world's best-selling Computer Science textbook authors.

About Deitel & Associates, Inc.

Deitel & Associates, Inc., is an internationally recognized corporate training and content-creation organization specializing in computer programming languages, Internet/World Wide Web software technology and object technology education. The company provides instructor-led courses on Internet and World Wide Web programming, object technology, and major programming languages and platforms, such as Java, Advanced Java, C, C++, .NET programming languages, XML, Perl, Python and more. The founders of Deitel & Associates, Inc., are Dr. Harvey M. Deitel and Paul J. Deitel. The company's clients include many of the world's largest computer companies, government agencies, branches of the military and business organizations. Through its 28-year publishing partnership with Prentice Hall, Deitel & Associates, Inc. publishes leading-edge programming textbooks, professional books, interactive multimedia *Cyber Classrooms*, *Complete Training Courses*, Web-based training courses and course management systems e-content for popular CMSs such as WebCT, Blackboard and Pearson's CourseCompass. Deitel & Associates, Inc., and the authors can be reached via e-mail at:

```
deitel@deitel.com
```

To learn more about Deitel & Associates, Inc., its publications and its worldwide Dive Into Series™ Corporate Training curriculum, see the last few pages of this book or visit:

```
www.deitel.com
```

and subscribe to the free *Deitel Buzz Online* e-mail newsletter at:

```
www.deitel.com/newsletter/subscribe.html
```

Individuals wishing to purchase Deitel books, Cyber Classrooms, Complete Training Courses and Web-based training courses can do so through:

```
www.deitel.com/books/index.html
```

Bulk orders by corporations and academic institutions should be placed directly with Prentice Hall. See the last few pages of this book for worldwide ordering details.

Before You Begin

Please follow the instructions in this section to ensure that Java is installed properly on your computer before you begin using this book.

Font and Naming Conventions

We use fonts to distinguish between on-screen components (such as menu names and menu items) and Java code or commands. Our convention is to emphasize on-screen components in a sans-serif bold **Helvetica** font (for example, **File** menu) and to emphasize Java code and commands in a sans-serif Lucida font (for example, System.out.println()).

Software and Other Resources on the CD That Accompanies *Small Java How to Program, Sixth Edition*

The CD that accompanies this book includes:

- BlueJ (version 1.3.5) for Windows/Linux
- jGRASP (version 1.7.0) and handbook, for Windows/Linux
- jEdit (version 4.1) for Windows/Linux
- JCreator LE (version 3.10) for Windows only
- NetBeans IDE (version 3.6) for Windows/Linux

The examples in this book were developed with the Java 2 Platform, Standard Edition Development Kit (JDK) version 5.0. At the time of this printing the JDK 5.0 was still in its final beta version, so the JDK is not included on the CD that accompanies this book. You can download the latest version of JDK 5.0 and its documentation from

```
java.sun.com/j2se/1.5.0/download.jsp
```

When Sun releases the final version of JDK 5.0, it will be included on the CD in future prints. If you have any questions, please feel free to email us at deitel@deitel.com. We will respond promptly.

Hardware and Software Requirements to Run JDK 5.0

To install and run JDK 5.0, Sun recommends that PCs meet the following minimum requirements:

- 500 MHz, Pentium III processor
- 256 MB RAM
- 100 MB of available disk space

[*Note:* the JDK is available for Windows, Linux and Solaris Operating Systems.]

Copying and Organizing Files

All of the examples for *Small Java How To Program, Sixth Edition* are included on the CD that accompanies this textbook. Follow the steps in the next section, *Copying the Book Examples from the CD*, to copy the examples directory from the CD onto your hard drive. We suggest that you work from your hard drive rather than your CD drive for two reasons: The CD is read-only, so you cannot save your applications to the book's CD, and files can be accessed faster from a hard drive than from a CD. The examples from the book are also available for download from:

```
www.deitel.com
www.prenhall.com/deitel
```

Screen shots in the following section might differ slightly from what you see on your computer, depending on whether you are using Windows 2000 or Windows XP, or your version of Internet Explorer.

Copying the Book Examples from the CD

1. ***Inserting the CD.*** Insert the CD that accompanies *Small Java How To Program, Sixth Edition* into your computer's CD drive. The window displayed in Fig. 1 should appear. If the page appears, proceed to *Step 3* of this section. If the page does not appear, proceed to *Step 2*.

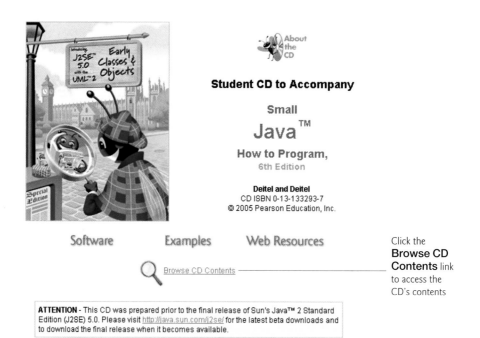

Fig. 1 | Welcome page for *Small Java How to Program* CD.

2. *Opening the CD directory using My Computer.* If the page shown in Fig. 1 does not appear, double click the **My Computer** icon on your desktop. In the **My Computer** window, double click your CD-ROM drive (Fig. 2) to access the CD's contents. Proceed to *Step 4.*

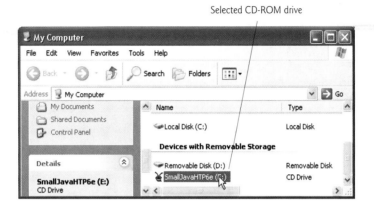

Fig.2 | Locating the CD-ROM drive.

3. *Opening the CD-ROM directory.* If the page in Fig. 1 does appear, click the **Browse CD Contents** link (Fig. 1) to access the CD's contents.

4. *Copying the* examples *directory.* Right click the examples directory (Fig. 3), then select **Copy**. Next, go to **My Computer** and double click the **C:** drive. Select the **Edit** menu's **Paste** option to copy the directory and its contents from the CD to your **C:** drive. [*Note*: We save the examples to the **C:** drive and refer to this drive throughout the text. You may choose to save your files to a different drive based on your computer's set up, the setup in your school's lab or personal preferences. If you are working in a computer lab, please see your instructor for more information to confirm where the examples should be saved.]

The book example files you copied onto your computer from the CD are read-only. Next, you will remove the read-only property so you can modify and run the examples.

Changing the Read-Only Property of Files

1. *Opening the Properties dialog.* Right click the examples directory and select **Properties** from the menu. The **examples Properties** dialog appears (Fig. 4).

2. *Changing the read-only property.* In the **Attributes** section of this dialog, click the box next to **Read-only** to remove the check mark (Fig. 5). Click **Apply** to apply the changes.

3. *Changing the property for all files.* Clicking **Apply** will display the **Confirm Attribute Changes** window (Fig. 6). In this window, click the radio button next to **Apply changes to this folder, subfolders and files** and click **OK** to remove the read-only property for all of the files and directories in the **examples** directory.

Right click the
examples directory   Select **Copy**

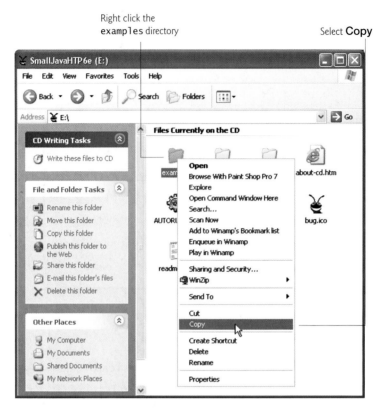

Fig.3 | Copying the **examples** directory.

Fig.4 | **examples Properties** dialog.

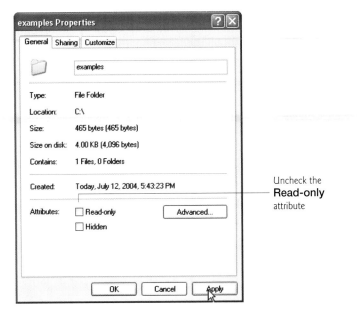

Uncheck the
Read-only
attribute

Fig.5 | Unchecking the **Read-only** check box.

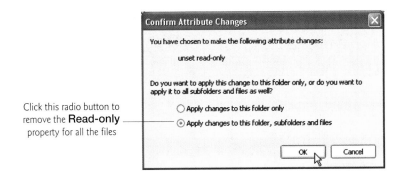

Click this radio button to
remove the **Read-only**
property for all the files

Fig.6 | Removing read-only for all the files in the **examples** directory.

Before you can run the applications in *Small Java How To Program, Sixth Edition* or build your own applications, you must install the Java Development Kit (JDK) 5.0 or another Java development tool. The following section describes how to install JDK 5.0.

Installing the J2SE Development Kit (JDK)

1. *Locating the JDK installer.* At the time of publication, the JDK 5.0 was still in beta releases and being updated frequently. As a result, the JDK installer might not be included on the CD that accompanies your book. If this is the case, you can download the most recent version of the installer from Sun's Web site. Go to java.sun.com/j2se/5.0/download.jsp and click the **DOWNLOAD** link in the **SDK** column. You must accept the license agreement before downloading. Once

you accept the license agreement, you are directed to a download page, where you can select and download the installer for your computer platform. Save the installer on your hard disk and keep track of where you save it. The following steps show the installation procedure on the Windows platform.

2. *Starting installation of the JDK.* After either downloading the JDK installer or locating it on the CD that accompanies the book, double click the installer program to begin installing the JDK. The **InstallShield Wizard** window (Fig. 7) is displayed. Wait for the wizard to finish the configuration.

3. *Accepting the license agreement.* Carefully read the license agreement. Select **Yes** to agree to the terms (Fig. 8). [*Note:* If you choose not to accept the license agreement, the software will not install and you will not be able to execute or create Java applications.]

4. *Choosing the installation directory for the JDK.* Select the directory in which you want the JDK to be installed (Fig. 9). If you change the default installation directory, be sure to write down the exact name and location of the directory you choose, as you will need this information later in the installation process. After selecting a directory, click the **Next >** button to install the development tool.

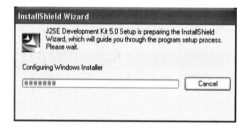

Fig.7 | **InstallShield Wizard** for the JDK.

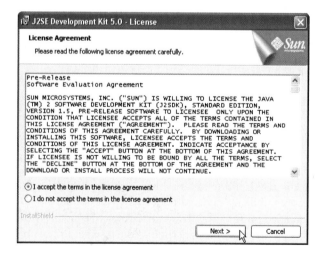

Fig.8 | JDK license agreement.

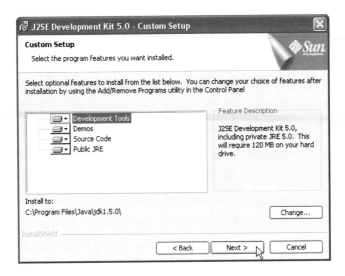

Fig.9 | Choosing the destination location.

5. ***Choosing the installation directory for the Java Runtime Environment (JRE).*** Select the directory in which you want the JRE to be installed (Fig. 10). We recommend that you choose the default installation directory. After you have selected a directory, click the **Next >** button to install the JRE.

6. ***Selecting browsers.*** As part of the installation, you have the option of making the Java plug-in the default Java runtime environment for Java programs called applets that run in Web browsers (Fig. 11). After you select the desired browsers click the **Next >** button.

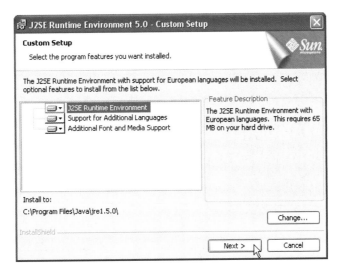

Fig.10 | Selecting the components of the JDK to install.

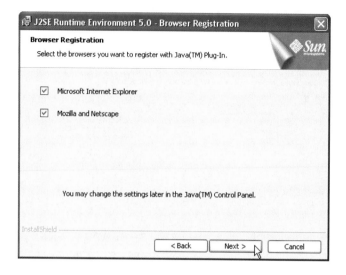

Fig. 11 | Selecting browsers.

7. *Finishing the installation.* The program will now install the JRE. Click the **Finish** button to complete the installation process (Fig. 12).

The PATH environment variable on your computer designates which directories the computer searches when looking for applications, such as the applications that enable you to compile and run your Java applications (called javac.exe and java.exe, respectively). You will now learn how to set the PATH environment variable on your computer.

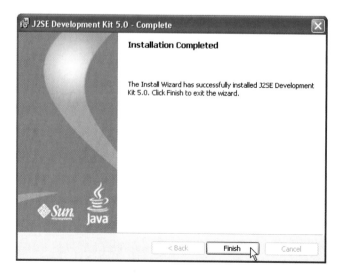

Fig. 12 | Completing the installation.

Setting the PATH Variable

The last step before you can use the JDK is to set the PATH environment variable to indicate where the JDK's tools are installed.

1. *Opening the* System Properties *dialog.* Right click on the **My Computer** icon on your desktop and select **Properties** from the menu. The **System Properties** dialog (Fig. 13) appears. [*Note*: Your **System Properties** dialog may appear different than the one shown in Fig. 13, depending on your version of Microsoft Windows. This particular dialog is from a computer running Microsoft Windows XP. Your dialog might include different information.]

2. *Opening the* Environment Variables *dialog.* Select the **Advanced** tab at the top of the **System Properties** dialog (Fig. 14). Click the **Environment Variables** button to display the **Environment Variables** dialog (Fig. 15).

3. *Editing the PATH variable.* Scroll down inside the **System variables** box to select the PATH variable. Click the **Edit** button. This will cause the **Edit System Variable** dialog to appear (Fig. 16).

4. *Changing the contents of the PATH variable.* Place the cursor inside the **Variable Value** field. Use the left-arrow key to move the cursor to the beginning of the list. At the beginning of the list, type the name of the directory in which you placed the JDK followed by \bin; (Fig. 17). If you chose the default installation directory in *Step 4* of the previous section, *Installing the J2SE Development Kit (JDK)*, you will add C:\Program Files\Java\jdk1.5.0\bin; to the PATH variable here.

Fig. 13 | **System Properties** dialog.

Click the **OK** button to complete the modification of the PATH variable. [*Note:* The default installation directory is named jdk1.5.0, even though the JDK is now called version 5.0.]

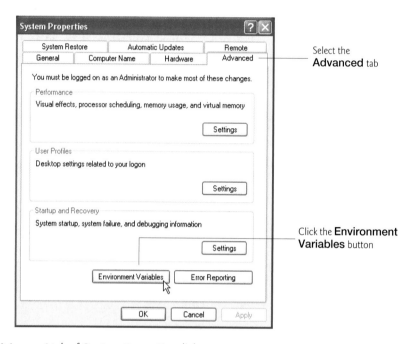

Fig. 14 | **Advanced** tab of **System Properties** dialog.

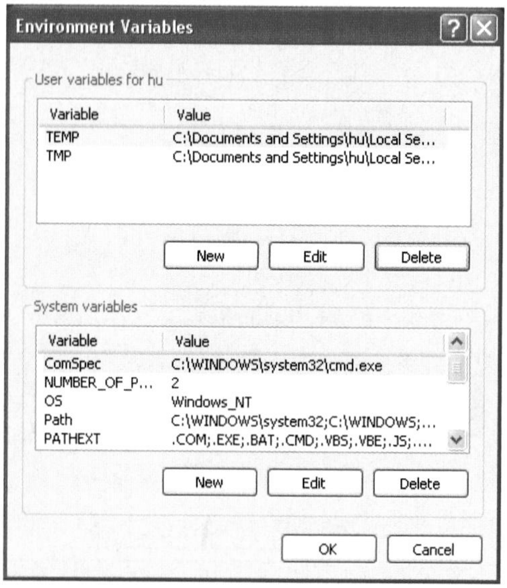

Fig. 15 | **Environment Variables** dialog.

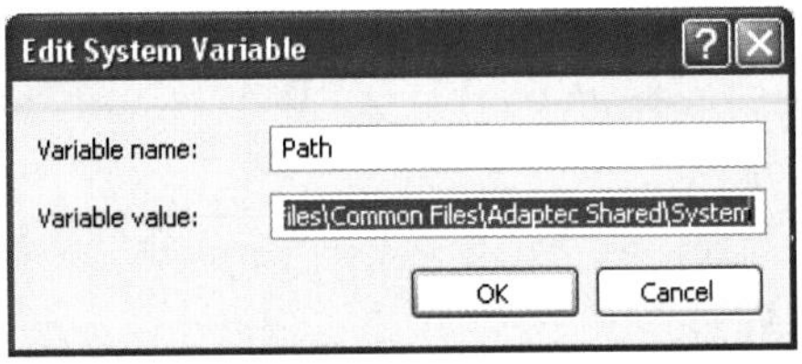

Fig.16 | Edit **System Variable** dialog.

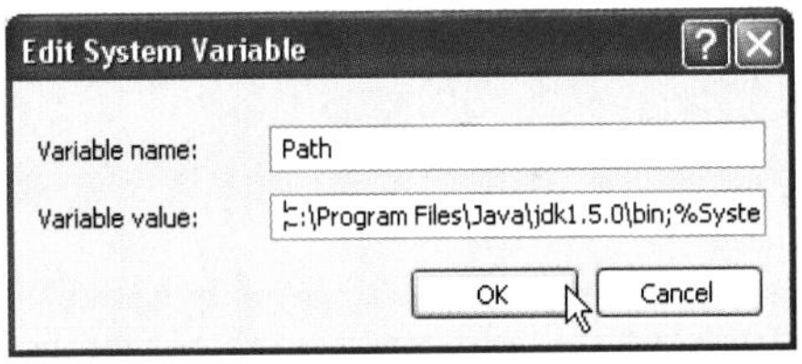

Fig.17 | Editing the PATH variable.

You are now ready to being your Java studies with *Small Java How to Program*. We hope you enjoy the book! You can reach us easily at `deitel@deitel.com`. We will respond promptly.

Introduction to Computers, the Internet and the World Wide Web

OBJECTIVES

In this chapter you will learn:

- Basic hardware and software concepts.
- Basic object technology concepts, such as classes, objects, attributes, behaviors, encapsulation, inheritance and polymorphism.
- The different types of programming languages.
- Which programming languages are most widely used.
- A typical Java development environment.
- Java's role in developing distributed client/server applications for the Internet and the Web.
- The history of the industry-standard object-oriented design language, the UML.
- The history of the Internet and the World Wide Web.
- To test-drive Java applications.

1.1 Introduction

Welcome to Java! We have worked hard to create what we hope you will find to be an informative, entertaining and challenging learning experience. Java is a powerful computer programming language that is fun for novices and appropriate for experienced programmers to use in building substantial information systems. *Small Java How to Program, Sixth Edition*, is an effective learning tool for each of these audiences.

The core of the book emphasizes achieving program *clarity* through the proven techniques of object-oriented programming. Nonprogrammers will learn programming the right way from the beginning. The presentation is clear, straightforward and abundantly illustrated. It includes scores of working Java programs and shows the outputs produced when those programs are run on a computer. We teach Java features in the context of complete working Java programs—we call this the live-code approach. The example programs are included on the CD that accompanies this book, or you may download them from www.deitel.com or www.prenhall.com/deitel.

The early chapters introduce the fundamentals of computers, computer programming and the Java computer programming language, providing a solid foundation for the deeper treatment of Java in the later chapters. Experienced programmers tend to read the early chapters quickly and find the treatment of Java in the later chapters rigorous and challenging.

Most people are familiar with the exciting tasks computers perform. Using this textbook, you will learn how to command computers to perform those tasks. It is software (i.e., the instructions you write to command computers to perform actions and make decisions) that controls computers (often referred to as hardware). Java, developed by Sun Microsystems, is one of today's most popular software development languages.

This book is based on Sun's Java 2 Platform, Standard Edition (J2SE). Sun provides an implementation of this platform, called the J2SE Development Kit (JDK), that includes the minimum set of tools you need to write software in Java. We used JDK version 5.0 to implement and test the programs in this book. When Sun makes the JDK available to publishers, it will be wrapped with the textbook on the accompanying CD. Sun updates the JDK on a regular basis to fix bugs. To download the most recent version of the JDK, visit `java.sun.com/j2se`.

Computer use is increasing in almost every field of endeavor. Computing costs have been decreasing dramatically due to rapid developments in both hardware and software technologies. Computers that might have filled large rooms and cost millions of dollars two decades ago can now be inscribed on silicon chips smaller than a fingernail, costing perhaps a few dollars each. Fortunately, silicon is one of the most abundant materials on earth—it is an ingredient in common sand. Silicon chip technology has made computing so economical that hundreds of millions of general-purpose computers are in use worldwide, helping people in business, industry and government, and in their personal lives. The number could easily double in the next few years.

Over the years, many programmers learned the programming methodology called structured programming. You will learn structured programming and an exciting newer methodology, object-oriented programming. Why do we teach both? Object orientation is the key programming methodology used by programmers today. You will create and work with many software objects in this text. But you will discover that their internal structure is often built using structured-programming techniques. Also, the logic of manipulating objects is occasionally expressed with structured programming.

Java has become the language of choice for implementing Internet-based applications and software for devices that communicate over a network. Before long the stereo and other devices in your home will be networked together by Java technology. Don't be surprised when your wireless devices, like cell phones, pagers and personal digital assistants (PDAs), begin to communicate over the so-called wireless Internet. According to Sun's Web site (`www.sun.com`), in 2003, over 267 million cell phones equipped with Java technology were shipped! Java has evolved rapidly into the large-scale applications arena. It is no longer used simply to make World Wide Web pages come alive—it has become the preferred language for meeting the enterprise-wide programming needs of many organizations.

Small Java How to Program, 6/e is based on the *Java 2 Platform, Standard Edition (J2SE) version 5.0.* Java has grown so large that it now has two other editions. The Java 2 Platform, Enterprise Edition (J2EE), is geared toward developing large-scale, distributed networking applications and Web-based applications. The Java 2 Platform, Micro Edition (J2ME) is geared toward developing applications for small, memory-constrained devices, such as cell phones, pagers and PDAs. *Advanced Java 2 Platform How to Program* emphasizes developing applications with J2EE and provides coverage of several high-end topics from the J2SE. *Advanced Java 2 Platform How to Program* also includes substantial materials on J2ME and wireless-application development.

You are embarking on a challenging and rewarding path. As you proceed, if you would like to communicate with us, please send e-mail to deitel@deitel.com

or browse our Web site at

    www.deitel.com

We will respond promptly. To keep up to date with Java developments at Deitel & Associates, please register for our free e-mail newsletter, *The Deitel Buzz Online,* at

    www.deitel.com/newsletter/subscribe.html

We hope that you will enjoy learning with *Small Java How to Program.*

1.2 What Is a Computer?

A computer is a device capable of performing computations and making logical decisions at speeds millions (even billions) of times faster than human beings can. For example, many of today's personal computers can perform a billion additions per second. A person operating a desk calculator could spend an entire lifetime performing calculations and still not complete as many calculations as a powerful personal computer can perform in one second. (Points to ponder: How would you know whether the person added the numbers correctly? How would you know whether the computer added the numbers correctly?) Today's fastest supercomputers can perform hundreds of billions of additions per second. And trillion-instructions-per-second computers are already functioning in research laboratories.

Computers process data under the control of sets of instructions called computer programs. These programs guide the computer through orderly sets of actions specified by people called computer programmers.

A computer consists of various devices referred to as hardware (e.g., the keyboard, screen, mouse, disks, memory, DVD, CD-ROM and processing units). The programs that run on a computer are referred to as software. Hardware costs have been declining dramatically in recent years, to the point that personal computers have become a commodity. Unfortunately, in the absence of significantly improved technology for software development, costs have been rising steadily as programmers develop ever more powerful and complex applications. In this book, you will learn a proven methodology that *can* reduce software development costs—object-oriented programming.

1.3 Computer Organization

Regardless of differences in physical appearance, virtually every computer may be envisioned as divided into six logical units or sections:

    1. *Input unit.* This is the "receiving" section of the computer. It obtains information (data and computer programs) from input devices and places this information at the disposal of the other units so that it can be processed. Most information is entered into computers through keyboards and mouse devices. Information also can be entered in many other ways, including by speaking to your computer, by scanning images and by having your computer receive information from a network, such as the Internet.

2. *Output unit.* This is the "shipping" section of the computer. It takes information that the computer has processed and places it on various output devices to make the information available for use outside the computer. Most information output from computers today is displayed on screens, printed on paper or used to control other devices. Computers also can output their information to networks, such as the Internet.

3. *Memory unit.* This is the rapid-access, relatively low-capacity "warehouse" section of the computer. It retains information that has been entered through the input unit, so that it will be immediately available for processing when needed. The memory unit also retains processed information until it can be placed on output devices by the output unit. Information in the memory unit is typically lost when the computer's power is turned off. The memory unit is often called either memory or primary memory.

4. *Arithmetic and logic unit (ALU).* This is the "manufacturing" section of the computer. It is responsible for performing calculations, such as addition, subtraction, multiplication and division. It contains the decision mechanisms that allow the computer, for example, to compare two items from the memory unit to determine whether they are equal.

5. *Central processing unit (CPU).* This is the "administrative" section of the computer. It coordinates and supervises the operation of the other sections. The CPU tells the input unit when information should be read into the memory unit, tells the ALU when information from the memory unit should be used in calculations and tells the output unit when to send information from the memory unit to certain output devices. Many of today's computers have multiple CPUs and, hence, can perform many operations simultaneously—such computers are called multiprocessors.

6. *Secondary storage unit.* This is the long-term, high-capacity "warehousing" section of the computer. Programs or data not actively being used by the other units normally are placed on secondary storage devices (e.g., your hard drive) until they are again needed, possibly hours, days, months or even years later. Information in secondary storage takes much longer to access than information in primary memory, but the cost per unit of secondary storage is much less than that of primary memory. Examples of secondary storage devices include CDs and DVDs, which can hold up to hundreds of millions of characters and billions of characters, respectively.

1.4 Early Operating Systems

Early computers could perform only one job or task at a time. This is often called single-user batch processing. The computer runs a single program at a time while processing data in groups or batches. In these early systems, users generally submitted their jobs to a computer center on decks of punched cards and often had to wait hours or even days before printouts were returned to their desks.

Software systems called operating systems were developed to make using computers more convenient. Early operating systems smoothed and speeded up the transition between jobs, and hence increased the amount of work, or throughput, computers could process.

As computers became more powerful, it became evident that single-user batch processing was inefficient, because so much time was spent waiting for slow input/output devices to complete their tasks. It was thought that many jobs or tasks could *share* the resources of the computer to achieve better utilization. This is called multiprogramming. Multiprogramming involves the simultaneous operation of many jobs that are competing to share the computer's resources. With early multiprogramming operating systems, users still submitted jobs on decks of punched cards and waited hours or days for results.

In the 1960s, several groups in industry and the universities pioneered timesharing operating systems. Timesharing is a special case of multiprogramming in which users access the computer through terminals, typically devices with keyboards and screens. Dozens or even hundreds of users share the computer at once. The computer actually does not run them all simultaneously. Rather, it runs a small portion of one user's job, then moves on to service the next user, perhaps providing service to each user several times per second. Thus, the users' programs *appear* to be running simultaneously. An advantage of timesharing is that user requests receive almost immediate responses.

1.5 Personal, Distributed and Client/Server Computing

In 1977, Apple Computer popularized personal computing. Computers became so economical that people could buy them for their own personal or business use. In 1981, IBM, the world's largest computer vendor, introduced the IBM Personal Computer. This quickly legitimized personal computing in business, industry and government organizations.

These computers were "standalone" units—people transported disks back and forth between them to share information (often called "sneakernet"). Although early personal computers were not powerful enough to timeshare several users, these machines could be linked together in computer networks, sometimes over telephone lines and sometimes in local area networks (LANs) within an organization. This led to the phenomenon of distributed computing, in which an organization's computing, instead of being performed only at some central computer installation, is distributed over networks to the sites where the organization's work is performed. Personal computers were powerful enough to handle the computing requirements of individual users as well as the basic communications tasks of passing information between computers electronically.

Today's personal computers are as powerful as the million-dollar machines of just two decades ago. The most powerful desktop machines—called workstations—provide individual users with enormous capabilities. Information is shared easily across computer networks where computers called file servers offer a common data store that may be used by client computers distributed throughout the network, hence the term client/server computing. Java has become widely used for writing software for computer networking and for distributed client/server applications. Today's popular operating systems, such as UNIX, Linux, Apple Mac OS X (pronounced "O-S ten") and Microsoft Windows, provide the kinds of capabilities discussed in this section.

1.6 The Internet and the World Wide Web

The Internet—a global network of computers—was developed almost four decades ago with funding supplied by the U.S. Department of Defense. Originally designed to connect the main computer systems of about a dozen universities and research organizations, the Internet today is accessible by hundreds of millions of computers worldwide.

With the introduction of the World Wide Web—which allows computer users to locate and view multimedia-based documents on almost any subject over the Internet—the Internet has exploded into one of the world's premier communication mechanisms.

The Internet and the World Wide Web are surely among humankind's most important and profound creations. In the past, most computer applications ran on computers that were not connected to one another. Today's applications can be written to communicate among the world's hundreds of millions of computers. The Internet mixes computing and communications technologies. It makes our work easier. It makes information instantly and conveniently accessible worldwide. It enables individuals and local small businesses to get worldwide exposure. It is changing the way business is done. People can search for the best prices on virtually any product or service. Special-interest communities can stay in touch with one another. Researchers can be made instantly aware of the latest breakthroughs.

Our larger book, *Java How to Program, 6/e*, presents programming techniques that allow Java applications to use the Internet and the Web to interact with other applications. These capabilities, and those discussed in our companion book, *Advanced Java 2 Platform How to Program*, allow Java programmers to develop the kind of enterprise-level distributed applications that are used in industry today. Java applications can be written to execute on every major type of computer, greatly reducing the time and cost of systems development for corporations. If you are interested in developing applications to run over the Internet and the Web, learning Java may be the key to rewarding career opportunities for you.

1.7 Machine Languages, Assembly Languages and High-Level Languages

Programmers write instructions in various programming languages, some directly understandable by computers and others requiring intermediate translation steps. Hundreds of computer languages are in use today. These may be divided into three general types:

1. Machine languages
2. Assembly languages
3. High-level languages

Any computer can directly understand only its own machine language. Machine language is the "natural language" of a computer and as such is defined by its hardware design. Machine languages generally consist of strings of numbers (ultimately reduced to 1s and 0s) that instruct computers to perform their most elementary operations one at a time. Machine languages are machine dependent (i.e., a particular machine language can be used on only one type of computer). Such languages are cumbersome for humans, as illustrated by the following section of an early machine-language program that adds overtime pay to base pay and stores the result in gross pay:

```
+1300042774
+1400593419
+1200274027
```

Machine-language programming was simply too slow and tedious for most programmers. Instead of using the strings of numbers that computers could directly understand, programmers began using English-like abbreviations to represent elementary operations. These abbreviations formed the basis of assembly languages. Translator programs called assemblers were developed to convert early assembly-language programs to machine language at computer speeds. The following section of an assembly-language program also adds overtime pay to base pay and stores the result in gross pay:

```
load    basepay
add     overpay
store   grosspay
```

Although such code is clearer to humans, it is incomprehensible to computers until translated to machine language.

Computer usage increased rapidly with the advent of assembly languages, but programmers still had to use many instructions to accomplish even the simplest tasks. To speed the programming process, high-level languages were developed in which single statements could be written to accomplish substantial tasks. Translator programs called compilers convert high-level language programs into machine language. High-level languages allow programmers to write instructions that look almost like everyday English and contain commonly used mathematical notations. A payroll program written in a high-level language might contain a statement such as

```
grossPay = basePay + overTimePay
```

Obviously, high-level languages are preferable to machine and assembly language from the programmer's standpoint. C, C++, Microsoft's .NET languages (e.g., Visual Basic .NET, Visual C++ .NET and C#) and Java are among the most widely used high-level programming languages.

The process of compiling a high-level language program into machine language can take a considerable amount of computer time. Interpreter programs were developed to execute high-level language programs directly, although much more slowly. Interpreters are popular in program-development environments in which new features are being added and errors corrected. Once a program is fully developed, a compiled version can be produced to run most efficiently.

You now know that there are ultimately two ways to translate a high-level language program into a form that the computer understands—compilation and interpretation. As you will learn in Section 1.13, Java uses a clever mixture of these technologies.

1.8 History of C and C++

Java evolved from C++, which evolved from C, which evolved from BCPL and B. BCPL was developed in 1967 by Martin Richards as a language for writing operating systems software and compilers. Ken Thompson modeled many features in his language B after their counterparts in BCPL, using B to create early versions of the UNIX operating system at Bell Laboratories in 1970.

The C language was evolved from B by Dennis Ritchie at Bell Laboratories and was originally implemented in 1972. It initially became widely known as the development language of the UNIX operating system. Today, most of the code for general-purpose operating systems (e.g., those found in laptops, desktops, workstations and small servers) is written in C or C++.

C++, an extension of C, was developed by Bjarne Stroustrup in the early 1980s at Bell Laboratories (now part of Lucent). C++ provides a number of features that "spruce up" the

C language, but more important, it provides capabilities for object-oriented programming (discussed in more detail in Section 1.16 and throughout this book). C++ is a hybrid language—it is possible to program in either a C-like style, an object-oriented style or both.

A revolution is brewing in the software community. Building software quickly, correctly and economically remains an elusive goal at a time when demands for new and more powerful software are soaring. Objects, or more precisely—as we will see in Section 1.16— the classes objects come from, are essentially reusable software components. There are date objects, time objects, audio objects, automobile objects, people objects and so on. In fact, almost any noun can be represented as a software object in terms of attributes (e.g., name, color and size) and behaviors (e.g., calculating, moving and communicating). Software developers are discovering that using a modular, object-oriented design and implementation approach can make software-development groups much more productive than was possible with earlier popular programming techniques like structured programming. Object-oriented programs are often easier to understand, correct and modify. Java is the world's most widely used object-oriented programming language.

1.9 History of Java

The microprocessor revolution's most important contribution to date is that it made possible the development of personal computers, which now number in the hundreds of millions worldwide. Personal computers have profoundly affected people's lives and the ways organizations conduct and manage their business.

Microprocessors are having a profound impact in intelligent consumer-electronic devices. Recognizing this, Sun Microsystems in 1991 funded an internal corporate research project code-named Green, which resulted in the development of a C++-based language that its creator, James Gosling, called Oak after an oak tree outside his window at Sun. It was later discovered that there already was a computer language called Oak. When a group of Sun people visited a local coffee shop, the name Java was suggested, and it stuck.

The Green project ran into some difficulties. The marketplace for intelligent consumer-electronic devices was not developing in the early 1990s as quickly as Sun had anticipated. The project was in danger of being canceled. By sheer good fortune, the World Wide Web exploded in popularity in 1993, and Sun people saw the immediate potential of using Java to add dynamic content, such as interactivity and animations, to Web pages. This breathed new life into the project.

Sun formally announced Java at a major conference in May 1995. Java garnered the attention of the business community because of the phenomenal interest in the World Wide Web. Java is now used to develop large-scale enterprise applications, to enhance the functionality of Web servers (the computers that provide the content we see in our Web browsers), to provide applications for consumer devices (e.g., cell phones, pagers and personal digital assistants) and for many other purposes.

1.10 Java Class Libraries

Java programs consist of pieces called classes. Classes include pieces called methods that perform tasks and return information when they complete them. Programmers can create each piece they need to form Java programs. However, most Java programmers take advantage of the rich collections of existing classes in the Java class libraries, which are also known as the Java APIs (Application Programming Interfaces). Thus, there are really two aspects to learning the Java "world." The first is the Java language itself, so that you can program your own classes, and the second is the classes in the extensive Java class libraries. Throughout this book, we discuss many library classes. Class libraries are provided primarily by compiler vendors, but many are supplied by independent software vendors (ISVs).

Software Engineering Observation 1.1

Use a building-block approach to create programs. Avoid reinventing the wheel—use existing pieces wherever possible. Called software reuse, *this practice is central to object-oriented programming.*

We include many tips such as these Software Engineering Observations throughout the book to explain concepts that affect and improve the overall architecture and quality of software systems. We also highlight other kinds of tips, including Good Programming Practices (to help you write programs that are clearer, more understandable, more maintainable and easier to test and debug—or remove programming errors), Common Programming Errors (problems to watch out for and avoid), Performance Tips (techniques for writing programs that run faster and use less memory), Portability Tips (techniques to help you write programs that can run, with little or no modification, on a variety of computers—these tips also include general observations about how Java achieves its high degree of portability), Error-Prevention Tips (techniques for removing bugs from your programs and, more important, techniques for writing bug-free programs in the first place) and Look and Feel Observations (techniques to help you design the "look" and "feel" of your applications' user interfaces for appearance and ease of use). Many of these are only guidelines. You will, no doubt, develop your own preferred programming style.

Software Engineering Observation 1.2

When programming in Java, you will typically use the following building blocks: Classes and methods from class libraries, classes and methods you create yourself and classes and methods that others create and make available to you.

The advantage of creating your own classes and methods is that you know exactly how they work and you can examine the Java code. The disadvantage is the time-consuming and potentially complex effort that is required.

Performance Tip 1.1

Using Java API classes and methods instead of writing your own versions can improve program performance, because they are carefully written to perform efficiently. This technique also shortens program development time.

Portability Tip 1.1

Using classes and methods from the Java API instead of writing your own improves program portability, because they are included in every Java implementation.

Software Engineering Observation 1.3

Extensive class libraries of reusable software components are available over the Internet and the Web, many at no charge.

To download the Java API documentation, go to the Sun Java site `java.sun.com/j2se/5.0/download.jsp`.

1.11 FORTRAN, COBOL, Pascal and Ada

Hundreds of high-level languages have been developed, but only a few have achieved broad acceptance. FORTRAN (FORmula TRANslator) was developed by IBM Corporation in the mid-1950s to be used for scientific and engineering applications that require complex mathematical computations. FORTRAN is still widely used, especially in engineering applications.

COBOL (COmmon Business Oriented Language) was developed in the late 1950s by computer manufacturers, the U.S. government and industrial computer users. COBOL is used for commercial applications that require precise and efficient manipulation of large amounts of data. Much business software is still programmed in COBOL.

During the 1960s, many large software-development efforts encountered severe difficulties. Software deliveries were typically late, costs greatly exceeded budgets and the finished products were unreliable. People began to realize that software development was a far more complex activity than they had imagined. Research in the 1960s resulted in the evolution of structured programming—a disciplined approach to writing programs that are clearer, easier to test and debug and easier to modify than large programs produced with previous techniques.

One of the more tangible results of this research was the development of the Pascal programming language by Professor Niklaus Wirth in 1971. Named after the seventeenth-century mathematician and philosopher Blaise Pascal, it was designed for teaching structured programming in academic environments and rapidly became the preferred programming language in most colleges. Pascal lacks many features needed to make it useful in commercial, industrial and government applications, so it has not been widely accepted in these environments.

The Ada programming language was developed under the sponsorship of the U.S. Department of Defense (DOD) during the 1970s and early 1980s. Hundreds of separate languages were being used to produce the DOD's massive command-and-control software systems. The DOD wanted a single language that would fill most of its needs. The Ada language was named after Lady Ada Lovelace, daughter of the poet Lord Byron. Lady Lovelace is credited with writing the world's first computer program in the early 1800s (for the Analytical Engine mechanical computing device designed by Charles Babbage). One important capability of Ada, called multitasking, allows programmers to specify that many activities are to occur in parallel. Java, through a technique called multithreading, also enables programmers to write programs with parallel activities.

1.12 BASIC, Visual Basic, Visual C++, C# and .NET

The BASIC (Beginner's All-Purpose Symbolic Instruction Code) programming language was developed in the mid-1960s at Dartmouth College as a means of writing simple programs. BASIC's primary purpose was to familiarize novices with programming techniques.

Microsoft's Visual Basic language was introduced in the early 1990s to simplify the development of Microsoft Windows applications and is one of the most popular programming languages in the world.

Microsoft's latest development tools are part of its corporate-wide strategy for integrating the Internet and the Web into computer applications. This strategy is implemented in Microsoft's .NET platform, which provides developers with the capabilities they need to create and run computer applications that can execute on computers distributed across the Internet. Microsoft's three primary programming languages are Visual Basic .NET (based on the original BASIC), Visual C++ .NET (based on C++) and C# (a new language based on C++ and Java that was developed expressly for the .NET platform). Developers using .NET can write software components in the language they are most familiar with and then form applications by combining those components with components written in any .NET language.

1.13 Typical Java Development Environment

We now explain the commonly used steps in creating and executing a Java application using a Java development environment (illustrated in Fig. 1.1).

Java programs normally go through five phases—*edit, compile, load, verify* and *execute*. We discuss these phases in the context of the *J2SE Development Kit (JDK) version 5.0* from Sun Microsystems, Inc., which will be wrapped with the book as an accompanying CD once Sun releases the final version of the JDK 5.0. If the CD for your book does not have the JDK on it, you can download both the JDK and its documentation now from `java.sun.com/j2se/5.0/download.jsp`. For help with the download, visit `servlet.java.sun.com/help/download`. *Carefully follow the installation instructions for the JDK provided on the CD (or at java.sun.com/j2se/5.0/install.html) to ensure that you set up your computer properly to compile and execute Java programs.* Complete installation instructions can also be found on Sun's Java Web site at

> `java.sun.com/learning/new2java/index.html`

[*Note:* This Web site provides installation instructions for Windows, UNIX/Linux and Mac OS X. If you are not using one of these operating systems, refer to the manuals for your system's Java environment or ask your instructor how to accomplish these tasks based on your computer's operating system. In addition, please keep in mind that Web links occasionally break as companies evolve their Web sites. If you encounter a problem with this link or any other links referenced in this book, please check our Web site (`www.deitel.com`) for errata and please notify us by e-mail at `deitel@deitel.com`. We will respond promptly.]

Phase 1: Creating a Program
Phase 1 consists of editing a file with an editor program (normally known simply as an editor). You type a Java program (typically referred to as source code) using the editor, make any necessary corrections and save the program on a secondary storage device, such as your hard drive. Java source-code file names end with the `.java` extension, which indicates that a file contains Java source code. We assume that the reader knows how to edit a file.

Two editors widely used on UNIX/Linux systems are `vi` and `emacs`. On Windows, a simple editing program like Windows Notepad will suffice. Many freeware and shareware editors are also available for download from the Internet on sites like `www.download.com`.

For organizations that develop substantial information systems, integrated development environments (IDEs) are available from many major software suppliers, including Sun Microsystems. IDEs provide many tools that support the software development process, including editors for writing and editing programs and debuggers for locating logic errors in programs.

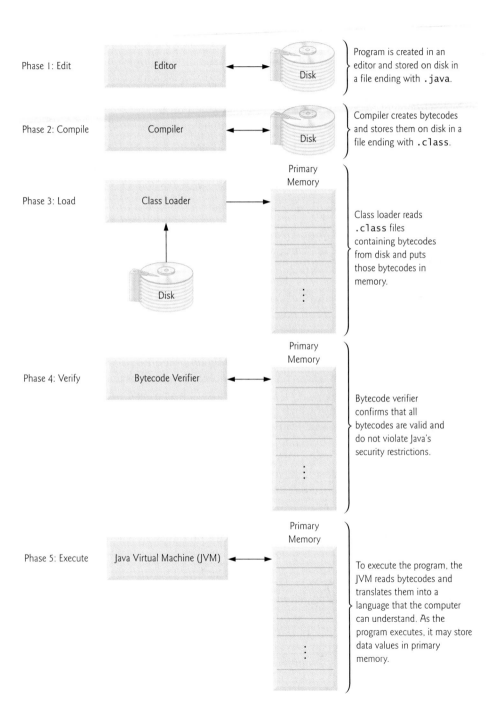

Fig. 1.1 | Typical Java development environment.

Several popular IDEs are NetBeans (www.netbeans.org), jEdit (www.jedit.org), Eclipse (www.eclipse.org), JBuilder (www.borland.com), JCreator (www.jcreator.com), BlueJ (www.blueJ.org) and jGRASP (www.jgrasp.org). Sun Microsystems has the Sun Java Studio (wwws.sun.com/software/sundev/jde/), which is an enhanced version of Net-Beans. [*Note:* NetBeans v. 3.6, jEdit v. 4.1, jGRASP v. 1.7 and BlueJ v. 1.3.5 are included on the CD that accompanies this book. These IDEs are designed to execute on most major platforms. Our example programs should operate properly with any Java integrated development environment that supports the JDK 5.0. We also provide free *Dive Into*™ guides for various IDEs on our Web site at www.deitel.com/books/sjhtp6/index.html.]

Phase 2: Compiling a Java Program into Bytecodes

In Phase 2, the programmer uses the command **javac** (the Java compiler) to compile a program. For example, to compile a program called Welcome.java, you would type

```
javac Welcome.java
```

in the command window of your system (i.e., the MS-DOS prompt in Windows 95/98/ME, the Command Prompt in Windows NT/2000/XP, the shell prompt in UNIX/Linux or the Terminal application in Mac OS X). If the program compiles, the compiler produces a .class file called Welcome.class that contains the compiled version of the program.

The Java compiler translates the Java source code into bytecodes that represent the tasks to be performed during the execution phase (Phase 5). Bytecodes are executed by the Java Virtual Machine (JVM)—a part of the JDK and the foundation of the Java platform. A virtual machine (VM) is a software application that simulates a computer, but hides the underlying operating system and hardware from the programs that interact with the VM. If the same VM is implemented on many computer platforms, applications that it executes can be used on all those platforms. The JVM is one of the most widely used virtual machines.

Unlike machine language, which is dependent on specific computer hardware, byte-codes are platform-independent instructions—they are not dependent on a particular hardware platform. So Java's bytecodes are portable—that is, the same bytecodes can execute on any platform containing a JVM that understands the version of Java in which the bytecodes were compiled. The JVM is invoked by the **java** command. For example, to execute a Java application called Welcome, you would type the command

```
java Welcome
```

in a command window to invoke the JVM, which would then initiate the steps necessary to execute the application. This begins Phase 3.

Phase 3: Loading a Program into Memory

In Phase 3, the program must be placed in memory before it can execute—a process known as loading. The class loader takes the .class files containing the program's bytecodes and transfers them to primary memory. The class loader also loads any of the .class files provided by Java that your program uses. The .class files can be loaded from a disk on your system or over a network (e.g., your local college or company network, or the Internet).

Phase 4: Bytecode Verification

In Phase 4, as the classes are loaded, the bytecode verifier examines their bytecodes to ensure that they are valid and do not violate Java's security restrictions. Java enforces strong security, to make sure that Java programs arriving over the network do not damage your files or your system (as computer viruses and worms might).

Phase 5: Execution

In Phase 5, the JVM executes the program's bytecodes, thus performing the actions specified by the program. In early Java versions, the JVM was simply an interpreter for Java bytecodes. This caused most Java programs to execute slowly because the JVM would interpret and execute one bytecode at a time. Today's JVMs typically execute bytecodes using a combination of interpretation and so-called just-in-time (JIT) compilation. In this process, The JVM analyzes the bytecodes as they are interpreted, searching for hot spots—parts of the bytecodes that execute frequently. For these parts, a just-in-time (JIT) compiler—known as the Java HotSpot compiler—translates the bytecodes into the underlying computer's machine language. When the JVM encounters these compiled parts again, the faster machine-language code executes. Thus Java programs actually go through two compilation phases—one in which source code is translated into bytecodes (for portability across JVMs on different computer platforms) and a second in which, during execution, the bytecodes are translated into machine language for the actual computer on which the program executes.

Problems That May Occur at Execution Time

Programs might not work on the first try. Each of the preceding phases can fail because of various errors that we will discuss throughout this book. For example, an executing program might attempt to divide by zero (an illegal operation for whole-number arithmetic in Java). This would cause the Java program to display an error message. If this occurs, you would have to return to the edit phase, make the necessary corrections and proceed through the remaining phases again to determine that the corrections fix the problem(s). [*Note:* Most programs in Java input or output data. When we say that a program displays a message, we normally mean that it displays that message on your computer's screen. Messages and other data may be output to other devices, such as disks and hardcopy printers, or even to a network for transmission to other computers.]

 Common Programming Error 1.1

Errors like division by zero occur as a program runs, so they are called runtime errors or execution-time errors. Fatal runtime errors cause programs to terminate immediately without having successfully performed their jobs. Nonfatal runtime errors allow programs to run to completion, often producing incorrect results.

1.14   Notes about Java and *Small Java How to Program, Sixth Edition*

Java is a powerful programming language. Experienced programmers sometimes take pride in creating weird, contorted, convoluted usage of a language. This is a poor programming practice. It makes programs more difficult to read, more likely to behave strangely, more difficult to test and debug, and more difficult to adapt to changing requirements. This book stresses *clarity*. The following is our first "good programming practice" tip.

 Good Programming Practice 1.1

Write your Java programs in a simple and straightforward manner. This is sometimes referred to as KIS ("keep it simple"). Do not "stretch" the language by trying bizarre usages.

You have heard that Java is a portable language and that programs written in Java can run on many different computers. For programming in general, *portability is an elusive goal.* The ANSI C standard document (located at www.ansi.org), which describes the C programming language, contains a lengthy list of portability issues. In fact, whole books have been written to discuss portability, such as Rex Jaeschke's *Portability and the C Language.*

Portability Tip 1.2

Although it is easier to write portable programs in Java than in other programming languages, differences between compilers, JVMs and computers can make portability difficult to achieve. Simply writing programs in Java does not guarantee portability.

Error-Prevention Tip 1.1

Always test your Java programs on all systems on which you intend to run them, to ensure that they will work correctly for their intended audiences.

We have audited our presentation against Sun's current Java documentation for completeness and accuracy. However, Java is a rich language, and no textbook can cover every topic. A Web-based version of the Java API documentation can be found at java.sun.com/j2se/5.0/docs/api/index.html or you can download this documentation to your own computer from java.sun.com/j2se/5.0/download.html. For additional technical details on Java, visit java.sun.com/reference/docs/index.html. This site provides detailed information about many aspects of Java development, including all three Java platforms.

Good Programming Practice 1.2

Read the documentation for the version of Java you are using. Refer to it frequently to be sure you are aware of the rich collection of Java features and are using them correctly.

Good Programming Practice 1.3

Your computer and compiler are good teachers. If, after carefully reading your Java documentation manual, you are not sure how a feature of Java works, experiment and see what happens. Study each error or warning message you get when you compile your programs (called compile-time errors or compilation errors), and correct the programs to eliminate these messages.

Software Engineering Observation 1.4

The J2SE Development Kit comes with the Java source code. Some programmers like to read the source code for the Java API classes to determine how the classes work and to learn additional programming techniques.

1.15 Test-Driving a Java Application

In this section, you will run and interact with your first Java application. You will begin by running an ATM application that simulates the transactions that take place when using an ATM machine (e.g., withdrawing money, making deposits and checking account balances). We borrowed this application from the optional, object-oriented case study found in our sister book, *Java How to Program, Sixth Edition.* Figure 1.10 at the end of this section suggests additional interesting applications that you may also want to test-drive after completing the ATM test-drive.

In the following steps, you will run the application and perform various transactions. The elements and functionality you see in this application are typical of what you will learn to program in this book. [*Note:* We use fonts to distinguish between features you see on a screen (e.g., the **Command Prompt**) and elements that are not directly related to a screen. Our convention is to emphasize screen features like titles and menus (e.g., the **File** menu) in a semibold sans-serif Helvetica font and to emphasize non-screen elements, such as file names or input (e.g., ProgramName.java) in a sans-serif Lucida font. As you have already noticed, the defining occurrence of each term is set in blue, heavy bold. In the figures in this section, we highlight in yellow the user input required by each step and point out significant parts of the application with lines and text. To make these features more visible, we have modified the background color of the **Command Prompt** windows.]

1. *Checking your setup.* Read the *For Students and Instructors: Important Information Before You Begin* section to confirm that you have set up Java properly on your computer and that you have copied the book's examples to your hard drive.

2. *Locating the completed application.* Open a **Command Prompt** window. For readers using Windows 95, 98 or 2000, this can be done by selecting **Start > Programs > Accessories > Command Prompt**. For Windows XP users, select **Start > All Programs > Accessories > Command Prompt**. Change to your completed ATM application directory by typing cd C:\examples\ch01\ATM and then pressing *Enter* (Fig. 1.2). The command cd is used to change directories.

3. *Running the ATM application.* Now that you are in the directory that contains the ATM application, type the command java ATMCaseStudy (Fig. 1.3) and press *Enter*. Remember from the preceding section that the java command, followed by the name of the application's .class file (in this case, ATMCaseStudy), executes the application. It is not necessary to specify the .class extension when using the java command. [*Note:* Java commands are case sensitive. It is important to type the name of this application with a capital A, T and M in "ATM," a capital C in "Case" and a capital S in "Study." Otherwise, the application will not execute.]

4. *Entering an account number.* When the application first executes, it displays a "Welcome!" greeting and prompts you for an account number. Type 12345 at the "Please enter your account number:" prompt (Fig. 1.4) and press *Enter*.

Using the cd command to change directories

File location of the ATM application

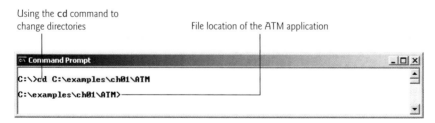

Fig. 1.2 | Opening a Windows XP **Command Prompt** and changing directories.

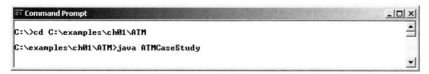

Fig. 1.3 | Using the java command to execute the ATM application.

ATM welcome message   Enter account number prompt

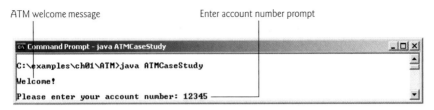

Fig. 1.4 | Prompting the user for an account number.

5. *Entering a PIN.* Once a valid account number is entered, the application displays the prompt "Enter your PIN:". Type "54321" as your valid PIN (Personal Identification Number) and press *Enter.* The ATM main menu containing a list of options will be displayed (Fig. 1.5).

6. *Viewing the account balance.* Select option 1, "View my balance", from the ATM menu. The application then displays two numbers—the Available balance ($1000.00) and the Total balance ($1,200.00). The available balance is the maximum amount of money in your account which is available for withdrawal at a given time. In some cases, certain funds, such as recent deposits, are not immediately available for the user to withdraw, so the available balance may be less than the total balance, as it is here. After the account balance information is shown, the application's main menu is displayed again (Fig. 1.6).

Enter valid PIN   ATM main menu

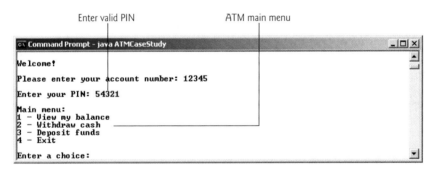

Fig. 1.5 | Entering a valid PIN number and displaying the ATM application's main menu.

Account balance information

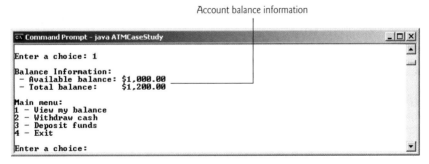

Fig. 1.6 | ATM application displaying user account balance information.

7. ***Withdrawing money from the account.*** Select option 2, `"Withdraw cash"`, from the application menu. You are then presented (Fig. 1.7) with a list of dollar amounts (e.g., 20, 40, 60, 100 and 200). You are also given the option to cancel the transaction and return to the main menu. Withdraw $100 by selecting option 4. The application displays `"Please take your cash now."` and returns to the main menu. [*Note:* Unfortunately, this application only *simulates* the behavior of a real ATM and thus does not actually dispense money.]

8. ***Confirming that the account information has been updated.*** From the main menu, select option 1 again to view your current account balance. Note that both the available balance and the total balance have been updated to reflect your withdrawal transaction (Fig. 1.8).

9. ***Ending the transaction.*** To end your current ATM session, select option 4, `"Exit"` from the main menu. The ATM will exit the system and display a goodbye message to the user. The application will then return to its original prompt asking for the next user's account number (Fig. 1.9).

ATM withdrawal menu

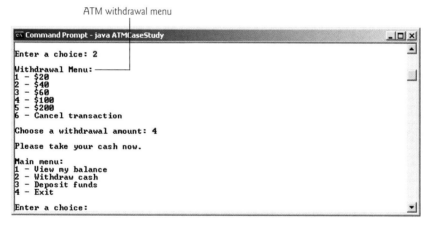

Fig. 1.7 | Withdrawing money from the account and returning to the main menu.

Confirming updated account balance
information after withdrawal transaction

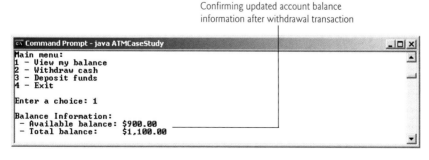

Fig. 1.8 | Checking new balance.

ATM goodbye message.   Account number prompt for next user

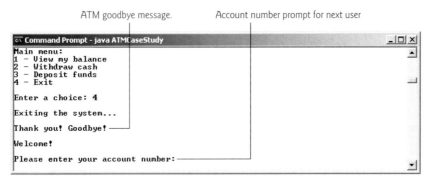

Fig. 1.9 | Ending an ATM transaction session.

10. *Exiting the ATM application and closing the* **Command Prompt** *window.* Most applications provide an option to exit and return to the **Command Prompt** directory from which the application was run. A real ATM does not provide a user with the option to turn off the ATM machine. Rather, when a user has completed all desired transactions and chooses the menu option to exit, the ATM resets itself and displays a prompt for the next user's account number. As Fig. 1.9 illustrates, the ATM application here behaves similarly. Choosing the menu option to exit ends only the current user's ATM session, not the entire ATM application. To actually exit the ATM application, click the close (**x**) button in the upper-right corner of the **Command Prompt** window. Closing the window causes the running application to terminate.

Additional Applications Found in **Small Java How to Program, 6/e**
We encourage you to practice running some of the Java applications featured in this textbook. Figure 1.10 lists a few of the hundreds of applications found in the examples and exercises in this text. Many of these programs simulate real-world applications and introduce the powerful and fun features of Java programming. Please feel free to run any or all of the programs listed to see some of the different types of applications you will learn how to build as you study the programming concepts in this textbook. The examples folder for Chapter 1 contains all the files required to run each application. You can do so by typing the commands listed in Fig. 1.10 in a **Command Prompt** window.

Application Name	Chapter Location	Commands to Run
Guessing Game	Chapter 6	`cd C:\examples\ch01\GuessGame` `java GuessGame`
Math Tutor	Chapter 6	`cd C:\examples\ch01\MathTutor` `java MathTutor`
Tic-Tac-Toe	Chapter 8	`cd C:\examples\ch01\Tic-Tac-Toe` `java TicTacToeTest`
Random Shapes	Chapter 9	`cd C:\examples\ch01\Shapes` `java Shapes`

Fig. 1.10 | Sample Java applications found in *Small Java How to Program, 6/e*.

1.16 Introduction to Object Technology and the UML

Now we begin our early introduction to object orientation, a natural way of thinking about the world and writing computer programs. Our goal here is to help you develop an object-oriented way of thinking and to introduce you to the Unified Modeling Language™ (UML™)—a graphical language that allows people who design software systems to use an industry standard notation to represent them.

Basic Object Technology Concepts

We begin our introduction to object orientation with some key terminology. Everywhere you look in the real world you see objects—people, animals, plants, cars, planes, buildings, computers and so on. Humans think in terms of objects. Telephones, houses, traffic lights, microwave ovens and water coolers are just a few more objects we see around us every day. Computer programs, such as the Java programs you will read in this book and the ones you will write, can also be viewed as objects, composed of lots of interacting software objects.

We sometimes divide objects into two categories: animate and inanimate. Animate objects are "alive" in some sense—they move around and do things. Inanimate objects, on the other hand, do not move on their own. Objects of both types, however, have some things in common. They all have attributes (e.g., size, shape, color and weight), and they all exhibit behaviors (e.g., a ball rolls, bounces, inflates and deflates; a baby cries, sleeps, crawls, walks and blinks; a car accelerates, brakes and turns; a towel absorbs water). We will study the kinds of attributes and behaviors that software objects have.

Humans learn about existing objects by studying their attributes and observing their behaviors. Different objects can have similar attributes and can exhibit similar behaviors. Comparisons can be made, for example, between babies and adults and between humans and chimpanzees.

Object-oriented design (OOD) models software in terms similar to those that people use to describe real-world objects. It takes advantage of class relationships, where objects of a certain class, such as a class of vehicles, have the same characteristics—cars, trucks, little red wagons and roller skates have much in common. OOD also takes advantage of inheritance relationships, where new classes of objects are derived by absorbing characteristics of existing classes and adding unique characteristics of their own. An object of class "convertible" certainly has the characteristics of the more general class "automobile," but more specifically, the roof goes up and down.

Object-oriented design provides a natural and intuitive way to view the software design process—namely, modeling objects by their attributes and behaviors just as we describe real-world objects. OOD also models communication between objects. Just as people send messages to one another (e.g., a sergeant commands a soldier to stand at attention), objects also communicate via messages. A bank account object may receive a message to decrease its balance by a certain amount because the customer has withdrawn that amount of money.

OOD encapsulates (i.e., wraps) attributes and operations (behaviors) into objects—an object's attributes and operations are intimately tied together. Objects have the property of information hiding. This means that objects may know how to communicate with one another across well-defined interfaces, but normally they are not allowed to know how other objects are implemented—implementation details are hidden within the objects themselves. We can drive a car effectively, for instance, without knowing the details of how engines, transmissions, brakes and exhaust systems work internally—as long as we know how to use the accelerator pedal, the brake pedal, the wheel and so on. Information hiding, as we will see, is crucial to good software engineering.

Languages like Java are object oriented. Programming in such a language is called object-oriented programming (OOP), and it allows computer programmers to implement an object-oriented design as a working system. Languages like C, on the other hand, are procedural, so programming tends to be action oriented. In C, the unit of programming is the function. Groups of actions that perform some common task are formed into functions, and functions are grouped to form programs. In Java, the unit of programming is the class from which objects are eventually instantiated (created). Java classes contain methods (which implement operations and are similar to functions in C) as well as fields (which implement attributes).

Java programmers concentrate on creating classes. Each class contains fields and the set of methods that manipulate the fields and provide services to clients (i.e., other classes that use the class). The programmer uses existing classes as the building blocks for constructing new classes.

Classes are to objects as blueprints are to houses. Just as we can build many houses from one blueprint, we can instantiate (create) many objects from one class. You cannot cook meals in the kitchen of a blueprint; you can cook meals in the kitchen of a house.

Classes can have relationships with other classes. For example, in an object-oriented design of a bank, the "bank teller" class needs to relate to the "customer" class, the "cash drawer" class, the "safe" class, and so on. These relationships are called associations.

Packaging software as classes makes it possible for future software systems to reuse the classes. Groups of related classes are often packaged as reusable components. Just as realtors often say that the three most important factors affecting the price of real estate are "location, location and location," people in the software community often say that the three most important factors affecting the future of software development are "reuse, reuse and reuse." Reuse of existing classes when building new classes and programs saves time and effort. Reuse also helps programmers build more reliable and effective systems, because existing classes and components often have gone through extensive testing, debugging and performance tuning.

Indeed, with object technology, you can build much of the software you will need by combining classes, just as automobile manufacturers combine interchangeable parts. Each new class you create will have the potential to become a valuable software asset that you and other programmers can use to speed and enhance the quality of future software development efforts.

Introduction to Object-Oriented Analysis and Design (OOAD)

Soon you will be writing programs in Java. How will you create the code for your programs? Perhaps, like many beginning programmers, you will simply turn on your computer and start typing. This approach may work for small programs (like the ones we present in the early chapters of the book), but what if you were asked to create a software system to control thousands of automated teller machines for a major bank? Or suppose you were asked to work on a team of 1,000 software developers building the next U.S. air traffic control system. For projects so large and complex, you could not sit down and simply start writing programs.

To create the best solutions, you should follow a detailed process for analyzing your project's requirements (i.e., determining *what* the system is supposed to do) and developing a design that satisfies them (i.e., deciding *how* the system should do it). Ideally, you would go through this process and carefully review the design (or have your design reviewed by other software professionals) before writing any code. If this process involves analyzing and designing your system from an object-oriented point of view, it is called an object-oriented analysis and design (OOAD) process. Experienced programmers know that analysis and design can save many hours by helping them to avoid an ill-planned system-development approach that has to be abandoned part of the way through its implementation, possibly wasting considerable time, money and effort.

OOAD is the generic term for the process of analyzing a problem and developing an approach for solving it. Small problems like the ones discussed in these first few chapters do not require an exhaustive OOAD process. It may be sufficient to write pseudocode before we begin writing Java code—pseudocode is an informal means of expressing program logic. It is not actually a programming language, but we can use it as a kind of outline to guide us as we write our code. We introduce pseudocode in Chapter 4.

As problems and the groups of people solving them increase in size, the methods of OOAD become more appropriate than pseudocode. Ideally, a group should agree on a strictly defined process for solving its problem and a uniform way of communicating the results of that process to one another. Although many different OOAD processes exist, a single graphical language for communicating the results of *any* OOAD process has come into wide use. This language, known as the Unified Modeling Language (UML), was developed in the mid-1990s under the initial direction of three software methodologists: Grady Booch, James Rumbaugh and Ivar Jacobson.

History of the UML

In the 1980s, increasing numbers of organizations began using OOP to build their applications, and a need developed for a standard OOAD process. Many methodologists—including Booch, Rumbaugh and Jacobson—individually produced and promoted separate processes to satisfy this need. Each process had its own notation, or "language" (in the form of graphical diagrams), to convey the results of analysis and design.

By the early 1990s, different organizations, and even divisions within the same organization, were using their own unique processes and notations. At the same time, these organizations also wanted to use software tools that would support their particular processes. Software vendors found it difficult to provide tools for so many processes. Clearly, a standard notation and standard processes were needed.

In 1994, James Rumbaugh joined Grady Booch at Rational Software Corporation (now a division of IBM), and the two began working to unify their popular processes. They soon were joined by Ivar Jacobson. In 1996, the group released early versions of the UML to the software engineering community and requested feedback. Around the same time, an organization known as the Object Management Group™ (OMG™) invited submissions for a common modeling language. The OMG (www.omg.org) is a nonprofit organization that promotes the standardization of object-oriented technologies by issuing guidelines and specifications, such as the UML. Several corporations—among them HP, IBM, Microsoft, Oracle and Rational Software—had already recognized the need for a common modeling language. In response to the OMG's request for proposals, these companies formed UML Partners—the consortium that developed the UML version 1.1 and submitted it to the OMG. The OMG accepted the proposal and, in 1997, assumed responsibility for the continuing maintenance and revision of the UML. In March 2003, the OMG released UML version 1.5. The UML version 2 now under development marks the first major revision of the UML since the 1997 version 1.1 standard. Owing to the forthcoming adoption of UML 2 by the OMG and the fact that many books, modeling tools and industry experts are already using UML 2, we present UML 2 terminology and notation throughout this book.

What Is the UML?

The Unified Modeling Language is now the most widely used graphical representation scheme for modeling object-oriented systems. It has indeed unified the various popular notational schemes. Those who design systems use the language (in the form of diagrams) to model their systems.

An attractive feature of the UML is its flexibility. The UML is extensible (i.e., capable of being enhanced with new features) and is independent of any particular OOAD process. UML modelers are free to use various processes in designing systems, but all developers can now express their designs with one standard set of graphical notations.

The UML is a complex, feature-rich graphical language. We use a simple, concise subset of these features to illustrate certain object-oriented programming concepts throughout the book.

Internet and Web UML Resources

For more information about the UML, refer to the following Web sites.

`www.uml.org`
This UML resource page from the Object Management Group (OMG) provides specification documents for the UML and other object-oriented technologies.

`www-306.ibm.com/software/rational/uml`
This is the UML resource page for IBM Rational—the successor to the Rational Software Corporation (the company that created the UML).

`www.softdocwiz.com/Dictionary.htm`
Hosts the Unified Modeling Language Dictionary, which lists and defines all terms used in the UML.

`www-306.ibm.com/software/rational/offerings/design.html`
Provides information about IBM Rational software available for designing systems. Provides downloads of 30-day trial versions of several products, such as IBM Rational Rose® XDE Developer.

`www.embarcadero.com/products/describe/index.html`
Provides a free 15-day license to download a trial version of Describe™—a UML modeling tool from Embarcadero Technologies®.

`www.borland.com/together/index.html`
Provides a free 30-day license to download a trial version of Borland® Together® Control-Center™—a software-development tool that supports the UML.

`www.ilogix.com/rhapsody/rhapsody.cfm`
Provides a free 30-day license to download a trial version of I-Logix Rhapsody®—a UML 2 based model-driven development environment.

`argouml.tigris.org`
Contains information and downloads for ArgoUML, a free open-source UML tool written in Java.

`www.objectsbydesign.com/books/booklist.html`
Lists books on the UML and object-oriented design.

`www.objectsbydesign.com/tools/umltools_byCompany.html`
Lists software tools that use the UML, such as IBM Rational Rose, Embarcadero Describe, Sparx Systems Enterprise Architect, I-Logix Rhapsody and Gentleware Poseidon for UML.

`www.ootips.org/ood-principles.html`
Provides answers to the question, "What Makes a Good Object-Oriented Design?"

`www.parlezuml.com/tutorials/java/class/index_files/frame.htm`
Provides a UML tutorial for Java developers that presents UML diagrams side by side with the Java code that implements them.

`www.cetus-links.org/oo_uml.html`
Introduces the UML and provides links to numerous UML resources.

`www.agilemodeling.com/essays/umlDiagrams.htm`
Provides in-depth descriptions and tutorials on each of the 13 UML 2 diagram types.

Recommended Readings

Many books on the UML have been published. The following recommended books provide information about object-oriented design with the UML.

Arlow, J., and I. Neustadt. *UML and the Unified Process: Practical Object-Oriented Analysis and Design.* London: Pearson Education Ltd., 2002.

Booch, G. *Object-Oriented Analysis and Design with Applications.* 3/e. Boston: Addison-Wesley, 2004.

Eriksson, H., et al. *UML 2 Toolkit.* New York: John Wiley, 2003.

Fowler, M. *UML Distilled, Third Edition: A Brief Guide to the Standard Object Modeling Language.* Boston: Addison-Wesley, 2004.

Kruchten, P. *The Rational Unified Process: An Introduction.* Boston: Addison-Wesley, 2004.

Larman, C. *Applying UML and Patterns: An Introduction to Object-Oriented Analysis and Design.* 2nd ed. Upper Saddle River, NJ: Prentice Hall, 2002.

Reed, P. *Developing Applications with Java and UML.* Boston: Addison-Wesley, 2002.

Roques, P. *UML in Practice: The Art of Modeling Software Systems Demonstrated Through Worked Examples and Solutions.* New York: John Wiley, 2004.

Rosenberg, D., and K. Scott. *Applying Use Case Driven Object Modeling with UML: An Annotated e-Commerce Example.* Reading, MA: Addison-Wesley, 2001.

Rumbaugh, J., I. Jacobson and G. Booch. *The Complete UML Training Course.* Upper Saddle River, NJ: Prentice Hall, 2000.

Rumbaugh, J., I. Jacobson and G. Booch. *The Unified Modeling Language Reference Manual.* Reading, MA: Addison-Wesley, 1999.

Rumbaugh, J., I. Jacobson and G. Booch. *The Unified Modeling Language User Guide.* Reading, MA: Addison-Wesley, 1999.

Rumbaugh, J., I. Jacobson and G. Booch. *The Unified Software Development Process.* Reading, MA: Addison-Wesley, 1999.

For additional books on the UML, please visit `www.amazon.com` or `www.bn.com`. IBM Rational, formerly Rational Software Corporation, also provides a recommended-reading list for UML books at `www.ibm.com/software/rational/info/technical/books.jsp`.

Section 1.16 Self-Review Exercises

1.1   List three examples of real-world objects that we did not mention. For each object, list several attributes and behaviors.

1.2   Pseudocode is _____.
   a)   another term for OOAD
   b)   a programming language used to display UML diagrams
   c)   an informal means of expressing program logic
   d)   a graphical representation scheme for modeling object-oriented systems

1.3   The UML is used primarily to _____.
   a)   test object-oriented systems
   b)   design object-oriented systems
   c)   implement object-oriented systems
   d)   Both a and b

Answers to Section 1.16 Self-Review Exercises

1.1   [*Note:* Answers may vary.] a) A television's attributes include the size of the screen, the number of colors it can display, its current channel and its current volume. A television turns on and off, changes channels, displays video and plays sounds. b) A coffee maker's attributes include the maximum volume of water it can hold, the time required to brew a pot of coffee and the temperature of the heating plate under the coffee pot. A coffee maker turns on and off, brews coffee and heats coffee. c) A turtle's attributes include its age, the size of its shell and its weight. A turtle walks, retreats into its shell, emerges from its shell and eats vegetation.

1.2   c.

1.3   b.

1.17 Wrap-Up

This chapter introduced basic hardware and software concepts, and basic object technology concepts, including classes, objects, attributes, behaviors, encapsulation, inheritance and polymorphism. We discussed the different types of programming languages and which programming languages are most widely used. You learned the steps for creating and executing a Java application using Sun's JDK 5.0. The chapter explored the history of the Internet and the World Wide Web and Java's role in developing distributed client/server applications for the Internet and the Web. You also learned about the history and purpose of the UML—the industry-standard graphical language for modeling software systems. Finally, you "test drove" a sample Java application similar to the types of applications you will learn to program in this book.

In the next chapter, you will create your first Java applications. You will see several examples that demonstrate how programs display messages and obtain information from the user for processing. We closely analyze and explain each example to help ease your way into Java programming.

1.18 Web Resources

This section provides many Web resources that will be useful to you as you learn Java. The sites include Java resources, Java development tools for students and professionals, and our own Web sites where you can find downloads and resources associated with this book. We also provide a link where you can subscribe to our free *Deitel Buzz Online* e-mail newsletter.

Deitel & Associates Web Sites

www.deitel.com/books/sjhtp6/index.html
The Deitel & Associates home page for *Small Java How to Program, Sixth Edition*. Here you will find links to the book's examples (also included on the CD that accompanies the book) and other resources, such as our free *Dive Into*™ guides that help you get started with several Java IDEs.

www.deitel.com
Please check the Deitel & Associates home page for updates, corrections and additional resources for all Deitel publications.

www.deitel.com/newsletter/subscribe.html
Please visit this site to subscribe to the free *Deitel Buzz Online* e-mail newsletter to follow the Deitel & Associates publishing program.

www.prenhall.com/deitel
Prentice Hall's home page for Deitel publications. Here you will find detailed product information, sample chapters and *Companion Web Sites* containing book- and chapter-specific resources for students and instructors.

Sun Microsystems Web Sites

java.sun.com
Sun's home page for Java technology. Here you will find downloads, reference guides for developers, community forums, online tutorials and many other valuable Java resources.

java.sun.com/j2se
The home page for the Java 2 Platform, Standard Edition.

java.sun.com/j2se/5.0/download.jsp
The download page for the Java 2 Platform, Standard Edition version 5.0 and its documentation. This development kit includes everything you need to compile and execute your Java applications. Please note that as Sun updates Java, the number 5.0 in the preceding URL will change. You can always go to java.sun.com/j2se to locate the most recent version of Java.

java.sun.com/j2se/5.0/install.html
Instructions for installing the JDK version 5.0 on Solaris, Windows and Linux platforms. Please check this site if you are having difficulty installing Java on your computer. Also please note that as Java is updated, 5.0 in the preceding URL will change. You can always go to java.sun.com/j2se to locate the most recent version of Java.

java.sun.com/learning/new2java/index.html
The "New to Java Center" on the Sun Microsystems Web site features online training resources to help you get started with Java programming.

java.sun.com/j2se/5.0/docs/api/index.html
This site provides the Java 2 Platform, Standard Edition version 5.0 API documentation. Refer to this site to learn about the Java class library's predefined classes and interfaces.

java.sun.com/reference/docs/index.html
Sun's documentation site for all Java technologies. Here you will find technical information on all Java technologies, including API (application programming interface) specifications for Java and related Sun technologies.

java.sun.com/products/hotspot
Product information page for Sun's HotSpot virtual machine and compiler, a standard component of the Java 2 Runtime Environment and the JDK.

developers.sun.com
Sun's home page for Java developers provides downloads, APIs, code samples, articles with technical advice and other resources on the best Java development practices.

Editors and Integrated Development Environments

www.download.com

A site that contains freeware and shareware application downloads. In particular, several editors are available at this site that can be used to edit Java source code.

www.eclipse.org

The home page for the Eclipse development environment, which can be used to develop code in any programming language. You can download the environment and several Java plug-ins to use this environment to develop your Java programs.

www.netbeans.org

The home page for the NetBeans IDE, one of the most widely used, freely distributed Java development tools.

borland.com/products/downloads/download_jbuilder.html

Borland provides a free Foundation Edition version of its popular Java IDE JBuilder. The site also provides 30-day trial versions of the Enterprise and Developer editions.

www.blueJ.org

The home page for the BlueJ environment—a tool designed to help teach object-oriented Java to new programmers. BlueJ is available as a free download.

www.jgrasp.org

The home page for jGRASP provides downloads, documentation and tutorials for this tool that displays visual representations of Java programs to aid comprehension.

www.jedit.org

The home page for jEdit—a text editor for programmers that is written in Java.

wwws.sun.com/software/sundev/jde/

The home page for Sun Java Studio—the Sun Microsystems enhanced version of NetBeans.

www.jcreator.com

The home page for JCreator—a popular Java IDE. JCreator Lite Edition is available as a free download. A 30-day trial version of JCreator Pro Edition is also available.

Additional Java Resource Sites

www.javalobby.org

Provides up-to-date Java news, forums where developers can exchange tips and advice, and a comprehensive Java knowledge base organizing articles and downloads from across the Web.

www.jguru.com

Provides forums, downloads, articles, online courses and a large collection of Java FAQs (Frequently Asked Questions).

www.javaworld.com

Provides resources for Java developers, such as articles, indices of popular Java books, tips and FAQs.

www.ftponline.com/javapro

The home page for the JavaPro magazine features monthly articles, programming tips, book reviews and more.

sys-con.com/java/

The home page for the Java Developer's Journal from Sys-Con Media, provides articles, e-books and other Java resources.

Summary

- The various devices that comprise a computer system (e.g., the keyboard, screen, disks, memory and processing units) are referred to as hardware.
- The computer programs that run on a computer are referred to as software.
- Java is one of today's most popular software development languages. Java is a fully object-oriented language with strong support for proper software-engineering techniques.
- A computer is a device capable of performing computations and making logical decisions at speeds millions, even billions, of times faster than humans can.
- Computers process data under the control of sets of instructions called computer programs. Computer programs guide the computer through actions specified by computer programmers.
- The input unit is the "receiving" section of the computer. It obtains information from input devices and places it at the disposal of other units for processing.
- The output unit is the "shipping" section of the computer. It takes information processed by the computer and places it on output devices to make it available for use outside the computer.
- The memory unit is the rapid-access, relatively low-capacity "warehouse" section of the computer. It retains information that has been entered through the input unit, making it immediately available for processing when needed, and retains information that has already been processed until that information can be placed on output devices by the output unit.
- The arithmetic and logic unit (ALU) is the "manufacturing" section of the computer. It is responsible for performing calculations and making decisions.
- The central processing unit (CPU) is the "administrative" section of the computer. It coordinates and supervises the operation of the other sections.
- The secondary storage unit is the long-term, high-capacity "warehousing" section of the computer. Programs or data not being used by the other units are normally placed on secondary storage devices (e.g., disks) until they are needed, possibly hours, days, months or even years later.
- Software systems called operating systems were developed to help make it more convenient to use computers.
- Multiprogramming involves the sharing of a computer's resources among the jobs competing for its attention, so that the jobs appear to run simultaneously.
- With distributed computing, an organization's computing is distributed over networks to the sites where the work of the organization is performed.
- Java has become the language of choice for developing Internet-based applications.
- Any computer can directly understand only its own machine language. Machine languages generally consist of strings of numbers (ultimately reduced to 1s and 0s) that instruct computers to perform their most elementary operations one at a time.
- English-like abbreviations form the basis of assembly languages. Translator programs called assemblers convert assembly-language programs to machine language.
- Compilers translate high-level language programs into machine-language programs. High-level languages (like Java) contain English words and conventional mathematical notations.
- Interpreter programs directly execute high-level language programs, eliminating the need to compile them into machine language.
- Java is used to create Web pages with dynamic and interactive content, develop large-scale enterprise applications, enhance the functionality of Web servers, provide applications for consumer devices and more.
- Java programs consist of pieces called classes. Classes include pieces called methods that perform tasks and return information when they complete their tasks.

- C++ is an extension of C developed by Bjarne Stroustrup in the early 1980s at Bell Laboratories. C++ provides a number of features that "spruce up" the C language, but more important, it provides capabilities for object-oriented programming.

- FORTRAN (FORmula TRANslator) was developed by IBM Corporation in the mid-1950s for scientific and engineering applications that require complex mathematical computations.

- COBOL (COmmon Business Oriented Language) was developed in the late 1950s by a group of computer manufacturers and government and industrial computer users. COBOL is used primarily for commercial applications that require precise and efficient data manipulation.

- Ada was developed under the sponsorship of the United States Department of Defense (DOD) during the 1970s and early 1980s. One important capability of Ada is multitasking—this allows programmers to specify that many activities are to occur in parallel. The Ada language was named after Lady Ada Lovelace, daughter of the poet Lord Byron. Lady Lovelace is credited with writing the world's first computer program in the early 1800s.

- The BASIC (Beginner's All-Purpose Symbolic Instruction Code) programming language was developed in the mid-1960s at Dartmouth College as a language for writing simple programs. BASIC's primary purpose was to familiarize novices with programming techniques.

- Microsoft's Visual Basic was introduced in the early 1990s to simplify the process of developing Microsoft Windows applications.

- Microsoft has a corporate-wide strategy for integrating the Internet and the Web into computer applications. This strategy is implemented in Microsoft's .NET platform, which provides developers with the capabilities they need to create and run computer applications that can execute on computers distributed across the Internet.

- The .NET platform's three primary programming languages are Visual Basic .NET (based on the original BASIC), Visual C++ .NET (based on C++) and C# (a new language based on C++ and Java that was developed expressly for the .NET platform).

- Developers using .NET can write software components in the language they are most familiar with and then form applications by combining those components with components written in any .NET language.

- Java, through a technique called multithreading, enables programmers to write programs with parallel activities.

- Java programs normally go through five phases—*edit, compile, load, verify* and *execute.*

- Java source code file names end with the .java extension.

- The Java compiler (javac) translates a Java program into bytecodes—instructions understood by the Java Virtual Machine (JVM), which executes Java programs. If a program compiles correctly, the compiler produces a file with the .class extension. This is the file containing the bytecodes that are executed by the JVM.

- A Java program must be placed in memory before it can execute. This is done by the class loader, which takes the .class file (or files) containing the bytecodes and transfers it to memory. The .class file can be loaded from a disk on your system or over a network.

- Object orientation is a natural way of thinking about the world and of writing computer programs.

- The Unified Modeling Language (UML) is a graphical language that allows people who build systems to represent their object-oriented designs in a common notation.

- Object-oriented design (OOD) models software components in terms of real-world objects. It takes advantage of class relationships, where objects of a certain class have the same characteristics. It also takes advantage of inheritance relationships, where newly created classes of objects are derived by absorbing characteristics of existing classes and adding unique characteristics of their own. OOD encapsulates data (attributes) and functions (behavior) into objects—the data and functions of an object are intimately tied together.

- Objects have the property of information hiding—objects normally are not allowed to know how other objects are implemented.

- Object-oriented programming (OOP) allows programmers to implement object-oriented designs as working systems.

- In Java, the unit of programming is the class from which objects are eventually instantiated. Java programmers concentrate on creating their own classes and reusing existing classes. Each class contains data and functions that manipulate that data. Function components are called methods.

- An instance of a class is called an object.

- Classes can have relationships with other classes. These relationships are called associations.

- With object technology, programmers can build much of the software they will need by combining standardized, interchangeable parts called classes.

- The process of analyzing and designing a system from an object-oriented point of view is called object-oriented analysis and design (OOAD).

Terminology

Ada
ALU (arithmetic and logic unit)
ANSI C
arithmetic and logic unit (ALU)
assembler
assembly language
attribute
BASIC
behavior
bytecode
bytecode verifier
C
C#
C++
central processing unit (CPU)
class
.class file
class libraries
class loader
client/server computing
COBOL
compile phase
compiler
compile-time error
computer
computer program
computer programmer
CPU (central processing unit)
disk
distributed computing
dynamic content

edit phase
editor
encapsulation
execute phase
execution-time error
fatal runtime error
file server
FORTRAN
hardware
high-level language
HotSpot™ compiler
HTML (Hypertext Markup Language)
IDE (Integrated Development Environment)
information hiding
inheritance
input device
input unit
input/output (I/O)
Internet
interpreter
Java
Java API (Java Application Programming Interface)
.java file-name extension
Java 2 Platform Standard Edition (J2SE)
Java 2 Platform Enterprise Edition (J2EE)
Java 2 Platform Micro Edition (J2ME)
J2SE Development Kit (JDK)
java interpreter
Java Virtual Machine (JVM)
javac compiler

JIT (just-in-time) compiler
KIS (keep it simple)
LAN (local area network)
legacy systems
live-code approach
load phase
machine language
memory unit
method
Microsoft Internet Explorer Web browser
modeling
multiprocessor
multiprogramming
multithreading
.NET
nonfatal runtime error
object
object-oriented design (OOD)
object-oriented programming (OOP)
operating system
output device
output unit
Pascal
personal computing

platform
portability
primary memory
problem statement
procedural programming
programmer-defined type
pseudocode
requirements document
reusable componentry
runtime error
secondary storage unit
software
software reuse
structured programming
Sun Microsystems
throughput
timesharing
translation
translator program
Unified Modeling Language (UML)
verify phase
Visual Basic .NET
Visual C++ .NET
World Wide Web

Self-Review Exercises

1.1   Fill in the blanks in each of the following statements:
    a) The company that popularized personal computing was _____.
    b) The computer that made personal computing legitimate in business and industry was the _____.
    c) Computers process data under the control of sets of instructions called _____.
    d) The six key logical units of the computer are the _____, _____, _____, _____, _____ and _____.
    e) The three classes of languages discussed in the chapter are _____, _____ and _____.
    f) The programs that translate high-level language programs into machine language are called _____.
    g) The _____ allows computer users to locate and view multimedia-based documents on almost any subject over the Internet.
    h) _____ allows a Java program to perform multiple activities in parallel.

1.2   Fill in the blanks in each of the following sentences about the Java environment:
    a) The _____ command from the J2SE Development Kit executes a Java application.
    b) The _____ command from the J2SE Development Kit compiles a Java program.
    c) A Java program file must end with the _____ file extension.
    d) When a Java program is compiled, the file produced by the compiler ends with the _____ file extension.
    e) The file produced by the Java compiler contains _____ that are executed by the Java Virtual Machine.

1.3   Fill in the blanks in each of the following statements (based on Section 1.16):

    a) Objects have the property of _____—although objects may know how to communicate with one another across well-defined interfaces, they normally are not allowed to know how other objects are implemented.

    b) Java programmers concentrate on creating _____, which contain fields and the set of methods that manipulate those fields and provide services to clients.

    c) Classes can have relationships with other classes. These relationships are called _____.

    d) The process of analyzing and designing a system from an object-oriented point of view is called _____.

    e) OOD also takes advantage of _____ relationships, where new classes of objects are derived by absorbing characteristics of existing classes then adding unique characteristics of their own.

    f) _____ is a graphical language that allows people who design software systems to use an industry standard notation to represent them.

    g) The size, shape, color and weight of an object are considered _____ of the object.

Answers to Self-Review Exercises

1.1   a) Apple. b) IBM Personal Computer. c) programs. d) input unit, output unit, memory unit, arithmetic and logic unit, central processing unit, secondary storage unit. e) machine languages, assembly languages, high-level languages. f) compilers. g) World Wide Web. h) Multithreading.

1.2   a) java. b) javac. c) .java. d) .class. e) bytecodes.

1.3   a) information hiding. b) classes. c) associations. d) object-oriented analysis and design (OOAD). e) inheritance. f) The Unified Modeling Language (UML). g) attributes.

Exercises

1.4   Categorize each of the following items as either hardware or software:

    a) CPU

    b) Java compiler

    c) JVM

    d) input unit

    e) editor

1.5   Fill in the blanks in each of the following statements:

    a) The logical unit of the computer that receives information from outside the computer for use by the computer is the _____.

    b) The process of instructing the computer to solve a problems is called _____.

    c) _____ is a type of computer language that uses English-like abbreviations for machine-language instructions.

    d) _____ is a logical unit of the computer that sends information which has already been processed to various devices so that it may be used outside the computer.

    e) _____ and _____ are logical units of the computer that retain information.

    f) _____ is a logical unit of the computer that performs calculations.

    g) _____ is a logical unit of the computer that makes logical decisions.

    h) _____ languages are most convenient to the programmer for writing programs quickly and easily.

    i) The only language that a computer can directly understand is that computer's _____.

    j) _____ is a logical unit of the computer that coordinates the activities of all the other logical units.

1.6   What is the difference between fatal errors and nonfatal errors? Why might you prefer to experience a fatal error rather than a nonfatal error?

1.7   Fill in the blanks in each of the following statements:
  a) _____ is now used to develop large-scale enterprise applications, to enhance the functionality of Web servers, to provide applications for consumer devices and for many other purposes.
  b) _____ was designed specifically for the .NET platform to enable programmers to migrate easily to .NET.
  c) _____ initially became widely known as the development language of the UNIX operating system.
  d) _____ was developed at Dartmouth College in the mid-1960s as a means of writing simple programs.
  e) _____ was developed by IBM Corporation in the mid-1950s to be used for scientific and engineering applications that require complex mathematical computations.
  f) _____ is used for commercial applications that require precise and efficient manipulation of large amounts of data.
  g) _____ was developed by Bjarne Stroustrup in the early 1980s at Bell Laboratories (now part of Lucent).

1.8   Fill in the blanks in each of the following statements (based on Section 1.13):
  a) Java programs normally go through five phases—_____, _____, _____, _____ and _____.
  b) A(n) _____ provides many tools that support the software development process, such as editors for writing and editing programs, debuggers for locating logic errors in programs and many other features.
  c) The command java invokes the _____, which executes Java programs.
  d) A(n) _____ is a software application that simulates a computer, but hides the underlying operating system and hardware from the programs that interact with the VM.
  e) A(n) _____ program can run on multiple platforms.
  f) The _____ takes the .class files containing the program's bytecodes and transfers them to primary memory.
  g) The _____ examines bytecodes to ensure that they are valid.

1.9   Explain the two compilation phases of Java programs.

Introduction to Java Applications

*What's in a name?
that which we call a rose
By any other name
would smell as sweet.*
—William Shakespeare

*When faced with a decision,
I always ask, "What would
be the most fun?"*
—Peggy Walker

*"Take some more tea," the
March Hare said to Alice,
very earnestly. "I've had
nothing yet, "Alice replied in
an offended tone: "so I can't
take more." "You mean you
can't take less," said the
Hatter: "it's very easy to take
more than nothing."*
—Lewis Carroll

OBJECTIVES

In this chapter you will learn:

- To write simple Java applications.

- To use input and output statements.

- Java's primitive types.

- Basic memory concepts.

- To use arithmetic operators.

- The precedence of arithmetic operators.

- To write decision-making statements.

- To use relational and equality operators.

2.1 Introduction

We now introduce Java application programming which facilitates a disciplined approach to program design. Most of the Java programs you will study in this book process information and display results. We present six examples that demonstrate how your programs can display messages and how they can obtain information from the user for processing. We begin with several examples that simply display messages on the screen. We then demonstrate a program that obtains two numbers from a user, calculates their sum and displays the result. You will learn how to perform various arithmetic calculations and save their results for later use. Many programs contain logic that requires the program to make decisions. The last example in this chapter demonstrates decision-making fundamentals by showing you how to compare numbers then display messages based on the comparison results. For example, the program displays a message indicating that two numbers are equal only if they have the same value. We analyze each example one line at a time to help you ease your way into Java programming. To help you apply the skills you learn here, we provide many fun and challenging problems in the chapter's exercises.

2.2 First Program in Java: Printing a Line of Text

Every time you use a computer, you execute various applications that perform tasks for you. For example, your e-mail application helps you send and receive e-mail, and your Web browser lets you view Web pages from Web sites around the world. Computer programmers create such applications by writing computer programs.

A Java application is a computer program that executes when you use the java command to launch the Java Virtual Machine (JVM). Let us consider a simple application that displays a line of text. (Later in this section we will discuss how to compile and run an application.) The program and its output are shown in Fig. 2.1. The output appears in the light blue box at the end of the program. The program illustrates several important Java language features. Java uses notations that may look strange to nonprogrammers. In addition, for your convenience, each program we present in this book includes line numbers, which are not part of actual Java programs. We will soon see that line 9 does the real work of the program—namely, displaying the phrase Welcome to Java Programming! on the screen. We now consider each line of the program in order.

```
 1   // Fig. 2.1: Welcome1.java
 2   // Text-printing program.
 3
 4   public class Welcome1
 5   {
 6      // main method begins execution of Java application
 7      public static void main( String args[] )
 8      {
 9         System.out.println( "Welcome to Java Programming!" );
10
11      } // end method main
12
13   } // end class Welcome1
```

```
Welcome to Java Programming!
```

Fig. 2.1 | Text-printing program.

Line 1

```
// Fig. 2.1: Welcome1.java
```

begins with //, indicating that the remainder of the line is a comment. Programmers insert comments to document programs and improve their readability. This helps other
people to read and understand programs. The Java compiler ignores comments, so they
do not cause the computer to perform any action when the program is run. We begin every
program with a comment indicating the figure number and file name.

A comment that begins with // is called an end-of-line (or single-line) comment,
because the comment terminates at the end of the line on which it appears. A // comment
also can begin in the middle of a line and continue until the end of that line (as in lines 11
and 13).

Traditional comments (also called multiple-line comments), such as

```
/* This is a traditional
   comment. It can be
   split over many lines */
```

can be spread over several lines. This type of comment begins with the delimiter /* and
ends with */. All text between the delimiters is ignored by the compiler. Java incorporated
traditional comments and end-of-line comments from the C and C++ programming languages, respectively. In this book, we use end-of-line comments.

Java also provides Javadoc comments that are delimited by /** and */. As with traditional comments, all text between the Javadoc comment delimiters is ignored by the
compiler. Javadoc comments enable programmers to embed program documentation
directly in their programs. Such comments are the preferred Java commenting format in
industry. The javadoc utility program (part of the J2SE Development Kit) reads Javadoc
comments and uses them to prepare your program's documentation in HTML format.
We demonstrate Javadoc comments and the javadoc utility in Appendix H. For complete
information, visit Sun's javadoc Tool Home Page at java.sun.com/j2se/javadoc.

Common Programming Error 2.1

Forgetting one of the delimiters of a traditional or Javadoc comment is a syntax error. The syntax of a programming language specifies the rules for creating a proper program in that language. A syntax error occurs when the compiler encounters code that violates Java's language rules (i.e., its syntax). In this case, the compiler does not produce a .class file. Instead, the compiler issues an error message to help the programmer identify and fix the incorrect code. Syntax errors are also called compiler errors, compile-time errors or compilation errors, because the compiler detects them during the compilation phase. You will be unable to execute your program until you correct all the syntax errors in it.

Line 2

```
// Text-printing program.
```

is an end-of-line comment that describes the purpose of the program.

Good Programming Practice 2.1

Every program should begin with a comment that explains the purpose of the program, the author and the date and time the program was last modified. (We are not showing the author, date and time in this book's programs because this information would be redundant.)

Line 3 is simply a blank line. Programmers use blank lines and space characters to make programs easier to read. Together, blank lines, space characters and tab characters are known as white space. (Space characters and tabs are known specifically as white-space characters.) White space is ignored by the compiler. In this chapter and the next several chapters, we discuss conventions for using white space to enhance program readability.

Good Programming Practice 2.2

Use blank lines and space characters to enhance program readability.

Line 4

```
public class Welcome1
```

begins a class declaration for class Welcome1. Every program in Java consists of at least one class declaration that is defined by you—the programmer. These are known as programmer-defined classes or user-defined classes. The class keyword introduces a class declaration in Java and is immediately followed by the class name (Welcome1). Keywords (sometimes called reserved words) are reserved for use by Java (we discuss the various keywords throughout the text) and are always spelled with all lowercase letters. The complete list of Java keywords is shown in Appendix C.

By convention, all class names in Java begin with a capital letter and capitalize the first letter of each word they include (e.g., SampleClassName). A Java class name is an identifier—a series of characters consisting of letters, digits, underscores (_) and dollar signs ($) that does not begin with a digit and does not contain spaces. Some valid identifiers are Welcome1, $value, _value, m_inputField1 and button7. The name 7button is not a valid identifier because it begins with a digit, and the name input field is not a valid identifier because it contains a space. Normally, an identifier that does not begin with a capital letter is not the name of a Java class. Java is case sensitive—that is, uppercase and lowercase letters are distinct, so a1 and A1 are different (but both valid) identifiers.

Good Programming Practice 2.3

By convention, always begin a class name's identifier with a capital letter and start each subsequent word in the identifier with a capital letter. Java programmers know that such identifiers normally represent Java classes, so naming your classes in this manner makes your programs more readable.

Common Programming Error 2.2

Java is case sensitive. Not using the proper uppercase and lowercase letters for an identifier normally causes a compilation error.

In Chapters 2–7, every class we define begins with the `public` keyword. For now, we will simply require this keyword. When you save your `public` class declaration in a file, the file name must be the class name followed by the ".`java`" file-name extension. For our application, the file name is `Welcome1.java`. You will learn more about `public` and non-`public` classes in Chapter 8.

Common Programming Error 2.3

It is an error for a `public` class to have a file name that is not identical to the class name (plus the .`java` extension) in terms of both spelling and capitalization.

Common Programming Error 2.4

It is an error not to end a file name with the .`java` extension for a file containing a class declaration. If that extension is missing, the Java compiler will not be able to compile the class declaration.

A left brace (at line 5 in this program), {, begins the body of every class declaration. A corresponding right brace (at line 13), }, must end each class declaration. Note that lines 6–11 are indented. This indentation is one of the spacing conventions mentioned earlier. We define each spacing convention as a Good Programming Practice.

Good Programming Practice 2.4

Whenever you type an opening left brace, {, in your program, immediately type the closing right brace, }, then reposition the cursor between the braces and indent to begin typing the body. This practice helps prevent errors due to missing braces.

Good Programming Practice 2.5

Indent the entire body of each class declaration one "level" of indentation between the left brace, {, and the right brace, }, that delimit the body of the class. This format emphasizes the class declaration's structure and makes it easier to read.

Good Programming Practice 2.6

Set a convention for the indent size you prefer, and then uniformly apply that convention. The Tab key may be used to create indents, but tab stops vary among text editors. We recommend using three spaces to form a level of indent.

Common Programming Error 2.5

It is a syntax error if braces do not occur in matching pairs.

Line 6

```
// main method begins execution of Java application
```

is an end-of-line comment indicating the purpose of lines 7–11 of the program. Line 7

```
public static void main( String args[] )
```

is the starting point of every Java application. The parentheses after the identifier main indicate that it is a program building block called a method. Java class declarations normally contain one or more methods. For a Java application, exactly one of the methods must be called main and must be defined as shown on line 7; otherwise, the JVM will not execute the application. Methods are able to perform tasks and return information when they complete their tasks. Keyword void indicates that this method will perform a task but will not return any information when it completes its task. Later, we will see that many methods return information when they complete their task. You will learn more about methods in Chapters 3 and 6. For now, simply mimic main's first line in your Java applications. In Line 7, the String args[] in parentheses is a required part of the method main's declaration. We discuss this in Chapter 7, Arrays.

The left brace, {, on line 8 begins the body of the method declaration. A corresponding right brace, }, must end the method declaration's body (line 11 of the program). Note that line 9 in the body of the method is indented between the braces.

Good Programming Practice 2.7

Indent the entire body of each method declaration one "level" of indentation between the left brace, {, and the right brace, }, that define the body of the method. This format makes the structure of the method stand out and makes the method declaration easier to read.

Line 9

```
System.out.println( "Welcome to Java Programming!" );
```

instructs the computer to perform an action—namely, to print the string of characters contained between the double quotation marks. A string is sometimes called a character string, a message or a string literal. We refer to characters between double quotation marks simply as strings. White-space characters in strings are not ignored by the compiler.

System.out is known as the standard output object. System.out allows Java applications to display sets of characters in the command window from which the Java application executes. In Microsoft Windows 95/98/ME, the command window is the MS-DOS prompt. In Microsoft Windows NT/2000/XP, the command window is the Command Prompt. In UNIX/Linux/Mac OS X, the command window is called a terminal window or a shell. Many programmers refer to the command window simply as the command line.

Method System.out.println displays (or prints) a line of text in the command window. The string in the parentheses on line 9 is the argument to the method. Method System.out.println performs its task by displaying (also called outputting) its argument in the command window. When System.out.println completes its task, it positions the output cursor (the location where the next character will be displayed) to the beginning of the next line in the command window. (This move of the cursor is similar to when a user presses the *Enter* key while typing in a text editor—the cursor appears at the beginning of the next line in the file.)

The entire line 9, including `System.out.println`, the argument `"Welcome to Java Programming!"` in the parentheses and the semicolon (;), is called a statement. Each statement ends with a semicolon. When the statement on line 9 of our program executes, it displays the message `Welcome to Java Programming!` in the command window. As we will see in subsequent programs, a method is typically composed of one or more statements that perform the method's task.

Common Programming Error 2.6

Omitting the semicolon at the end of a statement is a syntax error.

Error-Prevention Tip 2.1

When learning how to program, sometimes it is helpful to "break" a working program so you can familiarize yourself with the compiler's syntax-error messages. These messages do not always state the exact problem in the code. When you encounter such syntax-error messages in the future, you will have an idea of what caused the error. Try removing a semicolon or brace from the program of Fig. 2.1, then recompile the program to see the error messages generated by the omission.

Error-Prevention Tip 2.2

When the compiler reports a syntax error, the error may not be on the line number indicated by the error message. First, check the line for which the error was reported. If that line does not contain syntax errors, check several preceding lines.

Some programmers find it difficult when reading or writing a program to match the left and right braces ({ and }) that delimit the body of a class declaration or a method declaration. For this reason, some programmers include an end-of-line comment after a closing right brace (}) that ends a method declaration and after a closing right brace that ends a class declaration. For example, line 11

```
} // end method main
```

specifies the closing right brace (}) of method `main`, and line 13

```
} // end class Welcome1
```

specifies the closing right brace (}) of class `Welcome1`. Each comment indicates the method or class that the right brace terminates.

Good Programming Practice 2.8

Following the closing right brace (}) of a method body or class declaration with an end-of-line comment indicating the method or class declaration to which the brace belongs improves program readability.

Compiling and Executing Your First Java Application

We are now ready to compile and execute our program. For this purpose, we assume you are using the Sun Microsystems' J2SE Development Kit. On the **Downloads** page at our Web site (`www.deitel.com`), we provide Deitel® *Dive Into™ Series* publications to help you begin using several popular Java development tools.

To prepare to compile the program, open a command window and change to the directory where the program is stored. Most operating systems use the command `cd` to change directories. For example,

```
cd c:\examples\ch02\fig02_01
```

changes to the `fig02_01` directory on Windows. The command

```
cd ~/examples/ch02/fig02_01
```

changes to the `fig02_01` directory on UNIX/Linux/Max OS X.

To compile the program, type

```
javac Welcome1.java
```

If the program contains no syntax errors, the preceding command creates a new file called `Welcome1.class` (known as the class file for `Welcome1`) containing the Java bytecodes that represent our application. When we use the `java` command to execute the application, these bytecodes will be executed by the JVM.

Error-Prevention Tip 2.3

When attempting to compile a program, if you receive a message such as "bad command or file-name," "javac: command not found" or "'javac' is not recognized as an internal or external command, operable program or batch file," then your Java software installation was not completed properly. If you are using the J2SE Development Kit, this indicates that the system's PATH *environment variable was not set properly. Please review the J2SE Development Kit installation instructions at* java.sun.com/j2se/5.0/install.html *carefully. On some systems, after correcting the* PATH, *you may need to reboot your computer or open a new command window for these settings to take effect.*

Error-Prevention Tip 2.4

The Java compiler generates syntax-error messages when the syntax of a program is incorrect. Each error message contains the file name and line number where the error occurred. For example, Welcome1.java:6 *indicates that an error occurred in the file* Welcome1.java *at line 6. The remainder of the error message provides information about the syntax error.*

Error-Prevention Tip 2.5

*The compiler error message "*Public class ClassName must be defined in a file called *ClassName.java" indicates that the file name does not exactly match the name of the* public *class in the file or that you typed the class name incorrectly when compiling the class.*

Figure 2.2 shows the program of Fig. 2.1 executing in a Microsoft® Windows® XP **Command Prompt** window. To execute the program, type `java Welcome1`. This launches the JVM, which loads the ".class" file for class `Welcome1`. Note that the ".class" file-name extension is omitted from the preceding command; otherwise, the JVM will not execute the program. The JVM calls method `main`. Next, the statement at line 9 of `main` displays `"Welcome to Java Programming!"` [*Note:* Many environments show command prompts with black backgrounds and white text. We adjusted these settings in our environment to make our screen captures more readable.]

You type this command to execute
the application

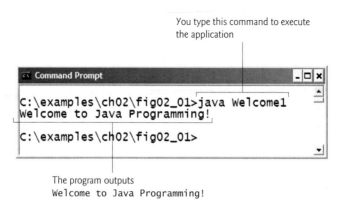

The program outputs
Welcome to Java Programming!

Fig. 2.2 | Executing Welcome1 in a Microsoft Windows XP **Command Prompt** window.

Error-Prevention Tip 2.6

When attempting to run a Java program, if you receive a message such as "Exception in thread "main" java.lang.NoClassDefFoundError: Welcome1," your CLASSPATH environment variable has not been set properly. Please review the J2SE Development Kit installation instructions carefully. On some systems, you may need to reboot your computer or open a new command window after configuring the CLASSPATH.

2.3 Modifying Our First Java Program

This section continues our introduction to Java programming with two examples that modify the example in Fig. 2.1 to print text on one line by using multiple statements and to print text on several lines by using a single statement.

Displaying a Single Line of Text with Multiple Statements

Welcome to Java Programming! can be displayed several ways. Class Welcome2, shown in Fig. 2.3, uses two statements to produce the same output as that shown in Fig. 2.1. From this point forward, we highlight the new and key features in each code listing, as shown in lines 9–10 of this program.

```
1   // Fig. 2.3: Welcome2.java
2   // Printing a line of text with multiple statements.
3
4   public class Welcome2
5   {
6      // main method begins execution of Java application
7      public static void main( String args[] )
8      {
9         System.out.print( "Welcome to " );
10        System.out.println( "Java Programming!" );
11
12     } // end method main
13
14  } // end class Welcome2
```

Fig. 2.3 | Printing a line of text with multiple statements. (Part 1 of 2.)

```
Welcome to Java Programming!
```

Fig. 2.3 | Printing a line of text with multiple statements. (Part 2 of 2.)

The program is almost identical to Fig. 2.1, so we discuss only the changes here. Line 2

```
// Printing a line of text with multiple statements.
```

is an end-of-line comment stating the purpose of this program. Line 4 begins the `Welcome2` class declaration.

Lines 9–10 of method `main`

```
System.out.print( "Welcome to " );
System.out.println( "Java Programming!" );
```

display one line of text in the command window. The first statement uses `System.out`'s method `print` to display a string. Unlike `println`, after displaying its argument, `print` does not position the output cursor at the beginning of the next line in the command window—the next character the program displays will appear immediately after the last character that `print` displays. Thus, line 10 positions the first character in its argument (the letter "J") immediately after the last character that line 9 displays (the space character before the string's closing double-quote character). Each `print` or `println` statement resumes displaying characters from where the last `print` or `println` statement stopped displaying characters.

Displaying Multiple Lines of Text with a Single Statement
A single statement can display multiple lines by using newline characters, which indicate to `System.out`'s `print` and `println` methods when they should position the output cursor at the beginning of the next line in the command window. Like blank lines, space characters and tab characters, newline characters are white-space characters. Figure 2.4 outputs four lines of text, using newline characters to determine when to begin each new line.

Most of the program is identical to those in Fig. 2.1 and Fig. 2.3, so we discuss only the changes here. Line 2

```
// Printing multiple lines of text with a single statement.
```

is a comment stating the purpose of this program. Line 4 begins the `Welcome3` class declaration.
Line 9

```
System.out.println( "Welcome\nto\nJava\nProgramming!" );
```

displays four separate lines of text in the command window. Normally, the characters in a string are displayed exactly as they appear in the double quotes. Note, however, that the two characters \ and n (repeated three times in the statement) do not appear on the screen. The backslash (\) is called an escape character. It indicates to `System.out`'s `print` and `println` methods that a "special character" is to be output. When a backslash appears in a string of characters, Java combines the next character with the backslash to form an escape sequence. The escape sequence \n represents the newline character. When a newline character appears in a string being output with `System.out`, the newline character causes the screen's output cursor to move to the beginning of the next line in the command window. Figure 2.5 lists several common escape sequences and describes how they affect the display of characters in the command window.

```
 1   // Fig. 2.4: Welcome3.java
 2   // Printing multiple lines of text with a single statement.
 3
 4   public class Welcome3
 5   {
 6      // main method begins execution of Java application
 7      public static void main( String args[] )
 8      {
 9         System.out.println( "Welcome\nto\nJava\nProgramming!" );
10
11      } // end method main
12
13   } // end class Welcome3
```

```
Welcome
to
Java
Programming!
```

Fig. 2.4 | Printing multiple lines of text with a single statement.

Escape sequence	Description
\n	Newline. Position the screen cursor at the beginning of the next line.
\t	Horizontal tab. Move the screen cursor to the next tab stop.
\r	Carriage return. Position the screen cursor at the beginning of the current line—do not advance to the next line. Any characters output after the carriage return overwrite the characters previously output on that line.
\\	Backslash. Used to print a backslash character.
\"	Double quote. Used to print a double-quote character. For example, `System.out.println( "\"in quotes\"" );` displays `"in quotes"`

Fig. 2.5 | Some common escape sequences.

2.4 Displaying Text with `printf`

A new feature of J2SE 5.0 is the `System.out.printf` method for displaying formatted data—the f in the name `printf` stands for "formatted." Figure 2.6 outputs the strings `"Welcome to"` and `"Java Programming!"` with `System.out.printf`.

Lines 9–10

```
System.out.printf( "%s\n%s\n",
   "Welcome to", "Java Programming!" );
```

```
 1   // Fig. 2.6: Welcome4.java
 2   // Printing multiple lines in a dialog box.
 3
 4   public class Welcome4
 5   {
 6      // main method begins execution of Java application
 7      public static void main( String args[] )
 8      {
 9         System.out.printf( "%s\n%s\n",
10            "Welcome to", "Java Programming!" );
11
12      } // end method main
13
14   } // end class Welcome4
```

```
Welcome to
Java Programming!
```

Fig. 2.6 | Displaying multiple lines with method `System.out.printf`.

call method `System.out.printf` to display the program's output. The method call specifies three arguments. When a method requires multiple arguments, the arguments are separated with commas (,)—this is known as a comma-separated list.

 Good Programming Practice 2.9

Place a space after each comma (,) in an argument list to make programs more readable.

Remember that all statements in Java end with a semicolon (;). Therefore, lines 9–10 represent only one statement. Java allows large statements to be split over many lines. However, you cannot split a statement in the middle of an identifier or in the middle of a string.

 Common Programming Error 2.7

Splitting a statement in the middle of an identifier or a string is a syntax error.

Method `printf`'s first argument is a format string that may consist of fixed text and format specifiers. Fixed text is output by `printf` just as it would be output by `print` or `println`. Each format specifier is a placeholder for a value and specifies the type of data to output. Format specifiers also may include optional formatting information.

Format specifiers begin with a percent sign (%) and are followed by a character that represents the data type. For example, the format specifier `%s` is a placeholder for a string. The format string in line 9 specifies that `printf` should output two strings and that each string should be followed by a newline character. At the first format specifier's position, `printf` substitutes the value of the first argument after the format string. At each subsequent format specifier's position, `printf` substitutes the value of the next argument in the argument list. So this example substitutes `"Welcome to"` for the first `%s` and `"Java Programming!"` for the second `%s`. The output shows that two lines of text were displayed.

We introduce various formatting features as they are needed in our examples. To learn more about formatting output with `printf`, see `java.sun.com/j2se/5.0/docs/api/java/util/Formatter.html`.

2.5 **Another Java Application: Adding Integers**

Our next application reads (or inputs) two integers (whole numbers, like –22, 7, 0 and 1024) typed by a user at the keyboard, computes the sum of the values and displays the result. This program must keep track of the numbers supplied by the user for the calculation later in the program. Programs remember numbers and other data in the computer's memory and access that data through program elements called variables. The program of Fig. 2.7 demonstrates these concepts. In the sample output, we use highlighting to differentiate between the user's input and the program's output.

Lines 1–2

```
// Fig. 2.7: Addition.java
// Addition program that displays the sum of two numbers.
```

state the figure number, file name and purpose of the program.

Line 3

```
import java.util.Scanner; // program uses class Scanner
```

```java
1   // Fig. 2.7: Addition.java
2   // Addition program that displays the sum of two numbers.
3   import java.util.Scanner; // program uses class Scanner
4
5   public class Addition
6   {
7      // main method begins execution of Java application
8      public static void main( String args[] )
9      {
10         // create Scanner to obtain input from command window
11         Scanner input = new Scanner( System.in );
12
13         int number1; // first number to add
14         int number2; // second number to add
15         int sum; // sum of number1 and number2
16
17         System.out.print( "Enter first integer: " ); // prompt
18         number1 = input.nextInt(); // read first number from user
19
20         System.out.print( "Enter second integer: " ); // prompt
21         number2 = input.nextInt(); // read second number from user
22
23         sum = number1 + number2; // add numbers
24
25         System.out.printf( "Sum is %d\n", sum ); // display sum
26
27      } // end method main
28
29   } // end class Addition
```

```
Enter first integer: 45
Enter second integer: 72
Sum is 117
```

Fig. 2.7 | Addition program that displays the sum of two numbers.

is an `import declaration` that helps the compiler locate a class that is used in this program. A great strength of Java is its rich set of predefined classes that programmers can reuse rather than "reinventing the wheel." These classes are grouped into packages—named collections of classes. Collectively, Java's packages are referred to as the Java class library, or the Java Application Programming Interface (Java API). Programmers use `import` declarations to identify the predefined classes used in a Java program. The `import` declaration in line 3 indicates that this example uses Java's predefined `Scanner` class (discussed shortly) from package `java.util`. Then the compiler attempts to ensure that you use class `Scanner` correctly.

Common Programming Error 2.8

All `import` declarations must appear before the first class declaration in the file. Placing an import declaration inside a class declaration's body or after a class declaration is a syntax error.

Error-Prevention Tip 2.7

Forgetting to include an `import` declaration for a class used in your program typically results in a compilation error containing a message such as "`cannot resolve symbol`." When this occurs, check that you provided the proper `import` declarations and that the names in the `import` declarations are spelled correctly, including proper use of uppercase and lowercase letters.

Line 5

```
public class Addition
```

begins the declaration of class `Addition`. The file name for this `public` class must be `Addition.java`. Remember that the body of each class declaration starts with an opening left brace (line 6), {, and ends with a closing right brace (line 29), }.

The application begins execution with method `main` (lines 8–27). The left brace (line 9) marks the beginning of `main`'s body, and the corresponding right brace (line 27) marks the end of `main`'s body. Note that method `main` is indented one level in the body of class `Addition` and that the code in the body of `main` is indented another level for readability.

Line 11

```
Scanner input = new Scanner( System.in );
```

is a variable declaration statement (also called a declaration) that specifies the name and type of a variable (`input`) that is used in this program. A variable is a location in the computer's memory where a value can be stored for use later in a program. All variables must be declared with a name and a type before they can be used. A variable's name enables the program to access the value of the variable in memory. A variable's name can be any valid identifier. (See Section 2.2 for identifier naming requirements.) A variable's type specifies what kind of information is stored at that location in memory. Like other statements, declaration statements end with a semicolon (;).

The declaration in line 11 specifies that the variable named `input` is of type `Scanner`. A `Scanner` enables a program to read data (e.g., numbers) for use in a program. The data can come from many sources, such as a file on disk or the user at the keyboard. Before using a `Scanner`, the program must create it and specify the source of the data.

The equal sign (=) in line 11 indicates that `Scanner` variable `input` should be initialized (i.e., prepared for use in the program) in its declaration with the result of the expression `new Scanner( System.in )` to the right of the equal sign. This expression creates a `Scanner` object that reads data typed by the user at the keyboard. Recall that the standard output object, `System.out`, allows Java applications to display characters in the command window. Similarly, the standard input object, `System.in`, enables Java applications to read information typed by the user. So, line 11 creates a `Scanner` that enables the application to read information typed by the user at the keyboard.

The variable declaration statements at lines 13–15

```
int number1; // first number to add
int number2; // second number to add
int sum; // sum of number1 and number2
```

declare that variables `number1`, `number2` and `sum` are data of type `int`—these variables will hold integer values (whole numbers such as 7, –11, 0 and 31,914). These variables are not yet initialized. The range of values for an `int` is –2,147,483,648 to +2,147,483,647. We will soon discuss types `float` and `double`, for specifying real numbers, and type `char`, for specifying character data. Real numbers are numbers that contain decimal points, such as 3.4, 0.0 and –11.19. Variables of type `char` represent individual characters, such as an uppercase letter (e.g., A), a digit (e.g., 7), a special character (e.g., * or %) or an escape sequence (e.g., the newline character, \n). Types such as `int`, `float`, `double` and `char` are often called primitive types or built-in types. Primitive-type names are keywords and therefore must appear in all lowercase letters. Appendix D summarizes the characteristics of the eight primitive types (`boolean`, `byte`, `char`, `short`, `int`, `long`, `float` and `double`).

Variable declaration statements can be split over several lines, with the variable names separated by commas (i.e., a comma-separated list of variable names). Several variables of the same type may be declared in one declaration or in multiple declarations. For example, lines 13–15 can also be written as follows:

```
int number1, // first number to add
    number2, // second number to add
    sum; // sum of number1 and number2
```

Note that we used end-of-line comments in lines 13–15. This use of comments is a common programming practice for indicating the purpose of each variable in the program.

Good Programming Practice 2.10

Declare each variable on a separate line. This format allows a descriptive comment to be easily inserted next to each declaration.

Good Programming Practice 2.11

Choosing meaningful variable names helps a program to be self-documenting (i.e., one can understand the program simply by reading it rather than by reading manuals or viewing an excessive number of comments).

Good Programming Practice 2.12

By convention, variable-name identifiers begin with a lowercase letter, and every word in the name after the first word begins with a capital letter. For example, variable-name identifier `firstNumber` *has a capital N in its second word,* `Number`.

Line 17

```
System.out.print( "Enter first integer: " ); // prompt
```

uses `System.out.print` to display the message `"Enter first integer: "`. This message is called a **prompt** because it directs the user to take a specific action. Recall from Section 2.2 that identifiers starting with capital letters represent class names. So, `System` is a class. Class `System` is part of package `java.lang`. Notice that class `System` is not imported with an `import` declaration at the beginning of the program.

Software Engineering Observation 2.1

By default, package `java.lang` is imported in every Java program; thus, `java.lang` is the only package in the Java API that does not require an `import` declaration.

Line 18

```
number1 = input.nextInt(); // read first number from user
```

uses `Scanner` object `input`'s `nextInt` method to obtain an integer from the user at the keyboard. At this point the program waits for the user to type the number and press the *Enter* key to submit the number to the program.

Technically, the user can type anything as the input value. Our program assumes that the user enters a valid integer value as requested. In this program, if the user types a non-integer value, a runtime logic error will occur and the program will terminate. Java has a technology called exception handling (beyond the scope of this book), which makes your programs more robust (**fault tolerant**) by enabling them to handle such errors.

In line 17, the result of the call to method `nextInt` (an `int` value) is placed in variable `number1` by using the **assignment operator**, `=`. The statement is read as "`number1` gets the value of `input.nextInt()`." Operator `=` is called a **binary operator** because it has two **operands**—`number1` and the result of the method call `input.nextInt()`. This statement is called an **assignment statement** because it is a statement that assigns a value to a variable. Everything to the right of the assignment operator, `=`, is always evaluated before the assignment is performed.

Good Programming Practice 2.13

Place spaces on either side of a binary operator to make it stand out and make the program more readable.

Line 20

```
System.out.print( "Enter second integer: " ); // prompt
```

prompts the user to input the second integer. Line 21

```
number2 = input.nextInt(); // read second number from user
```

reads the second integer and assigns it to variable `number2`.

Line 23

```
sum = number1 + number2; // add numbers
```

is an assignment statement that calculates the sum of the variables `number1` and `number2` and assigns the result to variable `sum` by using the assignment operator, `=`. The statement is read as "`sum` gets the value of `number1 + number2`." Most calculations are performed in assignment statements. When the program encounters the addition operation, it uses the values stored in the variables `number1` and `number2` to perform the calculation. In the preceding statement, the addition operator is a binary operator—its two *operands* are `number1` and `number2`. Portions of statements that contain calculations are called *expressions*. In fact, an expression is any portion of a statement that has a value associated with it. For example, the value of the expression `number1 + number2` is the sum of the numbers. Similarly, the value of the expression `input.nextInt()` is an integer typed by the user.

After the calculation has been performed, line 25

```
System.out.printf( "Sum is %d\n", sum ); // display sum
```

uses method `System.out.printf` to display the `sum`. The format specifier `%d` is a placeholder for an `int` value (in this case the value of `sum`)—the letter d stands for "decimal integer." Note that other than the `%d` format specifier, the remaining characters in the format string are all fixed text. So method `printf` displays `"Sum is "`, followed by the value of `sum` (in the position of the `%d` format specifier) and a newline.

Note that calculations can also be performed inside `printf` statements. We could have combined the statements at lines 23 and 25 into the statement

```
System.out.printf( "Sum is %d\n", ( number1 + number2 ) );
```

The parentheses around the expression `number1 + number2` are not required—they are included to emphasize that the value of the expression is output in the position of the `%d` format specifier.

Java API Documentation
For each new Java API class we use, we indicate the package in which it is located. This package information is important because it helps you locate descriptions of each package and class in the Java API documentation. A Web-based version of this documentation can be found at

```
java.sun.com/j2se/5.0/docs/api/
```

Also, you can download this documentation to your own computer from

```
java.sun.com/j2se/5.0/download.jsp
```

The download is approximately 40 megabytes (MB) in size. Appendix G provides an overview of using the Java API documentation.

2.6 Memory Concepts
Variable names such as `number1`, `number2` and `sum` actually correspond to *locations* in the computer's memory. Every variable has a *name*, a *type*, a *size* and a *value*.

In the addition program of Fig. 2.7, when the statement (line 18)

```
number1 = input.nextInt(); // read first number from user
```

executes, the number typed by the user is placed into a memory location to which the name `number1` has been assigned by the compiler. Suppose that the user enters 45. The computer places that integer value into location `number1`, as shown in Fig. 2.8. Whenever a value is placed in a memory location, the value replaces the previous value in that location. The previous value is lost.

number1   45

Fig. 2.8 | Memory location showing the name and value of variable `number1`.

When the statement (line 21)

```
number2 = input.nextInt(); // read second number from user
```

executes, suppose that the user enters 72. The computer places that integer value into location `number2`. The memory now appears as shown in Fig. 2.9.

After the program of Fig. 2.7 obtains values for `number1` and `number2`, it adds the values and places the sum into variable `sum`. The statement (line 23)

```
sum = number1 + number2; // add numbers
```

performs the addition, then replaces `sum`'s previous value. After `sum` has been calculated, memory appears as shown in Fig. 2.10. Note that the values of `number1` and `number2` appear exactly as they did before they were used in the calculation of `sum`. These values were used, but not destroyed, as the computer performed the calculation. Thus, when a value is read from a memory location, the process is nondestructive.

2.7 Arithmetic

Most programs perform arithmetic calculations. The arithmetic operators are summarized in Fig. 2.11. Note the use of various special symbols not used in algebra. The asterisk (*) indicates multiplication, and the percent sign (%) is the remainder operator (called-modulus in some languages), which we will discuss shortly. The arithmetic operators in Fig. 2.11 are binary operators because they each operate on two operands. For example, the expression f + 7 contains the binary operator + and the two operands f and 7.

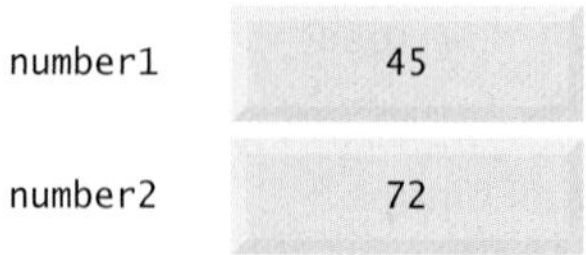

number1   45

number2   72

Fig. 2.9 | Memory locations after storing values for `number1` and `number2`.

number1   45

number2   72

sum   117

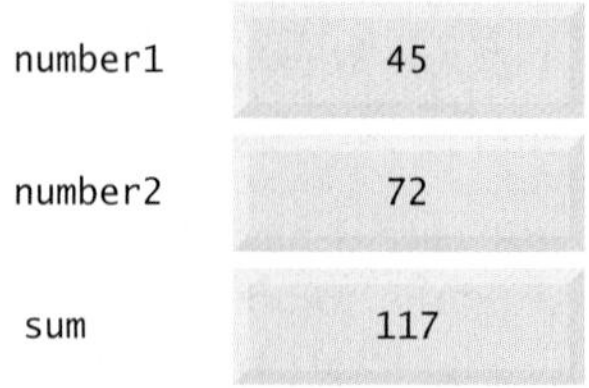

Fig. 2.10 | Memory locations after calculating and storing the sum of `number1` and `number2`.

Addition	+	$f + 7$	f + 7
Subtraction	–	$p - c$	p – c
Multiplication	*	bm	b * m
Division	/	$x / y\ \ or\ \dfrac{x}{y}\ \ or\ \ x \div y$	x / y
Remainder	%	$r \bmod s$	r % s

Fig. 2.11 | Arithmetic operators.

Integer division yields an integer quotient—for example, the expression 7 / 4 evaluates to 1, and the expression 17 / 5 evaluates to 3. Any fractional part in integer division is simply discarded (i.e., truncated)—no rounding occurs. Java provides the remainder operator, %, which yields the remainder after division. The expression x % y yields the remainder after x is divided by y. Thus, 7 % 4 yields 3, and 17 % 5 yields 2. This operator is most commonly used with integer operands, but can also be used with other arithmetic types. In this chapter's exercises and in later chapters, we consider several interesting applications of the remainder operator, such as determining whether one number is a multiple of another.

Arithmetic expressions in Java must be written in straight-line form to facilitate entering programs into the computer. Thus, expressions such as "a divided by b" must be written as a / b, so that all constants, variables and operators appear in a straight line. The following algebraic notation is generally not acceptable to compilers:

$$\frac{a}{b}$$

Parentheses are used to group terms in Java expressions in the same manner as in algebraic expressions. For example, to multiply a times the quantity b + c, we write

```
a * ( b + c )
```

If an expression contains nested parentheses, such as

```
( ( a + b ) * c )
```

the expression in the innermost set of parentheses (a + b in this case) is evaluated first.

Java applies the operators in arithmetic expressions in a precise sequence determined by the following rules of operator precedence, which are generally the same as those followed in algebra (Fig. 2.12):

1. Multiplication, division and remainder operations are applied first. If an expression contains several such operations, the operators are applied from left to right. Multiplication, division and remainder operators have the same level of precedence.

2. Addition and subtraction operations are applied next. If an expression contains several such operations, the operators are applied from left to right. Addition and subtraction operators have the same level of precedence.

These rules enable Java to apply operators in the correct order. When we say that operators are applied from left to right, we are referring to their associativity. You will see

Operator(s)	Operation(s)	Order of evaluation (precedence)
* / %	Multiplication Division Remainder	Evaluated first. If there are several operators of this type, they are evaluated from left to right.
+ -	Addition Subtraction	Evaluated next. If there are several operators of this type, they are evaluated from left to right.

Fig. 2.12 | Precedence of arithmetic operators.

that some operators associate from right to left. Figure 2.12 summarizes these rules of operator precedence. The table will be expanded as additional Java operators are introduced. A complete precedence chart is included in Appendix A.

Now let us consider several expressions in light of the rules of operator precedence. Each example lists an algebraic expression and its Java equivalent. The following is an example of an arithmetic mean (average) of five terms:

$Algebra:$ $m = \dfrac{a + b + c + d + e}{5}$

$Java:$ m = (a + b + c + d + e) / 5;

The parentheses are required because division has higher precedence than addition. The entire quantity (a + b + c + d + e) is to be divided by 5. If the parentheses are erroneously omitted, we obtain a + b + c + d + e / 5, which evaluates as

$$a + b + c + d + \frac{e}{5}$$

The following is an example of the equation of a straight line:

$Algebra:$ $y = mx + b$

$Java:$ y = m * x + b;

No parentheses are required. The multiplication operator is applied first because multiplication has a higher precedence than addition. The assignment occurs last because it has a lower precedence than multiplication or addition.

The following example contains remainder (%), multiplication, division, addition and subtraction operations:

$Algebra:$ $z = pr\%q + w/x - y$

$Java:$ z = p * r % q + w / x - y;
                  ⑥ ① ② ④ ③ ⑤

The circled numbers under the statement indicate the order in which Java applies the operators. The multiplication, remainder and division operations are evaluated first in left-to-right order (i.e., they associate from left to right), because they have higher precedence than addition and subtraction. The addition and subtraction operations are evaluated next. These operations are also applied from left to right.

To develop a better understanding of the rules of operator precedence, consider the evaluation of a second-degree polynomial ($y = ax^2 + bx + c$):

```
y  =  a  *  x  *  x  +  b  *  x  +  c;
   6     1     2     4     3     5
```

The circled numbers indicate the order in which Java applies the operators. The multiplication operations are evaluated first in left-to-right order (i.e., they associate from left to right), because they have higher precedence than addition. The addition operations are evaluated next and are applied from left to right. There is no arithmetic operator for exponentiation in Java, so x^2 is represented as x * x. Section 5.4 shows an alternative for performing exponentiation in Java.

Suppose that a, b, c and x in the preceding second-degree polynomial are initialized (given values) as follows: a = 2, b = 3, c = 7 and x = 5. Figure 2.13 illustrates the order in which the operators are applied.

As in algebra, it is acceptable to place unnecessary parentheses in an expression to make the expression clearer. These are called redundant parentheses. For example, the preceding assignment statement might be parenthesized as follows:

```
y = ( a * x * x ) + ( b * x ) + c;
```

 Good Programming Practice 2.14

Using parentheses for complex arithmetic expressions, even when the parentheses are not necessary, can make the arithmetic expressions easier to read.

Step 1.   y = 2 * 5 * 5 + 3 * 5 + 7;   *(Leftmost multiplication)*

2 * 5 is 10

Step 2.   y = 10 * 5 + 3 * 5 + 7;   *(Leftmost multiplication)*

10 * 5 is 50

Step 3.   y = 50 + 3 * 5 + 7;   *(Multiplication before addition)*

3 * 5 is 15

Step 4.   y = 50 + 15 + 7;   *(Leftmost addition)*

50 + 15 is 65

Step 5.   y = 65 + 7;   *(Last addition)*

65 + 7 is 72

Step 6.   y = 72   *(Last operation—place 72 in y)*

Fig. 2.13 | Order in which a second-degree polynomial is evaluated.

2.8 Decision Making: Equality and Relational Operators

A condition is an expression that can be either true or false. This section introduces a simple version of Java's if statement that allows a program to make a decision based on the value of a condition. For example, the condition "grade is greater than or equal to 60" determines whether a student passed a test. If the condition in an if statement is true, the body of the if statement executes. If the condition is false, the body does not execute. We will see an example shortly.

Conditions in if statements can be formed by using the equality operators (== and !=) and relational operators (>, <, >= and <=) summarized in Fig. 2.14. Both equality operators have the same level of precedence, which is lower than that of the relational operators. The equality operators associate from left to right. The relational operators all have the same level of precedence and also associate from left to right.

The application of Fig. 2.15 uses six if statements to compare two integers input by the user. If the condition in any of these if statements is true, the assignment statement associated with that if statement executes. The program uses a Scanner to input the two integers from the user and store them in variables number1 and number2. Then the program compares the numbers and displays the results of the comparisons that are true.

The declaration of class Comparison begins at line 6

```
public class Comparison
```

The class's main method (lines 9–41) begins the execution of the program.
Line 12

```
Scanner input = new Scanner( System.in );
```

declares Scanner variable input and assigns it a Scanner that inputs data from the standard input (i.e., the keyboard).

Standard algebraic equality or relational operator	Java equality or relational operator	Sample Java condition	Meaning of Java condition
Equality operators			
=	==	x == y	x is equal to y
≠	!=	x != y	x is not equal to y
Relational operators			
>	>	x > y	x is greater than y
<	<	x < y	x is less than y
≥	>=	x >= y	x is greater than or equal to y
≤	<=	x <= y	x is less than or equal to y

Fig. 2.14 | Equality and relational operators.

```
 1   // Fig. 2.15: Comparison.java
 2   // Compare integers using if statements, relational operators
 3   // and equality operators.
 4   import java.util.Scanner; // program uses class Scanner
 5
 6   public class Comparison
 7   {
 8      // main method begins execution of Java application
 9      public static void main( String args[] )
10      {
11         // create Scanner to obtain input from command window
12         Scanner input = new Scanner( System.in );
13
14         int number1; // first number to compare
15         int number2; // second number to compare
16
17         System.out.print( "Enter first integer: " ); // prompt
18         number1 = input.nextInt(); // read first number from user
19
20         System.out.print( "Enter second integer: " ); // prompt
21         number2 = input.nextInt(); // read second number from user
22
23         if ( number1 == number2 )
24            System.out.printf( "%d == %d\n", number1, number2 );
25
26         if ( number1 != number2 )
27            System.out.printf( "%d != %d\n", number1, number2 );
28
29         if ( number1 < number2 )
30            System.out.printf( "%d < %d\n", number1, number2 );
31
32         if ( number1 > number2 )
33            System.out.printf( "%d > %d\n", number1, number2 );
34
35         if ( number1 <= number2 )
36            System.out.printf( "%d <= %d\n", number1, number2 );
37
38         if ( number1 >= number2 )
39            System.out.printf( "%d >= %d\n", number1, number2 );
40
41      } // end method main
42
43   } // end class Comparison
```

```
Enter first integer: 777
Enter second integer: 777
777 == 777
777 <= 777
777 >= 777
```

Fig. 2.15 | Equality and relational operators. (Part 1 of 2.)

```
Enter first integer: 1000
Enter second integer: 2000
1000 != 2000
1000 < 2000
1000 <= 2000
```

```
Enter first integer: 2000
Enter second integer: 1000
2000 != 1000
2000 > 1000
2000 >= 1000
```

Fig. 2.15 | Equality and relational operators. (Part 2 of 2.)

Lines 14–15

```
int number1; // first number to compare
int number2; // second number to compare
```

declare the int variables used to store the values input from the user.

Lines 17–18

```
System.out.print( "Enter first integer: " ); // prompt
number1 = input.nextInt(); // read first number from user
```

prompt the user to enter the first integer and input the value, respectively. The input value is stored in variable number1.

Lines 20–21

```
System.out.print( "Enter second integer: " ); // prompt
number2 = input.nextInt(); // read second number from user
```

prompt the user to enter the second integer and input the value, respectively. The input value is stored in variable number2.

Lines 23–24

```
if ( number1 == number2 )
    System.out.printf( "%d == %d\n", number1, number2 );
```

declare an if statement that compares the values of the variables number1 and number2 to determine whether they are equal. An if statement always begins with keyword if, followed by a condition in parentheses. An if statement expects one statement in its body. The indentation of the body statement shown here is not required, but it improves the program's readability by emphasizing that the statement in line 24 is part of the if statement that begins on line 23. Line 24 executes only if the numbers stored in variables number1 and number2 are equal (i.e., the condition is true). The if statements at lines 26–27, 29–30, 32–33, 35–36 and 38–39 compare number1 and number2 with the operators !=, <, >, <= and >=, respectively. If the condition in any of the if statements is true, the corresponding body statement executes.

Common Programming Error 2.9

Forgetting the left and/or right parentheses for the condition in an if *statement is a syntax error—the parentheses are required.*

Common Programming Error 2.10

Confusing the equality operator, ==, with the assignment operator, =, can cause a logic error or a syntax error. The equality operator should be read as "is equal to," and the assignment operator should be read as "gets" or "gets the value of." To avoid confusion, some people read the equality operator as "double equals" or "equals equals."

Common Programming Error 2.11

It is a syntax error if the operators ==, !=, >= and <= contain spaces between their symbols, as in = =, ! =, > = and < =, respectively.

Common Programming Error 2.12

Reversing the operators !=, >= and <=, as in =!, => and =<, is a syntax error.

Good Programming Practice 2.15

Indent an if *statement's body to make it stand out and to enhance program readability.*

Good Programming Practice 2.16

Place only one statement per line in a program. This format enhances program readability.

Note that there is no semicolon (;) at the end of the first line of each if statement. Such a semicolon would result in a logic error at execution time. For example,

```
if ( number1 == number2 );   // logic error
   System.out.printf( "%d == %d\n", number1, number2 );
```

would actually be interpreted by Java as

```
if ( number1 == number2 )
   ; // empty statement

System.out.printf( "%d == %d\n", number1, number2 );
```

where the semicolon on the line by itself—called the empty statement—is the statement to execute if the condition in the if statement is true. When the empty statement executes, no task is performed in the program. The program then continues with the output statement, which always executes, regardless of whether the condition is true or false, because the output statement is not part of the if statement.

Common Programming Error 2.13

Placing a semicolon immediately after the right parenthesis of the condition in an if *statement is normally a logic error.*

Note the use of white space in Fig. 2.15. Recall that white-space characters, such as tabs, newlines and spaces, are normally ignored by the compiler. So statements may be split over several lines and may be spaced according to the programmer's preferences without affecting the meaning of a program. It is incorrect to split identifiers and strings. Ideally, statements should be kept small, but this is not always possible.

Good Programming Practice 2.17

A lengthy statement can be spread over several lines. If a single statement must be split across lines, choose breaking points that make sense, such as after a comma in a comma-separated list, or after an operator in a lengthy expression. If a statement is split across two or more lines, indent all subsequent lines until the end of the statement.

Figure 2.16 shows the precedence of the operators introduced in this chapter. The operators are shown from top to bottom in decreasing order of precedence. All these operators, with the exception of the assignment operator, =, associate from left to right. Addition is left associative, so an expression like x + y + z is evaluated as if it had been written as (x + y) + z. The assignment operator, =, associates from right to left, so an expression like x = y = 0 is evaluated as if it had been written as x = (y = 0), which, as we will soon see, first assigns the value 0 to variable y and then assigns the result of that assignment, 0, to x.

Good Programming Practice 2.18

Refer to the operator precedence chart (see the complete chart in Appendix A) when writing expressions containing many operators. Confirm that the operations in the expression are performed in the order you expect. If you are uncertain about the order of evaluation in a complex expression, use parentheses to force the order, exactly as you would do in algebraic expressions. Observe that some operators, such as assignment, =, associate from right to left rather than from left to right.

2.9 Wrap-Up

You learned many important features of Java in this chapter, including displaying data on the screen in a command prompt, inputting data from the keyboard, performing calculations and making decisions. The applications presented here were meant to introduce you to basic programming concepts. As you will see in Chapter 3, Java applications typically contain just a few lines of code in method main—these statements normally create the objects that perform the work of the application. In Chapter 3, you will learn how to implement your own classes and use objects of those classes in applications.

Operators				Associativity	Type
*	/	%		left to right	multiplicative
+	−			left to right	additive
<	<=	>	>=	left to right	relational
==	!=			left to right	equality
=				right to left	assignment

Fig. 2.16 | Precedence and associativity of operations discussed.

Summary

- Computer programmers create applications by writing computer programs. A Java application is a computer program that executes when you use the `java` command to launch the JVM.
- Programmers insert comments to document programs and improve their readability. The Java compiler ignores comments.
- A comment that begins with `//` is called an end-of-line (or single-line) comment because the comment terminates at the end of the line on which it appears.
- Traditional (multiple-line) comments can be spread over several lines and are delimited by `/*` and `*/`. All text between the delimiters is ignored by the compiler.
- Javadoc comments are delimited by `/**` and `*/`. Javadoc comments enable programmers to embed program documentation directly in their programs. The `javadoc` utility program generates HTML documentation based on Javadoc comments.
- A programming language's syntax specifies the rules for creating a proper program in that language.
- A syntax error (also called a compiler error, compile-time error or compilation error) occurs when the compiler encounters code that violates Java's language rules.
- Programmers use blank lines and space characters to make programs easier to read. Together, blank lines, space characters and tab characters are known as white space. Space characters and tabs are known specifically as white-space characters. White space is ignored by the compiler.
- Every program in Java consists of at least one class declaration that is defined by the programmer (also known as a programmer-defined class or a user-defined class).
- Keywords are reserved for use by Java and are always spelled with all lowercase letters.
- Keyword `class` introduces a class declaration and is immediately followed by the class name.
- By convention, all class names in Java begin with a capital letter and capitalize the first letter of each word they include (e.g., `SampleClassName`).
- A Java class name is an identifier—a series of characters consisting of letters, digits, underscores (`_`) and dollar signs (`$`) that does not begin with a digit and does not contain spaces. Normally, an identifier that does not begin with a capital letter is not the name of a Java class.
- Java is case sensitive—that is, uppercase and lowercase letters are distinct.
- The body of every class declaration is delimited by braces, `{` and `}`.
- A `public` class declaration must be saved in a file with the same name as the class followed by the "`.java`" file-name extension.
- Method `main` is the starting point of every Java application and must begin with

    ```
    public static void main( String args[] )
    ```

otherwise, the JVM will not execute the application.
- Methods are able to perform tasks and return information when they complete their tasks. Keyword `void` indicates that a method will perform a task but will not return any information.
- Statements instruct the computer to perform actions.
- A sequence of characters in double quotation marks is called a string, a character string, a message or a string literal.
- `System.out`, the standard output object, allows Java applications to display characters in the command window.
- Method `System.out.println` displays its argument in the command window followed by a new-line character to position the output cursor to the beginning of the next line.

- Every statement ends with a semicolon.
- Most operating systems use the command cd to change directories in the command window.
- You compile a program with the command javac. If the program contains no syntax errors, a class file containing the Java bytecodes that represent the application is created. These bytecodes are interpreted by the JVM when we execute the program.
- System.out.print displays its argument and positions the output cursor immediately after the last character displayed.
- A backslash (\) in a string is an escape character. It indicates that a "special character" is to be output. Java combines the next character with the backslash to form an escape sequence. The escape sequence \n represents the newline character, which positions the cursor on the next line.
- System.out.printf method (f means "formatted") displays formatted data.
- When a method requires multiple arguments, the arguments are separated with commas (,)—this is known as a comma-separated list.
- Method printf's first argument is a format string that may consist of fixed text and format specifiers. Fixed text is output by printf just as it would be output by print or println. Each format specifier is a placeholder for a value and specifies the type of data to output.
- Format specifiers begin with a percent sign (%) and are followed by a character that represents the (-) data type. The format specifier %s is a placeholder for a string.
- At the first format specifier's position, printf substitutes the value of the first argument after the format string. At each subsequent format specifier's position, printf substitutes the value of the next argument in the argument list.
- Integers are whole numbers, like –22, 7, 0 and 1024.
- An import declaration helps the compiler locate a class that is used in a program.
- Java provides a rich set of predefined classes that programmers can reuse rather than "reinventing the wheel." These classes are grouped into packages—named collections of classes.
- Collectively, Java's packages are referred to as the Java class library, or the Java Application Programming Interface (Java API).
- A variable declaration statement specifies the name and type of a variable.
- A variable is a location in the computer's memory where a value can be stored for use later in a program. All variables must be declared with a name and a type before they can be used.
- A variable's name enables the program to access the value of the variable in memory. A variable name can be any valid identifier.
- Like other statements, variable declaration statements end with a semicolon (;).
- A Scanner (package java.util) enables a program to read data for use in a program. The data can come from many sources, such as a file on disk or the user at the keyboard. Before using a Scanner, the program must create it and specify the source of the data.
- Variables should be initialized to prepare them for use in a program.
- The expression new Scanner(System.in) creates a Scanner that reads from the keyboard. The standard input object, System.in, enables Java applications to read data typed by the user.
- Data type int is used to declare variables that will hold integer values. The range of values for an int is –2,147,483,648 to +2,147,483,647.
- Types float and double specify real numbers, and type char specifies character data. Real numbers are numbers that contain decimal points, such as 3.4, 0.0 and –11.19. Variables of type char data represent individual characters, such as an uppercase letter (e.g., A), a digit (e.g., 7), a special character (e.g., * or %) or an escape sequence (e.g., the newline character, \n).

- Types such as int, float, double and char are often called primitive types or built-in types. Primitive-type names are keywords; thus, they must appear in all lowercase letters.
- A prompt directs the user to take a specific action.
- Scanner method nextInt obtains an integer for use in a program.
- The assignment operator, =, enables the program to give a value to a variable. Operator = is called a binary operator because it has two operands. An assignment statement uses an assignment operator to assign a value to a variable.
- Portions of statements that have values are called expressions.
- The format specifier %d is a placeholder for an int value.
- Variable names correspond to locations in the computer's memory. Every variable has a name, a type, a size and a value.
- Whenever a value is placed in a memory location, the value replaces the previous value in that location. The previous value is lost.
- Most programs perform arithmetic calculations. The arithmetic operators are + (addition), - (subtraction, * (multiplication), / (division) and % (remainder).
- Integer division yields an integer quotient.
- The remainder operator, %, yields the remainder after division.
- Arithmetic expressions in Java must be written in straight-line form.
- If an expression contains nested parentheses, the innermost set of parentheses is evaluated first.
- Java applies the operators in arithmetic expressions in a precise sequence determined by the rules of operator precedence.
- When we say that operators are applied from left to right, we are referring to their associativity. Some operators associate from right to left.
- Redundant parentheses in an expression can make an expression clearer.
- A condition is an expression that can be either true or false. Java's if statement allows a program to make a decision based on the value of a condition.
- Conditions in if statements can be formed by using the equality (== and !=) and relational (>, <, >= and <=) operators.
- An if statement always begins with keyword if, followed by a condition in parentheses, and expects one statement in its body.
- The empty statement is a statement that does not perform a task.

Terminology

addition operator (+)
application
argument
arithmetic operators (*, /, %, + and -)
assignment operator (=)
assignment statement
associativity of operators
backslash (\) escape character
binary operator
body of a class declaration
body of a method declaration
built-in type

case sensitive
char primitive type
character string
class declaration
class file
.class file extension
class keyword
class name
comma (,)
comma-separated list
command line
Command Prompt

command window
comment
compilation error
compiler error
compile-time error
condition
%d format specifier
decision
division operator (/)
document a program
double primitive type
empty statement (;)
end-of-line comment (//)
equality operators
    == "is equal to"
    != "is not equal to"
escape character
escape sequence
false
fault tolerant
fixed text in a format string
float primitive type
format specifier
format string
identifier
if statement
import declaration
int (integer) primitive type
integer
integer division
Java API documentation
Java Application Programming Interface (API)
Java class library
.java file extension
java command
javadoc utility program
javadoc tool home page
java.lang package
Javadoc comment (/** */)
left brace ({)
literal
location of a variable
main method
memory location
message
method
modulus operator (%)
multiple-line comment (/* */)
MS-DOS prompt
multiplication operator (*)

name of a variable
nested parentheses
newline character (\n)
object
operand
operator
optional package
output cursor
package
parentheses ()
perform an action
precedence
primitive type
programmer-defined class
prompt
public keyword
redundant parentheses
relational operators
    < "is less than"
    <= "is less than or equal to"
    > "is greater than"
    >= "is greater than or equal to"
remainder operator (%)
reserved words
right brace (})
rules of operator precedence
%s format specifier
Scanner class
self-documenting
semicolon (;)
shell
single-line comment (//)
size of a variable
standard input object (System.in)
standard output object (System.out)
statement
straight-line form
string
string literal
subtraction operator (-)
syntax error
System class
System.in (standard input) object
System.out (standard output) object
System.out.print method
System.out.printf method
System.out.println method
terminal window
traditional comment (/* */)
true
type of a variable
user-defined class

variable   variable value
variable declaration   void keyword
variable declaration statement   white space
variable name   white-space characters

Self-Review Exercises

2.1   Fill in the blanks in each of the following statements:
   a) A(n) _____ begins the body of every method, and a(n) _____ ends the body of every method.
   b) Every statement ends with a(n) _____.
   c) The _____ statement is used to make decisions.
   d) _____ begins an end-of-line comment.
   e) _____, _____, _____ and _____ are called white space.
   f) _____ are reserved for use by Java.
   g) Java applications begin execution at method _____.
   h) Methods _____, _____ and _____ display information in the command window.

2.2   State whether each of the following is *true* or *false*. If *false*, explain why.
   a) Comments cause the computer to print the text after the // on the screen when the program executes.
   b) All variables must be given a type when they are declared.
   c) Java considers the variables number and NuMbEr to be identical.
   d) The remainder operator (%) can be used only with integer operands.
   e) The arithmetic operators *, /, %, + and - all have the same level of precedence.

2.3   Write statements to accomplish each of the following tasks:
   a) Declare variables c, thisIsAVariable, q76354 and number to be of type int.
   b) Prompt the user to enter an integer.
   c) Input an integer and assign the result to int variable value. Assume Scanner variable input can be used to read a value from the keyboard.
   d) If the variable number is not equal to 7, display "The variable number is not equal to 7".
   e) Print "This is a Java program" on one line in the command window.
   f) Print "This is a Java program" on two lines in the command window. The first line should end with Java. Use method System.out.println.
   g) Print "This is a Java program" on two lines in the command window. The first line should end with Java. Use method System.out.printf and two %s format specifiers.

2.4   Identify and correct the errors in each of the following statements:
   a) ```
       if (c < 7);
          System.out.println("c is less than 7");
       ```
   b)  ```
       if ( c => 7 )
          System.out.println( "c is equal to or greater than 7" );
       ```

2.5   Write declarations, statements or comments that accomplish each of the following tasks:
   a) State that a program will calculate the product of three integers.
   b) Create a Scanner that reads values from the standard input.
   c) Declare the variables x, y, z and result to be of type int.
   d) Prompt the user to enter the first integer.
   e) Read the first integer from the user and store it in the variable x.
   f) Prompt the user to enter the second integer.
   g) Read the second integer from the user and store it in the variable y.
   h) Prompt the user to enter the third integer.

i) Read the third integer from the user and store it in the variable z.
j) Compute the product of the three integers contained in variables x, y and z, and assign the result to the variable result.
k) Display the message "Product is" followed by the value of the variable result.

2.6 Using the statements you wrote in Exercise 2.5, write a complete program that calculates and prints the product of three integers.

Answers to Self-Review Exercises

2.1 a) left brace ({), right brace (}). b) semicolon (;). c) if. d) //. e) Blank lines, space characters, newline characters and tab characters. f) Keywords. g) main. h) System.out.print, System.out.println and System.out.printf.

2.2 a) False. Comments do not cause any action to be performed when the program executes. They are used to document programs and improve their readability.
b) True.
c) False. Java is case sensitive, so these variables are distinct.
d) False. The remainder operator can also be used with noninteger operands in Java.
e) False. The operators *, / and % are on the same level of precedence, and the operators + and - are on a lower level of precedence.

2.3 a) `int c, thisIsAVariable, q76354, number;`
or
`int c;`
`int thisIsAVariable;`
`int q76354;`
`int number;`
b) `System.out.print( "Enter an integer: " );`
c) `value = input.nextInt();`
d) `if ( number != 7 )`
`    System.out.println( "The variable number is not equal to 7" );`
e) `System.out.println( "This is a Java program" );`
f) `System.out.println( "This is a Java\nprogram" );`
g) `System.out.printf( "%s\n%s\n", "This is a Java", "program" );`

2.4 The solutions to Self-Review Exercise 2.4 are as follows:
a) Error: Semicolon after the right parenthesis of the condition (c < 7) in the if.
Correction: Remove the semicolon after the right parenthesis. [*Note*: As a result, the output statement will execute regardless of whether the condition in the if is true.]
b) Error: The relational operator => is incorrect. Correction: Change => to >=.

2.5 a) `// Calculate the product of three integers`
b) `Scanner input = new Scanner( System.in );`
c) `int x, y, z, result;`
or
`int x;`
`int y;`
`int z;`
`int result;`
d) `System.out.print( "Enter first integer: " );`
e) `x = input.nextInt();`
f) `System.out.print( "Enter second integer: " );`
g) `y = input.nextInt();`
h) `System.out.print( "Enter third integer: " );`

i)   z = input.nextInt();
j)   result = x * y * z;
k) System.out.printf("Product is %d\n", result);

2.6   The solution to Exercise 2.6 is as follows:

```java
 1   // Ex. 2.6: Product.java
 2   // Calculate the product of three integers.
 3   import java.util.Scanner; // program uses Scanner
 4
 5   public class Product
 6   {
 7      public static void main( String args[] )
 8      {
 9         // create Scanner to obtain input from command window
10         Scanner input = new Scanner( System.in );
11
12         int x; // first number input by user
13         int y; // second number input by user
14         int z; // third number input by user
15         int result; // product of numbers
16
17         System.out.print( "Enter first integer: " ); // prompt for input
18         x = input.nextInt(); // read first integer
19
20         System.out.print( "Enter second integer: " ); // prompt for input
21         y = input.nextInt(); // read second integer
22
23         System.out.print( "Enter third integer: " ); // prompt for input
24         z = input.nextInt(); // read third integer
25
26         result = x * y * z; // calculate product of numbers
27
28         System.out.printf( "Product is %d\n", result );
29
30      } // end method main
31
32   } // end class Product
```

```
Enter first integer: 10
Enter second integer: 20
Enter third integer: 30
Product is 6000
```

Exercises

2.7   Fill in the blanks in each of the following statements:
a)   _____ are used to document a program and improve its readability.
b)   A decision can be made in a Java program with a(n) _____.
c)   Calculations are normally performed by _____ statements.
d)   The arithmetic operators with the same precedence as multiplication are _____ and
     _____.

e) When parentheses in an arithmetic expression are nested, the _____ set of parentheses is evaluated first.

f) A location in the computer's memory that may contain different values at various times throughout the execution of a program is called a(n) _____.

2.8   Write Java statements that accomplish each of the following tasks:

a) Display the message "Enter an integer: ", leaving the cursor on the same line.

b) Assign the product of variables b and c to variable a.

c) State that a program performs a sample payroll calculation (i.e., use text that helps to document a program).

2.9   State whether each of the following is *true* or *false*. If *false*, explain why.

a) Java operators are evaluated from left to right.

b) The following are all valid variable names: _under_bar_, m928134, t5, j7, her_sales$, his_$account_total, a, b$, c, z and z2.

c) A valid Java arithmetic expression with no parentheses is evaluated from left to right.

d) The following are all invalid variable names: 3g, 87, 67h2, h22 and 2h.

2.10   Assuming that x = 2 and y = 3, what does each of the following statements display?

a) `System.out.printf( "x = %d\n", x );`

b) `System.out.printf( "Value of %d + %d is %d\n", x, x, ( x + x ) );`

c) `System.out.printf( "x =" );`

d) `System.out.printf( "%d = %d\n", ( x + y ), ( y + x ) );`

2.11   Which of the following Java statements contain variables whose values are modified?

a) `p = i + j + k + 7;`

b) `System.out.println( "variables whose values are destroyed" );`

c) `System.out.println( "a = 5" );`

d) `value = input.nextInt();`

2.12   Given that $y = ax^3 + 7$, which of the following are correct Java statements for this equation?

a) `y = a * x * x * x + 7;`

b) `y = a * x * x * ( x + 7 );`

c) `y = ( a * x ) * x * ( x + 7 );`

d) `y = ( a * x ) * x * x + 7;`

e) `y = a * ( x * x * x ) + 7;`

f) `y = a * x * ( x * x + 7 );`

2.13   State the order of evaluation of the operators in each of the following Java statements, and show the value of x after each statement is performed:

a) `x = 7 + 3 * 6 / 2 - 1;`

b) `x = 2 % 2 + 2 * 2 - 2 / 2;`

c) `x = ( 3 * 9 * ( 3 + ( 9 * 3 / ( 3 ) ) ) );`

2.14   Write an application that displays the numbers 1 to 4 on the same line, with each pair of adjacent numbers separated by one space. Write the program using the following techniques:

a) Use one `System.out.println` statement.

b) Use four `System.out.print` statements.

c) Use one `System.out.printf` statement.

2.15   Write an application that asks the user to enter two integers, obtains them from the user and prints their sum, product, difference and quotient (division). Use the techniques shown in Fig. 2.7.

2.16   Write an application that asks the user to enter two integers, obtains them from the user and displays the larger number followed by the words "is larger". If the numbers are equal, print the message "These numbers are equal." Use the techniques shown in Fig. 2.15.

2.17   Write an application that inputs three integers from the user and displays the sum, average, product, smallest and largest of the numbers. Use the techniques shown in Fig. 2.15. [*Note*: The calculation of the average in this exercise should result in an integer representation of the average. So if the sum of the values is 7, the average should be 2, not 2.3333….]

2.18   Write an application that displays a box, an oval, an arrow and a diamond using asterisks (*), as follows:

```
*********      ***        *            *
*       *    *     *      ***         *  *
*       *   *       *    *****        *    *
*       *   *       *      *         *      *
*       *   *       *      *        *        *
*       *   *       *      *         *      *
*       *   *       *      *          *    *
*       *    *     *       *           *  *
*********      ***         *            *
```

2.19   What does the following code print?

```
System.out.println( "*\n**\n***\n****\n*****" );
```

2.20   What does the following code print?

```
System.out.println( "*" );
System.out.println( "***" );
System.out.println( "*****" );
System.out.println( "****" );
System.out.println( "**" );
```

2.21   What does the following code print?

```
System.out.print( "*" );
System.out.print( "***" );
System.out.print( "*****" );
System.out.print( "****" );
System.out.println( "**" );
```

2.22   What does the following code print?

```
System.out.print( "*" );
System.out.println( "***" );
System.out.println( "*****" );
System.out.print( "****" );
System.out.println( "**" );
```

2.23   What does the following code print?

```
System.out.printf( "%s\n%s\n%s\n", "*", "***", "*****" );
```

2.24   Write an application that reads five integers, determines and prints the largest and smallest integers in the group. Use only the programming techniques you learned in this chapter.

2.25   Write an application that reads an integer and determines and prints whether it is odd or even. [*Hint*: Use the remainder operator. An even number is a multiple of 2. Any multiple of 2 leaves a remainder of 0 when divided by 2.]

2.26   Write an application that reads two integers, determines whether the first is a multiple of the second and prints the result. [*Hint:* Use the remainder operator.]

2.27   Write an application that displays a checkerboard pattern, as follows:

```
* * * * * * * *
 * * * * * * * *
* * * * * * * *
 * * * * * * * *
* * * * * * * *
 * * * * * * * *
* * * * * * * *
 * * * * * * * *
```

2.28   Here's a peek ahead. In this chapter, you have learned about integers and the type `int`. Java can also represent floating-point numbers that contain decimal points, such as 3.14159. Write an application that inputs from the user the radius of a circle as an integer and prints the circle's diameter, circumference and area using the floating-point value 3.14159 for π. Use the techniques shown in Fig. 2.7. [*Note:* You may also use the predefined constant `Math.PI` for the value of π. This constant is more precise than the value 3.14159. Class `Math` is defined in package `java.lang`. Classes in that package are imported automatically, so you do not need to `import` class `Math` to use it.] Use the following formulas (*r* is the radius):

$$diameter = 2r$$
$$circumference = 2\pi r$$
$$area = \pi r^2$$

Do not store the results of each calculation in a variable. Rather, specify each calculation as the value that will be output in a `System.out.printf` statement. Note that the values produced by the circumference and area calculations are floating-point numbers. Such values can be output with the format specifier `%f` in a `System.out.printf` statement. You will learn more about floating-point numbers in Chapter 3.

2.29   Here's another peek ahead. In this chapter, you have learned about integers and the type `int`. Java can also represent uppercase letters, lowercase letters and a considerable variety of special symbols. Every character has a corresponding integer representation. The set of characters a computer uses and the corresponding integer representations for those characters is called that computer's character set. You can indicate a character value in a program simply by enclosing that character in single quotes, as in `'A'`.

You can determine the integer equivalent of a character by preceding that character with `(int)`, as in

```
(int) 'A'
```

This form is called a cast operator. (You will learn about cast operators in Chapter 4.) The following statement outputs a character and its integer equivalent:

```
System.out.printf(
   "The character %c has the value %d\n", 'A', ( (int) 'A' ) );
```

When the preceding statement executes, it displays the character A and the value 65 (from the so-called Unicode® character set) as part of the string. Note that the format specifier `%c` is a placeholder for a character (in this case, the character `'A'`).

Using statements similar to the one shown earlier in this exercise, write an application that displays the integer equivalents of some uppercase letters, lowercase letters, digits and special symbols. Display the integer equivalents of the following: A B C a b c 0 1 2 $ * + / and the blank character.

2.30   Write an application that inputs one number consisting of five digits from the user, separates the number into its individual digits and prints the digits separated from one another by three spaces each. For example, if the user types in the number 42339, the program should print

```
4    2    3    3    9
```

Assume that the user enters the correct number of digits. What happens when you execute the program and type a number with more than five digits? What happens when you execute the program and type a number with fewer than five digits? [*Hint*: It is possible to do this exercise with the techniques you learned in this chapter. You will need to use both division and remainder operations to "pick off" each digit.]

2.31   Using only the programming techniques you learned in this chapter, write an application that calculates the squares and cubes of the numbers from 0 to 10 and prints the resulting values in table format, as shown below. [*Note:* This program does not require any input from the user.]

```
number   square   cube
0        0        0
1        1        1
2        4        8
3        9        27
4        16       64
5        25       125
6        36       216
7        49       343
8        64       512
9        81       729
10       100      1000
```

2.32   Write a program that inputs five numbers and determines and prints the number of negative numbers input, the number of positive numbers input and the number of zeros input

Introduction to Classes and Objects

*You will see something new.
Two things. And I call them
Thing One and Thing Two.*
—Dr. Theodor Seuss Geisel

*Nothing can have value
without being an object of
utility.*
—Karl Marx

*Your public servants serve
you right.*
—Adlai E. Stevenson

*Knowing how to answer one
who speaks,
To reply to one who sends a
message.*
—Amenemope

OBJECTIVES

In this chapter you will learn:

■ What classes, objects, methods and instance variables are.

■ How to declare a class and use it to create an object.

■ How to declare methods in a class to implement the class's behaviors.

■ How to declare instance variables in a class to implement the class's attributes.

■ How to call an object's method to make that method perform its task.

■ The differences between instance variables of a class and local variables of a method.

■ How to use a constructor to ensure that an object's data is initialized when the object is created.

■ The differences between primitive and reference types.

3.1 Introduction

We introduced the basic terminology and concepts of object-oriented programming in Section 1.16. In Chapter 2, you began to use those concepts to create simple applications that displayed messages to the user, obtained information from the user, performed calculations and made decisions. One common feature of every application in Chapter 2 was that all the statements that performed tasks were located in method `main`. Typically, the applications you develop in this book will consist of two or more classes, each containing one or more methods. If you become part of a development team in industry, you might work on applications that contain hundreds, or even thousands, of classes. In this chapter, we present a simple framework for organizing object-oriented applications in Java.

First, we motivate the notion of classes with a real-world example. Then we present five complete working applications to demonstrate creating and using your own classes. The first four of these examples begin our case study on developing a grade-book class that instructors can use to maintain student test scores. This case study is enhanced over the next several chapters, culminating with the version presented in Chapter 7, Arrays. The last example in the chapter introduces floating-point numbers—that is, numbers containing decimal points, such as 0.0345, –7.23 and 100.7—in the context of a bank account class that maintains a customer's balance.

3.2 Classes, Objects, Methods and Instance Variables

Let's begin with a simple analogy to help you understand classes and their contents. Suppose you want to drive a car and make it go faster by pressing down on its accelerator pedal. What must happen before you can do this? Well, before you can drive a car, someone has to design the car. A car typically begins as engineering drawings, similar to the blueprints used to design a house. These engineering drawings include the design for an accelerator pedal to make the car go faster. The pedal "hides" the complex mechanisms that actually make the car go faster, just as the brake pedal "hides" the mechanisms that slow the car and the steering wheel "hides" the mechanisms that turn the car. This enables people with little or no knowledge of how engines work to drive a car easily.

Unfortunately, you cannot drive the engineering drawings of a car. Before you can drive a car, the car must be built from the engineering drawings that describe it. A completed car will have an actual accelerator pedal to make the car go faster, but even that's not enough—the car will not accelerate on its own, so the driver must press the accelerator pedal.

Now let's use our car example to introduce the key programming concepts of this section. Performing a task in a program requires a method. The method describes the mechanisms that actually perform its tasks. The method hides from its user the complex tasks that it performs, just as the accelerator pedal of a car hides from the driver the complex mechanisms of making the car go faster. In Java, we begin by creating a program unit called a class to house a method, just as a car's engineering drawings house the design of an accelerator pedal. In a class, you provide one or more methods that are designed to perform the class's tasks. For example, a class that represents a bank account might contain one method to deposit money to an account, another to withdraw money from an account and a third to inquire what the current balance is.

Just as you cannot drive an engineering drawing of a car, you cannot "drive" a class. Just as someone has to build a car from its engineering drawings before you can actually drive a car, you must build an object of a class before you can get a program to perform the tasks the class describes how to do. That is one reason Java is known as an object-oriented programming language.

When you drive a car, pressing its gas pedal sends a message to the car to perform a task—that is, make the car go faster. Similarly, you send messages to an object—each message is known as a method call and tells a method of the object to perform its task.

Thus far, we have used the car analogy to introduce classes, objects and methods. In addition to the capabilities a car provides, it also has many attributes, such as its color, the number of doors, the amount of gas in its tank, its current speed and its total miles driven (i.e., its odometer reading). Like the car's capabilities, these attributes are represented as part of a car's design in its engineering diagrams. As you drive a car, these attributes are always associated with the car. Every car maintains its own attributes. For example, each car knows how much gas is in its own gas tank, but not how much is in the tanks of other cars. Similarly, an object has attributes that are carried with the object as it is used in a program. These attributes are specified as part of the object's class. For example, a bank account object has a balance attribute that represents the amount of money in the account. Each bank account object knows the balance in the account it represents, but not the balances of the other accounts in the bank. Attributes are specified by the class's instance variables.

The remainder of this chapter presents examples that demonstrate the concepts we introduced in the context of the car analogy. The first four examples, summarized below, incrementally build a GradeBook class to demonstrate these concepts:

1. The first example presents a GradeBook class with one method that simply displays a welcome message when it is called. We then show how to create an object of that class and call the method so that it displays the welcome message.

2. The second example modifies the first by allowing the method to receive a course name as an argument and by displaying the name as part of the welcome message.

3. The third example shows how to store the course name in a GradeBook object. For this version of the class, we also show how to use methods to set the course name and obtain the course name.

4. The fourth example demonstrates how the data in a GradeBook object can be initialized when the object is created—the initialization is performed by the class's constructor.

The last example in the chapter presents an Account class that reinforces the concepts presented in the first four examples and introduces floating-point numbers—numbers containing decimal points, such as 0.0345, −7.23 and 100.7. For this purpose, we present an Account class that represents a bank account and maintains its balance as a floating-point number. The class contains two methods—one that credits a deposit to the account, thus increasing the balance, and another that retrieves the balance. The class's constructor allows the balance of each Account object to be initialized as the object is created. We create two Account objects and make deposits into each to show that each object maintains its own balance. The example also demonstrates how to input and display floating-point numbers.

3.3 Declaring a Class with a Method and Instantiating an Object of a Class

We begin with an example that consists of classes GradeBook (Fig. 3.1) and GradeBook-Test (Fig. 3.2). Class GradeBook (declared in file GradeBook.java) will be used to display a message on the screen (Fig. 3.2) welcoming the instructor to the grade-book application. Class GradeBookTest (declared in file GradeBookTest.java) is an application class in which the main method will use class GradeBook. Each class declaration that begins with keyword public must be stored in a file that has the same name as the class and ends with the .java file-name extension. Thus, classes GradeBook and GradeBookTest must be declared in separate files, because each class is declared public.

Common Programming Error 3.1

Declaring more than one public class in the same file is a compilation error.

Class *GradeBook*
The GradeBook class declaration (Fig. 3.1) contains a displayMessage method (lines 7–10) that displays a message on the screen. Line 9 of the class performs the work of displaying the message. Recall that a class is like a blueprint—we'll need to make an object of this class and call its method to get line 9 to execute and display its message.

```
1   // Fig. 3.1: GradeBook.java
2   // Class declaration with one method.
3
4   public class GradeBook
5   {
6      // display a welcome message to the GradeBook user
7      public void displayMessage()
8      {
9         System.out.println( "Welcome to the Grade Book!" );
10     } // end method displayMessage
11
12  } // end class GradeBook
```

Fig. 3.1 | Class declaration with one method.

The class declaration begins at line 4. The keyword public is an access modifier. For now, we will simply declare every class public. Every class declaration contains keyword class followed immediately by the class's name. Every class's body is enclosed in a pair of left and right braces ({ and }), as in lines 5 and 12 of class GradeBook.

In Chapter 2, each class we declared had one method named main. Class GradeBook also has one method—displayMessage (lines 7–10). Recall that main is a special method that is always called automatically by the Java Virtual Machine (JVM) when you execute an application. Most methods do not get called automatically. As you will soon see, you must call method displayMessage to tell it to perform its task.

The method declaration begins with keyword public to indicate that the method is "available to the public"—that is, it can be called from outside the class declaration's body by methods of other classes. Keyword void indicates that this method will perform a task but will not return (i.e., give back) any information to its calling method when it completes its task. You have already used methods that return information—for example, in Chapter 2 you used Scanner method nextInt to input an integer typed by the user at the keyboard. When nextInt inputs a value, it returns that value for use in the program.

The name of the method, displayMessage, follows the return type. By convention, method names begin with a lowercase first letter and all subsequent words in the name begin with a capital letter. The parentheses after the method name indicate that this is a method. An empty set of parentheses, as shown in line 7, indicates that this method does not require additional information to perform its task. Line 7 is commonly referred to as the method header. Every method's body is delimited by left and right braces ({ and }), as in lines 8 and 10.

The body of a method contains statement(s) that perform the method's task. In this case, the method contains one statement (line 9) that displays the message "Welcome to the Grade Book!" followed by a newline in the command window. After this statement executes, the method has completed its task.

Next, we'd like to use class GradeBook in an application. As you learned in Chapter 2, method main begins the execution of every application. A class that contains method main is a Java application. Such a class is special because the JVM can use main to begin execution. Class GradeBook is not an application because it does not contain main. Therefore, if you try to execute GradeBook by typing java GradeBook in the command window, you will get the error message:

```
Exception in thread "main" java.lang.NoSuchMethodError: main
```

This was not a problem in Chapter 2, because every class you declared had a main method. To fix this problem for the GradeBook, we must either declare a separate class that contains a main method or place a main method in class GradeBook. To help you prepare for the larger programs you will encounter later in this book and in industry, we use a separate class (GradeBookTest in this example) containing method main to test each new class we create in this chapter.

Class *GradeBookTest*

The GradeBookTest class declaration (Fig. 3.2) contains the main method that will control our application's execution. Any class that contains main declared as shown on line 7 can be used to execute an application. This class declaration begins at line 4 and ends at line 16. The class contains only a main method, which is typical of many classes that begin an application's execution.

```
 1   // Fig. 3.2: GradeBookTest.java
 2   // Create a GradeBook object and call its displayMessage method.
 3
 4   public class GradeBookTest
 5   {
 6      // main method begins program execution
 7      public static void main( String args[] )
 8      {
 9         // create a GradeBook object and assign it to myGradeBook
10         GradeBook myGradeBook = new GradeBook();
11
12         // call myGradeBook's displayMessage method
13         myGradeBook.displayMessage();
14      } // end main
15
16   } // end class GradeBookTest
```

```
Welcome to the Grade Book!
```

Fig. 3.2 | Creating an object of class GradeBook and calling its displayMessage method.

Lines 7–14 declare method main. Recall from Chapter 2 that the main header must appear as shown in line 7; otherwise, the application will not execute. A key part of enabling the JVM to locate and call method main to begin the application's execution is the static keyword (line 7), which indicates that main is a static method. A static method is special because it can be called without first creating an object of the class in which the method is declared. We thoroughly explain static methods in Chapter 6, Methods: A Deeper Look.

In this application, we'd like to call class GradeBook's displayMessage method to display the welcome message in the command window. Typically, you cannot call a method that belongs to another class until you create an object of that class, as shown in line 10. We begin by declaring variable myGradeBook. Note that the variable's type is GradeBook— the class we declared in Fig. 3.1. Each new class you create becomes a new type in Java that can be used to declare variables and create objects. Programmers can declare new class types as needed; this is one reason why Java is known as an extensible language.

Variable myGradeBook is initialized with the result of the class instance creation expression new GradeBook(). Keyword new creates a new object of the class specified to the right of the keyword (i.e., GradeBook). The parentheses to the right of the GradeBook are required. As you will learn in Section 3.7, those parentheses in combination with a class name represent a call to a constructor, which is similar to a method, but is used only at the time an object is created to initialize the object's data. In that section you will see that data can be placed in parentheses to specify initial values for the object's data. For now, we simply leave the parentheses empty.

Just as we can use object System.out to call methods print, printf and println, we can now use myGradeBook to call method displayMessage. Line 13 calls the method displayMessage (declared at lines 7–10 of Fig. 3.1) using variable myGradeBook followed by a dot separator (.), the method name displayMessage and an empty set of parentheses. This call causes the displayMessage method to perform its task. This method call differs from the method calls in Chapter 2 that displayed information in a command window—

each of those method calls provided arguments that specified the data to display. At the beginning of line 13, "myGradeBook." indicates that main should use the GradeBook object that was created on line 10. Line 7 of Fig. 3.1 indicates that method displayMessage has an empty parameter list—that is, displayMessage does not require additional information to perform its task. For this reason, the method call (line 13 of Fig. 3.2) specifies an empty set of parentheses after the method name to indicate that no arguments are being passed to method displayMessage. When method displayMessage completes its task, method main continues executing at line 14. This is the end of method main, so the program terminates.

Compiling an Application with Multiple Classes
You must compile the classes in Fig. 3.1 and Fig. 3.2 before you can execute the application. First, change to the directory that contains the application's source-code files. Next, type the command

```
javac GradeBook.java GradeBookTest.java
```

to compile both classes at once. If the directory containing the application includes only the files for this application, you can compile all the classes in the directory with the command

```
javac *.java
```

The asterisk (*) in *.java indicates that all files in the current directory that end with the file name extension ".java" should be compiled.

*UML Class Diagram for Class **GradeBook***
Figure 3.3 presents a UML class diagram for class GradeBook of Fig. 3.1. Recall from Section 1.16 that the UML is a graphical language used by programmers to represent their object-oriented systems in a standardized manner. In the UML, each class is modeled in a class diagram as a rectangle with three compartments. The top compartment contains the name of the class centered horizontally in boldface type. The middle compartment contains the class's attributes, which correspond to instance variables in Java. In Fig. 3.3, the middle compartment is empty because the version of class GradeBook in Fig. 3.1 does not have any attributes. The bottom compartment contains the class's operations, which correspond to methods in Java. The UML models operations by listing the operation name followed by a set of parentheses. Class GradeBook has one method, displayMessage, so the bottom compartment of Fig. 3.3 lists one operation with this name. Method displayMessage does not require additional information to perform its tasks, so the parentheses following displayMessage in the class diagram are empty, just as they were in the method's declaration in line 7 of Fig. 3.1. The plus sign (+) in front of the operation name indicates that displayMessage is a public operation in the UML (i.e., a public method in Java). We will often use UML class diagrams to summarize a class's attributes and operations.

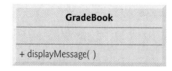

Fig. 3.3 | UML class diagram indicating that class GradeBook has a public displayMessage operation.

3.4 Declaring a Method with a Parameter

In our car analogy from Section 3.2, we discussed the fact that pressing a car's gas pedal sends a message to the car to perform a task—make the car go faster. But how fast should the car accelerate? As you know, the farther down you press the pedal, the faster the car accelerates. So the message to the car actually includes the task to perform and additional information that helps the car perform the task. This additional information is known as a parameter—the value of the parameter helps the car determine how fast to accelerate. Similarly, a method can require one or more parameters that represent additional information it needs to perform its task. A method call supplies values—called arguments—for each of the method's parameters. For example, the method System.out.println requires an argument that specifies the data to output in a command window. Similarly, to make a deposit into a bank account, a deposit method specifies a parameter that represents the deposit amount. When the deposit method is called, an argument value representing the deposit amount is assigned to the method's parameter. The method then makes a deposit of that amount.

Our next example declares class GradeBook (Fig. 3.4) with a displayMessage method that displays the course name as part of the welcome message. (See the sample execution in Fig. 3.5.) The new displayMessage method requires a parameter that represents the course name to output.

Before discussing the new features of class GradeBook, let's see how the new class is used from the main method of class GradeBookTest (Fig. 3.5). Line 12 creates a Scanner named input for reading the course name from the user. Line 15 creates an object of class Grade-Book and assigns it to variable myGradeBook. Line 18 prompts the user to enter a course name. Line 19 reads the name from the user and assigns it to the nameOfCourse variable, using Scanner method nextLine to perform the input. The user types the course name and presses *Enter* to submit the course name to the program. Note that pressing *Enter* inserts a newline character at the end of the characters typed by the user. Method nextLine reads characters typed by the user until the newline character is encountered, then returns a String containing the characters up to, but not including, the newline. The newline character is discarded. Note that Scanner provides a similar method—next—that reads individual words. When the user presses *Enter* after typing input, method next reads characters until a white-space character (such as a space, tab or newline) is encountered, then returns a String containing the characters up to, but not including, the white-space character (which is dis-

```
 1   // Fig. 3.4: GradeBook.java
 2   // Class declaration with a method that has a parameter.
 3
 4   public class GradeBook
 5   {
 6      // display a welcome message to the GradeBook user
 7      public void displayMessage( String courseName )
 8      {
 9         System.out.printf( "Welcome to the grade book for\n%s!\n",
10            courseName );
11      } // end method displayMessage
12
13   } // end class GradeBook
```

Fig. 3.4 | Class declaration with one method that has a parameter.

```
 1   // Fig. 3.5: GradeBookTest.java
 2   // Create GradeBook object and pass a String to
 3   // its displayMessage method.
 4   import java.util.Scanner; // program uses Scanner
 5
 6   public class GradeBookTest
 7   {
 8      // main method begins program execution
 9      public static void main( String args[] )
10      {
11         // create Scanner to obtain input from command window
12         Scanner input = new Scanner( System.in );
13
14         // create a GradeBook object and assign it to myGradeBook
15         GradeBook myGradeBook = new GradeBook();
16
17         // prompt for and input course name
18         System.out.println( "Please enter the course name:" );
19         String nameOfCourse = input.nextLine(); // read a line of text
20         System.out.println(); // outputs a blank line
21
22         // call myGradeBook's displayMessage method
23         // and pass nameOfCourse as an argument
24         myGradeBook.displayMessage( nameOfCourse );
25      } // end main
26
27   } // end class GradeBookTest
```

```
Please enter the course name:
CS101 Introduction to Java Programming

Welcome to the grade book for
CS101 Introduction to Java Programming!
```

Fig. 3.5 | Creating a GradeBook object and passing a String to its displayMessage method.

carded). All information after the first white-space character is not lost—it can be read by other statements that call the Scanner's methods later in the program.

Line 24 calls myGradeBooks's displayMessage method. The variable nameOfCourse in parentheses is the argument that is passed to method displayMessage so that the method can perform its task. The value of variable nameOfCourse in main becomes the value of method displayMessage's parameter courseName in line 7 of Fig. 3.4. When you execute this application, notice that method displayMessage outputs the name you type as part of the welcome message (Fig. 3.5).

Software Engineering Observation 3.1

Normally, objects are created with new. One exception is a string literal that is contained in quotes, such as "hello". String literals are references to String objects that are implicitly created by Java.

More on Arguments and Parameters

When you declare a method, you must specify in the method's declaration whether the method requires data to perform its task. To do so, you place additional information in the method's parameter list, which is located in the parentheses that follow the method name. The parameter list may contain any number of parameters, including none at all. Empty parentheses following the method name (as in Fig. 3.1, line 7) indicate that a method does not require any parameters. In Fig. 3.4, displayMessage's parameter list (line 7) declares that the method requires one parameter. Each parameter must specify a type and an identifier. In this case, the type String and the identifier courseName indicate that method displayMessage requires a String to perform its task. At the time the method is called, the argument value in the call is assigned to the corresponding parameter (in this case, courseName) in the method header. Then, the method body uses the parameter courseName to access the value. Lines 9–10 of Fig. 3.4 display parameter courseName's value, using the %s format specifier in printf's format string. Note that the parameter variable's name (Fig. 3.4, line 7) can be the same or different from the argument variable's name (Fig. 3.5, line 24).

A method can specify multiple parameters by separating each parameter from the next with a comma (we'll see an example of this in Chapter 6). The number of arguments in a method call must match the number of parameters in the parameter list of the called method's declaration. Also, the argument types in the method call must be consistent with the types of the corresponding parameters in the method's declaration. (As you will learn in subsequent chapters, an argument's type and its corresponding parameter's type are not always required to be identical.) In our example, the method call passes one argument of type String (nameOfCourse is declared as a String on line 19 of Fig. 3.5) and the method declaration specifies one parameter of type String (line 7 in Fig. 3.4). So the type of the argument in the method call exactly matches the type of the parameter in the method header.

Common Programming Error 3.2

A compilation error occurs if the number of arguments in a method call does not match the number of parameters in the method declaration.

Common Programming Error 3.3

A compilation error occurs if the types of the arguments in a method call are not consistent with the types of the corresponding parameters in the method declaration.

Updated UML Class Diagram for Class *GradeBook*

The UML class diagram of Fig. 3.6 models class GradeBook of Fig. 3.4. Like Fig. 3.1, this GradeBook class contains public operation displayMessage. However, this version of dis-

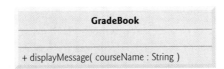

Fig. 3.6 | UML class diagram indicating that class GradeBook has a displayMessage operation with a courseName parameter of UML type String.

playMessage has a parameter. The UML models a parameter a bit differently from Java by listing the parameter name, followed by a colon and the parameter type in the parentheses following the operation name. The UML has its own data types similar to those of Java (but as you will see, not all the UML data types have the same names as the corresponding Java types). The UML type String does correspond to the Java type String. Method displayMessage of class GradeBook (Fig. 3.4) has a String parameter named courseName, so Fig. 3.6 lists courseName : String between the parentheses following displayMessage.

Notes on *import* Declarations

Notice the import declaration in Fig. 3.5 (line 4). This indicates to the compiler that the program uses class Scanner. Why do we need to import class Scanner, but not class System, String or class GradeBook? Most classes you will use in Java programs must be imported. Classes System and String are in package java.lang, which is implicitly imported into every Java program. Thus, all programs can use package java.lang's classes without explicitly importing them.

There is a special relationship between classes that are compiled in the same directory on disk, like classes GradeBook and GradeBookTest. By default, such classes are considered to be in the same package—known as the default package. Classes in the same package are implicitly imported into the source code files of other classes in the same package. Thus, an import declaration is not required when one class in a package uses another in the same package—such as when class GradeBookTest uses class GradeBook.

Actually, the import declaration at line 4 is not required if we always refer to class Scanner as java.util.Scanner, which includes the full package name and class name. This is known as the class's fully qualified class name. For example, line 12 could be written as

```
java.util.Scanner input = new java.util.Scanner( System.in );
```

Software Engineering Observation 3.2

The Java compiler does not require import declarations in a Java source code file if the fully qualified class name is specified every time a class name is used in the source code. But most Java programmers consider using fully qualified names to be cumbersome, and instead prefer to use import declarations.

3.5 Instance Variables, *set* Methods and *get* Methods

In Chapter 2, we declared all of an application's variables in the application's main method. Variables declared in the body of a particular method are known as local variables and can be used only in that method. When that method terminates, the values of its local variables are lost. Recall from Section 3.2 that an object has attributes that are carried with the object as it is used in a program. Such attributes exist before a method is called on an object and after the method completes execution.

A class normally consists of one or more methods that manipulate the attributes that belong to a particular object of the class. Attributes are represented as variables in a class declaration. Such variables are called fields and are declared inside a class declaration but outside the bodies of the class's method declarations. When each object of a class maintains its own copy of an attribute, the field that represents the attribute is also known as an instance variable—each object (instance) of the class has a separate instance of the variable in memory. The example in this section demonstrates a GradeBook class that contains a courseName instance variable to represent a particular GradeBook object's course name.

GradeBook *Class with an Instance Variable, a* set *Method and a* get *Method*

In our next application (Fig. 3.7–Fig. 3.8), class GradeBook (Fig. 3.7) maintains the course name as an instance variable so that it can be used or modified at any time during an application's execution. The class contains three methods—setCourseName, get-CourseName and displayMessage. Method setCourseName stores a course name in a GradeBook. Method getCourseName obtains a GradeBook's course name. Method displayMessage—which now specifies no parameters—still displays a welcome message that includes the course name. However, as you will see, the method now obtains the course name by calling another method in the same class—getCourseName.

A typical instructor teaches more than one course, each with its own course name. Line 7 declares that courseName is a variable of type String. Because the variable is declared in the body of the class (lines 6–30) but outside the bodies of the class's methods (lines 10–13, 16–19 and 22–28), line 7 is a declaration for an instance variable. Every instance (i.e., object) of class GradeBook contains one copy of each instance variable. For example, if there are two GradeBook objects, each object has its own copy of courseName

```
1   // Fig. 3.7: GradeBook.java
2   // GradeBook class that contains a courseName instance variable
3   // and methods to set and get its value.
4
5   public class GradeBook
6   {
7      private String courseName; // course name for this GradeBook
8
9      // method to set the course name
10     public void setCourseName( String name )
11     {
12        courseName = name; // store the course name
13     } // end method setCourseName
14
15     // method to retrieve the course name
16     public String getCourseName()
17     {
18        return courseName;
19     } // end method getCourseName
20
21     // display a welcome message to the GradeBook user
22     public void displayMessage()
23     {
24        // this statement calls getCourseName to get the
25        // name of the course this GradeBook represents
26        System.out.printf( "Welcome to the grade book for\n%s!\n",
27           getCourseName() );
28     } // end method displayMessage
29
30  } // end class GradeBook
```

Fig. 3.7 | GradeBook class that contains a courseName instance variable.

(one per object). A benefit of making `courseName` an instance variable is that all the methods of the class (in this case, `GradeBook`) can manipulate any instance variables that appear in the class (in this case, `courseName`).

Access Modifiers *public* and *private*

Most instance variable declarations are preceded with the `private` keyword (as in line 7). Like `public`, keyword `private` is an access modifier. Variables or methods declared with access modifier `private` are accessible only to methods of the class in which they are declared. Thus, variable `courseName` can be used only in methods `setCourseName`, `getCourseName` and `displayMessage` of (every object of) class `GradeBook`.

Software Engineering Observation 3.3

Precede every field and method declaration with an access modifier. As a rule of thumb, instance variables should be declared `private` and methods should be declared `public`. (We will see that it is appropriate to declare certain methods `private`, if they will be accessed only by other methods of the class.)

Good Programming Practice 3.1

We prefer to list the fields of a class first, so that, as you read the code, you see the names and types of the variables before you see them used in the methods of the class. It is possible to list the class's fields anywhere in the class outside its method declarations, but scattering them tends to lead to hard-to-read code.

Good Programming Practice 3.2

Place a blank line between method declarations to separate the methods and enhance program readability.

Declaring instance variables with access modifier `private` is known as data hiding. When a program creates (instantiates) an object of class `GradeBook`, variable `courseName` is encapsulated (hidden) in the object and can be accessed only by methods of the object's class. In class `GradeBook`, methods `setCourseName` and `getCourseName` manipulate the instance variable `courseName`.

Method `setCourseName` (lines 10–13) does not return any data when it completes its task, so its return type is `void`. The method receives one parameter—name—which represents the course name that will be passed to the method as an argument. Line 12 assigns name to instance variable `courseName`.

Method `getCourseName` (lines 16–19) returns a particular `GradeBook` object's course-Name. The method has an empty parameter list, so it does not require additional information to perform its task. The method specifies that it returns a `String`—this is known as the method's return type. When a method that specifies a return type is called and completes its task, the method returns a result to its calling method. For example, when you go to an automated teller machine (ATM) and request your account balance, you expect the ATM to give you back a value that represents your balance. Similarly, when a statement calls method `getCourseName` on a `GradeBook` object, the statement expects to receive the `GradeBook`'s course name (in this case, a `String`, as specified in the method declaration's return type). If you have a method square that returns the square of its argument, you would expect the statement

```
int result = square( 2 );
```

to return 4 from method `square` and assign 4 to variable `result`. If you have a method `maximum` that returns the largest of three integer arguments, you would expect the statement

```
int biggest = maximum( 27, 114, 51 );
```

to return 114 from method `maximum` and assign 114 to variable `biggest`.

Note that the statements at lines 12 and 18 each use `courseName` even though it was not declared in any of the methods. We can use `courseName` in the methods of class `GradeBook` because `courseName` is a field of the class. Also note that the order in which methods are declared in a class does not determine when they are called at execution time. So method `getCourseName` could be declared before method `setCourseName`.

Method `displayMessage` (lines 22–28) does not return any data when it completes its task, so its return type is `void`. The method does not receive parameters, so the parameter list is empty. Lines 26–27 output a welcome message that includes the value of instance variable `courseName`. Once again, we need to create an object of class `GradeBook` and call its methods before the welcome message can be displayed.

GradeBookTest Class That Demonstrates Class GradeBook

Class `GradeBookTest` (Fig. 3.8) creates one object of class `GradeBook` and demonstrates its methods. Line 11 creates a `Scanner` that will be used to obtain a course name from the user. Line 14 creates a `GradeBook` object and assigns it to local variable `myGradeBook` of type `GradeBook`. Lines 17–18 display the initial course name calling the object's `getCourseName` method. Note that the first line of the output shows the name "null." Unlike local variables, which are not automatically initialized, every field has a default initial value—a value provided by Java when the programmer does not specify the field's initial value. Thus, fields are not required to be explicitly initialized before they are used in a program—unless they must be initialized to values other than their default values. The default value for a field of type `String` (like `courseName` in this example) is `null`, which we say more about in Section 3.6.

Line 21 prompts the user to enter a course name. Local `String` variable `theName` (declared in line 22) is initialized with the course name entered by the user, which is returned by the call to the `nextLine` method of the `Scanner` object `input`. Line 23 calls object `myGradeBook`'s `setCourseName` method and supplies `theName` as the method's argument. When the method is called, the argument's value is assigned to parameter `name` (line 10, Fig. 3.7) of method `setCourseName` (lines 10–13, Fig. 3.7). Then the parameter's value is assigned to instance variable `courseName` (line 12, Fig. 3.7). Line 24 (Fig. 3.8) skips a line in the output, then line 27 calls object `myGradeBook`'s `displayMessage` method to display the welcome message containing the course name.

set *and* get *Methods*

A class's `private` fields can be manipulated only by methods of that class. So a client of an object—that is, any class that calls the object's methods—calls the class's `public` methods to manipulate the `private` fields of an object of the class. This is why the statements in method `main` (Fig. 3.8) call methods `setCourseName`, `getCourseName` and `displayMessage` on a `GradeBook` object. Classes often provide `public` methods to allow clients of the class to *set* (i.e., assign values to) or *get* (i.e., obtain the values of) `private` instance variables. The names of these methods need not begin with *set* or *get*, but this naming convention is highly recommended in Java and is required for special Java software components called JavaBeans that can simplify programming in many Java integrated development environments (IDEs). The

```
1   // Fig. 3.8: GradeBookTest.java
2   // Create and manipulate a GradeBook object.
3   import java.util.Scanner; // program uses Scanner
4
5   public class GradeBookTest
6   {
7      // main method begins program execution
8      public static void main( String args[] )
9      {
10        // create Scanner to obtain input from command window
11        Scanner input = new Scanner( System.in );
12
13        // create a GradeBook object and assign it to myGradeBook
14        GradeBook myGradeBook = new GradeBook();
15
16        // display initial value of courseName
17        System.out.printf( "Initial course name is: %s\n\n",
18           myGradeBook.getCourseName() );
19
20        // prompt for and read course name
21        System.out.println( "Please enter the course name:" );
22        String theName = input.nextLine(); // read a line of text
23        myGradeBook.setCourseName( theName ); // set the course name
24        System.out.println(); // outputs a blank line
25
26        // display welcome message after specifying course name
27        myGradeBook.displayMessage();
28     } // end main
29
30  } // end class GradeBookTest
```

```
Initial course name is: null

Please enter the course name:
CS101 Introduction to Java Programming

Welcome to the grade book for
CS101 Introduction to Java Programming!
```

Fig. 3.8 | Creating and manipulating a GradeBook object.

method that *sets* instance variable courseName in this example is called setCourseName, and the method that *gets* the value of instance variable courseName is called getCourseName.

GradeBook's UML Class Diagram with an Instance Variable and* set *and* get *Methods
Figure 3.9 contains an updated UML class diagram for the version of class GradeBook in Fig. 3.7. This diagram models class GradeBook's instance variable courseName as an attribute in the middle compartment of the class. The UML represents instance variables as attributes by listing the attribute name, followed by a colon and the attribute type. The UML type of attribute courseName is String. Instance variable courseName is private in Java, so the class diagram lists a minus sign (–) in front of the corresponding attribute's name. Class GradeBook contains three public methods, so the class diagram lists three op-

GradeBook
– courseName : String
+ setCourseName(name : String) + getCourseName( ) : String + displayMessage( )

Fig. 3.9 | UML class diagram indicating that class `GradeBook` has a `courseName` attribute of UML type `String` and three operations—`setCourseName` (with a `name` parameter of UML type `String`), `getCourseName` (returns UML type `String`) and `displayMessage`.

erations in the third compartment. Recall that the plus (+) sign before each operation name indicates that the operation is `public`. Operation `setCourseName` has a `String` parameter called `name`. The UML indicates the return type of an operation by placing a colon and the return type after the parentheses following the operation name. Method `getCourseName` of class `GradeBook` (Fig. 3.7) has a `String` return type in Java, so the class diagram shows a `String` return type in the UML. Note that operations `setCourseName` and `displayMessage` do not return values (i.e., they return `void`), so the UML class diagram does not specify a return type after the parentheses of these operations.

3.6 Primitive Types vs. Reference Types

Data types in Java are divided into two categories—primitive types and reference types (sometimes called nonprimitive types). The primitive types are `boolean`, `byte`, `char`, `short`, `int`, `long`, `float` and `double`. All nonprimitive types are reference types, so classes, which specify the types of objects, are reference types.

A primitive-type variable can store exactly one value of its declared type at a time. For example, an `int` variable can store one whole number (such as 7) at a time. When another value is assigned to that variable, its initial value is replaced. Primitive-type instance variables are initialized by default—variables of types `byte`, `char`, `short`, `int`, `long`, `float` and `double` are initialized to 0, and variables of type `boolean` are initialized to `false`. Programmers can specify their own initial values for primitive-type variables. Recall that local variables are *not* initialized by default.

Programs use variables of reference types (normally called references) to store the locations of objects in the computer's memory. Such variables are said to refer to objects in the program. Objects that are referenced may each contain many instance variables and methods. Line 14 of Fig. 3.8 creates an object of class `GradeBook`, and the variable `myGradeBook` contains a reference to that `GradeBook` object. Reference type instance variables are initialized by default to the value `null`—a reserved word that represents a "reference to nothing." This is why the first call to `getCourseName` in Fig. 3.8 returned `null`—the value of `courseName` had not been set, so the default initial value `null` was returned. The complete list of reserved words and keywords is listed in Appendix C, Keywords and Reserved Words.

A reference to an object is required to invoke (i.e., call) the object's methods. In the application of Fig. 3.8, the statements in method `main` use the variable `myGradeBook` to send messages to the `GradeBook` object. These messages are calls to methods (like `setCourseName` and `getCourseName`) that enable the program to interact with the `GradeBook` objects. For example, the statement (in line 23)

```
myGradeBook.setCourseName( theName ); // set the course name
```

uses myGradeBook to send the setCourseName message to the GradeBook object. The message includes the argument that setCourseName requires to perform its task. The GradeBook object uses this information to set the courseName instance variable. Note that primitive-type variables do not refer to objects, so such variables cannot be used to invoke methods.

Software Engineering Observation 3.4

A variable's declared type (e.g., int, double or GradeBook) indicates whether the variable is of a primitive or a reference type. If a variable's type is not one of the eight primitive types, then it is a reference type. For example, Account account1 indicates that account1 is a reference to an Account object).

3.7 Initializing Objects with Constructors

As mentioned in Section 3.5, when an object of class GradeBook (Fig. 3.7) is created, its instance variable courseName is initialized to null by default. What if you want to provide a course name when you create a GradeBook object? Each class you declare can provide a constructor that can be used to initialize an object of a class when the object is created. In fact, Java requires a constructor call for every object that is created. Keyword new calls the class's constructor to perform the initialization. The constructor call is indicated by the class name followed by parentheses. For example, line 14 of Fig. 3.8 first uses new to create a GradeBook object. The empty parentheses after "new GradeBook" indicate a call to the class's constructor without arguments. By default, the compiler provides a default constructor with no parameters in any class that does not explicitly include a constructor.

When you declare a class, you can provide your own constructor to specify custom initialization for objects of your class. For example, a programmer might want to specify a course name for a GradeBook object when the object is created, as in

```
GradeBook myGradeBook =
    new GradeBook( "CS101 Introduction to Java Programming" );
```

In this case, the argument "CS101 Introduction to Java Programming" is passed to the GradeBook object's constructor and used to initialize the courseName. The preceding statement requires that the class provide a constructor with a String parameter. Figure 3.10 contains a modified GradeBook class with such a constructor.

```
 1   // Fig. 3.10: GradeBook.java
 2   // GradeBook class with a constructor to initialize the course name.
 3
 4   public class GradeBook
 5   {
 6      private String courseName; // course name for this GradeBook
 7
 8      // constructor initializes courseName with String supplied as argument
 9      public GradeBook( String name )
10      {
11         courseName = name; // initializes courseName
12      } // end constructor
```

Fig. 3.10 | GradeBook class with a constructor that receives a course name. (Part 1 of 2.)

```
13
14      // method to set the course name
15      public void setCourseName( String name )
16      {
17         courseName = name; // store the course name
18      } // end method setCourseName
19
20      // method to retrieve the course name
21      public String getCourseName()
22      {
23         return courseName;
24      } // end method getCourseName
25
26      // display a welcome message to the GradeBook user
27      public void displayMessage()
28      {
29         // this statement calls getCourseName to get the
30         // name of the course this GradeBook represents
31         System.out.printf( "Welcome to the grade book for\n%s!\n",
32            getCourseName() );
33      } // end method displayMessage
34
35   } // end class GradeBook
```

Fig. 3.10 | GradeBook class with a constructor that receives a course name. (Part 2 of 2.)

Lines 9–12 declare the constructor for class GradeBook. A constructor must have the same name as its class. Like a method, a constructor specifies in its parameter list the data it requires to perform its task. When you create a new object, this data is placed in the parentheses that follow the class name. Line 9 indicates that class GradeBook's constructor has a parameter called name of type String. In line 11 of the constructor's body, the name passed to the constructor is assigned to instance variable courseName.

Figure 3.11 demonstrates initializing GradeBook objects using this constructor. Lines 11–12 create and initialize a GradeBook object. The constructor of class GradeBook is called with the argument "CS101 Introduction to Java Programming" to initialize the course name. The class instance creation expression to the right of = in lines 11–12 returns a reference to the new object, which is assigned to variable gradeBook1. Lines 13–14 repeat this process for another GradeBook object, this time passing the argument "CS102 Data Structures in Java" to initialize the course name for gradeBook2. Lines 17–20 use each object's getCourseName method to obtain the course names and show that they were indeed initialized when the objects were created. In the introduction to Section 3.5, you learned that each instance (i.e., object) of a class contains its own copy of the class's instance variables. The output confirms that each GradeBook maintains its own copy of instance variable courseName.

Like methods, constructors also can take arguments. However, an important difference between constructors and methods is that constructors cannot return values, so they cannot specify a return type (not even void). Normally, constructors are declared public. If a class does not include a constructor, the class's instance variables are initialized to their default values. If a programmer declares any constructors for a class, Java will not create a default constructor for that class.

```
1   // Fig. 3.11: GradeBookTest.java
2   // GradeBook constructor used to specify the course name at the
3   // time each GradeBook object is created.
4
5   public class GradeBookTest
6   {
7      // main method begins program execution
8      public static void main( String args[] )
9      {
10        // create GradeBook object
11        GradeBook gradeBook1 = new GradeBook(
12           "CS101 Introduction to Java Programming" );
13        GradeBook gradeBook2 = new GradeBook(
14           "CS102 Data Structures in Java" );
15
16        // display initial value of courseName for each GradeBook
17        System.out.printf( "gradeBook1 course name is: %s\n",
18           gradeBook1.getCourseName() );
19        System.out.printf( "gradeBook2 course name is: %s\n",
20           gradeBook2.getCourseName() );
21     } // end main
22
23  } // end class GradeBookTest
```

```
gradeBook1 course name is: CS101 Introduction to Java Programming
gradeBook2 course name is: CS102 Data Structures in Java
```

Fig. 3.11 | Constructor used to initialize GradeBook objects.

Error-Prevention Tip 3.1

Unless default initialization of your class's instance variables is acceptable, provide a constructor to ensure that your class's instance variables are properly initialized with meaningful values when each new object of your class is created.

Adding the Constructor to Class GradeBook's UML Class Diagram

The UML class diagram of Fig. 3.12 models class GradeBook of Fig. 3.10, which has a constructor that has a name parameter of type String. Like operations, the UML models constructors in the third compartment of a class in a class diagram. To distinguish a constructor from a class's operations, the UML places the word "constructor" between

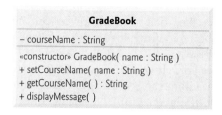

Fig. 3.12 | UML class diagram indicating that class GradeBook has a constructor that has a name parameter of UML type String.

guillemets (« and ») before the constructor's name. It is customary to list constructors before other operations in the third compartment.

3.8 Floating-Point Numbers and Type double

In our next application, we depart temporarily from our GradeBook case study to declare a class called Account that maintains the balance of a bank account. Most account balances are not whole numbers (e.g., 0, –22 and 1024). For this reason, class Account represents the account balance as a floating-point number (i.e., a number with a decimal point, such as 7.33, 0.0975 or 1000.12345). Java provides two primitive types for storing floating-point numbers in memory—float and double. The primary difference between them is that double variables can store numbers with larger magnitude and finer detail (i.e., more digits to the right of the decimal point—also known as the number's precision) than float variables.

Floating-Point Number Precision and Memory Requirements
Variables of type float represent single-precision floating-point numbers and have seven significant digits. Variables of type double represent double-precision floating-point numbers. These require twice as much memory as float variables and provide 15 significant digits—approximately double the precision of float variables. For the range of values required by most programs, variables of type float should suffice, but you can use double to "play it safe." In some applications, even variables of type double will be inadequate—such applications are beyond the scope of this book. Most programmers represent floating-point numbers with type double. In fact, Java treats all floating-point numbers you type in a program's source code (such as 7.33 and 0.0975) as double values by default. Such values in the source code are known as floating-point literals. See Appendix D, Primitive Types, for the ranges of values for floats and doubles.

Although floating-point numbers are not always 100% precise, they have numerous applications. For example, when we speak of a "normal" body temperature of 98.6, we do not need to be precise to a large number of digits. When we read the temperature on a thermometer as 98.6, it may actually be 98.5999473210643. Calling this number simply 98.6 is fine for most applications involving body temperatures. Due to the imprecise nature of floating-point numbers, type double is preferred over type float because double variables can represent floating-point numbers more accurately. For this reason, we use type double throughout the book.

Floating-point numbers also arise as a result of division. In conventional arithmetic, when we divide 10 by 3, the result is 3.3333333…, with the sequence of 3s repeating infinitely. The computer allocates only a fixed amount of space to hold such a value, so clearly the stored floating-point value can be only an approximation.

Common Programming Error 3.4

Using floating-point numbers in a manner that assumes they are represented precisely can lead to logic errors.

Account Class with an Instance Variable of Type double
Our next application (Fig. 3.13–Fig. 3.14) contains a class named Account (Fig. 3.13) that maintains the balance of a bank account. A typical bank services many accounts, each

```
1    // Fig. 3.13: Account.java
2    // Account class with a constructor to
3    // initialize instance variable balance.
4
5    public class Account
6    {
7       private double balance; // instance variable that stores the balance
8
9       // constructor
10      public Account( double initialBalance )
11      {
12         // validate that initialBalance is greater than 0.0;
13         // if it is not, balance is initialized to the default value 0.0
14         if ( initialBalance > 0.0 )
15            balance = initialBalance;
16      } // end Account constructor
17
18      // credit (add) an amount to the account
19      public void credit( double amount )
20      {
21         balance = balance + amount; // add amount to balance
22      } // end method credit
23
24      // return the account balance
25      public double getBalance()
26      {
27         return balance; // gives the value of balance to the calling method
28      } // end method getBalance
29
30   } // end class Account
```

Fig. 3.13 | Account class with an instance variable of type double.

with its own balance, so line 7 declares an instance variable named balance of type double. Variable balance is an instance variable because it is declared in the body of the class (lines 6–30) but outside the class's method declarations (lines 10–16, 19–22 and 25–28). Every instance (i.e., object) of class Account contains its own copy of balance.

Class Account contains a constructor and two methods. Since it is common for someone opening an account to place money in the account immediately, the constructor (lines 10–16) receives a parameter initialBalance of type double that represents the account's starting balance. Lines 14–15 ensure that initialBalance is greater than 0.0. If so, initialBalance's value is assigned to instance variable balance. Otherwise, balance remains at 0.0—its default initial value.

Method credit (lines 19–22) does not return any data when it completes its task, so its return type is void. The method receives one parameter named amount—a double value that will be added to the balance. Line 21 adds amount to the current value of balance, then assigns the result to balance (thus replacing the prior balance amount).

Method getBalance (lines 25–28) allows clients of the class (i.e., other classes that use this class) to obtain the value of a particular Account object's balance. The method specifies return type double and an empty parameter list.

Once again, note that the statements at lines 15, 21 and 27 use instance variable balance even though it was not declared in any of the methods. We can use balance in these methods because it is an instance variable of the class.

AccountTest Class to Use Class Account

Class AccountTest (Fig. 3.14) creates two Account objects (lines 10–11) and initializes them with 50.00 and -7.53, respectively. Lines 14–17 output the balance in each Account by calling the Account's getBalance method. When method getBalance is called for account1 from line 15, the value of account1's balance is returned from line 27 of Fig. 3.13 and displayed by the System.out.printf statement (Fig. 3.14, lines 14–15). Similarly, when method getBalance is called for account2 from line 17, the value of the account2's balance is returned from line 27 of Fig. 3.13 and displayed by the System.out.printf statement (Fig. 3.14, lines 16–17). Note that the balance of account2 is 0.00 because the constructor ensured that the account could not begin with a negative balance. The value is output by printf with the format specifier %.2f. The format specifier %f is used to output values of type float or double. The .2 between % and f represents the number of decimal places (2) that should be output to the right of the decimal point in the floating-point number—also known as the number's precision. Any floating point value output with %.2f will be rounded to the hundredths position—for example, 123.457 would be rounded to 123.46, and 27.333 would be rounded to 27.33.

```
1   // Fig. 3.14: AccountTest.java
2   // Create and manipulate an Account object.
3   import java.util.Scanner;
4
5   public class AccountTest
6   {
7      // main method begins execution of Java application
8      public static void main( String args[] )
9      {
10         Account account1 = new Account( 50.00 ); // create Account object
11         Account account2 = new Account( -7.53 ); // create Account object
12
13         // display initial balance of each object
14         System.out.printf( "account1 balance: $%.2f\n",
15            account1.getBalance() );
16         System.out.printf( "account2 balance: $%.2f\n\n",
17            account2.getBalance() );
18
19         // create Scanner to obtain input from command window
20         Scanner input = new Scanner( System.in );
21         double depositAmount; // deposit amount read from user
22
23         System.out.print( "Enter deposit amount for account1: " ); // prompt
24         depositAmount = input.nextDouble(); // obtain user input
25         System.out.printf( "\nadding %.2f to account1 balance\n\n",
26            depositAmount );
27         account1.credit( depositAmount ); // add to account1 balance
28
```

Fig. 3.14 | Inputting and outputting floating-point numbers with Account objects. (Part 1 of 2.)

```
29            // display balances
30            System.out.printf( "account1 balance: $%.2f\n",
31               account1.getBalance() );
32            System.out.printf( "account2 balance: $%.2f\n\n",
33               account2.getBalance() );
34
35            System.out.print( "Enter deposit amount for account2: " ); // prompt
36            depositAmount = input.nextDouble(); // obtain user input
37            System.out.printf( "\nadding %.2f to account2 balance\n\n",
38               depositAmount );
39            account2.credit( depositAmount ); // add to account2 balance
40
41            // display balances
42            System.out.printf( "account1 balance: $%.2f\n",
43               account1.getBalance() );
44            System.out.printf( "account2 balance: $%.2f\n",
45               account2.getBalance() );
46         } // end main
47
48      } // end class AccountTest
```

```
account1 balance: $50.00
account2 balance: $0.00

Enter deposit amount for account1: 25.53

adding 25.53 to account1 balance

account1 balance: $75.53
account2 balance: $0.00

Enter deposit amount for account2: 123.45

adding 123.45 to account2 balance

account1 balance: $75.53
account2 balance: $123.45
```

Fig. 3.14 | Inputting and outputting floating-point numbers with Account objects. (Part 2 of 2.)

Line 20 creates a Scanner that will be used to obtain deposit amounts from a user. Line 21 declares local variable depositAmount to store each deposit amount entered by the user. Unlike the instance variable balance in class Account, local variable depositAmount in main is not initialized to 0.0 by default. However, this variable does not need to be initialized here because its value will be determined by the user's input.

Line 23 prompts the user to enter a deposit amount for account1. Line 24 obtains the input from the user by calling Scanner object input's nextDouble method, which returns a double value entered by the user. Lines 25–26 display the deposit amount. Line 27 calls object account1's credit method and supplies depositAmount as the method's argument. When the method is called, the argument's value is assigned to parameter amount (line 19 of Fig. 3.13) of method credit (lines 19–22 of Fig. 3.13), then method credit adds that value to the balance (line 21 of Fig. 3.13). Lines 30–33 (Fig. 3.14) output the balances of both Accounts again to show that only account1's balance changed.

Line 35 prompts the user to enter a deposit amount for account2. Line 36 obtains the input from the user by calling Scanner object input's nextDouble method. Lines 37–38 display the deposit amount. Line 39 calls object account2's credit method and supplies depositAmount as the method's argument, then method credit adds that value to the balance. Finally, lines 42–45 output the balances of both Accounts again to show that only account2's balance changed.

UML Class Diagram for Class Account
The UML class diagram in Fig. 3.15 models class Account of Fig. 3.13. The diagram models the private attribute balance of UML type Double to correspond to the class's instance variable balance of Java type double. The diagram models class Account's constructor with a parameter initialBalance of UML type Double in the third compartment of the class. The class's two public methods are modeled as operations in the third compartment as well. The diagram models operation credit with an amount parameter of UML type Double (because the corresponding method has an amount parameter of Java type double) and operation getBalance with a return type of Double (because the corresponding Java method returns a double value).

3.9 (Optional) GUI and Graphics Case Study: Using Dialog Boxes

Introduction
This case study is designed for those who want to begin learning Java's powerful capabilities for creating graphical user interfaces (GUIs) and graphics. The GUI and Graphics Case Study appears in 8 brief sections (Fig. 3.16). Each section introduces a few basic concepts and provides visual, graphical examples and full source code. In the first few sections, you create your first graphical applications. In the following sections, you use the object-oriented programming concepts presented through Chapter 10 to create a drawing application that draws a variety of shapes. We hope you will find this case study informative and entertaining.

Displaying Text in a Dialog Box
Although the programs presented in this book thus far display output in the command window, many Java applications use windows or dialog boxes (also called dialogs) to display output. For example, World Wide Web browsers such as Netscape or Microsoft Internet Explorer display Web pages in their own windows. E-mail programs allow you to

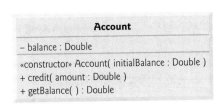

Fig. 3.15 | UML class diagram indicating that class Account has a private balance attribute of UML type Double, a constructor (with a parameter of UML type Double) and two public operations—credit (with an amount parameter of UML type Double) and getBalance (returns UML type Double).

type and read messages in a window. Typically, dialog boxes are windows in which programs display important messages to the user of the program. Class JOptionPane provides prepackaged dialog boxes that enable programs to display windows containing messages to users—such windows are called message dialogs. Figure 3.17 displays the string "Welcome\nto\nJava" in a message dialog.

Line 3 indicates that our program uses class JOptionPane from package javax.swing. This package contains many classes that help Java programmers create graphical user interfaces (GUIs) for applications. GUI components facilitate data entry by a program's user, and formatting or presenting data outputs to the user. In method main, line 10 calls method showMessageDialog of class JOptionPane to display a dialog box containing a message. The method requires two arguments. The first argument helps the Java application determine

Location	Title—Exercise(s)
Section 3.9	Using Dialog Boxes—Basic input and output with dialog boxes
Section 4.14	Creating Simple Drawings—Displaying and drawing lines on the screen
Section 5.10	Drawing Rectangles and Ovals—Using shapes to represent data
Section 6.13	Colors and Filled Shapes—Drawing a bull's-eye and random graphics
Section 7.13	Drawing Arcs—Drawing spirals with arcs
Section 8.18	Using Objects with Graphics—Storing shapes as objects
Section 9.8	Displaying Text and Images Using Labels—Providing status information
Section 10.8	Drawing with Polymorphism—Identifying the similarities between shapes

Fig. 3.16 | Summary of the GUI and Graphics Case Study in each chapter.

```
1   // Fig. 3.17: Dialog1.java
2   // Printing multiple lines in dialog box.
3   import javax.swing.JOptionPane; // import class JOptionPane
4
5   public class Dialog1
6   {
7      public static void main( String args[] )
8      {
9         // display a dialog with the message
10        JOptionPane.showMessageDialog( null, "Welcome\nto\nJava" );
11     } // end main
12  } // end class Dialog1
```

Fig. 3.17 | Using JOptionPane to display multiple lines in a dialog box.

where to position the dialog box. When the first argument is null, the dialog box appears in the center of the computer screen. The second argument is the String to display in the dialog box.

Method showMessageDialog is a special method of class JOptionPane called a static method. Such methods often define frequently used tasks that do not explicitly require creating an object. For example, many programs display messages to users in dialog boxes. Rather than require programmers to create code that performs this task, the designers of Java's JOptionPane class declared a static method for this purpose. Now, with a simple method call, all programmers can make a program display a dialog box containing a message. A static method typically is called by using its class name followed by a dot (.) and the method name, as in

ClassName.methodName(arguments)

Chapter 6, Methods: A Deeper Look will cover calling static methods in greater detail.

Entering Text in a Dialog Box

Our next application (Fig. 3.18) demonstrates input using dialogs. This program uses another predefined dialog box from class JOptionPane called an input dialog that allows the user to enter data for use in the program. The program asks for the user's name and responds with a greeting containing the name entered by the user.

```java
1   // Fig. 3.18: NameDialog.java
2   // Basic input with a dialog box.
3   import javax.swing.JOptionPane;
4
5   public class NameDialog
6   {
7      public static void main( String args[] )
8      {
9         // prompt user to enter name
10        String name =
11           JOptionPane.showInputDialog( "What is your name?" );
12
13        // create the message
14        String message =
15           String.format( "Welcome, %s, to Java Programming!", name );
16
17        // display the message to welcome the user by name
18        JOptionPane.showMessageDialog( null, message );
19     } // end main
20  } // end class NameDialog
```

Fig. 3.18 | Obtaining user input from a dialog.

Lines 10–11 use method `showInputDialog` of class `JOptionPane` to display a simple input dialog containing a prompt and a field for the user to enter text, known as a text field. The argument to `showInputDialog` is the prompt that indicates what the user should enter. The user types characters in the text field, then clicks the **OK** button or presses the *Enter* key to return the `String` to the program. Method `showInputDialog` returns a `String` containing the characters typed by the user, which we store in variable name. [*Note:* If you press the **Cancel** button in the dialog, the method returns `null` and the program displays the word "null" as the name.]

Lines 14–15 use `static` `String` method `format` to return a `String` containing a greeting with the name entered by the user. Method `format` is similar to method `System.out.printf`, except that `format` returns a formatted `String` rather than displaying it in a command window. Line 18 displays the greeting in a message dialog.

GUI and Graphics Case Study Exercise

3.1   Modify the addition program in Fig. 2.7 to use dialog-based input with `JOptionPane` instead of console-based input using `Scanner`. Since method `showInputDialog` only returns a `String`, you must convert the `String` the user enters to an `int` for use in calculations. Method `Integer.parseInt( String s )` takes a `String` argument representing an integer (e.g., the result of `JOptionPane.showInputDialog`) and returns the value as an `int`. If the `String` does not contain a valid integer, then the program will terminate with an error.

3.10 Wrap-Up

In this chapter, you learned the basic concepts of classes, objects, methods and instance variables—these will be used in most Java applications you create. In particular, you learned how to declare instance variables of a class to maintain data for each object of the class, and how to declare methods that operate on that data. You learned how to call a method to tell it to perform its task and how to pass information to methods as arguments. You learned the difference between a local variable of a method and an instance variable of a class and that only instance variables are initialized automatically. You also learned how to use a class's constructor to specify the initial values for an object's instance variables. Throughout the chapter, you saw how the UML can be used to create class diagrams that model the constructors, methods and attributes of classes. Finally, you learned about floating-point numbers—how to store them with variables of primitive type `double`, how to input them with a `Scanner` object and how to format them with `printf` and format specifier `%f` for display purposes. In the next chapter we begin our introduction to control statements, which specify the order in which a program's actions are performed. You will use these in your methods to specify how they should perform their tasks.

Summary

- Performing a task in a program requires a method. Inside the method you put the mechanisms that make the method do its tasks—that is, the method hides the implementation details of the tasks that it performs.

- The program unit that houses a method is called a class. A class may contain one or more methods that are designed to perform the class's tasks.

- A method can perform a task and return a result.

- A class can be used to create an instance of the class called an object. This is one of the reasons Java is known as an object-oriented programming language.

- Each message sent to an object is known as a method call and tells a method of the object to perform its task.
- Each method can specify parameters that represent additional information the method requires to perform its task correctly. A method call supplies values—called arguments—for the method's parameters.
- An object has attributes that are carried with the object as it is used in a program. These attributes are specified as part of the object's class. Attributes are specified in classes by fields.
- Each class declaration that begins with keyword `public` must be stored in a file that has exactly the same name as the class and ends with the `.java` file-name extension.
- Keyword `public` is an access modifier.
- Every class declaration contains keyword `class` followed immediately by the class's name.
- A method declaration that begins with keyword `public` indicates that the method is "available to the public"—that is, it can be called by other classes declared outside the class declaration.
- Keyword `void` indicates that a method will perform a task but will not return any information when it completes its task.
- By convention, method names begin with a lowercase first letter and all subsequent words in the name begin with a capital first letter.
- Empty parentheses following a method name indicate that the method does not require any parameters to perform its task.
- Every method's body is delimited by left and right braces ({ and }).
- The body of a method contains statements that perform the method's task. After the statements execute, the method has completed its task.
- When you attempt to execute a class, Java looks for the class's `main` method to begin execution.
- Any class that contains `public static void main( String args[] )` can be used to execute an application.
- Typically, you cannot call a method that belongs to another class until you create an object of that class.
- Class instance creation expressions beginning with keyword `new` create new objects.
- To call a method of an object, follow the variable name with a dot separator (.), the method name and a set of parentheses containing the method's arguments.
- Methods often require additional information to perform their tasks. Such additional information is provided to methods via arguments in method calls.
- `Scanner` method `nextLine` reads characters until a newline character is encountered, then returns the characters as a `String`.
- `Scanner` method `next` reads characters until any white-space character is encountered, then returns the characters as a `String`.
- A method that requires data to perform its task must specify this in its declaration by placing additional information in the method's parameter list.
- Each parameter must specify both a type and an identifier.
- At the time a method is called, its arguments are assigned to its parameters. Then the method body uses the parameter variables to access the argument values.
- A method can specify multiple parameters by separating each parameter from the next with a comma.

- The number of arguments in the method call must match the number of parameters in the method declaration's parameter list. Also, the argument types in the method call must be consistent with the types of the corresponding parameters in the method's declaration.

- Class `String` is in package `java.lang`, which is imported implicitly into all source-code files.

- There is a special relationship between classes that are compiled in the same directory on disk. By default, such classes are considered to be in the same package—known as the default package. Classes in the same package are implicitly imported into the source code files of other classes in the same package. Thus, an `import` declaration is not required when one class in a package uses another in the same package.

- An `import` declaration is not required if you always refer to a class with its fully qualified class name.

- Variables declared in the body of a particular method are known as local variables and can be used only in that method.

- A class normally consists of one or more methods that manipulate the attributes (data) that belong to a particular object of the class. Attributes are represented as fields in a class declaration. Such variables are called fields and are declared inside a class declaration but outside the bodies of the class's method declarations.

- When each object of a class maintains its own copy of an attribute, the field that represents the attribute is also known as an instance variable. Each object (instance) of the class has a separate instance of the variable in memory.

- Most instance variable declarations are preceded with the `private` access modifier. Variables or methods declared with access modifier `private` are accessible only to methods of the class in which they are declared.

- Declaring instance variables with access modifier `private` is known as data hiding.

- A benefit of fields is that all the methods of the class can use the fields. Another distinction between a field and a local variable is that a field has a default initial value provided by Java when the programmer does not specify the field's initial value, but a local variable does not.

- The default value for a field of type `String` is `null`.

- When a method that specifies a return type is called and completes its task, the method returns a result to its calling method.

- Classes often provide `public` methods to allow clients of the class to *set* or *get* `private` instance variables. The names of these methods need not begin with *set* or *get*, but this naming convention is highly recommended in Java and is required for special Java software components called Java-Beans.

- Types in Java are divided into two categories—primitive types and reference types (sometimes called nonprimitive types). The primitive types are `boolean`, `byte`, `char`, `short`, `int`, `long`, `float` and `double`. All other types are reference types, so classes, which specify the types of objects, are reference types.

- A primitive-type variable can store exactly one value of its declared type at a time.

- Primitive-type instance variables are initialized by default. Variables of types `byte`, `char`, `short`, `int`, `long`, `float` and `double` are initialized to 0. Variables of type `boolean` are initialized to `false`.

- Programs use variables of reference types (called references) to store the location of an object in the computer's memory. Such variables refer to objects in the program. The object that is referenced may contain many instance variables and methods.

- Reference-type fields are initialized by default to the value `null`.

- A reference to an object is required to invoke an object's instance methods. A primitive-type variable does not refer to an object and therefore cannot be used to invoke a method.
- A constructor can be used to initialize an object of a class when the object is created.
- Constructors can specify parameters but cannot specify return types.
- If no constructor is provided for a class, the compiler provides a default constructor with no parameters.
- A floating-point number is a number with a decimal point, such as 7.33, 0.0975 or 1000.12345. Java provides two primitive types for storing floating-point numbers in memory—`float` and `double`. The primary difference between these types is that `double` variables can store numbers with larger magnitude and finer detail (known as the number's precision) than `float` variables.
- Variables of type `float` represent single-precision floating-point numbers and have seven significant digits. Variables of type `double` represent double-precision floating-point numbers. These require twice as much memory as `float` variables and provide 15 significant digits—approximately double the precision of `float` variables.
- Floating-point values that appear in source code are known as floating-point literals and are type `double` by default.
- `Scanner` method `nextDouble` returns a `double` value.
- The format specifier `%f` is used to output values of type `float` or `double`. A precision can be specified between `%` and `f` to represent the number of decimal places that should be output to the right of the decimal point in the floating-point number.
- The default value for a field of type `double` is `0.0`, and the default value for a field of type `int` is `0`.
- In the UML, each class is modeled in a class diagram as a rectangle with three compartments. The top compartment contains the name of the class centered horizontally in boldface. The middle compartment contains the class's attributes, which correspond to fields in Java. The bottom compartment contains the class's operations, which correspond to methods and constructors in Java.
- The UML models operations by listing the operation name followed by a set of parentheses. A plus sign (+) in front of the operation name indicates that the operation is a `public` operation in the UML (i.e., a `public` method in Java).
- The UML models a parameter of an operation by listing the parameter name, followed by a colon and the parameter type between the parentheses following the operation name.
- The UML has its own data types similar to those of Java. Not all the UML data types have the same names as the corresponding Java types.
- The UML type `String` corresponds to the Java type `String`.
- The UML represents instance variables as attributes by listing the attribute name, followed by a colon and the attribute type.
- Private attributes are preceded by a minus sign (–) in the UML.
- The UML indicates the return type of an operation by placing a colon and the return type after the parentheses following the operation name.
- UML class diagrams do not specify return types for operations that do not return values.
- Like operations, the UML models constructors in the third compartment of a class diagram. To distinguish a constructor from a class's operations, the UML places the word "constructor" between guillemets (« and ») before the constructor's name.

Terminology

%f format specifier

access modifier

attribute (UML)

calling method

class

class declaration

class instance

class keyword

class instance creation expression

client of an object or a class

compartment in a class diagram (UML)

constructor

create an object

data hiding

default constructor

default package

default value

dot (.) separator

double-precision floating-point number

double primitive type

field

float primitive type

floating-point number

get method

guillemets, « and » (UML)

instance of a class (object)

instance variable

instantiate (or create) an object

invoke a method

.java file name extension

local variable

message

method

method header

new keyword

next method of class Scanner

nextDouble method of class Scanner

nextLine method of class Scanner

nonprimitive types

null reserved word

object (or instance)

operation (UML)

parameter

parameter list

precision of a floating-point value

precision of a formatted floating-point number

private access modifier

public access modifier

public method

refer to an object

reference

reference type

send a message

set method

single-precision floating-point number

UML class diagram

void keyword

Self-Review Exercises

3.1 Fill in the blanks in each of the following:
  a) A house is to a blueprint as a(n) _____ is to a class.
  b) Each class declaration that begins with keyword _____ must be stored in a file that has exactly the same name as the class and ends with the .java file-name extension.
  c) Every class declaration contains keyword _____ followed immediately by the class's name.
  d) Keyword _____ creates an object of the class specified to the right of the keyword.
  e) Each parameter must specify both a(n) _____ and a(n) _____.
  f) By default, classes that are compiled in the same directory are considered to be in the same package—known as the _____.
  g) When each object of a class maintains its own copy of an attribute, the field that represents the attribute is also known as a(n) _____.
  h) Java provides two primitive types for storing floating-point numbers in memory—_____ and _____.
  i) Variables of type double represent _____ floating-point numbers.
  j) Scanner method _____ returns a double value.
  k) Keyword public is a(n) _____.

l) Return type _____ indicates that a method will perform a task but will not return any information when it completes its task.

m) `Scanner` method _____ reads characters until a newline character is encountered, then returns those characters as a `String`.

n) Class `String` is in package _____.

o) A(n) _____ is not required if you always refer to a class with its fully qualified class name.

p) A(n) _____ is a number with a decimal point, such as 7.33, 0.0975 or 1000.12345.

q) Variables of type `float` represent _____ floating-point numbers.

r) The format specifier _____ is used to output values of type `float` or `double`.

s) Types in Java are divided into two categories—_____ types and _____ types.

3.2   State whether each of the following is *true* or *false*. If *false*, explain why.

a) By convention, method names begin with an uppercase first letter and all subsequent words in the name begin with a capital first letter.

b) An `import` declaration is not required when one class in a package uses another in the same package.

c) Empty parentheses following a method name in a method declaration indicate that the method does not require any parameters to perform its task.

d) Variables or methods declared with access modifier `private` are accessible only to methods of the class in which they are declared.

e) A primitive-type variable can be used to invoke a method.

f) Variables declared in the body of a particular method are known as instance variables and can be used in all methods of the class.

g) Every method's body is delimited by left and right braces ({ and }).

h) Primitive-type local variables are initialized by default.

i) Reference-type instance variables are initialized by default to the value `null`.

j) Any class that contains `public static void main( String args[] )` can be used to execute an application.

k) The number of arguments in the method call must match the number of parameters in the method declaration's parameter list.

l) Floating-point values that appear in source code are known as floating-point literals and are type `float` by default.

3.3   What is the difference between a local variable and a field?

3.4   Explain the purpose of a method parameter. What is the difference between a parameter and an argument?

Answers to Self-Review Exercises

3.1   a) object. b) `public`. c) `class`. d) `new`. e) type, name.   f) default package. g) instance variable.   h) `float`, `double`.   i) double-precision.   j) `nextDouble`.   k) access modifier.   l) `void`. m) `nextLine`. n) `java.lang`. o) `import` declaration.   p) floating-point number. q) single-precision. r) `%f`.   s) primitive, reference.

3.2   a) False. By convention, method names begin with a lowercase first letter and all subsequent words in the name begin with a capital first letter. b) True. c) True. d) True. e) False. A primitive-type variable cannot be used to invoke a method—a reference to an object is required to invoke the object's methods. f) False. Such variables are called local variables and can be used only in the method in which they are declared. g) True. h) False. Primitive-type instance variables are initialized by default. i) True. j) True. k) True. l) False. Such literals are of type `double` by default.

3.3 A local variable is declared in the body of a method and can be used only from the point at which it is declared through the end of the method declaration. A field is declared in a class, but not in the body of any of the class's methods. Every object (instance) of a class has a separate copy of the class's fields. Also, fields are accessible to all methods of the class. (We will see an exception to this in Chapter 8, Classes and Objects: A Deeper Look.)

3.4 A parameter represents additional information that a method requires to perform its task. Each parameter required by a method is specified in the method's declaration. An argument is the actual value for a method parameter. When a method is called, the argument values are passed to the method so that it can perform its task.

Exercises

3.5 What is the purpose of keyword new? Explain what happens when this keyword is used in an application.

3.6 What is a default constructor? How are an object's instance variables initialized if a class has only a default constructor?

3.7 Explain the purpose of an instance variable.

3.8 Most classes need to be imported before they can be used in an application. Why is every application allowed to use classes System and String without first importing them?

3.9 Explain how a program could use class Scanner without importing the class from package java.util.

3.10 Explain why a class might provide a *set* method and a *get* method for an instance variable.

3.11 Modify class GradeBook (Fig. 3.10) as follows:
 a) Include a second String instance variable that represents the name of the course's instructor.
 b) Provide a *set* method to change the instructor's name and a *get* method to retrieve it.
 c) Modify the constructor to specify two parameters—one for the course name and one for the instructor's name.
 d) Modify method displayMessage such that it first outputs the welcome message and course name, then outputs "This course is presented by: " followed by the instructor's name.

Use your modified class in a test application that demonstrates the class's new capabilities.

3.12 Modify class Account (Fig. 3.13) to provide a method called debit that withdraws money from an Account. Ensure that the debit amount does not exceed the Account's balance. If it does, the balance should be left unchanged and the method should print a message indicating "Debit amount exceeded account balance." Modify class AccountTest (Fig. 3.14) to test method debit.

3.13 Create a class called Invoice that a hardware store might use to represent an invoice for an item sold at the store. An Invoice should include four pieces of information as instance variables— a part number (type String), a part description (type String), a quantity of the item being purchased (type int) and a price per item (double). Your class should have a constructor that initializes the four instance variables. Provide a *set* and a *get* method for each instance variable. In addition, provide a method named getInvoiceAmount that calculates the invoice amount (i.e., multiplies the quantity by the price per item), then returns the amount as a double value. If the quantity is not positive, it should be set to 0. If the price per item is not positive, it should be set to 0.0. Write a test application named InvoiceTest that demonstrates class Invoice's capabilities.

3.14 Create a class called Employee that includes three pieces of information as instance variables—a first name (type String), a last name (type String) and a monthly salary (double). Your class should have a constructor that initializes the three instance variables. Provide a *set* and a *get* method for each instance variable. If the monthly salary is not positive, set it to 0.0. Write a test application named EmployeeTest that demonstrates class Employee's capabilities. Create two Employee objects and display each object's *yearly* salary. Then give each Employee a 10% raise and display each Employee's yearly salary again.

3.15   Create a class called Date that includes three pieces of information as instance variables—a month (type int), a day (type int) and a year (type int). Your class should have a constructor that initializes the three instance variables and assumes that the values provided are correct. Provide a *set* and a *get* method for each instance variable. Provide a method displayDate that displays the month, day and year separated by forward slashes (/). Write a test application named DateTest that demonstrates class Date's capabilities.

4

Control Statements: Part 1

OBJECTIVES

In this chapter you will learn:

- To use basic problem-solving techniques.
- To develop algorithms through the process of top-down, stepwise refinement.
- To use the `if` and `if...else` selection statements to choose among alternative actions.
- To use the `while` repetition statement to execute statements in a program repeatedly.
- To use counter-controlled repetition and sentinel-controlled repetition.
- To use the assignment, increment and decrement operators.

4.1 Introduction

Before writing a program to solve a problem, it is essential to have a thorough understanding of the problem and a carefully planned approach to solving it. When writing a program, it is also essential to understand the types of building blocks that are available and to employ proven program-construction techniques. In this chapter and in Chapter 5, Control Statements: Part 2, we discuss these issues in our presentation of the theory and principles of structured programming. The concepts presented here are crucial in building classes and manipulating objects.

In this chapter, we introduce Java's `if`, `if...else` and `while` statements, three of the building blocks that allow programmers to specify the logic required for methods to perform their tasks. We devote a portion of this chapter (and Chapters 5 and 7) to further developing the `GradeBook` class introduced in Chapter 3. In particular, we add a method to the `GradeBook` class that uses control statements to calculate the average of a set of student grades. Another example demonstrates additional ways to combine control statements to solve a similar problem. We introduce Java's compound assignment operators and explore Java's increment and decrement operators. These additional operators abbreviate and simplify many program statements. Finally, we present an overview of the primitive data types available to programmers.

4.2 Algorithms

Any computing problem can be solved by executing a series of actions in a specific order. A procedure for solving a problem in terms of

1. the *actions* to execute and
2. the *order* in which these actions execute

is called an algorithm. The following example demonstrates that correctly specifying the order in which the actions execute is important.

Consider the "rise-and-shine algorithm" followed by one executive for getting out of bed and going to work: (1) Get out of bed; (2) take off pajamas; (3) take a shower; (4) get dressed; (5) eat breakfast; (6) carpool to work. This routine gets the executive to work well prepared to make critical decisions. Suppose that the same steps are performed in a slightly different order: (1) Get out of bed; (2) take off pajamas; (3) get dressed; (4) take a shower; (5) eat breakfast; (6) carpool to work. In this case, our executive shows up for work soaking wet.

Specifying the order in which statements (actions) execute in a program is called program control. This chapter investigates program control using Java's control statements.

4.3 Pseudocode

Pseudocode is an informal language that helps programmers develop algorithms without having to worry about the strict details of Java language syntax. The pseudocode we present is particularly useful for developing algorithms that will be converted to structured portions of Java programs. Pseudocode is similar to everyday English—it is convenient and user friendly, but it is not an actual computer programming language.

Pseudocode does not execute on computers. Rather, it helps the programmer "think out" a program before attempting to write it in a programming language, such as Java. This chapter provides several examples of how to use pseudocode to develop Java programs.

The style of pseudocode we present consists purely of characters, so programmers can type pseudocode conveniently, using any text-editor program. A carefully prepared pseudocode program can easily be converted to a corresponding Java program. In many cases, this simply requires replacing pseudocode statements with Java equivalents.

Pseudocode normally describes only statements representing the actions that occur after a programmer converts a program from pseudocode to Java and the program is run on a computer. Such actions might include input, output or a calculation. We typically do not include variable declarations in our pseudocode. However, some programmers choose to list variables and mention their purposes at the beginning of their pseudocode.

4.4 Control Structures

Normally, statements in a program are executed one after the other in the order in which they are written. This process is called sequential execution. Various Java statements, which we will soon discuss, enable the programmer to specify that the next statement to execute is not necessarily the next one in sequence. This is called transfer of control.

During the 1960s, it became clear that the indiscriminate use of transfers of control was the root of much difficulty experienced by software development groups. The blame was pointed at the **goto** statement (used in most programming languages of the time), which allows the programmer to specify a transfer of control to one of a very wide range of possible destinations in a program. The notion of so-called structured programming became almost synonymous with "goto elimination." [*Note:* Java does not have a goto statement; however, the word goto is reserved by Java and should not be used as an identifier in programs.]

The research of Bohm and Jacopini[1] had demonstrated that programs could be written without any goto statements. The challenge of the era for programmers was to shift their styles to "goto-less programming." Not until the 1970s did programmers start taking structured programming seriously. The results were impressive. Software development groups reported shorter development times, more frequent on-time delivery of systems and more frequent within-budget completion of software projects. The key to these successes was that structured programs were clearer, easier to debug and modify, and more likely to be bug free in the first place.

Bohm and Jacopini's work demonstrated that all programs could be written in terms of only three control structures—the sequence structure, the selection structure and the repetition structure. The term "control structures" comes from the field of computer science. When we introduce Java's implementations of control structures, we will refer to them in the terminology of the *Java Language Specification* as "control statements."

Sequence Structure in Java

The sequence structure is built into Java. Unless directed otherwise, the computer executes Java statements one after the other in the order in which they are written, that is, in sequence. The activity diagram in Fig. 4.1 illustrates a typical sequence structure in which two calculations are performed in order. Java lets us have as many actions as we want in a sequence structure. As we will soon see, anywhere a single action may be placed, we may place several actions in sequence.

Activity diagrams are part of the UML. An activity diagram models the workflow (also called the activity) of a portion of a software system. Such workflows may include a portion of an algorithm, such as the sequence structure in Fig. 4.1. Activity diagrams are composed of special-purpose symbols, such as action-state symbols (rectangles with their left and right sides replaced with arcs curving outward), diamonds and small circles. These symbols are connected by transition arrows, which represent the flow of the activity, that is, the order in which the actions should occur

Like pseudocode, activity diagrams help programmers develop and represent algorithms, although many programmers prefer pseudocode. Activity diagrams clearly show how control structures operate.

Consider the activity diagram for the sequence structure in Fig. 4.1. It contains two action states that represent actions to perform. Each action state contains an action expression—for example, "add grade to total" or "add 1 to counter"—that specifies a particular action to perform. Other actions might include calculations or input/output operations. The arrows in the activity diagram represent transitions, which indicate the order in which the actions represented by the action states occur. The program that implements the activities illustrated by the diagram in Fig. 4.1 first adds grade to total, then adds 1 to counter.

The solid circle located at the top of the activity diagram represents the activity's initial state—the beginning of the workflow before the program performs the modeled actions. The solid circle surrounded by a hollow circle that appears at the bottom of the diagram represents the final state—the end of the workflow after the program performs its actions.

Figure 4.1 also includes rectangles with the upper-right corners folded over. These are UML notes (like comments in Java)—explanatory remarks that describe the purpose of symbols in the diagram. Figure 4.1 uses UML notes to show the Java code associated with each action state in the activity diagram. A dotted line connects each note with the ele-

---

1. Bohm, C., and G. Jacopini, "Flow Diagrams, Turing Machines, and Languages with Only Two Formation Rules," *Communications of the ACM*, Vol. 9, No. 5, May 1966, pp. 336–371.

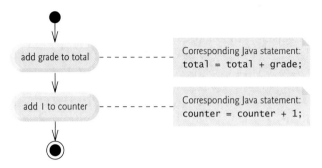

Fig. 4.1 | Sequence structure activity diagram.

ment that the note describes. Activity diagrams normally do not show the Java code that implements the activity. We use notes for this purpose here to illustrate how the diagram relates to Java code. For more information on the UML, please visit www.uml.org.

Selection Statements in Java

Java has three types of selection statements (discussed in this chapter and Chapter 5). The if statement either performs (selects) an action if a condition is true or skips the action, if the condition is false. The if...else statement performs an action if a condition is true and performs a different action if the condition is false. The switch statement (Chapter 5) performs one of many different actions, depending on the value of an expression.

The if statement is a single-selection statement because it selects or ignores a single action (or, as we will soon see, a single group of actions). The if...else statement is called a double-selection statement because it selects between two different actions (or groups of actions). The switch statement is called a multiple-selection statement because it selects among many different actions (or groups of actions).

Repetition Statements in Java

Java provides three repetition statements (also called looping statements) that enable programs to perform statements repeatedly as long as a condition (called the loop-continuation condition) remains true. The repetition statements are the while, do...while and for statements. (Chapter 5 presents the do...while and for statements.) The while and for statements perform the action (or group of actions) in their bodies zero or more times—if the loop-continuation condition is initially false, the action (or group of actions) will not execute. The do...while statement performs the action (or group of actions) in its body one or more times.

The words if, else, switch, while, do and for are Java keywords. Recall that keywords are used to implement various Java features, such as control statements. Keywords cannot be used as identifiers, such as variable names. A complete list of Java keywords appears in Appendix C.

Summary of Control Statements in Java

Java has only three kinds of control structures, which from this point forward we refer to as control statements: the sequence statement, selection statements (three types) and repetition statements (three types). Every program is formed by combining as many sequence, selection and repetition statements as is appropriate for the algorithm the program implements. As with the sequence statement in Fig. 4.1, we can model each control statement as an activity diagram. Each diagram contains an initial state and a final state that represent a control statement's entry point and exit point, respectively. Single-entry/single-exit control statements make it easy to build programs—the control statements are "attached" to one another by connecting the exit point of one to the entry point of the next. This procedure is similar to the way in which a child stacks building blocks, so we call it control-statement stacking. We will learn that there is only one other way in which control statements may be connected—control-statement nesting—in which a control statement appears inside another control statement. Thus, algorithms in Java programs are constructed from only three kinds of control statements, combined in only two ways. This is the essence of simplicity.

4.5 if Single-Selection Statement

Programs use selection statements to choose among alternative courses of action. For example, suppose that the passing grade on an exam is 60. The pseudocode statement

> *If student's grade is greater than or equal to 60*
>   *Print "Passed"*

determines whether the condition "student's grade is greater than or equal to 60" is true or false. If the condition is true, "Passed" is printed, and the next pseudocode statement in order is "performed." (Remember that pseudocode is not a real programming language.) If the condition is false, the *Print* statement is ignored, and the next pseudocode statement in order is performed. The indentation of the second line of this selection statement is optional, but recommended, because it emphasizes the inherent structure of structured programs.

The preceding pseudocode *If* statement may be written in Java as

```
if ( studentGrade >= 60 )
    System.out.println( "Passed" );
```

Note that the Java code corresponds closely to the pseudocode. This is one of the properties of pseudocode that makes it such a useful program development tool.

Figure 4.2 illustrates the single-selection if statement. This activity diagram contains what is perhaps the most important symbol in an activity diagram—the diamond, or decision symbol, which indicates that a decision is to be made. The workflow will continue along a path determined by the symbol's associated guard conditions, which can be true or false. Each transition arrow emerging from a decision symbol has a guard condition (specified in square brackets next to the transition arrow). If a guard condition is true, the workflow enters the action state to which the transition arrow points. In Fig. 4.2, if the grade is greater than or equal to 60, the program prints "Passed," then transitions to the final state of this activity. If the grade is less than 60, the program immediately transitions to the final state without displaying a message.

The if statement is a single-entry/single-exit control statement. We will see that the activity diagrams for the remaining control statements also contain initial states, transition arrows, action states that indicate actions to perform, decision symbols (with associated guard conditions) that indicate decisions to be made and final states. This is consistent with the action/decision model of programming we have been emphasizing.

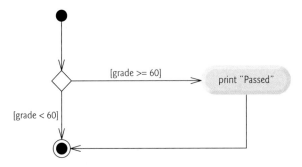

Fig. 4.2 | `if` single-selection statement UML activity diagram.

Envision seven bins, each containing only one type of Java control statement. The control statements are all empty. Your task is to assemble a program from as many of each type of control statement as the algorithm demands, combining the control statements in only two possible ways (stacking or nesting), then filling in the action states and decisions with action expressions and guard conditions appropriate for the algorithm. We will discuss the variety of ways in which actions and decisions can be written.

4.6 `if...else` Double-Selection Statement

The `if` single-selection statement performs an indicated action only when the condition is `true`; otherwise, the action is skipped. The `if...else` double-selection statement allows the programmer to specify an action to perform when the condition is true and a different action when the condition is false. For example, the pseudocode statement

> *If student's grade is greater than or equal to 60*
> > *Print "Passed"*
> *Else*
> > *Print "Failed"*

prints "Passed" if the student's grade is greater than or equal to 60, but prints "Failed" if it is less than 60. In either case, after printing occurs, the next pseudocode statement in sequence is "performed."

The preceding *If...Else* pseudocode statement can be written in Java as

```
if ( grade >= 60 )
   System.out.println( "Passed" );
else
   System.out.println( "Failed" );
```

Note that the body of the `else` is also indented. Whatever indentation convention you choose should be applied consistently throughout your programs. It is difficult to read programs that do not obey uniform spacing conventions.

Good Programming Practice 4.1

Indent both body statements of an `if...else` *statement.*

Good Programming Practice 4.2

If there are several levels of indentation, each level should be indented the same additional amount of space.

Figure 4.3 illustrates the flow of control in the if...else statement. Once again, the symbols in the UML activity diagram (besides the initial state, transition arrows and final state) represent action states and decisions. We continue to emphasize this action/decision model of computing. Imagine again a deep bin containing as many empty if...else statements as might be needed to build any Java program. Your job is to assemble these if...else statements (by stacking and nesting) with any other control statements required by the algorithm. You fill in the action states and decision symbols with action expressions and guard conditions appropriate to the algorithm you are developing.

Conditional Operator (?:)

Java provides the conditional operator (?:) that can be used in place of an if...else statement. This is Java's only ternary operator—this means that it takes three operands. Together, the operands and the ?: symbol form a conditional expression. The first operand (to the left of the ?) is a boolean expression (i.e., a condition that evaluates to a boolean value—true or false), the second operand (between the ? and :) is the value of the conditional expression if the boolean expression is true and the third operand (to the right of the :) is the value of the conditional expression if the boolean expression evaluates to false. For example, the statement

```
System.out.println( studentGrade >= 60 ? "Passed" : "Failed" );
```

prints the value of println's conditional-expression argument. The conditional expression in this statement evaluates to the string "Passed" if the boolean expression studentGrade >= 60 is true and evaluates to the string "Failed" if the boolean expression is false. Thus, this statement with the conditional operator performs essentially the same function as the if...else statement shown earlier in this section. The precedence of the conditional operator is low, so the entire conditional expression is normally placed in parentheses. We will see that conditional expressions can be used in some situations where if...else statements cannot.

Good Programming Practice 4.3

Conditional expressions are more difficult to read than if...else statements and should be used to replace only simple if...else statements that choose between two values.

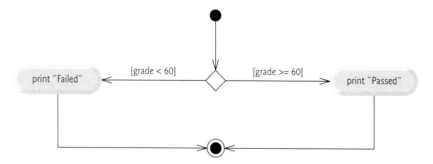

Fig. 4.3 | if...else double-selection statement UML activity diagram.

Nested if...else Statements

A program can test multiple cases by placing if...else statements inside other if...else statements to create nested if...else statements. For example, the following pseudocode represents a nested if...else that prints A for exam grades greater than or equal to 90, B for grades in the range 80 to 89, C for grades in the range 70 to 79, D for grades in the range 60 to 69 and F for all other grades:

> *If student's grade is greater than or equal to 90*
>> *Print "A"*
> *else*
>> *If student's grade is greater than or equal to 80*
>>> *Print "B"*
>> *else*
>>> *If student's grade is greater than or equal to 70*
>>>> *Print "C"*
>>> *else*
>>>> *If student's grade is greater than or equal to 60*
>>>>> *Print "D"*
>>>> *else*
>>>>> *Print "F"*

This pseudocode may be written in Java as

```
if ( studentGrade >= 90 )
   System.out.println( "A" );
else
   if ( studentGrade >= 80 )
      System.out.println( "B" );
   else
      if ( studentGrade >= 70 )
         System.out.println( "C" );
      else
         if ( studentGrade >= 60 )
            System.out.println( "D" );
         else
            System.out.println( "F" );
```

If studentGrade is greater than or equal to 90, the first four conditions will be true, but only the statement in the if-part of the first if...else statement will execute. After that statement executes, the else-part of the "outermost" if...else statement is skipped. Most Java programmers prefer to write the preceding if...else statement as

```
if ( studentGrade >= 90 )
   System.out.println( "A" );
else if ( studentGrade >= 80 )
   System.out.println( "B" );
else if ( studentGrade >= 70 )
   System.out.println( "C" );
else if ( studentGrade >= 60 )
   System.out.println( "D" );
else
   System.out.println( "F" );
```

The two forms are identical except for the spacing and indentation, which the compiler ignores. The latter form is popular because it avoids deep indentation of the code to the right. Such indentation often leaves little room on a line of code, forcing lines to be split and decreasing program readability.

Dangling-*else* Problem

The Java compiler always associates an else with the immediately preceding if unless told to do otherwise by the placement of braces ({ and }). This behavior can lead to what is referred to as the dangling-else problem. For example,

```
if ( x > 5 )
   if ( y > 5 )
      System.out.println( "x and y are > 5" );
else
   System.out.println( "x is <= 5" );
```

appears to indicate that if x is greater than 5, the nested if statement determines whether y is also greater than 5. If so, the string "x and y are > 5" is output. Otherwise, it appears that if x is not greater than 5, the else part of the if...else outputs the string "x is <= 5".

Beware! This nested if...else statement does not execute as it appears. The compiler actually interprets the statement as

```
if ( x > 5 )
   if ( y > 5 )
      System.out.println( "x and y are > 5" );
   else
      System.out.println( "x is <= 5" );
```

in which the body of the first if is a nested if...else. The outer if statement tests whether x is greater than 5. If so, execution continues by testing whether y is also greater than 5. If the second condition is true, the proper string—"x and y are > 5"—is displayed. However, if the second condition is false, the string "x is <= 5" is displayed, even though we know that x is greater than 5.

To force the nested if...else statement to execute as it was originally intended, we must write it as follows:

```
if ( x > 5 )
{
   if ( y > 5 )
      System.out.println( "x and y are > 5" );
}
else
   System.out.println( "x is <= 5" );
```

The braces ({}) indicate to the compiler that the second if statement is in the body of the first if and that the else is associated with the first if. Exercise 4.27 and Exercise 4.28 investigate the dangling-else problem further.

Blocks

The if statement normally expects only one statement in its body. To include several statements in the body of an if (or the body of an else for an if...else statement), enclose the statements in braces ({ and }). A set of statements contained within a pair of braces is called a block. A block can be placed anywhere in a program that a single statement can be placed.

The following example includes a block in the else-part of an if...else statement:

```
if ( grade >= 60 )
    System.out.println( "Passed" );
else
{
    System.out.println( "Failed" );
    System.out.println( "You must take this course again." );
}
```

In this case, if grade is less than 60, the program executes both statements in the body of the else and prints

```
Failed.
You must take this course again.
```

Note the braces surrounding the two statements in the else clause. These braces are important. Without the braces, the statement

```
System.out.println( "You must take this course again." );
```

would be outside the body of the else-part of the if...else statement and would execute regardless of whether the grade was less than 60.

Syntax errors (e.g., when one brace in a block is left out of the program) are caught by the compiler. A logic error (e.g., when both braces in a block are left out of the program) has its effect at execution time. A fatal logic error causes a program to fail and terminate prematurely. A nonfatal logic error allows a program to continue executing, but causes the program to produce incorrect results.

Common Programming Error 4.1

Forgetting one or both of the braces that delimit a block can lead to syntax errors or logic errors in a program.

Good Programming Practice 4.4

Always using braces in an if...else (or other) statement helps prevent their accidental omission, especially when adding statements to the if-part or the else-part at a later time. To avoid omitting one or both of the braces, some programmers type the beginning and ending braces of blocks before typing the individual statements within the braces.

Just as a block can be placed anywhere a single statement can be placed, it is also possible to have an empty statement. Recall from Section 2.8 that the empty statement is represented by placing a semicolon (;) where a statement would normally be.

Common Programming Error 4.2

Placing a semicolon after the condition in an if or if...else statement leads to a logic error in single-selection if statements and a syntax error in double-selection if...else statements (when the if-part contains an actual body statement).

4.7 while Repetition Statement

A repetition statement (also called a looping statement or a loop) allows the programmer to specify that a program should repeat an action while some condition remains true. The pseudocode statement

> *While there are more items on my shopping list*
> *Purchase next item and cross it off my list*

describes the repetition that occurs during a shopping trip. The condition "there are more items on my shopping list" may be true or false. If it is true, then the action "Purchase next item and cross it off my list" is performed. This action will be performed repeatedly while the condition remains true. The statement(s) contained in the *While* repetition statement constitute the body of the *While* repetition statement, which may be a single statement or a block. Eventually, the condition will become false (when the last item on the shopping list has been purchased and crossed off the list). At this point, the repetition terminates, and the first statement after the repetition statement executes.

As an example of Java's while repetition statement, consider a program segment designed to find the first power of 3 larger than 100. Suppose that the int variable product is initialized to 3. When the following while statement finishes executing, product contains the result:

```
int product = 3;

while ( product <= 100 )
    product = 3 * product;
```

When this while statement begins execution, the value of variable product is 3. Each iteration of the while statement multiplies product by 3, so product takes on the values 9, 27, 81 and 243 successively. When variable product becomes 243, the while statement condition—product <= 100—becomes false. This terminates the repetition, so the final value of product is 243. At this point, program execution continues with the next statement after the while statement.

Common Programming Error 4.3

Not providing, in the body of a while statement, an action that eventually causes the condition in the while to become false normally results in a logic error called an infinite loop, in which the loop never terminates.

The UML activity diagram in Fig. 4.4 illustrates the flow of control that corresponds to the preceding while statement. Once again, the symbols in the diagram (besides the initial state, transition arrows, a final state and three notes) represent an action state and a decision. This diagram also introduces the UML's merge symbol. The UML represents both the merge symbol and the decision symbol as diamonds. The merge symbol joins two flows of activity into one. In this diagram, the merge symbol joins the transitions from the initial state and from the action state, so they both flow into the decision that determines whether the loop should begin (or continue) executing. The decision and merge symbols can be distinguished by the number of "incoming" and "outgoing" transition arrows. A decision symbol has one transition arrow pointing to the diamond and two or more transition arrows pointing out from the diamond to indicate possible transitions from that

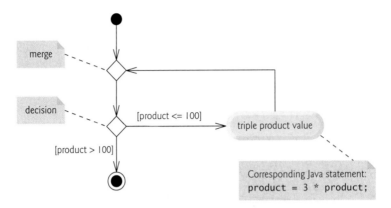

Fig. 4.4 | `while` repetition statement UML activity diagram.

point. In addition, each transition arrow pointing out of a decision symbol has a guard condition next to it. A merge symbol has two or more transition arrows pointing to the diamond and only one transition arrow pointing from the diamond, to indicate multiple activity flows merging to continue the activity. None of the transition arrows associated with a merge symbol have guard conditions.

Figure 4.4 clearly shows the repetition of the `while` statement discussed earlier in this section. The transition arrow emerging from the action state points back to the merge, from which program flow transitions back to the decision that is tested at the beginning of each iteration of the loop. The loop continues to execute until the guard condition `product > 100` becomes true. Then the `while` statement exits (reaches its final state), and control passes to the next statement in sequence in the program.

4.8 Formulating Algorithms: Counter-Controlled Repetition

To illustrate how algorithms are developed, we modify the GradeBook class of Chapter 3 to solve two variations of a problem that averages student grades. Consider the following problem statement:

> *A class of ten students took a quiz. The grades (integers in the range 0 to 100) for this quiz are available to you. Determine the class average on the quiz.*

The class average is equal to the sum of the grades divided by the number of students. The algorithm for solving this problem on a computer must input each grade, keep track of the total of all grades input, perform the averaging calculation and print the result.

Pseudocode Algorithm with Counter-Controlled Repetition
Let's use pseudocode to list the actions to execute and specify the order in which they should execute. We use counter-controlled repetition to input the grades one at a time. This technique uses a variable called a counter (or control variable) to control the number of times a set of statements will execute. Counter-controlled repetition is often called definite repetition, because the number of repetitions is known before the loop begins executing. In this example, repetition terminates when the counter exceeds 10. This section presents a fully developed pseudocode algorithm (Fig. 4.5) and a version of class Grade-

```
 1   Set total to zero
 2   Set grade counter to one
 3
 4   While grade counter is less than or equal to ten
 5       Prompt the user to enter the next grade
 6       Input the next grade
 7       Add the grade into the total
 8       Add one to the grade counter
 9
10   Set the class average to the total divided by ten
11   Print the class average
```

Fig. 4.5 | Pseudocode algorithm that uses counter-controlled repetition to solve the class-average problem.

Book (Fig. 4.6) that implements the algorithm in a Java method. The section then presents an application (Fig. 4.7) that demonstrates the algorithm in action. In Section 4.9, we demonstrate how to use pseudocode to develop such an algorithm from scratch.

Software Engineering Observation 4.1

Experience has shown that the most difficult part of solving a problem on a computer is developing the algorithm for the solution. Once a correct algorithm has been specified, the process of producing a working Java program from the algorithm is normally straightforward.

Note the references in the algorithm of Fig. 4.5 to a total and a counter. A total is a variable used to accumulate the sum of several values. A counter is a variable used to count—in this case, the grade counter indicates which of the 10 grades is about to be entered by the user. Variables used to store totals are normally initialized to zero before being used in a program.

Implementing Counter-Controlled Repetition in Class *GradeBook*

Class GradeBook (Fig. 4.6) contains a constructor (lines 11–14) that assigns a value to the class's instance variable courseName (declared in line 8). Lines 17–20, 23–26 and 29–34 declare methods setCourseName, getCourseName and displayMessage, respectively. Lines 37–66 declare method determineClassAverage, which implements the class-averaging algorithm described by the pseudocode in Fig. 4.5.

Line 40 declares and initializes Scanner variable input, which is used to read values entered by the user. Lines 42–45 declare local variables total, gradeCounter, grade and average to be of type int. Variable grade stores the user input.

Note that the declarations (in lines 42–45) appear in the body of method determineClassAverage. Recall that variables declared in a method body are local variables and can be

```
 1   // Fig. 4.6: GradeBook.java
 2   // GradeBook class that solves class-average problem using
 3   // counter-controlled repetition.
 4   import java.util.Scanner; // program uses class Scanner
 5
```

Fig. 4.6 | Counter-controlled repetition: Class-average problem. (Part 1 of 3.)

```
6   public class GradeBook
7   {
8      private String courseName; // name of course this GradeBook represents
9
10     // constructor initializes courseName
11     public GradeBook( String name )
12     {
13        courseName = name; // initializes courseName
14     } // end constructor
15
16     // method to set the course name
17     public void setCourseName( String name )
18     {
19        courseName = name; // store the course name
20     } // end method setCourseName
21
22     // method to retrieve the course name
23     public String getCourseName()
24     {
25        return courseName;
26     } // end method getCourseName
27
28     // display a welcome message to the GradeBook user
29     public void displayMessage()
30     {
31        // getCourseName gets the name of the course
32        System.out.printf( "Welcome to the grade book for\n%s!\n\n",
33           getCourseName() );
34     } // end method displayMessage
35
36     // determine class average based on 10 grades entered by user
37     public void determineClassAverage()
38     {
39        // create Scanner to obtain input from command window
40        Scanner input = new Scanner( System.in );
41
42        int total; // sum of grades entered by user
43        int gradeCounter; // number of the grade to be entered next
44        int grade; // grade value entered by user
45        int average; // average of grades
46
47        // initialization phase
48        total = 0; // initialize total
49        gradeCounter = 1; // initialize loop counter
50
51        // processing phase
52        while ( gradeCounter <= 10 ) // loop 10 times
53        {
54           System.out.print( "Enter grade: " ); // prompt
55           grade = input.nextInt(); // input next grade
56           total = total + grade; // add grade to total
57           gradeCounter = gradeCounter + 1; // increment counter by 1
58        } // end while
```

Fig. 4.6 | Counter-controlled repetition: Class-average problem. (Part 2 of 3.)

```
59
60          // termination phase
61          average = total / 10; // integer division yields integer result
62
63          // display total and average of grades
64          System.out.printf( "\nTotal of all 10 grades is %d\n", total );
65          System.out.printf( "Class average is %d\n", average );
66       } // end method determineClassAverage
67
68   } // end class GradeBook
```

Fig. 4.6 | Counter-controlled repetition: Class-average problem. (Part 3 of 3.)

used only from the line of their declaration in the method to the closing right brace (}) of the method declaration. A local variable's declaration must appear before the variable is used in that method. A local variable cannot be accessed outside the method in which it is declared.

In the versions of class GradeBook in this chapter, we simply read and process a set of grades. The averaging calculation is performed in method determineClassAverage using local variables—we do not preserve any information about student grades in instance variables of the class. In later versions of the class (in Chapter 7, Arrays), we maintain the grades in memory using an instance variable that refers to a data structure known as an array. This allows a GradeBook object to perform various calculations on the same set of grades without requiring the user to enter the grades multiple times.

Good Programming Practice 4.5

Separate declarations from other statements in methods with a blank line for readability.

The assignments (in lines 48–49) initialize total to 0 and gradeCounter to 1. Note that these initializations occur before the variables are used in calculations. Variables grade and average (for the user input and calculated average, respectively) need not be initialized here—their values will be assigned as they are input or calculated later in the method.

Common Programming Error 4.4

Using the value of a local variable before it is initialized results in a compilation error. All local variables must be initialized before their values are used in expressions.

Error-Prevention Tip 4.1

Initialize each counter and total, either in its declaration or in an assignment statement. Totals are normally initialized to 0. Counters are normally initialized to 0 or 1, depending on how they are used (we will show examples of when to use 0 and when to use 1).

Line 52 indicates that the while statement should continue looping (also called iterating) as long as the value of gradeCounter is less than or equal to 10. While this condition remains true, the while statement repeatedly executes the statements between the braces that delimit its body (lines 53–58).

Line 54 displays the prompt "Enter grade: " at the command line. Line 55 reads the grade entered by the user and assigns it to variable grade. Then line 56 adds the new grade entered by the user to the total and assigns the result to total, which replaces its previous value.

Line 57 adds 1 to gradeCounter to indicate that the program has processed a grade and is ready to input the next grade from the user. Incrementing gradeCounter eventually causes gradeCounter to exceed 10. At that point the while loop terminates because its condition (line 52) becomes false.

When the loop terminates, line 61 performs the averaging calculation and assigns its result to the variable average. Line 64 uses System.out's printf method to display the text "Total of all 10 grades is " followed by variable total's value. Line 65 then uses printf to display the text "Class average is " followed by variable average's value. Method determineClassAverage returns control to the calling method (i.e., main in GradeBookTest of Fig. 4.7) after reaching line 66.

Class *GradeBookTest*

Class GradeBookTest (Fig. 4.7) creates an object of class GradeBook (Fig. 4.6) and demonstrates its capabilities. Lines 10–11 of Fig. 4.7 create a new GradeBook object and assign it to variable myGradeBook. The String in line 11 is passed to the GradeBook constructor (lines 11–14 of Fig. 4.6). Line 13 calls myGradeBook's displayMessage method to display a welcome message to the user. Line 14 then calls myGradeBook's determineClassAverage method to allow the user to enter 10 grades, for which the method then calculates and prints the average—the method performs the algorithm shown in Fig. 4.5.

Notes on Integer Division and Truncation

The averaging calculation performed by method determineClassAverage in response to the method call at line 14 in Fig. 4.7 produces an integer result. The program's output indicates that the sum of the grade values in the sample execution is 846, which, when divided by 10, should yield the floating-point number 84.6. However, the result of the calculation total / 10 (line 61 of Fig. 4.6) is the integer 84, because total and 10 are both integers. Dividing two integers results in integer division—any fractional part of the calculation is lost (i.e., truncated). We will see how to obtain a floating-point result from the averaging calculation in the next section.

```
1   // Fig. 4.7: GradeBookTest.java
2   // Create GradeBook object and invoke its determineClassAverage method.
3
4   public class GradeBookTest
5   {
6      public static void main( String args[] )
7      {
8         // create GradeBook object myGradeBook and
9         // pass course name to constructor
10        GradeBook myGradeBook = new GradeBook(
11           "CS101 Introduction to Java Programming" );
12
13        myGradeBook.displayMessage(); // display welcome message
14        myGradeBook.determineClassAverage(); // find average of 10 grades
15     } // end main
16
17   } // end class GradeBookTest
```

Fig. 4.7 | GradeBookTest class creates an object of class GradeBook (Fig. 4.6) and invokes its determineClassAverage method. (Part I of 2.)

```
Welcome to the grade book for
CS101 Introduction to Java Programming!

Enter grade: 67
Enter grade: 78
Enter grade: 89
Enter grade: 67
Enter grade: 87
Enter grade: 98
Enter grade: 93
Enter grade: 85
Enter grade: 82
Enter grade: 100

Total of all 10 grades is 846
Class average is 84
```

Fig. 4.7 | `GradeBookTest` class creates an object of class `GradeBook` (Fig. 4.6) and invokes its `determineClassAverage` method. (Part 2 of 2.)

 Common Programming Error 4.5

Assuming that integer division rounds (rather than truncates) can lead to incorrect results. For example, 7 ÷ 4, which yields 1.75 in conventional arithmetic, truncates to 1 in integer arithmetic, rather than rounding to 2.

4.9 Formulating Algorithms: Sentinel-Controlled Repetition

Let us generalize Section 4.8's class-average problem. Consider the following problem:

> *Develop a class-averaging program that processes grades for an arbitrary number of students each time it is run.*

In the previous class-average example, the problem statement specified the number of students, so the number of grades (10) was known in advance. In this example, no indication is given of how many grades the user will enter during the program's execution. The program must process an arbitrary number of grades. How can it determine when to stop the input of grades? How will it know when to calculate and print the class average?

One way to solve this problem is to use a special value called a sentinel value (also called a signal value, a dummy value or a flag value) to indicate "end of data entry." The user enters grades until all legitimate grades have been entered. The user then types the sentinel value to indicate that no more grades will be entered. Sentinel-controlled repetition is often called indefinite repetition because the number of repetitions is not known before the loop begins executing.

Clearly, a sentinel value must be chosen that cannot be confused with an acceptable input value. Grades on a quiz are nonnegative integers, so –1 is an acceptable sentinel value for this problem. Thus, a run of the class-average program might process a stream of inputs such as 95, 96, 75, 74, 89 and –1. The program would then compute and print the class average for the grades 95, 96, 75, 74 and 89. Since –1 is the sentinel value, it should not enter into the averaging calculation.

Common Programming Error 4.6

Choosing a sentinel value that is also a legitimate data value is a logic error.

Developing the Pseudocode Algorithm with Top-Down, Stepwise Refinement: The Top and First Refinement

We approach the class-average program with a technique called top-down, stepwise refinement, which is essential to the development of well-structured programs. We begin with a pseudocode representation of the *top*—a single statement that conveys the overall function of the program:

> *Determine the class average for the quiz*

The top is, in effect, a *complete* representation of a program. Unfortunately, the top rarely conveys sufficient detail from which to write a Java program. So we now begin the refinement process. We divide the top into a series of smaller tasks and list these in the order in which they will be performed. This results in the following first refinement:

> *Initialize variables*
> *Input, sum and count the quiz grades*
> *Calculate and print the class average*

This refinement uses only the sequence structure—the steps listed should execute in order, one after the other.

Software Engineering Observation 4.2

Each refinement, as well as the top itself, is a complete specification of the algorithm—only the level of detail varies.

Software Engineering Observation 4.3

Many programs can be divided logically into three phases: an initialization phase that initializes the variables; a processing phase that inputs data values and adjusts program variables (e.g., counters and totals) accordingly; and a termination phase that calculates and outputs the final results.

Proceeding to the Second Refinement

The preceding *Software Engineering Observation* is often all you need for the first refinement in the top-down process. To proceed to the next level of refinement, that is, the second refinement, we commit to specific variables. In this example, we need a running total of the numbers, a count of how many numbers have been processed, a variable to receive the value of each grade as it is input by the user and a variable to hold the calculated average. The pseudocode statement

> *Initialize variables*

can be refined as follows:

> *Initialize total to zero*
> *Initialize counter to zero*

Only the variables *total* and *counter* need to be initialized before they are used. The variables *average* and *grade* (for the calculated average and the user input, respectively) need not be initialized, because their values will be replaced as they are calculated or input.

The pseudocode statement

   Input, sum and count the quiz grades

requires a repetition structure (i.e., a loop) that successively inputs each grade. We do not know in advance how many grades are to be processed, so we will use sentinel-controlled repetition. The user enters grades one at a time. After entering the last grade, the user enters the sentinel value. The program tests for the sentinel value after each grade is input and terminates the loop when the user enters the sentinel value. The second refinement of the preceding pseudocode statement is then

   Prompt the user to enter the first grade
   Input the first grade (possibly the sentinel)

   While the user has not yet entered the sentinel
      Add this grade into the running total
      Add one to the grade counter
      Prompt the user to enter the next grade
      Input the next grade (possibly the sentinel)

In pseudocode, we do not use braces around the statements that form the body of the *While* structure. We simply indent the statements under the *While* to show that they belong to the *While*. Again, pseudocode is only an informal program-development aid.

   The pseudocode statement

   Calculate and print the class average

can be refined as follows:

   If the counter is not equal to zero
      Set the average to the total divided by the counter
      Print the average
   else
      Print "No grades were entered"

We are careful here to test for the possibility of division by zero—normally a logic error that, if undetected, would cause the program to fail or produce invalid output. The complete second refinement of the pseudocode for the class-average problem is shown in Fig. 4.8.

Error-Prevention Tip 4.2

When performing division by an expression whose value could be zero, explicitly test for this possibility and handle it appropriately in your program (e.g., by printing an error message) rather than allow the error to occur

1 *Initialize total to zero*
2 *Initialize counter to zero*
3
4 *Prompt the user to enter the first grade*
5 *Input the first grade (possibly the sentinel)*
6

Fig. 4.8 | Class-average problem pseudocode algorithm with sentinel-controlled repetition. (Part 1 of 2.)

```
 7    While the user has not yet entered the sentinel
 8        Add this grade into the running total
 9        Add one to the grade counter
10        Prompt the user to enter the next grade
11        Input the next grade (possibly the sentinel)
12
13    If the counter is not equal to zero
14        Set the average to the total divided by the counter
15        Print the average
16    else
17        Print "No grades were entered"
```

Fig. 4.8 | Class-average problem pseudocode algorithm with sentinel-controlled repetition. (Part 2 of 2.)

In Fig. 4.5 and Fig. 4.8, we included some completely blank lines and indentation in the pseudocode to make it more readable. The blank lines separate the pseudocode algorithms into their various phases and set off control statements, and the indentation emphasizes the bodies of the control statements.

The pseudocode algorithm in Fig. 4.8 solves the more general class-averaging problem. This algorithm was developed after only two refinements. Sometimes more refinements are necessary.

Software Engineering Observation 4.4

Terminate the top-down, stepwise refinement process when you have specified the pseudocode algorithm in sufficient detail for you to convert the pseudocode to Java. Normally, implementing the Java program is then straightforward.

Software Engineering Observation 4.5

Some experienced programmers write programs without ever using program-development tools like pseudocode. They feel that their ultimate goal is to solve the problem on a computer and that writing pseudocode merely delays the production of final outputs. Although this method may work for simple and familiar problems, it can lead to serious errors and delays in large, complex projects.

Implementing Sentinel-Controlled Repetition in Class *GradeBook*

Figure 4.9 shows the Java class GradeBook containing method determineClassAverage that implements the pseudocode algorithm of Fig. 4.8. Although each grade is an integer, the averaging calculation is likely to produce a number with a decimal point—in other words, a real number or floating-point number. The type int cannot represent such a number, so this class uses type double to do so.

```
1   // Fig. 4.9: GradeBook.java
2   // GradeBook class that solves class-average program using
3   // sentinel-controlled repetition.
4   import java.util.Scanner; // program uses class Scanner
5
```

Fig. 4.9 | Sentinel-controlled repetition: Class-average problem. (Part 1 of 3.)

```java
6  public class GradeBook
7  {
8     private String courseName; // name of course this GradeBook represents
9
10    // constructor initializes courseName
11    public GradeBook( String name )
12    {
13       courseName = name; // initializes courseName
14    } // end constructor
15
16    // method to set the course name
17    public void setCourseName( String name )
18    {
19       courseName = name; // store the course name
20    } // end method setCourseName
21
22    // method to retrieve the course name
23    public String getCourseName()
24    {
25       return courseName;
26    } // end method getCourseName
27
28    // display a welcome message to the GradeBook user
29    public void displayMessage()
30    {
31       // getCourseName gets the name of the course
32       System.out.printf( "Welcome to the grade book for\n%s!\n\n",
33          getCourseName() );
34    } // end method displayMessage
35
36    // determine the average of an arbitrary number of grades
37    public void determineClassAverage()
38    {
39       // create Scanner to obtain input from command window
40       Scanner input = new Scanner( System.in );
41
42       int total; // sum of grades
43       int gradeCounter; // number of grades entered
44       int grade; // grade value
45       double average; // number with decimal point for average
46
47       // initialization phase
48       total = 0; // initialize total
49       gradeCounter = 0; // initialize loop counter
50
51       // processing phase
52       // prompt for input and read grade from user
53       System.out.print( "Enter grade or -1 to quit: " );
54       grade = input.nextInt();
55
56       // loop until sentinel value read from user
57       while ( grade != -1 )
58       {
```

Fig. 4.9 | Sentinel-controlled repetition: Class-average problem. (Part 2 of 3.)

```
59          total = total + grade; // add grade to total
60          gradeCounter = gradeCounter + 1; // increment counter
61
62          // prompt for input and read next grade from user
63          System.out.print( "Enter grade or -1 to quit: " );
64          grade = input.nextInt();
65       } // end while
66
67       // termination phase
68       // if user entered at least one grade...
69       if ( gradeCounter != 0 )
70       {
71          // calculate average of all grades entered
72          average = (double) total / gradeCounter;
73
74          // display total and average (with two digits of precision)
75          System.out.printf( "\nTotal of the %d grades entered is %d\n",
76             gradeCounter, total );
77          System.out.printf( "Class average is %.2f\n", average );
78       } // end if
79       else // no grades were entered, so output appropriate message
80          System.out.println( "No grades were entered" );
81    } // end method determineClassAverage
82
83 } // end class GradeBook
```

Fig. 4.9 | Sentinel-controlled repetition: Class-average problem. (Part 3 of 3.)

In this example, we see that control statements may be stacked on top of one another (in sequence) just as a child stacks building blocks. The while statement (lines 57–65) is followed in sequence by an if...else statement (lines 69–80). Much of the code in this program is identical to the code in Fig. 4.6, so we concentrate on the new features and issues.

Line 45 declares double variable average. This variable allows us to store the calculated class average as a floating-point number. Line 49 initializes gradeCounter to 0, because no grades have been entered yet. Remember that this program uses sentinel-controlled repetition to input the grades from the user. To keep an accurate record of the number of grades entered, the program increments gradeCounter only when the user inputs a valid grade value.

Program Logic for Sentinel-Controlled Repetition vs. Counter-Controlled Repetition

Compare the program logic for sentinel-controlled repetition in this application with that for counter-controlled repetition in Fig. 4.6. In counter-controlled repetition, each iteration of the while statement (e.g., lines 52–58 of Fig. 4.6) reads a value from the user, for the specified number of iterations. In sentinel-controlled repetition, the program reads the first value (lines 53–54 of Fig. 4.9) before reaching the while. This value determines whether the program's flow of control should enter the body of the while. If the condition of the while is false, the user entered the sentinel value, so the body of the while does not execute (i.e., no grades were entered). If, on the other hand, the condition is true, the body begins execution, and the loop adds the grade value to the total (line 59). Then lines 63–64 in the loop's body input the next value from the user. Next, program control reaches the closing right brace (}) of the body at line 65, so execution continues with the test of the while's condition (line 57). The condition uses the most recent grade input by the user to determine whether the loop's body should execute again. Note that the value of variable grade is always input from the user immediately before the program tests the while condition. This allows the program to determine whether the value just input is the sentinel value *before* the program processes that value (i.e., adds it to the total). If the sentinel value is input, the loop terminates, and the program does not add –1 to the total.

Good Programming Practice 4.6

In a sentinel-controlled loop, the prompts requesting data entry should explicitly remind the user of the sentinel value.

After the loop terminates, the if...else statement at lines 69–80 executes. The condition at line 69 determines whether any grades were input. If none were input, the else part (lines 79–80) of the if...else statement executes and displays the message "No grades were entered" and the method returns control to the calling method.

Notice the while statement's block in Fig. 4.9 (lines 58–65). Without the braces, the loop would consider its body to be only the first statement, which adds the grade to the total. The last three statements in the block would fall outside the loop's body, causing the computer to interpret the code incorrectly as follows:

```
while ( grade != -1 )
   total = total + grade; // add grade to total
gradeCounter = gradeCounter + 1; // increment counter

// prompt for input and read next grade from user
System.out.print( "Enter grade or -1 to quit: " );
grade = input.nextInt();
```

The preceding code would cause an infinite loop in the program if the user did not input the sentinel -1 at line 54 (before the while statement).

Common Programming Error 4.7

Omitting the braces that delimit a block can lead to logic errors, such as infinite loops. To prevent this problem, some programmers enclose the body of every control statement in braces even if the body contains only a single statement.

Explicitly and Implicitly Converting Between Primitive Types
If at least one grade was entered, line 72 of Fig. 4.9 calculates the average of the grades. Recall from Fig. 4.6 that integer division yields an integer result. Even though variable average is declared as a double (line 45), the calculation

```
average = total / gradeCounter;
```

loses the fractional part of the quotient before the result of the division is assigned to average. This occurs because total and gradeCounter are both integers and integer division yields an integer result. To perform a floating-point calculation with integer values, we must temporarily treat these values as floating-point numbers for use in the calculation. Java provides the unary cast operator to accomplish this task. Line 72 uses the (double) cast operator—a unary operator—to create a *temporary* floating-point copy of its operand `total` (which appears to the right of the operator). Using a cast operator in this manner is called explicit conversion. The value stored in `total` is still an integer.

The calculation now consists of a floating-point value (the temporary `double` version of `total`) divided by the integer `gradeCounter`. Java knows how to evaluate only arithmetic expressions in which the operands' types are identical. To ensure that the operands are of the same type, Java performs an operation called promotion (or implicit conversion) on selected operands. For example, in an expression containing values of the types `int` and `double`, the `int` values are promoted to `double` values for use in the expression. In this example, the value of `gradeCounter` is promoted to type `double`, then the floating-point division is performed and the result of the calculation is assigned to `average`. As long as the `(double)` cast operator is applied to any variable in the calculation, the calculation will yield a `double` result. Later in this chapter, we discuss all the primitive types. You will learn more about the promotion rules in Section 6.7.

Common Programming Error 4.8

The cast operator can be used to convert between primitive numeric types, such as `int` and `double`, and between related reference types (as we discuss in Chapter 10, Object-Oriented Programming: Polymorphism). Casting to the wrong type may cause compilation errors or runtime errors.

Cast operators are available for any type. The cast operator is formed by placing parentheses around the name of a type. The operator is a unary operator (i.e., an operator that takes only one operand). In Chapter 2, we studied the binary arithmetic operators. Java also supports unary versions of the plus (+) and minus (–) operators, so the programmer can write expressions like -7 or +5. Cast operators associate from right to left and have the same precedence as other unary operators, such as unary + and unary -. This precedence is one level higher than that of the multiplicative operators *, / and %. (See the operator precedence chart in Appendix A.) We indicate the cast operator with the notation (*type*) in our precedence charts, to indicate that any type name can be used to form a cast operator.

Line 77 outputs the class average using `System.out`'s `printf` method. In this example, we decided that we'd like to display the class average rounded to the nearest hundredth and output the average with exactly two digits to the right of the decimal point. The format specifier %.2f in `printf`'s format control string (line 77) indicates that variable `average`'s value should be displayed with two digits of precision to the right of the decimal point—indicated by .2 in the format specifier. The three grades entered during the sample execution of class `GradeBookTest` (Fig. 4.10) total 257, which yields the average 85.666666.... Method `printf` uses the precision in the format specifier to round the value to the specified number of digits. In this program, the average is rounded to the hundredths position and the average is displayed as 85.67.

4.10 Formulating Algorithms: Nested Control Statements

For the next example, we once again formulate an algorithm by using pseudocode and top-down, stepwise refinement, and write a corresponding Java program. We have seen that control statements can be stacked on top of one another (in sequence) just as a child stacks building blocks. In this case study, we examine the only other structured way control statements can be connected, namely, by nesting one control statement within another.

```
 1   // Fig. 4.10: GradeBookTest.java
 2   // Create GradeBook object and invoke its determineClassAverage method.
 3
 4   public class GradeBookTest
 5   {
 6      public static void main( String args[] )
 7      {
 8         // create GradeBook object myGradeBook and
 9         // pass course name to constructor
10         GradeBook myGradeBook = new GradeBook(
11            "CS101 Introduction to Java Programming" );
12
13         myGradeBook.displayMessage(); // display welcome message
14         myGradeBook.determineClassAverage(); // find average of grades
15      } // end main
16
17   } // end class GradeBookTest
```

```
Welcome to the grade book for
CS101 Introduction to Java Programming!

Enter grade or -1 to quit: 97
Enter grade or -1 to quit: 88
Enter grade or -1 to quit: 72
Enter grade or -1 to quit: -1

Total of the 3 grades entered is 257
Class average is 85.67
```

Fig. 4.10 | GradeBookTest class creates an object of class GradeBook (Fig. 4.9) and invokes its determineClassAverage method.

Consider the following problem statement:

A college offers a course that prepares students for the state licensing exam for real estate brokers. Last year, ten of the students who completed this course took the exam. The college wants to know how well its students did on the exam. You have been asked to write a program to summarize the results. You have been given a list of these 10 students. Next to each name is written a 1 if the student passed the exam or a 2 if the student failed.

Your program should analyze the results of the exam as follows:

1. *Input each test result (i.e., a 1 or a 2). Display the message "Enter result" on the screen each time the program requests another test result.*

2. *Count the number of test results of each type.*

3. *Display a summary of the test results indicating the number of students who passed and the number who failed.*

4. *If more than eight students passed the exam, print the message "Raise tuition."*

After reading the problem statement carefully, we make the following observations:

1. The program must process test results for 10 students. A counter-controlled loop can be used because the number of test results is known in advance.

2. Each test result has a numeric value—either a 1 or a 2. Each time the program reads a test result, the program must determine whether the number is a 1 or a 2. We test for a 1 in our algorithm. If the number is not a 1, we assume that it is a 2. (Exercise 4.24 considers the consequences of this assumption.)

3. Two counters are used to keep track of the exam results—one to count the number of students who passed the exam and one to count the number of students who failed the exam.

4. After the program has processed all the results, it must decide whether more than eight students passed the exam.

Let us proceed with top-down, stepwise refinement. We begin with a pseudocode representation of the top:

Analyze exam results and decide whether tuition should be raised

Once again, the top is a *complete* representation of the program, but several refinements are likely to be needed before the pseudocode can evolve naturally into a Java program. Our first refinement is

Initialize variables
Input the 10 exam results, and count passes and failures
Print a summary of the exam results and decide whether tuition should be raised

Here, too, even though we have a complete representation of the entire program, further refinement is necessary. We now commit to specific variables. Counters are needed to record the passes and failures, a counter will be used to control the looping process and a variable is needed to store the user input. The variable in which the user input will be stored is not initialized at the start of the algorithm, because its value is read from the user during each iteration of the loop.

The pseudocode statement

Initialize variables

can be refined as follows:

Initialize passes to zero
Initialize failures to zero
Initialize student counter to one

Notice that only the counters are initialized at the start of the algorithm.

The pseudocode statement

Input the 10 exam results, and count passes and failures

requires a loop that successively inputs the result of each exam. We know in advance that there are precisely 10 exam results, so counter-controlled looping is appropriate. Inside the loop (i.e., nested within the loop), a double-selection structure will determine whether each exam result is a pass or a failure and will increment the appropriate counter. The refinement of the preceding pseudocode statement is then

> *While student counter is less than or equal to 10*
>> *Prompt the user to enter the next exam result*
>> *Input the next exam result*
>
>> *If the student passed*
>>> *Add one to passes*
>> *Else*
>>> *Add one to failures*
>
>> *Add one to student counter*

We use blank lines to isolate the *If…Else* control structure, which improves readability. The pseudocode statement

> *Print a summary of the exam results and decide whether tuition should be raised*

can be refined as follows:

> *Print the number of passes*
> *Print the number of failures*
>
> *If more than eight students passed*
>> *Print "Raise tuition"*

Complete Second Refinement of Pseudocode and Conversion to Class `Analysis`

The complete second refinement of the pseudocode appears in Fig. 4.11. Notice that blank lines are also used to set off the *While* structure for program readability. This pseudocode is now sufficiently refined for conversion to Java. The Java class that implements the pseudocode algorithm is shown in Fig. 4.12, and two sample executions appear in Fig. 4.13.

```
 1   Initialize passes to zero
 2   Initialize failures to zero
 3   Initialize student counter to one
 4
 5   While student counter is less than or equal to 10
 6       Prompt the user to enter the next exam result
 7       Input the next exam result
 8
 9       If the student passed
10           Add one to passes
11       Else
12           Add one to failures
13
14       Add one to student counter
15
16   Print the number of passes
17   Print the number of failures
18
19   If more than eight students passed
20       Print "Raise tuition"
```

Fig. 4.11 | Pseudocode for examination-results problem.

```
1   // Fig. 4.12: Analysis.java
2   // Analysis of examination results.
3   import java.util.Scanner; // class uses class Scanner
4
5   public class Analysis
6   {
7      public void processExamResults
8      {
9         // create Scanner to obtain input from command window
10        Scanner input = new Scanner( System.in );
11
12        // initializing variables in declarations
13        int passes = 0; // number of passes
14        int failures = 0; // number of failures
15        int studentCounter = 1; // student counter
16        int result; // one exam result (obtains value from user)
17
18        // process 10 students using counter-controlled loop
19        while ( studentCounter <= 10 )
20        {
21           // prompt user for input and obtain value from user
22           System.out.print( "Enter result (1 = pass, 2 = fail): " );
23           result = input.nextInt();
24
25           // if...else nested in while
26           if ( result == 1 )          // if result 1,
27              passes = passes + 1;     // increment passes;
28           else                        // else result is not 1, so
29              failures = failures + 1; // increment failures
30
31           // increment studentCounter so loop eventually terminates
32           studentCounter = studentCounter + 1;
33        } // end while
34
35        // termination phase; prepare and display results
36        System.out.printf( "Passed: %d\nFailed: %d\n", passes, failures );
37
38        // determine whether more than 8 students passed
39        if ( passes > 8 )
40           System.out.println( "Raise Tuition" );
41     } // end method processExamResults
42
43  } // end class Analysis
```

Fig. 4.12 | Nested control structures: Examination-results problem.

Lines 13–16 of Fig. 4.12 declare the variables that method processExamResults of class Analysis uses to process the examination results. Several of these declarations use Java's ability to incorporate variable initialization into declarations (passes is assigned 0, failures is assigned 0 and studentCounter is assigned 1). Looping programs may require initialization at the beginning of each repetition—such reinitialization would normally be performed by assignment statements rather than in declarations.

The `while` statement (lines 19–33) loops 10 times. During each iteration, the loop inputs and processes one exam result. Notice that the `if...else` statement (lines 26–29) for processing each result is nested in the `while` statement. If the `result` is 1, the `if...else` statement increments `passes`; otherwise, it assumes the `result` is 2 and increments `failures`. Line 32 increments `studentCounter` before the loop condition is tested again at line 19. After 10 values have been input, the loop terminates and line 36 displays the number of `passes` and the number of `failures`. The `if` statement at lines 39–40 determines whether more than eight students passed the exam and, if so, outputs the message `"Raise Tuition"`.

Error-Prevention Tip 4.3

Initializing local variables when they are declared helps the programmer avoid any compilation errors that might arise from attempts to use uninitialized data. While Java does not require that local variable initializations be incorporated into declarations, it does require that local variables be initialized before their values are used in an expression.

AnalysisTest Class That Demonstrates Class Analysis

Class `AnalysisTest` (Fig. 4.13) creates an `Analysis` object (line 8) and invokes the object's `processExamResults` method (line 9) to process a set of exam results entered by the user. Figure 4.13 shows the input and output from two sample executions of the program. During the first sample execution, the condition at line 39 of method `processExamResults` in Fig. 4.12 is true—more than eight students passed the exam, so the program outputs a message indicating that the tuition should be raised.

```
1   // Fig. 4.13: AnalysisTest.java
2   // Test program for class Analysis.
3
4   public class AnalysisTest
5   {
6      public static void main( String args[] )
7      {
8         Analysis application = new Analysis(); // create Analysis object
9         application.processExamResults(); // call method to process results
10     } // end main
11
12  } // end class AnalysisTest
```

```
Enter result (1 = pass, 2 = fail): 1
Enter result (1 = pass, 2 = fail): 2
Enter result (1 = pass, 2 = fail): 1
Enter result (1 = pass, 2 = fail): 1
Enter result (1 = pass, 2 = fail): 1
Enter result (1 = pass, 2 = fail): 1
Enter result (1 = pass, 2 = fail): 1
Enter result (1 = pass, 2 = fail): 1
Enter result (1 = pass, 2 = fail): 1
Enter result (1 = pass, 2 = fail): 1
Passed: 9
Failed: 1
Raise Tuition
```

Fig. 4.13 | Test program for class `Analysis` (Fig. 4.12). (Part 1 of 2.)

```
Enter result (1 = pass, 2 = fail): 1
Enter result (1 = pass, 2 = fail): 2
Enter result (1 = pass, 2 = fail): 1
Enter result (1 = pass, 2 = fail): 2
Enter result (1 = pass, 2 = fail): 1
Enter result (1 = pass, 2 = fail): 2
Enter result (1 = pass, 2 = fail): 2
Enter result (1 = pass, 2 = fail): 1
Enter result (1 = pass, 2 = fail): 1
Enter result (1 = pass, 2 = fail): 1
Passed: 6
Failed: 4
```

Fig. 4.13 | Test program for class `Analysis` (Fig. 4.12). (Part 2 of 2.)

4.11 Compound Assignment Operators

Java provides several compound assignment operators for abbreviating assignment expressions. Any statement of the form

> *variable = variable   operator   expression*;

where *operator* is one of the binary operators +, -, *, / or % (or others we discuss later in the text) can be written in the form

> *variable   operator= expression*;

For example, you can abbreviate the statement

```
c = c + 3;
```

with the addition compound assignment operator, +=, as

```
c += 3;
```

The += operator adds the value of the expression on the right of the operator to the value of the variable on the left of the operator and stores the result in the variable on the left of the operator. Thus, the assignment expression c += 3 adds 3 to c. Figure 4.14 shows the arithmetic compound assignment operators, sample expressions using the operators and explanations of what the operators do.

Assignment operator	Sample expression	Explanation	Assigns
Assume: int c = 3, d = 5, e = 4, f = 6, g = 12;			
+=	c += 7	c = c + 7	10 to c
-=	d -= 4	d = d - 4	1 to d
*=	e *= 5	e = e * 5	20 to e
/=	f /= 3	f = f / 3	2 to f
%=	g %= 9	g = g % 9	3 to g

Fig. 4.14 | Arithmetic compound assignment operators.

4.12 **Increment and Decrement Operators**

Java provides two unary operators for adding 1 to or subtracting 1 from the value of a numeric variable. These are the unary increment operator, ++, and the unary decrement operator, --, which are summarized in Fig. 4.15. A program can increment by 1 the value of a variable called c using the increment operator, ++, rather than the expression c = c + 1 or c += 1. An increment or decrement operator that is prefixed to (placed before) a variable is referred to as the prefix increment or prefix decrement operator, respectively. An increment or decrement operator that is postfixed to (placed after) a variable is referred to as the postfix increment or postfix decrement operator, respectively.

Using the prefix increment (or decrement) operator to add (or subtract) 1 from a variable is known as preincrementing (or predecrementing) the variable. Preincrementing (or predecrementing) a variable causes the variable to be incremented (decremented) by 1, and then the new value of the variable is used in the expression in which it appears. Using the postfix increment (or decrement) operator to add (or subtract) 1 from a variable is known as postincrementing (or postdecrementing) the variable. Postincrementing (or postdecrementing) the variable causes the current value of the variable to be used in the expression in which it appears, and then the variable's value is incremented (decremented) by 1.

Good Programming Practice 4.7

Unlike binary operators, the unary increment and decrement operators should be placed next to their operands, with no intervening spaces.

Figure 4.16 demonstrates the difference between the prefix increment and postfix increment versions of the ++ increment operator. The decrement operator (--) works similarly. Note that this example contains only one class, with method main performing all the class's work. In this chapter and in Chapter 3, you have seen examples consisting of two classes—one class containing methods that perform useful tasks and one containing method main, which creates an object of the other class and calls its methods. In this example, we simply want to show the mechanics of the ++ operator, so we use only one

Operator	Called	Sample expression	Explanation
++	prefix increment	++a	Increment a by 1, then use the new value of a in the expression in which a resides.
++	postfix increment	a++	Use the current value of a in the expression in which a resides, then increment a by 1.
--	prefix decrement	--b	Decrement b by 1, then use the new value of b in the expression in which b resides.
--	postfix decrement	b--	Use the current value of b in the expression in which b resides, then decrement b by 1.

Fig. 4.15 | Increment and decrement operators.

```
1    // Fig. 4.16: Increment.java
2    // Prefix increment and postfix increment operators.
3
4    public class Increment
5    {
6       public static void main( String args[] )
7       {
8          int c;
9
10         // demonstrate postfix increment operator
11         c = 5; // assign 5 to c
12         System.out.println( c );    // print 5
13         System.out.println( c++ ); // print 5 then postincrement
14         System.out.println( c );     // print 6
15
16         System.out.println(); // skip a line
17
18         // demonstrate prefix increment operator
19         c = 5; // assign 5 to c
20         System.out.println( c );    // print 5
21         System.out.println( ++c ); // preincrement then print 6
22         System.out.println( c );     // print 6
23
24      } // end main
25
26   } // end class Increment
```

```
5
5
6

5
6
6
```

Fig. 4.16 | Preincrementing and postincrementing.

class declaration containing method `main`. Occasionally, when it does not make sense to try to create a reusable class to demonstrate a simple concept, we will use a mechanical example contained entirely within the `main` method of a single class.

Line 11 initializes the variable c to 5, and line 12 outputs c's initial value. Line 13 outputs the value of the expression c++. This expression postincrements the variable c, so c's original value (5) is output, then c's value is incremented. Thus, line 13 outputs c's initial value (5) again. Line 14 outputs c's new value (6) to prove that the variable's value was indeed incremented in line 13.

Line 19 resets c's value to 5, and line 20 outputs c's value. Line 21 outputs the value of the expression ++c. This expression preincrements c, so its value is incremented, then the new value (6) is output. Line 22 outputs c's value again to show that the value of c is still 6 after line 21 executes.

The arithmetic compound assignment operators and the increment and decrement operators can be used to simplify program statements. For example, the three assignment statements in Fig. 4.12 (lines 27, 29 and 32)

```
passes = passes + 1;
failures = failures + 1;
studentCounter = studentCounter + 1;
```

can be written more concisely with compound assignment operators as

```
passes += 1;
failures += 1;
studentCounter += 1;
```

with prefix increment operators as

```
++passes;
++failures;
++studentCounter;
```

or with postfix increment operators as

```
passes++;
failures++;
studentCounter++;
```

When incrementing or decrementing a variable in a statement by itself, the prefix increment and postfix increment forms have the same effect, and the prefix decrement and postfix decrement forms have the same effect. It is only when a variable appears in the context of a larger expression that preincrementing and postincrementing the variable have different effects (and similarly for predecrementing and postdecrementing).

Common Programming Error 4.9

Attempting to use the increment or decrement operator on an expression other than one to which a value can be assigned is a syntax error. For example, writing ++(x + 1) is a syntax error because (x + 1) is not a variable.

Figure 4.17 shows the precedence and associativity of the operators we have introduced to this point. The operators are shown from top to bottom in decreasing order of precedence. The second column describes the associativity of the operators at each level of precedence. The conditional operator (?:); the unary operators increment (++), decrement (--), plus (+) and minus (-); the cast operators and the assignment operators =, +=, -=, *=, /= and %= associate from right to left. All the other operators in the operator precedence chart in Fig. 4.17 associate from left to right. The third column names the groups of operators.

4.13 Primitive Types

The table in Appendix D, Primitive Types, lists the eight primitive types in Java. Like its predecessor languages C and C++, Java requires all variables to have a type. For this reason, Java is referred to as a strongly typed language.

Operators						Associativity	Type
++	--					right to left	unary postfix
++	--	+	-	(*type*)		right to left	unary prefix
*	/	%				left to right	multiplicative
+	-					left to right	additive
<	<=	>	>=			left to right	relational
==	!=					left to right	equality
?:						right to left	conditional
=	+=	-=	*=	/=	%=	right to left	assignment

Fig. 4.17 | Precedence and associativity of the operators discussed so far.

In C and C++, programmers frequently have to write separate versions of programs to support different computer platforms, because the primitive types are not guaranteed to be identical from computer to computer. For example, an int value on one machine might be represented by 16 bits (2 bytes) of memory, while an int value on another machine might be represented by 32 bits (4 bytes) of memory. In Java, int values are always 32 bits (4 bytes).

 Portability Tip 4.1

Unlike C and C++, the primitive types in Java are portable across all computer platforms that support Java. Thanks to this and Java's many other portability features, a programmer can write a program once and be certain that it will execute on any computer platform that supports Java. This capability is sometimes referred to as WORA (Write Once, Run Anywhere).

Each type in Appendix D is listed with its size in bits (there are eight bits to a byte) and its range of values. Because the designers of Java want it to be maximally portable, they use internationally recognized standards for both character formats (Unicode; for more information, visit www.unicode.org) and floating-point numbers (IEEE 754; for more information, visit grouper.ieee.org/groups/754/).

Recall from Section 3.5 that variables of primitive types declared outside of a method as fields of a class are automatically assigned default values unless explicitly initialized. Instance variables of types char, byte, short, int, long, float and double are all given the value 0 by default. Instance variables of type boolean are given the value false by default. Similarly, reference type instance variables are initialized by default to the value null.

4.14 (Optional) GUI and Graphics Case Study: Creating Simple Drawings

One of Java's appealing features is its graphics support that enables programmers to visually enhance their applications. This section introduces one of Java's graphical capabilities—drawing lines. It also covers the basics of creating a window to display a drawing on the computer screen.

To begin drawing in Java, you must first understand Java's coordinate system (Fig. 4.18), a scheme for identifying every point on the screen. By default, the upper-left corner of a GUI component has the coordinates (0, 0). A coordinate pair is composed of an *x*-coordinate (the horizontal coordinate) and a *y*-coordinate (the vertical coordinate). The *x*-coordinate is the horizontal location moving from left to right. The *y*-coordinate is the vertical location moving top to bottom. The *x*-axis describes every horizontal coordinate, and the *y*-axis every vertical coordinate.

Coordinates are used to indicate where graphics should be displayed on a screen. Coordinate units are measured in pixels. A pixel is a display monitor's smallest unit of resolution. (The term pixel stands for "picture element.")

Our first drawing application simply draws two lines from the corners. Class Draw-Panel (Fig. 4.19) performs the actual drawing, while class DrawPanelTest (Fig. 4.20) creates a window to display the drawing. In class DrawPanel, the import statements in lines 3–4 allow us to use class Graphics (from package java.awt), which provides various methods for drawing text and shapes onto the screen, and class JPanel (from package javax.swing), which provides an area on which we can draw.

Line 6 uses the keyword extends to indicate that class DrawPanel is an enhanced type of JPanel. The keyword extends represents a so-called inheritance relationship in which our new class DrawPanel begins with the existing members (data and methods) from class JPanel. The class from which DrawPanel inherits, JPanel, appears to the right of keyword extends. In this inheritance relationship, JPanel is called the superclass and DrawPanel is called the subclass. This results in a DrawPanel class that has the attributes (data) and behaviors (methods) of class JPanel as well as the new features we are adding in our Draw-Panel class declaration (specifically, the ability to draw two lines along the diagonals of the panel). Inheritance will be explained in more detail in Chapter 9.

Every JPanel, including our DrawPanel, has a paintComponent method (lines 9–22), which the system automatically calls every time it needs to display the JPanel. Method paintComponent must be declared as shown on line 9—otherwise, the system will not call the method. This method is called when a JPanel is first displayed on the screen, when it is covered then uncovered by a window on the screen and when the window in which it appears is resized. Method paintComponent requires one argument, a Graphics object, that is provided for you by the system when it calls paintComponent.

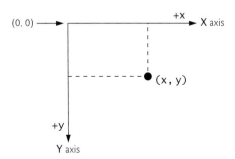

Fig. 4.18 | Java coordinate system. Units are measured in pixels.

```
1    // Fig. 4.19: DrawPanel.java
2    // Draws two crossing lines on a panel.
3    import java.awt.Graphics;
4    import javax.swing.JPanel;
5
6    public class DrawPanel extends JPanel
7    {
8       // draws an X from the corners of the panel
9       public void paintComponent( Graphics g )
10      {
11         // call paintComponent to ensure the panel displays correctly
12         super.paintComponent( g );
13
14         int width = getWidth(); // total width
15         int height = getHeight(); // total height
16
17         // draw a line from the upper-left to the lower-right
18         g.drawLine( 0, 0, width, height );
19
20         // draw a line from the lower-left to the upper-right
21         g.drawLine( 0, height, width, 0 );
22      } // end method paintComponent
23   } // end class DrawPanel
```

Fig. 4.19 | Using drawLine to connect the corners of a panel.

The first statement in every paintComponent method you create should always be

```
super.paintComponent( g );
```

This will ensure that the panel is properly rendered on the screen before we begin drawing on it. Next, lines 14 and 15 call two methods that class DrawPanel inherits from class JPanel. Because DrawPanel extends JPanel, DrawPanel can use any public methods that are declared in JPanel. Methods getWidth and getHeight return the width and the height of the JPanel respectively. Lines 14–15 store these values in the local variables width and height. Finally, lines 18 and 21 use the Graphics reference g to call method drawLine to draw the two lines. Method drawLine draws a line between two points represented by its four arguments. The first two arguments are the x- and y-coordinates for one endpoint of the line, and the last two arguments are the coordinates for the other endpoint of the line. If you resize the window, the lines will scale accordingly because the arguments are based on the width and height of the panel. Note that resizing the window in this application causes the system to call paintComponent to redraw the DrawPanel's contents.

To display the DrawPanel on the screen, we must place it in a window. You create a window with an object of class JFrame. In DrawPanelTest.java (Fig. 4.20), line 3 imports class JFrame from package javax.swing. Line 10 in the main method of class DrawPanelTest creates an instance of class DrawPanel, which contains our drawing, and line 13 creates a new JFrame that can hold and display our panel. Line 16 calls method setDefaultCloseOperation with the argument JFrame.EXIT_ON_CLOSE to indicate that the application should terminate when the user closes the window. Line 18 uses JFrame's add method to attach the DrawPanel containing our drawing to the JFrame. Line 19 sets the size

```
1   // Fig. 4.20: DrawPanelTest.java
2   // Application to display a DrawPanel.
3   import javax.swing.JFrame;
4
5   public class DrawPanelTest
6   {
7      public static void main( String args[] )
8      {
9         // create a panel that contains our drawing
10        DrawPanel panel = new DrawPanel();
11
12        // create a new frame to hold the panel
13        JFrame application = new JFrame();
14
15        // set the frame to exit when it is closed
16        application.setDefaultCloseOperation( JFrame.EXIT_ON_CLOSE );
17
18        application.add( panel ); // add the panel to the frame
19        application.setSize( 250, 250 ); // set the size of the frame
20        application.setVisible( true ); // make the frame visible
21     } // end main
22  } // end class DrawPanelTest
```

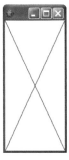

Fig. 4.20 | Creating JFrame to display DrawPanel.

of the JFrame. Method setSize takes two parameters—the first parameter is the width of the JFrame, and the second is the height. Finally, line 20 displays the JFrame. When the JFrame is displayed, the DrawPanel's paintComponent method (lines 9–22 of Fig. 4.19) is called, and the two lines are drawn (see the sample outputs in Fig. 4.20). Try resizing the window to see that the lines always draw based on the window's current width and height.

For the next several GUI and graphics sections, there will be very few changes required in the main method. As we introduce additional drawing capabilities, most of the changes will come in the class that extends JPanel, since that is where the drawing takes place.

GUI and Graphics Case Study Exercises

4.1   Using loops and control statements to draw lines can lead to many interesting designs.
   a) Create the design in the left screen capture of Fig. 4.21. This design draws lines from the top-left corner, fanning out the lines until they cover the upper-left half of the panel. One approach is to divide the width and height into an equal number of steps (we found 15 steps worked well). The first endpoint of a line will always be in the top-left corner

(0, 0). The second endpoint can be found by starting at the bottom-left corner and moving up one vertical step and moving right one horizontal step. Draw a line between the two endpoints. Continue moving up and to the right one step to find each successive endpoint. The figure should scale accordingly as you resize the window.

b) Modify your answer in part (a) to have lines fan out from all four corners, as shown in the right screen capture of Fig. 4.21. Lines from opposite corners should intersect along the middle.

4.2   Figure 4.22 displays two additional designs created using `while` loops and `drawLine`.

a) Create the design in the left screen capture of Fig. 4.22. Begin by dividing each edge into an equal number of increments (we chose 15 again). The first line starts in the top-left corner and ends one step right on the bottom edge. For each successive line, move down one increment on the left edge and right one increment on the bottom edge. Continue drawing lines until you reach the bottom-right corner. The figure should scale as you resize the window so that the endpoints always touch the edges.

b) Modify your answer in part (a) to mirror the design in all four corners, as shown in the right screen capture of Fig. 4.22.

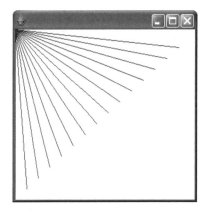
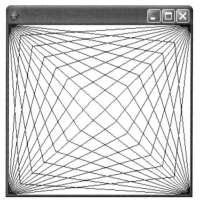

Fig. 4.21 | Lines fanning from a corner.

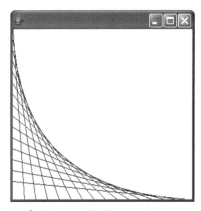
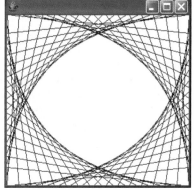

Fig. 4.22 | Line art with loops and `drawLine`.

4.15 Wrap-Up

This chapter presented basic problem-solving strategies that programmers use in building classes and developing methods for these classes. We demonstrated how to construct an algorithm (i.e., an approach to solving a problem), then how to refine the algorithm through several phases of pseudocode development, resulting in Java code that can be executed as part of a method. The chapter showed how to use top-down, stepwise refinement to plan out the specific actions that a method must perform and the order in which the method must perform these actions.

Only three types of control structures—sequence, selection and repetition—are needed to develop any problem-solving algorithm. Specifically, this chapter demonstrated the if single-selection statement, the if...else double-selection statement and the while repetition statement. These are some of the building blocks used to construct solutions to many problems. We used control-statement stacking to total and compute the average of a set of student grades with counter- and sentinel-controlled repetition, and we used control-statement nesting to analyze and make decisions based on a set of exam results. We introduced Java's compound assignment operators, as well as its increment and decrement operators. Finally, we discussed the primitive types available to Java programmers. In Chapter 5, Control Statements: Part 2, we continue our discussion of control statements, introducing the for, do...while and switch statements.

Summary

- An algorithm is a procedure for solving a problem in terms of the actions to execute and the order in which the actions execute.
- Specifying the order in which statements (actions) execute in a program is called program control.
- Pseudocode helps a programmer think out a program before attempting to write it in a programming language.
- Activity diagrams are part of the Unified Modeling Language (UML)—an industry standard for modeling software systems.
- An activity diagram models the workflow (also called the activity) of a software system.
- Activity diagrams are composed of special-purpose symbols, such as action-state symbols, diamonds and small circles. These symbols are connected by transition arrows that represent the flow of the activity.
- Like pseudocode, activity diagrams help programmers develop and represent algorithms.
- An action state is represented as a rectangle with its left and right sides replaced with arcs curving outward. The action expression appears inside the action state.
- The arrows in an activity diagram represent transitions, which indicate the order in which the actions represented by action states occur.
- The solid circle located at the top of an activity diagram represents the initial state—the beginning of the workflow before the program performs the modeled actions.
- The solid circle surrounded by a hollow circle that appears at the bottom of the activity diagram represents the final state—the end of the workflow after the program performs its actions.
- Rectangles with the upper-right corners folded over are called notes in the UML. Notes are explanatory remarks that describe the purpose of symbols in the diagram. A dotted line connects each note with the element that the note describes.

- A diamond or decision symbol in an activity diagram indicates that a decision is to be made. The workflow will continue along a path determined by the symbol's associated guard conditions, which can be true or false. Each transition arrow emerging from a decision symbol has a guard condition (specified in square brackets next to the transition arrow). If a guard condition is true, the workflow enters the action state to which the transition arrow points.

- A diamond in an activity diagram also represents the merge symbol, which joins two flows of activity into one. A merge symbol has two or more transition arrows pointing to the diamond and only one transition arrow pointing from the diamond, to indicate multiple activity flows merging to continue the activity.

- Top-down, stepwise refinement is a process for refining pseudocode by maintaining a complete representation of the program during each refinement.

- There are three types of control structures—sequence, selection and repetition.

- The sequence structure is built into Java—by default, statements execute in the order they appear.

- A selection structure chooses among alternative courses of action.

- The `if` single-selection statement either performs (selects) an action if a condition is true, or skips the action if the condition is false.

- The `if...else` double-selection statement performs (selects) an action if a condition is true and performs a different action if the condition is false.

- To include several statements in an `if`'s body (or the body of `else` for an `if...else` statement), enclose the statements in braces (`{` and `}`). A set of statements contained within a pair of braces is called a block. A block can be placed anywhere in a program that a single statement can be placed.

- An empty statement, indicating that no action is to be taken, is indicated by a semicolon (`;`).

- A repetition statement specifies that an action is to be repeated while some condition remains true.

- The format for the `while` repetition statement is

      while (*condition*)
          statement

- Counter-controlled repetition is used when the number of repetitions is known before a loop begins executing.

- The unary cast operator (`double`) creates a temporary floating-point copy of its operand.

- Sentinel-controlled repetition is used when the number of repetitions is not known before a loop begins executing.

- A nested control statement appears in the body of another control statement.

- Java provides the arithmetic compound assignment operators `+=`, `-=`, `*=`, `/=` and `%=` for abbreviating assignment expressions.

- The increment operator, `++`, and the decrement operator, `--`, increment or decrement a variable by 1, respectively. If the operator is prefixed to the variable, the variable is incremented or decremented by 1 first, and then its new value is used in the expression in which it appears. If the operator is postfixed to the variable, the variable is first used in the expression in which it appears, and then the variable's value is incremented or decremented by 1.

- The primitive types (`boolean`, `char`, `byte`, `short`, `int`, `long`, `float` and `double`) are portable across all computer platforms that support Java.

- Java is a strongly typed language—it requires all variables to have a type.

- Local variables are declared inside methods and are not assigned default values.

- Variables declared outside of methods as fields are assigned default values. Instance variables of types `char`, `byte`, `short`, `int`, `long`, `float` and `double` are all given the value 0 by default. Instance variables of type `boolean` are given the value `false` by default. Reference-type instance variables are initialized by default to the value `null`.

Terminology

-- operator
?: operator
++ operator
action
action/decision model of programming
action expression (in the UML)
action state (in the UML)
action-state symbol (in the UML)
activity (in the UML)
activity diagram (in the UML)
addition compound assignment operator (+=)
algorithm
arithmetic compound assignment operators:
    +=, -=, *=, /= and %=
block
`boolean` primitive type
body of a loop
cast operator, (*type*)
compound assignment operator
conditional expression
conditional operator (?:)
control statement
control-statement nesting
control-statement stacking
control variable
counter
counter-controlled repetition
creating an instance of a class
dangling-`else` problem
decision
decision symbol (in the UML)
decrement operator (--)
definite repetition
diamond (in the UML)
dotted line
double-selection statement
dummy value
explicit conversion
`false`
fatal logic error
final state (in the UML)
first refinement
flag value
`goto` statement
guard condition (in the UML)
`if` statement
`if...else` statement
implicit conversion
increment operator (++)

indefinite repetition
infinite loop
initial state (in the UML)
initialization
integer division
instantiate an object
iteration
logic error
loop
loop-continuation condition
loop counter
looping statement
merge symbol (in the UML)
multiple-selection statement
multiplicative operator
nested control statements
nested `if...else` statements
`new` keyword
nonfatal logic error
note (in the UML)
order in which actions should execute
postdecrement a variable
postfix decrement operator
postfix increment operator
postincrement a variable
predecrement a variable
prefix decrement operator
prefix increment operator
preincrement a variable
primitive types
procedure
program control
promotion
pseudocode
repetition
repetition structure
second refinement
selection structure
sentinel-controlled repetition
sentinel value
sequence structure
sequential execution
signal value
single-entry/single-exit control statements
single-selection statement
small circle (in the UML)
solid circle (in the UML)

solid circle surrounded by a hollow circle (in the UML)	transfer of control
	transition (in the UML)
stacked control statements	transition arrow (in the UML)
strongly typed language	true
structured programming	truncate
syntax error	unary cast operator
ternary operator	unary operator
top-down stepwise refinement	while statement
top	WORA (write once, run anywhere)
total	workflow

Self-Review Exercises

4.1　Fill in the blanks in each of the following statements:

a) All programs can be written in terms of three types of control structures: _____, _____ and _____.

b) The _____ statement is used to execute one action when a condition is true and another when that condition is false.

c) Repeating a set of instructions a specific number of times is called _____ repetition.

d) When it is not known in advance how many times a set of statements will be repeated, a(n) _____ value can be used to terminate the repetition.

e) The _____ structure is built into Java—by default, statements execute in the order they appear.

f) Instance variables of types char, byte, short, int, long, float and double are all given the value _____ by default.

g) Java is a _____ language—it requires all variables to have a type.

h) If the increment operator is _____ to a variable, the variable is incremented by 1 first, then its new value is used in the expression.

4.2　State whether each of the following is *true* or *false*. If *false*, explain why.

a) An algorithm is a procedure for solving a problem in terms of the actions to execute and the order in which these actions execute.

b) A set of statements contained within a pair of parentheses is called a block.

c) A selection statement specifies that an action is to be repeated while some condition remains true.

d) A nested control statement appears in the body of another control statement.

e) Java provides the arithmetic compound assignment operators +=, -=, *=, /= and %= for abbreviating assignment expressions.

f) The primitive types (boolean, char, byte, short, int, long, float and double) are portable across only Windows platforms.

g) Specifying the order in which statements (actions) execute in a program is called program control.

h) The unary cast operator (double) creates a temporary integer copy of its operand.

i) Instance variables of type boolean are given the value true by default.

j) Pseudocode helps a programmer think out a program before attempting to write it in a programming language.

4.3　Write four different Java statements that each add 1 to integer variable x.

4.4　Write Java statements to accomplish each of the following tasks:

a) Assign the sum of x and y to z, and increment x by 1 after the calculation. Use only one statement.

b) Test whether variable count is greater than 10. If it is, print "Count is greater than 10".

c) Decrement the variable x by 1, then subtract it from the variable total. Use only one statement.

d) Calculate the remainder after q is divided by divisor, and assign the result to q. Write this statement in two different ways.

4.5 Write a Java statement to accomplish each of the following tasks:
a) Declare variables sum and x to be of type int.
b) Assign 1 to variable x.
c) Assign 0 to variable sum.
d) Add variable x to variable sum, and assign the result to variable sum.
e) Print "The sum is: ", followed by the value of variable sum.

4.6 Combine the statements that you wrote in Exercise 4.5 into a Java application that calculates and prints the sum of the integers from 1 to 10. Use a while statement to loop through the calculation and increment statements. The loop should terminate when the value of x becomes 11.

4.7 Determine the value of the variables in the following statement after the calculation is performed. Assume that when the statement begins executing, all variables are type int and have the value 5.

```
product *= x++;
```

4.8 Identify and correct the errors in each of the following sets of code:
a)
```
while ( c <= 5 )
   {
      product *= c;
      ++c;
```
b)
```
if ( gender == 1 )
      System.out.println( "Woman" );
   else;
      System.out.println( "Man" );
```

4.9 What is wrong with the following while statement?

```
while ( z >= 0 )
   sum += z;
```

Answers to Self-Review Exercises

4.1 a) sequence, selection, repetition. b) if…else. c) counter-controlled (or definite). d) sentinel, signal, flag or dummy. e) sequence. f) 0 (zero). g) strongly typed. h) prefixed.

4.2 a) True. b) False. A set of statements contained within a pair of braces ({ and }) is called a block. c) False. A repetition statement specifies that an action is to be repeated while some condition remains true. d) True. e) True. f) False. The primitive types (boolean, char, byte, short, int, long, float and double) are portable across all computer platforms that support Java. g) True. h) False. The unary cast operator (double) creates a temporary floating-point copy of its operand. i) False. Instance variables of type boolean are given the value false by default. j) True.

4.3
```
x = x + 1;
x += 1;
++x;
x++;
```

4.4 a)
```
z = x++ + y;
```
b)
```
if ( count > 10 )
      System.out.println( "Count is greater than 10" );
```

c) total -= --x;
d) q %= divisor;
    q = q % divisor;

4.5   a) int sum, x;
b) x = 1;
c) sum = 0;
d) sum += x; or sum = sum + x;
e) System.out.printf("The sum is: %d\n", sum);

4.6   The program is as follows:

```
1   // Calculate the sum of the integers from 1 to 10
2   public class Calculate
3   {
4      public static void main( String args[] )
5      {
6         int sum;
7         int x;
8
9         x = 1;   // initialize x to 1 for counting
10        sum = 0; // initialize sum to 0 for totaling
11
12        while ( x <= 10 ) // while x is less than or equal to 10
13        {
14           sum += x; // add x to sum
15           ++x; // increment x
16        } // end while
17
18        System.out.printf( "The sum is: %d\n", sum );
19     } // end main
20
21  } // end class Calculate
```

```
The sum is: 55
```

4.7   product = 25, x = 6

4.8   a) Error: The closing right brace of the while statement's body is missing.
    Correction: Add a closing right brace after the statement ++c;.
b) Error: The semicolon after else results in a logic error. The second output statement will always be executed.
    Correction: Remove the semicolon after else.

4.9   The value of the variable z is never changed in the while statement. Therefore, if the loop-continuation condition (z >= 0) is true, an infinite loop is created. To prevent an infinite loop from occurring, z must be decremented so that it eventually becomes less than 0.

Exercises

4.10   Compare and contrast the if single-selection statement and the while repetition statement. How are these two statements similar? How are they different?

4.11   Explain what happens when a Java program attempts to divide one integer by another. What happens to the fractional part of the calculation? How can a programmer avoid that outcome?

4.12 Describe the two ways in which control statements can be combined.

4.13 What type of repetition would be appropriate for calculating the sum of the first 100 positive integers? What type of repetition would be appropriate for calculating the sum of an arbitrary number of positive integers? Briefly describe how each of these tasks could be performed.

4.14 What is the difference between preincrementing a variable and postincrementing a variable?

4.15 Identify and correct the errors in each of the following pieces of code. [*Note:* There may be more than one error in each piece of code.]

```
a) if ( age >= 65 );
      System.out.println( "Age greater than or equal to 65" );
   else
      System.out.println( "Age is less than 65 )";
b) int x = 1, total;
   while ( x <= 10 )
   {
      total += x;
      ++x;
   }
c) while ( x <= 100 )
      total += x;
      ++x;
d) while ( y > 0 )
   {
      System.out.println( y );
      ++y;
```

4.16 What does the following program print?

```
 1  public class Mystery
 2  {
 3     public static void main( String args[] )
 4     {
 5        int y;
 6        int x = 1;
 7        int total = 0;
 8
 9        while ( x <= 10 )
10        {
11           y = x * x;
12           System.out.println( y );
13           total += y;
14           ++x;
15        } // end while
16
17        System.out.printf( "Total is %d\n", total );
18     } // end main
19
20  } // end class Mystery
```

For Exercise 4.17 through Exercise 4.20, perform each of the following steps:

    a) Read the problem statement.
    b) Formulate the algorithm using pseudocode and top-down, stepwise refinement.
    c) Write a Java program.
    d) Test, debug and execute the Java program.
    e) Process three complete sets of data.

4.17   Drivers are concerned with the mileage their automobiles get. One driver has kept track of several tankfuls of gasoline by recording the miles driven and gallons used for each tankful. Develop a Java application that will input the miles driven and gallons used (both as integers) for each tankful. The program should calculate and display the miles per gallon obtained for each tankful and print the combined miles per gallon obtained for all tankfuls up to this point. All averaging calculations should produce floating-point results. Use class `Scanner` and sentinel-controlled repetition to obtain the data from the user.

4.18   Develop a Java application that will determine whether any of several department-store customers has exceeded the credit limit on a charge account. For each customer, the following facts are available:

    a) account number
    b) balance at the beginning of the month
    c) total of all items charged by the customer this month
    d) total of all credits applied to the customer's account this month
    e) allowed credit limit

The program should input all these facts as integers, calculate the new balance (= *beginning balance + charges − credits*), display the new balance and determine whether the new balance exceeds the customer's credit limit. For those customers whose credit limit is exceeded, the program should display the message `"Credit limit exceeded"`.

4.19   A large company pays its salespeople on a commission basis. The salespeople receive $200 per week plus 9% of their gross sales for that week. For example, a salesperson who sells $5,000 worth of merchandise in a week receives $200 plus 9% of $5,000, or a total of $650. You have been supplied with a list of the items sold by each salesperson. The values of these items are as follows:

Item	Value
1	239.99
2	129.75
3	99.95
4	350.89

Develop a Java application that inputs one salesperson's items sold for last week and calculates and displays that salesperson's earnings. There is no limit to the number of items that can be sold by a salesperson.

4.20   Develop a Java application that will determine the gross pay for each of three employees. The company pays straight time for the first 40 hours worked by each employee and time and a half for all hours worked in excess of 40 hours. You are given a list of the employees of the company, the number of hours each employee worked last week and the hourly rate of each employee. Your program should input this information for each employee and should determine and display the employee's gross pay. Use class `Scanner` to input the data.

4.21   The process of finding the largest value (i.e., the maximum of a group of values) is used frequently in computer applications. For example, a program that determines the winner of a sales contest would input the number of units sold by each salesperson. The salesperson who sells the most units wins the contest. Write a pseudocode program and then a Java application that inputs a series of 10 integers and determines and prints the largest integer. Your program should use at least the following three variables:

    a) `counter`: A counter to count to 10 (i.e., to keep track of how many numbers have been input and to determine when all 10 numbers have been processed).

    b) `number`: The integer most recently input by the user.

    c) `largest`: The largest number found so far.

4.22   Write a Java application that uses looping to print the following table of values:

N	10*N	100*N	1000*N
1	10	100	1000
2	20	200	2000
3	30	300	3000
4	40	400	4000
5	50	500	5000

4.23   Using an approach similar to that for Exercise 4.21, find the *two* largest values of the 10 values entered. [*Note*: You may input each number only once.]

4.24   Modify the program in Fig. 4.12 to validate its inputs. For any input, if the value entered is other than 1 or 2, keep looping until the user enters a correct value.

4.25   What does the following program print?

```
1   public class Mystery2
2   {
3      public static void main( String args[] )
4      {
5         int count = 1;
6
7         while ( count <= 10 )
8         {
9            System.out.println( count % 2 == 1 ? "*****" : "++++++++" );
10           ++count;
11        } // end while
12     } // end main
13
14  } // end class Mystery2
```

4.26   What does the following program print?

```
1   public class Mystery3
2   {
3      public static void main( String args[] )
4      {
5         int row = 10;
6         int column;
7
```

```
8           while ( row >= 1 )
9           {
10             column = 1;
11
12             while ( column <= 10 )
13             {
14                System.out.print( row % 2 == 1 ? "<" : ">" );
15                ++column;
16             } // end while
17
18             --row;
19             System.out.println();
20          } // end while
21       } // end main
22
23  } // end class Mystery3
```

4.27 *(Dangling-else Problem)* Determine the output for each of the given sets of code when x is 9 and y is 11 and when x is 11 and y is 9. Note that the compiler ignores the indentation in a Java program. Also, the Java compiler always associates an else with the immediately preceding if unless told to do otherwise by the placement of braces ({}). On first glance, the programmer may not be sure which if an else matches—this situation is referred to as the "dangling-else problem." We have eliminated the indentation from the following code to make the problem more challenging. [*Hint*: Apply the indentation conventions you have learned.]

a)
```
if ( x < 10 )
if ( y > 10 )
System.out.println( "*****" );
else
System.out.println( "#####" );
System.out.println( "$$$$$" );
```

b)
```
if ( x < 10 )
{
if ( y > 10 )
System.out.println( "*****" );
}
else
{
System.out.println( "#####" );
System.out.println( "$$$$$" );
}
```

4.28 *(Another Dangling-else Problem)* Modify the given code to produce the output shown in each part of the problem. Use proper indentation techniques. Make no changes other than inserting braces and changing the indentation of the code. The compiler ignores indentation in a Java program. We have eliminated the indentation from the given code to make the problem more challenging. [*Note*: It is possible that no modification is necessary for some of the parts.]

```
if ( y == 8 )
if ( x == 5 )
System.out.println( "@@@@@" );
else
System.out.println( "#####" );
System.out.println( "$$$$$" );
System.out.println( "&&&&&" );
```

a) Assuming that x = 5 and y = 8, the following output is produced:

```
@@@@@
$$$$$
&&&&&
```

b) Assuming that x = 5 and y = 8, the following output is produced:

```
@@@@@
```

c) Assuming that x = 5 and y = 8, the following output is produced:

```
@@@@@
&&&&&
```

d) Assuming that x = 5 and y = 7, the following output is produced. [*Note*: The last three output statements after the `else` are all part of a block.]

```
#####
$$$$$
&&&&&
```

4.29 Write an application that prompts the user to enter the size of the side of a square, then displays a hollow square of that size made of asterisks. Your program should work for squares of all side lengths between 1 and 20.

4.30 *(Palindromes)* A palindrome is a sequence of characters that reads the same backward as forward. For example, each of the following five-digit integers is a palindrome: 12321, 55555, 45554 and 11611. Write an application that reads in a five-digit integer and determines whether it is a palindrome. If the number is not five digits long, display an error message and allow the user to enter a new value.

4.31 Write an application that inputs an integer containing only 0s and 1s (i.e., a binary integer) and prints its decimal equivalent. [*Hint*: Use the remainder and division operators to pick off the binary number's digits one at a time, from right to left. In the decimal number system, the rightmost digit has a positional value of 1 and the next digit to the left has a positional value of 10, then 100, then 1000, and so on. The decimal number 234 can be interpreted as 4 * 1 + 3 * 10 + 2 * 100. In the binary number system, the rightmost digit has a positional value of 1, the next digit to the left has a positional value of 2, then 4, then 8, and so on. The decimal equivalent of binary 1101 is 1 * 1 + 0 * 2 + 1 * 4 + 1 * 8, or 1 + 0 + 4 + 8 or, 13.]

4.32 Write an application that uses only the output statements

```
System.out.print( "* " );
System.out.print( " " );
System.out.println();
```

to display the checkerboard pattern that follows. Note that a `System.out.println` method call with no arguments causes the program to output a single newline character. [*Hint*: Repetition statements are required.]

```
* * * * * * * *
 * * * * * * * *
* * * * * * * *
 * * * * * * * *
* * * * * * * *
 * * * * * * * *
* * * * * * * *
 * * * * * * * *
```

4.33   Write an application that keeps displaying in the command window the multiples of the integer 2—namely, 2, 4, 8, 16, 32, 64, and so on. Your loop should not terminate (i.e., create an infinite loop). What happens when you run this program?

4.34   What is wrong with the following statement? Provide the correct statement to add one to the sum of x and y.

```
System.out.println( ++(x + y) );
```

4.35   Write an application that reads three nonzero values entered by the user and determines and prints whether they could represent the sides of a triangle.

4.36   Write an application that reads three nonzero integers and determines and prints whether they could represent the sides of a right triangle.

4.37   A company wants to transmit data over the telephone, but is concerned that its phones may be tapped. It has asked you to write a program that will encrypt the data so that it may be transmitted more securely. All the data is transmitted as four-digit integers. Your application should read a four-digit integer entered by the user and encrypt it as follows: Replace each digit with the result of adding 7 to the digit and getting the remainder after dividing the new value by 10. Then swap the first digit with the third, and swap the second digit with the fourth. Then print the encrypted integer. Write a separate application that inputs an encrypted four-digit integer and decrypts it to form the original number.

4.38   The factorial of a nonnegative integer n is written as $n!$ (pronounced "n factorial") and is defined as follows:

$$n! = n \cdot (n-1) \cdot (n-2) \cdot \ldots \cdot 1 \quad \text{(for values of } n \text{ greater than or equal to 1)}$$

and

$$n! = 1 \quad \text{(for } n = 0\text{)}$$

For example, $5! = 5 \cdot 4 \cdot 3 \cdot 2 \cdot 1$, which is 120.

  a) Write an application that reads a nonnegative integer and computes and prints its factorial.

  b) Write an application that estimates the value of the mathematical constant e by using the formula

$$e = 1 + \frac{1}{1!} + \frac{1}{2!} + \frac{1}{3!} + \ldots$$

  c) Write an application that computes the value of e^x by using the formula

$$e^x = 1 + \frac{x}{1!} + \frac{x^2}{2!} + \frac{x^3}{3!} + \ldots$$

5

Control Statements: Part 2

OBJECTIVES

In this chapter you will learn:

- The essentials of counter-controlled repetition.
- To use the **for** and **do...while** repetition statements to execute statements in a program repeatedly.
- To understand multiple selection using the **switch** selection statement.
- To use the **break** and **continue** program control statements to alter the flow of control.
- To use the logical operators to form complex conditional expressions in control statements.

5.1 Introduction

Chapter 4 began our introduction to the types of building blocks that are available for problem solving. We used those building blocks to employ proven program-construction techniques. In this chapter, we continue our presentation of the theory and principles of structured programming by introducing Java's remaining control statements. The control statements we study here and in Chapter 4 are helpful in building and manipulating objects.

In this chapter, we demonstrate Java's for, do…while and switch statements. Through a series of short examples using while and for, we explore the essentials of counter-controlled repetition. We devote a portion of the chapter (and Chapter 7) to expanding the GradeBook class presented in Chapters 3–4. In particular, we create a version of class GradeBook that uses a switch statement to count the number of A, B, C, D and F grade equivalents in a set of numeric grades entered by the user. We introduce the break and continue program control statements. We discuss Java's logical operators, which enable programmers to use more complex conditional expressions in control statements. Finally, we summarize Java's control statements and the proven problem-solving techniques presented in this chapter and Chapter 4.

5.2 Essentials of Counter-Controlled Repetition

This section uses the while repetition statement introduced in Chapter 4 to formalize the elements required to perform counter-controlled repetition. Counter-controlled repetition requires

1. a control variable (or loop counter)

2. the initial value of the control variable

3. the increment (or decrement) by which the control variable is modified each time through the loop (also known as each iteration of the loop)

4. the loop-continuation condition that determines whether looping should continue.

To see these elements of counter-controlled repetition, consider the application of Fig. 5.1, which uses a loop to display the numbers from 1 through 10. Note that Fig. 5.1 contains only one method, main, which does all of the class's work. For most applications in Chapters 3–4, we have encouraged the use of two separate files—one that declares a reusable class (e.g., Account) and one that instantiates one or more objects of that class (e.g., AccountTest) and demonstrates its (their) functionality. Occasionally, however, it is more appropriate simply to create one class whose main method concisely illustrates a basic concept. Throughout this chapter, we use several one-class examples like Fig. 5.1 to demonstrate the mechanics of Java's control statements.

In main of Fig. 5.1 (lines 6–17), the elements of counter-controlled repetition are defined in lines 8, 10 and 13. Line 8 declares the control variable (counter) as an int, reserves space for it in memory and sets its initial value to 1. Variable counter could also have been declared and initialized with the following local-variable declaration and assignment statements:

```
int counter; // declare counter
counter = 1; // initialize counter to 1
```

Line 12 in the while statement displays control variable counter's value during each iteration of the loop. Line 13 increments the control variable by 1 for each iteration of the loop. The loop-continuation condition in the while (line 10) tests whether the value of the control variable is less than or equal to 10 (the final value for which the condition is true). Note that the program performs the body of this while even when the control variable is 10. The loop terminates when the control variable exceeds 10 (i.e., counter becomes 11).

Common Programming Error 5.1

Because floating-point values may be approximate, controlling loops with floating-point variables may result in imprecise counter values and inaccurate termination tests.

```
1   // Fig. 5.1: WhileCounter.java
2   // Counter-controlled repetition with the while repetition statement.
3
4   public class WhileCounter
5   {
6      public static void main( String args[] )
7      {
8         int counter = 1; // declare and initialize control variable
9
10        while ( counter <= 10 ) // loop-continuation condition
11        {
12           System.out.printf( "%d  ", counter );
13           ++counter; // increment control variable by 1
14        } // end while
15
16        System.out.println(); // output a newline
17     } // end main
18  } // end class WhileCounter
```

```
1  2  3  4  5  6  7  8  9  10
```

Fig. 5.1 | Counter-controlled repetition with the while repetition statement.

Error-Prevention Tip 5.1

Control counting loops with integers.

Good Programming Practice 5.1

Place blank lines above and below repetition and selection control statements, and indent the statement bodies to enhance readability.

The program in Fig. 5.1 can be made more concise by initializing counter to 0 in line 8 and preincrementing counter in the while condition as follows:

```
while ( ++counter <= 10 ) // loop-continuation condition
    System.out.printf( "%d  ", counter );
```

This code saves a statement (and eliminates the need for braces around the loop's body), because the while condition performs the increment before testing the condition. (Recall from Section 4.12 that the precedence of ++ is higher than that of <=.) Coding in such a condensed fashion takes practice and might make code more difficult to read, debug, modify and maintain, and typically should be avoided.

Software Engineering Observation 5.1

"Keep it simple" remains good advice for most of the code you will write.

5.3 for Repetition Statement

Section 5.2 presented the essentials of counter-controlled repetition. The while statement can be used to implement any counter-controlled loop. Java also provides the for repetition statement, which specifies the counter-controlled-repetition details in a single line of code. Figure 5.2 reimplements the application in Fig. 5.1 using for.

```
1   // Fig. 5.2: ForCounter.java
2   // Counter-controlled repetition with the for repetition statement.
3
4   public class ForCounter
5   {
6      public static void main( String args[] )
7      {
8         // for statement header includes initialization,
9         // loop-continuation condition and increment
10        for ( int counter = 1; counter <= 10; counter++ )
11           System.out.printf( "%d  ", counter );
12
13        System.out.println(); // output a newline
14     } // end main
15  } // end class ForCounter
```

```
1  2  3  4  5  6  7  8  9  10
```

Fig. 5.2 | Counter-controlled repetition with the for repetition statement.

The application's `main` method operates as follows: When the `for` statement (lines 10–11) begins executing, the control variable `counter` is declared and initialized to 1. (Recall from Section 5.2 that the first two elements of counter-controlled repetition are the control variable and its initial value.) Next, the program checks the loop-continuation condition, `counter <= 10`, which is between the two required semicolons. Because the initial value of `counter` is 1, the condition initially is true. Therefore, the body statement (line 11) displays control variable `counter`'s value, namely 1. After executing the loop's body, the program increments `counter` in the expression `counter++`, which appears to the right of the second semicolon. Then the loop-continuation test is performed again to determine whether the program should continue with the next iteration of the loop. At this point, the control variable value is 2, so the condition is still true (the final value is not exceeded)—thus, the program performs the body statement again (i.e., the next iteration of the loop). This process continues until the numbers 1 through 10 have been displayed and the `counter`'s value becomes 11, causing the loop-continuation test to fail and repetition to terminate (after 10 repetitions of the loop body at line 11). Then the program performs the first statement after the `for`—in this case, line 13.

Note that Fig. 5.2 uses (in line 10) the loop-continuation condition `counter <= 10`. If the programmer incorrectly specified `counter < 10` as the condition, the loop would iterate only nine times. This mistake is a common logic error called an off-by-one error.

Common Programming Error 5.2

Using an incorrect relational operator or an incorrect final value of a loop counter in the loop-continuation condition of a repetition statement can cause an off-by-one error.

Good Programming Practice 5.2

Using the final value in the condition of a `while` *or* `for` *statement and using the* `<=` *relational operator helps avoid off-by-one errors. For a loop that prints the values 1 to 10, the loop-continuation condition should be* `counter <= 10` *rather than* `counter < 10` *(which causes an off-by-one error) or* `counter < 11` *(which is correct). Many programmers prefer so-called zero-based counting, in which to count 10 times,* `counter` *would be initialized to zero and the loop-continuation test would be* `counter < 10`.

Figure 5.3 takes a closer look at the `for` statement in Fig. 5.2. The `for`'s first line (including the keyword `for` and everything in parentheses after `for`)—line 10 in Fig. 5.2—is sometimes called the for statement header, or simply the for header. Note that the `for` header "does it all"—it specifies each of the items needed for counter-controlled repetition with a control variable. If there is more than one statement in the body of the `for`, braces ({ and }) are required to define the body of the loop.

The general format of the `for` statement is

```
for ( initialization; loopContinuationCondition; increment )
     statement
```

where the *initialization* expression names the loop's control variable and provides its initial value, *loopContinuationCondition* is the condition that determines whether the loop should continue executing and *increment* modifies the control variable's value (possibly an increment or decrement), so that the loop-continuation condition eventually becomes false. The two semicolons in the `for` header are required.

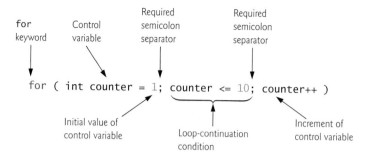

Fig. 5.3 | for statement header components.

 Common Programming Error 5.3

Using commas instead of the two required semicolons in a for header is a syntax error.

In most cases, the for statement can be represented with an equivalent while statement as follows:

initialization;

```
while ( loopContinuationCondition )
{
    statement
    increment;
}
```

In Section 5.7, we show a case in which a for statement cannot be represented with an equivalent while statement.

Typically, for statements are used for counter-controlled repetition and while statements are used for sentinel-controlled repetition. However, while and for can each be used for either repetition type.

If the *initialization* expression in the for header declares the control variable (i.e., the control variable's type is specified before the variable name, as in Fig. 5.2), the control variable can be used only in that for statement—it will not exist outside the for statement. This restricted use of the name of the control variable is known as the variable's scope. The scope of a variable defines where it can be used in a program. For example, a local variable can be used only in the method that declares the variable and only from the point of declaration through the end of the method. Scope is discussed in detail in Chapter 6, Methods: A Deeper Look.

 Common Programming Error 5.4

When a for statement's control variable is declared in the initialization section of the for's header, using the control variable after the for's body is a compilation error.

All three expressions in a for header are optional. If the *loopContinuationCondition* is omitted, Java assumes that the loop-continuation condition is always true, thus creating an infinite loop. You might omit the *initialization* expression if the program initializes the control variable before the loop. You might omit the *increment* expression if the program calculates the increment with statements in the loop's body or if no increment is needed. The increment expression in a for acts as if it were a stand-alone statement at the end of the for's body. Therefore, the expressions

```
counter = counter + 1
counter += 1
++counter
counter++
```

are equivalent increment expressions in a for statement. Many programmers prefer counter++ because it is concise and because a for loop evaluates its increment expression after its body executes. Therefore, the postfix increment form seems more natural. In this case, the variable being incremented does not appear in a larger expression, so preincrementing and postincrementing actually have the same effect.

Performance Tip 5.1

There is a slight performance advantage to preincrementing, but if you choose to postincrement because it seems more natural (as in a for header), optimizing compilers will generate Java bytecode that uses the more efficient form anyway.

Good Programming Practice 5.3

In the most cases, preincrementing and postincrementing are both used to add 1 to a variable in a statement by itself. In these cases, the effect is exactly the same, except that preincrementing has a slight performance advantage. Given that the compiler typically optimizes your code to help you get the best performance, use the idiom with which you feel most comfortable in these situations.

Common Programming Error 5.5

Placing a semicolon immediately to the right of the right parenthesis of a for header makes that for's body an empty statement. This is normally a logic error.

Error-Prevention Tip 5.2

Infinite loops occur when the loop-continuation condition in a repetition statement never becomes false. To prevent this situation in a counter-controlled loop, ensure that the control variable is incremented (or decremented) during each iteration of the loop. In a sentinel-controlled loop, ensure that the sentinel value is eventually input.

The initialization, loop-continuation condition and increment portions of a for statement can contain arithmetic expressions. For example, assume that x = 2 and y = 10. If x and y are not modified in the body of the loop, the statement

```
for ( int j = x; j <= 4 * x * y; j += y / x )
```

is equivalent to the statement

```
for ( int j = 2; j <= 80; j += 5 )
```

The increment of a for statement may also be negative, in which case it is really a decrement, and the loop counts downward.

If the loop-continuation condition is initially false, the program does not execute the for statement's body. Instead, execution proceeds with the statement following the for.

Programs frequently display the control variable value or use it in calculations in the loop body, but this use is not required. The control variable is commonly used to control repetition without mentioning the control variable in the body of the for.

Error-Prevention Tip 5.3

Although the value of the control variable can be changed in the body of a for loop, avoid doing so, because this practice can lead to subtle errors.

The for statement's UML activity diagram is similar to that of the while statement (Fig. 4.4). Figure 5.4 shows the activity diagram of the for statement in Fig. 5.2. The diagram makes it clear that initialization occurs once before the loop-continuation test is evaluated the first time, and that incrementing occurs each time through the loop after the body statement executes.

5.4 Examples Using the for Statement

The following examples show techniques for varying the control variable in a for statement. In each case, we write the appropriate for header. Note the change in the relational operator for loops that decrement the control variable.

a) Vary the control variable from 1 to 100 in increments of 1.

```
for ( int i = 1; i <= 100; i++ )
```

b) Vary the control variable from 100 to 1 in decrements of 1.

```
for ( int i = 100; i >= 1; i-- )
```

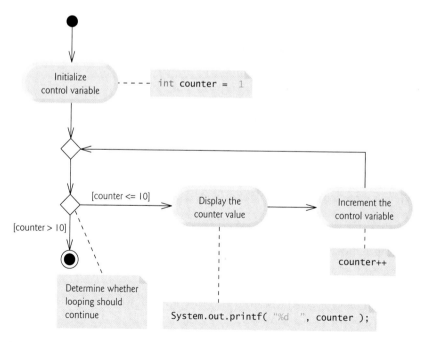

Fig. 5.4 | UML activity diagram for the for statement in Fig. 5.2.

c) Vary the control variable from 7 to 77 in increments of 7.

```
for ( int i = 7; i <= 77; i += 7 )
```

d) Vary the control variable from 20 to 2 in decrements of 2.

```
for ( int i = 20; i >= 2; i -= 2 )
```

e) Vary the control variable over the following sequence of values: 2, 5, 8, 11, 14, 17, 20.

```
for ( int i = 2; i <= 20; i += 3 )
```

f) Vary the control variable over the following sequence of values: 99, 88, 77, 66, 55, 44, 33, 22, 11, 0.

```
for ( int i = 99; i >= 0; i -= 11 )
```

 Common Programming Error 5.6

Not using the proper relational operator in the loop-continuation condition of a loop that counts downward (e.g., using i <= 1 instead of i >= 1 in a loop counting down to 1) is usually a logic error.

Application: Summing the Even Integers from 2 to 20

We now consider two sample applications that demonstrate simple uses of for. The application in Fig. 5.5 uses a for statement to sum the even integers from 2 to 20 and store the result in an int variable called total.

The *initialization* and *increment* expressions can be comma-separated lists of expressions that enable the programmer to use multiple initialization expressions or multiple increment expressions. For example, the body of the for statement in lines 11–12 of Fig. 5.5 could be merged into the increment portion of the for header by using a comma as follows:

```
for ( int number = 2; number <= 20; total += number, number += 2 )
   ; // empty statement
```

```
1   // Fig. 5.5: Sum.java
2   // Summing integers with the for statement.
3
4   public class Sum
5   {
6      public static void main( String args[] )
7      {
8         int total = 0; // initialize total
9
10        // total even integers from 2 through 20
11        for ( int number = 2; number <= 20; number += 2 )
12           total += number;
13
14        System.out.printf( "Sum is %d\n", total ); // display results
15     } // end main
16  } // end class Sum
```

```
Sum is 110
```

Fig. 5.5 | Summing integers with the for statement.

Good Programming Practice 5.4

Limit the size of control statement headers to a single line if possible.

Good Programming Practice 5.5

Place only expressions involving the control variables in the initialization and increment sections of a for statement. Manipulations of other variables should appear either before the loop (if they execute only once, like initialization statements) or in the body of the loop (if they execute once per iteration of the loop, like increment or decrement statements).

Application: Compound Interest Calculations

The next application uses the for statement to compute compound interest. Consider the following problem:

> *A person invests $1,000 in a savings account yielding 5% interest. Assuming that all the interest is left on deposit, calculate and print the amount of money in the account at the end of each year for 10 years. Use the following formula to determine the amounts:*
>
> $$a = p\,(1 + r\,)^{n}$$
>
> *where*
>
> p is the original amount invested (i.e., the principal)
> r is the annual interest rate (e.g., use 0.05 for 5%)
> n is the number of years
> a is the amount on deposit at the end of the nth year.

This problem involves a loop that performs the indicated calculation for each of the 10 years the money remains on deposit. The solution is the application shown in Fig. 5.6. Lines 8–10 in method main declare double variables amount, principal and rate, and initialize principal to 1000.0 and rate to 0.05. Java treats floating-point constants like 1000.0 and 0.05 as type double. Similarly, Java treats whole number constants like 7 and -22 as type int.

Line 13 outputs the headers for this application's two columns of output. The first column displays the year, and the second column displays the amount on deposit at the end of that year. Note that we use the format specifier %20s to output the String "Amount on Deposit". The integer 20 between the % and the conversion character s indicates that the value output should be displayed with a field width of 20—that is, printf displays the value with at least 20 character positions. If the value to be output is less than 20 character positions wide (17 characters in this example), the value is right justified in the field by default. If the year value to be output were more than four character positions wide, the field width would be extended to the right to accommodate the entire value—this would push the amount field to the right, upsetting the neat columns of our tabular output. To indicate that values should be output left justified, simply precede the field width with the minus sign (–) formatting flag.

The for statement (lines 16–23) executes its body 10 times, varying control variable year from 1 to 10 in increments of 1. This loop terminates when control variable year becomes 11. (Note that year represents n in the problem statement.)

Classes provide methods that perform common tasks on objects. In fact, most methods must be called on a specific object. For example, to output text in Fig. 5.6, line 13 calls method printf on the System.out object. Many classes also provide methods that perform

```
1   // Fig. 5.6: Interest.java
2   // Compound-interest calculations with for.
3
4   public class Interest
5   {
6      public static void main( String args[] )
7      {
8         double amount; // amount on deposit at end of each year
9         double principal = 1000.0; // initial amount before interest
10        double rate = 0.05; // interest rate
11
12        // display headers
13        System.out.printf( "%s%20s\n", "Year", "Amount on deposit" );
14
15        // calculate amount on deposit for each of ten years
16        for ( int year = 1; year <= 10; year++ )
17        {
18           // calculate new amount for specified year
19           amount = principal * Math.pow( 1.0 + rate, year );
20
21           // display the year and the amount
22           System.out.printf( "%4d%,20.2f\n", year, amount );
23        } // end for
24     } // end main
25  } // end class Interest
```

```
Year    Amount on deposit
  1              1,050.00
  2              1,102.50
  3              1,157.63
  4              1,215.51
  5              1,276.28
  6              1,340.10
  7              1,407.10
  8              1,477.46
  9              1,551.33
 10              1,628.89
```

Fig. 5.6 | Compound-interest calculations with for.

common tasks and do not require objects. Such methods are called static methods. For example, Java does not include an exponentiation operator, so the designers of Java's Math class defined static method pow for raising a value to a power. You can call a static method by specifying the class name followed by a dot (.) and the method name, as in

ClassName.methodName(arguments)

In Chapter 6, you will learn how to implement static methods in your own classes.

We use static method pow of class Math to perform the compound interest calculation in Fig. 5.6. Math.pow(x, y) calculates the value of x raised to the yth power. The method receives two double arguments and returns a double value. Line 19 performs the calculation $a = p (1 + r)^n$, where a is amount, p is principal, r is rate and n is year.

After each calculation, line 22 outputs the year and the amount on deposit at the end of that year. The year is output in a field width of four characters (as specified by %4d). The amount is output as a floating-point number with the format specifier %,20.2f. The comma (,) formatting flag indicates that the floating-point value should be output with a thousands separator. The actual separator used is specific to the user's locale (i.e., country). For example, in the United States, the number will be output using commas to separate the thousands and a decimal point to separate the fractional part of the number, as in 1,234.45. The number 20 in the format specification indicates that the value should be output right justified in a field width of 20 characters. The .2 specifies the formatted number's precision—in this case, the number is rounded to the nearest hundredth and output with two digits to the right of the decimal point.

We declared variables amount, principal and rate to be of type double in this example. We are dealing with fractional parts of dollars and thus need a type that allows decimal points in its values. Unfortunately, floating-point numbers can cause trouble. Here is a simple explanation of what can go wrong when using double (or float) to represent dollar amounts (assuming that dollar amounts are displayed with two digits to the right of the decimal point): Two double dollar amounts stored in the machine could be 14.234 (which would normally be rounded to 14.23 for display purposes) and 18.673 (which would normally be rounded to 18.67 for display purposes). When these amounts are added, they produce the internal sum 32.907, which would normally be rounded to 32.91 for display purposes. Thus, your output could appear as

```
    14.23
  + 18.67
    -------
    32.91
```

but a person adding the individual numbers as displayed would expect the sum to be 32.90. You have been warned!

Good Programming Practice 5.6

Do not use variables of type double (or float) to perform precise monetary calculations. The imprecision of floating-point numbers can cause errors that will result in incorrect monetary values. In the exercises, we explore the use of integers to perform monetary calculations. [Note: Some third-party vendors provide for-sale class libraries that perform precise monetary calculations. In addition, the Java API provides class java.math.BigDecimal for performing calculations with arbitrary precision floating-point values.]

Note that the body of the for statement contains the calculation 1.0 + rate, which appears as an argument to the Math.pow method. In fact, this calculation produces the same result each time through the loop, so repeating the calculation every iteration of the loop is wasteful.

Performance Tip 5.2

In loops, avoid calculations for which the result never changes—such calculations should typically be placed before the loop. [Note: Many of today's sophisticated optimizing compilers will place such calculations outside loops in the compiled code.]

5.5 do...while Repetition Statement

The do...while repetition statement is similar to the while statement. In the while, the program tests the loop-continuation condition at the beginning of the loop, before executing the loop's body. If the condition is false, the body never executes. The do...while statement tests the loop-continuation condition *after* executing the loop's body; therefore, the body always executes at least once. When a do...while statement terminates, execution continues with the next statement in sequence. Figure 5.7 uses a do...while (lines 10–14) to output the numbers 1–10.

Line 8 declares and initializes control variable counter. Upon entering the do...while statement, line 12 outputs counter's value and line 13 increments counter. Then the program evaluates the loop-continuation test at the bottom of the loop (line 14). If the condition is true, the loop continues from the first body statement in the do...while (line 12). If the condition is false, the loop terminates and the program continues with the next statement after the loop.

Figure 5.8 contains the UML activity diagram for the do...while statement. This diagram makes it clear that the loop-continuation condition is not evaluated until after the loop performs the action state at least once. Compare this activity diagram with that of the while statement (Fig. 4.4). It is not necessary to use braces in the do...while repetition statement if there is only one statement in the body. However, most programmers include the braces, to avoid confusion between the while and do...while statements. For example,

    while (*condition*)

is normally the first line of a while statement. A do...while statement with no braces around a single-statement body appears as:

```
1   // Fig. 5.7: DoWhileTest.java
2   // do...while repetition statement.
3
4   public class DoWhileTest
5   {
6      public static void main( String args[] )
7      {
8         int counter = 1; // initialize counter
9
10        do
11        {
12           System.out.printf( "%d  ", counter );
13           ++counter;
14        } while ( counter <= 10 ); // end do...while
15
16        System.out.println(); // outputs a newline
17     } // end main
18  } // end class DoWhileTest
```

```
1 2  3  4  5  6  7  8  9  10
```

Fig. 5.7 | do...while repetition statement.

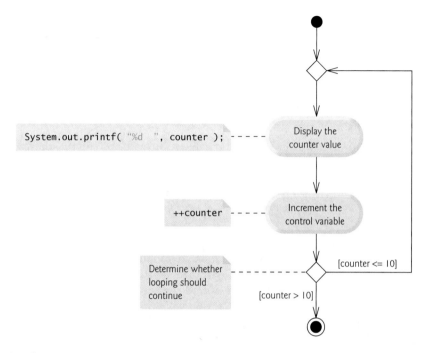

Fig. 5.8 | do...while repetition statement UML activity diagram.

```
do
    statement
while ( condition );
```

which can be confusing. A reader may misinterpret the last line—while(*condition*);— as a while statement containing an empty statement (the semicolon by itself). Thus, the do...while statement with one body statement is usually written as follows:

```
do
{
    statement
} while ( condition );
```

Good Programming Practice 5.7

Always include braces in a do...while statement, even if they are not necessary. This helps eliminate ambiguity between the while statement and a do...while statement containing only one statement.

5.6 switch Multiple-Selection Statement

We discussed the if single-selection statement and the if...else double-selectionstate-ment in Chapter 4. Java provides the switch multiple-selection statement to perform dif-ferent actions based on the possible values of an integer variable or expression. Each action. is associated with the value of a constant integral expression (i.e., a constant value of type byte, short, int or char, but not long) that the variable or expression on which the switch is based may assume.

***GradeBook* Class with *switch* Statement to Count A, B, C, D and F Grades.**
Figure 5.9 contains an enhanced version of the GradeBook class introduced in Chapter 3 and
further developed in Chapter 4. The version of the class we now present not only calculates
the average of a set of numeric grades entered by the user, but uses a switch statement to
determine whether each grade is the equivalent of an A, B, C, D or F and to increment the
appropriate grade counter. The class also displays a summary of the number of students who
received each grade. Please refer to Fig. 5.10 for sample input and output of the GradeBook-
Test application that uses class GradeBook to process a set of grades.

```java
 1   // Fig. 5.9: GradeBook.java
 2   // GradeBook class uses switch statement to count A, B, C, D and F grades.
 3   import java.util.Scanner; // program uses class Scanner
 4
 5   public class GradeBook
 6   {
 7      private String courseName; // name of course this GradeBook represents
 8      private int total; // sum of grades
 9      private int gradeCounter; // number of grades entered
10      private int aCount; // count of A grades
11      private int bCount; // count of B grades
12      private int cCount; // count of C grades
13      private int dCount; // count of D grades
14      private int fCount; // count of F grades
15
16      // constructor initializes courseName;
17      // int instance variables are initialized to 0 by default
18      public GradeBook( String name )
19      {
20         courseName = name; // initializes courseName
21      } // end constructor
22
23      // method to set the course name
24      public void setCourseName( String name )
25      {
26         courseName = name; // store the course name
27      } // end method setCourseName
28
29      // method to retrieve the course name
30      public String getCourseName()
31      {
32         return courseName;
33      } // end method getCourseName
34
35      // display a welcome message to the GradeBook user
36      public void displayMessage()
37      {
38         // getCourseName gets the name of the course
39         System.out.printf( "Welcome to the grade book for\n%s!\n\n",
40            getCourseName() );
41      } // end method displayMessage
42
```

Fig. 5.9 | GradeBook class uses switch statement to count A, B, C, D and F grades. (Part 1 of 3.)

```
43      // input arbitrary number of grades from user
44      public void inputGrades()
45      {
46         Scanner input = new Scanner( System.in );
47
48         int grade; // grade entered by user
49
50         System.out.printf( "%s\n%s\n   %s\n   %s\n",
51            "Enter the integer grades in the range 0-100.",
52            "Type the end-of-file indicator to terminate input:",
53            "On UNIX/Linux/Mac OS X type <ctrl> d then press Enter",
54            "On Windows type <ctrl> z then press Enter" );
55
56         // loop until user enters the end-of-file indicator
57         while ( input.hasNext() )
58         {
59            grade = input.nextInt(); // read grade
60            total += grade; // add grade to total
61            ++gradeCounter; // increment number of grades
62
63            // call method to increment appropriate counter
64            incrementLetterGradeCounter( grade );
65         } // end while
66      } // end method inputGrades
67
68      // add 1 to appropriate counter for specified grade
69      public void incrementLetterGradeCounter( int numericGrade )
70      {
71         // determine which grade was entered
72         switch ( grade / 10 )
73         {
74            case 9:  // grade was between 90
75            case 10: // and 100
76               ++aCount; // increment aCount
77               break; // necessary to exit switch
78
79            case 8: // grade was between 80 and 89
80               ++bCount; // increment bCount
81               break; // exit switch
82
83            case 7: // grade was between 70 and 79
84               ++cCount; // increment cCount
85               break; // exit switch
86
87            case 6: // grade was between 60 and 69
88               ++dCount; // increment dCount
89               break; // exit switch
90
91            default: // grade was less than 60
92               ++fCount; // increment fCount
93               break; // optional; will exit switch anyway
94         } // end switch
95      } // end method incrementLetterGradeCounter
```

Fig. 5.9 | GradeBook class uses switch statement to count A, B, C, D and F grades. (Part 2 of 3.)

```
 96
 97      // display a report based on the grades entered by user
 98      public void displayGradeReport()
 99      {
100         System.out.println( "\nGrade Report:" );
101
102         // if user entered at least one grade...
103         if ( gradeCounter != 0 )
104         {
105            // calculate average of all grades entered
106            double average = (double) total / gradeCounter;
107
108            // output summary of results
109            System.out.printf( "Total of the %d grades entered is %d\n",
110               gradeCounter, total );
111            System.out.printf( "Class average is %.2f\n", average );
112            System.out.printf( "%s\n%s%d\n%s%d\n%s%d\n%s%d\n%s%d\n",
113               "Number of students who received each grade:",
114               "A: ", aCount,    // display number of A grades
115               "B: ", bCount,    // display number of B grades
116               "C: ", cCount,    // display number of C grades
117               "D: ", dCount,    // display number of D grades
118               "F: ", fCount );  // display number of F grades
119         } // end if
120         else // no grades were entered, so output appropriate message
121            System.out.println( "No grades were entered" );
122      } // end method displayGradeReport
123   } // end class GradeBook
```

Fig. 5.9 | GradeBook class uses switch statement to count A, B, C, D and F grades. (Part 3 of 3.)

Like earlier versions of the class, class GradeBook (Fig. 5.9) declares instance variable courseName (line 7) and contains methods setCourseName (lines 24–27), getCourseName (lines 30–33) and displayMessage (lines 36–41), which set the course name, store the course name and display a welcome message to the user, respectively. The class also contains a constructor (lines 18–21) that initializes the course name.

Class GradeBook also declares instance variables total (line 8) and gradeCounter (line 9), which keep track of the sum of the grades entered by the user and the number of grades entered, respectively. Lines 10–14 declare counter variables for each grade category. Class GradeBook maintains total, gradeCounter and the five letter-grade counters as instance variables so that these variables can be used or modified in any of the class's methods. Note that the class's constructor (lines 18–21) sets only the course name, because the remaining seven instance variables are ints and are initialized to 0 by default.

Class GradeBook (Fig. 5.9) contains three additional methods—inputGrades, incrementLetterGradeCounter and displayGradeReport. Method inputGrades (lines 44–66) reads an arbitrary number of integer grades from the user using sentinel-controlled repetition and updates instance variables total and gradeCounter. Method inputGrades calls method incrementLetterGradeCounter (lines 69–95) to update the appropriate letter-grade counter for each grade entered. Class GradeBook also contains method displayGradeReport (lines 98–122), which outputs a report containing the total of all grades entered, the average of the grades and the number of students who received each letter grade. Let's examine these methods in more detail.

Line 48 in method `inputGrades` declares variable `grade`, which will store the user's input. Lines 50–54 prompt the user to enter integer grades and to type the end-of-file indicator to terminate the input. The end-of-file indicator is a system-dependent keystroke combination which the user enters to indicate that there is no more data to input.

On UNIX/Linux/Mac OS X systems, end-of-file is entered by typing the sequence

  <ctrl> d

on a line by itself. This notation means to simultaneously press both the *ctrl* key and the *d* key. On Windows systems, end-of-file can be entered by typing

  <ctrl> z

[*Note:* On some systems, you must press *Enter* after typing the end-of-file key sequence. Also, Windows typically displays the characters ^Z on the screen when the end-of-file indicator is typed, as is shown in the output of Fig. 5.9.]

Portability Tip 5.1

The keystroke combinations for entering end-of-file are system dependent.

The `while` statement (lines 57–65) obtains the user input. The condition at line 57 calls `Scanner` method **hasNext** to determine whether there is more data to input. This method returns the `boolean` value `true` if there is more data; otherwise, it returns `false`. The returned value is then used as the condition in the `while` statement. As long as the end-of-file indicator has not been typed, method `hasNext` will return `true`.

Line 59 inputs a grade value from the user. Line 60 uses the += operator to add `grade` to `total`. Line 61 increments `gradeCounter`. The class's `displayGradeReport` method uses these variables to compute the average of the grades. Line 64 calls the class's `incrementLetterGradeCounter` method (declared in lines 69–95) to increment the appropriate letter-grade counter based on the numeric grade entered.

Method `incrementLetterGradeCounter` contains a `switch` statement (lines 72–94) that determines which counter to increment. In this example, we assume that the user enters a valid grade in the range 0–100. A grade in the range 90–100 represents A, 80–89 represents B, 70–79 represents C, 60–69 represents D and 0–59 represents F. The `switch` statement consists of a block that contains a sequence of **case** labels and an optional **default** case. These are used in this example to determine which counter to increment based on the grade.

When the flow of control reaches the `switch`, the program evaluates the expression in the parentheses (`grade / 10`) following keyword `switch`. This is called the controlling expression of the `switch`. The program compares the value of the controlling expression (which must evaluate to an integral value of type `byte`, `char`, `short` or `int`) with each `case` label. The controlling expression in line 72 performs integer division, which truncates the fractional part of the result. Thus, when we divide any value for 0–100 by 10, the result is always a value from 0 to 10. We use several of these values in our `case` labels. For example, if the user enters the integer 85, the controlling expression evaluates to the `int` value 8. The `switch` compares 8 with each `case`. If a match occurs (`case 8:` at line 79), the program executes the statements for that `case`. For the integer 8, line 80 increments `bCount`, because a grade in the 80s is a B. The `break` statement (line 81) causes program control to proceed with the first statement after the `switch`—in this program, we reach the end of method `incrementLetterGradeCounter`'s body, so control returns to line 65 in method `input-Grades` (the first line after the call to `incrementLetterGradeCounter`). This line marks the end of the body of the `while` loop that inputs grades (lines 57–65), so control flows to the `while`'s condition (line 57) to determine whether the loop should continue executing.

The `cases` in our `switch` explicitly test for the values 10, 9, 8, 7 and 6. Note the cases at lines 74–75 that test for the values 9 and 10 (both of which represent the grade A). Listing cases consecutively in this manner with no statements between them enables the cases to perform the same set of statements—when the controlling expression evaluates to 9 or 10, the statements in lines 76–77 will execute. The `switch` statement does not provide a mechanism for testing ranges of values, so every value that must be tested should be listed in a separate `case` label. Note that each `case` can have multiple statements. The `switch` statement differs from other control statements in that it does not require braces around multiple statements in each `case`.

Without `break` statements, each time a match occurs in the `switch`, the statements for that case and subsequent cases execute until a `break` statement or the end of the `switch` is encountered. This is often referred to as "falling through" to the statements in subsequent `cases`. (This feature is perfect for writing a concise program that displays the iterative song "The Twelve Days of Christmas" in Exercise 5.29.)

Common Programming Error 5.7

Forgetting a break *statement when one is needed in a* switch *is a logic error.*

If no match occurs between the controlling expression's value and a `case` label, the `default` case (lines 91–93) executes. We use the `default` case in this example to process all controlling-expression values that are less than 6, that is, all failing grades. If no match occurs and the `switch` does not contain a `default` case, program control simply continues with the first statement after the `switch`.

GradeBookTest Class That Demonstrates Class GradeBook

Class `GradeBookTest` (Fig. 5.10) creates a `GradeBook` object (lines 10–11). Line 13 invokes the object's `displayMessage` method to output a welcome message to the user. Line 14 invokes the object's `inputGrades` method to read a set of grades from the user and keep track of the sum of all the grades entered and the number of grades. Recall that method `inputGrades` also calls method `incrementLetterGradeCounter` to keep track of the number of students who received each letter grade. Line 15 invokes method `displayGradeReport` of class `GradeBook`, which outputs a report based on the grades entered (as in the input/output window in Fig. 5.10). Line 103 of class `GradeBook` (Fig. 5.9) determines whether the user entered at least one grade—this helps us avoid dividing by zero. If so, line 106 calculates the average of the grades. Lines 109–118 then output the total of all the grades, the class average and the number of students who received each letter grade. If no grades were entered, line 121 outputs an appropriate message. The output in Fig. 5.10 shows a sample grade report based on 10 grades.

```
1    // Fig. 5.10: GradeBookTest.java
2    // Create GradeBook object, input grades and display grade report.
3
4    public class GradeBookTest
5    {
6       public static void main( String args[] )
7       {
8          // create GradeBook object myGradeBook and
9          // pass course name to constructor
10         GradeBook myGradeBook = new GradeBook(
11            "CS101 Introduction to Java Programming" );
12
13         myGradeBook.displayMessage(); // display welcome message
14         myGradeBook.inputGrades(); // read grades from user
15         myGradeBook.displayGradeReport(); // display report based on grades
16      } // end main
17   } // end class GradeBookTest
```

```
Welcome to the grade book for
CS101 Introduction to Java Programming!

Enter the integer grades in the range 0-100.
Type the end-of-file indicator to terminate input:
   On UNIX/Linux/Mac OS X type <ctrl> d then press Enter
   On Windows type <ctrl> z then press Enter
99
92
45
57
63
71
76
85
90
100
^Z

Grade Report:
Total of the 10 grades entered is 778
Class average is 77.80
Number of students who received each grade:
A: 4
B: 1
C: 2
D: 1
F: 2
```

Fig. 5.10 | GradeBookTest creates a GradeBook object and invokes its methods.

Note that class GradeBookTest (Fig. 5.10) does not directly call GradeBook method incrementLetterGradeCounter (lines 69–95 of Fig. 5.9). This method is used exclusively by method inputGrades of class GradeBook to update the appropriate letter-grade counter as each new grade is entered by the user. Method incrementLetterGradeCounter exists solely to support the operations of class GradeBook's other methods and thus could be declared private. Recall from Chapter 3 that methods declared with access modifier private can be called only by other methods of the class in which the private methods are declared. Such methods are commonly referred to as utility methods or helper methods because they can be called only by other methods of that class and are used to support the operation of those methods.

switch *Statement UML Activity Diagram*

Figure 5.11 shows the UML activity diagram for the general switch statement. Most switch statements use a break in each case to terminate the switch statement after processing the case. Figure 5.11 emphasizes this by including break statements in the activity diagram. The diagram makes it clear that the break statement at the end of a case causes control to exit the switch statement immediately.

The break statement is not required for the switch's last case (or the default case, when it appears last), because execution continues with the next statement after the switch.

Software Engineering Observation 5.2

Provide a default case in switch statements. Including a default case focuses you on the need to process exceptional conditions.

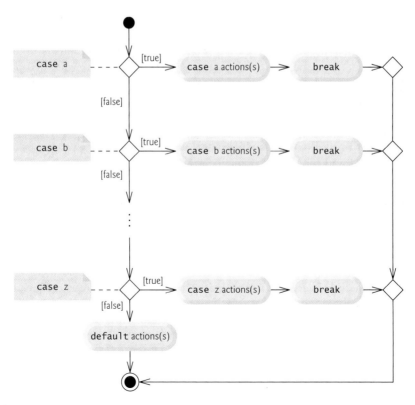

Fig. 5.11 | switch multiple-selection statement UML activity diagram with **break** statements.

Good Programming Practice 5.8

Although each case and the default case in a switch can occur in any order, place the default case last. When the default case is listed last, the break for that case is not required. Some programmers include this break for clarity and symmetry with other cases.

When using the switch statement, remember that the expression after each case can be only a constant integral expression—that is, any combination of integer constants that evaluates to a constant integer value (e.g., -7, 0 or 221). An integer constant is simply an integer value. In addition, you can use character constants—specific characters in single quotes, such as 'A', '7' or '$'—which represent the integer values of characters. (Appendix B, ASCII Character Set shows the integer values of the characters in the ASCII character set, which is a subset of the Unicode character set used by Java.)

The expression in each case also can be a constant variable—a variable that contains a value which does not change for the entire program. Such a variable is declared with keyword final (discussed in Chapter 6, Methods: A Deeper Look). J2SE 5.0 has a new feature called enumerations, which we also present in Chapter 6. Enumeration constants can also be used in case labels. In Chapter 10, Object-Oriented Programming: Polymorphism, we present a more elegant way to implement switch logic—we use a technique called polymorphism to create programs that are often clearer, easier to maintain and easier to extend than programs using switch logic.

5.7 break and continue Statements

In addition to selection and repetition statements, Java provides statements break and continue (presented in this section and Appendix K, Labeled break and continue Statements) to alter the flow of control. The preceding section showed how break can be used to terminate a switch statement's execution. This section discusses how to use break in a repetition statement.

In addition to the break and continue statements discussed in this section, Java provides the labeled break and continue statements for use in cases in which a programmer needs to conveniently alter the flow of control in nested control statements. We discuss the labeled break and continue statements in Appendix K.

break Statement

The break statement, when executed in a while, for, do...while or switch, causes immediate exit from that statement. Execution continues with the first statement after the control statement. Common uses of the break statement are to escape early from a loop or to skip the remainder of a switch (as in Fig. 5.9). Figure 5.12 demonstrates a break statement exiting a for.

When the if nested at line 11 in the for statement (lines 9–15) detects that count is 5, the break statement at line 12 executes. This terminates the for statement, and the program proceeds to line 17 (immediately after the for statement), which displays a message indicating the value of the control variable when the loop terminated. The loop fully executes its body only four times instead of 10.

continue Statement

The continue statement, when executed in a while, for or do...while, skips the remaining statements in the loop body and proceeds with the next iteration of the loop. In while

```
 1   // Fig. 5.12: BreakTest.java
 2   // break statement exiting a for statement.
 3   public class BreakTest
 4   {
 5      public static void main( String args[] )
 6      {
 7         int count; // control variable also used after loop terminates
 8
 9         for ( count = 1; count <= 10; count++ ) // loop 10 times
10         {
11            if ( count == 5 ) // if count is 5,
12               break;          // terminate loop
13
14            System.out.printf( "%d ", count );
15         } // end for
16
17         System.out.printf( "\nBroke out of loop at count = %d\n", count );
18      } // end main
19   } // end class BreakTest
```

```
1 2 3 4
Broke out of loop at count = 5
```

Fig. 5.12 | break statement exiting a for statement.

and do…while statements, the program evaluates the loop-continuation test immediately after the continue statement executes. In a for statement, the increment expression executes, then the program evaluates the loop-continuation test.

Figure 5.13 uses the continue statement in a for to skip the statement at line 12 when the nested if (line 9) determines that the value of count is 5. When the continue statement executes, program control continues with the increment of the control variable in the for statement (line 7).

```
 1   // Fig. 5.13: ContinueTest.java
 2   // continue statement terminating an iteration of a for statement.
 3   public class ContinueTest
 4   {
 5      public static void main( String args[] )
 6      {
 7         for ( int count = 1; count <= 10; count++ ) // loop 10 times
 8         {
 9            if ( count == 5 ) // if count is 5,
10               continue;       // skip remaining code in loop
11
12            System.out.printf( "%d ", count );
13         } // end for
14
15         System.out.println( "\nUsed continue to skip printing 5" );
16      } // end main
17   } // end class ContinueTest
```

Fig. 5.13 | continue statement terminating an iteration of a for statement. (Part 1 of 2.)

```
1 2 3 4 6 7 8 9 10
Used continue to skip printing 5
```

Fig. 5.13 | `continue` statement terminating an iteration of a `for` statement. (Part 2 of 2.)

In Section 5.3, we stated that `while` could be used in most cases in place of `for`. The one exception occurs when the increment expression in the `while` follows a `continue` statement. In this case, the increment does not execute before the program evaluates the repetition-continuation condition, so the `while` does not execute in the same manner as the `for`.

Software Engineering Observation 5.3

Some programmers feel that break *and* continue *violate structured programming. Since the same effects are achievable with structured programming techniques, these programmers do not use* break *or* continue.

Software Engineering Observation 5.4

There is a tension between achieving quality software engineering and achieving the best-performing software. Often, one of these goals is achieved at the expense of the other. For all but the most performance-intensive situations, apply the following rule of thumb: First, make your code simple and correct; then make it fast and small, but only if necessary.

5.8 Logical Operators

The `if`, `if...else`, `while`, `do...while` and `for` statements each require a condition to determine how to continue a program's flow of control. So far, we have studied only simple conditions, such as `count <= 10`, `number != sentinelValue` and `total > 1000`. Simple conditions are expressed in terms of the relational operators `>`, `<`, `>=` and `<=` and the equality operators `==` and `!=`, and each expression tests only one condition. To test multiple conditions in the process of making a decision, we performed these tests in separate statements or in nested `if` or `if...else` statements. Sometimes, control statements require more complex conditions to determine a program's flow of control.

Java provides logical operators to enable programmers to form more complex conditions by combining simple conditions. The logical operators are `&&` (conditional AND), `||` (conditional OR), `&` (boolean logical AND), `|` (boolean logical inclusive OR), `^` (boolean logical exclusive OR) and `!` (logical NOT).

Conditional AND (&&) Operator
Suppose that we wish to ensure at some point in a program that two conditions are *both* true before we choose a certain path of execution. In this case, we can use the `&&` (conditional AND) operator, as follows:

```
if ( gender == FEMALE && age >= 65 )
    ++seniorFemales;
```

This `if` statement contains two simple conditions. The condition `gender == FEMALE` compares variable `gender` to the constant `FEMALE`. This might be evaluated, for example, to determine whether a person is female. The condition `age >= 65` might be evaluated to determine whether a person is a senior citizen. The `if` statement considers the combined condition

> `gender == FEMALE && age >= 65`

which is true if and only if both simple conditions are true. If the combined condition is true, the `if` statement's body increments `seniorFemales` by 1. If either or both of the simple conditions are false, the program skips the increment. Some programmers find that the preceding combined condition is more readable when redundant parentheses are added, as in:

> `( gender == FEMALE ) && ( age >= 65 )`

The table in Fig. 5.14 summarizes the `&&` operator. The table shows all four possible combinations of `false` and `true` values for *expression1* and *expression2*. Such tables are called truth tables. Java evaluates to `false` or `true` all expressions that include relational operators, equality operators or logical operators.

Conditional OR (||) Operator

Now suppose that we wish to ensure that either *or* both of two conditions are true before we choose a certain path of execution. In this case, we use the `||` (conditional OR) operator, as in the following program segment:

```
if ( ( semesterAverage >= 90 ) || ( finalExam >= 90 ) )
    System.out.println ( "Student grade is A" );
```

This statement also contains two simple conditions. The condition `semesterAverage >= 90` evaluates to determine whether the student deserves an A in the course because of a solid performance throughout the semester. The condition `finalExam >= 90` evaluates to determine whether the student deserves an A in the course because of an outstanding performance on the final exam. The `if` statement then considers the combined condition

> `( semesterAverage >= 90 ) || ( finalExam >= 90 )`

and awards the student an A if either or both of the simple conditions are true. The only time the message `"Student grade is A"` is *not* printed is when both of the simple conditions are false. Figure 5.15 is a truth table for operator conditional OR (`||`). Operator `&&` has a higher precedence than operator `||`. Both operators associate from left to right.

expression1	expression2	expression1 && expression2
false	false	false
false	true	false
true	false	false
true	true	true

Fig. 5.14 | `&&` (conditional AND) operator truth table.

expression1	expression2	expression1 || expression2
false	false	false
false	true	true
true	false	true
true	true	true

Fig. 5.15 | \|\| (conditional OR) operator truth table.

Short-Circuit Evaluation of Complex Conditions

The parts of an expression containing && or || operators are evaluated only until it is known whether the condition is true or false. Thus, evaluation of the expression

```
( gender == FEMALE ) && ( age >= 65 )
```

stops immediately if gender is not equal to FEMALE (i.e., the entire expression is false) and continues if gender *is* equal to FEMALE (i.e., the entire expression could still be true if the condition age >= 65 is true). This feature of conditional AND and conditional OR expressions is called short-circuit evaluation.

Common Programming Error 5.8

In expressions using operator &&, a condition—we will call this the dependent condition—may require another condition to be true for the evaluation of the dependent condition to be meaningful. In this case, the dependent condition should be placed after the other condition, or an error might occur. For example, in the expression (i != 0) && (10 / i == 2), the second condition must appear after the first condition, or a divide-by-zero error might occur.

Boolean Logical AND (&) and Boolean Logical OR (|) Operators

The boolean logical AND (&) and boolean logical inclusive OR (|) operators work identically to the && (conditional AND) and || (conditional OR) operators, with one exception: The boolean logical operators always evaluate both of their operands (i.e., they do not perform short-circuit evaluation). Therefore, the expression

```
( gender == 1 ) & ( age >= 65 )
```

evaluates age >= 65 regardless of whether gender is equal to 1. This is useful if the right operand of the boolean logical AND or boolean logical inclusive OR operator has a required side effect—a modification of a variable's value. For example, the expression

```
( birthday == true ) | ( ++age >= 65 )
```

guarantees that the condition ++age >= 65 will be evaluated. Thus, the variable age is incremented in the preceding expression, regardless of whether the overall expression is true or false.

Error-Prevention Tip 5.4

For clarity, avoid expressions with side effects in conditions. The side effects may look clever, but they can make it harder to understand code and can lead to subtle logic errors.

Boolean Logical Exclusive OR (∧)

A simple condition containing the boolean logical exclusive OR (∧) operator is true *if and only if one of its operands is* true *and the other is* false. If both operands are true or both are false, the entire condition is false. Figure 5.16 is a truth table for the boolean logical exclusive OR operator (∧). This operator is also guaranteed to evaluate both of its operands.

Logical Negation (!) Operator

The ! (logical NOT, also called logical negation or logical complement) operator enables a programmer to "reverse" the meaning of a condition. Unlike the logical operators &&, ||, &, | and ∧, which are binary operators that combine two conditions, the logical negation operator is a unary operator that has only a single condition as an operand. The logical negation operator is placed before a condition to choose a path of execution if the original condition (without the logical negation operator) is false, as in the program segment

```
if ( ! ( grade == sentinelValue ) )
    System.out.printf( "The next grade is %d\n", grade );
```

which executes the printf call only if grade is not equal to sentinelValue. The parentheses around the condition grade == sentinelValue are needed because the logical negation operator has a higher precedence than the equality operator.

In most cases, the programmer can avoid using logical negation by expressing the condition differently with an appropriate relational or equality operator. For example, the previous statement may also be written as follows:

```
if ( grade != sentinelValue )
    System.out.printf( "The next grade is %d\n", grade );
```

This flexibility can help a programmer express a condition in a more convenient manner. Figure 5.17 is a truth table for the logical negation operator.

expression1	expression2	expression1 ∧ expression2
false	false	false
false	true	true
true	false	true
true	true	false

Fig. 5.16 | ∧ (boolean logical exclusive OR) operator truth table.

expression	!expression
false	true
true	false

Fig. 5.17 | ! (logical negation, or logical NOT) operator truth table.

Logical Operators Example

Figure 5.18 demonstrates the logical operators and boolean logical operators by producing their truth tables. The output shows the expression that was evaluated and the boolean result of that expression. The values of the boolean expressions are displayed with printf using the %b format specifier, which outputs the word "true" or the word "false" based on the expression's value. Lines 9–13 produce the truth table for &&. Lines 16–20 produce the truth table for ||. Lines 23–27 produce the truth table for &. Lines 30–35 produce the truth table for |. Lines 38–43 produce the truth table for ^. Lines 46–47 produce the truth table for !.

Figure 5.19 shows the precedence and associativity of the Java operators introduced so far. The operators are shown from top to bottom in decreasing order of precedence.

```
1   // Fig. 5.18: LogicalOperators.java
2   // Logical operators.
3
4   public class LogicalOperators
5   {
6      public static void main( String args[] )
7      {
8         // create truth table for && (conditional AND) operator
9         System.out.printf( "%s\n%s: %b\n%s: %b\n%s: %b\n%s: %b\n\n",
10           "Conditional AND (&&)", "false && false", ( false && false ),
11           "false && true", ( false && true ),
12           "true && false", ( true && false ),
13           "true && true", ( true && true ) );
14
15        // create truth table for || (conditional OR) operator
16        System.out.printf( "%s\n%s: %b\n%s: %b\n%s: %b\n%s: %b\n\n",
17           "Conditional OR (||)", "false || false", ( false || false ),
18           "false || true", ( false || true ),
19           "true || false", ( true || false ),
20           "true || true", ( true || true ) );
21
22        // create truth table for & (boolean logical AND) operator
23        System.out.printf( "%s\n%s: %b\n%s: %b\n%s: %b\n%s: %b\n\n",
24           "Boolean logical AND (&)", "false & false", ( false & false ),
25           "false & true", ( false & true ),
26           "true & false", ( true & false ),
27           "true & true", ( true & true ) );
28
29        // create truth table for | (boolean logical inclusive OR) operator
30        System.out.printf( "%s\n%s: %b\n%s: %b\n%s: %b\n%s: %b\n\n",
31           "Boolean logical inclusive OR (|)",
32           "false | false", ( false | false ),
33           "false | true", ( false | true ),
34           "true | false", ( true | false ),
35           "true | true", ( true | true ) );
36
37        // create truth table for ^ (boolean logical exclusive OR) operator
38        System.out.printf( "%s\n%s: %b\n%s: %b\n%s: %b\n%s: %b\n\n",
39           "Boolean logical exclusive OR (^)",
40           "false ^ false", ( false ^ false ),
```

Fig. 5.18 | Logical operators. (Part 1 of 2.)

```
41            "false ^ true", ( false ^ true ),
42            "true ^ false", ( true ^ false ),
43            "true ^ true", ( true ^ true ) );
44
45         // create truth table for ! (logical negation) operator
46         System.out.printf( "%s\n%s: %b\n%s: %b\n", "Logical NOT (!)",
47            "!false", ( !false ), "!true", ( !true ) );
48      } // end main
49   } // end class LogicalOperators
```

```
Conditional AND (&&)
false && false: false
false && true: false
true && false: false
true && true: true

Conditional OR (||)
false || false: false
false || true: true
true || false: true
true || true: true

Boolean logical AND (&)
false & false: false
false & true: false
true & false: false
true & true: true

Boolean logical inclusive OR (|)
false | false: false
false | true: true
true | false: true
true | true: true

Boolean logical exclusive OR (^)
false ^ false: false
false ^ true: true
true ^ false: true
true ^ true: false

Logical NOT (!)
!false: true
!true: false
```

Fig. 5.18 | Logical operators. (Part 2 of 2.)

Operators	Associativity	Type
++ --	right to left	unary postfix
++ -- + - ! (*type*)	right to left	unary prefix
* / %	left to right	multiplicative

Fig. 5.19 | Precedence/associativity of the operators discussed so far. (Part 1 of 2.)

Operators					Associativity	Type
+	–				left to right	additive
<	<=	>	>=		left to right	relational
==	!=				left to right	equality
&					left to right	boolean logical AND
^					left to right	boolean logical exclusive OR
|					left to right	boolean logical inclusive OR
&&					left to right	conditional AND
||					left to right	conditional OR
?:					right to left	conditional
=	+=	-=	*=	/= %=	right to left	assignment

Fig. 5.19 | Precedence/associativity of the operators discussed so far. (Part 2 of 2.)

5.9 Structured Programming Summary

Just as architects design buildings by employing the collective wisdom of their profession, so should programmers design programs. Our field is younger than architecture, and our collective wisdom is considerably sparser. We have learned that structured programming produces programs that are easier than unstructured programs to understand, test, debug, modify and even prove correct in a mathematical sense.

Figure 5.20 uses UML activity diagrams to summarize Java's control statements. The initial and final states indicate the single entry point and the single exit point of each control statement. Arbitrarily connecting individual symbols in an activity diagram can lead to unstructured programs. Therefore, the programming profession has chosen a limited set of control statements that can be combined in only two simple ways to build structured programs.

For simplicity, only single-entry/single-exit control statements are used—there is only one way to enter and only one way to exit each control statement. Connecting control statements in sequence to form structured programs is simple. The final state of one control statement is connected to the initial state of the next control statement—that is, the control statements are placed one after another in a program in sequence. We call this "control-statement stacking." The rules for forming structured programs also allow for control statements to be nested.

Figure 5.21 shows the rules for forming structured programs. The rules assume that action states may be used to indicate any action. The rules also assume that we begin with the simplest activity diagram (Fig. 5.22) consisting of only an initial state, an action state, a final state and transition arrows.

Applying the rules in Fig. 5.21 always results in a properly structured activity diagram with a neat, building-block appearance. For example, repeatedly applying rule 2 to the simplest activity diagram results in an activity diagram containing many action states in sequence (Fig. 5.23). Rule 2 generates a stack of control statements, so let us call rule 2 the stacking rule. [*Note:* The vertical dashed lines in Fig. 5.23 are not part of the UML. We use them to separate the four activity diagrams that demonstrate rule 2 of Fig. 5.21 being applied.]

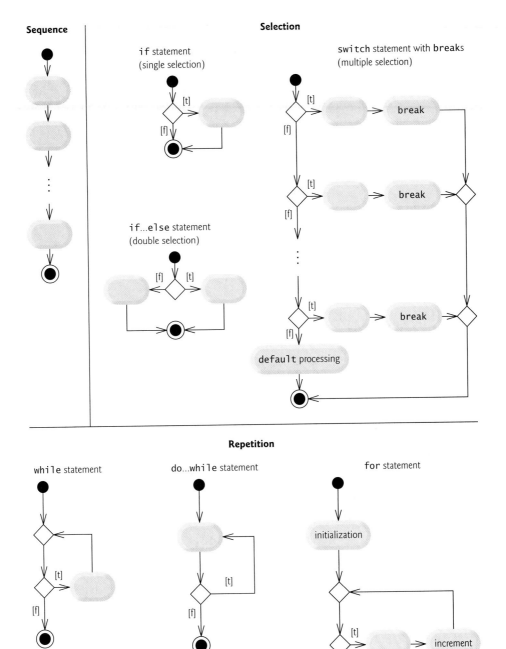

Fig. 5.20 | Java's single-entry/single-exit sequence, selection and repetition statements.

Rules for Forming Structured Programs
1 Begin with the simplest activity diagram (Fig. 5.22).
2 Any action state can be replaced by two action states in sequence.
3 Any action state can be replaced by any control statement (sequence of action states, `if`, `if...else`, `switch`, `while`, `do...while` or `for`).
4 Rules 2 and 3 can be applied as often as you like and in any order.

Fig. 5.21 | Rules for forming structured programs.

Fig. 5.22 | Simplest activity diagram.

Rule 3 is called the nesting rule. Repeatedly applying rule 3 to the simplest activity diagram results in an activity diagram with neatly nested control statements. For example, in Fig. 5.24, the action state in the simplest activity diagram is replaced with a double-selection (`if...else`) statement. Then rule 3 is applied again to the action states in the double-selection statement, replacing each of these action states with a double-selection statement. The dashed action-state symbols around each of the double-selection statements represent the action state that was replaced. [*Note:* The dashed arrows and dashed action state symbols shown in Fig. 5.24 are not part of the UML. They are used here to illustrate that any action state can be replaced with a control statement.]

Rule 4 generates larger, more involved and more deeply nested statements. The diagrams that emerge from applying the rules in Fig. 5.21 constitute the set of all possible structured activity diagrams and hence the set of all possible structured programs. The beauty of the structured approach is that we use only seven simple single-entry/single-exit control statements and assemble them in only two simple ways.

If the rules in Fig. 5.21 are followed, an "unstructured' activity diagram (like the one in Fig. 5.25) cannot be created. If you are uncertain about whether a particular diagram is structured, apply the rules of Fig. 5.21 in reverse to reduce the diagram to the simplest activity diagram. If you can reduce it, the original diagram is structured; otherwise, it is not.

Structured programming promotes simplicity. Bohm and Jacopini have given us the result that only three forms of control are needed to implement an algorithm:

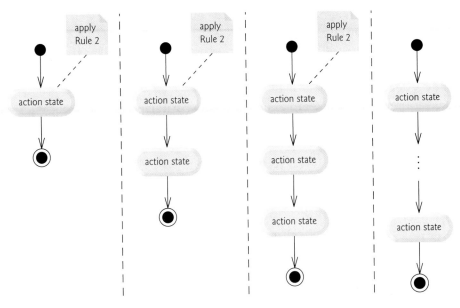

Fig. 5.23 | Repeatedly applying the stacking rule (rule 2) of Fig. 5.21 to the simplest activity diagram.

- Sequence
- Selection
- Repetition

The sequence structure is trivial. Simply list the statements to execute in the order in which they should execute. Selection is implemented in one of three ways:

- `if` statement (single selection)
- `if...else` statement (double selection)
- `switch` statement (multiple selection)

In fact, it is straightforward to prove that the simple `if` statement is sufficient to provide any form of selection—everything that can be done with the `if...else` statement and the `switch` statement can be implemented by combining `if` statements (although perhaps not as clearly and efficiently).

Repetition is implemented in one of three ways:

- `while` statement
- `do...while` statement
- `for` statement

It is straightforward to prove that the `while` statement is sufficient to provide any form of repetition. Everything that can be done with the `do...while` statement and the `for` statement can be done with the `while` statement (although perhaps not as conveniently).

Combining these results illustrates that any form of control ever needed in a Java program can be expressed in terms of

- sequence
- if statement (selection)
- while statement (repetition)

and that these can be combined in only two ways—stacking and nesting. indeed, structured programming is the essence of simplicity.

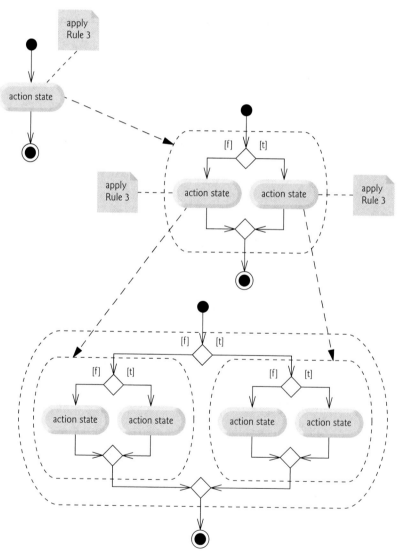

Fig. 5.24 | Repeatedly applying the nesting rule (rule 3) of Fig. 5.21 to the simplest activity diagram.

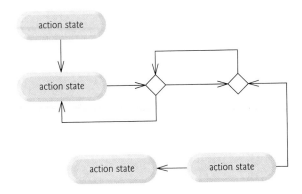

Fig. 5.25 | "Unstructured" activity diagram.

5.10 (Optional) GUI and Graphics Case Study: Drawing Rectangles and Ovals

This section introduces two other shapes you can draw using the graphics features in Java—rectangles and ovals. To draw rectangles and ovals, we call Graphics methods drawRect and drawOval, respectively, as demonstrated in Fig. 5.26.

Line 6 begins the class declaration for Shapes, which extends JPanel. Shapes contains one instance variable, choice, declared on line 8, that determines whether paint-Component should draw rectangles or ovals. The Shapes constructor at lines 11–14 initializes choice with the value passed in parameter userChoice.

Method paintComponent (lines 17–36) performs the actual drawing. Remember, the first statement in every paintComponent method should be a call to super.paintComponent, as in line 19. The for statement (lines 21–35) loops 10 times to draw 10 shapes. The switch statement (Lines 24–34) chooses between drawing rectangles and drawing ovals.

If choice is 1, then the program draws a rectangle. Lines 27–28 call Graphics method drawRect. Method drawRect requires four arguments. The first two arguments represent the x- and y-coordinates of the upper-left corner of the rectangle. The next two represent the width and the height of the rectangle. In this example, we start at a position 10 pixels down and 10 pixels right of the top-left corner, and every iteration of the loop moves the upper-left corner another 10 pixels down and to the right. The width and the height of the rectangle start at 50 pixels and increase by 10 pixels in each iteration.

If choice is 2, then the program performs a similar operation, drawing an oval instead of a rectangle. When drawing an oval, an imaginary rectangle called a bounding rectangle is created, and an oval that touches the midpoints of all four sides of the bounding rectangle is placed inside. Method drawOval (lines 31–32) requires the same four arguments as method drawRect. The arguments specify the position and size of the bounding rectangle for the oval. The values passed to drawOval in this example are exactly the same as the values passed to drawRect in lines 27–28. Since the width and height of the bounding rectangle are identical in this example, lines 27–28 draw a circle. You may modify the program to draw both rectangles and ovals to see how drawOval and drawRect are related.

Figure 5.27 is responsible for handling input from the user and creating a window to display the appropriate drawing based on the user's response. Line 3 imports JFrame to handle the display, and Line 4 imports JOptionPane to handle the input.

Lines 11–13 prompt the user with an input dialog and store the user's response in variable input. Line 15 uses Integer method parseInt to convert the String entered by the user to an int and stores the result in variable choice. An instance of class Shapes is created at line 18, with the user's choice passed to the constructor. Lines 20–25 perform the standard operations for creating and setting up a window—creating a frame, setting it to exit the application when closed, adding the drawing to the frame, setting the frame size and making it visible.

```
1   // Fig. 5.26: Shapes.java
2   // Demonstrates drawing different shapes.
3   import java.awt.Graphics;
4   import javax.swing.JPanel;
5
6   public class Shapes extends JPanel
7   {
8      private int choice; // user's choice of which shape to draw
9
10     // constructor sets the user's choice
11     public Shapes( int userChoice )
12     {
13        choice = userChoice;
14     } // end Shapes constructor
15
16     // draws a cascade of shapes starting from the top left corner
17     public void paintComponent( Graphics g )
18     {
19        super.paintComponent( g );
20
21        for ( int i = 0; i < 10; i++ )
22        {
23           // pick the shape based on the user's choice
24           switch ( choice )
25           {
26              case 1: // draw rectangles
27                 g.drawRect( 10 + i * 10, 10 + i * 10,
28                    50 + i * 10, 50 + i * 10 );
29                 break;
30              case 2: // draw ovals
31                 g.drawOval( 10 + i * 10, 10 + i * 10,
32                    50 + i * 10, 50 + i * 10 );
33                 break;
34           } // end switch
35        } // end for
36     } // end method paintComponent
37  } // end class Shapes
```

Fig. 5.26 | Drawing a cascade of shapes based on the user's choice.

```
1   // Fig. 5.27: ShapesTest.java
2   // Test application that displays class Shapes.
3   import javax.swing.JFrame;
4   import javax.swing.JOptionPane;
5
6   public class ShapesTest
7   {
8      public static void main( String args[] )
9      {
10        // obtain user's choice
11        String input = JOptionPane.showInputDialog(
12           "Enter 1 to draw rectangles\n" +
13           "Enter 2 to draw ovals" );
14
15        int choice = Integer.parseInt( input ); // convert input to int
16
17        // create the panel with the user's input
18        Shapes panel = new Shapes( choice );
19
20        JFrame application = new JFrame(); // creates a new JFrame
21
22        application.setDefaultCloseOperation( JFrame.EXIT_ON_CLOSE );
23        application.add( panel ); // add the panel to the frame
24        application.setSize( 300, 300 ); // set the desired size
25        application.setVisible( true ); // show the frame
26     } // end main
27  } // end class ShapesTest
```

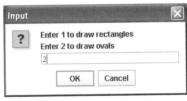

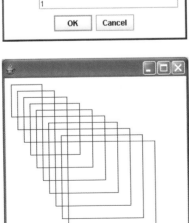

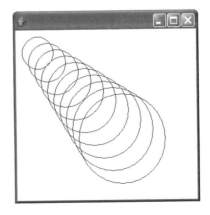

Fig. 5.27 | Obtaining user input and creating a JFrame to display Shapes.

GUI and Graphics Case Study Exercises

5.1   Draw 12 concentric circles in the center of a JPanel (Fig. 5.28). The innermost circle should have a radius of 10 pixels, and each successive circle should have a radius 10 pixels larger than the previous one. Begin by finding the center of the JPanel. To get the upper-left corner of a circle, move up one radius and to the left one radius from the center. The width and height of the bounding rectangle is the diameter of the circle (twice the radius).

5.2   Modify Exercise 5.16 from the end-of-chapter exercises to read input using dialogs and to display the bar chart using rectangles of varying lengths.

5.11 Wrap-Up

In this chapter, we completed our introduction to Java's control statements, which enable programmers to control the flow of execution in methods. Chapter 4 discussed Java's if, if...else and while statements. The current chapter demonstrated Java's remaining control statements—for, do...while and switch. We have shown that any algorithm can be developed using combinations of the sequence structure (i.e., statements listed in the order in which they should execute), the three types of selection statements—if, if...else and switch—and the three types of repetition statements—while, do...while and for. In this chapter and Chapter 4, we have discussed how programmers can combine these building blocks to utilize proven program-construction and problem-solving techniques. This chapter also introduced Java's logical operators, which enable programmers to use more complex conditional expressions in control statements.

In Chapter 3, we introduced the basic concepts of objects, classes and methods. Chapter 4 and this chapter provided a thorough introduction to the types of control statements that programmers use to specify program logic in methods. In Chapter 6, we examine methods in greater depth.

Fig. 5.28 | Drawing concentric circles.

Summary

- The `for` repetition statement specifies the details of counter-controlled-repetition. The general format of the `for` statement is

      for (*initialization*; *loopContinuationCondition*; *increment*)
          statement

  where the *initialization* expression names the loop's control variable and provides its initial value, *loopContinuationCondition* is the condition that determines whether the loop should continue executing and *increment* modifies the control variable's value, so that the loop-continuation condition eventually becomes false.

- Typically, `for` statements are used for counter-controlled repetition and `while` statements are used for sentinel-controlled repetition.

- The scope of a variable defines where it can be used in a program. For example, a local variable can be used only in the method that declares the variable and only from the point of declaration through the end of the method.

- The initialization, loop-continuation condition and increment portions of a `for` statement can contain arithmetic expressions. The increment of a `for` statement may also be negative, in which case it is really a decrement, and the loop counts downward.

- If the loop-continuation condition in a `for` header is initially `false`, the program does not execute the `for` statement's body. Instead, execution proceeds with the statement following the `for`.

- The format specifier `%20s` outputs a `String` with a field width of 20 (i.e., at least 20 character positions). If the value to be output is less than 20 character positions wide, the value is right justified in the field by default. A value can be output left justified by simply preceding the field width with the minus sign (–) formatting flag.

- Methods that perform common tasks and do not require objects are called `static` methods.

- Java does not include an exponentiation operator. Instead, `Math.pow(x, y)` can be used to calculate the value of x raised to the yth power. The method receives two `double` arguments and returns a `double` value.

- The comma (,) formatting flag in a format specifier (e.g., `%,20.2f`) indicates that a value should be output with a thousands separator.

- The do...`while` statement tests the loop-continuation condition *after* executing the loop's body; therefore, the body always executes at least once. The format for the do...`while` statement is

      do
      {
          statement
      } while (*condition*);

- The `switch` multiple-selection statement performs different actions based on the possible values of an integer variable or expression. Each action is associated with the value of a constant integral expression (i.e., a constant value of type `byte`, `short`, `int` or `char`, but not `long`) that the variable or expression on which the `switch` is based may assume. The `switch` statement consists of a block containing a sequence of `case` labels and an optional `default` case.

- The expression in parentheses following keyword `switch` is called the controlling expression of the `switch`. A program compares the value of the controlling expression with each `case` label, and if a match occurs, the program executes the statements for that `case`.

- The `switch` statement does not provide a mechanism for testing ranges of values, so every value that must be tested should be listed in a separate `case` label.

- Listing cases consecutively with no statements between them enables those cases to perform the same set of statements.

- Each case can have multiple statements. The switch statement differs from other control statements in that it does not require braces around multiple statements in each case.

- Most switch statements use a break in each case to terminate the switch statement after processing the case.

- The end-of-file indicator is a system-dependent keystroke combination which indicates that there is no more data to input.

- Scanner method hasNext determines whether there is more data to input. This method returns the boolean value true if there is more data; otherwise, it returns false.

- The break statement, when executed in one of the repetition statements, causes immediate exit from that statement. Execution continues with the first statement after the control statement.

- The continue statement, when executed in a while, for or do...while, skips the remaining statements in the loop body and proceeds with the next iteration of the loop.

- Logical operators enable programmers to form complex conditions by combining simple conditions. The logical operators are && (conditional AND), || (conditional OR), & (boolean logical AND), | (boolean logical inclusive OR), ∧ (boolean logical exclusive OR) and ! (logical NOT).

- The && (conditional AND) operator can be used to ensure that two conditions are *both* true before choosing a certain path of execution.

- The || (conditional OR) operator can be used to ensure that either *or* both of two conditions are true before choosing a certain path of execution.

- The parts of an expression containing && or || operators are evaluated only until it is known whether the condition is true or false. This feature of conditional AND and conditional OR expressions is called short-circuit evaluation.

- The boolean logical AND (&) and boolean logical inclusive OR (|) operators work identically to the && (conditional AND) and || (conditional OR) operators, with one exception: The boolean logical operators always evaluate both of their operands (i.e., they do not perform short-circuit evaluation).

- A simple condition containing the boolean logical exclusive OR (∧) operator is true if and only if one of its operands is true and the other is false. If both operands are true or both are false, the entire condition is false.

- The ! (logical NOT, also called logical negation or logical complement) operator enables a programmer to "reverse" the meaning of a condition. The logical negation operator is placed before a condition to choose a path of execution if the original condition (without the logical negation operator) is false. In most cases, the programmer can avoid using logical negation by expressing the condition differently with an appropriate relational or equality operator.

- Unlike the logical operators &&, ||, &, | and ∧, which are binary operators that combine two conditions, the logical negation operator is a unary operator that has only a single condition as an operand.

- The %b format specifier causes the value of a boolean expression to be output as the word "true" or the word "false" based on the expression's value.

- Any form of control ever needed in a Java program can be expressed in terms of sequence, selection and repetition statements, and these can be combined in only two ways—stacking and nesting.

Terminology

!, logical not operator	for repetition statement
&, boolean logical AND operator	for statement header
&&, conditional AND operator	increment a control variable
|, boolean logical OR operator	initial value
||, conditional OR operator	iteration of a loop
∧, boolean logical exclusive OR operator	logical complement (!)
boolean logical AND (&)	logical negation (!)
boolean logical exclusive OR (∧)	logical operators
boolean logical inclusive OR (|)	loop-continuation condition
break statement	multiple selection
case label	nested control statements
character constant	nesting rule
conditional AND (&&)	off-by-one error
conditional OR (||)	repetition statement
constant integral expression	scope of a variable
constant variable	short-circuit evaluation
continue statement	side effect
control variable	simple condition
controlling expression of a switch	single-entry/single-exit control statements
decrement a control variable	stacked control statements
default case in switch	stacking rule
do...while repetition statement	static method
final keyword	switch selection statement
for header	truth table

Self-Review Exercises

5.1 Fill in the blanks in each of the following statements:

a) Typically, _____ statements are used for counter-controlled repetition and _____ statements are used for sentinel-controlled repetition.

b) The do...while statement tests the loop-continuation condition _____ executing the loop's body; therefore, the body always executes at least once.

c) The _____ statement selects among multiple actions based on the possible values of an integer variable or expression.

d) The _____ statement, when executed in a repetition statement, skips the remaining statements in the loop body and proceeds with the next iteration of the loop.

e) The _____ operator can be used to ensure that two conditions are *both* true before choosing a certain path of execution.

f) If the loop-continuation condition in a for header is initially _____, the program does not execute the for statement's body.

g) Methods that perform common tasks and do not require objects are called _____ methods.

5.2 State whether each of the following is *true* or *false*. If *false*, explain why.

a) The default case is required in the switch selection statement.

b) The break statement is required in the last case of a switch selection statement.

c) The expression ((x > y) && (a < b)) is true if either x > y is true or a < b is true.

d) An expression containing the || operator is true if either or both of its operands are true.

e) The comma (,) formatting flag in a format specifier (e.g., %,20.2f) indicates that a value should be output with a thousands separator.

f) To test for a range of values in a switch statement, use a hyphen (-) between the start and end values of the range in a case label.

g) Listing cases consecutively with no statements between them enables the cases to perform the same set of statements.

5.3   Write a Java statement or a set of Java statements to accomplish each of the following tasks:

a) Sum the odd integers between 1 and 99, using a for statement. Assume that the integer variables sum and count have been declared.

b) Calculate the value of 2.5 raised to the power of 3, using the pow method.

c) Print the integers from 1 to 20, using a while loop and the counter variable i. Assume that the variable i has been declared, but not initialized. Print only five integers per line. [*Hint*: Use the calculation i % 5. When the value of this expression is 0, print a newline character; otherwise, print a tab character. Assume that this code is an application. Use the System.out.println() method to output the newline character, and use the System.out.print('\t') method to output the tab character.]

d) Repeat part (c), using a for statement.

5.4   Find the error in each of the following code segments, and explain how to correct it:

a) i = 1;

```
while ( i <= 10 );
    i++;
}
```

b)
```
for ( k = 0.1; k != 1.0; k += 0.1 )
    System.out.println( k );
```

c)
```
switch ( n )
{
    case 1:
        System.out.println( "The number is 1" );
    case 2:
        System.out.println( "The number is 2" );
        break;
    default:
        System.out.println( "The number is not 1 or 2" );
        break;
}
```

d) The following code should print the values 1 to 10:
```
n = 1;

while ( n < 10 )
    System.out.println( n++ );
```

Answers to Self-Review Exercises

5.1   a) for, while. b) after. c) switch. d) continue. e) && (conditional AND). f) false. g) static.

5.2   a) False. The default case is optional. If no default action is needed, then there is no need for a default case. b) False. The break statement is used to exit the switch statement. The break statement is not required for the last case in a switch statement. c) False. Both of the relational expressions must be true for the entire expression to be true when using the && operator. d) True. e) True. f) False. The switch statement does not provide a mechanism for testing ranges of values, so every value that must be tested should be listed in a separate case label. g) True.

5.3   a) ```
sum = 0;
for (count = 1; count <= 99; count += 2)
   sum += count;
```
       b) ```
double result = Math.pow( 2.5, 3 );
```
       c) ```
i = 1;

while (i <= 20)
{
   System.out.print(i);

   if (i % 5 == 0)
      System.out.println();
   else
      System.out.print('\t');

   ++i;
}
```
       d) ```
for ( i = 1; i <= 20; i++ )
{
    System.out.print( i );

    if ( i % 5 == 0 )
       System.out.println();
    else
       System.out.print( '\t' );
}
```

5.4   a) Error: The semicolon after the `while` header causes an infinite loop, and there is a missing left brace.
          Correction: Replace the semicolon by a {, or remove both the ; and the }.
       b) Error: Using a floating-point number to control a `for` statement may not work, because floating-point numbers are represented only approximately by most computers.
          Correction: Use an integer, and perform the proper calculation in order to get the values you desire:
          ```
for ( k = 1; k != 10; k++ )
    System.out.println( (double) k / 10 );
```
       c) Error: The missing code is the `break` statement in the statements for the first case.
          Correction: Add a `break` statement at the end of the statements for the first case. Note that this omission is not necessarily an error if the programmer wants the statement of case 2: to execute every time the case 1: statement executes.
       d) Error: An improper relational operator is used in the `while` repetition-continuation condition.
          Correction: Use <= rather than <, or change 10 to 11.

Exercises

5.5   Describe the four basic elements of counter-controlled repetition.

5.6   Compare and contrast the `while` and `for` repetition statements.

5.7   Discuss a situation in which it would be more appropriate to use a do...while statement than a `while` statement. Explain why.

5.8   Compare and contrast the `break` and `continue` statements.

5.9   Find and correct the error(s) in each of the following segments of code:
       a) ```
for (i = 100, i >= 1, i++)
     System.out.println(i);
```
       b) The following code should print whether integer `value` is odd or even:
```

```
switch ( value % 2 )
{
    case 0:
        System.out.println( "Even integer" );

    case 1:
        System.out.println( "Odd integer" );
}
```

c) The following code should output the odd integers from 19 to 1:

```
for ( i = 19; i >= 1; i += 2 )
    System.out.println( i );
```

d) The following code should output the even integers from 2 to 100:

```
counter = 2;

do
{
    System.out.println( counter );
    counter += 2;
} While ( counter < 100 );
```

5.10 What does the following program do?

```
 1  public class Printing
 2  {
 3      public static void main( String args[] )
 4      {
 5          for ( int i = 1; i <= 10; i++ )
 6          {
 7              for ( int j = 1; j <= 5; j++ )
 8                  System.out.print( '@' );
 9
10              System.out.println();
11          } // end outer for
12      } // end main
13  } // end class Printing
```

5.11 Write an application that finds the smallest of several integers. Assume that the first value read specifies the number of values to input from the user.

5.12 Write an application that calculates the product of the odd integers from 1 to 15.

5.13 *Factorials* are used frequently in probability problems. The factorial of a positive integer *n* (written *n!* and pronounced "*n* factorial") is equal to the product of the positive integers from 1 to *n*. Write an application that evaluates the factorials of the integers from 1 to 5. Display the results in tabular format. What difficulty might prevent you from calculating the factorial of 20?

5.14 Modify the compound-interest application of Fig. 5.6 to repeat its steps for interest rates of 5, 6, 7, 8, 9 and 10%. Use a for loop to vary the interest rate.

5.15 Write an application that displays the following patterns separately, one below the other. Use for loops to generate the patterns. All asterisks (*) should be printed by a single statement of the form System.out.print('*'); which causes the asterisks to print side by side. A statement of the form System.out.println(); can be used to move to the next line. A statement of the form System.out.print(' '); can be used to display a space for the last two patterns. There should be no other output statements in the program. [*Hint:* The last two patterns require that each line begin with an appropriate number of blank spaces.]

(a)	(b)	(c)	(d)
*	**********	**********	*
**	*********	*********	**
***	********	********	***
****	*******	*******	****
*****	******	******	*****
******	*****	*****	******
*******	****	****	*******
********	***	***	********
*********	**	**	*********
**********	*	*	**********

5.16   One interesting application of computers is to display graphs and bar charts. Write an application that reads five numbers between 1 and 30. For each number that is read, your program should display the same number of adjacent asterisks. For example, if your program reads the number 7, it should display *******.

5.17   A mail-order house sells five products whose retail prices are as follows: Product 1, $2.98; product 2, $4.50; product 3, $9.98; product 4, $4.49 and product 5, $6.87. Write an application that reads a series of pairs of numbers as follows:
   a)   product number
   b)   quantity sold

Your program should use a `switch` statement to determine the retail price for each product. It should calculate and display the total retail value of all products sold. Use a sentinel-controlled loop to determine when the program should stop looping and display the final results.

5.18   Modify the application in Fig. 5.6 to use only integers to calculate the compound interest. [*Hint*: Treat all monetary amounts as integral numbers of pennies. Then break the result into its dollars and cents portions by using the division and remainder operations, respectively. Insert a period between the dollars and the cents portions.]

5.19   Assume that i = 1, j = 2, k = 3 and m = 2. What does each of the following statements print?
   a)   `System.out.println( i == 1 );`
   b)   `System.out.println( j == 3 );`
   c)   `System.out.println( ( i >= 1 ) && ( j < 4 ) );`
   d)   `System.out.println( ( m <= 99 ) & ( k < m ) );`
   e)   `System.out.println( ( j >= i ) || ( k == m ) );`
   f)   `System.out.println( ( k + m < j ) | ( 3 - j >= k ) );`
   g)   `System.out.println( !( k > m ) );`

5.20   Calculate the value of π from the infinite series

$$\pi = 4 - \frac{4}{3} + \frac{4}{5} - \frac{4}{7} + \frac{4}{9} - \frac{4}{11} + \cdots$$

Print a table that shows the value of π approximated by computing one term of this series, by two terms, by three terms, and so on. How many terms of this series do you have to use before you first get 3.14? 3.141? 3.1415? 3.14159?

5.21   (*Pythagorean Triples*) A right triangle can have sides whose lengths are all integers. The set of three integer values for the lengths of the sides of a right triangle is called a Pythagorean triple. The lengths of the three sides must satisfy the relationship that the sum of the squares of two of the sides is equal to the square of the hypotenuse. Write an application to find all Pythagorean triples for side1, side2 and the hypotenuse, all no larger than 500. Use a triple-nested `for` loop that tries all possibilities. This method is an example of "brute-force" computing. You will learn in more advanced computer science courses that there are large numbers of interesting problems for which there is no known algorithmic approach other than using sheer brute force.

5.22 Modify Exercise 5.15 to combine your code from the four separate triangles of asterisks such that all four patterns print side by side. Make clever use of nested for loops.

5.23 (*De Morgan's Laws*) In this chapter, we have discussed the logical operators &&, &, ||, |, ^ and !. De Morgan's Laws can sometimes make it more convenient for us to express a logical expression. These laws state that the expression !(*condition1* && *condition2*) is logically equivalent to the expression (!*condition1* || !*condition2*). Also, the expression !(*condition1* || *condition2*) is logically equivalent to the expression (!*condition1* && !*condition2*). Use De Morgan's Laws to write equivalent expressions for each of the following, then write an application to show that both the original expression and the new expression in each case produce the same value:

a) !(x < 5) && !(y >= 7)
b) !(a == b) || !(g != 5)
c) !((x <= 8) && (y > 4))
d) !((i > 4) || (j <= 6))

5.24 Write an application that prints the following diamond shape. You may use output statements that print a single asterisk (*), a single space or a single newline character. Maximize your use of repetition (with nested for statements), and minimize the number of output statements.

```
    *
   ***
  *****
 *******
*********
 *******
  *****
   ***
    *
```

5.25 Modify the application you wrote in Exercise 5.24 to read an odd number in the range 1 to 19 to specify the number of rows in the diamond. Your program should then display a diamond of the appropriate size.

5.26 A criticism of the break statement and the continue statement is that each is unstructured. Actually, break statements and continue statements can always be replaced by structured statements, although doing so can be awkward. Describe in general how you would remove any break statement from a loop in a program and replace that statement with some structured equivalent. [*Hint*: The break statement exits a loop from the body of the loop. The other way to exit is by failing the loop-continuation test. Consider using in the loop-continuation test a second test that indicates "early exit because of a 'break' condition."] Use the technique you develop here to remove the break statement from the application in Fig. 5.12.

5.27 What does the following program segment do?

```java
for ( i = 1; i <= 5; i++ )
{
    for ( j = 1; j <= 3; j++ )
    {
        for ( k = 1; k <= 4; k++ )
            System.out.print( '*' );

        System.out.println();
    } // end inner for

    System.out.println();
} // end outer for
```

5.28   Describe in general how you would remove any `continue` statement from a loop in a program and replace it with some structured equivalent. Use the technique you develop here to remove the `continue` statement from the program in Fig. 5.13.

5.29   (*"The Twelve Days of Christmas" Song*) Write an application that uses repetition and `switch` statements to print the song "The Twelve Days of Christmas." One `switch` statement should be used to print the day (i.e., "First," "Second," etc.). A separate `switch` statement should be used to print the remainder of each verse. Visit the Web site `www.12days.com/library/carols/12daysofxmas.htm` for the complete lyrics of the song.

6

Methods:
A Deeper Look

OBJECTIVES

In this chapter you will learn:

- How **static** methods and fields are associated with an entire class rather than specific instances of the class.

- To use common **Math** methods available in the Java API.

- To understand the mechanisms for passing information between methods.

- How the method call/return mechanism is supported by the method call stack and activation records.

- How packages group related classes.

- How to use random-number generation to implement game-playing applications.

- To understand how the visibility of declarations is limited to specific regions of programs.

- What method overloading is and how to create overloaded methods.

6.1 Introduction

Most computer programs that solve real-world problems are much larger than the programs presented in the first few chapters of this book. Experience has shown that the best way to develop and maintain a large program is to construct it from small, simple pieces, or modules. This technique is called divide and conquer. We introduced methods in Chapter 3. In Chapter 6, we study methods in more depth. We emphasize how to declare and use methods to facilitate the design, implementation, operation and maintenance of large programs.

You will see that it is possible for certain methods, called `static` methods, to be called without the need for an object of the class to exist. You will learn how to declare a method with more than one parameter. You will also learn how Java is able to keep track of which method is currently executing, how local variables of methods are maintained in memory and how a method knows where to return after it completes execution.

We will take a brief diversion into simulation techniques with random-number generation and develop a version of the casino dice game called craps that will use most of the programming techniques you have used to this point in the book. In addition, you will learn two techniques for declaring values that cannot change (i.e., constants) in your programs.

Many of the classes you will use or create while developing applications will have more than one method of the same name. This technique, called overloading, is used by programmers to implement methods that perform similar tasks for arguments of different types or possibly for different numbers of arguments.

6.2 Program Modules in Java

Three kinds of modules exist in Java—methods, classes and packages. Java programs are written by combining new methods and classes that the programmer writes with predefined methods and classes available in the Java Application Programming Interface (also referred to as the Java API or Java class library) and in various other class libraries. Related classes are typically grouped into packages so that they can be imported into programs and reused. You will learn how to group your own classes into packages in Chapter 8. The Java API provides a rich collection of predefined classes that contain methods for performing common mathematical calculations, string manipulations, character manipulations, input/output operations, database operations, networking operations, file processing, error checking and many other useful operations. The Java API classes are part of the J2SE Development Kit (JDK) 5.0.

Good Programming Practice 6.1

Familiarize yourself with the rich collection of classes and methods provided by the Java API (java.sun.com/j2se/5.0/docs/api/index.html). In Section 6.8, we present an overview of several common packages. In Appendix G, we explain how to navigate the Java API documentation.

Software Engineering Observation 6.1

Don't try to reinvent the wheel. When possible, reuse Java API classes and methods. This reduces program development time and avoids introducing programming errors.

Methods (called functions or procedures in other programming languages) allow the programmer to modularize a program by separating its tasks into self-contained units. You have declared methods in every program you have written. These methods are sometimes referred to as programmer-declared methods. The actual statements in the method bodies are written only once, reused from perhaps several locations in a program and are hidden from other methods.

There are several motivations for modularizing a program by means of methods. One is the divide-and-conquer approach, which makes program development more manageable by constructing programs from small, simple pieces. Another is software reusability—using existing methods as building blocks to create new programs. Often, you can create programs mostly from standardized methods rather than by building customized code. For example, in earlier programs, we did not have to define how to read data values from the keyboard—Java provides these capabilities in class Scanner. A third motivation is to avoid repeating code. Dividing a program into meaningful methods makes the program easier to debug and maintain.

Software Engineering Observation 6.2

To promote software reusability, every method should be limited to performing a single, well-defined task, and the name of the method should express that task effectively. Such methods make programs easier to write, debug, maintain and modify.

Error-Prevention Tip 6.1

A small method that performs one task is easier to test and debug than a larger method that performs many tasks.

> **Software Engineering Observation 6.3**
>
> *If you cannot choose a concise name that expresses a method's task, your method might be attempting to perform too many diverse tasks. It is usually best to break such a method into several smaller method declarations.*

As you know, a method is invoked by a method call, and when the called method completes its task, it either returns a result or simply control to the caller. An analogy to this program structure is the hierarchical form of management (Figure 6.1). A boss (the caller) asks a worker (the called method) to perform a task and report back (i.e., return) the results after completing the task. The boss method does not know how the worker method performs its designated tasks. The worker may also call other worker methods, unbeknownst to the boss. This "hiding" of implementation details promotes good software engineering. Figure 6.1 shows the boss method communicating with several worker methods in a hierarchical manner. The boss method divides the responsibilities among the various worker methods. Note that worker1 acts as a "boss method" to worker4 and worker5.

6.3 static Methods, static Fields and Class Math

As you know, every class provides methods that perform common tasks on objects of the class. For example, to input data from the keyboard, you have called methods on a Scanner object that was initialized in its constructor to obtain input from the standard input stream (System.in). Java also allows you to initialize a Scanner to obtain input from other sources, such as a file on disk. One program could have a Scanner object that inputs information from the standard input stream and a second Scanner that inputs information from a file. Each input method called on the standard input stream Scanner would obtain input from the keyboard, and each input method called on the file Scanner would obtain input from the specified file on disk.

Although most methods execute in response to method calls on specific objects, this is not always the case. Sometimes a method performs a task that does not depend on the contents of any object. Such a method applies to the class in which it is declared as a whole and is known as a static method or a class method. It is not uncommon for a class to contain a group of convenient static methods to perform common tasks. For example, recall that we used static method pow of class Math to raise a value to a power in Fig. 5.6.

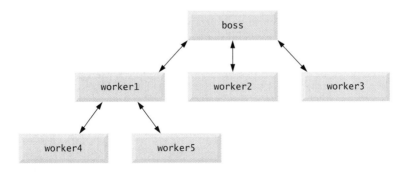

Fig. 6.1 | Hierarchical boss-method/worker-method relationship.

To declare a method as static, place the keyword static before the return type in the method's declaration. You can call any static method by specifying the name of the class in which the method is declared, followed by a dot (.) and the method name, as in

>   *ClassName.methodName(arguments)*

   We use various Math class methods here to present the concept of static methods. Class Math provides a collection of methods that enable you to perform common mathematical calculations. For example, you can calculate the square root of 900.0 with the static method call

>   Math.sqrt(900.0)

The preceding expression evaluates to 30.0. Method sqrt takes an argument of type double and returns a result of type double. To output the value of the preceding method call in the command window, you might write the statement

>   System.out.println(Math.sqrt(900.0));

In this statement, the value that sqrt returns becomes the argument to method println. Note that there was no need to create a Math object before calling method sqrt. Also note that *all* Math class methods are static—therefore, each is called by preceding the name of the method with the class name Math and a dot (.) separator.

Software Engineering Observation 6.4

Class Math is part of the java.lang package, which is implicitly imported by the compiler, so it is not necessary to import class Math to use its methods.

   Method arguments may be constants, variables or expressions. If c = 13.0, d = 3.0 and f = 4.0, then the statement

>   System.out.println(Math.sqrt(c + d * f));

calculates and prints the square root of 13.0 + 3.0 * 4.0 = 25.0—namely, 5.0. Figure 6.2 summarizes several Math class methods. In the figure, *x* and *y* are of type double.

Math Class Constants PI and E

Class Math also declares two fields that represent commonly used mathematical constants: Math.PI and Math.E. The constant Math.PI (3.14159265358979323846) is the ratio of a circle's circumference to its diameter. The constant Math.E (2.7182818284590452354) is the base value for natural logarithms (calculated with static Math method log). These fields are declared in class Math with the modifiers public, final and static. Making them public allows other programmers to use these fields in their own classes. Any field declared with keyword final is constant—its value cannot be changed after the field is initialized. Both PI and E are declared final because their values never change. Making these fields static allows them to be accessed via the class name Math and a dot (.) separator, just like class Math's methods. Recall from Section 3.5 that when each object of a class maintains its own copy of an attribute, the field that represents the attribute is also known as an instance variable—each object (instance) of the class has a separate instance of the variable in memory. There are fields for which each object of a class does not have a separate instance of the field. That is the case with static fields, which are also known as class variables. When objects of a class containing static fields are created, all the objects of that class share one copy of the class's

Method	Description	Example
abs(x)	absolute value of x	abs(23.7) is 23.7 abs(0.0) is 0.0 abs(-23.7) is 23.7
ceil(x)	rounds x to the smallest integer not less than x	ceil(9.2) is 10.0 ceil(-9.8) is -9.0
cos(x)	trigonometric cosine of x (x in radians)	cos(0.0) is 1.0
exp(x)	exponential method e^x	exp(1.0) is 2.71828 exp(2.0) is 7.38906
floor(x)	rounds x to the largest integer not greater than x	floor(9.2) is 9.0 floor(-9.8) is -10.0
log(x)	natural logarithm of x (base e)	log(Math.E) is 1.0 log(Math.E * Math.E) is 2.0
max(x, y)	larger value of x and y	max(2.3, 12.7) is 12.7 max(-2.3, -12.7) is -2.3
min(x, y)	smaller value of x and y	min(2.3, 12.7) is 2.3 min(-2.3, -12.7) is -12.7
pow(x, y)	x raised to the power y (i.e., x^y)	pow(2.0, 7.0) is 128.0 pow(9.0, 0.5) is 3.0
sin(x)	trigonometric sine of x (x in radians)	sin(0.0) is 0.0
sqrt(x)	square root of x	sqrt(900.0) is 30.0
tan(x)	trigonometric tangent of x (x in radians)	tan(0.0) is 0.0

Fig. 6.2 | Math class methods.

static fields. Together the class variables and instance variables represent the fields of a class. You will learn more about static fields in Section 8.11.

Why Is Method main Declared static?

Why must main be declared static? When you execute the Java Virtual Machine (JVM) with the java command, the JVM attempts to invoke the main method of the class you specify—when no objects of the class have been created. Declaring main as static allows the JVM to invoke main without creating an instance of the class. Method main is usually declared with the header:

```
public static void main( String args[] )
```

When you execute your application, you specify its class name as an argument to the command java, as in

```
java ClassName argument1 argument2 ...
```

The JVM loads the class specified by *ClassName* and uses that class name to invoke method main. In the preceding command, *ClassName* is a command-line argument to the JVM that tells it which class to execute. Following the *ClassName*, you can also specify a list of `Strings` (separated by spaces) as command-line arguments that the JVM will pass to your application. Such arguments might be used to specify options (e.g., a file name) to run the application. As you will learn in Chapter 7, Arrays, your application can access those command-line arguments and use them to customize the application.

Additional Comments about Method `main`

In earlier chapters, every application had one class that contained only `main` and possibly a second class that was used by `main` to create and manipulate objects. Actually, any class can contain a `main` method. In fact, each of our two-class examples could have been implemented as one class. For example, in the application in Fig. 5.9 and Fig. 5.10, method `main` (lines 6–16 of Fig. 5.10) could have been taken as is and placed in class `GradeBook` (Fig. 5.9). You would then execute the application by typing the command `java Grade-Book` in the command window—the application results would be identical to those of the two-class version. You can place a `main` method in every class you declare. The JVM invokes the `main` method only in the class used to execute the application. Some programmers take advantage of this to build a small test program into each class they declare.

6.4 Declaring Methods with Multiple Parameters

Chapters 3–5 presented classes containing simple methods that had at most one parameter. Methods often require more than one piece of information to perform their tasks. We now consider how programmers write their own methods with multiple parameters.

The application in Fig. 6.3 and Fig. 6.4 uses a programmer-declared method called `maximum` to determine and return the largest of three `double` values that are input by the user. When the application begins execution, class `MaximumFinderTest`'s `main` method (lines 7–11 of Fig. 6.4) creates one object of class `MaximumFinder` (line 9) and calls the object's `determineMaximum` method (line 10) to produce the program's output. In class `MaximumFinder` (Fig. 6.3), lines 14–18 of method `determineMaximum` prompt the user to enter three `double` values and read them from the user. Line 21 calls method `maximum` (declared in lines 28–41) to determine the largest of the three `double` values passed as arguments to the method. When method `maximum` returns the result to line 21, the program assigns `maximum`'s return value to local variable `result`. Then line 24 outputs the maximum value. At the end of this section, we'll discuss the use of operator + in line 24.

Consider the declaration of method `maximum` (lines 28–41). Line 28 indicates that the method returns a `double` value, that the method's name is `maximum` and that the method requires three `double` parameters (x, y and z) to accomplish its task. When a method has more than one parameter, the parameters are specified as a comma-separated list. When `maximum` is called from line 21, the parameter x is initialized with the value of the argument `number1`, the parameter y is initialized with the value of the argument `number2` and the parameter z is initialized with the value of the argument `number3`. There must be one argument in the method call for each parameter (sometimes called a formal parameter) in the method declaration. Also, each argument must be consistent with the type of the corresponding parameter. For example, a parameter of type `double` can receive values like 7.35, 22 or –0.03456, but not `Strings` like `"hello"`. Section 6.7 discusses the argument types that can be provided in a method call for each parameter of a primitive type.

```
1   // Fig. 6.3: MaximumFinder.java
2   // Programmer-declared method maximum.
3   import java.util.Scanner;
4
5   public class MaximumFinder
6   {
7      // obtain three floating-point values and locate the maximum value
8      public void determineMaximum()
9      {
10        // create Scanner for input from command window
11        Scanner input = new Scanner( System.in );
12
13        // obtain user input
14        System.out.print(
15           "Enter three floating-point values separated by spaces: " );
16        double number1 = input.nextDouble(); // read first double
17        double number2 = input.nextDouble(); // read second double
18        double number3 = input.nextDouble(); // read third double
19
20        // determine the maximum value
21        double result = maximum( number1, number2, number3 );
22
23        // display maximum value
24        System.out.println( "Maximum is: " + result );
25     } // end method determineMaximum
26
27     // returns the maximum of its three double parameters
28     public double maximum( double x, double y, double z )
29     {
30        double maximumValue = x; // assume x is the largest to start
31
32        // determine whether y is greater than maximumValue
33        if ( y > maximumValue )
34           maximumValue = y;
35
36        // determine whether z is greater than maximumValue
37        if ( z > maximumValue )
38           maximumValue = z;
39
40        return maximumValue;
41     } // end method maximum
42  } // end class MaximumFinder
```

Fig. 6.3 | Programmer-declared method `maximum` that has three `double` parameters.

To determine the maximum value, we begin with the assumption that parameter x contains the largest value, so line 30 declares local variable `maximumValue` and initializes it with the value of parameter x. Of course, it is possible that parameter y or z contains the actual largest value, so we must compare each of these values with `maximumValue`. The `if` statement at lines 33–34 determines whether y is greater than `maximumValue`. If so, line 34 assigns y to `maximumValue`. The `if` statement at lines 37–38 determines whether z is greater than `maximumValue`. If so, line 38 assigns z to `maximumValue`. At this point the largest of the three values resides in `maximumValue`, so line 40 returns that value to line 21. When program con-

```
 1   // Fig. 6.4: MaximumFinderTest.java
 2   // Application to test class MaximumFinder.
 3
 4   public class MaximumFinderTest
 5   {
 6      // application starting point
 7      public static void main( String args[] )
 8      {
 9         MaximumFinder maximumFinder = new MaximumFinder();
10         maximumFinder.determineMaximum();
11      } // end main
12   } // end class MaximumFinderTest
```

```
Enter three floating-point values separated by spaces: 9.35 2.74 5.1
Maximum is: 9.35
```

```
Enter three floating-point values separated by spaces: 5.8 12.45 8.32
Maximum is: 12.45
```

```
Enter three floating-point values separated by spaces: 6.46 4.12 10.54
Maximum is: 10.54
```

Fig. 6.4 | Application to test class `MaximumFinder`.

trol returns to the point in the program where maximum was called, maximum's parameters x, y and z no longer exist in memory. Note that methods can return at most one value, but the returned value could be a reference to an object that contains many values.

Note that result is a local variable in determineMaximum because it is declared in the block that represents the method's body. Variables should be declared as fields of a class only if they are required for use in more than one method of the class or if the program should save their values between calls to the class's methods.

Common Programming Error 6.1

Declaring method parameters of the same type as float x, y *instead of* float x, float y *is a syntax error—a type is required for each parameter in the parameter list.*

Software Engineering Observation 6.5

A method that has many parameters may be performing too many tasks. Consider dividing the method into smaller methods that perform the separate tasks. As a guideline, try to fit the method header on one line if possible.

Implementing Method `maximum` by Reusing Method `Math.max`

Recall from Fig. 6.2 that class Math has a max method that can determine the larger of two values. The entire body of our maximum method could also be implemented with two calls to Math.max, as follows:

```
return Math.max( x, Math.max( y, z ) );
```

The first call to `Math.max` specifies arguments x and `Math.max( y, z )`. Before any method can be called, all its arguments must be evaluated to determine their values. If an argument is a method call, the method call must be performed to determine its return value. So, in the preceding statement, `Math.max( y, z )` is evaluated first to determine the maximum of y and z. Then the result is passed as the second argument to the other call to `Math.max`, which returns the larger of its two arguments. Using `Math.max` in this manner is a good example of software reuse—we find the largest of three values by reusing `Math.max`, which finds the largest of two values. Note how concise this code is compared to lines 30–40 of Fig. 6.3.

Assembling Strings with String Concatenation

Java allows `String` objects to be created by assembling smaller strings into larger strings using operator + (or the compound assignment operator +=). This is known as string concatenation. When both operands of operator + are `String` objects, operator + creates a new `String` object in which the characters of the right operand are placed at the end of those in the left operand. For example, the expression `"hello "` + `"there"` creates the `String` `"hello there"`.

In line 24 of Fig. 6.3, the expression `"Maximum is: "` + `result` uses operator + with operands of types `String` and `double`. Every primitive value and object in Java has a `String` representation. When one of the + operator's operands is a `String`, the other is converted to a `String`, then the two are concatenated. In line 24, the `double` value is converted to its `String` representation and placed at the end of the `String` `"Maximum is: "`. If there are any trailing zeros in a `double` value, these will be discarded when the number is converted to a `String`. Thus, the number 9.3500 would be represented as 9.35 in the resulting `String`.

For primitive values used in string concatenation, the primitive values are converted to `Strings`. If a `boolean` is concatenated with a `String`, the `boolean` is converted to the `String` `"true"` or `"false"`. All objects have a method named `toString` that returns a `String` representation of the object. When an object is concatenated with a `String`, the object's `toString` method is implicitly called to obtain the `String` representation of the object. You will learn more about method `toString` in Chapter 7, Arrays.

When a large `String` literal is typed into a program's source code, programmers sometimes prefer to break that `String` into several smaller `Strings` and place them on multiple lines of code for readability. In this case, the `Strings` can be reassembled using concatenation.

Common Programming Error 6.2

It is a syntax error to break a `String` *literal across multiple lines in a program. If a* `String` *does not fit on one line, split the* `String` *into several smaller* `Strings` *and use concatenation to form the desired* `String`.

Common Programming Error 6.3

Confusing the + operator used for string concatenation with the + operator used for addition can lead to strange results. Java evaluates the operands of an operator from left to right. For example, if integer variable y has the value 5, the expression `"y + 2 = "` *+ y + 2 results in the string* `"y + 2 = 52"`, *not* `"y + 2 = 7"`, *because first the value of y (5) is concatenated with the string* `"y + 2 = "`, *then the value 2 is concatenated with the new larger string* `"y + 2 = 5"`. *The expression* `"y + 2 = "` *+ (y + 2) produces the desired result* `"y + 2 = 7"`.

6.5 Notes on Declaring and Using Methods

There are three ways to call a method:

1. Using a method name by itself to call another method of the same class—such as maximum(number1, number2, number3) in line 21 of Fig. 6.3.

2. Using a variable that contains a reference to an object, followed by a dot (.) and the method name to call a method of the referenced object—such as the method call in line 10 of Fig. 6.4, maximumFinder.determineMaximum(), which calls a method of class MaximumFinder from the main method of MaximumFinderTest.

3. Using the class name and a dot (.) to call a static method of a class—such as Math.sqrt(900.0) in Section 6.3.

Note that a static method can call only other static methods of the same class directly (i.e., using the method name by itself) and can manipulate only static fields in the same class directly. To access the class's non-static members, a static method must use a reference to an object of the class. Recall that static methods relate to a class as a whole, whereas non-static methods are associated with a specific instance (object) of the class and may manipulate the instance variables of that object. Many objects of a class, each with its own copies of the instance variables, may exist at the same time. Suppose a static method were to invoke a non-static method directly. How would the method know which object's instance variables to manipulate? What would happen if no objects of the class existed at the time the non-static method was invoked? Clearly, such a situation would be problematic. Thus, Java does not allow a static method to access non-static members of the same class directly.

There are three ways to return control to the statement that calls a method. If the method does not return a result, control returns when the program flow reaches the method-ending right brace or when the statement

```
return;
```

is executed. If the method returns a result, the statement

```
return expression;
```

evaluates the *expression*, then returns the result to the caller.

Common Programming Error 6.4

Declaring a method outside the body of a class declaration or inside the body of another method is a syntax error.

Common Programming Error 6.5

Omitting the return-value-type *in a method declaration is a syntax error.*

Common Programming Error 6.6

Placing a semicolon after the right parenthesis enclosing the parameter list of a method declaration is a syntax error.

Common Programming Error 6.7

Redeclaring a method parameter as a local variable in the method's body is a compilation error.

Common Programming Error 6.8

Forgetting to return a value from a method that should return a value is a compilation error. If a return value type other than void *is specified, the method must contain a* return *statement that returns a value consistent with the method's* return-value-type. *Returning a value from a method whose return type has been declared* void *is a compilation error.*

6.6 Method Call Stack and Activation Records

To understand how Java performs method calls, we first need to consider a data structure (i.e., collection of related data items) known as a stack. Students can think of a stack as analogous to a pile of dishes. When a dish is placed on the pile, it is normally placed at the top (referred to as pushing the dish onto the stack). Similarly, when a dish is removed from the pile, it is always removed from the top (referred to as popping the dish off the stack). Stacks are known as last-in, first-out (LIFO) data structures—the last item pushed (inserted) on the stack is the first item popped (removed) from the stack.

When a program calls a method, the called method must know how to return to its caller, so the return address of the calling method is pushed onto the program execution stack (sometimes referred to as the method call stack). If a series of method calls occurs, the successive return addresses are pushed onto the stack in last-in, first-out order so that each method can return to its caller.

The program execution stack also contains the memory for the local variables used in each invocation of a method during a program's execution. This data, stored as a portion of the program execution stack, is known as the activation record or stack frame of the method call. When a method call is made, the activation record for that method call is pushed onto the program execution stack. When the method returns to its caller, the activation record for this method call is popped off the stack and those local variables are no longer known to the program. If a local variable holding a reference to an object is the only variable in the program with a reference to that object, when the activation record containing that local variable is popped off the stack, the object can no longer be accessed by the program and will eventually be deleted from memory by the JVM during "garbage collection." We'll discuss garbage collection in Section 8.10.

Of course, the amount of memory in a computer is finite, so only a certain amount of memory can be used to store activation records on the program execution stack. If more method calls occur than can have their activation records stored on the program execution stack, an error known as a stack overflow occurs.

6.7 Argument Promotion and Casting

Another important feature of method calls is argument promotion—converting an argument's value to the type that the method expects to receive in its corresponding parameter. For example, a program can call Math method sqrt with an integer argument even though the method expects to receive a double argument (but, as we will soon see, not vice versa). The statement

```
System.out.println( Math.sqrt( 4 ) );
```

correctly evaluates `Math.sqrt( 4 )` and prints the value `2.0`. The method declaration's parameter list causes Java to convert the `int` value 4 to the `double` value `4.0` before passing the value to `sqrt`. Attempting these conversions may lead to compilation errors if Java's promotion rules are not satisfied. The promotion rules specify which conversions are allowed, that is, which conversions can be performed without losing data. In the `sqrt` example above, an `int` is converted to a `double` without changing its value. However, converting a `double` to an `int` truncates the fractional part of the `double` value—thus, part of the value is lost. Converting large integer types to small integer types (e.g., `long` to `int`) may also result in changed values.

The promotion rules apply to expressions containing values of two or more primitive types and to primitive-type values passed as arguments to methods. Each value is promoted to the "highest" type in the expression. (Actually, the expression uses a temporary copy of each value—the types of the original values remain unchanged.) Figure 6.5 lists the primitive types and the types to which each can be promoted. Note that the valid promotions for a given type are always to a type higher in the table. For example, an `int` can be promoted to the higher types `long`, `float` and `double`.

Converting values to types lower in the table of Fig. 6.5 will result in different values if the lower type cannot represent the value of the higher type (e.g., the `int` value 2000000 cannot be represented as a `short`, and any floating-point number with digits after its decimal point cannot be represented in an integer type such as `long`, `int` or `short`). Therefore, in cases where information may be lost due to conversion, the Java compiler requires the programmer to use a cast operator (introduced in Section 4.9) to explicitly force the conversion to occur—otherwise a compilation error occurs. This enables the programmer to "take control" from the compiler. The programmer essentially says, "I know this conversion might cause loss of information, but for my purposes here, that's fine." Suppose method `square` calculates the square of an integer and thus requires an `int` argument. To call `square` with a `double` argument named `doubleValue`, we would be required to write the method call as `square( (int) doubleValue )`. This method call explicitly casts (converts) the value of `doubleValue` to an integer for use in method `square`. Thus, if `doubleValue`'s value is `4.5`, the method receives the value 4 and returns 16, not `20.25`.

Type	Valid promotions
`double`	None
`float`	`double`
`long`	`float` or `double`
`int`	`long`, `float` or `double`
`char`	`int`, `long`, `float` or `double`
`short`	`int`, `long`, `float` or `double` (but not `char`)
`byte`	`short`, `int`, `long`, `float` or `double` (but not `char`)
`boolean`	None (`boolean` values are not considered to be numbers in Java)

Fig. 6.5 | Promotions allowed for primitive types.

Common Programming Error 6.9

Converting a primitive-type value to another primitive type may change the value if the new type is not a valid promotion. For example, converting a floating-point value to an integral value may introduce truncation errors (loss of the fractional part) into the result.

6.8 Java API Packages

As we have seen, Java contains many predefined classes that are grouped into categories of related classes called packages. Together, we refer to these packages as the Java Application Programming Interface (Java API), or the Java class library.

Throughout the text, `import` declarations specify the classes required to compile a Java program. For example, a program includes the declaration

```
import java.util.Scanner;
```

to specify that the program uses class `Scanner` from the `java.util` package. This allows programmers to use the simple class name `Scanner`, rather than the fully qualified class name `java.util.Scanner`, in the code. A great strength of Java is the large number of classes in the packages of the Java API. Some key Java API packages are described in Fig. 6.6, which represents only a small portion of the reusable components in the Java API. When learning Java, spend a portion of your time browsing the packages and classes in the Java API documentation (`java.sun.com/j2se/5.0/docs/api/index.html`).

The set of packages available in the J2SE Development Kit (JDK) is quite large. In addition to the packages summarized in Fig. 6.6, the JDK includes packages for complex graphics, advanced graphical user interfaces, printing, advanced networking, security, database processing, multimedia, accessibility (for people with disabilities) and many other capabilities. For an overview of the packages in the JDK 5.0, visit

```
java.sun.com/j2se/5.0/docs/api/overview-summary.html
```

Many other packages are also available for download at `java.sun.com`.

Package	Description
`java.applet`	The Java Applet Package contains a class and several interfaces required to create Java applets—programs that execute in Web browsers. (Interfaces are discussed in Chapter 10, Object-Oriented Programming: Polymorphism.)
`java.awt`	The Java Abstract Window Toolkit Package contains the classes and interfaces required to create and manipulate GUIs in Java 1.0 and 1.1. In current versions of Java, the Swing GUI components of the `javax.swing` packages are often used instead. (Some elements of the `java.awt` package are discussed in Section 4.14, Section 5.10, Section 6.13, Section 7.13, Section 8.18 and Section 10.8 in the optional GUI and Graphics Case Study.)

Fig. 6.6 | Java API packages (a subset). (Part 1 of 2.)

Package	Description
`java.awt.event`	The Java Abstract Window Toolkit Event Package contains classes and interfaces that enable event handling for GUI components in both the `java.awt` and `javax.swing` packages.
`java.io`	The Java Input/Output Package contains classes and interfaces that enable programs to input and output data.
`java.lang`	The Java Language Package contains classes and interfaces (discussed throughout this text) that are required by many Java programs. This package is imported by the compiler into all programs, so the programmer does not need to do so.
`java.net`	The Java Networking Package contains classes and interfaces that enable programs to communicate via computer networks like the Internet.
`java.text`	The Java Text Package contains classes and interfaces that enable programs to manipulate numbers, dates, characters and strings. The package provides internationalization capabilities that enable a program to be customized to a specific locale (e.g., a program may display strings in different languages, based on the user's country).
`java.util`	The Java Utilities Package contains utility classes and interfaces that enable such actions as date and time manipulations, random-number processing (class `Random`), the storing and processing of large amounts of data and the breaking of strings into smaller pieces called tokens (class `StringTokenizer`).
`javax.swing`	The Java Swing GUI Components Package contains classes and interfaces for Java's Swing GUI components that provide support for portable GUIs. (You will learn more about some elements of this package in Section 3.9, Section 9.8 and Section 10.8 in the optional GUI and Graphics Case Study.)
`javax.swing.event`	The Java Swing Event Package contains classes and interfaces that enable event handling (e.g., responding to button clicks) for GUI components in package `javax.swing`.

Fig. 6.6 | Java API packages (a subset). (Part 2 of 2.)

You can locate additional information about a predefined Java class's methods in the Java API documentation at `java.sun.com/j2se/5.0/docs/api/index.html`. When you visit this site, click the **Index** link to see an alphabetical listing of all the classes and methods in the Java API. Locate the class name and click its link to see the online description of the class. Click the **METHOD** link to see a table of the class's methods. Each `static` method will be listed with the word `"static"` preceding the method's return type. For a more detailed overview of navigating the Java API documentation, see Appendix G, Using the Java API Documentation.

Good Programming Practice 6.2

The online Java API documentation is easy to search and provides many details about each class. As you learn a class in this book, you should get in the habit of looking at the class in the online documentation for additional information.

6.9 Case Study: Random-Number Generation

We now take a brief and, hopefully, entertaining diversion into a popular type of programming application—simulation and game playing. In this and the next section, we develop a nicely structured game-playing program with multiple methods. The program uses most of the control statements presented thus far in the book and introduces several new programming concepts.

There is something in the air of a casino that invigorates people—from the high rollers at the plush mahogany-and-felt craps tables to the quarter poppers at the one-armed bandits. It is the element of chance, the possibility that luck will convert a pocketful of money into a mountain of wealth. The element of chance can be introduced in a program via an object of class `Random` (package `java.util`) or via the `static` method `random` of class Math. Objects of class `Random` can produce random `boolean`, `byte`, `float`, `double`, `int`, `long` and Gaussian values, whereas `Math` method `random` can produce only `double` values in the range $0.0 \leq x < 1.0$, where x is the value returned by method `random`. In the next several examples, we use objects of class Random to produce random values.

A new random-number generator object can be created as follows:

```
Random randomNumbers = new Random();
```

The random-number generator object can then be used to generate random `boolean`, `byte`, `float`, `double`, `int`, `long` and Gaussian values—we discuss only random `int` values here. For more information on the `Random` class, see `java.sun.com/j2se/5.0/docs/api/java/util/Random.html`.

Consider the following statement:

```
int randomValue = randomNumbers.nextInt();
```

Method `nextInt` of class Random generates a random `int` value in the range –2,147,483,648 to +2,147,483,647. If the `nextInt` method truly produces values at random, then every value in that range should have an equal chance (or probability) of being chosen each time method `nextInt` is called. The values returned by `nextInt` are actually pseudorandom numbers—a sequence of values produced by a complex mathematical calculation. The calculation uses the current time of day (which, of course, changes constantly) to seed the random-number generator such that each execution of a program yields a different sequence of random values.

The range of values produced directly by method `nextInt` often differs from the range of values required in a particular Java application. For example, a program that simulates coin tossing might require only 0 for "heads" and 1 for "tails." A program that simulates the rolling of a six-sided die might require random integers in the range 1–6. A program that randomly predicts the next type of spaceship (out of four possibilities) that will fly across the horizon in a video game might require random integers in the range 1–4. For cases like these, class Random provides another version of method `nextInt` that receives an `int` argument and returns a value from 0 up to, but not including, the argument's value. For example, to simulate coin tossing, you might use the statement

```
int randomValue = randomNumbers.nextInt( 2 );
```

which returns 0 or 1.

Rolling a Six-Sided Die

To demonstrate random numbers, let us develop a program that simulates 20 rolls of a six-sided die and displays the value of each roll. We begin by using `nextInt` to produce random values in the range 0–5, as follows:

```
face = randomNumbers.nextInt( 6 );
```

The argument 6—called the scaling factor—represents the number of unique values that `nextInt` should produce (in this case six—0, 1, 2, 3, 4 and 5). This manipulation is called scaling the range of values produced by `Random` method `nextInt`.

A six-sided die has the numbers 1–6 on its faces, not 0–5. So we shift the range of numbers produced by adding a shifting value—in this case 1—to our previous result, as in

```
face = 1 + randomNumbers.nextInt( 6 );
```

The shifting value (1) specifies the first value in the desired set of random integers. The preceding statement assigns `face` a random integer in the range 1–6.

Figure 6.7 shows two sample outputs which confirm that the results of the preceding calculation are integers in the range 1–6, and that each run of the program can produce a different sequence of random numbers. Line 3 imports class `Random` from the `java.util` package. Line 9 creates the `Random` object `randomNumbers` to produce random values. Line 16 executes 20 times in a loop to roll the die. The `if` statement (lines 21–22) in the loop starts a new line of output after every five numbers, so the results can be presented on multiple lines.

Rolling a Six-Sided Die 6000 Times

To show that the numbers produced by `nextInt` occur with approximately equal likelihood, let us simulate 6000 rolls of a die with the application in Fig. 6.8. Each integer from 1 to 6 should appear approximately 1000 times.

As the two sample outputs show, scaling and shifting the values produced by method `nextInt` enables the program to realistically simulate rolling a six-sided die. The application uses nested control statements (the `switch` is nested inside the `for`) to determine the number of times each side of the die occurred. The `for` statement (lines 21–47) iterates 6000 times. During each iteration, line 23 produces a random value from 1 to 6. That value is then used as the controlling expression (line 26) of the `switch` statement (lines 26–46). Based on the `face` value, the `switch` statement increments one of the six counter variables during each iteration of the loop. (When we study arrays in Chapter 7, we will show an elegant way to replace the entire `switch` statement in this program with a single statement!) Note that the `switch` statement has no `default` case because we have a `case` for every possible die value that the expression in line 23 could produce. Run the program several times, and observe the results. As you will see, every time you execute this program, it produces different results.

```
1   // Fig. 6.7: RandomIntegers.java
2   // Shifted and scaled random integers.
3   import java.util.Random; // program uses class Random
4
5   public class RandomIntegers
6   {
7      public static void main( String args[] )
8      {
9         Random randomNumbers = new Random(); // random number generator
10        int face; // stores each random integer generated
11
12        // loop 20 times
13        for ( int counter = 1; counter <= 20; counter++ )
14        {
15           // pick random integer from 1 to 6
16           face = 1 + randomNumbers.nextInt( 6 );
17
18           System.out.printf( "%d  ", face ); // display generated value
19
20           // if counter is divisible by 5, start a new line of output
21           if ( counter % 5 == 0 )
22              System.out.println();
23        } // end for
24     } // end main
25  } // end class RandomIntegers
```

```
1  5  3  6  2
5  2  6  5  2
4  4  4  2  6
3  1  6  2  2
```

```
6  5  4  2  6
1  2  5  1  3
6  3  2  2  1
6  4  2  6  4
```

Fig. 6.7 | Shifted and scaled random integers.

```
1   // Fig. 6.8: RollDie.java
2   // Roll a six-sided die 6000 times.
3   import java.util.Random;
4
5   public class RollDie
6   {
7      public static void main( String args[] )
8      {
9         Random randomNumbers = new Random(); // random number generator
10
11        int frequency1 = 0; // maintains count of 1s rolled
```

Fig. 6.8 | Rolling a six-sided die 6000 times. (Part I of 3.)

```
12          int frequency2 = 0; // count of 2s rolled
13          int frequency3 = 0; // count of 3s rolled
14          int frequency4 = 0; // count of 4s rolled
15          int frequency5 = 0; // count of 5s rolled
16          int frequency6 = 0; // count of 6s rolled
17
18          int face; // stores most recently rolled value
19
20          // summarize results of 6000 rolls of a die
21          for ( int roll = 1; roll <= 6000; roll++ )
22          {
23             face = 1 + randomNumbers.nextInt( 6 ); // number from 1 to 6
24
25             // determine roll value 1-6 and increment appropriate counter
26             switch ( face )
27             {
28                case 1:
29                   ++frequency1; // increment the 1s counter
30                   break;
31                case 2:
32                   ++frequency2; // increment the 2s counter
33                   break;
34                case 3:
35                   ++frequency3; // increment the 3s counter
36                   break;
37                case 4:
38                   ++frequency4; // increment the 4s counter
39                   break;
40                case 5:
41                   ++frequency5; // increment the 5s counter
42                   break;
43                case 6:
44                   ++frequency6; // increment the 6s counter
45                   break; // optional at end of switch
46             } // end switch
47          } // end for
48
49          System.out.println( "Face\tFrequency" ); // output headers
50          System.out.printf( "1\t%d\n2\t%d\n3\t%d\n4\t%d\n5\t%d\n6\t%d\n",
51             frequency1, frequency2, frequency3, frequency4,
52             frequency5, frequency6 );
53       } // end main
54    } // end class RollDie
```

Face	Frequency
1	982
2	1001
3	1015
4	1005
5	1009
6	988

Fig. 6.8 | Rolling a six-sided die 6000 times. (Part 2 of 3.)

Face	Frequency
1	1029
2	994
3	1017
4	1007
5	972
6	981

Fig. 6.8 | Rolling a six-sided die 6000 times. (Part 3 of 3.)

6.9.1 Generalized Scaling and Shifting of Random Numbers

Previously, we demonstrated the statement

```
face = 1 + randomNumbers.nextInt( 6 );
```

which simulates the rolling of a six-sided die. This statement always assigns to variable `face` an integer in the range $1 \leq face \leq 6$. The width of this range (i.e., the number of consecutive integers in the range) is 6, and the starting number in the range is 1. Referring to the preceding statement, we see that the width of the range is determined by the number 6 that is passed as an argument to Random method `nextInt`, and the starting number of the range is the number 1 that is added to `randomNumberGenerator.nextInt( 6 )`. We can generalize this result as

```
number = shiftingValue + randomNumbers.nextInt( scalingFactor );
```

where *shiftingValue* specifies the first number in the desired range of consecutive integers and *scalingFactor* specifies how many numbers are in the range.

It is also possible to choose integers at random from sets of values other than ranges of consecutive integers. For example, to obtain a random value from the sequence 2, 5, 8, 11 and 14, you could use the statement

```
number = 2 + 3 * randomNumbers.nextInt( 5 );
```

In this case, `randomNumberGenerator.nextInt( 5 )` produces values in the range 0–4. Each value produced is multiplied by 3 to produce a number in the sequence 0, 3, 6, 9 and 12. We then add 2 to that value to shift the range of values and obtain a value from the sequence 2, 5, 8, 11 and 14. We can generalize this result as

```
number = shiftingValue +
         differenceBetweenValues * randomNumbers.nextInt( scalingFactor );
```

where *shiftingValue* specifies the first number in the desired range of values, *difference-BetweenValues* represents the difference between consecutive numbers in the sequence and *scalingFactor* specifies how many numbers are in the range.

6.9.2 Random-Number Repeatability for Testing and Debugging

As we mentioned earlier in Section 6.9, the methods of class Random actually generate pseudorandom numbers based on complex mathematical calculations. Repeatedly calling any of Random's methods produces a sequence of numbers that appears to be random. The calculation that produces the pseudorandom numbers uses the time of day as a seed value to change the sequence's starting point. Each new Random object seeds itself with a value based on the computer system's clock at the time the object is created, enabling each execution of a program to produce a different sequence of random numbers.

When debugging an application, it is sometimes useful to repeat the exact same sequence of pseudorandom numbers during each execution of the program. This repeatability enables you to prove that your application is working for a specific sequence of random numbers before you test the program with different sequences of random numbers. When repeatability is important, you can create a Random object as follows:

```
Random randomNumbers = new Random( seedValue );
```

The seedValue argument (type long) seeds the random-number calculation. If the same seedValue is used every time, the Random object produces the same sequence of random numbers. You can set a Random object's seed at any time during program execution by calling the object's setSeed method, as in

```
randomNumbers.setSeed( seedValue );
```

Error-Prevention Tip 6.2

While a program is under development, create the Random object with a specific seed value to produce a repeatable sequence of random numbers each time the program executes. If a logic error occurs, fix the error and test the program again with the same seed value—this allows you to reconstruct the same sequence of random numbers that caused the error. Once the logic errors have been removed, create the Random object without using a seed value, causing the Random object to generate a new sequence of random numbers each time the program executes.

6.10 Case Study: A Game of Chance (Introducing Enumerations)

A popular game of chance is a dice game known as "craps," which is played in casinos and back alleys throughout the world. The rules of the game are straightforward:

You roll two dice. Each die has six faces, which contain one, two, three, four, five and six spots, respectively. After the dice have come to rest, the sum of the spots on the two upward faces is calculated. If the sum is 7 or 11 on the first throw, you win. If the sum is 2, 3 or 12 on the first throw (called "craps"), you lose (i.e., the "house" wins). If the sum is 4, 5, 6, 8, 9 or 10 on the first throw, that sum becomes your "point." To win, you must continue rolling the dice until you "make your point" (i.e., roll that same point value). You lose by rolling a 7 before making the point.

The application in Fig. 6.9 and Fig. 6.10 simulates the game of craps, using methods to define the logic of the game. In the main method of class CrapsTest (Fig. 6.10), line 8 creates an object of class Craps (Fig. 6.9) and line 9 calls its play method to start the game. The play method (Fig. 6.9, lines 21–65) calls the rollDice method (Fig. 6.9, lines 68–81) as necessary to roll the two dice and compute their sum. Four sample outputs in Fig. 6.10 show winning on the first roll, losing on the first roll, winning on a subsequent roll and losing on a subsequent roll, respectively.

Let's discuss the declaration of class Craps in Fig. 6.9. In the rules of the game, the player must roll two dice on the first roll, and must do the same on all subsequent rolls.

We declare method rollDice (lines 68–81) to roll the dice and compute and print their sum. Method rollDice is declared once, but it is called from two places (lines 26 and 50) in method play, which contains the logic for one complete game of craps. Method roll-Dice takes no arguments, so it has an empty parameter list. Each time it is called, rollDice returns the sum of the dice, so the return type int is indicated in the method header (line 68). Although lines 71 and 72 look the same (except for the die names), they do not necessarily produce the same result. Each of these statements produces a random value in the range 1–6. Note that randomNumbers (used in lines 71–72) is not declared in the method. Rather it is declared as a private instance variable of the class and initialized in line 8. This enables us to create one Random object that is reused in each call to rollDice.

```java
 1   // Fig. 6.9: Craps.java
 2   // Craps class simulates the dice game craps.
 3   import java.util.Random;
 4
 5   public class Craps
 6   {
 7      // create random number generator for use in method rollDice
 8      private Random randomNumbers = new Random();
 9
10      // enumeration with constants that represent the game status
11      private enum Status { CONTINUE, WON, LOST };
12
13      // constants that represent common rolls of the dice
14      private final static int SNAKE_EYES = 2;
15      private final static int TREY = 3;
16      private final static int SEVEN = 7;
17      private final static int YO_LEVEN = 11;
18      private final static int BOX_CARS = 12;
19
20      // plays one game of craps
21      public void play()
22      {
23         int myPoint = 0; // point if no win or loss on first roll
24         Status gameStatus; // can contain CONTINUE, WON or LOST
25
26         int sumOfDice = rollDice(); // first roll of the dice
27
28         // determine game status and point based on first roll
29         switch ( sumOfDice )
30         {
31            case SEVEN: // win with 7 on first roll
32            case YO_LEVEN: // win with 11 on first roll
33               gameStatus = Status.WON;
34               break;
35            case SNAKE_EYES: // lose with 2 on first roll
36            case TREY: // lose with 3 on first roll
37            case BOX_CARS: // lose with 12 on first roll
38               gameStatus = Status.LOST;
39               break;
```

Fig. 6.9 | Craps class simulates the dice game craps. (Part 1 of 2.)

```
40              default: // did not win or lose, so remember point
41                 gameStatus = Status.CONTINUE; // game is not over
42                 myPoint = sumOfDice; // remember the point
43                 System.out.printf( "Point is %d\n", myPoint );
44                 break; // optional at end of switch
45           } // end switch
46
47           // while game is not complete
48           while ( gameStatus == Status.CONTINUE ) // not WON or LOST
49           {
50              sumOfDice = rollDice(); // roll dice again
51
52              // determine game status
53              if ( sumOfDice == myPoint ) // win by making point
54                 gameStatus = Status.WON;
55              else
56                 if ( sumOfDice == SEVEN ) // lose by rolling 7 before point
57                    gameStatus = Status.LOST;
58           } // end while
59
60           // display won or lost message
61           if ( gameStatus == Status.WON )
62              System.out.println( "Player wins" );
63           else
64              System.out.println( "Player loses" );
65        } // end method play
66
67        // roll dice, calculate sum and display results
68        public int rollDice()
69        {
70           // pick random die values
71           int die1 = 1 + randomNumbers.nextInt( 6 ); // first die roll
72           int die2 = 1 + randomNumbers.nextInt( 6 ); // second die roll
73
74           int sum = die1 + die2; // sum of die values
75
76           // display results of this roll
77           System.out.printf( "Player rolled %d + %d = %d\n",
78              die1, die2, sum );
79
80           return sum; // return sum of dice
81        } // end method rollDice
82     } // end class Craps
```

Fig. 6.9 | Craps class simulates the dice game craps. (Part 2 of 2.)

The game is reasonably involved. The player may win or lose on the first roll, or may win or lose on any subsequent roll. Method play (lines 21–65) uses local variable myPoint (line 23) to store the "point" if the player does not win or lose on the first roll, local variable gameStatus (line 24) to keep track of the overall game status and local variable sumOfDice (line 26) to maintain the sum of the dice for the most recent roll. Note that myPoint is initialized to 0 to ensure that the application will compile. If you do not initialize myPoint, the compiler issues an error, because myPoint is not assigned a value in every branch of the switch

```
1   // Fig. 6.10: CrapsTest.java
2   // Application to test class Craps.
3
4   public class CrapsTest
5   {
6      public static void main( String args[] )
7      {
8         Craps game = new Craps();
9         game.play(); // play one game of craps
10     } // end main
11   } // end class CrapsTest
```

```
Player rolled 5 + 6 = 11
Player wins
```

```
Player rolled 1 + 2 = 3
Player loses
```

```
Player rolled 5 + 4 = 9
Point is 9
Player rolled 2 + 2 = 4
Player rolled 2 + 6 = 8
Player rolled 4 + 2 = 6
Player rolled 3 + 6 = 9
Player wins
```

```
Player rolled 2 + 6 = 8
Point is 8
Player rolled 5 + 1 = 6
Player rolled 2 + 1 = 3
Player rolled 1 + 6 = 7
Player loses
```

Fig. 6.10 | Application to test class Craps.

statement, and thus the program could try to use myPoint before it is assigned a value. By contrast, gameStatus does not require initialization because it *is* assigned a value in every branch of the switch statement—thus, it is guaranteed to be initialized before it is used.

Note that local variable gameStatus is declared to be of a new type called Status, which we declared at line 11. Type Status is declared as a private member of class Craps, because Status will be used only in that class. Status is a programmer-declared type called an enumeration, which, in its simplest form, declares a set of constants represented by identifiers. An enumeration is a special kind of class that is introduced by the keyword enum (new to J2SE 5.0) and a type name (in this case, Status). As with any class, braces ({ and }) delimit the body of an enum declaration. Inside the braces is a comma-separated list of enumeration constants, each representing a unique value. The identifiers in an enum must be unique. (You will learn more about enumerations in Chapter 8.)

Good Programming Practice 6.3

Use only uppercase letters in the names of constants. This makes the constants stand out in a program and reminds the programmer that enumeration constants are not variables.

Variables of type `Status` can be assigned only one of the three constants declared in the enumeration or a compilation error will occur. When the game is won, the program sets local variable `gameStatus` to `Status.WON` (lines 33 and 54). When the game is lost, the program sets local variable `gameStatus` to `Status.LOST` (lines 38 and 57). Otherwise, the program sets local variable `gameStatus` to `Status.CONTINUE` (line 41) to indicate that the dice must be rolled again.

Good Programming Practice 6.4

Using enumeration constants (like `Status.WON`, `Status.LOST` and `Status.CONTINUE`) rather than literal integer values (such as 0, 1 and 2) can make programs easier to read and maintain.

Line 26 in method `play` calls `rollDice`, which picks two random values from 1 to 6, displays the value of the first die, the value of the second die and the sum of the dice, and returns the sum of the dice. Method `play` next enters the `switch` statement at lines 29–45, which uses the `sumOfDice` value from line 26 to determine whether the game has been won or lost, or whether it should continue with another roll. The sums of the dice that would result in a win or loss on the first roll are declared as `public final static int` constants in lines 14–18. These are used in the `cases` of the `switch` statement. The identifier names use casino parlance for these sums. Note that these constants, like `enum` constants, are declared with all capital letters by convention, to make them stand out in the program. Lines 31–34 determine whether the player won on the first roll with `SEVEN` (7) or `YO_LEVEN` (11). Lines 35–39 determine whether the player lost on the first roll with `SNAKE_EYES` (2), `TREY` (3), or `BOX_CARS` (12). After the first roll, if the game is not over, the `default` case (lines 40–44) saves `sumOfDice` in `myPoint` (line 42) and displays the point (line 43).

If we are still trying to "make our point" (i.e., the game is continuing from a prior roll), the loop in lines 48–58 executes. Line 50 rolls the dice again. In line 53, if `sumOfDice` matches `myPoint`, line 54 sets `gameStatus` to `Status.WON`, then the loop terminates because the game is complete. In line 56, if `sumOfDice` is equal to `SEVEN` (7), line 57 sets `gameStatus` to `Status.LOST`, and the loop terminates because the game is complete. When the game completes, lines 61–64 display a message indicating whether the player won or lost and the program terminates.

Note the use of the various program-control mechanisms we have discussed. The `Craps` class uses three methods—`main`, `play` (called from `main`) and `rollDice` (called twice from `play`)—and the `switch`, `while`, `if...else` and nested `if` control statements. Note also the use of multiple `case` labels in the `switch` statement to execute the same statements for sums of `SEVEN` and `YO_LEVEN` (lines 31–32) and for sums of `SNAKE_EYES`, `TREY` and `BOX_CARS` (lines 35–37).

You might be wondering why we declared the sums of the dice as `public final static int` constants rather than as `enum` constants. The answer lies in the fact that the program must compare `int sumOfDice` (line 26) to these constants to determine the outcome of each roll. Suppose we were to declare `enum Sum` containing constants (e.g., `Sum.SNAKE_EYES`) representing the five sums used in the game, then use these constants in place of the `final` variables in the `cases` of the `switch` statement (lines 29–45). Doing so would prevent us from using `sumOfDice` as the `switch` statement's controlling expression—Java does not allow an `int` to be compared to an enumeration constant. To achieve the same functionality as the current program, we would have to use a variable `currentSum` of type `Sum` as the `switch`'s controlling expression. Unfortunately, Java does not provide an easy way to convert an `int` value to a particular `enum` constant. To translate an `int` into an `enum` constant would require a separate `switch` statement. Clearly this would be cumbersome and not improve the readability of the program (thus defeating the purpose of using an `enum`), so we are better off using `public final static int` constants to represent the sums of the dice.

6.11 Scope of Declarations

You have seen declarations of various Java entities, such as classes, methods, variables and parameters. Declarations introduce names that can be used to refer to such Java entities. The scope of a declaration is the portion of the program that can refer to the declared entity by its name. Such an entity is said to be "in scope" for that portion of the program. This section introduces several important scope issues. (For more scope information, see the *Java Language Specification, Section 6.3: Scope of a Declaration*, at `java.sun.com/docs/books/jls/second_edition/html/names.doc.html#103228`.)

The basic scope rules are as follows:

1. The scope of a parameter declaration is the body of the method in which the declaration appears.

2. The scope of a local-variable declaration is from the point at which the declaration appears to the end of that block.

3. The scope of a local-variable declaration that appears in the initialization section of a `for` statement's header is the body of the `for` statement and the other expressions in the header.

4. The scope of a method or field of a class is the entire body of the class. This enables non-`static` methods of a class to use the class's fields and other methods.

Any block may contain variable declarations. If a local variable or parameter in a method has the same name as a field, the field is "hidden" until the block terminates execution—this is called shadowing. In Chapter 8, we discuss how to access shadowed fields.

Common Programming Error 6.10

A compilation error occurs when a local variable is declared more than once in a method.

Error-Prevention Tip 6.3

Use different names for fields and local variables to help prevent subtle logic errors that occur when a method is called and a local variable of the method shadows a field of the same name in the class.

The application in Fig. 6.11 and Fig. 6.12 demonstrates scoping issues with fields and local variables. When the application begins execution, class `ScopeTest`'s `main` method (Fig. 6.12, lines 7–11) creates an object of class `Scope` (line 9) and calls the object's `begin` method (line 10) to produce the program's output (shown in Fig. 6.12).

```
1   // Fig. 6.11: Scope.java
2   // Scope class demonstrates field and local variable scopes.
3
4   public class Scope
5   {
6      // field that is accessible to all methods of this class
7      private int x = 1;
8
9      // method begin creates and initializes local variable x
10     // and calls methods useLocalVariable and useField
11     public void begin()
12     {
13        int x = 5; // method's local variable x shadows field x
14
15        System.out.printf( "local x in method begin is %d\n", x );
16
17        useLocalVariable(); // useLocalVariable has local x
18        useField(); // useField uses class Scope's field x
19        useLocalVariable(); // useLocalVariable reinitializes local x
20        useField(); // class Scope's field x retains its value
21
22        System.out.printf( "\nlocal x in method begin is %d\n", x );
23     } // end method begin
24
25     // create and initialize local variable x during each call
26     public void useLocalVariable()
27     {
28        int x = 25; // initialized each time useLocalVariable is called
29
30        System.out.printf(
31           "\nlocal x on entering method useLocalVariable is %d\n", x );
32        ++x; // modifies this method's local variable x
33        System.out.printf(
34           "local x before exiting method useLocalVariable is %d\n", x );
35     } // end method useLocalVariable
36
37     // modify class Scope's field x during each call
38     public void useField()
39     {
40        System.out.printf(
41           "\nfield x on entering method useField is %d\n", x );
42        x *= 10; // modifies class Scope's field x
43        System.out.printf(
44           "field x before exiting method useField is %d\n", x );
45     } // end method useField
46  } // end class Scope
```

Fig. 6.11 | Scope class demonstrating scopes of a field and local variables.

In class Scope, line 7 declares and initializes the field x to 1. This field is shadowed (hidden) in any block (or method) that declares a local variable named x. Method begin (lines 11–23) declares a local variable x (line 13) and initializes it to 5. This local variable's

```
 1   // Fig. 6.12: ScopeTest.java
 2   // Application to test class Scope.
 3
 4   public class ScopeTest
 5   {
 6      // application starting point
 7      public static void main( String args[] )
 8      {
 9         Scope testScope = new Scope();
10         testScope.begin();
11      } // end main
12   } // end class ScopeTest
```

```
local x in method begin is 5

local x on entering method useLocalVariable is 25
local x before exiting method useLocalVariable is 26

field x on entering method useField is 1
field x before exiting method useField is 10

local x on entering method useLocalVariable is 25
local x before exiting method useLocalVariable is 26

field x on entering method useField is 10
field x before exiting method useField is 100

local x in method begin is 5
```

Fig. 6.12 | Application to test class Scope.

value is output to show that the field x (whose value is 1) is shadowed in method begin. The program declares two other methods—useLocalVariable (lines 26–35) and use-Field (lines 38–45)—that each take no arguments and do not return results. Method begin calls each method twice (lines 17–20). Method useLocalVariable declares local variable x (line 28). When useLocalVariable is first called (line 17), it creates local variable x and initializes it to 25 (line 28), outputs the value of x (lines 30–31), increments x (line 32) and outputs the value of x again (lines 33–34). When use1LocalVariable is called a second time (line 19), it re-creates local variable x and re-initializes it to 25, so the output of each useLocalVariable call is identical.

Method useField does not declare any local variables. Therefore, when it refers to x, field x (line 7) of the class is used. When method useField is first called (line 18), it outputs the value (1) of field x (lines 40–41), multiplies the field x by 10 (line 42) and outputs the value (10) of field x again (lines 43–44) before returning. The next time method use-Field is called (line 20), the field has its modified value, 10, so the method outputs 10, then 100. Finally, in method begin, the program outputs the value of local variable x again (line 22) to show that none of the method calls modified start's local variable x, because the methods all referred to variables named x in other scopes.

6.12 Method Overloading

Methods of the same name can be declared in the same class, as long as they have different sets of parameters (determined by the number, types and order of the parameters)—this is called method overloading. When an overloaded method is called, the Java compiler selects the appropriate method by examining the number, types and order of the arguments in the call. Method overloading is commonly used to create several methods with the same name that perform the same or similar tasks, but on different types or different numbers of arguments. For example, Math methods abs, min and max (summarized in Section 6.3) are overloaded with four versions each:

1. One with two double parameters.

2. One with two float parameters.

3. One with two int parameters.

4. One with two long parameters.

Our next example demonstrates declaring and invoking overloaded methods. You will see examples of overloaded constructors in Chapter 8.

Declaring Overloaded Methods

In our class MethodOverload (Fig. 6.13), we include two overloaded versions of a method called square—one that calculates the square of an int (and returns an int) and one that calculates the square of a double (and returns a double). Although these methods have the same name and similar parameter lists and bodies, you can think of them simply as *different* methods. It may help to think of the method names as "square of int" and "square of double," respectively. When the application begins execution, class MethodOverloadTest's main method (Fig. 6.14, lines 6–10) creates an object of class MethodOverload (line 8) and calls the object's method testOverloadedMethods (line 9) to produce the program's output (Fig. 6.14).

In Fig. 6.13, line 9 invokes method square with the argument 7. Literal integer values are treated as type int, so the method call on line 9 invokes the version of square at lines 14–19 that specifies an int parameter. Similarly, line 10 invokes method square with the argument 7.5. Literal floating-point values are treated as type double, so the method call on line 10 invokes the version of square at lines 22–27 that specifies a double parameter. Each method first outputs a line of text to prove that the proper method was called in each case. In line 10, note that the argument value and return value are displayed with the format specifier %f and that we did not specify a precision in either case. By default, floating-point values are displayed with six digits of precision if the precision is not specified in the format specifier.

Distinguishing Between Overloaded Methods

The compiler distinguishes overloaded methods by their signature—a combination of the method's name and the number, types and order of its parameters. If the compiler looked only at method names during compilation, the code in Fig. 6.13 would be ambiguous—the compiler would not know how to distinguish between the two square methods (lines 14–19 and 22–27). Internally, the compiler uses longer method names that include the original method name, the types of each parameter and the exact order of the parameters to determine whether the methods in a class are unique in that class.

```
 1   // Fig. 6.13: MethodOverload.java
 2   // Overloaded method declarations.
 3
 4   public class MethodOverload
 5   {
 6      // test overloaded square methods
 7      public void testOverloadedMethods()
 8      {
 9         System.out.printf( "Square of integer 7 is %d\n", square( 7 ) );
10         System.out.printf( "Square of double 7.5 is %f\n", square( 7.5 ) );
11      } // end method testOverloadedMethods
12
13      // square method with int argument
14      public int square( int intValue )
15      {
16         System.out.printf( "\nCalled square with int argument: %d\n",
17            intValue );
18         return intValue * intValue;
19      } // end method square with int argument
20
21      // square method with double argument
22      public double square( double doubleValue )
23      {
24         System.out.printf( "\nCalled square with double argument: %f\n",
25            doubleValue );
26         return doubleValue * doubleValue;
27      } // end method square with double argument
28   } // end class MethodOverload
```

Fig. 6.13 | Overloaded method declarations.

```
 1   // Fig. 6.14: MethodOverloadTest.java
 2   // Application to test class MethodOverload.
 3
 4   public class MethodOverloadTest
 5   {
 6      public static void main( String args[] )
 7      {
 8         MethodOverload methodOverload = new MethodOverload();
 9         methodOverload.testOverloadedMethods();
10      } // end main
11   } // end class MethodOverloadTest
```

```
Called square with int argument: 7
Square of integer 7 is 49

Called square with double argument: 7.500000
Square of double 7.5 is 56.250000
```

Fig. 6.14 | Overloaded method declarations.

For example, in Fig. 6.13, the compiler might use the logical name "square of int" for the square method that specifies an int parameter and "square of double" for the square method that specifies a double parameter (the actual names the compiler uses are messier). If method1's declaration begins as

```
void method1( int a, float b )
```

then the compiler might use the logical name "method1 of int and float." If the parameters are specified as

```
void method1( float a, int b )
```

then the compiler might use the logical name "method1 of float and int." Note that the order of the parameter types is important—the compiler considers the preceding two method1 headers to be distinct.

Return Types of Overloaded Methods

In discussing the logical names of methods used by the compiler, we did not mention the return types of the methods. This is because method *calls* cannot be distinguished by return type. The program in Fig. 6.15 illustrates the compiler errors generated when two methods have the same signature and different return types. Overloaded methods can have different return types if the methods have different parameter lists. Also, overloaded methods need not have the same number of parameters.

```java
 1   // Fig. 6.15: MethodOverloadError.java
 2   // Overloaded methods with identical signatures
 3   // cause compilation errors, even if return types are different.
 4
 5   public class MethodOverloadError
 6   {
 7      // declaration of method square with int argument
 8      public int square( int x )
 9      {
10         return x * x;
11      }
12
13      // second declaration of method square with int argument
14      // causes compilation error even though return types are different
15      public double square( int y )
16      {
17         return y * y;
18      }
19   } // end class MethodOverloadError
```

```
MethodOverloadError.java:15: square(int) is already defined in
MethodOverloadError
   public double square( int y )
                    ^
1 error
```

Fig. 6.15 | Overloaded method declarations with identical signatures cause compilation errors, even if the return types are different.

Common Programming Error 6.11

Declaring overloaded methods with identical parameter lists is a compilation error regardless of whether the return types are different.

6.13 (Optional) GUI and Graphics Case Study: Colors and Filled Shapes

Although you can create many interesting designs with just lines and basic shapes, class `Graphics` provides many more capabilities. The next two features we introduce are colors and filled shapes. Adding color brings another dimension to the drawings a user sees on the computer screen. Filled shapes fill entire regions with solid colors, rather than just drawing outlines.

Colors displayed on computer screens are defined by their red, green, and blue components. These components, called RGB values, have integer values from 0 to 255. The higher the value of a particular component, the brighter the particular shade will be in the final color. Java uses class `Color` in package `java.awt` to represent colors using their RGB values. For convenience, the `Color` object contains 13 predefined `static Color` objects—`Color.BLACK`, `Color.BLUE`, `Color.CYAN`, `Color.DARK_GRAY`, `Color.GRAY`, `Color.GREEN`, `Color.LIGHT_GRAY`, `Color.MAGENTA`, `Color.ORANGE`, `Color.PINK`, `Color.RED`, `Color.WHITE` and `Color.YELLOW`. Class `Color` also contains a constructor of the form:

```
public Color( int r, int g, int b )
```

so you can create custom colors by specifying values for the individual red, green and blue components of a color.

Filled rectangles and filled ovals are drawn using `Graphics` methods `fillRect` and `fillOval`, respectively. These two methods have the same parameters as their unfilled counterparts `drawRect` and `drawOval`; the first two parameters are the coordinates for the upper-left corner of the shape, while the next two parameters determine its width and height. The example in Fig. 6.16 and Fig. 6.17 demonstrates colors and filled shapes by drawing and displaying a yellow smiley face on the screen.

The `import` statements in lines 3–5 of Fig. 6.16 import `Color`, `Graphics` and `JPanel`. Class `DrawSmiley` uses class `Color` to specify drawing colors and class `Graphics` to draw. Class `JPanel` again provides the area in which we draw. Line 14 in method `paintComponent` uses `Graphics` method `setColor` to set the current drawing color to `Color.YELLOW`. Method `setColor` requires one argument, the `Color` to set as the drawing color. In this case, we use the predefined object `Color.YELLOW`. Line 15 draws a circle with diameter 200 to represent the face—when the width and height arguments are identical, method `fillOval` draws a circle. Next, line 18 sets the color to `Color.Black`, and lines 19–20 draw the eyes. Line 23 draws the mouth as an oval, but this is not quite what we want. To create a happy face, we will "touch up" the mouth. Line 26 sets the color to `Color.YELLOW`, so any shapes we draw will blend in with the face. Line 27 draws a rectangle that is half the mouth's height. This "erases" the top half of the mouth, leaving just the bottom half. To create a better smile, line 28 draws another oval to slightly cover the upper portion of the mouth. Class `DrawSmileyTest` (Fig. 6.17) creates and displays a `JFrame` containing the drawing, resulting in the system calling method `paintComponent` to draw the smiley face.

```
1   // Fig. 6.16: DrawSmiley.java
2   // Demonstrates filled shapes.
3   import java.awt.Color;
4   import java.awt.Graphics;
5   import javax.swing.JPanel;
6
7   public class DrawSmiley extends JPanel
8   {
9      public void paintComponent( Graphics g )
10     {
11        super.paintComponent( g );
12
13        // draw the face
14        g.setColor( Color.YELLOW );
15        g.fillOval( 10, 10, 200, 200 );
16
17        // draw the eyes
18        g.setColor( Color.BLACK );
19        g.fillOval( 55, 65, 30, 30 );
20        g.fillOval( 135, 65, 30, 30 );
21
22        // draw the mouth
23        g.fillOval( 50, 110, 120, 60 );
24
25        // "touch up" the mouth into a smile
26        g.setColor( Color.YELLOW );
27        g.fillRect( 50, 110, 120, 30 );
28        g.fillOval( 50, 120, 120, 40 );
29     } // end method paintComponent
30  } // end class DrawSmiley
```

Fig. 6.16 | Drawing a smiley face using colors and filled shapes.

```
1   // Fig. 6.17: DrawSmileyTest.java
2   // Test application that displays a smiley face.
3   import javax.swing.JFrame;
4
5   public class DrawSmileyTest
6   {
7      public static void main( String args[] )
8      {
9         DrawSmiley panel = new DrawSmiley();
10        JFrame application = new JFrame();
11
12        application.setDefaultCloseOperation( JFrame.EXIT_ON_CLOSE );
13        application.add( panel );
14        application.setSize( 230, 250 );
15        application.setVisible( true );
16     } // end main
17  } // end class DrawSmileyTest
```

Fig. 6.17 | Creating JFrame to display a smiley face. (Part 1 of 2.)

Fig. 6.17 | Creating JFrame to display a smiley face. (Part 2 of 2.)

GUI and Graphics Case Study Exercises

6.1   Using method fillOval, draw a bull's-eye that alternates between two random colors, as in Fig. 6.18. Use the constructor Color(int r, int g, int b) with random arguments to generate random colors.

6.2   Create a program that draws 10 random filled shapes in random colors and at random positions (Fig. 6.19). Method paintComponent should contain a loop that iterates 10 times. In each iteration, the loop should determine whether to draw a filled rectangle or an oval, create a random color and choose coordinates and dimensions at random. The coordinates should be chosen based on the panel's width and height. Lengths of sides should be limited to half the width or height of the window. What happens each time paintComponent is called (i.e., the window is resized, uncovered, etc.)? We will resolve this issue in Chapter 8.

6.14 Wrap-Up

In this chapter, you learned more about the details of method declarations. You also learned the difference between non-static and static methods and how to call static methods by preceding the method name with the name of the class in which it appears and a dot (.). You learned how to use operator + to perform string concatenations. You learned how to declare named constants using both enum types and public final static variables. You saw how to use class Random to generate sets of random numbers that can be used for simulations. You also learned about the scope of fields and local variables in a class. Finally, you learned that multiple methods in one class can be overloaded by providing methods with the same name and different signatures. Such methods can be used to perform the same or similar tasks using different types or different numbers of parameters.

In Chapter 7, you will learn how to maintain lists and tables of data in arrays. You will see a more elegant implementation of the application that rolls a die 6000 times and two enhanced versions of our GradeBook case study that you studied in Chapters 3–5. You will also learn how to access an application's command-line arguments that are passed to method main when an application begins execution.

Fig. 6.18 | A bull's-eye with two alternating, random colors.

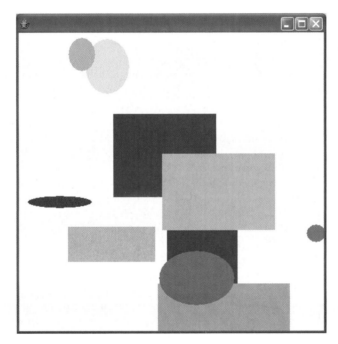

Fig. 6.19 | Randomly generated shapes.

Summary

- Experience has shown that the best way to develop and maintain a large program is to construct it from small, simple pieces, or modules. This technique is called divide and conquer.
- There are three kinds of modules in Java—methods, classes and packages. Methods are declared within classes. Classes are typically grouped into packages so that they can be imported into programs and reused.
- Methods allow the programmer to modularize a program by separating its tasks into self-contained units. The statements in a method are written only once and hidden from other methods.

- Using existing methods as building blocks to create new programs is a form of software reusability that allows programmers to avoid repeating code within a program.

- A method call specifies the name of the method to call and provides the arguments that the called method requires to perform its task. When the method call completes, the method returns either a result or simply control to its caller.

- A class may contain static methods to perform common tasks that do not require an object of the class. Any data a static method might require to perform its tasks can be sent to the method as arguments in a method call. A static method is called by specifying the name of the class in which the method is declared followed by a dot (.) and the method name, as in

    ClassName.*methodName*(*arguments*)

- Method arguments may be constants, variables or expressions.

- Class Math provides static methods for performing common mathematical calculations. Class Math declares two fields that represent commonly used mathematical constants: Math.PI and Math.E. The constant Math.PI (3.14159265358979323846) is the ratio of a circle's circumference to its diameter. The constant Math.E (2.7182818284590452354) is the base value for natural logarithms (calculated with static Math method log).

- Math.PI and Math.E are declared with the modifiers public, final and static. Making them public allows other programmers to use these fields in their own classes. Any field declared with keyword final is constant—its value cannot be changed after the field is initialized. Both PI and E are declared final because their values never change. Making these fields static allows them to be accessed via the class name Math and a dot (.) separator, just like class Math's methods.

- When objects of a class containing static fields (class variables) are created, all the objects of that class share one copy of the class's static fields. Together the class variables and instance variables represent the fields of a class. You will learn more about static fields in Section 8.11.

- When you execute the Java Virtual Machine (JVM) with the java command, the JVM attempts to invoke the main method of the class you specify. The JVM loads the class specified by *ClassName* and uses that class name to invoke method main. You can specify an optional list of Strings (separated by spaces) as command-line arguments that the JVM will pass to your application.

- You can place a main method in every class you declare—only the main method in the class you use to execute the application will be called. Some programmers take advantage of this to build a small test program into each class they declare.

- When a method is called, the program makes a copy of the method's argument values and assigns them to the method's corresponding parameters, which are created and initialized when the method is called. When program control returns to the point in the program where the method was called, the method's parameters are removed from memory.

- A method can return at most one value, but the returned value could be a reference to an object that contains many values.

- Variables should be declared as fields of a class only if they are required for use in more than one method of the class or if the program should save their values between calls to the class's methods.

- There are three ways to call a method—using a method name by itself to call another method of the same class; using a variable that contains a reference to an object, followed by a dot (.) and the method name to call a method of the referenced object; and using the class name and a dot (.) to call a static method of a class.

- There are three ways to return control to a statement that calls a method. If the method does not return a result, control returns when the program flow reaches the method-ending right brace or when the statement

```
return;
```

is executed. If the method returns a result, the statement

```
return expression;
```

evaluates the *expression*, then immediately returns the resulting value to the caller.

- When a method has more than one parameter, the parameters are specified as a comma-separated list. There must be one argument in the method call for each parameter in the method declaration. Also, each argument must be consistent with the type of the corresponding parameter. If a method does not accept arguments, the parameter list is empty.

- Strings can be concatenated using operator +, which places the characters of the right operand at the end of those in the left operand.

- Every primitive value and object in Java has a String representation. When an object is concatenated with a String, the object is converted to a String, then the two Strings are concatenated.

- For primitive values used in string concatenation, the JVM handles the conversion of the primitive values to Strings. If a boolean is concatenated with a String, the word "true" or the word "false" is used to represent the boolean value. If there are any trailing zeros in a floating-point value, these will be discarded when the number is concatenated to a String.

- All objects in Java have a special method named toString that returns a String representation of the object's contents. When an object is concatenated with a String, the JVM implicitly calls the object's toString method to obtain the string representation of the object.

- When a large String literal is typed into a program's source code, programmers sometimes break that String into several smaller Strings and place them on multiple lines of code for readability, then reassemble the Strings using concatenation.

- Stacks are known as last-in, first-out (LIFO) data structures—the last item pushed (inserted) on the stack is the first item popped (removed) from the stack.

- A called method must know how to return to its caller, so the return address of the calling method is pushed onto the program execution stack when the method is called. If a series of method calls occurs, the successive return addresses are pushed onto the stack in last-in, first-out order so that the last method to execute will be the first to return to its caller.

- The program execution stack contains the memory for the local variables used in each invocation of a method during a program's execution. This data is known as the activation record or stack frame of the method call. When a method call is made, the activation record for that method call is pushed onto the program execution stack. When the method returns to its caller, the activation record for this method call is popped off the stack and those local variables are no longer known to the program. If a local variable holding a reference to an object is the only variable in the program with a reference to that object, when the activation record containing that local variable is popped off the stack, the object can no longer be accessed by the program and will eventually be deleted from memory by the JVM during "garbage collection."

- The amount of memory in a computer is finite, so only a certain amount of memory can be used to store activation records on the program execution stack. If there are more method calls than can have their activation records stored on the program execution stack, an error known as a stack overflow occurs. The application will compile correctly, but its execution causes a stack overflow.

- An important feature of method calls is argument promotion—converting an argument's value to the type that the method expects to receive in its corresponding parameter.

- A set of promotion rules apply to expressions containing values of two or more primitive types and to primitive-type values passed as arguments to methods. Each value is promoted to the "highest" type in the expression. In cases where information may be lost due to conversion, the Java compiler requires the programmer to use a cast operator to explicitly force the conversion to occur.

- Objects of class `Random` (package `java.util`) can produce random `int`, `long`, `float` or `double` values. `Math` method `random` can produce `double` values in the range $0.0 \leq x < 1.0$, where x is the value returned by method `random`.

- `Random` method `nextInt` generates a random `int` value in the range $-2,147,483,648$ to $+2,147,483,647$. The values returned by `nextInt` are actually pseudorandom numbers—a sequence of values produced by a complex mathematical calculation. That calculation uses the current time of day to seed the random-number generator such that each execution of a program yields a different sequence of random values.

- Class `Random` provides another version of method `nextInt` that receives an `int` argument and returns a value from 0 up to, but not including, the argument's value.

- Random numbers in a range can be generated with

      number = *shiftingValue* + randomNumbers.nextInt(*scalingFactor*);

  where *shiftingValue* specifies the first number in the desired range of consecutive integers, and *scalingFactor* specifies how many numbers are in the range.

- Random numbers can be chosen from nonconsecutive integer ranges, as in

      number = *shiftingValue* +
          differenceBetweenValues * randomNumbers.nextInt(*scalingFactor*);

  where *shiftingValue* specifies the first number in the range of values, *differenceBetweenValues* represents the difference between consecutive numbers in the sequence and *scalingFactor* specifies how many numbers are in the range.

- For debugging, it is sometimes useful to repeat the same sequence of pseudorandom numbers during each program execution to prove that your application is working for a specific sequence of random numbers before testing the program with different sequences of random numbers. When repeatability is important, you can create a `Random` object by passing a `long` integer value to the constructor. If the same seed is used every time the program executes, the `Random` object produces the same sequence of random numbers. You can also set a `Random` object's seed at any time by calling the object's `setSeed` method.

- An enumeration is introduced by the keyword `enum` (new to J2SE 5.0) and a type name. As with any class, braces (`{` and `}`) delimit the body of an `enum` declaration. Inside the braces is a comma-separated list of enumeration constants, each representing a unique value. The identifiers in an `enum` must be unique. Variables of an `enum` type can be assigned only constants of that `enum` type.

- Constants can also be declared as `public final static` variables. Such constants are declared with all capital letters by convention to make them stand out in the program.

- Scope is the portion of the program in which an entity, such as a variable or a method, can be referred to by its name. Such an entity is said to be "in scope" for that portion of the program.

- The scope of a parameter declaration is the body of the method in which the declaration appears.

- The scope of a local-variable declaration is from the point at which the declaration appears to the end of that block.

- The scope of a label in a labeled `break` or `continue` statement is the labeled statement's body.

- The scope of a local-variable declaration that appears in the initialization section of a `for` statement's header is the body of the `for` statement and the other expressions in the header.

- The scope of a method or field of a class is the entire body of the class. This enables a class's methods to use simple names to call the class's other methods and to access the class's fields.

- Any block may contain variable declarations. If a local variable or parameter in a method has the same name as a field, the field is shadowed until the block terminates execution.

- Java allows several methods of the same name to be declared in a class, as long as the methods have different sets of parameters (determined by the number, order and types of the parameters). This technique is called method overloading.

- Overloaded methods are distinguished by their signatures—combinations of the methods' names and the number, types and order of their parameters. Methods cannot be distinguished by return type.

Terminology

activation record
application programming interface
argument promotion
block
class variable
class method
comma-separated list of parameters
command-line argument
divide-and-conquer approach
element of chance
enum keyword
enumeration
enumeration constant
final keyword
formal parameter
function
"hidden" fields
hide implementation details
hierarchical boss method/worker method
    relationship
invoke a method
Java API documentation
Java Application Programming Interface (API)
last-in, first-out (LIFO) data structure
local variable
make your point (game of craps)
method call
method call stack
method declaration
method overloading
modularizing a program with methods
module

nextInt method of Random
overload method
package
parameter
parameter list
popping (from a stack)
primitive type promotions
procedure
program execution stack
programmer-declared method
promotion rules
pushing (onto a stack)
pseudorandom number
Random class
random method of Math
random numbers
return keyword
reusable software components
scaling factor (random numbers)
scope of a declaration
seed value (random numbers)
setSeed method of Random
shadow a field
shift a range (random numbers)
shifting value (random numbers)
signature of a method
simulation
software reuse
stack
stack frame
stack overflow
string concatenation

Self-Review Exercises

6.1 Fill in the blanks in each of the following statements:
  a) A method is invoked with a(n) _____.
  b) A variable known only within the method in which it is declared is called a(n) _____.

c) The _____ statement in a called method can be used to pass the value of an expression back to the calling method.

d) The keyword _____ indicates that a method does not return a value.

e) Data can be added or removed only from the _____ of a stack.

f) Stacks are known as _____ data structures—the last item pushed (inserted) on the stack is the first item popped (removed) from the stack.

g) The three ways to return control from a called method to a caller are _____, _____ and _____.

h) An object of class _____ produces random numbers.

i) The program execution stack contains the memory for local variables on each invocation of a method during a program's execution. This data, stored as a portion of the program execution stack, is known as the _____ or _____ of the method call.

j) If there are more method calls than can be stored on the program execution stack, an error known as a(n) _____ occurs.

k) The _____ of a declaration is the portion of a program that can refer to the entity in the declaration by name.

l) In Java, it is possible to have several methods with the same name that each operate on different types or numbers of arguments. This feature is called method _____.

m) The program execution stack is also referred to as the _____ stack.

6.2   For the class Craps in Fig. 6.9, state the scope of each of the following entities:
a) the variable randomNumbers.
b) the variable die1.
c) the method rollDice.
d) the method play.
e) the variable sumOfDice.

6.3   Write an application that tests whether the examples of the Math class method calls shown in Fig. 6.2 actually produce the indicated results.

6.4   Give the method header for each of the following methods:
a) Method hypotenuse, which takes two double-precision, floating-point arguments side1 and side2 and returns a double-precision, floating-point result.
b) Method smallest, which takes three integers x, y and z and returns an integer.
c) Method instructions, which does not take any arguments and does not return a value. [*Note*: Such methods are commonly used to display instructions to a user.]
d) Method intToFloat, which takes an integer argument number and returns a floating-point result.

6.5   Find the error in each of the following program segments. Explain how to correct the error.
a)
```java
int g()
{
    System.out.println( "Inside method g" );
    int h()
    {
        System.out.println( "Inside method h" );
    }
}
```
b)
```java
int sum( int x, int y )
{
    int result;
    result = x + y;
}
```

c) void f(float a);
```
    {
       float a;
       System.out.println( a );
    }
```
d) void product()
```
    {
       int a = 6, b = 5, c = 4, result;
       result = a * b * c;
       System.out.printf( "Result is %d\n", result );
       return result;
    }
```

6.6   Write a complete Java application to prompt the user for the `double` radius of a sphere, and call method `sphereVolume` to calculate and display the volume of the sphere. Use the following statement to calculate the volume:

```
double volume = ( 4.0 / 3.0 ) * Math.PI * Math.pow( radius, 3 )
```

Answers to Self-Review Exercises

6.1   a) method call. b) local variable. c) `return`. d) `void`. e) top. f) last-in, first-out (LIFO).
g) `return;` or `return` *expression*; or encountering the closing right brace of a method. h) `Random`.
i) activation record, stack frame. j) stack overflow. k) scope. l) overloading. m) method call.

6.2   a) class body. b) block that defines method `rollDice`'s body. c) class body. d) class body.
e) block that defines method `play`'s body.

6.3   The following solution demonstrates the `Math` class methods in Fig. 6.2:

```
1   // Exercise 6.3: MathTest.java
2   // Testing the Math class methods.
3
4   public class MathTest
5   {
6      public static void main( String args[] )
7      {
8         System.out.printf( "Math.abs( 23.7 ) = %f\n", Math.abs( 23.7 ) );
9         System.out.printf( "Math.abs( 0.0 ) = %f\n", Math.abs( 0.0 ) );
10        System.out.printf( "Math.abs( -23.7 ) = %f\n", Math.abs( -23.7 ) );
11        System.out.printf( "Math.ceil( 9.2 ) = %f\n", Math.ceil( 9.2 ) );
12        System.out.printf( "Math.ceil( -9.8 ) = %f\n", Math.ceil( -9.8 ) );
13        System.out.printf( "Math.cos( 0.0 ) = %f\n", Math.cos( 0.0 ) );
14        System.out.printf( "Math.exp( 1.0 ) = %f\n", Math.exp( 1.0 ) );
15        System.out.printf( "Math.exp( 2.0 ) = %f\n", Math.exp( 2.0 ) );
16        System.out.printf( "Math.floor( 9.2 ) = %f\n", Math.floor( 9.2 ) );
17        System.out.printf( "Math.floor( -9.8 ) = %f\n",
18           Math.floor( -9.8 ) );
19        System.out.printf( "Math.log( Math.E ) = %f\n",
20           Math.log( Math.E ) );
21        System.out.printf( "Math.log( Math.E * Math.E ) = %f\n",
22           Math.log( Math.E * Math.E ) );
23        System.out.printf( "Math.max( 2.3, 12.7 ) = %f\n",
24           Math.max( 2.3, 12.7 ) );
```

```
25        System.out.printf( "Math.max( -2.3, -12.7 ) = %f\n",
26           Math.max( -2.3, -12.7 ) );
27        System.out.printf( "Math.min( 2.3, 12.7 ) = %f\n",
28           Math.min( 2.3, 12.7 ) );
29        System.out.printf( "Math.min( -2.3, -12.7 ) = %f\n",
30           Math.min( -2.3, -12.7 ) );
31        System.out.printf( "Math.pow( 2.0, 7.0 ) = %f\n",
32           Math.pow( 2.0, 7.0 ) );
33        System.out.printf( "Math.pow( 9.0, 0.5 ) = %f\n",
34           Math.pow( 9.0, 0.5 ) );
35        System.out.printf( "Math.sin( 0.0 ) = %f\n", Math.sin( 0.0 ) );
36        System.out.printf( "Math.sqrt( 900.0 ) = %f\n",
37           Math.sqrt( 900.0 ) );
38        System.out.printf( "Math.sqrt( 9.0 ) = %f\n", Math.sqrt( 9.0 ) );
39        System.out.printf( "Math.tan( 0.0 ) = %f\n", Math.tan( 0.0 ) );
40     } // end main
41  } // end class MathTest
```

```
Math.abs( 23.7 ) = 23.700000
Math.abs( 0.0 ) = 0.000000
Math.abs( -23.7 ) = 23.700000
Math.ceil( 9.2 ) = 10.000000
Math.ceil( -9.8 ) = -9.000000
Math.cos( 0.0 ) = 1.000000
Math.exp( 1.0 ) = 2.718282
Math.exp( 2.0 ) = 7.389056
Math.floor( 9.2 ) = 9.000000
Math.floor( -9.8 ) = -10.000000
Math.log( Math.E ) = 1.000000
Math.log( Math.E * Math.E ) = 2.000000
Math.max( 2.3, 12.7 ) = 12.700000
Math.max( -2.3, -12.7 ) = -2.300000
Math.min( 2.3, 12.7 ) = 2.300000
Math.min( -2.3, -12.7 ) = -12.700000
Math.pow( 2.0, 7.0 ) = 128.000000
Math.pow( 9.0, 0.5 ) = 3.000000
Math.sin( 0.0 ) = 0.000000
Math.sqrt( 900.0 ) = 30.000000
Math.sqrt( 9.0 ) = 3.000000
Math.tan( 0.0 ) = 0.000000
```

6.4   a) `double hypotenuse( double side1, double side2 )`
       b) `int smallest( int x, int y, int z )`
       c) `void instructions()`
       d) `float intToFloat( int number )`

6.5   a) Error: Method h is declared within method g.
           Correction: Move the declaration of h outside the declaration of g.
       b) Error: The method is supposed to return an integer, but does not.
           Correction: Delete the variable `result`, and place the statement
               `return x + y;`
           in the method, or add the following statement at the end of the method body:
               `return result;`

c) Error: The semicolon after the right parenthesis of the parameter list is incorrect, and the parameter a should not be redeclared in the method.
Correction: Delete the semicolon after the right parenthesis of the parameter list, and delete the declaration float a;.

d) Error: The method returns a value when it is not supposed to.
Correction: Change the return type from void to int.

6.6   The following solution calculates the volume of a sphere, using the radius entered by the user:

```java
1   // Exercise 6.6: Sphere.java
2   // Calculate the volume of a sphere.
3   import java.util.Scanner;
4
5   public class Sphere
6   {
7      // obtain radius from user and display volume of sphere
8      public void determineSphereVolume()
9      {
10        Scanner input = new Scanner( System.in );
11
12        System.out.print( "Enter radius of sphere: " );
13        double radius = input.nextDouble();
14
15        System.out.printf( "Volume is %f\n", sphereVolume( radius ) );
16     } // end method determineSphereVolume
17
18     // calculate and return sphere volume
19     public double sphereVolume( double radius )
20     {
21        double volume = ( 4.0 / 3.0 ) * Math.PI * Math.pow( radius, 3 );
22        return volume;
23     } // end method sphereVolume
24  } // end class Sphere
```

```java
1   // Exercise 6.6: SphereTest.java
2   // Calculate the volume of a sphere.
3
4   public class SphereTest
5   {
6      // application starting point
7      public static void main( String args[] )
8      {
9         Sphere mySphere = new Sphere();
10        mySphere.determineSphereVolume();
11     } // end main
12  } // end class SphereTest
```

```
Enter radius of sphere: 4
Volume is 268.082573
```

Exercises

6.7 What is the value of x after each of the following statements is executed?
a) x = Math.abs(7.5);
b) x = Math.floor(7.5);
c) x = Math.abs(0.0);
d) x = Math.ceil(0.0);
e) x = Math.abs(-6.4);
f) x = Math.ceil(-6.4);
g) x = Math.ceil(-Math.abs(-8 + Math.floor(-5.5)));

6.8 A parking garage charges a $2.00 minimum fee to park for up to three hours. The garage charges an additional $0.50 per hour for each hour *or part thereof* in excess of three hours. The maximum charge for any given 24-hour period is $10.00. Assume that no car parks for longer than 24 hours at a time. Write an application that calculates and displays the parking charges for each customer who parked in the garage yesterday. You should enter the hours parked for each customer. The program should display the charge for the current customer and should calculate and display the running total of yesterday's receipts. The program should use the method calculateCharges to determine the charge for each customer.

6.9 An application of method Math.floor is rounding a value to the nearest integer. The statement

    y = Math.floor(x + 0.5);

will round the number x to the nearest integer and assign the result to y. Write an application that reads double values and uses the preceding statement to round each of the numbers to the nearest integer. For each number processed, display both the original number and the rounded number.

6.10 Math.floor may be used to round a number to a specific decimal place. The statement

    y = Math.floor(x * 10 + 0.5) / 10;

rounds x to the tenths position (i.e., the first position to the right of the decimal point). The statement

    y = Math.floor(x * 100 + 0.5) / 100;

rounds x to the hundredths position (i.e., the second position to the right of the decimal point). Write an application that defines four methods for rounding a number x in various ways:
a) roundToInteger(number)
b) roundToTenths(number)
c) roundToHundredths(number)
d) roundToThousandths(number)

For each value read, your program should display the original value, the number rounded to the nearest integer, the number rounded to the nearest tenth, the number rounded to the nearest hundredth and the number rounded to the nearest thousandth.

6.11 Answer each of the following questions:
a) What does it mean to choose numbers "at random?"
b) Why is the Math.random method useful for simulating games of chance?
c) Why is it often necessary to scale or shift the values produced by a Random object?
d) Why is computerized simulation of real-world situations a useful technique?

6.12 Write statements that assign random integers to the variable n in the following ranges:
a) $1 \leq n \leq 2$
b) $1 \leq n \leq 100$

    c) $0 \leq n \leq 9$
    d) $1000 \leq n \leq 1112$
    e) $-1 \leq n \leq 1$
    f) $-3 \leq n \leq 11$

6.13   For each of the following sets of integers, write a single statement that will display a number at random from the set:
    a) 2, 4, 6, 8, 10.
    b) 3, 5, 7, 9, 11.
    c) 6, 10, 14, 18, 22.

6.14   Write a method `integerPower( base, exponent )` that returns the value of

    $base^{\,exponent}$

For example, `integerPower( 3, 4 )` calculates 3^4 (or 3 * 3 * 3 * 3). Assume that exponent is a positive, nonzero integer and that base is an integer. Method `integerPower` should use a `for` or `while` loop to control the calculation. Do not use any math-library methods. Incorporate this method into an application that reads integer values for base and exponent and performs the calculation with the `integerPower` method.

6.15   Define a method `hypotenuse` that calculates the length of the hypotenuse of a right triangle when the lengths of the other two sides are given. (Use the sample data in Fig. 6.20.) The method should take two arguments of type `double` and return the hypotenuse as a `double`. Incorporate this method into an application that reads values for `side1` and `side2` and performs the calculation with the `hypotenuse` method. Determine the length of the hypotenuse for each of the triangles in Fig. 6.20.

6.16   Write a method `multiple` that determines, for a pair of integers, whether the second integer is a multiple of the first. The method should take two integer arguments and return `true` if the second is a multiple of the first and `false` otherwise. Incorporate this method into an application that inputs a series of pairs of integers (one pair at a time) and determines whether the second value in each pair is a multiple of the first.

6.17   Write a method `isEven` that uses the remainder operator (%) to determine whether an integer is even. The method should take an integer argument and return `true` if the integer is even and `false` otherwise. Incorporate this method into an application that inputs a sequence of integers (one at a time) and determines whether each is even or odd.

6.18   Write a method `squareOfAsterisks` that displays a solid square (the same number of rows and columns) of asterisks whose side is specified in integer parameter `side`. For example, if `side` is 4, the method should display

```
****
****
****
****
```

Triangle	Side 1	Side 2
1	3.0	4.0
2	5.0	12.0
3	8.0	15.0

Fig. 6.20 | Values for the sides of triangles in Exercise 6.15.

Incorporate this method into an application that reads an integer value for side from the user and outputs the asterisks with the squareOfAsterisks method.

6.19   Modify the method created in Exercise 6.18 to form the square out of whatever character is contained in character parameter fillCharacter. Thus, if side is 5 and fillCharacter is "#", the method should display

```
#####
#####
#####
#####
#####
```

6.20   Write an application that prompts the user for the radius of a circle and uses a method called circleArea to calculate the area of the circle.

6.21   Write program segments that accomplish each of the following tasks:
   a)   Calculate the integer part of the quotient when integer a is divided by integer b.
   b)   Calculate the integer remainder when integer a is divided by integer b.
   c)   Use the program pieces developed in parts (a) and (b) to write a method displayDigits that receives an integer between 1 and 99999 and displays it as a sequence of digits, separating each pair of digits by two spaces. For example, the integer 4562 should appear as

```
4   5   6   2
```

   d)   Incorporate the method developed in part (c) into an application that inputs an integer and calls displayDigits by passing the method the integer entered. Display the results.

6.22   Implement the following integer methods:
   a)   Method celsius returns the Celsius equivalent of a Fahrenheit temperature, using the calculation

```
C = 5.0 / 9.0 * ( F - 32 );
```

   b)   Method fahrenheit returns the Fahrenheit equivalent of a Celsius temperature, using the calculation

```
F = 9.0 / 5.0 * C + 32;
```

   c)   Use the methods from parts (a) and (b) to write an application that enables the user either to enter a Fahrenheit temperature and display the Celsius equivalent or to enter a Celsius temperature and display the Fahrenheit equivalent.

6.23   Write a method minimum3 that returns the smallest of three floating-point numbers. Use the Math.min method to implement minimum3. Incorporate the method into an application that reads three values from the user, determines the smallest value and displays the result.

6.24   An integer number is said to be a *perfect number* if its factors, including 1 (but not the number itself), sum to the number. For example, 6 is a perfect number, because 6 = 1 + 2 + 3. Write a method perfect that determines whether parameter number is a perfect number. Use this method in an application that determines and displays all the perfect numbers between 1 and 1000. Display the factors of each perfect number to confirm that the number is indeed perfect. Challenge the computing power of your computer by testing numbers much larger than 1000. Display the results.

6.25   An integer is said to be *prime* if it is divisible by only 1 and itself. For example, 2, 3, 5 and 7 are prime, but 4, 6, 8 and 9 are not.
   a)   Write a method that determines whether a number is prime.
   b)   Use this method in an application that determines and displays all the prime numbers less than 10,000. How many numbers up to 10,000 do you have to test to ensure that you have found all the primes?

c) Initially, you might think that *n*/2 is the upper limit for which you must test to see whether a number is prime, but you need only go as high as the square root of *n*. Why? Rewrite the program, and run it both ways. Estimate the performance improvement.

6.26   Write a method that takes an integer value and returns the number with its digits reversed. For example, given the number 7631, the method should return 1367. Incorporate the method into an application that reads a value from the user and displays the result.

6.27   The *greatest common divisor* (*GCD*) of two integers is the largest integer that evenly divides each of the two numbers. Write a method gcd that returns the greatest common divisor of two integers. Incorporate the method into an application that reads two values from the user and displays the result.

6.28   Write a method qualityPoints that inputs a student's average and returns 4 if the student's average is 90–100, 3 if the average is 80–89, 2 if the average is 70–79, 1 if the average is 60–69 and 0 if the average is lower than 60. Incorporate the method into an application that reads a value from the user and displays the result.

6.29   Write an application that simulates coin tossing. Let the program toss a coin each time the user chooses the "Toss Coin" menu option. Count the number of times each side of the coin appears. Display the results. The program should call a separate method flip that takes no arguments and returns false for tails and true for heads. [*Note*: If the program realistically simulates coin tossing, each side of the coin should appear approximately half the time.]

6.30   Computers are playing an increasing role in education. Write a program that will help an elementary school student learn multiplication. Use a Random object to produce two positive one-digit integers. The program should then prompt the user with a question, such as

```
How much is 6 times 7?
```

The student then inputs the answer. Next, the program checks the student's answer. If it is correct, display the message "Very good!" and ask another multiplication question. If the answer is wrong, display the message "No. Please try again." and let the student try the same question repeatedly until the student finally gets it right. A separate method should be used to generate each new question. This method should be called once when the application begins execution and each time the user answers the question correctly.

6.31   The use of computers in education is referred to as *computer-assisted instruction* (*CAI*). One problem that develops in CAI environments is student fatigue. This problem can be eliminated by varying the computer's responses to hold the student's attention. Modify the program of Exercise 6.30 so that the various comments are displayed for each correct answer and each incorrect answer as follows:

Responses to a correct answer:

```
Very good!
Excellent!
Nice work!
Keep up the good work!
```

Responses to an incorrect answer:

```
No. Please try again.
Wrong. Try once more.
Don't give up!
No. Keep trying.
```

Use random-number generation to choose a number from 1 to 4 that will be used to select an appropriate response to each answer. Use a switch statement to issue the responses.

6.32 More sophisticated computer-assisted instruction systems monitor the student's performance over a period of time. The decision to begin a new topic is often based on the student's success with previous topics. Modify the program of Exercise 6.31 to count the number of correct and incorrect responses typed by the student. After the student types 10 answers, your program should calculate the percentage of correct responses. If the percentage is lower than 75%, display Please ask your instructor for extra help and reset the program so another student can try it.

6.33 Write an application that plays "guess the number" as follows: Your program chooses the number to be guessed by selecting a random integer in the range 1 to 1000. The application displays the prompt Guess a number between 1 and 1000. The player inputs a first guess. If the player's guess is incorrect, your program should display Too high. Try again. or Too low. Try again. to help the player "zero in" on the correct answer. The program should prompt the user for the next guess. When the user enters the correct answer, display Congratulations. You guessed the number!, and allow the user to choose whether to play again. [*Note*: The guessing technique employed in this problem is similar to that used in a binary search.]

6.34 Modify the program of Exercise 6.33 to count the number of guesses the player makes. If the number is 10 or fewer, display Either you know the secret or you got lucky! If the player guesses the number in 10 tries, display Aha! You know the secret! If the player makes more than 10 guesses, display You should be able to do better! Why should it take no more than 10 guesses? Well, with each "good guess," the player should be able to eliminate half of the numbers. Now show why any number from 1 to 1000 can be guessed in 10 or fewer tries.

6.35 Exercise 6.30 through Exercise 6.32 developed a computer-assisted instruction program to teach an elementary school student multiplication. Perform the following enhancements:

a) Modify the program to allow the user to enter a school grade-level capability. A grade level of 1 means that the program should use only single-digit numbers in the problems, a grade level of 2 means that the program should use numbers as large as two digits, and so on.

b) Modify the program to allow the user to pick the type of arithmetic problems he or she wishes to study. An option of 1 means addition problems only, 2 means subtraction problems only, 3 means multiplication problems only, 4 means division problems only and 5 means a random mixture of problems of all these types.

6.36 Write method distance to calculate the distance between two points ($x1$, $y1$) and ($x2$, $y2$). All numbers and return values should be of type double. Incorporate this method into an application that enables the user to enter the coordinates of the points.

6.37 Modify the craps program of Fig. 6.9 to allow wagering. Initialize variable bankBalance to 1000 dollars. Prompt the player to enter a wager. Check that wager is less than or equal to bankBalance, and if it is not, have the user reenter wager until a valid wager is entered. After a correct wager is entered, run one game of craps. If the player wins, increase bankBalance by wager and display the new bankBalance. If the player loses, decrease bankBalance by wager, display the new bankBalance, check whether bankBalance has become zero and, if so, display the message "Sorry. You busted!" As the game progresses, display various messages to create some "chatter," such as "Oh, you're going for broke, huh?" or "Aw c'mon, take a chance!" or "You're up big. Now's the time to cash in your chips!". Implement the "chatter" as a separate method that randomly chooses the string to display.

6.38 Write an application that displays a table of the binary, octal, and hexadecimal equivalents of the decimal numbers in the range 1 through 256. If you are not familiar with these number systems, read Appendix E first.

7

Arrays

OBJECTIVES

In this chapter you will learn:

- What arrays are.
- To use arrays to store data in and retrieve data from lists and tables of values.
- To declare an array, initialize an array and refer to individual elements of an array.
- To use the enhanced **for** statement to iterate through arrays.
- To pass arrays to methods.
- To declare and manipulate multidimensional arrays.
- To write methods that use variable-length argument lists.
- To read command-line arguments into a program.

7.1 Introduction

This chapter introduces the important topic of data structures—collections of related data items. Arrays are data structures consisting of related data items of the same type. Arrays are fixed-length entities—they remain the same length once they are created, although an array variable may be reassigned such that it refers to a new array of a different length.

After discussing how arrays are declared, created and initialized, this chapter presents a series of practical examples that demonstrate several common array manipulations. We also present a case study that examines how arrays can help simulate the shuffling and dealing of playing cards for use in an application that implements a card game. The chapter then introduces Java's enhanced `for` statement, which allows a program to access the data in an array more easily than the counter-controlled `for` statement presented in Section 5.3 does. Two sections of the chapter enhance the case study of class `GradeBook` in Chapters 3–5. In particular, we use arrays to enable the class to maintain a set of grades in memory and analyze student grades from multiple exams in a semester—two capabilities that were absent from previous versions of the class. These and other chapter examples demonstrate the ways in which arrays allow programmers to organize and manipulate data.

7.2 Arrays

An array is a group of variables (called elements or components) containing values that all have the same type. Recall that types are divided into two categories—primitive types and reference types. Arrays are objects, so they are considered reference types. As you will soon see, what we typically think of as an array is actually a reference to an array object in memory. The elements of an array can be either primitive types or reference types (including arrays, as we will see in Section 7.9). To refer to a particular element in an array, we specify the name of the reference to the array and the position number of the element in the array. The position number of the element is called the element's index or subscript.

Figure 7.1 shows a logical representation of an integer array called c. This array contains 12 elements. A program refers to any one of these elements with an array-access expression that includes the name of the array followed by the index of the particular element in square brackets ([]). The first element in every array has index zero and is sometimes called the zeroth element. Thus, the elements of array c are c[0], c[1], c[2] and so on. The highest index in array c is 11, which is 1 less than 12—the number of elements in the array. Array names follow the same conventions as other variable names.

An index must be a nonnegative integer. A program can use an expression as an index. For example, if we assume that variable a is 5 and variable b is 6, then the statement

```
c[ a + b ] += 2;
```

adds 2 to array element c[11]. Note that an indexed array name is an array-access expression. Such expressions can be used on the left side of an assignment to place a new value into an array element.

Common Programming Error 7.1

Using a value of type long as an array index results in a compilation error. An index must be an int value or a value of a type that can be promoted to int—namely, byte, short or char, but not long.

Let us examine array c in Fig. 7.1 more closely. The name of the array is c. Every array object knows its own length and maintains this information in a length field. The expression c.length accesses array c's length field to determine the length of the array. Note that, even though the length member of an array is public, it cannot be changed because it is a final variable. This array's 12 elements are referred to as c[0], c[1], c[2], ..., c[11]. The value of c[0] is -45, the value of c[1] is 6, the value of c[2] is 0, the value

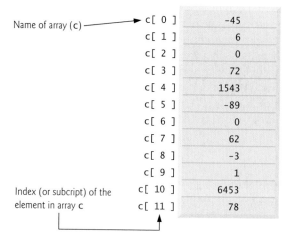

c[0]	−45
c[1]	6
c[2]	0
c[3]	72
c[4]	1543
c[5]	−89
c[6]	0
c[7]	62
c[8]	−3
c[9]	1
c[10]	6453
c[11]	78

Name of array (c)

Index (or subcript) of the element in array c

Fig. 7.1 | A 12-element array.

of c[7] is 62 and the value of c[11] is 78. To calculate the sum of the values contained in the first three elements of array c and store the result in variable sum, we would write

```
sum = c[ 0 ] + c[ 1 ] + c[ 2 ];
```

To divide the value of c[6] by 2 and assign the result to the variable x, we would write

```
x = c[ 6 ] / 2;
```

7.3 Declaring and Creating Arrays

Array objects occupy space in memory. Like other objects, arrays are created with keyword new. To create an array object, the programmer specifies the type of the array elements and the number of elements as part of an array-creation expression that uses keyword new. Such an expression returns a reference that can be stored in an array variable. The following declaration and array-creation expression create an array object containing 12 int elements and store the array's reference in variable c:

```
int c[] = new int[ 12 ];
```

This expression can be used to create the array shown in Fig. 7.1. This task also can be performed in two steps as follows:

```
int c[];            // declare the array variable
c = new int[ 12 ];  // create the array; assign to array variable
```

In the declaration, the square brackets following the variable name c indicate that c is a variable that will refer to an array (i.e., the variable will store an array reference). In the assignment statement, the array variable c receives the reference to a new array of 12 int elements. When an array is created, each element of the array receives a default value—zero for the numeric primitive-type elements, false for boolean elements and null for references (any nonprimitive type). As we will soon see, we can provide specific, nondefault initial element values when we create an array.

Common Programming Error 7.2

In an array declaration, specifying the number of elements in the square brackets of the declaration (e.g., int c[12];*) is a syntax error.*

A program can create several arrays in a single declaration. The following String array declaration reserves 100 elements for b and 27 elements for x:

```
String b[] = new String[ 100 ], x[] = new String[ 27 ];
```

In this case, the class name String applies to each variable in the declaration. For readability, we prefer to declare only one variable per declaration, as in:

```
String b[] = new String[ 100 ]; // create array b
String x[] = new String[ 27 ]; // create array x
```

Good Programming Practice 7.1

For readability, declare only one variable per declaration. Keep each declaration on a separate line, and include a comment describing the variable being declared.

When an array is declared, the type of the array and the square brackets can be combined at the beginning of the declaration to indicate that all the identifiers in the declaration are array variables. For example, the declaration

```
double[] array1, array2;
```

indicates that `array1` and `array2` are "array of `double`" variables. The preceding declaration is equivalent to:

```
double array1[];
double array2[];
```

or

```
double[] array1;
double[] array2;
```

The preceding pairs of declarations are equivalent—when only one variable is declared in each declaration, the square brackets can be placed either after the type or after the array variable name.

Common Programming Error 7.3

Declaring multiple array variables in a single declaration can lead to subtle errors. Consider the declaration `int[] a, b, c;`. If a, b and c should be declared as array variables, then this declaration is correct—placing square brackets directly following the type indicates that all the identifiers in the declaration are array variables. However, if only a is intended to be an array variable, and b and c are intended to be individual `int` variables, then this declaration is incorrect—the declaration `int a[], b, c;` would achieve the desired result.

A program can declare arrays of any type. Every element of a primitive-type array contains a value of the array's declared type. Similarly, in an array of a reference type, every element is a reference to an object of the array's declared type. For example, every element of an `int` array is an `int` value, and every element of a `String` array is a reference to a `String` object.

7.4 Examples Using Arrays

This section presents several examples that demonstrate declaring arrays, creating arrays, initializing arrays and manipulating array elements.

Creating and Initializing an Array

The application of Fig. 7.2 uses keyword `new` to create an array of 10 `int` elements, which are initially zero (the default for `int` variables).

Line 8 declares `array`—a reference capable of referring to an array of `int` elements. Line 10 creates the array object and assigns its reference to variable `array`. Line 12 outputs the column headings. The first column contains the index (0–9) of each array element, and the second column contains the default value (0) of each array element.

The `for` statement in lines 15–16 outputs the index number (represented by `counter`) and value of each array element (represented by `array[ counter ]`). Note that the loop control variable `counter` is initially 0—index values start at 0, so using zero-based counting allows the loop to access every element of the array. The `for`'s loop-continuation condition uses the expression `array.length` (line 15) to determine the length of the array. In this example, the length of the array is 10, so the loop continues executing as long as

```
 1   // Fig. 7.2: InitArray.java
 2   // Creating an array.
 3
 4   public class InitArray
 5   {
 6      public static void main( String args[] )
 7      {
 8         int array[]; // declare array named array
 9
10         array = new int[ 10 ]; // create the space for array
11
12         System.out.printf( "%s%8s\n", "Index", "Value" ); // column headings
13
14         // output each array element's value
15         for ( int counter = 0; counter < array.length; counter++ )
16            System.out.printf( "%5d%8d\n", counter, array[ counter ] );
17      } // end main
18   } // end class InitArray
```

```
Index   Value
    0       0
    1       0
    2       0
    3       0
    4       0
    5       0
    6       0
    7       0
    8       0
    9       0
```

Fig. 7.2 | Initializing the elements of an array to default values of zero.

the value of control variable counter is less than 10. The highest index value of a 10-element array is 9, so using the less-than operator in the loop-continuation condition guarantees that the loop does not attempt to access an element beyond the end of the array (i.e., during the final iteration of the loop, counter is 9). We will soon see what Java does when it encounters such an out-of-range index at execution time.

Using an Array Initializer

A program can create an array and initialize its elements with an array initializer, which is a comma-separated list of expressions (called an initializer list) enclosed in braces ({ and }). In this case, the array length is determined by the number of elements in the initializer list. For example, the declaration

```
int n[] = { 10, 20, 30, 40, 50 };
```

creates a five-element array with index values 0, 1, 2, 3 and 4. Element n[0] is initialized to 10, n[1] is initialized to 20, and so on. This declaration does not require new to create the array object. When the compiler encounters an array declaration that includes an initializer list, the compiler counts the number of initializers in the list to determine the size of the array, then sets up the appropriate new operation "behind the scenes."

The application in Fig. 7.3 initializes an integer array with 10 values (line 9) and displays the array in tabular format. The code for displaying the array elements (lines 14–15) is identical to that in Fig. 7.2 (lines 15–16).

Calculating a Value to Store in Each Array Element

Some programs calculate the value stored in each array element. The application in Fig. 7.4 creates a 10-element array and assigns to each element one of the even integers from 2 to 20 (2, 4, 6, ..., 20). Then the application displays the array in tabular format. The for statement at lines 12–13 calculates an array element's value by multiplying the current value of the for loop's control variable counter by 2, then adding 2.

Line 8 uses the modifier final to declare the constant variable ARRAY_LENGTH, whose value is 10. Constant variables (also known as final variables) must be initialized before they are used and cannot be modified thereafter. If an attempt is made to modify a final variable after it is initialized in its declaration (as in line 8), the compiler issues the error message

```
cannot assign a value to final variable variableName
```

```
 1   // Fig. 7.3: InitArray.java
 2   // Initializing the elements of an array with an array initializer.
 3
 4   public class InitArray
 5   {
 6      public static void main( String args[] )
 7      {
 8         // initializer list specifies the value for each element
 9         int array[] = { 32, 27, 64, 18, 95, 14, 90, 70, 60, 37 };
10
11         System.out.printf( "%s%8s\n", "Index", "Value" ); // column headings
12
13         // output each array element's value
14         for ( int counter = 0; counter < array.length; counter++ )
15            System.out.printf( "%5d%8d\n", counter, array[ counter ] );
16      } // end main
17   } // end class InitArray
```

```
Index   Value
    0      32
    1      27
    2      64
    3      18
    4      95
    5      14
    6      90
    7      70
    8      60
    9      37
```

Fig. 7.3 | Initializing the elements of an array with an array initializer.

```
1   // Fig. 7.4: InitArray.java
2   // Calculating values to be placed into elements of an array.
3
4   public class InitArray
5   {
6      public static void main( String args[] )
7      {
8         final int ARRAY_LENGTH = 10; // declare constant
9         int array[] = new int[ ARRAY_LENGTH ]; // create array
10
11         // calculate value for each array element
12         for ( int counter = 0; counter < array.length; counter++ )
13            array[ counter ] = 2 + 2 * counter;
14
15         System.out.printf( "%s%8s\n", "Index", "Value" ); // column headings
16
17         // output each array element's value
18         for ( int counter = 0; counter < array.length; counter++ )
19            System.out.printf( "%5d%8d\n", counter, array[ counter ] );
20      } // end main
21   } // end class InitArray
```

```
Index   Value
    0       2
    1       4
    2       6
    3       8
    4      10
    5      12
    6      14
    7      16
    8      18
    9      20
```

Fig. 7.4 | Calculating values to be placed into elements of an array.

If an attempt is made to access the value of a `final` variable before it is initialized, the compiler issues the error message

    variable *variableName* might not have been initialized

Good Programming Practice 7.2

Constant variables also are called named constants or read-only variables. Such variables often make programs more readable than programs that use literal values (e.g., 10)—a named constant such as ARRAY_LENGTH clearly indicates its purpose, whereas a literal value could have different meanings based on the context in which it is used.

Common Programming Error 7.4

Assigning a value to a constant after the variable has been initialized is a compilation error.

Common Programming Error 7.5

Attempting to use a constant before it is initialized is a compilation error.

Summing the Elements of an Array

Often, the elements of an array represent a series of values to be used in a calculation. For example, if the elements of an array represent exam grades, a professor may wish to total the elements of the array and use that sum to calculate the class average for the exam. The examples using class GradeBook later in the chapter, namely Fig. 7.14 and Fig. 7.18, use this technique.

The application in Fig. 7.5 sums the values contained in a 10-element integer array. The program declares, creates and initializes the array at line 8. The for statement performs the calculations. [*Note:* The values supplied as array initializers are often read into a program rather than specified in an initializer list. For example, an application could input the values from a user or from a file on disk. Reading the data into a program makes the program more reusable, because it can be used with different sets of data.]

Using Bar Charts to Display Array Data Graphically

Many programs present data to users in a graphical manner. For example, numeric values are often displayed as bars in a bar chart. In such a chart, longer bars represent proportionally larger numeric values. One simple way to display numeric data graphically is with a bar chart that shows each numeric value as a bar of asterisks (*).

Professors often like to examine the distribution of grades on an exam. A professor might graph the number of grades in each of several categories to visualize the grade distribution for the exam. Suppose the grades on an exam were 87, 68, 94, 100, 83, 78, 85, 91, 76 and 87. Note that there was one grade of 100, two grades in the 90s, four grades in the 80s, two grades in the 70s, one grade in the 60s and no grades below 60. Our next applica-

```java
 1    // Fig. 7.5: SumArray.java
 2    // Computing the sum of the elements of an array.
 3
 4    public class SumArray
 5    {
 6       public static void main( String args[] )
 7       {
 8          int array[] = { 87, 68, 94, 100, 83, 78, 85, 91, 76, 87 };
 9          int total = 0;
10
11          // add each element's value to total
12          for ( int counter = 0; counter < array.length; counter++ )
13             total += array[ counter ];
14
15          System.out.printf( "Total of array elements: %d\n", total );
16       } // end main
17    } // end class SumArray
```

```
Total of array elements: 849
```

Fig. 7.5 | Computing the sum of the elements of an array.

```
1   // Fig. 7.6: BarChart.java
2   // Bar chart printing program.
3
4   public class BarChart
5   {
6      public static void main( String args[] )
7      {
8         int array[] = { 0, 0, 0, 0, 0, 0, 1, 2, 4, 2, 1 };
9
10        System.out.println( "Grade distribution:" );
11
12        // for each array element, output a bar of the chart
13        for ( int counter = 0; counter < array.length; counter++ )
14        {
15           // output bar label ( "00-09: ", ..., "90-99: ", "100: " )
16           if ( counter == 10 )
17              System.out.printf( "%5d: ", 100 );
18           else
19              System.out.printf( "%02d-%02d: ",
20                 counter * 10, counter * 10 + 9 );
21
22           // print bar of asterisks
23           for ( int stars = 0; stars < array[ counter ]; stars++ )
24              System.out.print( "*" );
25
26           System.out.println(); // start a new line of output
27        } // end outer for
28     } // end main
29  } // end class BarChart
```

```
Grade distribution:
00-09:
10-19:
20-29:
30-39:
40-49:
50-59:
60-69: *
70-79: **
80-89: ****
90-99: **
  100: *
```

Fig. 7.6 | Bar chart printing program.

tion (Fig. 7.6) stores this grade distribution data in an array of 11 elements, each corresponding to a category of grades. For example, array[0] indicates the number of grades in the range 0–9, array[7] indicates the number of grades in the range 70–79 and array[10] indicates the number of 100 grades. The two versions of class GradeBook later in the chapter (Fig. 7.14 and Fig. 7.18) contain code that calculates these grade frequencies based on a set of grades. For now, we manually create the array by looking at the set of grades.

The application reads the numbers from the array and graphs the information as a bar chart. The program displays each grade range followed by a bar of asterisks indicating the number of grades in that range. To label each bar, lines 16–20 output a grade range (e.g., "70-79: ") based on the current value of counter. When counter is 10, line 17 outputs 100 with a field width of 5, followed by a colon and a space, to align the label "100: " with the other bar labels. The nested for statement (lines 23–24) outputs the bars. Note the loop-continuation condition at line 23 (stars < array[counter]). Each time the program reaches the inner for, the loop counts from 0 up to array[counter], thus using a value in array to determine the number of asterisks to display. In this example, array[0]– array[5] contain zeroes because no students received a grade below 60. Thus, the program displays no asterisks next to the first six grade ranges. Note that line 19 uses the format specifier %02d to output the numbers in a grade range. This specifier indicates that an int value should be formatted as a field of two digits. The 0 flag in the format specifier indicates that values with fewer digits than the field width (2) should begin with a leading 0.

Using the Elements of an Array as Counters

Sometimes, programs use counter variables to summarize data, such as the results of a survey. In Fig. 6.8, we used separate counters in our die-rolling program to track the number of occurrences of each side of a die as the program rolled the die 6000 times. An array version of the application in Fig. 6.8 is shown in Fig. 7.7.

```java
1   // Fig. 7.7: RollDie.java
2   // Roll a six-sided die 6000 times.
3   import java.util.Random;
4
5   public class RollDie
6   {
7      public static void main( String args[] )
8      {
9         Random randomNumbers = new Random(); // random number generator
10        int frequency[] = new int[ 7 ]; // array of frequency counters
11
12        // roll die 6000 times; use die value as frequency index
13        for ( int roll = 1; roll <= 6000; roll++ )
14           ++frequency[ 1 + randomNumbers.nextInt( 6 ) ];
15
16        System.out.printf( "%s%10s\n", "Face", "Frequency" );
17
18        // output each array element's value
19        for ( int face = 1; face < frequency.length; face++ )
20           System.out.printf( "%4d%10d\n", face, frequency[ face ] );
21     } // end main
22  } // end class RollDie
```

```
Face Frequency
   1       988
   2       963
   3      1018
   4      1041
   5       978
   6      1012
```

Fig. 7.7 | Die-rolling program using arrays instead of switch.

Fig. 7.7 uses the array frequency (line 10) to count the occurrences of each side of the die. *The single statement in line 14 of this program replaces lines 23–46 of Fig. 6.8.* Line 14 uses the random value to determine which frequency element to increment during each iteration of the loop. The calculation in line 14 produces random numbers from 1 to 6, so array frequency must be large enough to store six counters. However, we use a seven-element array in which we ignore frequency[0]—it is more logical to have the face value 1 increment frequency[1] than frequency[0]. Thus, each face value is used as an index for array frequency. We also replaced lines 50–52 from Fig. 6.8 by looping through array frequency to output the results (lines 19–20).

Using Arrays to Analyze Survey Results

Our next example uses arrays to summarize the results of data collected in a survey:

> *Forty students were asked to rate the quality of the food in the student cafeteria on a scale of 1 to 10 (where 1 means awful and 10 means excellent). Place the 40 responses in an integer array, and summarize the results of the poll.*

This is a typical array-processing application (see Fig. 7.8). We wish to summarize the number of responses of each type (i.e., 1 through 10). The array responses (lines 9–11) is a 40-element integer array of the students' responses to the survey. We use an 11-element array frequency (line 12) to count the number of occurrences of each response. Each element of the array is used as a counter for one of the survey responses and is initialized to zero by default. As in Fig. 7.7, we ignore frequency[0].

```
1   // Fig. 7.8: StudentPoll.java
2   // Poll analysis program.
3
4   public class StudentPoll
5   {
6      public static void main( String args[] )
7      {
8         // array of survey responses
9         int responses[] = { 1, 2, 6, 4, 8, 5, 9, 7, 8, 10, 1, 6, 3, 8, 6,
10           10, 3, 8, 2, 7, 6, 5, 7, 6, 8, 6, 7, 5, 6, 6, 5, 6, 7, 5, 6,
11           4, 8, 6, 8, 10 };
12        int frequency[] = new int[ 11 ]; // array of frequency counters
13
14        // for each answer, select responses element and use that value
15        // as frequency index to determine element to increment
16        for ( int answer = 0; answer < responses.length; answer++ )
17           ++frequency[ responses[ answer ] ];
18
19        System.out.printf( "%s%10s", "Rating", "Frequency" );
20
21        // output each array element's value
22        for ( int rating = 1; rating < frequency.length; rating++ )
23           System.out.printf( "%d%10d", rating, frequency[ rating ] );
24     } // end main
25  } // end class StudentPoll
```

Fig. 7.8 | Poll analysis program. (Part 1 of 2.)

```
Rating Frequency
    1        2
    2        2
    3        2
    4        2
    5        5
    6       11
    7        5
    8        7
    9        1
   10        3
```

Fig. 7.8 | Poll analysis program. (Part 2 of 2.)

The for loop at lines 16–17 takes the responses one at a time from array responses and increments one of the 10 counters in the frequency array (frequency[1] to frequency[10]). The key statement in the loop is line 17, which increments the appropriate frequency counter, depending on the value of responses[answer].

Let's consider several iterations of the for loop. When control variable answer is 0, the value of responses[answer] is the value of responses[0] (i.e., 1), so the program interprets ++frequency[responses[answer]] as

        ++frequency[1]

which increments the value in array element 1. To evaluate the expression, start with the value in the innermost set of square brackets (answer). Once you know answer's value (which is the value of the loop control variable in line 16), plug it into the expression and evaluate the next outer set of square brackets (i.e., responses[answer], which is a value selected from the responses array in lines 9–11). Then use the resulting value as the index for the frequency array to specify which counter to increment.

When answer is 1, responses[answer] is the value of responses[1] (2), so the program interprets ++frequency[responses[answer]] as

        ++frequency[2]

which increments array element 2.

When answer is 2, responses[answer] is the value of responses[2] (6), so the program interprets ++frequency[responses[answer]] as

        ++frequency[6]

which increments array element 6, and so on. Regardless of the number of responses processed in the survey, the program requires only an 11-element array (ignoring element zero) to summarize the results, because all the response values are between 1 and 10 and the index values for an 11-element array are 0 through 10.

If the data in the responses array had contained invalid values, such as 13, the program would have attempted to add 1 to frequency[13], which is outside the bounds of the array. Java disallows this. When a Java program executes, the JVM checks array indices to ensure that they are valid (i.e., they must be greater than or equal to 0 and less than the length of the array). If a program uses an invalid index, Java generates a so-called exception to indicate that an error occurred in the program at execution time. A control statement can be used to prevent such an "out-of-bounds" error from occurring. For example, the condition in a control statement could determine whether an index is valid before allowing it to be used in an array-access expression.

Error-Prevention Tip 7.1

An exception indicates that an error has occurred in a program. A programmer often can write code to recover from an exception and continue program execution, rather than abnormally terminating the program. When a program attempts to access an element outside the array bounds, an `ArrayIndexOutOfBoundsException` *occurs.*

Error-Prevention Tip 7.2

When writing code to loop through an array, ensure that the array index is always greater than or equal to 0 and less than the length of the array. The loop-continuation condition should prevent the accessing of elements outside this range.

7.5 Case Study: Card Shuffling and Dealing Simulation

The examples in the chapter thus far have used arrays containing elements of primitive types. Recall from Section 7.2 that the elements of an array can be either primitive types or reference types. This section uses random number generation and an array of reference-type elements, namely objects representing playing cards, to develop a class that simulates card shuffling and dealing. This class can then be used to implement applications that play specific card games. The exercises at the end of the chapter use the classes developed here to build a simple poker application.

We first develop class `Card` (Fig. 7.9), which represents a playing card that has a face (e.g., `"Ace"`, `"Deuce"`, `"Three"`, …, `"Jack"`, `"Queen"`, `"King"`) and a suit (e.g., `"Hearts"`, `"Diamonds"`, `"Clubs"`, `"Spades"`). Next, we develop the `DeckOfCards` class (Fig. 7.10), which creates a deck of 52 playing cards in which each element is a `Card` object. We then build a test application (Fig. 7.11) that demonstrates class `DeckOfCards`'s card shuffling and dealing capabilities.

Class *Card*

Class `Card` (Fig. 7.9) contains two `String` instance variables—`face` and `suit`—that are used to store references to the face name and suit name for a specific `Card`. The constructor for the class (lines 10–14) receives two `Strings` that it uses to initialize `face` and `suit`. Method `toString` (lines 17–20) creates a `String` consisting of the `face` of the card, the `String " of "` and the `suit` of the card. Recall from Chapter 6 that the + operator can be used to concatenate (i.e., combine) several `Strings` to form one larger `String`. `Card`'s `toString` method can be invoked explicitly to obtain a string representation of a `Card` object (e.g., `"Ace of Spades"`). The `toString` method of an object is called implicitly when the object is used where a `String` is expected (e.g., when `printf` outputs the object as a `String` using the `%s` format specifier or when the object is concatenated to a `String` using the + operator). For this behavior to occur, `toString` must be declared with the header shown in Fig. 7.9.

```
 1    // Fig. 7.9: Card.java
 2    // Card class represents a playing card.
 3
 4    public class Card
 5    {
 6       private String face; // face of card ("Ace", "Deuce", ...)
 7       private String suit; // suit of card ("Hearts", "Diamonds", ...)
 8
 9       // two-argument constructor initializes card's face and suit
10       public Card( String cardFace, String cardSuit )
11       {
12          face = cardFace; // initialize face of card
13          suit = cardSuit; // initialize suit of card
14       } // end two-argument Card constructor
15
16       // return String representation of Card
17       public String toString()
18       {
19          return face + " of " + suit;
20       } // end method toString
21    } // end class Card
```

Fig. 7.9 | Card class represents a playing card.

Class DeckOfCards

Class DeckOfCards (Fig. 7.10) declares an instance variable array named deck of Card objects (line 7). Like primitive-type array declarations, the declaration of an array of objects includes the type of the elements in the array, followed by the name of the array variable and square brackets (e.g., Card deck[]). Class DeckOfCards also declares an integer instance variable currentCard (line 8) representing the next Card to be dealt from the deck array and a named constant NUMBER_OF_CARDS (line 9) indicating the number of Cards in the deck (52).

```
 1    // Fig. 7.10: DeckOfCards.java
 2    // DeckOfCards class represents a deck of playing cards.
 3    import java.util.Random;
 4
 5    public class DeckOfCards
 6    {
 7       private Card deck[]; // array of Card objects
 8       private int currentCard; // index of next Card to be dealt
 9       private final int NUMBER_OF_CARDS = 52; // constant number of Cards
10       private Random randomNumbers; // random number generator
11
12       // constructor fills deck of Cards
13       public DeckOfCards()
14       {
15          String faces[] = { "Ace", "Deuce", "Three", "Four", "Five", "Six",
16             "Seven", "Eight", "Nine", "Ten", "Jack", "Queen", "King" };
17          String suits[] = { "Hearts", "Diamonds", "Clubs", "Spades" };
```

Fig. 7.10 | DeckOfCards class represents a deck of playing cards that can be shuffled and dealt one at a time. (Part I of 2.)

```
18
19        deck = new Card[ NUMBER_OF_CARDS ]; // create array of Card objects
20        currentCard = 0; // set currentCard so first Card dealt is deck[ 0 ]
21        randomNumbers = new Random(); // create random number generator
22
23        // populate deck with Card objects
24        for ( int count = 0; count < deck.length; count++ )
25           deck[ count ] =
26              new Card( faces[ count % 13 ], suits[ count / 13 ] );
27     } // end DeckOfCards constructor
28
29     // shuffle deck of Cards with one-pass algorithm
30     public void shuffle()
31     {
32        // after shuffling, dealing should start at deck[ 0 ] again
33        currentCard = 0; // reinitialize currentCard
34
35        // for each Card, pick another random Card and swap them
36        for ( int first = 0; first < deck.length; first++ )
37        {
38           // select a random number between 0 and 51
39           int second =  randomNumbers.nextInt( NUMBER_OF_CARDS );
40
41           // swap current Card with randomly selected Card
42           Card temp = deck[ first ];
43           deck[ first ] = deck[ second ];
44           deck[ second ] = temp;
45        } // end for
46     } // end method shuffle
47
48     // deal one Card
49     public Card dealCard()
50     {
51        // determine whether Cards remain to be dealt
52        if ( currentCard < deck.length )
53           return deck[ currentCard++ ]; // return current Card in array
54        else
55           return null; // return null to indicate that all Cards were dealt
56     } // end method dealCard
57  } // end class DeckOfCards
```

Fig. 7.10 | DeckOfCards class represents a deck of playing cards that can be shuffled and dealt one at a time. (Part 2 of 2.)

The class's constructor instantiates the deck array (line 19) to be of size NUMBER_OF_CARDS. When first created, the elements of the deck array are null by default, so the constructor uses a for statement (lines 24–26) to fill the deck array with Cards. The for statement initializes control variable count to 0 and loops while count is less than deck.length, causing count to take on each integer value from 0 to 51 (the indices of the deck array). Each Card is instantiated and initialized with two Strings—one from the faces array (which contains the Strings "Ace" through "King") and one from the suits array (which contains the Strings "Hearts", "Diamonds", "Clubs" and "Spades"). The calculation count % 13 always results in a value from 0 to 12 (the 13 indices of the faces array in lines 15–16), and the calculation count / 13 always results in a value from 0 to 3 (the four indices of the suits array in line 17). When the deck array is initialized, it contains the Cards with faces "Ace" through "King" in order for each suit.

Method shuffle (lines 30–46) shuffles the Cards in the deck. The method loops through all 52 Cards (array indices 0 to 51). For each Card, a number between 0 and 51 is picked randomly to select another Card. Next, the current Card object and the randomly selected Card object are swapped in the array. This exchange is performed by the three assignments in lines 42–44. The extra variable temp temporarily stores one of the two Card objects being swapped. The swap cannot be performed with only the two statements

```
deck[ first ] = deck[ second ];
deck[ second ] = deck[ first ];
```

If deck[first] is the "Ace" of "Spades" and deck[second] is the "Queen" of "Hearts", after the first assignment, both array elements contain the "Queen" of "Hearts" and the "Ace" of "Spades" is lost—hence, the extra variable temp is needed. After the for loop terminates, the Card objects are randomly ordered. A total of only 52 swaps are made in a single pass of the entire array, and the array of Card objects is shuffled!

Method dealCard (lines 49–56) deals one Card in the array. Recall that currentCard indicates the index of the next Card to be dealt (i.e., the Card at the top of the deck). Thus, line 52 compares currentCard to the length of the deck array. If the deck is not empty (i.e., currentCard is less than 52), line 53 returns the top Card and increments current-Card to prepare for the next call to dealCard—otherwise, null is returned. Recall from Chapter 3 that null represents a "reference to nothing."

Shuffling and Dealing Cards

The application of Fig. 7.11 demonstrates the card dealing and shuffling capabilities of class DeckOfCards (Fig. 7.10). Line 9 creates a DeckOfCards object named myDeckOfCards. Recall that the DeckOfCards constructor creates the deck with the 52 Card objects in order by suit and face. Line 10 invokes myDeckOfCards's shuffle method to rearrange the Card objects. The for statement in lines 13–19 deals all 52 Cards in the deck and prints them in four columns of 13 Cards each. Lines 16–18 deal and print four Card objects, each obtained by invoking myDeckOfCards's dealCard method. When printf outputs a Card with the %-20s format specifier, the Card's toString method (declared in lines 17–20 of Fig. 7.9) is implicitly invoked, and the result is output left justified in a field of width 20.

7.6 Enhanced for Statement

In previous examples, we demonstrated how to use counter-controlled for statements to iterate through the elements in an array. In this section, we introduce a feature new in J2SE 5.0—the enhanced for statement, which iterates through the elements of an array without using a counter. The syntax of an enhanced for statement is:

for (*parameter* : *arrayName*)
   statement

```
 1   // Fig. 7.11: DeckOfCardsTest.java
 2   // Card shuffling and dealing application.
 3
 4   public class DeckOfCardsTest
 5   {
 6      // execute application
 7      public static void main( String args[] )
 8      {
 9         DeckOfCards myDeckOfCards = new DeckOfCards();
10         myDeckOfCards.shuffle(); // place Cards in random order
11
12         // print all 52 Cards in the order in which they are dealt
13         for ( int i = 0; i < 13; i++ )
14         {
15            // deal and print 4 Cards
16            System.out.printf( "%-20s%-20s%-20s%-20s\n",
17               myDeckOfCards.dealCard(), myDeckOfCards.dealCard(),
18               myDeckOfCards.dealCard(), myDeckOfCards.dealCard() );
19         } // end for
20      } // end main
21   } // end class DeckOfCardsTest
```

Six of Spades	Eight of Spades	Six of Clubs	Nine of Hearts
Queen of Hearts	Seven of Clubs	Nine of Spades	King of Hearts
Three of Diamonds	Deuce of Clubs	Ace of Hearts	Ten of Spades
Four of Spades	Ace of Clubs	Seven of Diamonds	Four of Hearts
Three of Clubs	Deuce of Hearts	Five of Spades	Jack of Diamonds
King of Clubs	Ten of Hearts	Three of Hearts	Six of Diamonds
Queen of Clubs	Eight of Diamonds	Deuce of Diamonds	Ten of Diamonds
Three of Spades	King of Diamonds	Nine of Clubs	Six of Hearts
Ace of Spades	Four of Diamonds	Seven of Hearts	Eight of Clubs
Deuce of Spades	Eight of Hearts	Five of Hearts	Queen of Spades
Jack of Hearts	Seven of Spades	Four of Clubs	Nine of Diamonds
Ace of Diamonds	Queen of Diamonds	Five of Clubs	King of Spades
Five of Diamonds	Ten of Clubs	Jack of Spades	Jack of Clubs

Fig. 7.11 | Card shuffling and dealing.

where *parameter* has two parts—a type and an identifier (e.g., int number), and *arrayName* is the array through which to iterate. The type of the parameter must match the type of the elements in the array. As the next example illustrates, the identifier represents successive values in the array on successive iterations of the enhanced for statement.

Figure 7.12 uses the enhanced for statement to calculate the sum of the integers in an array of student grades (lines 12–13). The type specified in the parameter to the enhanced for is int, because array is an array containing int values—therefore, the loop will select one int value from the array during each iteration. The enhanced for statement iterates through successive values in the array one-by-one. The enhanced for header can be read concisely as "for each iteration, assign the next element of array to int variable number, then execute the following statement." Thus, for each iteration, identifier number represents an int value in array. Lines 12–13 are equivalent to the following counter-controlled repetition used in lines 12–13 of Fig. 7.5 to total the integers in array:

```
 1   // Fig. 7.12: EnhancedForTest.java
 2   // Using enhanced for statement to total integers in an array.
 3
 4   public class EnhancedForTest
 5   {
 6      public static void main( String args[] )
 7      {
 8         int array[] = { 87, 68, 94, 100, 83, 78, 85, 91, 76, 87 };
 9         int total = 0;
10
11         // add each element's value to total
12         for ( int number : array )
13            total += number;
14
15         System.out.printf( "Total of array elements: %d\n", total );
16      } // end main
17   } // end class EnhancedForTest
```

```
Total of array elements: 849
```

Fig. 7.12 | Using the enhanced for statement to total integers in an array.

```
for ( int counter = 0; counter < array.length; counter++ )
   total += array[ counter ];
```

The enhanced for statement simplifies the code for iterating through an array. Note, however, that the enhanced for statement can be used only to access array elements—it cannot be used to modify elements. If your program needs to modify elements, use the traditional counter-controlled for statement.

The enhanced for statement can be used in place of the counter-controlled for statement whenever code looping through an array does not require access to the counter indicating the index of the current array element. For example, totalling the integers in an array requires access only to the element values—the index of each element is irrelevant. However, if a program must use a counter for some reason other than simply to loop through an array (e.g., to print an index number next to each array element value, as in the examples earlier in this chapter), use the counter-controlled for statement.

7.7 Passing Arrays to Methods

This section demonstrates how to pass arrays and array elements as arguments to methods. At the end of the section, we discuss how all types of arguments are passed to methods. To pass an array argument to a method, specify the name of the array without any brackets. For example, if array hourlyTemperatures is declared as

```
double hourlyTemperatures[] = new double[ 24 ];
```

then the method call

```
modifyArray( hourlyTemperatures );
```

passes the reference of array `hourlyTemperatures` to method `modifyArray`. Every array object "knows" its own length (via its `length` field). Thus, when we pass an array object's reference into a method, we need not pass the array length as an additional argument.

For a method to receive an array reference through a method call, the method's parameter list must specify an array parameter. For example, the method header for method `modifyArray` might be written as

```
void modifyArray( int b[] )
```

indicating that `modifyArray` receives the reference of an integer array in parameter `b`. The method call passes array `hourlyTemperature`'s reference, so when the called method uses the array variable `b`, it refers to the same array object as `hourlyTemperatures` in the calling method.

When an argument to a method is an entire array or an individual array element of a reference type, the called method receives a copy of the reference. However, when an argument to a method is an individual array element of a primitive type, the called method receives a copy of the element's value. Such primitive values are called scalars or scalar quantities. To pass an individual array element to a method, use the indexed name of the array as an argument in the method call.

Figure 7.13 demonstrates the difference between passing an entire array and passing a primitive-type array element to a method. The enhanced `for` statement at lines 16–17 outputs the five elements of `array` (an array of `int` values). Line 19 invokes method `modifyArray`, passing `array` as an argument. Method `modifyArray` (lines 36–40) receives a copy of `array`'s reference and uses the reference to multiply each of `array`'s elements by 2. To prove that `array`'s elements were modified, the `for` statement at lines 23–24 outputs the five elements of `array` again. As the output shows, method `modifyArray` doubled the value of each element.

```java
1   // Fig. 7.13: PassArray.java
2   // Passing arrays and individual array elements to methods.
3
4   public class PassArray
5   {
6      // main creates array and calls modifyArray and modifyElement
7      public static void main( String args[] )
8      {
9         int array[] = { 1, 2, 3, 4, 5 };
10
11         System.out.println(
12            "Effects of passing reference to entire array:\n" +
13            "The values of the original array are:" );
14
15         // output original array elements
16         for ( int value : array )
17            System.out.printf( "   %d", value );
18
19         modifyArray( array ); // pass array reference
20         System.out.println( "\n\nThe values of the modified array are:" );
```

Fig. 7.13 | Passing arrays and individual array elements to methods. (Part 1 of 2.)

```
21
22          // output modified array elements
23          for ( int value : array )
24             System.out.printf( "   %d", value );
25
26          System.out.printf(
27             "\n\nEffects of passing array element value:\n" +
28             "array[3] before modifyElement: %d\n", array[ 3 ] );
29
30          modifyElement( array[ 3 ] ); // attempt to modify array[ 3 ]
31          System.out.printf(
32             "array[3] after modifyElement: %d\n", array[ 3 ] );
33       } // end main
34
35       // multiply each element of an array by 2
36       public static void modifyArray( int array2[] )
37       {
38          for ( int counter = 0; counter < array2.length; counter++ )
39             array2[ counter ] *= 2;
40       } // end method modifyArray
41
42       // multiply argument by 2
43       public static void modifyElement( int element )
44       {
45          element *= 2;
46          System.out.printf(
47             "Value of element in modifyElement: %d\n", element );
48       } // end method modifyElement
49    } // end class PassArray
```

```
Effects of passing reference to entire array:
The values of the original array are:
   1   2   3   4   5

The values of the modified array are:
   2   4   6   8   10

Effects of passing array element value:
array[3] before modifyElement: 8
Value of element in modifyElement: 16
array[3] after modifyElement: 8
```

Fig. 7.13 | Passing arrays and individual array elements to methods. (Part 2 of 2.)

Figure 7.13 next demonstrates that when a copy of an individual primitive-type array element is passed to a method, modifying the copy in the called method does not affect the original value of that element in the calling method's array. To show the value of array[3] before invoking method modifyElement, lines 26–28 output the value of array[3] (8). Line 30 calls method modifyElement and passes array[3] as an argument. Remember that array[3] is actually one int value (8) in array. Therefore, the program passes a copy of the value of array[3]. Method modifyElement (lines 43–48) multiplies the value received as an argument by 2, stores the result in its parameter element, then outputs the value of element (16). Since method parameters, like local variables, cease to exist when the method in which they are declared completes execution, the method parameter element is destroyed when method modifyElement terminates. Thus, when the program returns control to main, lines 31–32 output the unmodified value of array[3] (i.e., 8).

Notes on Passing Arguments to Methods

The preceding example demonstrated the different ways that arrays and primitive-type array elements are passed as arguments to methods. We now take a closer look at how arguments in general are passed to methods. Two ways to pass arguments in method calls in many programming languages are pass-by-value and pass-by-reference (also called call-by-value and call-by-reference). When an argument is passed by value, a copy of the argument's value is passed to the called method. The called method works exclusively with the copy. Changes to the called method's copy do not affect the original variable's value in the caller.

When an argument is passed by reference, the called method can access the argument's value in the caller directly and modify that data, if necessary. Pass-by-reference improves performance by eliminating the need to copy possibly large amounts of data.

Unlike some other languages, Java does not allow programmers to choose pass-by-value or pass-by-reference—all arguments are passed by value. A method call can pass two types of values to a method—copies of primitive values (e.g., values of type int and double) and copies of references to objects (including references to arrays). Objects themselves cannot be passed to methods. When a method modifies a primitive-type parameter, changes to the parameter have no effect on the original argument value in the calling method. For example, when line 30 in main of Fig. 7.13 passes array[3] to method modifyElement, the statement in line 45 that doubles the value of parameter element has no effect on the value of array[3] in main. This is also true for reference-type parameters. If you modify a reference-type parameter by assigning it the reference of another object, the parameter refers to the new object, but the reference stored in the caller's variable still refers to the original object.

Although an object's reference is passed by value, a method can still interact with the referenced object by calling its public methods using the copy of the object's reference. Since the reference stored in the parameter is a copy of the reference that was passed as an argument, the parameter in the called method and the argument in the calling method refer to the same object in memory. For example, in Fig. 7.13, both parameter array2 in method modifyArray and variable array in main refer to the same array object in memory. Any changes made using the parameter array2 are carried out on the same object that is referenced by the variable that was passed as an argument in the calling method. In Fig. 7.13, the changes made in modifyArray using array2 affect the contents of the array object referenced by array in main. Thus, with a reference to an object, the called method can manipulate the caller's object directly.

Performance Tip 7.1

Passing arrays by reference makes sense for performance reasons. If arrays were passed by value, a copy of each element would be passed. For large, frequently passed arrays, this would waste time and consume considerable storage for the copies of the arrays.

7.8 Case Study: Class GradeBook Using an Array to Store Grades

This section further evolves class GradeBook, introduced in Chapter 3 and expanded in Chapters 4–5. Recall that this class represents a grade book used by a professor to store and analyze a set of student grades. Previous versions of the class process a set of grades entered by the user, but do not maintain the individual grade values in instance variables of the class. Thus, repeat calculations require the user to reenter the same grades. One way to solve this problem would be to store each grade entered in an individual instance of the class. For example, we could create instance variables grade1, grade2, ..., grade10 in class GradeBook to store 10 student grades. However, the code to total the grades and determine the class average would be cumbersome, and the class would not be able to process any more than 10 grades at a time. In this section, we solve this problem by storing grades in an array.

*Storing Student Grades in an Array in Class **GradeBook***
The version of class GradeBook (Fig. 7.14) presented here uses an array of integers to store the grades of several students on a single exam. This eliminates the need to repeatedly input the same set of grades. Array grades is declared as an instance variable in line 7—therefore, each GradeBook object maintains its own set of grades. The class's constructor (lines 10–14) has two parameters—the name of the course and an array of grades. When an application (e.g., class GradeBookTest in Fig. 7.15) creates a GradeBook object, the application passes an existing int array to the constructor, which assigns the array's reference to instance variable grades (line 13). The size of the array grades is determined by the class that passes the array to the constructor. Thus, a GradeBook object can process a variable number of grades. The grade values in the passed array could have been input from a user or read from a file on disk (as discussed in Chapter 14). In our test application, we simply initialize an array with a set of grade values (Fig. 7.15, line 10). Once the grades are

```
 1   // Fig. 7.14: GradeBook.java
 2   // Grade book using an array to store test grades.
 3
 4   public class GradeBook
 5   {
 6      private String courseName; // name of course this GradeBook represents
 7      private int grades[]; // array of student grades
 8
 9      // two-argument constructor initializes courseName and grades array
10      public GradeBook( String name, int gradesArray[] )
11      {
12         courseName = name; // initialize courseName
13         grades = gradesArray; // store grades
14      } // end two-argument GradeBook constructor
15
16      // method to set the course name
17      public void setCourseName( String name )
18      {
19         courseName = name; // store the course name
20      } // end method setCourseName
```

Fig. 7.14 | GradeBook class using an array to store test grades. (Part 1 of 4.)

```
21
22      // method to retrieve the course name
23      public String getCourseName()
24      {
25         return courseName;
26      } // end method getCourseName
27
28      // display a welcome message to the GradeBook user
29      public void displayMessage()
30      {
31         // getCourseName gets the name of the course
32         System.out.printf( "Welcome to the grade book for\n%s!\n\n",
33            getCourseName() );
34      } // end method displayMessage
35
36      // perform various operations on the data
37      public void processGrades()
38      {
39         // output grades array
40         outputGrades();
41
42         // call method getAverage to calculate the average grade
43         System.out.printf( "\nClass average is %.2f\n", getAverage() );
44
45         // call methods getMinimum and getMaximum
46         System.out.printf( "Lowest grade is %d\nHighest grade is %d\n\n",
47            getMinimum(), getMaximum() );
48
49         // call outputBarChart to print grade distribution chart
50         outputBarChart();
51      } // end method processGrades
52
53      // find minimum grade
54      public int getMinimum()
55      {
56         int lowGrade = grades[ 0 ]; // assume grades[ 0 ] is smallest
57
58         // loop through grades array
59         for ( int grade : grades )
60         {
61            // if grade lower than lowGrade, assign it to lowGrade
62            if ( grade < lowGrade )
63               lowGrade = grade; // new lowest grade
64         } // end for
65
66         return lowGrade; // return lowest grade
67      } // end method getMinimum
68
69      // find maximum grade
70      public int getMaximum()
71      {
72         int highGrade = grades[ 0 ]; // assume grades[ 0 ] is largest
73
```

Fig. 7.14 | GradeBook class using an array to store test grades. (Part 2 of 4.)

```
74        // loop through grades array
75        for ( int grade : grades )
76        {
77           // if grade greater than highGrade, assign it to highGrade
78           if ( grade > highGrade )
79              highGrade = grade; // new highest grade
80        } // end for
81
82        return highGrade; // return highest grade
83     } // end method getMaximum
84
85     // determine average grade for test
86     public double getAverage()
87     {
88        int total = 0; // initialize total
89
90        // sum grades for one student
91        for ( int grade : grades )
92           total += grade;
93
94        // return average of grades
95        return (double) total / grades.length;
96     } // end method getAverage
97
98     // output bar chart displaying grade distribution
99     public void outputBarChart()
100    {
101       System.out.println( "Grade distribution:" );
102
103       // stores frequency of grades in each range of 10 grades
104       int frequency[] = new int[ 11 ];
105
106       // for each grade, increment the appropriate frequency
107       for ( int grade : grades )
108          ++frequency[ grade / 10 ];
109
110       // for each grade frequency, print bar in chart
111       for ( int count = 0; count < frequency.length; count++ )
112       {
113          // output bar label ( "00-09: ", ..., "90-99: ", "100: " )
114          if ( count == 10 )
115             System.out.printf( "%5d: ", 100 );
116          else
117             System.out.printf( "%02d-%02d: ",
118                count * 10, count * 10 + 9  );
119
120          // print bar of asterisks
121          for ( int stars = 0; stars < frequency[ count ]; stars++ )
122             System.out.print( "*" );
123
124          System.out.println(); // start a new line of output
125       } // end outer for
126    } // end method outputBarChart
```

Fig. 7.14 | GradeBook class using an array to store test grades. (Part 3 of 4.)

```
127
128     // output the contents of the grades array
129     public void outputGrades()
130     {
131        System.out.println( "The grades are:\n" );
132
133        // output each student's grade
134        for ( int student = 0; student < grades.length; student++ )
135           System.out.printf( "Student %2d: %3d\n",
136              student + 1, grades[ student ] );
137     } // end method outputGrades
138  } // end class GradeBook
```

Fig. 7.14 | GradeBook class using an array to store test grades. (Part 4 of 4.)

stored in instance variable grades of class GradeBook, all the class's methods can access the elements of grades as needed to perform various calculations.

Method processGrades (lines 37–51) contains a series of method calls that result in the output of a report summarizing the grades. Line 40 calls method outputGrades to print the contents of the array grades. Lines 134–136 in method outputGrades use a for statement to output each student's grade. A counter-controlled for must be used in this case, because lines 135–136 use counter variable student's value to output each grade next to a particular student number (see Fig. 7.15). Although array indices start at 0, a professor would typically number students starting at 1. Thus, lines 135–136 output student + 1 as the student number to produce grade labels "Student 1: ", "Student 2: ", and so on.

Method processGrades next calls method getAverage (line 43) to obtain the average of the grades in the array. Method getAverage (lines 86–96) uses an enhanced for statement to total the values in array grades before calculating the average. The parameter in the enhanced for's header (e.g., int grade) indicates that for each iteration, the int variable grade takes on a value in the array grades. Note that the averaging calculation in line 95 uses grades.length to determine the number of grades being averaged.

Lines 46–47 in method processGrades calls methods getMinimum and getMaximum to determine the lowest and highest grades of any student on the exam, respectively. Each of these methods uses an enhanced for statement to loop through array grades. Lines 59–64 in method getMinimum loop through the array, and lines 62–63 compare each grade to lowGrade. If a grade is less than lowGrade, lowGrade is set to that grade. When line 66 executes, lowGrade contains the lowest grade in the array. Method getMaximum (lines 70–83) works the same way as method getMinimum.

Finally, line 50 in method processGrades calls method outputBarChart to print a distribution chart of the grade data using a technique similar to that in Fig. 7.6. In that example, we manually calculated the number of grades in each category (i.e., 0–9, 10–19, …, 90–99 and 100) by simply looking at a set of grades. In this example, lines 107–108 use a technique similar to that in Fig. 7.7 and Fig. 7.8 to calculate the frequency of grades in each category. Line 104 declares and creates array frequency of 11 ints to store the frequency of grades in each grade category. For each grade in array grades, lines 107–108 increment the appropriate element of the frequency array. To determine which element to increment, line 108 divides the current grade by 10 using integer division. For example, if grade is 85, line 108 increments frequency[8] to update the count of grades in the range 80–89. Lines 111–125 next print the bar chart (see Fig. 7.15) based on the values in array frequency. Like lines 23–24 of Fig. 7.6, lines 121–122 of Fig. 7.14 use a value in array frequency to determine the number of asterisks to display in each bar.

Class *GradeBookTest* That Demonstrates Class *GradeBook*

The application of Fig. 7.15 creates an object of class GradeBook (Fig. 7.14) using the int array gradesArray (declared and initialized in line 10). Lines 12–13 pass a course name and gradesArray to the GradeBook constructor. Line 14 displays a welcome message, and line 15 invokes the GradeBook object's processGrades method. The output reveals the summary of the 10 grades in myGradeBook.

> **Software Engineering Observation 7.1**
>
> *A test harness (or test application) is responsible for creating an object of the class being tested and providing it with data. This data could come from any of several sources. Test data can be placed directly into an array with an array initializer, it can come from the user at the keyboard, it can come from a file, or it can come from a network. After passing this data to the class's constructor to instantiate the object, the test harness should call upon the object to test its methods and manipulate its data. Gathering data in the test harness like this allows the class to manipulate data from several sources.*

7.9 Multidimensional Arrays

Multidimensional arrays with two dimensions are often used to represent tables of values consisting of information arranged in rows and columns. To identify a particular table element, we must specify two indices. By convention, the first identifies the element's row and the second its column. Arrays that require two indices to identify a particular element are called two-dimensional arrays. (Multidimensional arrays can have more than two dimensions.) Java does not support multidimensional arrays directly, but it does allow the

```
1  // Fig. 7.15: GradeBookTest.java
2  // Creates GradeBook object using an array of grades.
3
4  public class GradeBookTest
5  {
6     // main method begins program execution
7     public static void main( String args[] )
8     {
9        // array of student grades
10       int gradesArray[] = { 87, 68, 94, 100, 83, 78, 85, 91, 76, 87 };
11
12       GradeBook myGradeBook = new GradeBook(
13          "CS101 Introduction to Java Programming", gradesArray );
14       myGradeBook.displayMessage();
15       myGradeBook.processGrades();
16    } // end main
17 } // end class GradeBookTest
```

Fig. 7.15 | GradeBookTest creates a GradeBook object using an array of grades, then invokes method processGrades to analyze them. (Part 1 of 2.)

```
Welcome to the grade book for
CS101 Introduction to Java Programming!

The grades are:

Student  1:   87
Student  2:   68
Student  3:   94
Student  4:  100
Student  5:   83
Student  6:   78
Student  7:   85
Student  8:   91
Student  9:   76
Student 10:   87

Class average is 84.90
Lowest grade is 68
Highest grade is 100

Grade distribution:
00-09:
10-19:
20-29:
30-39:
40-49:
50-59:
60-69: *
70-79: **
80-89: ****
90-99: **
  100: *
```

Fig. 7.15 | GradeBookTest creates a GradeBook object using an array of grades, then invokes method processGrades to analyze them. (Part 2 of 2.)

programmer to specify one-dimensional arrays whose elements are also one-dimensional arrays, thus achieving the same effect. Figure 7.16 illustrates a two-dimensional array a that contains three rows and four columns (i.e., a three-by-four array). In general, an array with *m* rows and *n* columns is called an *m-by-n array*.

Every element in array a is identified in Fig. 7.16 by an array-access expression of the form a[row][column]; a is the name of the array, and row and column are the indices that uniquely identify each element in array a by row and column number. Note that the names of the elements in row 0 all have a first index of 0, and the names of the elements in column 3 all have a second index of 3.

Arrays of One-Dimensional Arrays

Like one-dimensional arrays, multidimensional arrays can be initialized with array initializers in declarations. A two-dimensional array b with two rows and two columns could be declared and initialized with nested array initializers as follows:

```
int b[][] = { { 1, 2 }, { 3, 4 } };
```

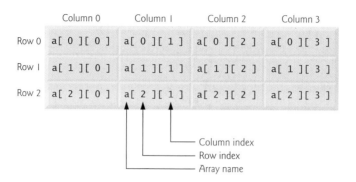

Fig. 7.16 | Two-dimensional array with three rows and four columns.

The initializer values are grouped by row in braces. So 1 and 2 initialize b[0][0] and b[0][1], respectively, and 3 and 4 initialize b[1][0] and b[1][1], respectively. The compiler counts the number of nested array initializers (represented by sets of braces within the outer braces) in the array declaration to determine the number of rows in array b. The compiler counts the initializer values in the nested array initializer for a row to determine the number of columns in that row. As we will see momentarily, this means that rows can have different lengths.

Multidimensional arrays are maintained as arrays of one-dimensional arrays. Therefore array b in the preceding declaration is actually composed of two separate one-dimensional arrays—one containing the values in the first nested initializer list { 1, 2 } and one containing the values in the second nested initializer list { 3, 4 }. Thus, array b itself is an array of two elements, each a one-dimensional array of int values.

Two-Dimensional Arrays with Rows of Different Lengths
The manner in which multidimensional arrays are represented makes them quite flexible. In fact, the lengths of the rows in array b are not required to be the same. For example,

```
int b[][] = { { 1, 2 }, { 3, 4, 5 } };
```

creates integer array b with two elements (determined by the number of nested array initializers) that represent the rows of the two-dimensional array. Each element of b is a reference to a one-dimensional array of int variables. The int array for row 0 is a one-dimensional array with two elements (1 and 2), and the int array for row 1 is a one-dimensional array with three elements (3, 4 and 5).

Creating Two-Dimensional Arrays with Array-Creation Expressions
A multidimensional array with the same number of columns in every row can be created with an array-creation expression. For example, the following lines declare array b and assign it a reference to a three-by-four array:

```
int b[][];
b = new int[ 3 ][ 4 ];
```

In this case, we use the literal values 3 and 4 to specify the number of rows and number of columns, respectively, but this is not required. Programs can also use variables to specify array dimensions. As with one-dimensional arrays, the elements of a multidimensional array are initialized when the array object is created.

A multidimensional array in which each row has a different number of columns can be created as follows:

```
int b[][];
b = new int[ 2 ][ ];    // create 2 rows
b[ 0 ] = new int[ 5 ]; // create 5 columns for row 0
b[ 1 ] = new int[ 3 ]; // create 3 columns for row 1
```

The preceding statements create a two-dimensional array with two rows. Row 0 has five columns, and row 1 has three columns.

Two-Dimensional Array Example: Displaying Element Values

Figure 7.17 demonstrates initializing two-dimensional arrays with array initializers and using nested for loops to traverse the arrays (i.e., manipulate every element of each array).

```
 1   // Fig. 7.17: InitArray.java
 2   // Initializing two-dimensional arrays.
 3
 4   public class InitArray
 5   {
 6      // create and output two-dimensional arrays
 7      public static void main( String args[] )
 8      {
 9         int array1[][] = { { 1, 2, 3 }, { 4, 5, 6 } };
10         int array2[][] = { { 1, 2 }, { 3 }, { 4, 5, 6 } };
11
12         System.out.println( "Values in array1 by row are" );
13         outputArray( array1 ); // displays array1 by row
14
15         System.out.println( "\nValues in array2 by row are" );
16         outputArray( array2 ); // displays array2 by row
17      } // end main
18
19      // output rows and columns of a two-dimensional array
20      public static void outputArray( int array[][] )
21      {
22         // loop through array's rows
23         for ( int row = 0; row < array.length; row++ )
24         {
25            // loop through columns of current row
26            for ( int column = 0; column < array[ row ].length; column++ )
27               System.out.printf( "%d  ", array[ row ][ column ] );
28
29            System.out.println(); // start new line of output
30         } // end outer for
31      } // end method outputArray
32   } // end class InitArray
```

Fig. 7.17 | Initializing two-dimensional arrays. (Part I of 2.)

```
Values in array1 by row are
1  2  3
4  5  6

Values in array2 by row are
1  2
3
4  5  6
```

Fig. 7.17 | Initializing two-dimensional arrays. (Part 2 of 2.)

Class `InitArray`'s main declares two arrays. The declaration of array1 (line 9) uses nested array initializers to initialize the first row of the array to the values 1, 2 and 3, and the second row to the values 4, 5 and 6. The declaration of array2 (line 10) uses nested initializers of different lengths. In this case, the first row is initialized to have two elements with values 1 and 2, respectively. The second row is initialized to have one element with value 3. The third row is initialized to have three elements with the values 4, 5 and 6, respectively.

Lines 13 and 16 call method `outputArray` (lines 20–31) to output the elements of array1 and array2, respectively. Method `outputArray` specifies the array parameter as `int array[][]` to indicate that the method receives a two-dimensional array. The for statement (lines 23–30) outputs the rows of a two-dimensional array. In the loop-continuation condition of the outer for statement, the expression `array.length` determines the number of rows in the array. In the inner for statement, the expression `array[ row ].length` determines the number of columns in the current row of the array. This condition enables the loop to determine the exact number of columns in each row.

Common Multidimensional-Array Manipulations Performed with for Statements
Many common array manipulations use for statements. As an example, the following for statement sets all the elements in row 2 of array a in Fig. 7.16 to zero:

```
for ( int column = 0; column < a[ 2 ].length; column++)
   a[ 2 ][ column ] = 0;
```

We specified row 2; therefore, we know that the first index is always 2 (0 is the first row, and 1 is the second row). This for loop varies only the second index (i.e., the column index). The preceding for statement is equivalent to the assignment statements

```
a[ 2 ][ 0 ] = 0;
a[ 2 ][ 1 ] = 0;
a[ 2 ][ 2 ] = 0;
a[ 2 ][ 3 ] = 0;
```

The following nested for statement totals the values of all the elements in array a:

```
int total = 0;

for ( int row = 0; row < a.length; row++ )
{
   for ( int column = 0; column < a[ row ].length; column++ )
      total += a[ row ][ column ];
} // end outer for
```

This nested for statements total the array elements one row at a time. The outer for statement begins by setting the row index to 0 so that the first row's elements may be totaled by the inner for statement. The outer for then increments row to 1 so that the second row can be totaled. Then, the outer for increments row to 2 so that the third row can be totaled. The variable total can be displayed when the outer for statement terminates. In the next example, we show how to process a two-dimensional array in a similar manner using nested enhanced for statements.

7.10 Case Study: Class GradeBook Using a Two-Dimensional Array

In Section 7.8, we presented class GradeBook (Fig. 7.14), which used a one-dimensional array to store student grades on a single exam. In most semesters, students take several exams. Professors are likely to want to analyze grades across the entire semester, both for a single student and for the class as a whole.

Storing Student Grades in a Two-Dimensional Array in Class GradeBook

Figure 7.18 contains a version of class GradeBook that uses a two-dimensional array grades to store the grades of a number of students on multiple exams. Each row of the array represents a single student's grades for the entire course, and each column represents a grade on one of the exams the students took during the course. An application such as GradeBookTest (Fig. 7.19) passes the array as an argument to the GradeBook constructor. In this example, we use a ten-by-three array containing ten students' grades on three exams. Five methods perform array manipulations to process the grades. Each method is similar to its counterpart in the earlier one-dimensional array version of class GradeBook (Fig. 7.14). Method getMinimum (lines 52–70) determines the lowest grade of any student for the semester. Method getMaximum (lines 73–91) determines the highest grade of any student for the semester. Method getAverage (lines 94–104) determines a particular student's semester average. Method outputBarChart (lines 107–137) outputs a bar chart of the distribution of all student grades for the semester. Method outputGrades (lines 140–164) outputs the two-dimensional array in a tabular format, along with each student's semester average.

```
 1   // Fig. 7.18: GradeBook.java
 2   // Grade book using a two-dimensional array to store grades.
 3
 4   public class GradeBook
 5   {
 6      private String courseName; // name of course this grade book represents
 7      private int grades[][]; // two-dimensional array of student grades
 8
 9      // two-argument constructor initializes courseName and grades array
10      public GradeBook( String name, int gradesArray[][] )
11      {
12         courseName = name; // initialize courseName
13         grades = gradesArray; // store grades
14      } // end two-argument GradeBook constructor
15
```

Fig. 7.18 | GradeBook class using a two-dimensional array to store grades. (Part 1 of 4.)

```
16      // method to set the course name
17      public void setCourseName( String name )
18      {
19         courseName = name; // store the course name
20      } // end method setCourseName
21
22      // method to retrieve the course name
23      public String getCourseName()
24      {
25         return courseName;
26      } // end method getCourseName
27
28      // display a welcome message to the GradeBook user
29      public void displayMessage()
30      {
31         // getCourseName gets the name of the course
32         System.out.printf( "Welcome to the grade book for\n%s!\n\n",
33            getCourseName() );
34      } // end method displayMessage
35
36      // perform various operations on the data
37      public void processGrades()
38      {
39         // output grades array
40         outputGrades();
41
42         // call methods getMinimum and getMaximum
43         System.out.printf( "\n%s %d\n%s %d\n\n",
44            "Lowest grade in the grade book is", getMinimum(),
45            "Highest grade in the grade book is", getMaximum() );
46
47         // output grade distribution chart of all grades on all tests
48         outputBarChart();
49      } // end method processGrades
50
51      // find minimum grade
52      public int getMinimum()
53      {
54         // assume first element of grades array is smallest
55         int lowGrade = grades[ 0 ][ 0 ];
56
57         // loop through rows of grades array
58         for ( int studentGrades[] : grades )
59         {
60            // loop through columns of current row
61            for ( int grade : studentGrades )
62            {
63               // if grade less than lowGrade, assign it to lowGrade
64               if ( grade < lowGrade )
65                  lowGrade = grade;
66            } // end inner for
67         } // end outer for
```

Fig. 7.18 | GradeBook class using a two-dimensional array to store grades. (Part 2 of 4.)

```
68
69          return lowGrade; // return lowest grade
70      } // end method getMinimum
71
72      // find maximum grade
73      public int getMaximum()
74      {
75          // assume first element of grades array is largest
76          int highGrade = grades[ 0 ][ 0 ];
77
78          // loop through rows of grades array
79          for ( int studentGrades[] : grades )
80          {
81              // loop through columns of current row
82              for ( int grade : studentGrades )
83              {
84                  // if grade greater than highGrade, assign it to highGrade
85                  if ( grade > highGrade )
86                      highGrade = grade;
87              } // end inner for
88          } // end outer for
89
90          return highGrade; // return highest grade
91      } // end method getMaximum
92
93      // determine average grade for particular set of grades
94      public double getAverage( int setOfGrades[] )
95      {
96          int total = 0; // initialize total
97
98          // sum grades for one student
99          for ( int grade : setOfGrades )
100             total += grade;
101
102         // return average of grades
103         return (double) total / setOfGrades.length;
104     } // end method getAverage
105
106     // output bar chart displaying overall grade distribution
107     public void outputBarChart()
108     {
109         System.out.println( "Overall grade distribution:" );
110
111         // stores frequency of grades in each range of 10 grades
112         int frequency[] = new int[ 11 ];
113
114         // for each grade in GradeBook, increment the appropriate frequency
115         for ( int studentGrades[] : grades )
116         {
117             for ( int grade : studentGrades )
118                 ++frequency[ grade / 10 ];
119         } // end outer for
```

Fig. 7.18 | GradeBook class using a two-dimensional array to store grades. (Part 3 of 4.)

```
120
121         // for each grade frequency, print bar in chart
122         for ( int count = 0; count < frequency.length; count++ )
123         {
124            // output bar label ( "00-09: ", ..., "90-99: ", "100: " )
125            if ( count == 10 )
126               System.out.printf( "%5d: ", 100 );
127            else
128               System.out.printf( "%02d-%02d: ",
129                  count * 10, count * 10 + 9 );
130
131            // print bar of asterisks
132            for ( int stars = 0; stars < frequency[ count ]; stars++ )
133               System.out.print( "*" );
134
135            System.out.println(); // start a new line of output
136         } // end outer for
137      } // end method outputBarChart
138
139      // output the contents of the grades array
140      public void outputGrades()
141      {
142         System.out.println( "The grades are:\n" );
143         System.out.print( "            " ); // align column heads
144
145         // create a column heading for each of the tests
146         for ( int test = 0; test < grades[ 0 ].length; test++ )
147            System.out.printf( "Test %d  ", test + 1 );
148
149         System.out.println( "Average" ); // student average column heading
150
151         // create rows/columns of text representing array grades
152         for ( int student = 0; student < grades.length; student++ )
153         {
154            System.out.printf( "Student %2d", student + 1 );
155
156            for ( int test : grades[ student ] ) // output student's grades
157               System.out.printf( "%8d", test );
158
159            // call method getAverage to calculate student's average grade;
160            // pass row of grades as the argument to getAverage
161            double average = getAverage( grades[ student ] );
162            System.out.printf( "%9.2f\n", average );
163         } // end outer for
164      } // end method outputGrades
165   } // end class GradeBook
```

Fig. 7.18 | GradeBook class using a two-dimensional array to store grades. (Part 4 of 4.)

Methods getMinimum, getMaximum, outputBarChart and outputGrades each loop through array grades by using nested for statements—for example, the nested enhanced for statement from the declaration of method getMinimum (lines 58–67). The outer enhanced for statement iterates through the two-dimensional array grades, assigning successive rows to parameter studentGrades on successive iterations. The square brackets following the parameter name indicate that studentGrades refers to a one-dimensional int array—namely, a row in array grades containing one student's grades. To find the lowest overall grade, the inner for statement compares the elements of the current one-dimensional array studentGrades to variable lowGrade. For example, on the first iteration of the outer for, row 0 of grades is assigned to parameter studentGrades. The inner enhanced for statement then loops through studentGrades and compares each grade value with lowGrade. If a grade is less than lowGrade, lowGrade is set to that grade. On the second iteration of the outer enhanced for statement, row 1 of grades is assigned to studentGrades, and the elements of this row are compared with variable lowGrade. This repeats until all rows of grades have been traversed. When execution of the nested statement is complete, lowGrade contains the lowest grade in the two-dimensional array. Method getMaximum works similarly to method getMinimum.

Method outputBarChart in Fig. 7.18 is nearly identical to the one in Fig. 7.14. However, to output the overall grade distribution for a whole semester, the method here uses a nested enhanced for statement (lines 115–119) to create the one-dimensional array frequency based on all the grades in the two-dimensional array. The rest of the code in each of the two outputBarChart methods that displays the chart is identical.

Method outputGrades (lines 140–164) also uses nested for statements to output values of the array grades, in addition to each student's semester average. The output in Fig. 7.19 shows the result, which resembles the tabular format of a professor's physical grade book. Lines 146–147 print the column headings for each test. We use a counter-controlled for statement here so that we can identify each test with a number. Similarly, the for statement in lines 152–163 first outputs a row label using a counter variable to identify each student (line 154). Although array indices start at 0, note that lines 147 and 154 output test + 1 and student + 1, respectively, to produce test and student numbers starting at 1 (see Fig. 7.19). The inner for statement in lines 156–157 uses the outer for statement's counter variable student to loop through a specific row of array grades and output each student's test grade. Note that an enhanced for statement can be nested in a counter-controlled for statement, and vice versa. Finally, line 161 obtains each student's semester average by passing the current row of grades (i.e., grades[student]) to method getAverage.

Method getAverage (lines 94–104) takes one argument—a one-dimensional array of test results for a particular student. When line 161 calls getAverage, the argument is grades[student], which specifies that a particular row of the two-dimensional array grades should be passed to getAverage. For example, based on the array created in Fig. 7.19, the argument grades[1] represents the three values (a one-dimensional array of grades) stored in row 1 of the two-dimensional array grades. Remember that a two-dimensional array is an array whose elements are one-dimensional arrays. Method getAverage calculates the sum of the array elements, divides the total by the number of test results and returns the floating-point result as a double value (line 103).

Class *GradeBookTest* That Demonstrates Class *GradeBook*

The application in Fig. 7.19 creates an object of class GradeBook (Fig. 7.18) using the two-dimensional array of ints named gradesArray (declared and initialized in lines 10–19). Lines 21–22 pass a course name and gradesArray to the GradeBook constructor. Lines 23–24 then invoke myGradeBook's displayMessage and processGrades methods to display a welcome message and obtain a report summarizing the students' grades for the semester, respectively.

```
1    // Fig. 7.19: GradeBookTest.java
2    // Creates GradeBook object using a two-dimensional array of grades.
3
4    public class GradeBookTest
5    {
6       // main method begins program execution
7       public static void main( String args[] )
8       {
9          // two-dimensional array of student grades
10         int gradesArray[][] = { { 87, 96, 70 },
11                                 { 68, 87, 90 },
12                                 { 94, 100, 90 },
13                                 { 100, 81, 82 },
14                                 { 83, 65, 85 },
15                                 { 78, 87, 65 },
16                                 { 85, 75, 83 },
17                                 { 91, 94, 100 },
18                                 { 76, 72, 84 },
19                                 { 87, 93, 73 } };
20
21         GradeBook myGradeBook = new GradeBook(
22            "CS101 Introduction to Java Programming", gradesArray );
23         myGradeBook.displayMessage();
24         myGradeBook.processGrades();
25      } // end main
26   } // end class GradeBookTest
```

```
Welcome to the grade book for
CS101 Introduction to Java Programming!

The grades are:

            Test 1  Test 2  Test 3  Average
Student  1     87      96      70    84.33
Student  2     68      87      90    81.67
Student  3     94     100      90    94.67
Student  4    100      81      82    87.67
Student  5     83      65      85    77.67
Student  6     78      87      65    76.67
Student  7     85      75      83    81.00
Student  8     91      94     100    95.00
Student  9     76      72      84    77.33
Student 10     87      93      73    84.33

Lowest grade in the grade book is 65
Highest grade in the grade book is 100

Overall grade distribution:
00-09:
10-19:
20-29:
```
(continued top of next page...)

Fig. 7.19 | Creates GradeBook object using a two-dimensional array of grades, then invokes method processGrades to analyze them. (Part 1 of 2.)

(continued from previous page...)

```
30-39:
40-49:
50-59:
60-69: ***
70-79: ******
80-89: ***********
90-99: *******
  100: ***
```

Fig. 7.19 | Creates GradeBook object using a two-dimensional array of grades, then invokes method processGrades to analyze them. (Part 2 of 2.)

7.11 Variable-Length Argument Lists

Variable-length argument lists are a new feature in J2SE 5.0. Programmers can create methods that receive an unspecified number of arguments. An argument type followed by an ellipsis (...) in a method's parameter list indicates that the method receives a variable number of arguments of that particular type. This use of the ellipsis can occur only once in a parameter list, and the ellipsis, together with its type, must be placed at the end of the parameter list. While programmers can use method overloading and array passing to accomplish much of what is accomplished with "varargs," or variable-length argument lists, using an ellipsis in a method's parameter list is more concise.

Figure 7.20 demonstrates method average (lines 7–16), which receives a variable-length sequence of doubles. Java treats the variable-length argument list as an array whose elements are all of the same type. Hence, the method body can manipulate the parameter numbers as an array of doubles. Lines 12–13 use the enhanced for loop to walk through the array and calculate the total of the doubles in the array. Line 15 accesses numbers.length to obtain the size of the numbers array for use in the averaging calculation. Lines 29, 31 and 33 in main call method average with two, three and four arguments, respectively. Method average has a variable-length argument list, so it can average as many double arguments as the caller passes. The output reveals that each call to method average returns the correct value.

```
1   // Fig. 7.20: VarargsTest.java
2   // Using variable-length argument lists.
3
4   public class VarargsTest
5   {
6      // calculate average
7      public static double average( double... numbers )
8      {
9         double total = 0.0; // initialize total
10
11        // calculate total using the enhanced for statement
12        for ( double d : numbers )
13           total += d;
14
```

Fig. 7.20 | Using variable-length argument lists. (Part 1 of 2.)

```
15          return total / numbers.length;
16      } // end method average
17
18      public static void main( String args[] )
19      {
20          double d1 = 10.0;
21          double d2 = 20.0;
22          double d3 = 30.0;
23          double d4 = 40.0;
24
25          System.out.printf( "d1 = %.1f\nd2 = %.1f\nd3 = %.1f\nd4 = %.1f\n\n",
26              d1, d2, d3, d4 );
27
28          System.out.printf( "Average of d1 and d2 is %.1f\n",
29              average( d1, d2 ) );
30          System.out.printf( "Average of d1, d2 and d3 is %.1f\n",
31              average( d1, d2, d3 ) );
32          System.out.printf( "Average of d1, d2, d3 and d4 is %.1f\n",
33              average( d1, d2, d3, d4 ) );
34      } // end main
35  } // end class VarargsTest
```

```
d1 = 10.0
d2 = 20.0
d3 = 30.0
d4 = 40.0

Average of d1 and d2 is 15.0
Average of d1, d2 and d3 is 20.0
Average of d1, d2, d3 and d4 is 25.0
```

Fig. 7.20 | Using variable-length argument lists. (Part 2 of 2.)

Common Programming Error 7.6

Placing an ellipsis in the middle of a method parameter list is a syntax error. An ellipsis may be placed only at the end of the parameter list.

7.12 Using Command-Line Arguments

On many systems it is possible to pass arguments from the command line (these are known as command-line arguments) to an application by including a parameter of type String[] (i.e., an array of Strings) in the parameter list of main, exactly as we have done in every application in the book. By convention, this parameter is named args. When an application is executed using the java command, Java passes the command-line arguments that appear after the class name in the java command to the application's main method as Strings in the array args. The number of arguments passed in from the command line is obtained by accessing the array's length attribute. For example, the command "java MyClass a b" passes two command-line arguments to application MyClass. Note that command-line arguments are separated by white space, not commas. When this command executes, MyClass's main method receives the two-element array args (i.e., args.length is 2) in which args[0] contains the String "a" and args[1] contains the

String "b". Common uses of command-line arguments include passing options and file names to applications.

Figure 7.21 uses three command-line arguments to initialize an array. When the program executes, if args.length is not 3, the program prints an error message and terminates (lines 9–12). Otherwise, lines 14–32 initialize and display the array based on the values of the command-line arguments.

The command-line arguments become available to main as Strings in args. Line 16 gets args[0]—a String that specifies the array size—and converts it to an int value that the program uses to create the array in line 17. The static method **parseInt** of class Integer converts its String argument to an int.

```java
1   // Fig. 7.21: InitArray.java
2   // Using command-line arguments to initialize an array.
3
4   public class InitArray
5   {
6      public static void main( String args[] )
7      {
8         // check number of command-line arguments
9         if ( args.length != 3 )
10           System.out.println(
11              "Error: Please re-enter the entire command, including\n" +
12              "an array size, initial value and increment." );
13        else
14        {
15           // get array size from first command-line argument
16           int arrayLength = Integer.parseInt( args[ 0 ] );
17           int array[] = new int[ arrayLength ]; // create array
18
19           // get initial value and increment from command-line argument
20           int initialValue = Integer.parseInt( args[ 1 ] );
21           int increment = Integer.parseInt( args[ 2 ] );
22
23           // calculate value for each array element
24           for ( int counter = 0; counter < array.length; counter++ )
25              array[ counter ] = initialValue + increment * counter;
26
27           System.out.printf( "%s%8s\n", "Index", "Value" );
28
29           // display array index and value
30           for ( int counter = 0; counter < array.length; counter++ )
31              System.out.printf( "%5d%8d\n", counter, array[ counter ] );
32        } // end else
33     } // end main
34  } // end class InitArray
```

```
java InitArray
Error: Please re-enter the entire command, including
an array size, initial value and increment.
```

Fig. 7.21 | Initializing an array using command-line arguments. (Part 1 of 2.)

```
java InitArray 5 0 4
Index   Value
   0       0
   1       4
   2       8
   3      12
   4      16
```

```
java InitArray 10 1 2
Index   Value
   0       1
   1       3
   2       5
   3       7
   4       9
   5      11
   6      13
   7      15
   8      17
   9      19
```

Fig. 7.21 | Initializing an array using command-line arguments. (Part 2 of 2.)

Lines 20–21 convert the `args[ 1 ]` and `args[ 2 ]` command-line arguments to `int` values and store them in `initialValue` and `increment`, respectively. Lines 24–25 calculate the value for each array element.

The output of the first sample execution indicates that the application received an insufficient number of command-line arguments. The second sample execution uses command-line arguments 5, 0 and 4 to specify the size of the array (5), the value of the first element (0) and the increment of each value in the array (4), respectively. The corresponding output indicates that these values create an array containing the integers 0, 4, 8, 12 and 16. The output from the third sample execution illustrates that the command-line arguments 10, 1 and 2 produce an array whose 10 elements are the nonnegative odd integers from 1 to 19.

7.13 (Optional) GUI and Graphics Case Study: Drawing Arcs

Using Java's graphics features, we can create complex drawings that would be more tedious to code line by line. In Fig. 7.22 and Fig. 7.23, we use arrays and repetition statements to draw a rainbow by using `Graphics` method `fillArc`. Drawing arcs in Java is similar to drawing ovals—an arc is simply a section of an oval.

Figure 7.22 begins with the usual `import` statements for creating drawings (lines 3–5). Lines 9–10 declare and create two new colors—`VIOLET` and `INDIGO`. As you may know, the colors of a rainbow are red, orange, yellow, green, blue, indigo and violet. Java only has predefined constants for the first five colors. Lines 15–17 initialize an array with the colors of the rainbow, starting with the innermost arcs first. The array begins with two `Color.WHITE` elements, which, as you will soon see, are for drawing the empty arcs at the center of the rainbow. Note that the instance variables can be initialized when they are declared, as shown in lines 10–17. The constructor (lines 20–23) contains a single state-ment that calls method **setBackground** (which is inherited from class JPanel) with the

```
1   // Fig. 7.22: DrawRainbow.java
2   // Demonstrates using colors in an array.
3   import java.awt.Color;
4   import java.awt.Graphics;
5   import javax.swing.JPanel;
6
7   public class DrawRainbow extends JPanel
8   {
9      // Define indigo and violet
10     final Color VIOLET = new Color( 128, 0, 128 );
11     final Color INDIGO = new Color( 75, 0, 130 );
12
13     // colors to use in the rainbow, starting from the innermost
14     // The two white entries result in an empty arc in the center
15     private Color colors[] =
16        { Color.WHITE, Color.WHITE, VIOLET, INDIGO, Color.BLUE,
17          Color.GREEN, Color.YELLOW, Color.ORANGE, Color.RED };
18
19     // constructor
20     public DrawRainbow()
21     {
22        setBackground( Color.WHITE ); // set the background to white
23     } // end DrawRainbow constructor
24
25     // draws a rainbow using concentric circles
26     public void paintComponent( Graphics g )
27     {
28        super.paintComponent( g );
29
30        int radius = 20; // radius of an arch
31
32        // draw the rainbow near the bottom-center
33        int centerX = getWidth() / 2;
34        int centerY = getHeight() - 10;
35
36        // draws filled arcs starting with the outermost
37        for ( int counter = colors.length; counter > 0; counter-- )
38        {
39           // set the color for the current arc
40           g.setColor( colors[ counter - 1 ] );
41
42           // fill the arc from 0 to 180 degrees
43           g.fillArc( centerX - counter * radius,
44              centerY - counter * radius,
45              counter * radius * 2, counter * radius * 2, 0, 180 );
46        } // end for
47     } // end method paintComponent
48  } // end class DrawRainbow
```

Fig. 7.22 | Drawing a rainbow using arcs and an array of colors.

```
 1   // Fig. 7.23: DrawRainbowTest.java
 2   // Test application to display a rainbow.
 3   import javax.swing.JFrame;
 4
 5   public class DrawRainbowTest
 6   {
 7      public static void main( String args[] )
 8      {
 9         DrawRainbow panel = new DrawRainbow();
10         JFrame application = new JFrame();
11
12         application.setDefaultCloseOperation( JFrame.EXIT_ON_CLOSE );
13         application.add( panel );
14         application.setSize( 400, 250 );
15         application.setVisible( true );
16      } // end main
17   } // end class DrawRainbowTest
```

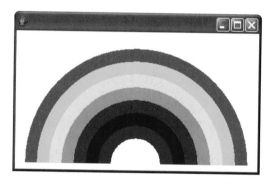

Fig. 7.23 | Creating JFrame to display a rainbow.

parameter Color.WHITE. Method setBackground takes a single Color argument and sets the background of the component to that color.

Line 30 in paintComponent declares local variable radius, which determines the thickness of each arc. Local variables centerX and centerY (lines 33–34) determine the location of the midpoint on the base of the rainbow. The loop at lines 37–46 uses control variable counter to count backwards from the end of the array, drawing the largest arcs first and placing each successive smaller arc on top of the previous one. Line 40 sets the color to draw the current arc from the array. The reason we have Color.WHITE entries at the beginning of the array is to create the empty arc in the center. Otherwise, the center of the rainbow would just be a solid violet semicircle. [*Note:* You can change the individual colors and the number of entries in the array to create new designs.]

The fillArc method call at lines 43–45 draws a filled semicircle. Method fillArc requires six parameters. The first four represent the bounding rectangle in which the arc will be drawn. The first two specify the coordinates for the upper-left corner of the bounding rectangle, and the next two specify its width and height. The fifth parameter is the starting angle on the oval, and the sixth specifies the sweep, or the amount of arc to cover. The starting angle and sweep are measured in degrees, with zero degrees pointing right. A positive sweep draws the arc counter-clockwise, while a negative sweep draws the arc clockwise. A method similar to fillArc is drawArc—it requires the same parameters as fillArc, but draws the edge of the arc rather than filling it.

Class DrawRainbowTest (Fig. 7.23) creates and sets up a JFrame to display the rainbow. Once the program makes the JFrame visible, the system calls the paintComponent method in class DrawRainbow to draw the rainbow on the screen.

GUI and Graphics Case Study Exercise

7.1   (*Drawing Spirals*) In this exercise, you will draw spirals with methods drawLine and drawArc.

a) Draw a square-shaped spiral (as in the left screen capture of Fig. 7.24), centered on the panel, using method drawLine. One technique is to use a loop that increases the line length after drawing every second line. The direction in which to draw the next line should follow a distinct pattern, such as down, left, up, right.

b) Draw a circular spiral (as in the right screen capture of Fig. 7.24), using method drawArc to draw one semicircle at a time. Each successive semicircle should have a larger radius (as specified by the bounding rectangle's width) and should continue drawing where the previous semicircle finished.

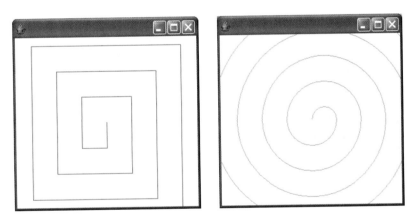

Fig. 7.24 | Drawing a spiral using drawLine (left) and drawArc (right).

7.14 Wrap-Up

This chapter began our introduction to data structures, exploring the use of arrays to store data in and retrieve data from lists and tables of values. The chapter examples demonstrated how to declare an array, initialize an array and refer to individual elements of an array. The chapter introduced the enhanced for statement to iterate through arrays. We also illustrated how to pass arrays to methods and how to declare and manipulate multidimensional arrays. Finally, the chapter showed how to write methods that use variable-length argument lists and how to read arguments passed to a program from the command line.

We have now introduced the basic concepts of classes, objects, control statements, methods and arrays. In Chapter 8, we take a deeper look at classes and objects.

Summary

- Arrays are data structures consisting of related data items of the same type. Arrays are fixed-length entities—they remain the same length once they are created, although an array variable may be reassigned the reference of a new array of a different length.

- An array is a group of variables (called elements or components) containing values that all have the same type. Arrays are objects, so they are considered reference types. The elements of an array can be either primitive types or reference types (including arrays).

- To refer to a particular element in an array, we specify the name of the reference to the array and the index (subscript) of the element in the array.

- A program refers to any one of an array's elements with an array-access expression that includes the name of the array followed by the index of the particular element in square brackets ([]).

- The first element in every array has index zero and is sometimes called the zeroth element.

- An index must be a nonnegative integer. A program can use an expression as an index.

- Every array object knows its own length and maintains this information in a `length` field. The expression *array*.`length` accesses *array*'s `length` field to determine the length of the array.

- To create an array object, the programmer specifies the type of the array elements and the number of elements as part of an array-creation expression that uses keyword `new`. The following array-creation expression creates an array of 100 `int` values:

      int b[] = new int[100];

- When an array is created, each element of the array receives a default value—zero for numeric primitive-type elements, `false` for boolean elements and `null` for references (any nonprimitive type).

- When an array is declared, the type of the array and the square brackets can be combined at the beginning of the declaration to indicate that all the identifiers in the declaration are array variables, as in

      double[] array1, array2;

- A program can declare arrays of any type. Every element of a primitive-type array contains a variable of the array's declared type. Similarly, in an array of a reference type, every element is a reference to an object of the array's declared type.

- A program can create an array and initialize its elements with an array initializer (i.e., an initializer list enclosed in braces).

- Constant variables (also called named constants or read-only variables) must be initialized before they are used and cannot be modified thereafter.

- When a Java program executes, the JVM checks array indices to ensure that they are valid (i.e., they must be greater than or equal to 0 and less than the length of the array). If a program uses an invalid index, Java generates a so-called exception to indicate that an error occurred in the program at execution time.

- The enhanced `for` statement allows programmers to iterate through the elements of an array or a collection without using a counter. The syntax of an enhanced `for` statement is:

      for (parameter : arrayName)
         statement

  where *parameter* has two parts—a type and an identifier (e.g., int number), and *arrayName* is the array through which to iterate.

- The enhanced `for` statement cannot be used to modify elements in an array. If a program needs to modify elements, use the traditional counter-controlled `for` statement.

- When an argument is passed by value, a copy of the argument's value is made and passed to the called method. The called method works exclusively with the copy.

- When an argument is passed by reference, the called method can access the argument's value in the caller directly and possibly modify it.

- Java does not allow programmers to choose between pass-by-value and pass-by-reference—all arguments are passed by value. A method call can pass two types of values to a method—copies of primitive values (e.g., values of type int and double) and copies of references to objects. Although an object's reference is passed by value, a method can still interact with the referenced object by calling its public methods using the copy of the object's reference.

- To pass an object reference to a method, simply specify in the method call the name of the variable that refers to the object.

- When an argument to a method is an entire array or an individual array element of a reference type, the called method receives a copy of the array or element's reference. When an argument to a method is an individual array element of a primitive type, the called method receives a copy of the element's value.

- To pass an individual array element to a method, use the indexed name of the array as an argument in the method call.

- Multidimensional arrays with two dimensions are often used to represent tables of values consisting of information arranged in rows and columns.

- Arrays that require two indices to identify a particular element are called two-dimensional arrays. An array with m rows and n columns is called an m-by-n array. A two-dimensional array can be initialized with an array initializer of the form

    arrayType arrayName[][] = { { *row1 initializer* }, { *row2 initializer* }, ... };

- Multidimensional arrays are maintained as arrays of separate one-dimensional arrays. As a result, the lengths of the rows in a two-dimensional array are not required to be the same.

- A multidimensional array with the same number of columns in every row can be created with an array-creation expression of the form

    arrayType arrayName[][] = new *arrayType*[*numRows*][*numColumns*];

- An argument type followed by an ellipsis (. . .) in a method's parameter list indicates that the method receives a variable number of arguments of that particular type. The ellipsis can occur only once in a method's parameter list and it must be at the end of the parameter list.

- A variable-length argument list is treated as an array within the method body. The number of arguments in the array can be obtained using the array's length field.

- Passing arguments to main in a Java application from the command line is achieved by including a parameter of type String[] in the parameter list of main. By convention, main's parameter is named args.

- Java passes the command-line arguments that appear after the class name in the java command to the application's main method as Strings in the array args. The number of arguments passed in from the command line is obtained by accessing the array's length attribute.

- The static method parseInt of class Integer converts its String argument to an int.

Terminology

0 flag (in a format specifier)	array
a[i]	array-access expression
a[i][j]	array-creation expression

array initializer	nested array initializers
bounds checking	off-by-one error
column index	one-dimensional array
column of an array	`parseInt` method of class `Integer`
command-line arguments	pass-by-reference
component of an array	pass-by-value
constant variable	passing arrays to methods
data structure	position number
declare an array	read-only variable
element of an array	row index
ellipsis (. . .) in a method's parameter list	row of an array
enhanced `for` statement	scalar
`final` keyword	scalar quantity
index	square brackets, `[]`
index zero	subscript
initialize an array	table of values
initializer list	tabular format
length field of an array	traverse an array
m-by-*n* array	two-dimensional array
multidimensional array	value of an element
name of an array	variable-length argument list
named constant	zeroth element

Self-Review Exercises

7.1 Fill in the blank(s) in each of the following statements:
a) Lists and tables of values can be stored in _____.
b) An array is a group of _____ (called elements or components) containing values that all have the same _____.
c) The _____ allows programmers to iterate through the elements in an array without using a counter.
d) The number used to refer to a particular element of an array is called the element's _____.
e) An array that uses two indices is referred to as a(n) _____ array.
f) Use the enhanced `for` statement _____ to walk through `double` array `numbers`.
g) Command-line arguments are stored in _____.
h) Use the expression _____ to receive the total number of arguments in a command line. Assume that command-line arguments are stored in `String args[]`.
i) Given the command `java MyClass test`, the first command-line argument is _____.
j) A(/n) _____ in the parameter list of a method indicates that the method can receive a variable number of arguments.

7.2 Determine whether each of the following is *true* or *false*. If *false*, explain why.
a) An array can store many different types of values.
b) An array index should normally be of type `float`.
c) An individual array element that is passed to a method and modified in that method will contain the modified value when the called method completes execution.
d) Command-line arguments are separated by commas.
e) Expression `array.length` is used to access the number of arguments of a variable-length argument called `array`.

7.3   Perform the following tasks for an array called `fractions`:
    a) Declare a constant `ARRAY_SIZE` that is initialized to 10.
    b) Declare an array with `ARRAY_SIZE` elements of type `double`, and initialize the elements to 0.
    c) Name the fourth element of the array.
    d) Refer to array element 4.
    e) Assign the value `1.667` to array element 9.
    f) Assign the value `3.333` to the seventh element of the array.
    g) Sum all the elements of the array, using a `for` statement. Declare the integer variable x as a control variable for the loop.

7.4   Perform the following tasks for an array called `table`:
    a) Declare and create the array as an integer array that has three rows and three columns. Assume that the constant `ARRAY_SIZE` has been declared to be 3.
    b) How many elements does the array contain?
    c) Use a `for` statement to initialize each element of the array to the sum of its indices. Assume that the integer variables x and y are declared as control variables.

7.5   Find and correct the error in each of the following program segments:
    a) `final int ARRAY_SIZE = 5;`
        `ARRAY_SIZE = 10;`
    b) Assume `int b[] = new int[ 10 ];`
        `for ( int i = 0; i <= b.length; i++ )`
          `b[ i ] = 1;`
    c) Assume `int a[][] = { { 1, 2 }, { 3, 4 } };`
        `a[ 1, 1 ] = 5;`

Answers to Self-Review Exercises

7.1   a) arrays. b) variables, type. c) enhanced `for` statement. d) index (or subscript or position number). e) two-dimensional. f) `for ( double d : numbers )`. g) an array of `String`s, usually called `args`. h) `args.length`. i) `test`. j) ellipsis (`...`).

7.2   a) False. An array can store only values of the same type.
    b) False. An array index must be an integer or an integer expression.
    c) For individual primitive-type elements of an array: False. A called method receives and manipulates a copy of the value of such an element, so modifications do not affect the original value. If the reference of an array is passed to a method, however, modifications to the array elements made in the called method are indeed reflected in the original. For individual elements of a nonprimitive type: True. A called method receives a copy of the reference of such an element, and changes to the referenced object will be reflected in the original array element.
    d) False. Command-line arguments are separated by white space.
    e) True.

7.3   a) `final int ARRAY_SIZE = 10;`
    b) `double fractions[] = new double[ ARRAY_SIZE ];`
    c) `fractions[ 3 ]`
    d) `fractions[ 4 ]`
    e) `fractions[ 9 ] = 1.667;`
    f) `fractions[ 6 ] = 3.333;`
    g) `double total = 0.0;`
        `for ( int x = 0; x < fractions.length; x++ )`
          `total += fractions[ x ];`

7.4   a)   `int table[][] = new int[ ARRAY_SIZE ][ ARRAY_SIZE ];`
      b)   Nine.
      c)
```
for ( int x = 0; x < table.length; x++ )
    for ( int y = 0; y < table[ x ].length; y++ )
        table[ x ][ y ] = x + y;
```

7.5   a)   Error: Assigning a value to a constant after it has been initialized.
           Correction: Assign the correct value to the constant in a `final int ARRAY_SIZE`
           declaration or declare another variable.
      b)   Error: Referencing an array element outside the bounds of the array (`b[10]`).
           Correction: Change the `<=` operator to `<`.
      c)   Error: Array indexing is performed incorrectly.
           Correction: Change the statement to `a[ 1 ][ 1 ] = 5;`.

Exercises

7.6   Fill in the blanks in each of the following statements:
      a)   One-dimensional array p contains four elements. The names of those elements are
           _____, _____, _____ and _____.
      b)   Naming an array, stating its type and specifying the number of dimensions in the array
           is called _____ the array.
      c)   In a two-dimensional array, the first index identifies the _____ of an element and
           the second index identifies the _____ of an element.
      d)   An *m-by-n* array contains _____ rows, _____ columns and _____ el-
           ements.
      e)   The name of the element in row 3 and column 5 of array d is _____.

7.7   Determine whether each of the following is *true* or *false*. If *false*, explain why.
      a)   To refer to a particular location or element within an array, we specify the name of the
           array and the value of the particular element.
      b)   An array declaration reserves space for the array.
      c)   To indicate that 100 locations should be reserved for integer array p, the programmer
           writes the declaration
               `p[ 100 ];`
      d)   An application that initializes the elements of a 15-element array to zero must contain
           at least one `for` statement.
      e)   An application that totals the elements of a two-dimensional array must contain nested
           `for` statements.

7.8   Write Java statements to accomplish each of the following tasks:
      a)   Display the value of the seventh element of character array f.
      b)   Initialize each of the five elements of one-dimensional integer array g to 8.
      c)   Total the 100 elements of floating-point array c.
      d)   Copy 11-element array a into the first portion of array b, which contains 34 elements.
      e)   Determine and display the smallest and largest values contained in 99-element floating-
           point array w.

7.9   Consider a two-by-three integer array t.
      a)   Write a statement that declares and creates t.
      b)   How many rows does t have?
      c)   How many columns does t have?
      d)   How many elements does t have?
      e)   Write the names of all the elements in the second row of t.
      f)   Write the names of all the elements in the third column of t.

g) Write a single statement that sets the element of t in row 1 and column 2 to zero.
h) Write a series of statements that initializes each element of t to zero. Do not use a repetition statement.
i) Write a nested for statement that initializes each element of t to zero.
j) Write a nested for statement that inputs the values for the elements of t from the user.
k) Write a series of statements that determines and displays the smallest value in t.
l) Write a statement that displays the elements of the first row of t.
m) Write a statement that totals the elements of the third column of t.
n) Write a series of statements that displays the contents of t in tabular format. List the column indices as headings across the top, and list the row indices at the left of each row.

7.10 *(Sales Commissions)* Use a one-dimensional array to solve the following problem: A company pays its salespeople on a commission basis. The salespeople receive $200 per week plus 9% of their gross sales for that week. For example, a salesperson who grosses $5000 in sales in a week receives $200 plus 9% of $5000, or a total of $650. Write an application (using an array of counters) that determines how many of the salespeople earned salaries in each of the following ranges (assume that each salesperson's salary is truncated to an integer amount):
a) $200–299
b) $300–399
c) $400–499
d) $500–599
e) $600–699
f) $700–799
g) $800–899
h) $900–999
i) $1000 and over

Summarize the results in tabular format.

7.11 Write statements that perform the following one-dimensional-array operations:
a) Set the 10 elements of integer array counts to zero.
b) Add one to each of the 15 elements of integer array bonus.
c) Display the five values of integer array bestScores in column format.

7.12 *(Duplicate Elimination)* Use a one-dimensional array to solve the following problem: Write an application that inputs five numbers, each of which is between 10 and 100, inclusive. As each number is read, display it only if it is not a duplicate of a number already read. Provide for the "worst case," in which all five numbers are different. Use the smallest possible array to solve this problem. Display the complete set of unique values input after the user inputs each new value.

7.13 Label the elements of three-by-five two-dimensional array sales to indicate the order in which they are set to zero by the following program segment:

```
for ( int row = 0; row < sales.length; row++ )
{
   for ( int col = 0; col < sales[ row ].length; col++ )
   {
      sales[ row ][ col ] = 0;
   }
}
```

7.14 Write an application that calculates the product of a series of integers that are passed to method product using a variable-length argument list. Test your method with several calls, each with a different number of arguments.

7.15 Rewrite Fig. 7.2 so that the size of the array is specified by the first command-line argument. If no command-line argument is supplied, use 10 as the default size of the array.

7.16 Write an application that uses an enhanced for statement to sum the double values passed by the command-line arguments. [*Hint:* Use the static method parseDouble of class Double to convert a String to a double value.]

7.17 *(Dice Rolling)* Write an application to simulate the rolling of two dice. The application should use an object of class Random once to roll the first die and again to roll the second die. The sum of the two values should then be calculated. Each die can show an integer value from 1 to 6, so the sum of the values will vary from 2 to 12, with 7 being the most frequent sum and 2 and 12 being the least frequent sums. Figure 7.25 shows the 36 possible combinations of the two dice. Your application should roll the dice 36,000 times. Use a one-dimensional array to tally the number of times each possible sum appears. Display the results in tabular format. Determine whether the totals are reasonable (e.g., there are six ways to roll a 7, so approximately one-sixth of the rolls should be 7).

7.18 *(Game of Craps)* Write an application that runs 1000 games of craps (Fig. 6.9) and answers the following questions:
   a) How many games are won on the first roll, second roll, …, twentieth roll and after the twentieth roll?
   b) How many games are lost on the first roll, second roll, …, twentieth roll and after the twentieth roll?
   c) What are the chances of winning at craps? [*Note:* You should discover that craps is one of the fairest casino games. What do you suppose this means?]
   d) What is the average length of a game of craps?
   e) Do the chances of winning improve with the length of the game?

7.19 *(Airline Reservations System)* A small airline has just purchased a computer for its new automated reservations system. You have been asked to develop the new system. You are to write an application to assign seats on each flight of the airline's only plane (capacity: 10 seats).

Your application should display the following alternatives: Please type 1 for First Class and Please type 2 for Economy. If the user types 1, your application should assign a seat in the first-class section (seats 1–5). If the user types 2, your application should assign a seat in the economy section (seats 6–10). Your application should then display a boarding pass indicating the person's seat number and whether it is in the first-class or economy section of the plane. Use a one-dimensional array of primitive type boolean to represent the seating chart of the plane. Initialize all the elements of the array to false to indicate that all the seats are empty. As each seat is assigned, set the corresponding elements of the array to true to indicate that the seat is no longer available.

Your application should never assign a seat that has already been assigned. When the economy section is full, your application should ask the person if it is acceptable to be placed in the first-class section (and vice versa). If yes, make the appropriate seat assignment. If no, display the message "Next flight leaves in 3 hours."

	1	2	3	4	5	6
1	2	3	4	5	6	7
2	3	4	5	6	7	8
3	4	5	6	7	8	9
4	5	6	7	8	9	10
5	6	7	8	9	10	11
6	7	8	9	10	11	12

Fig. 7.25 | The 36 possible sums of two dice.

7.20 *(Total Sales)* Use a two-dimensional array to solve the following problem: A company has four salespeople (1 to 4) who sell five different products (1 to 5). Once a day, each salesperson passes in a slip for each type of product sold. Each slip contains the following:

a) The salesperson number
b) The product number
c) The total dollar value of that product sold that day

Thus, each salesperson passes in between 0 and 5 sales slips per day. Assume that the information from all the slips for last month is available. Write an application that will read all this information for last month's sales and summarize the total sales by salesperson and by product. All totals should be stored in the two-dimensional array `sales`. After processing all the information for last month, display the results in tabular format, with each column representing a particular salesperson and each row representing a particular product. Cross-total each row to get the total sales of each product for last month. Cross-total each column to get the total sales by salesperson for last month. Your tabular output should include these cross-totals to the right of the totaled rows and to the bottom of the totaled columns.

7.21 *(Turtle Graphics)* The Logo language made the concept of *turtle graphics* famous. Imagine a mechanical turtle that walks around the room under the control of a Java application. The turtle holds a pen in one of two positions, up or down. While the pen is down, the turtle traces out shapes as it moves, and while the pen is up, the turtle moves about freely without writing anything. In this problem, you will simulate the operation of the turtle and create a computerized sketchpad.

Use a 20-by-20 array `floor` that is initialized to zeros. Read commands from an array that contains them. Keep track of the current position of the turtle at all times and whether the pen is currently up or down. Assume that the turtle always starts at position (0, 0) of the floor with its pen up. The set of turtle commands your application must process are shown in Fig. 7.26.

Suppose that the turtle is somewhere near the center of the floor. The following "program" would draw and display a 12-by-12 square, leaving the pen in the up position:

```
2
5,12
3
5,12
3
5,12
3
5,12
1
6
9
```

Command	Meaning
1	Pen up
2	Pen down
3	Turn right
4	Turn left
5,10	Move forward 10 spaces (replace 10 for a different number of spaces)
6	Display the 20-by-20 array
9	End of data (sentinel)

Fig. 7.26 | Turtle graphics commands.

As the turtle moves with the pen down, set the appropriate elements of array floor to 1s. When the 6 command (display the array) is given, wherever there is a 1 in the array, display an asterisk or any character you choose. Wherever there is a 0, display a blank.

Write an application to implement the turtle graphics capabilities discussed here. Write several turtle graphics programs to draw interesting shapes. Add other commands to increase the power of your turtle graphics language.

7.22   (*Knight's Tour*) One of the more interesting puzzlers for chess buffs is the Knight's Tour problem, originally proposed by the mathematician Euler. Can the chess piece called the knight move around an empty chessboard and touch each of the 64 squares once and only once? We study this intriguing problem in depth here.

The knight makes only L-shaped moves (two spaces in one direction and one space in a perpendicular direction). Thus, as shown in Fig. 7.27, from a square near the middle of an empty chessboard, the knight (labeled K) can make eight different moves (numbered 0 through 7).

 a) Draw an eight-by-eight chessboard on a sheet of paper, and attempt a Knight's Tour by hand. Put a 1 in the starting square, a 2 in the second square, a 3 in the third, and so on. Before starting the tour, estimate how far you think you will get, remembering that a full tour consists of 64 moves. How far did you get? Was this close to your estimate?

 b) Now let us develop an application that will move the knight around a chessboard. The board is represented by an eight-by-eight two-dimensional array board. Each square is initialized to zero. We describe each of the eight possible moves in terms of their horizontal and vertical components. For example, a move of type 0, as shown in Fig. 7.27, consists of moving two squares horizontally to the right and one square vertically upward. A move of type 2 consists of moving one square horizontally to the left and two squares vertically upward. Horizontal moves to the left and vertical moves upward are indicated with negative numbers. The eight moves may be described by two one-dimensional arrays, horizontal and vertical, as follows:

```
horizontal[ 0 ] = 2      vertical[ 0 ] = -1
horizontal[ 1 ] = 1      vertical[ 1 ] = -2
horizontal[ 2 ] = -1     vertical[ 2 ] = -2
horizontal[ 3 ] = -2     vertical[ 3 ] = -1
horizontal[ 4 ] = -2     vertical[ 4 ] = 1
horizontal[ 5 ] = -1     vertical[ 5 ] = 2
horizontal[ 6 ] = 1      vertical[ 6 ] = 2
horizontal[ 7 ] = 2      vertical[ 7 ] = 1
```

Fig. 7.27 | The eight possible moves of the knight.

Let the variables `currentRow` and `currentColumn` indicate the row and column, respectively, of the knight's current position. To make a move of type `moveNumber`, where `moveNumber` is between 0 and 7, your application should use the statements

```
currentRow += vertical[ moveNumber ];
currentColumn += horizontal[ moveNumber ];
```

Write an application to move the knight around the chessboard. Keep a counter that varies from 1 to 64. Record the latest count in each square the knight moves to. Test each potential move to see if the knight has already visited that square. Test every potential move to ensure that the knight does not land off the chessboard. Run the application. How many moves did the knight make?

c) After attempting to write and run a Knight's Tour application, you have probably developed some valuable insights. We will use these insights to develop a *heuristic* (or "rule of thumb") for moving the knight. Heuristics do not guarantee success, but a carefully developed heuristic greatly improves the chance of success. You may have observed that the outer squares are more troublesome than the squares nearer the center of the board. In fact, the most troublesome or inaccessible squares are the four corners.

Intuition may suggest that you should attempt to move the knight to the most troublesome squares first and leave open those that are easiest to get to, so that when the board gets congested near the end of the tour, there will be a greater chance of success.

We could develop an "accessibility heuristic" by classifying each of the squares according to how accessible it is and always moving the knight (using the knight's L-shaped moves) to the most inaccessible square. We label a two-dimensional array `accessibility` with numbers indicating from how many squares each particular square is accessible. On a blank chessboard, each of the 16 squares nearest the center is rated as 8, each corner square is rated as 2, and the other squares have accessibility numbers of 3, 4 or 6 as follows:

```
2  3  4  4  4  4  3  2
3  4  6  6  6  6  4  3
4  6  8  8  8  8  6  4
4  6  8  8  8  8  6  4
4  6  8  8  8  8  6  4
4  6  8  8  8  8  6  4
3  4  6  6  6  6  4  3
2  3  4  4  4  4  3  2
```

Write a new version of the Knight's Tour, using the accessibility heuristic. The knight should always move to the square with the lowest accessibility number. In case of a tie, the knight may move to any of the tied squares. Therefore, the tour may begin in any of the four corners. [*Note:* As the knight moves around the chessboard, your application should reduce the accessibility numbers as more squares become occupied. In this way, at any given time during the tour, each available square's accessibility number will remain equal to precisely the number of squares from which that square may be reached.] Run this version of your application. Did you get a full tour? Modify the application to run 64 tours, one starting from each square of the chessboard. How many full tours did you get?

d) Write a version of the Knight's Tour application that, when encountering a tie between two or more squares, decides what square to choose by looking ahead to those squares reachable from the "tied" squares. Your application should move to the tied square for which the next move would arrive at a square with the lowest accessibility number.

7.23 (*Knight's Tour: Brute-Force Approaches*) In part (c) of Exercise 7.22, we developed a solution to the Knight's Tour problem. The approach used, called the "accessibility heuristic," generates many solutions and executes efficiently.

As computers continue to increase in power, we will be able to solve more problems with sheer computer power and relatively unsophisticated algorithms. Let us call this approach "brute-force" problem solving.

a) Use random-number generation to enable the knight to walk around the chessboard (in its legitimate L-shaped moves) at random. Your application should run one tour and display the final chessboard. How far did the knight get?

b) Most likely, the application in part (a) produced a relatively short tour. Now modify your application to attempt 1000 tours. Use a one-dimensional array to keep track of the number of tours of each length. When your application finishes attempting the 1000 tours, it should display this information in neat tabular format. What was the best result?

c) Most likely, the application in part (b) gave you some "respectable" tours, but no full tours. Now let your application run until it produces a full tour. (*Caution:* This version of the application could run for hours on a powerful computer.) Once again, keep a table of the number of tours of each length, and display this table when the first full tour is found. How many tours did your application attempt before producing a full tour? How much time did it take?

d) Compare the brute-force version of the Knight's Tour with the accessibility-heuristic version. Which required a more careful study of the problem? Which algorithm was more difficult to develop? Which required more computer power? Could we be certain (in advance) of obtaining a full tour with the accessibility-heuristic approach? Could we be certain (in advance) of obtaining a full tour with the brute-force approach? Argue the pros and cons of brute-force problem solving in general.

7.24 (*Eight Queens*) Another puzzler for chess buffs is the Eight Queens problem, which asks the following: Is it possible to place eight queens on an empty chessboard so that no queen is "attacking" any other (i.e., no two queens are in the same row, in the same column or along the same diagonal)? Use the thinking developed in Exercise 7.22 to formulate a heuristic for solving the Eight Queens problem. Run your application. (*Hint:* It is possible to assign a value to each square of the chessboard to indicate how many squares of an empty chessboard are "eliminated" if a queen is placed in that square. Each of the corners would be assigned the value 22, as demonstrated by Fig. 7.28. Once these "elimination numbers" are placed in all 64 squares, an appropriate heuristic might be as follows: Place the next queen in the square with the smallest elimination number. Why is this strategy intuitively appealing?

Fig. 7.28 | The 22 squares eliminated by placing a queen in the upper left corner.

7.25 (*Eight Queens: Brute-Force Approaches*) In this exercise, you will develop several brute-force approaches to solving the Eight Queens problem introduced in Exercise 7.24.

  a) Use the random brute-force technique developed in Exercise 7.23 to solve the Eight Queens problem.

  b) Use an exhaustive technique (i.e., try all possible combinations of eight queens on the chessboard) to solve the Eight Queens problem.

  c) Why might the exhaustive brute-force approach not be appropriate for solving the Knight's Tour problem?

  d) Compare and contrast the random brute-force and exhaustive brute-force approaches.

7.26 (*Knight's Tour: Closed-Tour Test*) In the Knight's Tour (Exercise 7.22), a full tour occurs when the knight makes 64 moves, touching each square of the chessboard once and only once. A closed tour occurs when the 64th move is one move away from the square in which the knight started the tour. Modify the application you wrote in Exercise 7.22 to test for a closed tour if a full tour has occurred.

7.27 (*Sieve of Eratosthenes*) A prime number is any integer greater than one that is evenly divisible only by itself and 1. The Sieve of Eratosthenes is a method of finding prime numbers. It operates as follows:

  a) Create a primitive type `boolean` array with all elements initialized to `true`. Array elements with prime indices will remain `true`. All other array elements will eventually be set to `false`.

  b) Starting with array index 2, determine whether a given element is `true`. If so, loop through the remainder of the array and set to `false` every element whose index is a multiple of the index for the element with value `true`. Then continue the process with the next element with value `true`. For array index 2, all elements beyond element 2 in the array that have indices which are multiples of 2 (indices 4, 6, 8, 10, etc.) will be set to `false`; for array index 3, all elements beyond element 3 in the array that have indices which are multiples of 3 (indices 6, 9, 12, 15, etc.) will be set to `false`; and so on.

When this process completes, the array elements that are still `true` indicate that the index is a prime number. These indices can be displayed. Write an application that uses an array of 1000 elements to determine and display the prime numbers between 2 and 999. Ignore array elements 0 and 1.

7.28 (*Simulation: The Tortoise and the Hare*) In this problem, you will re-create the classic race of the tortoise and the hare. You will use random-number generation to develop a simulation of this memorable event.

  Our contenders begin the race at square 1 of 70 squares. Each square represents a possible position along the race course. The finish line is at square 70. The first contender to reach or pass square 70 is rewarded with a pail of fresh carrots and lettuce. The course weaves its way up the side of a slippery mountain, so occasionally the contenders lose ground.

  A clock ticks once per second. With each tick of the clock, your application should adjust the position of the animals according to the rules in Fig. 7.29. Use variables to keep track of the positions of the animals (i.e., position numbers are 1–70). Start each animal at position 1 (the "starting gate"). If an animal slips left before square 1, move it back to square 1.

  Generate the percentages in Fig. 7.29 by producing a random integer i in the range $1 \leq i \leq 10$. For the tortoise, perform a "fast plod" when $1 \leq i \leq 5$, a "slip" when $6 \leq i \leq 7$ or a "slow plod" when $8 \leq i \leq 10$. Use a similar technique to move the hare.

  Begin the race by displaying

```
BANG !!!!!
AND THEY'RE OFF !!!!!
```

Then, for each tick of the clock (i.e., each repetition of a loop), display a 70-position line showing the letter T in the position of the tortoise and the letter H in the position of the hare. Occasionally,

Animal	Move type	Percentage of the time	Actual move
Tortoise	Fast plod	50%	3 squares to the right
	Slip	20%	6 squares to the left
	Slow plod	30%	1 square to the right
Hare	Sleep	20%	No move at all
	Big hop	20%	9 squares to the right
	Big slip	10%	12 squares to the left
	Small hop	30%	1 square to the right
	Small slip	20%	2 squares to the left

Fig. 7.29 | Rules for adjusting the positions of the tortoise and the hare.

the contenders will land on the same square. In this case, the tortoise bites the hare, and your application should display OUCH!!! beginning at that position. All output positions other than the T, the H or the OUCH!!! (in case of a tie) should be blank.

After each line is displayed, test for whether either animal has reached or passed square 70. If so, display the winner and terminate the simulation. If the tortoise wins, display TORTOISE WINS!!! YAY!!! If the hare wins, display Hare wins. Yuch. If both animals win on the same tick of the clock, you may want to favor the tortoise (the "underdog"), or you may want to display It's a tie. If neither animal wins, perform the loop again to simulate the next tick of the clock. When you are ready to run your application, assemble a group of fans to watch the race. You'll be amazed at how involved your audience gets!

7.29 *(Fibonacci Series)* The Fibonacci series

0, 1, 1, 2, 3, 5, 8, 13, 21, …

begins with the terms 0 and 1 and has the property that each succeeding term is the sum of the two preceding terms.

   a) Write a method fibonacci(n) that calculates the nth Fibonacci number. Incorporate this method into an application that enables the user to enter the value of n.
   b) Determine the largest Fibonacci number that can be displayed on your system.
   c) Modify the application you wrote in part (a) to use double instead of int to calculate and return Fibonacci numbers, and use this modified application to repeat part (b).

Exercise 7.30–Exercise 7.33 are reasonably challenging. Once you have done these problems, you ought to be able to implement most popular card games easily.

7.30 *(Card Shuffling and Dealing)* Modify the application of Fig. 7.11 to deal a five-card poker hand. Then modify class DeckOfCards of Fig. 7.10 to include methods that determine whether a hand contains

   a) a pair
   b) two pairs
   c) three of a kind (e.g., three jacks)
   d) four of a kind (e.g., four aces)

e) a flush (i.e., all five cards of the same suit)

f) a straight (i.e., five cards of consecutive face values)

g) a full house (i.e., two cards of one face value and three cards of another face value)

[*Hint:* Add methods `getFace` and `getSuit` to class `Card` of Fig. 7.9.]

7.31 *(Card Shuffling and Dealing)* Use the methods developed in Exercise 7.30 to write an application that deals two five-card poker hands, evaluates each hand and determines which is the better hand.

7.32 *(Card Shuffling and Dealing)* Modify the application developed in Exercise 7.31 so that it can simulate the dealer. The dealer's five-card hand is dealt "face down," so the player cannot see it. The application should then evaluate the dealer's hand, and, based on the quality of the hand, the dealer should draw one, two or three more cards to replace the corresponding number of unneeded cards in the original hand. The application should then reevaluate the dealer's hand. [*Caution*: This is a difficult problem!]

7.33 *(Card Shuffling and Dealing)* Modify the application developed in Exercise 7.32 so that it can handle the dealer's hand automatically, but the player is allowed to decide which cards of the player's hand to replace. The application should then evaluate both hands and determine who wins. Now use this new application to play 20 games against the computer. Who wins more games, you or the computer? Have a friend play 20 games against the computer. Who wins more games? Based on the results of these games, refine your poker-playing application. (This, too, is a difficult problem.) Play 20 more games. Does your modified application play a better game?

Special Section: Building Your Own Computer

In the next several problems, we take a temporary diversion from the world of high-level language programming. To "peel open" a computer and look at its internal structure. We introduce machine-language programming and write several machine-language programs. To make this an especially valuable experience, we then build a computer (through the technique of software-based *simulation*) on which you can execute your machine-language programs.

7.34 *(Machine-Language Programming)* Let us create a computer called the Simpletron. As its name implies, it is a simple, but powerful, machine. The Simpletron runs programs written in the only language it directly understands: Simpletron Machine Language, or SML for short.

The Simpletron contains an *accumulator*—a special register in which information is put before the Simpletron uses that information in calculations or examines it in various ways. All the information in the Simpletron is handled in terms of *words*. A word is a signed four-digit decimal number, such as +3364, -1293, +0007 and -0001. The Simpletron is equipped with a 100-word memory, and these words are referenced by their location numbers 00, 01, ..., 99.

Before running an SML program, we must *load*, or place, the program into memory. The first instruction (or statement) of every SML program is always placed in location 00. The simulator will start executing at this location.

Each instruction written in SML occupies one word of the Simpletron's memory (and hence instructions are signed four-digit decimal numbers). We shall assume that the sign of an SML instruction is always plus, but the sign of a data word may be either plus or minus. Each location in the Simpletron's memory may contain an instruction, a data value used by a program or an unused (and hence undefined) area of memory. The first two digits of each SML instruction are the *operation code* specifying the operation to be performed. SML operation codes are summarized in Fig. 7.30.

The last two digits of an SML instruction are the *operand*—the address of the memory location containing the word to which the operation applies. Let's consider several simple SML programs.

The first SML program (Fig. 7.31) reads two numbers from the keyboard and computes and displays their sum. The instruction +1007 reads the first number from the keyboard and places it into location 07 (which has been initialized to 0). Then instruction +1008 reads the next number

Operation code	Meaning
Input/output operations:	
`final int READ = 10;`	Read a word from the keyboard into a specific location in memory.
`final int WRITE = 11;`	Write a word from a specific location in memory to the screen.
Load/store operations:	
`final int LOAD = 20;`	Load a word from a specific location in memory into the accumulator.
`final int STORE = 21;`	Store a word from the accumulator into a specific location in memory.
Arithmetic operations:	
`final int ADD = 30;`	Add a word from a specific location in memory to the word in the accumulator (leave the result in the accumulator).
`final int SUBTRACT = 31;`	Subtract a word from a specific location in memory from the word in the accumulator (leave the result in the accumulator).
`final int DIVIDE = 32;`	Divide a word from a specific location in memory into the word in the accumulator (leave result in the accumulator).
`final int MULTIPLY = 33;`	Multiply a word from a specific location in memory by the word in the accumulator (leave the result in the accumulator).
Transfer of control operations:	
`final int BRANCH = 40;`	Branch to a specific location in memory.
`final int BRANCHNEG = 41;`	Branch to a specific location in memory if the accumulator is negative.
`final int BRANCHZERO = 42;`	Branch to a specific location in memory if the accumulator is zero.
`final int HALT = 43;`	Halt. The program has completed its task.

Fig. 7.30 | Simpletron Machine Language (SML) operation codes.

into location 08. The *load* instruction, +2007, puts the first number into the accumulator, and the *add* instruction, +3008, adds the second number to the number in the accumulator. *All SML arithmetic instructions leave their results in the accumulator.* The *store* instruction, +2109, places the result back into memory location 09, from which the *write* instruction, +1109, takes the number and displays it (as a signed four-digit decimal number). The *halt* instruction, +4300, terminates execution.

The second SML program (Fig. 7.32) reads two numbers from the keyboard and determines and displays the larger value. Note the use of the instruction +4107 as a conditional transfer of control, much the same as Java's if statement.

Location	Number	Instruction
00	+1007	(Read A)
01	+1008	(Read B)
02	+2007	(Load A)
03	+3008	(Add B)
04	+2109	(Store C)
05	+1109	(Write C)
06	+4300	(Halt)
07	+0000	(Variable A)
08	+0000	(Variable B)
09	+0000	(Result C)

Fig. 7.31 | SML program that reads two integers and computes their sum.

Location	Number	Instruction
00	+1009	(Read A)
01	+1010	(Read B)
02	+2009	(Load A)
03	+3110	(Subtract B)
04	+4107	(Branch negative to 07)
05	+1109	(Write A)
06	+4300	(Halt)
07	+1110	(Write B)
08	+4300	(Halt)
09	+0000	(Variable A)
10	+0000	(Variable B)

Fig. 7.32 | SML program that reads two integers and determines the larger.

Now write SML programs to accomplish each of the following tasks:
a) Use a sentinel-controlled loop to read 10 positive numbers. Compute and display their sum.
b) Use a counter-controlled loop to read seven numbers, some positive and some negative, and compute and display their average.
c) Read a series of numbers, and determine and display the largest number. The first number read indicates how many numbers should be processed.

7.35 (*Computer Simulator*) In this problem, you are going to build your own computer. No, you will not be soldering components together. Rather, you will use the powerful technique of *software-based simulation* to create an object-oriented *software model* of the Simpletron of Exercise 7.34. Your Simpletron simulator will turn the computer you are using into a Simpletron, and you will actually be able to run, test and debug the SML programs you wrote in Exercise 7.34.

When you run your Simpletron simulator, it should begin by displaying:

```
*** Welcome to Simpletron! ***
*** Please enter your program one instruction  ***
*** (or data word) at a time into the input    ***
*** text field. I will display the location    ***
*** number and a question mark (?). You then    ***
*** type the word for that location. Press the ***
*** Done button to stop entering your program. ***
```

Your application should simulate the memory of the Simpletron with a one-dimensional array memory that has 100 elements. Now assume that the simulator is running, and let us examine the dialog as we enter the program of Fig. 7.32 (Exercise 7.34):

```
00 ? +1009
01 ? +1010
02 ? +2009
03 ? +3110
04 ? +4107
05 ? +1109
06 ? +4300
07 ? +1110
08 ? +4300
09 ? +0000
10 ? +0000
11 ? -99999
```

Your program should display the memory location followed by a question mark. Each of the values to the right of a question mark is input by the user. When the sentinel value -99999 is input, the program should display the following:

```
*** Program loading completed ***
*** Program execution begins  ***
```

The SML program has now been placed (or loaded) in array memory. Now the Simpletron executes the SML program. Execution begins with the instruction in location 00 and, as in Java, continues sequentially, unless directed to some other part of the program by a transfer of control.

Use the variable accumulator to represent the accumulator register. Use the variable instructionCounter to keep track of the location in memory that contains the instruction being performed. Use the variable operationCode to indicate the operation currently being performed (i.e., the left two digits of the instruction word). Use the variable operand to indicate the memory location on which the current instruction operates. Thus, operand is the rightmost two digits of the instruction currently being performed. Do not execute instructions directly from memory. Rather, transfer the next instruction to be performed from memory to a variable called instructionRegister. Then "pick off" the left two digits and place them in operationCode, and "pick off" the right two digits and place them in operand. When the Simpletron begins execution, the special registers are all initialized to zero.

Now, let us "walk through" execution of the first SML instruction, +1009 in memory location 00. This procedure is called an *instruction execution cycle*.

The instructionCounter tells us the location of the next instruction to be performed. We *fetch* the contents of that location from memory by using the Java statement

```
instructionRegister = memory[ instructionCounter ];
```

The operation code and the operand are extracted from the instruction register by the statements

```
operationCode = instructionRegister / 100;
operand = instructionRegister % 100;
```

Now the Simpletron must determine that the operation code is actually a *read* (versus a *write*, a *load*, etc.). A switch differentiates among the 12 operations of SML. In the switch statement, the behavior of various SML instructions is simulated as shown in Fig. 7.33. We discuss branch instructions shortly and leave the others to you.

When the SML program completes execution, the name and contents of each register as well as the complete contents of memory should be displayed. Such a printout is often called a computer dump (no, a computer dump is not a place where old computers go). To help you program your dump method, a sample dump format is shown in Fig. 7.34. Note that a dump after executing a Simpletron program would show the actual values of instructions and data values at the moment execution terminated.

Let us proceed with the execution of our program's first instruction—namely, the +1009 in location 00. As we have indicated, the switch statement simulates this task by prompting the user to enter a value, reading the value and storing it in memory location memory[operand]. The value is then read into location 09. At this point, simulation of the first instruction is completed. All that remains is to prepare the Simpletron to execute the next instruction. Since the instruction just performed was not a transfer of control, we need merely increment the instruction-counter register as follows:

```
instructionCounter++;
```

Instruction	Description
read:	Display the prompt "Enter an integer", then input the integer and store it in location memory[operand].
load:	accumulator = memory[operand];
add:	accumulator += memory[operand];
halt:	This instruction displays the message *** Simpletron execution terminated ***

Fig. 7.33 | Behavior of several SML instructions in the Simpletron.

```
REGISTERS:
accumulator            +0000
instructionCounter        00
instructionRegister    +0000
operationCode             00
operand                   00

MEMORY:
        0      1      2      3      4      5      6      7      8      9
 0  +0000  +0000  +0000  +0000  +0000  +0000  +0000  +0000  +0000  +0000
10  +0000  +0000  +0000  +0000  +0000  +0000  +0000  +0000  +0000  +0000
20  +0000  +0000  +0000  +0000  +0000  +0000  +0000  +0000  +0000  +0000
30  +0000  +0000  +0000  +0000  +0000  +0000  +0000  +0000  +0000  +0000
40  +0000  +0000  +0000  +0000  +0000  +0000  +0000  +0000  +0000  +0000
50  +0000  +0000  +0000  +0000  +0000  +0000  +0000  +0000  +0000  +0000
60  +0000  +0000  +0000  +0000  +0000  +0000  +0000  +0000  +0000  +0000
70  +0000  +0000  +0000  +0000  +0000  +0000  +0000  +0000  +0000  +0000
80  +0000  +0000  +0000  +0000  +0000  +0000  +0000  +0000  +0000  +0000
90  +0000  +0000  +0000  +0000  +0000  +0000  +0000  +0000  +0000  +0000
```

Fig. 7.34 | A sample dump.

This action completes the simulated execution of the first instruction. The entire process (i.e., the instruction execution cycle) begins anew with the fetch of the next instruction to execute.

Now let us consider how the branching instructions—the transfers of control—are simulated. All we need to do is adjust the value in the instruction counter appropriately. Therefore, the unconditional branch instruction (40) is simulated within the `switch` as

```
instructionCounter = operand;
```

The conditional "branch if accumulator is zero" instruction is simulated as

```
if ( accumulator == 0 )
    instructionCounter = operand;
```

At this point, you should implement your Simpletron simulator and run each of the SML programs you wrote in Exercise 7.34. If you desire, you may embellish SML with additional features and provide for these features in your simulator.

Your simulator should check for various types of errors. During the program-loading phase, for example, each number the user types into the Simpletron's `memory` must be in the range -9999 to +9999. Your simulator should test that each number entered is in this range and, if not, keep prompting the user to reenter the number until the user enters a correct number.

During the execution phase, your simulator should check for various serious errors, such as attempts to divide by zero, attempts to execute invalid operation codes, and accumulator overflows (i.e., arithmetic operations resulting in values larger than +9999 or smaller than -9999). Such serious errors are called *fatal errors*. When a fatal error is detected, your simulator should display an error message, such as

```
*** Attempt to divide by zero ***
*** Simpletron execution abnormally terminated ***
```

and should display a full computer dump in the format we discussed previously. This treatment will help the user locate the error in the program.

7.36 (*Simpletron Simulator Modifications*) In Exercise 7.35, you wrote a software simulation of a computer that executes programs written in Simpletron Machine Language (SML). In this exercise, we propose several modifications and enhancements to the Simpletron Simulator.

a) Extend the Simpletron Simulator's memory to contain 1000 memory locations to enable the Simpletron to handle larger programs.

b) Allow the simulator to perform remainder calculations. This modification requires an additional SML instruction.

c) Allow the simulator to perform exponentiation calculations. This modification requires an additional SML instruction.

d) Modify the simulator to use hexadecimal values rather than integer values to represent SML instructions.

e) Modify the simulator to allow output of a newline. This modification requires an additional SML instruction.

f) Modify the simulator to process floating-point values in addition to integer values.

g) Modify the simulator to handle string input. [*Hint:* Each Simpletron word can be divided into two groups, each holding a two-digit integer. Each two-digit integer represents the ASCII (see Appendix B) decimal equivalent of a character. Add a machine-language instruction that will input a string and store the string, beginning at a specific Simpletron memory location. The first half of the word at that location will be a count of the number of characters in the string (i.e., the length of the string). Each succeeding half-word contains one ASCII character expressed as two decimal digits. The machine-language instruction converts each character into its ASCII equivalent and assigns it to a half-word.]

h) Modify the simulator to handle output of strings stored in the format of part (g). [*Hint:* Add a machine-language instruction that will display a string, beginning at a certain Simpletron memory location. The first half of the word at that location is a count of the number of characters in the string (i.e., the length of the string). Each succeeding half-word contains one ASCII character expressed as two decimal digits. The machine-language instruction checks the length and displays the string by translating each two-digit number into its equivalent character.]

8

Classes and Objects: A Deeper Look

OBJECTIVES

In this chapter you will learn:

- Encapsulation and data hiding.
- The notions of data abstraction and abstract data types (ADTs).
- To use keyword **this**.
- To use **static** variables and methods.
- To import **static** members of a class.
- To use the **enum** type to create sets of constants with unique identifiers.
- How to declare **enum** constants with parameters.

Instead of this absurd
division into sexes, they
ought to class people as
static and dynamic.
—Evelyn Waugh

Is it a world to hide virtues
in?
—William Shakespeare

But what, to serve
our private ends,
Forbids the cheating
of our friends?
—Charles Churchill

This above all: to thine own
self be true.
—William Shakespeare

Don't be "consistent,"
but be simply true.
—Oliver Wendell Holmes, Jr.

Outline

8.1 **Introduction**

In our discussions of object-oriented programs in the preceding chapters, we introduced many basic concepts and terminology that relate to Java object-oriented programming (OOP). We also discussed our program development methodology: We selected appropriate variables and methods for each program and specified the manner in which an object of our class collaborated with objects of Java API classes to accomplish the program's overall goals.

In this chapter, we take a deeper look at building classes, controlling access to members of a class and creating constructors. We discuss composition—a capability that allows a class to have references to objects of other classes as members. We reexamine the use of *set* and *get* methods and further explore the new J2SE 5.0 class type enum (introduced in Section 6.10) that enables programmers to declare and manipulate sets of unique identifiers that represent constant values. In Section 6.10, we introduced the basic enum type, which appeared within another class and simply declared a set of constants. In this chapter, we discuss the relationship between enum types and classes, demonstrating that an enum, like a class, can be declared in its own file with constructors, methods and fields. The chapter also discusses static class members and final instance variables in detail. We investigate issues such as software reusability, data abstraction and encapsulation. Finally, we explain how to organize classes in packages to help manage large applications and promote reuse, then show a special relationship between classes in the same package.

Chapter 9, Object-Oriented Programming: Inheritance, and Chapter 10, Object-Oriented Programming: Polymorphism, introduce inheritance and polymorphism, respectively—two additional key object-oriented programming technologies.

8.2 Time Class Case Study

Time1 Class Declaration

Our first example consists of two classes—Time1 (Fig. 8.1) and Time1Test (Fig. 8.2). Class Time1 represents the time of day. Class Time1Test is an application class in which the main method creates one object of class Time1 and invokes its methods. These classes must be declared in separate files because they are both public classes. The output of this program appears in Fig. 8.2.

Class Time1 contains three private instance variables of type int (Fig. 8.1, lines 6–8)—hour, minute and second—that represent the time in universal-time format (24-hour clock format in which hours are in the range 0–23). Class Time1 contains public methods setTime (lines 12–17), toUniversalString (lines 20–23) and toString (lines 26–31). These methods are also called the **public services** or the **public interface** that the class provides to its clients.

In this example, class Time1 does not declare a constructor, so the class has a default constructor that is supplied by the compiler. Each instance variable implicitly receives the default value 0 for an int. Note that instance variables also can be initialized when they are declared in the class body using the same initialization syntax as with a local variable.

Method setTime (lines 12–17) is a public method that declares three int parameters and uses them to set the time. A conditional expression tests each argument to determine whether the value is in a specified range. For example, the hour value (line 14) must be greater than or equal to 0 and less than 24, because universal-time format represents hours as integers from 0 to 23 (e.g., 1 PM is hour 13 and 11 PM is hour 23; midnight is hour 0 and noon is hour 12). Similarly, both minute and second values (lines 15 and 16) must be greater than or equal to 0 and less than 60. Any values outside these ranges are set to zero to ensure that a Time1 object always contains consistent data—that is, the object's data values are always kept in range, even if the values provided as arguments to method setTime were incorrect. In this example, zero is a consistent value for hour, minute and second.

A value passed to setTime is a correct value if that value is in the allowed range for the member it is initializing. So, any number in the range 0–23 would be a correct value for the hour. A correct value is always a consistent value. However, a consistent value is not necessarily a correct value. If setTime sets hour to 0 because the argument received was out of range, then setTime is taking an incorrect value and making it consistent, so the object remains in a consistent state at all times. In this case, the program might want to indicate that the object is incorrect.

Software Engineering Observation 8.1

Methods that modify the values of private *variables should verify that the intended new values are proper. If they are not, the set methods should place the* private *variables into an appropriate consistent state.*

```
 1   // Fig. 8.1: Time1.java
 2   // Time1 class declaration maintains the time in 24-hour format.
 3
 4   public class Time1
 5   {
 6      private int hour;   // 0 - 23
 7      private int minute; // 0 - 59
 8      private int second; // 0 - 59
 9
10      // set a new time value using universal time; ensure that
11      // the data remains consistent by setting invalid values to zero
12      public void setTime( int h, int m, int s )
13
14         hour = ( ( h >= 0 && h < 24 ) ? h : 0 );   // validate hour
15         minute = ( ( m >= 0 && m < 60 ) ? m : 0 ); // validate minute
16         second = ( ( s >= 0 && s < 60 ) ? s : 0 ); // validate second
17      } // end method setTime
18
19      // convert to String in universal-time format (HH:MM:SS)
20      public String toUniversalString()
21      {
22         return String.format( "%02d:%02d:%02d", hour, minute, second );
23      } // end method toUniversalString
24
25      // convert to String in standard-time format (H:MM:SS AM or PM)
26      public String toString()
27      {
28         return String.format( "%d:%02d:%02d %s",
29            ( ( hour == 0 || hour == 12 ) ? 12 : hour % 12 ),
30            minute, second, ( hour < 12 ? "AM" : "PM" ) );
31      } // end method toString
32   } // end class Time1
```

Fig. 8.1 | Time1 class declaration maintains the time in 24-hour format.

Method toUniversalString (lines 20–23) takes no arguments and returns a String in universal-time format, consisting of six digits—two for the hour, two for the minute and two for the second. For example, if the time were 1:30:07 PM, method toUniversalString would return 13:30:07. The return statement (line 22) uses static method format of class String to return a String containing the formatted hour, minute and second values, each with two digits and possibly a leading 0 (specified with the 0 flag). Method format is similar to method System.out.printf except that format returns a formatted String rather than displaying it in a command window. The formatted String is returned by method toUniversalString.

Method toString (lines 26–31) takes no arguments and returns a String in standard-time format, consisting of the hour, minute and second values separated by colons and followed by an AM or PM indicator (e.g., 1:27:06 PM). Like method toUniversalString, method toString uses static String method format to format the minute and second as two-digit values with leading zeros if necessary. Line 29 uses a conditional operator (?:) to determine the value for hour in the string—if the hour is 0 or 12 (AM or PM), it appears as 12—otherwise, the hour appears as a value from 1 to 11. The conditional operator in line 30 determines whether AM or PM will be returned as part of the String.

Recall from Section 6.4 that all objects in Java have a toString method that returns a String representation of the object. We chose to return a String containing the time in standard-time format. Method toString can be called implicitly whenever a Time1 object appears in the code where a String is needed, such as the value to output with a %s format specifier in a call to System.out.printf.

Using Class *Time1*

As you learned in Chapter 3, each class you declare represents a new type in Java. Therefore, after declaring class Time1, we can use it as a type in declarations such as

```
Time1 sunset; // sunset can hold a reference to a Time1 object
```

The Time1Test application class (Fig. 8.2) uses class Time1. Line 9 declares and creates a Time1 object and assigns it to local variable time. Note that new implicitly invokes class Time1's default constructor, since Time1 does not declare any constructors. Lines 12–16 output the time first in universal-time format (by invoking time's toUniversalString method in line 13), then in standard-time format (by explicitly invoking time's toString method in line 15) to confirm that the Time1 object was initialized properly.

Line 19 invokes method setTime of the time object to change the time. Then lines 20–24 output the time again in both formats to confirm that the time was set correctly.

To illustrate that method setTime maintains the object in a consistent state, line 27 calls method setTime with arguments of 99 for the hour, minute and second. Lines 28–32 output the time again in both formats to confirm that setTime maintained the object's consistent state, then the program terminates. The last two lines of the application's output show that the time is reset to midnight—the initial value of a Time1 object—after an attempt to set the time with three out-of-range values.

Notes on the *Time1* Class Declaration

Consider several issues of class design with respect to class Time1. The instance variables hour, minute and second are each declared private. The actual data representation used within the class is of no concern to the class's clients. For example, it would be perfectly reasonable for Time1 to represent the time internally as the number of seconds since midnight or the number of minutes and seconds since midnight. Clients could use the same public methods and get the same results without being aware of this. (Exercise 8.5 asks you to represent the time in class Time1 as the number of seconds since midnight and show that there is indeed no change visible to the clients of the class.)

Software Engineering Observation 8.2

Classes simplify programming, because the client can use only the public methods exposed by the class. Such methods are usually client oriented rather than implementation oriented. Clients are neither aware of, nor involved in, a class's implementation. Clients generally care about what the class does but not how the class does it.

Software Engineering Observation 8.3

Interfaces change less frequently than implementations. When an implementation changes, implementation-dependent code must change accordingly. Hiding the implementation reduces the possibility that other program parts will become dependent on class-implementation details.

```
 1    // Fig. 8.2: Time1Test.java
 2    // Time1 object used in an application.
 3
 4    public class Time1Test
 5    {
 6       public static void main( String args[] )
 7       {
 8          // create and initialize a Time1 object
 9          Time1 time = new Time1(); // invokes Time1 constructor
10
11          // output string representations of the time
12          System.out.print( "The initial universal time is: " );
13          System.out.println( time.toUniversalString() );
14          System.out.print( "The initial standard time is: " );
15          System.out.println( time.toString() );
16          System.out.println(); // output a blank line
17
18          // change time and output updated time
19          time.setTime( 13, 27, 6 );
20          System.out.print( "Universal time after setTime is: " );
21          System.out.println( time.toUniversalString() );
22          System.out.print( "Standard time after setTime is: " );
23          System.out.println( time.toString() );
24          System.out.println(); // output a blank line
25
26          // set time with invalid values; output updated time
27          time.setTime( 99, 99, 99 );
28          System.out.println( "After attempting invalid settings:" );
29          System.out.print( "Universal time: " );
30          System.out.println( time.toUniversalString() );
31          System.out.print( "Standard time: " );
32          System.out.println( time.toString() );
33       } // end main
34    } // end class Time1Test
```

```
The initial universal time is: 00:00:00
The initial standard time is: 12:00:00 AM

Universal time after setTime is: 13:27:06
Standard time after setTime is: 1:27:06 PM

After attempting invalid settings:
Universal time: 00:00:00
Standard time: 12:00:00 AM
```

Fig. 8.2 | Time1 object used in an application.

8.3 Controlling Access to Members

The access modifiers public and private control access to a class's variables and methods. (In Chapter 9, we will introduce the additional access modifier protected.) As we stated in Section 8.2, the primary purpose of public methods is to present to the class's clients a view of the services the class provides (the class's public interface). Clients of the class need not be concerned with how the class accomplishes its tasks. For this reason, the private variables and private methods of a class (i.e., the class's implementation details) are not directly accessible to the class's clients.

Figure 8.3 demonstrates that private class members are not directly accessible outside the class. Lines 9–11 attempt to access directly the private instance variables hour, minute and second of the Time1 object time. When this program is compiled, the compiler generates error messages stating that these private members are not accessible. [*Note:* This program assumes that the Time1 class from Fig. 8.1 is used.]

Common Programming Error 8.1

An attempt by a method that is not a member of a class to access a private member of that class is a compilation error.

8.4 Referring to the Current Object's Members with the this Reference

Every object can access a reference to itself with keyword **this** (sometimes called the **this reference**). When a non-static method is called for a particular object, the method's body implicitly uses keyword this to refer to the object's instance variables and other methods. As you will see in Fig. 8.4, you can also use keyword this explicitly in a non-static meth-

```
1   // Fig. 8.3: MemberAccessTest.java
2   // Private members of class Time1 are not accessible.
3   public class MemberAccessTest
4   {
5      public static void main( String args[] )
6      {
7         Time1 time = new Time1(); // create and initialize Time1 object
8
9         time.hour = 7;    // error: hour has private access in Time1
10        time.minute = 15; // error: minute has private access in Time1
11        time.second = 30; // error: second has private access in Time1
12     } // end main
13   } // end class MemberAccessTest
```

```
MemberAccessTest.java:9: hour has private access in Time1
      time.hour = 7;     // error: hour has private access in Time1
          ^
MemberAccessTest.java:10: minute has private access in Time1
      time.minute = 15; // error: minute has private access in Time1
          ^
MemberAccessTest.java:11: second has private access in Time1
      time.second = 30; // error: second has private access in Time1
          ^
3 errors
```

Fig. 8.3 | Private members of class Time1 are not accessible.

od's body. Section 8.5 shows another interesting use of keyword this. Section 8.11 explains why keyword this cannot be used in a static method.

We now demonstrate implicit and explicit use of the this reference to enable class ThisTest's main method to display the private data of a class SimpleTime object (Fig. 8.4). Note that this example is the first in which we declare two classes in one file—class ThisTest is declared in lines 4–11, and class SimpleTime is declared in lines 14–47. We did this to demonstrate that when you compile a .java file that contains more than one class, the compiler produces a separate class file with the .class extension for every compiled class. In this case two separate files are produced—one for SimpleTime and one for ThisTest. When one source-code (.java) file contains multiple class declarations, the class files for those classes are placed in the same directory by the compiler. Also, note that only class ThisTest is declared public in Fig. 8.4. A source-code file can contain only one public class—otherwise, a compilation error occurs.

Class SimpleTime (lines 14–47) declares three private instance variables—hour, minute and second (lines 16–18). The constructor (lines 23–28) receives three int arguments to initialize a SimpleTime object. Note that we used parameter names for the constructor (line 23) that are identical to the class's instance variable names (lines 16–18). We don't recommend this practice, but we did it here to shadow (hide) the corresponding instance variables so that we could illustrate explicit use of the this reference. If a method

```
1   // Fig. 8.4: ThisTest.java
2   // this used implicitly and explicitly to refer to members of an object.
3
4   public class ThisTest
5   {
6      public static void main( String args[] )
7      {
8         SimpleTime time = new SimpleTime( 15, 30, 19 );
9         System.out.println( time.buildString() );
10     } // end main
11  } // end class ThisTest
12
13  // class SimpleTime demonstrates the "this" reference
14  class SimpleTime
15  {
16     private int hour;    // 0-23
17     private int minute;  // 0-59
18     private int second;  // 0-59
19
20     // if the constructor uses parameter names identical to
21     // instance variable names the "this" reference is
22     // required to distinguish between names
23     public SimpleTime( int hour, int minute, int second )
24     {
25        this.hour = hour;       // set "this" object's hour
26        this.minute = minute;   // set "this" object's minute
27        this.second = second;   // set "this" object's second
28     } // end SimpleTime constructor
```

Fig. 8.4 | this used implicitly and explicitly to refer to members of an object. (Part 1 of 2.)

```
29
30        // use explicit and implicit "this" to call toUniversalString
31        public String buildString()
32        {
33           return String.format( "%24s: %s\n%24s: %s",
34              "this.toUniversalString()", this.toUniversalString(),
35              "toUniversalString()", toUniversalString() );
36        } // end method buildString
37
38        // convert to String in universal-time format (HH:MM:SS)
39        public String toUniversalString()
40        {
41           // "this" is not required here to access instance variables,
42           // because method does not have local variables with same
43           // names as instance variables
44           return String.format( "%02d:%02d:%02d",
45              this.hour, this.minute, this.second );
46        } // end method toUniversalString
47     } // end class SimpleTime
```

```
this.toUniversalString(): 15:30:19
    toUniversalString(): 15:30:19
```

Fig. 8.4 | `this` used implicitly and explicitly to refer to members of an object. (Part 2 of 2.)

contains a local variable with the same name as a field, that method will refer to the local variable rather than the field. In this case, the local variable shadows the field in the method's scope. However, the method can use the `this` reference to refer to the shadowed field explicitly, as shown in lines 25–27 for `SimpleTime`'s shadowed instance variables.

Method `buildString` (lines 31–36) returns a `String` created by a statement that uses the `this` reference explicitly and implicitly. Line 34 uses the `this` reference explicitly to call method `toUniversalString`. Line 35 uses the `this` reference implicitly to call the same method. Note that both lines perform the same task. Programmers typically do not use `this` explicitly to reference other methods within the current object. Also, note that line 45 in method `toUniversalString` explicitly uses the `this` reference to access each instance variable. This is not necessary here, because the method does not have any local variables that shadow the instance variables of the class.

Common Programming Error 8.2

It is often a logic error when a method contains a parameter or local variable that has the same name as a field of the class. In this case, use reference `this` if you wish to access the field of the class—otherwise, the method parameter or local variable will be referenced.

Error-Prevention Tip 8.1

Avoid method parameter names or local variable names that conflict with field names. This helps prevent subtle, hard-to-locate bugs.

Application class `ThisTest` (lines 4–11) demonstrates class `SimpleTime`. Line 8 creates an instance of class `SimpleTime` and invokes its constructor. Line 9 invokes the object's `buildString` method, then displays the results.

> **Performance Tip 8.1**
>
> *Java conserves storage by maintaining only one copy of each method per class—this method is invoked by every object of the class. Each object, on the other hand, has its own copy of the class's instance variables (i.e., non-static fields). Each method of the class implicitly uses this to determine the specific object of the class to manipulate.*

8.5 Time Class Case Study: Overloaded Constructors

As you know, you can declare your own constructor to specify how objects of a class should be initialized. Next, we demonstrate a class with several overloaded constructors that enable objects of that class to be initialized in different ways. To overload constructors, simply provide multiple constructor declarations with different signatures. Recall from Section 6.12 that the compiler differentiates signatures by the number and types of the parameters in each signature.

Class *Time2* with Overloaded Constructors

The default constructor for class Time1 (Fig. 8.1) initialized hour, minute and second to their default 0 values (which is midnight in universal time). The default constructor does not enable the class's clients to initialize the time with specific non-zero values. Class Time2 (Fig. 8.5) contains five overloaded constructors that provide convenient ways to initialize objects of the new class Time2. Every object each constructor initializes begins in a consistent state. In this program, four of the constructors invoke a fifth constructor, which, in turn, calls method setTime to ensure that the value supplied for hour is in the range 0 to 23 and that the values for minute and second are each in the range 0 to 59. If a value is out of range, it is set to zero by setTime (once again ensuring that each instance variable remains in a consistent state). The compiler invokes the appropriate constructor by matching the number and types of the arguments specified in the constructor call with the num-

```
1   // Fig. 8.5: Time2.java
2   // Time2 class declaration with overloaded constructors.
3
4   public class Time2
5   {
6      private int hour;    // 0 - 23
7      private int minute;  // 0 - 59
8      private int second;  // 0 - 59
9
10     // Time2 no-argument constructor: initializes each instance variable
11     // to zero; ensures that Time2 objects start in a consistent state
12     public Time2()
13     {
14        this( 0, 0, 0 ); // invoke Time2 constructor with three arguments
15     } // end Time2 no-argument constructor
16
17     // Time2 constructor: hour supplied, minute and second defaulted to 0
18     public Time2( int h )
19     {
20        this( h, 0, 0 ); // invoke Time2 constructor with three arguments
21     } // end Time2 one-argument constructor
22
```

Fig. 8.5 | Time2 class with overloaded constructors. (Part 1 of 3.)

```
23    // Time2 constructor: hour and minute supplied, second defaulted to 0
24    public Time2( int h, int m )
25    {
26       this( h, m, 0 ); // invoke Time2 constructor with three arguments
27    } // end Time2 two-argument constructor
28
29    // Time2 constructor: hour, minute and second supplied
30    public Time2( int h, int m, int s )
31    {
32       setTime( h, m, s ); // invoke setTime to validate time
33    } // end Time2 three-argument constructor
34
35    // Time2 constructor: another Time2 object supplied
36    public Time2( Time2 time )
37    {
38       // invoke Time2 three-argument constructor
39       this( time.getHour(), time.getMinute(), time.getSecond() );
40    } // end Time2 constructor with a Time2 object argument
41
42    // Set Methods
43    // set a new time value using universal time; ensure that
44    // the data remains consistent by setting invalid values to zero
45    public void setTime( int h, int m, int s )
46    {
47       setHour( h );   // set the hour
48       setMinute( m ); // set the minute
49       setSecond( s ); // set the second
50    } // end method setTime
51
52    // validate and set hour
53    public void setHour( int h )
54    {
55       hour = ( ( h >= 0 && h < 24 ) ? h : 0 );
56    } // end method setHour
57
58    // validate and set minute
59    public void setMinute( int m )
60    {
61       minute = ( ( m >= 0 && m < 60 ) ? m : 0 );
62    } // end method setMinute
63
64    // validate and set second
65    public void setSecond( int s )
66    {
67       second = ( ( s >= 0 && s < 60 ) ? s : 0 );
68    } // end method setSecond
69
70    // Get Methods
71    // get hour value
72    public int getHour()
73    {
74       return hour;
75    } // end method getHour
```

Fig. 8.5 | Time2 class with overloaded constructors. (Part 2 of 3.)

```
76
77      // get minute value
78      public int getMinute()
79      {
80         return minute;
81      } // end method getMinute
82
83      // get second value
84      public int getSecond()
85      {
86         return second;
87      } // end method getSecond
88
89      // convert to String in universal-time format (HH:MM:SS)
90      public String toUniversalString()
91      {
92         return String.format(
93            "%02d:%02d:%02d", getHour(), getMinute(), getSecond() );
94      } // end method toUniversalString
95
96      // convert to String in standard-time format (H:MM:SS AM or PM)
97      public String toString()
98      {
99         return String.format( "%d:%02d:%02d %s",
100           ( (getHour() == 0 || getHour() == 12) ? 12 : getHour() % 12 ),
101           getMinute(), getSecond(), ( getHour() < 12 ? "AM" : "PM" ) );
102     } // end method toString
103  } // end class Time2
```

Fig. 8.5 | Time2 class with overloaded constructors. (Part 3 of 3.)

ber and types of the parameters specified in each constructor declaration. Note that class Time2 also provides *set* and *get* methods for each instance variable.

Class Time2's Constructors

Lines 12–15 declare a so-called no-argument constructor—that is, a constructor invoked without arguments. Such a constructor simply initializes the object as specified in the constructor's body. In the body, we introduce a use of the this reference that is allowed only as the first statement in a constructor's body. Line 14 uses this in method-call syntax to invoke the Time2 constructor that takes three arguments (lines 30–33). The no-argument constructor passes values of 0 for the hour, minute and second to the constructor with three parameters. Using the this reference as shown here is a popular way to reuse initialization code provided by another of the class's constructors rather than defining similar code in the no-argument constructor's body. We use this syntax in four of the five Time2 constructors to make the class easier to maintain and modify. If we need to change how objects of class Time2 are initialized, only the constructor that the class's other constructors call would need to be modified. In fact, even that constructor might not need modification in this example. That constructor simply calls the setTime method to perform the actual initialization, so it is possible that the changes the class might require would be localized to the *set* methods.

Common Programming Error 8.3

It is a syntax error when this *is used in a constructor's body to call another constructor of the same class if that call is not the first statement in the constructor. It is also a syntax error when a method attempts to invoke a constructor directly via* this.

Lines 18–21 declare a Time2 constructor with a single int parameter representing the hour, which is passed with 0 for the minute and second to the constructor at lines 30–33. Lines 24–27 declare a Time2 constructor that receives two int parameters representing the hour and minute, which are passed with 0 for the second to the constructor at lines 30–33. Like the no-argument constructor, each of these constructors invokes the constructor at lines 30–33 to minimize code duplication. Lines 30–33 declare the Time2 constructor that receives three int parameters representing the hour, minute and second. This constructor calls setTime to initialize the instance variables to consistent values.

Common Programming Error 8.4

A constructor can call methods of the class. Be aware that the instance variables might not yet be in a consistent state, because the constructor is in the process of initializing the object. Using instance variables before they have been initialized properly is a logic error.

Lines 36–40 declare a Time2 constructor that receives a Time2 reference to another Time2 object. In this case, the values from the Time2 argument are passed to the three-argument constructor at lines 30–33 to initialize the hour, minute and second. Note that line 39 could have directly accessed the hour, minute and second values of the constructor's argument time with the expressions time.hour, time.minute and time.second—even though hour, minute and second are declared as private variables of class Time2. This is due to a special relationship between objects of the same class.

Software Engineering Observation 8.4

When one object of a class has a reference to another object of the same class, the first object can access all the second object's data and methods (including those that are private).

Notes Regarding Class *Time2*'s Set *and* Get *Methods and Constructors*
Note that Time2's *set* and *get* methods are called throughout the body of the class. In particular, method setTime calls methods setHour, setMinute and setSecond in lines 47–49, and methods toUniversalString and toString call methods getHour, getMinute and getSecond in line 93 and lines 100–101, respectively. In each case, these methods could have accessed the class's private data directly without calling the *set* and *get* methods. However, consider changing the representation of the time from three int values (requiring 12 bytes of memory) to a single int value representing the total number of seconds that have elapsed since midnight (requiring only 4 bytes of memory). If we make such a change, only the bodies of the methods that access the private data directly would need to change—in particular, the individual *set* and *get* methods for the hour, minute and second. There would be no need to modify the bodies of methods setTime, toUniversalString or toString because they do not access the data directly. Designing the class in this manner reduces the likelihood of programming errors when altering the class's implementation.

Similarly, each Time2 constructor could be written to include a copy of the appropriate statements from method setTime. Doing so may be slightly more efficient, because the extra constructor call and call to setTime are eliminated. However, duplicating statements in multiple methods or constructors makes changing the class's internal data representation more difficult. Having the Time2 constructors call the constructor with three arguments (or even call setTime directly) requires any changes to the implementation of setTime to be made only once.

Software Engineering Observation 8.5

When implementing a method of a class, use the class's set *and* get *methods to access the class's private data. This simplifies code maintenance and reduces the likelihood of errors.*

Using Class *Time2*'s Overloaded Constructors

Class Time2Test (Fig. 8.6) creates six Time2 objects (lines 8–13) to invoke the overloaded Time2 constructors. Line 8 shows that the no-argument constructor (lines 12–15 of Fig. 8.5) is invoked by placing an empty set of parentheses after the class name when allocating a Time2 object with new. Lines 9–13 of the program demonstrate passing arguments to the other Time2 constructors. Java invokes the appropriate overloaded constructor by matching the number and types of the arguments specified in the constructor call with the number and types of the parameters specified in each constructor declaration. Line 9 invokes the constructor at lines 18–21 of Fig. 8.5. Line 10 invokes the constructor at lines 24–27 of Fig. 8.5. Lines 11–12 invoke the constructor at lines 30–33 of Fig. 8.5. Line 13 invokes the constructor at lines 36–40 of Fig. 8.5. The application displays the String representation of each initialized Time2 object to confirm that it was initialized properly.

```java
1   // Fig. 8.6: Time2Test.java
2   // Overloaded constructors used to initialize Time2 objects.
3
4   public class Time2Test
5   {
6      public static void main( String args[] )
7      {
8         Time2 t1 = new Time2();              // 00:00:00
9         Time2 t2 = new Time2( 2 );           // 02:00:00
10        Time2 t3 = new Time2( 21, 34 );      // 21:34:00
11        Time2 t4 = new Time2( 12, 25, 42 );  // 12:25:42
12        Time2 t5 = new Time2( 27, 74, 99 );  // 00:00:00
13        Time2 t6 = new Time2( t4 );          // 12:25:42
14
15        System.out.println( "Constructed with:" );
16        System.out.println( "t1: all arguments defaulted" );
17        System.out.printf( "   %s\n", t1.toUniversalString() );
18        System.out.printf( "   %s\n", t1.toString() );
19
20        System.out.println(
21           "t2: hour specified; minute and second defaulted" );
22        System.out.printf( "   %s\n", t2.toUniversalString() );
23        System.out.printf( "   %s\n", t2.toString() );
24
```

Fig. 8.6 | Overloaded constructors used to initialize Time2 objects. (Part 1 of 2.)

```
25          System.out.println(
26             "t3: hour and minute specified; second defaulted" );
27          System.out.printf( "   %s\n", t3.toUniversalString() );
28          System.out.printf( "   %s\n", t3.toString() );
29
30          System.out.println( "t4: hour, minute and second specified" );
31          System.out.printf( "   %s\n", t4.toUniversalString() );
32          System.out.printf( "   %s\n", t4.toString() );
33
34          System.out.println( "t5: all invalid values specified" );
35          System.out.printf( "   %s\n", t5.toUniversalString() );
36          System.out.printf( "   %s\n", t5.toString() );
37
38          System.out.println( "t6: Time2 object t4 specified" );
39          System.out.printf( "   %s\n", t6.toUniversalString() );
40          System.out.printf( "   %s\n", t6.toString() );
41       } // end main
42    } // end class Time2Test
```

```
t1: all arguments defaulted
   00:00:00
   12:00:00 AM
t2: hour specified; minute and second defaulted
   02:00:00
   2:00:00 AM
t3: hour and minute specified; second defaulted
   21:34:00
   9:34:00 PM
t4: hour, minute and second specified
   12:25:42
   12:25:42 PM
t5: all invalid values specified
   00:00:00
   12:00:00 AM
t6: Time2 object t4 specified
   12:25:42
   12:25:42 PM
```

Fig. 8.6 | Overloaded constructors used to initialize `Time2` objects. (Part 2 of 2.)

8.6 Default and No-Argument Constructors

Every class must have at least one constructor. As you learned in Section 3.7, if you do not provide any constructors in a class's declaration, the compiler creates a default constructor that takes no arguments when it is invoked. The default constructor initializes the instance variables to the initial values specified in their declarations or to their default values (zero for primitive numeric types, `false` for `boolean` values and `null` for references). In Section 9.4.1, you will learn that the default constructor performs another task in addition to initializing instance variables to their default value.

If your class declares constructors, the compiler will not create a default constructor for your class. In this case, to specify the default initialization for objects of your class, you must declare a no-argument constructor—as in lines 12–15 of Fig. 8.5. Like a default constructor, a no-argument constructor is invoked with empty parentheses. Note that the

`Time2` no-argument constructor explicitly initializes a `Time2` object by passing to the three-argument constructor 0 for each parameter. Since 0 is the default value for `int` instance variables, the no-argument constructor in this example could actually be declared with an empty body. In this case, each instance variable would receive its default value when the no-argument constructor is called. If we omit the no-argument constructor, clients of this class would not be able to create a `Time2` object with the expression `new Time2()`.

Common Programming Error 8.5

If a class has constructors, but none of the `public` constructors are no-argument constructors, and a program attempts to call a no-argument constructor to initialize an object of the class, a compilation error occurs. A constructor can be called with no arguments only if the class does not have any constructors (in which case the default constructor is called) or if the class has a `public` no-argument constructor.

Software Engineering Observation 8.6

Java allows other methods of the class besides its constructors to have the same name as the class and to specify return types. Such methods are not constructors and will not be called when an object of the class is instantiated. Java determines which methods are constructors by locating the methods that have the same name as the class and do not specify a return type.

8.7 Notes on *Set* and *Get* Methods

As you know, a class's `private` fields can be manipulated only by methods of that class. A typical manipulation might be the adjustment of a customer's bank balance (e.g., a `private` instance variable of a class `BankAccount`) by a method `computeInterest`. Classes often provide `public` methods to allow clients of the class to *set* (i.e., assign values to) or *get* (i.e., obtain the values of) `private` instance variables.

As a naming example, a method that sets instance variable `interestRate` would typically be named `setInterestRate` and a method that gets the `interestRate` would typically be called `getInterestRate`. *Set* methods are also commonly called mutator methods, because they typically change a value. *Get* methods are also commonly called accessor methods or query methods.

Set *and* Get *Methods vs.* `public` *Data*

It would seem that providing *set* and *get* capabilities is essentially the same as making the instance variables `public`. This is a subtlety of Java that makes the language so desirable for software engineering. A `public` instance variable can be read or written by any method that has a reference to an object that contains the instance variable. If an instance variable is declared `private`, a `public` *get* method certainly allows other methods to access the variable, but the *get* method can control how the client can access the variable. For example, a *get* method might control the format of the data it returns and thus shield the client code from the actual data representation. A `public` *set* method can—and should—carefully scrutinize attempts to modify the variable's value to ensure that the new value is appropriate for that data item. For example, an attempt to *set* the day of the month to 37 would be rejected, an attempt to *set* a person's weight to a negative value would be rejected, and so on. Thus, although *set* and *get* methods provide access to `private` data, the access is restricted by the programmer's implementation of the methods. This helps promote good software engineering.

Validity Checking in Set *Methods*

The benefits of data integrity are not automatic simply because instance variables are declared `private`—the programmer must provide validity checking. Java enables programmers to design better programs in a convenient manner. A class's *set* methods can return values indicating that attempts were made to assign invalid data to objects of the class. A client of the class can test the return value of a *set* method to determine whether the client's attempt to modify the object was successful and to take appropriate action.

Software Engineering Observation 8.7

When necessary, provide `public` *methods to change and retrieve the values of* `private` *instance variables. This architecture helps hide the implementation of a class from its clients, which improves program modifiability.*

Software Engineering Observation 8.8

Class designers need not provide set *or* get *methods for each* `private` *field. These capabilities should be provided only when it makes sense.*

Predicate Methods

Another common use for accessor methods is to test whether a condition is true or false—such methods are often called predicate methods. An example of a predicate method would be an `isEmpty` method for a container class—a class capable of holding many objects, such as a linked list, a stack or a queue. A program might test `isEmpty` before attempting to read another item from a container object. A program might test `isFull` before attempting to insert another item into a container object.

Using Set *and* Get *Methods to Create a Class That Is Easier to Debug and Maintain*

If only one method performs a particular task, such as setting the hour in a `Time2` object, it is easier to debug and maintain the class. If the `hour` is not being set properly, the code that actually modifies instance variable `hour` is localized to one method's body—`setHour`. Thus, your debugging efforts can be focused on method `setHour`.

8.8 Composition

A class can have references to objects of other classes as members. Such a capability is called composition and is sometimes referred to as a *has-a* relationship. For example, an object of class `AlarmClock` needs to know the current time and the time when it is supposed to sound its alarm, so it is reasonable to include two references to `Time` objects as members of the `AlarmClock` object.

Software Engineering Observation 8.9

One form of software reuse is composition, in which a class has as members references to objects of other classes.

Our example of composition contains three classes—`Date` (Fig. 8.7), `Employee` (Fig. 8.8) and `EmployeeTest` (Fig. 8.9). Class `Date` (Fig. 8.7) declares instance variables month, day and year (lines 6–8) to represent a date. The constructor receives three `int`

```
 1    // Fig. 8.7: Date.java
 2    // Date class declaration.
 3
 4    public class Date
 5    {
 6       private int month; // 1-12
 7       private int day;   // 1-31 based on month
 8       private int year;  // any year
 9
10       // constructor: call checkMonth to confirm proper value for month;
11       // call checkDay to confirm proper value for day
12       public Date( int theMonth, int theDay, int theYear )
13       {
14          month = checkMonth( theMonth ); // validate month
15          year = theYear; // could validate year
16          day = checkDay( theDay ); // validate day
17
18          System.out.printf(
19             "Date object constructor for date %s\n", this );
20       } // end Date constructor
21
22       // utility method to confirm proper month value
23       private int checkMonth( int testMonth )
24       {
25          if ( testMonth > 0 && testMonth <= 12 ) // validate month
26             return testMonth;
27          else // month is invalid
28          {
29             System.out.printf(
30                "Invalid month (%d) set to 1.", testMonth );
31             return 1; // maintain object in consistent state
32          } // end else
33       } // end method checkMonth
34
35       // utility method to confirm proper day value based on month and year
36       private int checkDay( int testDay )
37       {
38          int daysPerMonth[] =
39             { 0, 31, 28, 31, 30, 31, 30, 31, 31, 30, 31, 30, 31 };
40
41          // check if day in range for month
42          if ( testDay > 0 && testDay <= daysPerMonth[ month ] )
43             return testDay;
44
45          // check for leap year
46          if ( month == 2 && testDay == 29 && ( year % 400 == 0 ||
47             ( year % 4 == 0 && year % 100 != 0 ) ) )
48             return testDay;
49
50          System.out.printf( "Invalid day (%d) set to 1.", testDay );
51          return 1;  // maintain object in consistent state
52       } // end method checkDay
53
```

Fig. 8.7 | Date class declaration. (Part 1 of 2.)

```
54      // return a String of the form month/day/year
55      public String toString()
56      {
57         return String.format( "%d/%d/%d", month, day, year );
58      } // end method toString
59   } // end class Date
```

Fig. 8.7 | Date class declaration. (Part 2 of 2.)

parameters. Line 14 invokes utility method checkMonth (lines 23–33) to validate the month—an out-of-range value is set to 1 to maintain a consistent state. Line 15 assumes that the value for year is correct and does not validate it. Line 16 invokes utility method checkDay (lines 36–52) to validate the value for day based on the current month and year. Lines 42–43 determine whether the day is correct based on the number of days in the particular month. If the day is not correct, lines 46–47 determine whether the month is February, the day is 29 and the year is a leap year. If lines 42–48 do not return a correct value for day, line 51 returns 1 to maintain the Date in a consistent state. Note that lines 18–19 in the constructor output the this reference as a String. Since this is a reference to the current Date object, the object's toString method (lines 55–58) is called implicitly to obtain the object's String representation.

Class Employee (Fig. 8.8) has instance variables firstName, lastName, birthDate and hireDate. Members birthDate and hireDate (lines 8–9) are references to Date objects. This demonstrates that a class can have as instance variables references to objects of other classes. The Employee constructor (lines 12–19) takes four parameters—first, last, dateOfBirth and dateOfHire. The objects referenced by the parameters dateOfBirth and dateOfHire are assigned to the Employee object's birthDate and hireDate instance variables, respectively. Note that when class Employee's toString method is called, it returns a String containing the String representations of the two Date objects. Each of these Strings is obtained with an implicit call to the Date class's toString method.

Class EmployeeTest (Fig. 8.9) creates two Date objects (lines 8–9) to represent an Employee's birthday and hire date, respectively. Line 10 creates an Employee and initializes its instance variables by passing to the constructor two Strings (representing the Employee's first and last names) and two Date objects (representing the birthday and hire date). Line 12 implicitly invokes the Employee's toString method to display the values of its instance variables and demonstrate that the object was initialized properly.

8.9 Enumerations

In Fig. 6.9 (Craps.java), we introduced the basic enum type which defines a set of constants that are represented as unique identifiers. In that program, the enum constants represented the game's status. In this section, we discuss the relationship between enum types and classes. Like classes, all enum types are reference types, which means that you can refer to an object of an enum type with a reference. An enum type is declared with an **enum declaration**, which is a comma-separated list of enum constants—the declaration may optionally include other components of traditional classes, such as constructors, fields and methods. Each enum declaration declares an enum class with the following restrictions:

```
1   // Fig. 8.8: Employee.java
2   // Employee class with references to other objects.
3
4   public class Employee
5   {
6      private String firstName;
7      private String lastName;
8      private Date birthDate;
9      private Date hireDate;
10
11     // constructor to initialize name, birth date and hire date
12     public Employee( String first, String last, Date dateOfBirth,
13        Date dateOfHire )
14     {
15        firstName = first;
16        lastName = last;
17        birthDate = dateOfBirth;
18        hireDate = dateOfHire;
19     } // end Employee constructor
20
21     // convert Employee to String format
22     public String toString()
23     {
24        return String.format( "%s, %s  Hired: %s  Birthday: %s",
25           lastName, firstName, hireDate, birthDate );
26     } // end method toString
27  } // end class Employee
```

Fig. 8.8 | Employee class with references to other objects.

```
1   // Fig. 8.9: EmployeeTest.java
2   // Composition demonstration.
3
4   public class EmployeeTest
5   {
6      public static void main( String args[] )
7      {
8         Date birth = new Date( 7, 24, 1949 );
9         Date hire = new Date( 3, 12, 1988 );
10        Employee employee = new Employee( "Bob", "Blue", birth, hire );
11
12        System.out.println( employee );
13     } // end main
14  } // end class EmployeeTest
```

```
Date object constructor for date 7/24/1949
Date object constructor for date 3/12/1988
Blue, Bob  Hired: 3/12/1988  Birthday: 7/24/1949
```

Fig. 8.9 | Composition demonstration.

1. enum types are implicitly `final`, because they declare constants that should not be modified.

2. enum constants are implicitly `static`.

3. Any attempt to create an object of an enum type with operator `new` results in a compilation error.

The enum constants can be used anywhere constants can be used, such as in the `case` labels of `switch` statements and to control enhanced `for` statements.

Figure 8.10 illustrates how to declare instance variables, a constructor and methods in an enum type. The enum declaration (lines 5–37) contains two parts—the enum constants and the other members of the enum type. The first part (lines 8–13) declares six enum constants.

```java
1   // Fig. 8.10: Book.java
2   // Declaring an enum type with constructor and explicit instance fields
3   // and accessors for these field
4
5   public enum Book
6   {
7      // declare constants of enum type
8      JHTP6( "Java How to Program 6e", "2005" ),
9      CHTP4( "C How to Program 4e", "2004" ),
10     IW3HTP3( "Internet & World Wide Web How to Program 3e", "2004" ),
11     CPPHTP4( "C++ How to Program 4e", "2003" ),
12     VBHTP2( "Visual Basic .NET How to Program 2e", "2002" ),
13     CSHARPHTP( "C# How to Program", "2002" );
14
15     // instance fields
16     private final String title; // book title
17     private final String copyrightYear; // copyright year
18
19     // enum constructor
20     Book( String bookTitle, String year )
21     {
22        title = bookTitle;
23        copyrightYear = year;
24     } // end enum Book constructor
25
26     // accessor for field title
27     public String getTitle()
28     {
29        return title;
30     } // end method getTitle
31
32     // accessor for field copyrightYear
33     public String getCopyrightYear()
34     {
35        return copyrightYear;
36     } // end method getCopyrightYear
37  } // end enum Book
```

Fig. 8.10 | Declaring `enum` type with instance fields, constructor and methods.

Each enum constant is optionally followed by arguments which are passed to the enum constructor (lines 20–24). Like the constructors you have seen in classes, an enum constructor can specify any number of parameters and can be overloaded. In this example, the enum constructor has two `String` parameters, hence each enum constant is followed by parentheses containing two `String` arguments. The second part (lines 16–36) declares the other members of the enum type—two instance variables (lines 16–17), a constructor (lines 20–24) and two methods (lines 27–30 and 33–36).

Lines 16–17 declare the instance variables `title` and `copyrightYear`. Each enum constant in Book is actually an object of type Book that has its own copy of instance variables `title` and `copyrightYear`. The constructor (lines 20–24) takes two `String` parameters, one that specifies the book title and one that specifies the copyright year of the book. Lines 22–23 assign these parameters to the instance variables. Lines 27–36 declare two methods, which return the book title and copyright year, respectively. Figure 8.11 tests the enum type declared in Fig. 8.10 and illustrates how to iterate through a range of enum constants.

For every enum, the compiler generates a `static` method called `values` (called in line 12) that returns an array of the enum's constants in the order in which they were declared. Recall from Section 7.6 that the enhanced `for` statement can be used to iterate through an array. Lines 12–14 use the enhanced `for` statement to display all the constants declared in the enum Book. Line 14 invokes the enum Book's `getTitle` and `getCopyrightYear` methods to get the title and copyright year associated with the constant. Note that when an enum constant is converted to a `String` (e.g., book in line 13), the constant's identifier is used as the `String` representation (e.g., JHTP6 for the first enum constant).

```java
1   // Fig. 8.11: EnumTest.java
2   // Testing enum type Book.
3   import java.util.EnumSet;
4
5   public class EnumTest
6   {
7      public static void main( String args[] )
8      {
9         System.out.println( "All books:\n" );
10
11         // print all books in enum Book
12         for ( Book book : Book.values() )
13            System.out.printf( "%-10s%-45s%s\n", book,
14               book.getTitle(), book.getCopyrightYear() );
15
16         System.out.println( "\nDisplay a range of enum constants:\n" );
17
18         // print first four books
19         for ( Book book : EnumSet.range( Book.JHTP6, Book.CPPHTP4 ) )
20            System.out.printf( "%-10s%-45s%s\n", book,
21               book.getTitle(), book.getCopyrightYear() );
22      } // end main
23   } // end class EnumTest
```

Fig. 8.11 | Testing an enum type. (Part 1 of 2.)

```
All books:

JHTP6      Java How to Program 6e                          2005
CHTP4      C How to Program 4e                             2004
IW3HTP3    Internet & World Wide Web How to Program 3e     2004
CPPHTP4    C++ How to Program 4e                           2003
VBHTP2     Visual Basic .NET How to Program 2e             2002
CSHARPHTP  C# How to Program                               2002

Display a range of enum constants:

JHTP6      Java How to Program 6e                          2005
CHTP4      C How to Program 4e                             2004
IW3HTP3    Internet & World Wide Web How to Program 3e     2004
CPPHTP4    C++ How to Program 4e                           2003
```

Fig. 8.11 | Testing an enum type. (Part 2 of 2.)

Lines 19–21 use the static method range of class EnumSet (declared in package java.util) to display a range of the enum Book's constants. Method range takes two parameters—the first enum constant in the range and the last enum constant in the range—and returns an EnumSet that contains all the constants between these two constants, inclusive. For example, EnumSet.range(Book.JHTP6, Book.CPPHTP4) returns an EnumSet containing Book.JHTP6, Book.CHTP4, Book.IW3HTP3 and Book.CPPHTP4. The enhanced for statement can be used with an EnumSet just as it can with an array, so lines 19–21 use the enhanced for statement to display the title and copyright year of every book in the EnumSet. Class EnumSet provides several other static methods for creating sets of enum constants from the same enum type. For more details of class EnumSet, visit java.sun.com/j2se/5.0/docs/api/java/util/EnumSet.html.

 Common Programming Error 8.6

In an enum declaration, it is a syntax error to declare enum constants after the enum type's constructors, fields and methods in the enum declaration.

8.10 Garbage Collection and Method finalize

Every class in Java has the methods of class Object (package java.lang), one of which is the finalize method. This method is rarely used. In fact, we searched over 6500 source-code files for the Java API classes and found fewer than 50 declarations of the finalize method. Nevertheless, because this method is part of every class, we discuss it here to help you understand its intended purpose in case you encounter it in your studies or in industry. The complete details of the finalize method are beyond the scope of this book, and most programmers should not use it—you'll soon see why. You will learn more about class Object in Chapter 9, Object-Oriented Programming: Inheritance.

Every object you create uses various system resources, such as memory. We need a disciplined way to give resources back to the system when they are no longer needed to avoid "resource leaks." The Java Virtual Machine (JVM) performs automatic garbage collection to reclaim the memory occupied by objects that are no longer in use. When there are no more references to an object, the object is marked for garbage collection by the JVM. The memory for such an object can be reclaimed when the JVM executes its garbage collector, which is responsible for retrieving the memory of objects that are no longer used so the memory can be used for other objects. Therefore, memory leaks that are common in other languages like C and C++ (because memory is not automatically reclaimed in those languages) are less likely in Java (but some can still happen in subtle ways). Other types of resource leaks can occur. For example, an application could open a file on disk to modify the file's contents. If the application does not close the file, no other application can use the file until the application that opened the file completes.

The finalize method is called by the garbage collector to perform termination housekeeping on an object just before the garbage collector reclaims the object's memory. Method finalize does not take parameters and has return type void. A problem with method finalize is that the garbage collector is not guaranteed to execute at a specified time. In fact, the garbage collector may never execute before a program terminates. Thus, it is unclear if, or when, method finalize will be called. For this reason, most programmers should avoid method finalize. In Section 8.11, we demonstrate a situation in which method finalize is called by the garbage collector.

Software Engineering Observation 8.10

A class that uses system resources, such as files on disk, should provide a method to eventually release the resources. Many Java API classes provide close or dispose methods for this purpose. For example, class Scanner (java.sun.com/j2se/5.0/docs/api/java/util/Scanner.html) has a close method.

8.11 static Class Members

Every object has its own copy of all the instance variables of the class. In certain cases, only one copy of a particular variable should be shared by all objects of a class. A static field—called a class variable—is used in such cases. A static variable represents classwide information—all objects of the class share the same piece of data. The declaration of a static variable begins with the keyword static.

Let's motivate static data with an example. Suppose that we have a video game with Martians and other space creatures. Martians tend to be brave and willing to attack other space creatures when the Martian is aware that there are at least four other Martians present. If fewer than five Martians are present, become cowardly. Thus each Martian needs to know the martianCount. We could endow class Martian with martianCount as an instance variable. If we do this, then every Martian will have a separate copy of the instance variable, and every time we create a new Martian, we will have to update the instance variable martianCount in every Martian. This wastes space with the redundant copies, wastes time in updating the separate copies and is error prone. Instead, we declare martianCount to be static, making martianCount classwide data. Every Martian can see the martianCount as if it were an instance variable of class Martian, but only one copy of the static martianCount is maintained. This saves space. We save time by having the Martian constructor increment the static martianCount—there is only one copy, so we do not have to increment separate copies of martianCount for each Martian object.

Software Engineering Observation 8.11

Use a static variable when all objects of a class must use the same copy of the variable.

Static variables have class scope. A class's `public static` members can be accessed through a reference to any object of the class, or they can be accessed by qualifying the member name with the class name and a dot (`.`), as in `Math.random()`. A class's `private static` class members can be accessed only through methods of the class. Actually, `static` class members exist even when no objects of the class exist—they are available as soon as the class is loaded into memory at execution time. To access a `public static` member when no objects of the class exist (and even when they do), prefix the class name and a dot (`.`) to the `static` member, as in `Math.PI`. To access a `private static` member when no objects of the class exist, a `public static` method must be provided and the method must be called by qualifying its name with the class name and a dot.

Software Engineering Observation 8.12

Static class variables and methods exist, and can be used, even if no objects of that class have been instantiated.

Our next program declares two classes—`Employee` (Fig. 8.12) and `EmployeeTest` (Fig. 8.13). Class `Employee` declares `private static` variable `count` (Fig. 8.12, line 9), and `public static` method `getCount` (lines 46–49). The `static` variable `count` is initialized to zero in line 9. If a `static` variable is not initialized, the compiler assigns a default value to the variable—in this case `0`, the default value for type `int`. Variable `count` maintains a count of the number of objects of class `Employee` that currently reside in memory. This includes objects that have already been marked for garbage collection by the JVM, but have not yet been reclaimed by the garbage collector.

When `Employee` objects exist, member `count` can be used in any method of an `Employee` object—this example increments `count` in the constructor (line 18) and decrements it in the `finalize` method (line 28). When no objects of class `Employee` exist, member `count` can still be referenced, but only through a call to `public static` method `getCount` (lines 46–49), as in `Employee.getCount()`, which returns the number of `Employee` objects currently in memory. When objects exist, method `getCount` can also be called through any reference to an `Employee` object, as in the call `e1.getCount()`.

```
1   // Fig. 8.12: Employee.java
2   // Static variable used to maintain a count of the number of
3   // Employee objects in memory.
4
5   public class Employee
6   {
7      private String firstName;
8      private String lastName;
9      private static int count = 0; // number of objects in memory
10
11     // initialize employee, add 1 to static count and
12     // output String indicating that constructor was called
13     public Employee( String first, String last )
14     {
```

Fig. 8.12 | `static` variable used to maintain a count of the number of `Employee` objects in memory. (Part 1 of 2.)

```
15        firstName = first;
16        lastName = last;
17
18        count++;  // increment static count of employees
19        System.out.printf( "Employee constructor: %s %s; count = %d\n",
20           firstName, lastName, count );
21     } // end Employee constructor
22
23     // subtract 1 from static count when garbage
24     // collector calls finalize to clean up object;
25     // confirm that finalize was called
26     protected void finalize()
27     {
28        count--; // decrement static count of employees
29        System.out.printf( "Employee finalizer: %s %s; count = %d\n",
30           firstName, lastName, count );
31     } // end method finalize
32
33     // get first name
34     public String getFirstName()
35     {
36        return firstName;
37     } // end method getFirstName
38
39     // get last name
40     public String getLastName()
41     {
42        return lastName;
43     } // end method getLastName
44
45     // static method to get static count value
46     public static int getCount()
47     {
48        return count;
49     } // end method getCount
50  } // end class Employee
```

Fig. 8.12 | static variable used to maintain a count of the number of Employee objects in memory. (Part 2 of 2.)

```
1  // Fig. 8.13: EmployeeTest.java
2  // Static member demonstration.
3
4  public class EmployeeTest
5  {
6     public static void main( String args[] )
7     {
8        // show that count is 0 before creating Employees
9        System.out.printf( "Employees before instantiation: %d\n",
10          Employee.getCount() );
11
```

Fig. 8.13 | static member demonstration. (Part 1 of 2.)

```
12          // create two Employees; count should be 2
13          Employee e1 = new Employee( "Susan", "Baker" );
14          Employee e2 = new Employee( "Bob", "Blue" );
15
16          // show that count is 2 after creating two Employees
17          System.out.println( "\nEmployees after instantiation: " );
18          System.out.printf( "via e1.getCount(): %d\n", e1.getCount() );
19          System.out.printf( "via e2.getCount(): %d\n", e2.getCount() );
20          System.out.printf( "via Employee.getCount(): %d\n",
21             Employee.getCount() );
22
23          // get names of Employees
24          System.out.printf( "\nEmployee 1: %s %s\nEmployee 2: %s %s\n\n",
25             e1.getFirstName(), e1.getLastName(),
26             e2.getFirstName(), e2.getLastName() );
27
28          // in this example, there is only one reference to each Employee,
29          // so the following two statements cause the JVM to mark each
30          // Employee object for garbage collection
31          e1 = null;
32          e2 = null;
33
34          System.gc(); // ask for garbage collection to occur now
35
36          // show Employee count after calling garbage collector; count
37          // displayed may be 0, 1 or 2 based on whether garbage collector
38          // executes immediately and number of Employee objects collected
39          System.out.printf( "\nEmployees after System.gc(): %d\n",
40             Employee.getCount() );
41    } // end main
42 } // end class EmployeeTest
```

```
Employees before instantiation: 0
Employee constructor: Susan Baker; count = 1
Employee constructor: Bob Blue; count = 2

Employees after instantiation:
via e1.getCount(): 2
via e2.getCount(): 2
via Employee.getCount(): 2

Employee 1: Susan Baker
Employee 2: Bob Blue

Employee finalizer: Bob Blue; count = 1
Employee finalizer: Susan Baker; count = 0

Employees after System.gc(): 0
```

Fig. 8.13 | static member demonstration. (Part 2 of 2.)

Good Programming Practice 8.1

Invoke every static *method by using the class name and a dot (.) to emphasize that the method being called is a* static *method.*

Note that the Employee class has a finalize method (lines 26–31). This method is included only to show when the garbage collector executes in this program. Method finalize is normally declared protected, so it is not part of the public services of a class. We will discuss the protected member access modifier in detail in Chapter 9.

EmployeeTest method main (Fig. 8.13) instantiates two Employee objects (lines 13–14). When each Employee object's constructor is invoked, lines 15–16 of Fig. 8.12 assign the Employee's first name and last name to instance variables firstName and lastName. Note that these two statements do not make copies of the original String arguments. Actually, String objects in Java are immutable—they cannot be modified after they are created. Therefore, it is safe to have many references to one String object. This is not normally the case for objects of most other classes in Java. If String objects are immutable, you might wonder why are we able to use operators + and += to concatenate String objects. String concatenation operations actually result in a new Strings object containing the concatenated values. The original String objects are not modified.

When main has finished using the two Employee objects, the references e1 and e2 are set to null at lines 31–32. At this point, references e1 and e2 no longer refer to the objects that were instantiated on lines 13–14. This "marks the objects for garbage collection" because there are no more references to the objects in the program.

Eventually, the garbage collector might reclaim the memory for these objects (or the operating system surely will reclaim the memory when the program terminates). The JVM does not guarantee when the garbage collector will execute (or even whether it will execute), so this program explicitly calls the garbage collector in line 34 using static method gc of class System (package java.lang) to indicate that the garbage collector should make a best-effort attempt to reclaim objects that are eligible for garbage collection. This is just a best effort—it is possible that no objects or only a subset of the eligible objects will be collected. In Fig. 8.13's sample output, the garbage collector did execute before lines 39–40 displayed current Employee count. The last output line indicates that the number of Employee objects in memory is 0 after the call to System.gc(). The third- and second-to-last lines of the output show that the Employee object for Bob Blue was finalized before the Employee object for Susan Baker. The output on your system may differ, because the garbage collector is not guaranteed to execute when System.gc() is called, nor is it guaranteed to collect objects in a specific order.

[*Note:* A method declared static cannot access non-static class members, because a static method can be called even when no objects of the class have been instantiated. For the same reason, the this reference cannot be used in a static method—the this reference must refer to a specific object of the class, and when a static method is called, there might not be any objects of its class in memory. The this reference is required to allow a method of a class to access other non-static members of the same class.]

Common Programming Error 8.7

A compilation error occurs if a static method calls an instance (non-static) method in the same class by using only the method name. Similarly, a compilation error occurs if a static method attempts to access an instance variable in the same class by using only the variable name.

Common Programming Error 8.8

Referring to this in a static method is a syntax error.

8.12 static Import

In Section 6.3, you learned about the static fields and methods of class Math. We invoked class Math's static fields and methods by preceding each with the class name Math and a dot (.). A **static import** declaration (a new feature of J2SE 5.0) enables programmers to refer to imported static members as if they were declared in the class that uses them—the class name and a dot (.) are not required to use an imported static member.

A static import declaration has two forms—one that imports a particular static member (which is known as single static import) and one that imports all static members of a class (which is known as static import on demand). The following syntax imports a particular static member:

> import static *packageName*.*ClassName*.*staticMemberName*;

where *packageName* is the package of the class (e.g., java.lang), *ClassName* is the name of the class (e.g., Math) and *staticMemberName* is the name of the static field or method (e.g., PI or abs). The following syntax imports all static members of a class:

> import static *packageName*.*ClassName*.*;

where *packageName* is the package of the class (e.g., java.lang) and *ClassName* is the name of the class (e.g., Math). The asterisk (*) indicates that *all* static members of the specified class should be available for use in the class(es) declared in the file. Note that static import declarations import only static class members. Regular import statements should be used to specify the classes used in a program.

Figure 8.14 demonstrates a static import. Line 3 is a static import declaration, that imports all static fields and methods of class Math from package java.lang. Lines 9–12 access the Math class's static field E (line 11) and the static methods sqrt (line 9), ceil (line 10), log (line 11) and cos (line 12) without preceding the field name or method names with class name Math and a dot.

```
 1  // Fig. 8.14: StaticImportTest.java
 2  // Using static import to import static methods of class Math.
 3  import static java.lang.Math.*;
 4
 5  public class StaticImportTest
 6  {
 7     public static void main( String args[] )
 8     {
 9        System.out.printf( "sqrt( 900.0 ) = %.1f\n", sqrt( 900.0 ) );
10        System.out.printf( "ceil( -9.8 ) = %.1f\n", ceil( -9.8 ) );
11        System.out.printf( "log( E ) = %.1f\n", log( E ) );
12        System.out.printf( "cos( 0.0 ) = %.1f\n", cos( 0.0 ) );
13     } // end main
14  } // end class StaticImportTest
```

```
sqrt( 900.0 ) = 30.0
ceil( -9.8 ) = -9.0
log( E ) = 1.0
cos( 0.0 ) = 1.0
```

Fig. 8.14 | Static import Math methods.

Common Programming Error 8.9

A compilation error occurs if a program attempts to import static methods that have the same signature or static fields that have the same name from two or more classes.

8.13 final Instance Variables

The principle of least privilege is fundamental to good software engineering. In the context of an application, the principle states that code should be granted only the amount of privilege and access that the code needs to accomplish its designated task, but no more. Let us see how this principle applies to instance variables.

Some instance variables need to be modifiable and some do not. You can use the keyword final to specify that a variable is not modifiable (i.e., it is a constant) and that any attempt to modify it is an error. For example,

```
private final int INCREMENT;
```

declares a final (constant) instance variable INCREMENT of type int. Although constants can be initialized when they are declared, this is not required. Constants can be initialized by each of the class's constructors.

Software Engineering Observation 8.13

Declaring an instance variable as final helps enforce the principle of least privilege. If an instance variable should not be modified, declare it to be final to prevent modification.

Our next example contains two classes—class Increment (Fig. 8.15) and class IncrementTest (Fig. 8.16). Class Increment contains a final instance variable of type int named INCREMENT (Fig. 8.15, line 7). Note that the final variable is not initialized in its declaration, so it must be initialized by the class's constructor (lines 9–13). If the class provided multiple constructors, every constructor would be required to initialize the final variable. The constructor receives int parameter incrementValue and assigns its value to INCREMENT (line 12). A final variable cannot be modified by assignment after it is initialized. Application class IncrementTest creates an object of class Increment (Fig. 8.16, line 8) and provides as the argument to the constructor the value 5 to be assigned to the constant INCREMENT.

```
 1   // Fig. 8.15: Increment.java
 2   // final instance variable in a class.
 3
 4   public class Increment
 5   {
 6      private int total = 0; // total of all increments
 7      private final int INCREMENT; // constant variable (uninitialized)
 8
 9      // constructor initializes final instance variable INCREMENT
10      public Increment( int incrementValue )
11      {
12         INCREMENT = incrementValue; // initialize constant variable (once)
13      } // end Increment constructor
14
```

Fig. 8.15 | final instance variable in a class. (Part 1 of 2.)

```
15      // add INCREMENT to total
16      public void addIncrementToTotal()
17      {
18         total += INCREMENT;
19      } // end method addIncrementToTotal
20
21      // return String representation of an Increment object's data
22      public String toString()
23      {
24         return String.format( "total = %d", total );
25      } // end method toIncrementString
26   } // end class Increment
```

Fig. 8.15 | `final` instance variable in a class. (Part 2 of 2.)

```
 1   // Fig. 8.16: IncrementTest.java
 2   // final variable initialized with a constructor argument.
 3
 4   public class IncrementTest
 5   {
 6      public static void main( String args[] )
 7      {
 8         Increment value = new Increment( 5 );
 9
10         System.out.printf( "Before incrementing: %s\n\n", value );
11
12         for ( int i = 1; i <= 3; i++ )
13         {
14            value.addIncrementToTotal();
15            System.out.printf( "After increment %d: %s\n", i, value );
16         } // end for
17      } // end main
18   } // end class IncrementTest
```

```
Before incrementing: total = 0

After increment 1: total = 5
After increment 2: total = 10
After increment 3: total = 15
```

Fig. 8.16 | `final` variable initialized with a constructor argument.

Common Programming Error 8.10

Attempting to modify a `final` instance variable after it is initialized is a compilation error.

Error-Prevention Tip 8.2

Attempts to modify a `final` instance variable are caught at compilation time rather than causing execution-time errors. It is always preferable to get bugs out at compilation time, if possible, rather than allow them to slip through to execution time (where studies have found that the cost of repair is often many times more expensive).

Software Engineering Observation 8.14

A final *field should also be declared* static *if it is initialized in its declaration. Once a* final *field is initialized in its declaration, its value can never change. Therefore, it is not necessary to have a separate copy of the field for every object of the class. Making the field* static *enables all objects of the class to share the* final *field.*

If a final variable is not initialized, a compilation error occurs. To demonstrate this, we placed line 12 of Fig. 8.15 in a comment and recompiled the class. Fig. 8.17 shows the error message produced by the compiler.

Common Programming Error 8.11

Not initializing a final *instance variable in its declaration or in every constructor of the class yields a compilation error indicating that the variable might not have been initialized. The same error occurs if the class initializes the variable in some, but not all, of the class's constructors.*

8.14 Software Reusability

Java programmers concentrate on crafting new classes and reusing existing classes. Many class libraries exist, and others are being developed worldwide. Software is then constructed from existing, well-defined, carefully tested, well-documented, portable, widely available components. This kind of software reusability speeds the development of powerful, high-quality software. Rapid application development (RAD) is of great interest today.

Java programmers now have thousands of classes in the Java API from which to choose to help them implement Java programs. Indeed, Java is not just a programming language. It is a framework in which Java developers can work to achieve true reusability and rapid application development. Java programmers can focus on the task at hand when developing their programs and leave the lower-level details to the classes of the Java API. For example, to write a program that draws graphics, a Java programmer does not require knowledge of graphics on every computer platform where the program will execute. Instead, the programmer can concentrate on learning Java's graphics capabilities (which are quite substantial and growing) and write a Java program that draws the graphics, using Java's API classes, such as Graphics. When the program executes on a given computer, it is the job of the JVM to translate Java commands into commands that the local computer can understand.

The Java API classes enable Java programmers to bring new applications to market faster by using preexisting, tested components. Not only does this reduce development time, it also improves the programmer's ability to debug and maintain applications. To take advantage of Java's many capabilities, it is essential that programmers familiarize themselves with the variety of packages and classes in the Java API. There are many Web-based resources at java.sun.com to help you with this task. The primary resource for learning about the Java API is the Java API documentation, which can be found at

        java.sun.com/j2se/5.0/docs/api/index.html

```
Increment.java:13: variable INCREMENT might not have been initialized
   } // end Increment constructor
   ^
1 error
```

Fig. 8.17 | final variable INCREMENT must be initialized.

We overview how to use the documentation in Appendix G, Using the Java API Documentation. You can download the API documentation from

```
java.sun.com/j2se/5.0/download.html
```

In addition, `java.sun.com` provides many other resources, including tutorials, articles and sites specific to individual Java topics.

Good Programming Practice 8.2

Avoid reinventing the wheel. Study the capabilities of the Java API. If the API contains a class that meets your program's requirements, use that class rather than create your own.

To realize the full potential of software reusability, we need to improve cataloging schemes, licensing schemes, protection mechanisms which ensure that master copies of classes are not corrupted, description schemes that system designers use to determine whether existing objects meet their needs, browsing mechanisms that determine what classes are available and how closely they meet software developer requirements, and the like. Many interesting research and development problems have been solved and many more need to be solved. These problems will likely be solved because the potential value of increased software reuse is enormous.

8.15 Data Abstraction and Encapsulation

Classes normally hide the details of their implementation from their clients. This is called information hiding. As an example, let us consider the stack data structure introduced in Section 6.6. Recall that a stack is a last-in, first-out (LIFO) data structure—the last item pushed (inserted) on the stack is the first item popped (removed) from the stack.

Stacks can be implemented with arrays and with other data structures, such as linked lists. A client of a stack class need not be concerned with the stack's implementation. The client knows only that when data items are placed in the stack, they will be recalled in last-in, first-out order. The client cares about what functionality a stack offers, not about how that functionality is implemented. This concept is referred to as data abstraction. Although programmers might know the details of a class's implementation, they should not write code that depends on these details. This enables a particular class (such as one that implements a stack and its operations, *push* and *pop*) to be replaced with another version without affecting the rest of the system. As long as the `public` services of the class do not change (i.e., every original method still has the same name, return type and parameter list in the new class declaration), the rest of the system is not affected.

Most programming languages emphasize actions. In these languages, data exists to support the actions that programs must take. Data is "less interesting" than actions. Data is "crude." Only a few primitive types exist, and it is difficult for programmers to create their own types. Java and the object-oriented style of programming elevate the importance of data. The primary activities of object-oriented programming in Java are the creation of types (e.g., classes) and the expression of the interactions among objects of those types. To create languages that emphasize data, the programming-languages community needed to formalize some notions about data. The formalization we consider here is the notion of abstract data types (ADTs), which improve the program-development process.

Consider primitive type `int`, which most people would associate with an integer in mathematics. Rather, an `int` is an abstract representation of an integer. Unlike mathematical integers, computer `int`s are fixed in size. For example, type `int` in Java is limited to the range –2,147,483,648 to +2,147,483,647. If the result of a calculation falls outside this range, an error occurs, and the computer responds in some machine-dependent manner. It might, for example, "quietly" produce an incorrect result, such as a value too large to fit in an `int` variable (commonly called arithmetic overflow). Mathematical integers do not have this problem. Therefore, the notion of a computer `int` is only an approximation of the notion of a real-world integer. The same is true of `float` and other built-in types.

We have taken the notion of `int` for granted until this point, but we now consider it from a new perspective. Types like `int`, `float`, and `char` are all examples of abstract data types. They are representations of real-world notions to some satisfactory level of precision within a computer system.

An ADT actually captures two notions: A data representation and the operations that can be performed on that data. For example, in Java, an `int` contains an integer value (data) and provides addition, subtraction, multiplication, division and remainder operations—division by zero is undefined. Java programmers use classes to implement abstract data types.

Software Engineering Observation 8.15

Programmers create types through the class mechanism. New types can be designed to be convenient to use as the built-in types. This marks Java as an extensible language. Although the language is easy to extend via new types, the programmer cannot alter the base language itself.

Another abstract data type we discuss is a queue, which is similar to a "waiting line." Computer systems use many queues internally. A queue offers well-understood behavior to its clients: Clients place items in a queue one at a time via an *enqueue* operation, then get them back one at a time via a *dequeue* operation. A queue returns items in first-in, first-out (FIFO) order, which means that the first item inserted in a queue is the first item removed from the queue. Conceptually, a queue can become infinitely long, but real queues are finite.

The queue hides an internal data representation that keeps track of the items currently waiting in line, and it offers operations to its clients (*enqueue* and *dequeue*). The clients are not concerned about the implementation of the queue—they simply depend on the queue to operate "as advertised." When a client enqueues an item, the queue should accept that item and place it in some kind of internal FIFO data structure. Similarly, when the client wants the next item from the front of the queue, the queue should remove the item from its internal representation and deliver it in FIFO order (i.e., the item that has been in the queue the longest should be the next one returned by the next dequeue operation).

The queue ADT guarantees the integrity of its internal data structure. Clients cannot manipulate this data structure directly—only the queue ADT has access to its internal data. Clients are able to perform only allowable operations on the data representation—the ADT rejects operations that its public interface does not provide.

8.16 Time Class Case Study: Creating Packages

We have seen in almost every example in the text that classes from preexisting libraries, such as the Java API, can be imported into a Java program. Each class in the Java API belongs to a package that contains a group of related classes. As applications become more complex, packages help programmers manage the complexity of application components. Packages also facilitate software reuse by enabling programs to import classes from other packages (as we have done in most examples). Another benefit of packages is that they provide a convention for unique class names, which helps prevent class-name conflicts (discussed later in this section). This section introduces how to create your own packages.

Steps for Declaring a Reusable Class

Before a class can be imported into multiple applications, it must be placed in a package to make it reusable. Figure 8.18 shows how to specify the package in which a class should be placed. Figure 8.19 shows how to import our packaged class so that it can be used in an application. The steps for creating a reusable class are:

1. Declare a `public` class. If the class is not `public`, it can be used only by other classes in the same package.

2. Choose a package name and add a package declaration to the source-code file for the reusable class declaration. There can be only one `package` declaration in each Java source-code file, and it must precede all other declarations and statements in the file. Note that comments are not statements, so comments can be placed before a `package` statement in a file.

3. Compile the class so that it is placed in the appropriate package directory structure.

4. Import the reusable class into a program and use the class.

Steps 1 and 2: Creating a **public** Class and Adding the **package** Statement

For *Step 1*, we modify the `public` class `Time1` declared in Fig. 8.1. The new version is shown in Fig. 8.18. No modifications have been made to the implementation of the class, so we will not discuss its implementation details again here.

For *Step 2*, we add a `package` declaration (line 3) that declares a `package` named `com.deitel.sjhtp6.ch08`. Placing a `package` declaration at the beginning of a Java source file indicates that the class declared in the file is part of the specified package. Only `package` declarations, `import` declarations and comments can appear outside the braces of a class declaration. A Java source-code file must have the following order:

1. a `package` declaration (if any),

2. `import` declarations (if any), then

3. class declarations.

Only one of the class declarations in a particular file can be `public`. Other classes in the file are placed in the package and can be used only by the other classes in the package. Non-`public` classes are in a package to support the reusable classes in the package.

In an effort to provide unique names for every package, Sun Microsystems specifies a convention for package naming that all Java programmers should follow. Every package name should start with your Internet domain name in reverse order. For example, our domain name is `deitel.com`, so our package names begin with `com.deitel`. For the domain name *yourcollege*.edu, the package name should begin with edu.*yourcollege*. After the domain name is reversed, you can choose any other names you want for your package. If you are part of a company with many divisions or a university with many schools, you

```java
// Fig. 8.18: Time1.java
// Time1 class declaration maintains the time in 24-hour format.
package com.deitel.sjhtp6.ch08;

public class Time1
{
   private int hour;   // 0 - 23
   private int minute; // 0 - 59
   private int second; // 0 - 59

   // set a new time value using universal time; perform
   // validity checks on the data; set invalid values to zero
   public void setTime( int h, int m, int s )
   {
      hour = ( ( h >= 0 && h < 24 ) ? h : 0 );   // validate hour
      minute = ( ( m >= 0 && m < 60 ) ? m : 0 ); // validate minute
      second = ( ( s >= 0 && s < 60 ) ? s : 0 ); // validate second
   } // end method setTime

   // convert to String in universal-time format (HH:MM:SS)
   public String toUniversalString()
   {
      return String.format( "%02d:%02d:%02d", hour, minute, second );
   } // end method toUniversalString

   // convert to String in standard-time format (H:MM:SS AM or PM)
   public String toString()
   {
      return String.format( "%d:%02d:%02d %s",
         ( ( hour == 0 || hour == 12 ) ? 12 : hour % 12 ),
         minute, second, ( hour < 12 ? "AM" : "PM" ) );
   } // end method toString
} // end class Time1
```

Fig. 8.18 | Packaging class Time1 for reuse.

may want to use the name of your division or school as the next name in the package. We chose to use sjhtp6 as the next name in our package name to indicate that this class is from *Small Java How to Program, Sixth Edition*. The last name in our package name specifies that this package is for Chapter 8 (ch08).

Step 3: Compiling the Packaged Class

Step 3 is to compile the class so that it is stored in the appropriate package. When a Java file containing a package declaration is compiled, the resulting class file is placed in the directory specified by the package declaration. The package declaration in Fig. 8.18 indicates that class Time1 should be placed in the directory

```
com
   deitel
      sjhtp6
         ch08
```

The directory names in the package declaration specify the exact location of the classes in the package.

When compiling a class in a package, the javac command-line option -d causes the javac compiler to create appropriate directories based on the class's package declaration. The option also specifies where the directories should be stored. For example, in a command window, we used the compilation command

```
javac -d . Time1.java
```

to specify that the first directory in our package name should be placed in the current directory. The period (.) after -d in the preceding command represents the current directory on the Windows, UNIX and Linux operating systems (and several others as well). After executing the compilation command, the current directory contains a directory called com, com contains a directory called deitel, deitel contains a directory called sjhtp6 and sjhtp6 contains a directory called ch08. In the ch08 directory, you can find the file Time1.class. [*Note:* If you do not use the -d option, then you must copy or move the class file to the appropriate package directory after compiling it.]

The package name is part of the fully qualified class name, so the name of class Time1 is actually com.deitel.sjhtp6.ch08.Time1. You can use this fully qualified name in your programs, or you can import the class and use its simple name (the class name by itself—Time1) in the program. If another package also contains a Time1 class, the fully qualified class names can be used to distinguish between the classes in the program and prevent a name conflict (also called a name collision).

Step 4: Importing the Reusable Class
Once the class is compiled and stored in its package, the class can be imported into programs (*Step 4*). In the Time1PackageTest application of Fig. 8.19, line 3 specifies that class Time1 should be imported for use in class Time1PackageTest. Class Time1PackageTest is in the default package because the class's .java file does not contain a package declaration. Since the two classes are in different packages, the import at line 3 is required so that class Time1PackageTest can use class Time1.

Line 3 is known as a single-type-import declaration—that is, the import declaration specifies one class to import. When your program uses multiple classes from the same package, you can import those classes with a single import declaration. For example, the import declaration

```
import java.util.*; // import classes from package java.util
```

uses an asterisk (*) at the end of the import declaration to inform the compiler that all classes from the java.util package are available for use in the program. This is known as a type-import-on-demand declaration. Only the classes from package java.util that are used in the program are loaded by the JVM. The preceding import allows you to use the simple name of any class from the java.util package in the program. Throughout this book, we use single-type-import declarations for clarity.

 Common Programming Error 8.12

Using the import declaration import java.; causes a compilation error. You must specify the exact name of the package from which you want to import classes.*

```
1    // Fig. 8.19: Time1PackageTest.java
2    // Time1 object used in an application.
3    import com.deitel.sjhtp6.ch08.Time1; // import class Time1
4
5    public class Time1PackageTest
6    {
7       public static void main( String args[] )
8       {
9          // create and initialize a Time1 object
10         Time1 time = new Time1(); // calls Time1 constructor
11
12         // output string representations of the time
13         System.out.print( "The initial universal time is: " );
14         System.out.println( time.toUniversalString() );
15         System.out.print( "The initial standard time is: " );
16         System.out.println( time.toString() );
17         System.out.println(); // output a blank line
18
19         // change time and output updated time
20         time.setTime( 13, 27, 6 );
21         System.out.print( "Universal time after setTime is: " );
22         System.out.println( time.toUniversalString() );
23         System.out.print( "Standard time after setTime is: " );
24         System.out.println( time.toString() );
25         System.out.println(); // output a blank line
26
27         // set time with invalid values; output updated time
28         time.setTime( 99, 99, 99 );
29         System.out.println( "After attempting invalid settings:" );
30         System.out.print( "Universal time: " );
31         System.out.println( time.toUniversalString() );
32         System.out.print( "Standard time: " );
33         System.out.println( time.toString() );
34      } // end main
35   } // end class Time1PackageTest
```

```
The initial universal time is: 00:00:00
The initial standard time is: 12:00:00 AM

Universal time after setTime is: 13:27:06
Standard time after setTime is: 1:27:06 PM

After attempting invalid settings:
Universal time: 00:00:00
Standard time: 12:00:00 AM
```

Fig. 8.19 | Time1 object used in an application.

Specifying the Classpath During Compilation

When compiling Time1PackageTest, javac must locate the .class file for Time1 to ensure that class Time1PackageTest uses class Time1 correctly. The compiler uses a special
object called a class loader to locate the classes it needs. The class loader begins by search-

ing the standard Java classes that are bundled with the JDK. Then it searches for optional packages. Java provides an extension mechanism that enables new (optional) packages to be added to Java for development and execution purposes. [*Note:* The extension mechanism is beyond the scope of this book. For more information, visit `java.sun.com/j2se/5.0/docs/guide/extensions`.] If the class is not found in the standard Java classes or in the extension classes, the class loader searches the classpath, which contains a list of locations in which classes are stored. The classpath consists of a list of directories or archive files, each separated by a directory separator—a semicolon (;) on Windows or a colon (:) on UNIX/Linux/Mac OS X. Archive files are individual files that contain directories of other files, typically in a compressed format. For example, the standard classes used by your programs are contained in the archive file `rt.jar`, which is installed with the JDK. Archive files normally end with the `.jar` or `.zip` file-name extensions. The directories and archive files specified in the classpath contain the classes you wish to make available to the Java compiler and the JVM.

By default, the classpath consists only of the current directory. However, the classpath can be modified by

1. providing the `-classpath` option to the `javac` compiler or

2. setting the `CLASSPATH` environment variable (a special variable that you define and the operating system maintains so that applications can search for classes in the specified locations).

For more information on the classpath, visit `java.sun.com/j2se/5.0/docs/tooldocs/tools.html`. The section entitled "General Information" contains information on setting the classpath for UNIX/Linux and Windows.

 Common Programming Error 8.13

Specifying an explicit classpath eliminates the current directory from the classpath. This prevents classes in the current directory (including packages in the current directory) from loading properly. If classes must be loaded from the current directory, include a dot (.) in the classpath to specify the current directory.

 Software Engineering Observation 8.16

In general, it is a better practice to use the `-classpath` option of the compiler, rather than the `CLASSPATH` *environment variable, to specify the classpath for a program. This enables each application to have its own classpath.*

 Error-Prevention Tip 8.3

Specifying the classpath with the `CLASSPATH` *environment variable can cause subtle and difficult-to-locate errors in programs that use different versions of the same package.*

For the example of Fig. 8.18 and Fig. 8.19, we did not specify an explicit classpath. Thus, to locate the classes in the `com.deitel.sjhtp6.ch08` package from this example, the class loader looks in the current directory for the first name in the package—com. Next, the class loader navigates the directory structure. Directory `com` contains the subdirectory `deitel`. Directory `deitel` contains the subdirectory `sjhtp6`. Finally, directory `sjhtp6` contains subdirectory `ch08`. In the `ch08` directory is the file `Time1.class`, which is loaded by the class loader to ensure that the class is used properly in our program.

Specifying the Classpath When Executing an Application
When you execute an application, the JVM must be able to locate the classes used in that application. Like the compiler, the `java` command uses a class loader that searches the standard classes and extension classes first, then searches the classpath (the current directory by default). The classpath for the JVM can be specified explicitly by using either of the techniques discussed for the compiler. As with the compiler, it is better to specify an individual program's classpath via command-line options to the JVM. You can specify the classpath in the `java` command via the `-classpath` or `-cp` command-line options, followed by a list of directories or archive files separated by semicolons (`;`) on Microsoft Windows or by colons (`:`) on UNIX/Linux/Mac OS X. Again, if classes must be loaded from the current directory, be sure to include a dot (`.`) in the classpath to specify the current directory.

8.17 Package Access

If no access modifier (`public`, `protected` or `private`—`protected` is discussed in Chapter 9) is specified for a method or variable when it is declared in a class, the method or variable is considered to have package access. In a program that consists of one class declaration, this has no specific effect. However, if a program uses multiple classes from the same package (i.e., a group of related classes), these classes can access each other's package-access members directly through references to objects of the appropriate classes.

The application in Fig. 8.20 demonstrates package access. The application contains two classes in one source-code file—the `PackageDataTest` application class (lines 5–21) and the `PackageData` class (lines 24–41). When you compile this program, the compiler produces two separate .class files—`PackageDataTest.class` and `PackageData.class`. The compiler places the two `.class` files in the same directory, so the classes are considered to be part of the same package. Since they are part of the same package, class `PackageDataTest` is allowed to modify the package-access data of `PackageData` objects.

In the `PackageData` class declaration, lines 26–27 declare the instance variables `number` and `string` with no access modifiers—therefore, these are package-access instance variables. The `PackageDataTest` application's `main` method creates an instance of the `PackageData` class (line 9) to demonstrate the ability to modify the `PackageData` instance variables directly (as shown on lines 15–16). The results of the modification can be seen in the output window.

8.18 (Optional) GUI and Graphics Case Study: Using Objects with Graphics

Most of the graphics you have seen to this point did not vary each time you executed the program. However, Exercise 6.2 asked you to create a program that generated shapes and colors at random. In that exercise, the drawing changed every time the system called `paintComponent` to redraw the panel. To create a more consistent drawing that remains the same each time it is drawn, we must store information about the displayed shapes so that we can reproduce them exactly each time the system calls `paintComponent`.

```
1    // Fig. 8.20: PackageDataTest.java
2    // Package-access members of a class are accessible by other classes
3    // in the same package.
4
5    public class PackageDataTest
6    {
7       public static void main( String args[] )
8       {
9          PackageData packageData = new PackageData();
10
11         // output String representation of packageData
12         System.out.printf( "After instantiation:\n%s\n", packageData );
13
14         // change package access data in packageData object
15         packageData.number = 77;
16         packageData.string = "Goodbye";
17
18         // output String representation of packageData
19         System.out.printf( "\nAfter changing values:\n%s\n", packageData );
20      } // end main
21   } // end class PackageDataTest
22
23   // class with package access instance variables
24   class PackageData
25   {
26      int number; // package-access instance variable
27      String string; // package-access instance variable
28
29      // constructor
30      public PackageData()
31      {
32         number = 0;
33         string = "Hello";
34      } // end PackageData constructor
35
36      // return PackageData object String representation
37      public String toString()
38      {
39         return String.format( "number: %d; string: %s", number, string );
40      } // end method toString
41   } // end class PackageData
```

```
After instantiation:
number: 0; string: Hello

After changing values:
number: 77; string: Goodbye
```

Fig. 8.20 | Package-access members of a class are accessible by other classes in the same package.

To do this, we will create a set of shape classes that store information about each shape. We will make these classes "smart" by allowing objects of these classes to draw themselves if provided with a Graphics object. Figure 8.21 declares class MyLine, which has all these capabilities.

Class MyLine imports Color and Graphics (lines 3–4). Lines 8–11 declare instance variables for the coordinates needed to draw a line, and line 12 declares the instance variable that stores the color of the line. The constructor at lines 15–22 takes five parameters, one for each instance variable that it initializes. Method draw at lines 25–29 requires a Graphics object and uses it to draw the line in the proper color and at the proper coordinates.

In Fig. 8.22, we declare class DrawPanel, which will generate random objects of class MyLine. Line 12 declares a MyLine array to store the lines to draw. Inside the constructor (lines 15–37), line 17 sets the background color to Color.WHITE. Line 19 creates the array with a random length between 5 and 9. The loop at lines 22–36 creates a new MyLine for every element in the array. Lines 25–28 generate random coordinates for each line's endpoints, and lines 31–32 generate a random color for the line. Line 35 creates a new MyLine object with the randomly generated values and stores it in the array.

```
1   // Fig. 8.21: MyLine.java
2   // Declaration of class MyLine.
3   import java.awt.Color;
4   import java.awt.Graphics;
5
6   public class MyLine
7   {
8      private int x1; // x coordinate of first endpoint
9      private int y1; // y coordinate of first endpoint
10     private int x2; // x coordinate of second endpoint
11     private int y2; // y coordinate of second endpoint
12     private Color myColor; // color of this shape
13
14     // constructor with input values
15     public MyLine( int x1, int y1, int x2, int y2, Color color )
16     {
17        this.x1 = x1; // set x coordinate of first endpoint
18        this.y1 = y1; // set y coordinate of first endpoint
19        this.x2 = x2; // set x coordinate of second endpoint
20        this.y2 = y2; // set y coordinate of second endpoint
21        myColor = color; // set the color
22     } // end MyLine constructor
23
24     // Draw the line in the specified color
25     public void draw( Graphics g )
26     {
27        g.setColor( myColor );
28        g.drawLine( x1, y1, x2, y2 );
29     } // end method draw
30  } // end class MyLine
```

Fig. 8.21 | MyLine class represents a line.

```java
1   // Fig. 8.22: DrawPanel.java
2   // Program that uses class MyLine
3   // to draw random lines.
4   import java.awt.Color;
5   import java.awt.Graphics;
6   import java.util.Random;
7   import javax.swing.JPanel;
8
9   public class DrawPanel extends JPanel
10  {
11     private Random randomNumbers = new Random();
12     private MyLine lines[]; // array of lines
13
14     // constructor, creates a panel with random shapes
15     public DrawPanel()
16     {
17        setBackground( Color.WHITE );
18
19        lines = new MyLine[ 5 + randomNumbers.nextInt( 5 ) ];
20
21        // create lines
22        for ( int count = 0; count < lines.length; count++ )
23        {
24           // generate random coordinates
25           int x1 = randomNumbers.nextInt( 300 );
26           int y1 = randomNumbers.nextInt( 300 );
27           int x2 = randomNumbers.nextInt( 300 );
28           int y2 = randomNumbers.nextInt( 300 );
29
30           // generate a random color
31           Color color = new Color( randomNumbers.nextInt( 256 ),
32              randomNumbers.nextInt( 256 ), randomNumbers.nextInt( 256 ) );
33
34           // add the line to the list of lines to be displayed
35           lines[ count ] = new MyLine( x1, y1, x2, y2, color );
36        } // end for
37     } // end DrawPanel constructor
38
39     // for each shape array, draw the individual shapes
40     public void paintComponent( Graphics g )
41     {
42        super.paintComponent( g );
43
44        // draw the lines
45        for ( MyLine line : lines )
46           line.draw( g );
47     } // end method paintComponent
48  } // end class DrawPanel
```

Fig. 8.22 | Creating random MyLine objects.

Method paintComponent iterates through the MyLine objects in array lines using an enhanced for statement (lines 45–46). Each iteration calls the draw method of the current

```
1   // Fig. 8.23: TestDraw.java
2   // Test application to display a DrawPanel.
3   import javax.swing.JFrame;
4
5   public class TestDraw
6   {
7      public static void main( String args[] )
8      {
9         DrawPanel panel = new DrawPanel();
10        JFrame application = new JFrame();
11
12        application.setDefaultCloseOperation( JFrame.EXIT_ON_CLOSE );
13        application.add( panel );
14        application.setSize( 300, 300 );
15        application.setVisible( true );
16     } // end main
17  } // end class TestDraw
```

Fig. 8.23 | Creating JFrame to display DrawPanel.

MyLine object and passes it the Graphics object for drawing on the panel. Class TestDraw in Fig. 8.23 sets up a new window to display our drawing. Since we are setting the coordinates for the lines only once in the constructor, the drawing does not change if paint-Component is called to refresh the drawing on the screen.

GUI and Graphics Case Study Exercise

8.1   Extend the program in Fig. 8.21–Fig. 8.23 to randomly draw rectangles and ovals. Create classes MyRectangle and MyOval. Both of these classes should include *x1, y1, x2, y2* coordinates, a color and a boolean flag to determine whether the shape is a filled shape. Declare a constructor in each class with arguments for initializing all the instance variables. To help draw rectangles and ovals, each class should provide methods getUpperLeftX, getUpperLeftY, getWidth and getHeight that calculate the upper-left *x*-coordinate, upper-left *y*-coordinate, width and height, respectively. The upper-left *x*-coordinate is the smaller of the two *x*-coordinate values, the upper-left *y*-coordinate is the smaller of the two *y*-coordinate values, the width is the absolute value of the difference between the two *x*-coordinate values, and the height is the absolute value of the difference between the two *y*-coordinate values.

Class `DrawPanel`, which extends `JPanel` and handles the creation of the shapes, should declare three arrays, one for each shape type. The length of each array should be a random number between 1 and 5. The constructor of class `DrawPanel` will fill each of the arrays with shapes of random position, size, color and fill.

In addition, modify all three shape classes to include the following:

a) A constructor with no arguments that sets all the coordinates of the shape to 0, the color of the shape to `Color.BLACK`, and the filled property to `false` (`MyRect` and `MyOval` only).

b) *Set* methods for the instance variables in each class. The methods that set a coordinate value should verify that the argument is greater than or equal to zero before setting the coordinate—if it is not, they should set the coordinate to zero. The constructor should call the *set* methods rather than initialize the local variables directly.

c) *Get* methods for the instance variables in each class. Method `draw` should reference the coordinates by the *get* methods rather than access them directly.

8.19 Wrap-Up

In this chapter, we presented additional class concepts. The `Time` class case study presented a complete class declaration consisting of `private` data, overloaded `public` constructors for initialization flexibility, *set* and *get* methods for manipulating the class's data, and methods that returned `String` representations of a `Time` object in two different formats. You also learned that every class can declare a `toString` method that returns a `String` representation of an object of the class and that method `toString` can be called implicitly whenever an object of a class appears in the code where a `String` is expected.

You learned that the `this` reference is used implicitly in a class's non-`static` methods to access the class's instance variables and other non-`static` methods. You also saw explicit uses of the `this` reference to access the class's members (including shadowed fields) and how to use keyword `this` in a constructor to call another constructor of the class.

The chapter discussed the differences between default constructors provided by the compiler and no-argument constructors provided by the programmer. You learned that a class can have references to objects of other classes as members—a concept known as composition. You saw the new `enum` class type introduced in J2SE 5.0 and learned how it can be used to create a set of constants for use in a program. You learned about Java's garbage collection capability and how it reclaims the memory of objects that are no longer used. The chapter explained the motivation for `static` fields in a class and demonstrated how to declare and use `static` fields and methods in your own classes. You also learned how to declare and initialize `final` variables.

You learned how to package your own classes for reuse and how to import those classes into an application. Finally, you learned that fields declared without an access modifier are given package access by default. You saw the relationship between classes in the same package that allows each class in a package to access the package-access members of other classes in the package.

In the next chapter, you will learn about an important aspect of object-oriented programming in Java—inheritance. You will see that all classes in Java are related directly or indirectly to the class called `Object`. You will also begin to understand how the relationships between classes enable you to build more powerful applications.

Summary

- Every class you declare represents a new type in Java.

- The `public` methods of a class are also known as the class's `public` services or `public` interface. The primary purpose of `public` methods is to present to the class's clients a view of the services the class provides. Clients of the class need not be concerned with how the class accomplishes its tasks. For this reason, `private` class members are not directly accessible to the class's clients.

- An object that contains consistent data has data values that are always kept in range.

- A value passed to a method to modify an instance variable is a correct value if that value is in the instance variable's allowed range. A correct value is always a consistent value, but a consistent value is not correct if a method receives an out-of-range value and sets it to a consistent value to maintain the object in a consistent state.

- `String` class `static` method `format` is similar to method `System.out.printf` except that `format` returns a formatted `String` rather than displaying it in a command window.

- All objects in Java have a `toString` method that returns a `String` representation of the object. Method `toString` is called implicitly when an object appears in code where a `String` is needed.

- A non-`static` method of an object implicitly uses keyword `this` to refer to the object's instance variables and other methods. Keyword `this` can also be used explicitly.

- The compiler produces a separate file with the `.class` extension for every compiled class.

- If a method contains a local variable with the same name as one of its class's fields, the local variable shadows the field in the method's scope. The method can use the `this` reference to refer to the shadowed field explicitly.

- Overloaded constructors enable objects of a class to be initialized in different ways. The compiler differentiates overloaded constructors by their signatures.

- Every class must have at least one constructor. If none are provided, the compiler creates a default constructor that initializes the instance variables to the initial values specified in their declarations or to their default values.

- If a class declares constructors, the compiler will not create a default constructor. To specify the default initialization for objects of a class with multiple constructors, the programmer must declare a no-argument constructor.

- *Set* methods are commonly called mutator methods because they typically change a value. *Get* methods are commonly called accessor methods or query methods. A predicate method tests whether a condition is true or false.

- A class can have references to objects of other classes as members. Such a capability is called composition and is sometimes referred to as a *has-a* relationship.

- All enum types are reference types. An enum type is declared with an enum declaration, which is a comma-separated list of enum constants. The declaration may optionally include other components of traditional classes, such as constructors, fields and methods.

- enum types are implicitly `final`, because they declare constants that should not be modified.

- enum constants are implicitly `static`.

- Any attempt to create an object of an enum type with operator new results in a compilation error.

- enum constants can be used anywhere constants can be used, such as in the case labels of `switch` statements and to control enhanced `for` statements.

- Each enum constant in an enum declaration is optionally followed by arguments which are passed to the enum constructor.

- For every enum, the compiler generates a static method called values that returns an array of the enum's constants in the order in which they were declared.

- EnumSet static method range takes two parameters—the first enum constant in a range and the last enum constant in a range—and returns an that EnumSet contain all the constants between these two constants, inclusive.

- Every class in Java has the methods of class Object, one of which is the finalize method.

- The Java Virtual Machine (JVM) performs automatic garbage collection to reclaim the memory occupied by objects that are no longer in use. When there are no more references to an object, the object is marked for garbage collection by the JVM. The memory for such an object can be reclaimed when the JVM executes its garbage collector.

- The finalize method is called by the garbage collector just before it reclaims the object's memory. Method finalize does not take parameters and has return type void.

- The garbage collector may never execute before a program terminates. Thus, it is unclear if, or when, method finalize will be called.

- A static variable represents classwide information that is shared among all objects of the class.

- Static variables have class scope. A class's public static members can be accessed through a reference to any object of the class, or they can be accessed by qualifying the member name with the class name and a dot (.). A class's private static class members can be accessed only through methods of the class.

- static class members exist even when no objects of the class exist—they are available as soon as the class is loaded into memory at execution time. To access a private static member when no objects of the class exist, a public static method must be provided.

- System class static method gc indicates that the garbage collector should make a best-effort attempt to reclaim objects that are eligible for garbage collection.

- A method declared static cannot access non-static class members, because a static method can be called even when no objects of the class have been instantiated.

- The this reference cannot be used in a static method.

- A static import declaration enables programmers to refer to imported static members without the class name and a dot (.). A single static import declaration imports one static member, and a static import on demand imports all static members of a class.

- In the context of an application, the principle of least privilege states that code should be granted only the amount of privilege and access that the code needs to accomplish its designated task.

- Keyword final specifies that a variable is not modifiable—in other words, it is constant. Constants can be initialized when they are declared or by each of a class's constructors. If a final variable is not initialized, a compilation error occurs.

- Software is constructed from existing, well-defined, carefully tested, well-documented, portable, widely available components. Software reusability speeds the development of powerful, high-quality software. Rapid application development (RAD) is of great interest today.

- Java programmers now have thousands of classes in the Java API from which to choose to help them implement Java programs. The Java API classes enable Java programmers to bring new applications to market faster by using preexisting, tested components.

- The client of a class cares about the functionality the class offers, but not about how the functionality is implemented. This is referred to as data abstraction. Although programmers may know the details of a class's implementation, they should not write code that depends on these details. This enables a class to be replaced with another version without affecting the rest of the system.

- An abstract data type (ADT) consists of a data representation and the operations that can be performed on that data.
- Each class in the Java API belongs to a package that contains a group of related classes. Packages help manage the complexity of application components and facilitate software reuse.
- Packages provide a convention for unique class names that helps prevent class name conflicts.
- Before a class can be imported into multiple applications, the class must be placed in a package. There can be only one package declaration in each Java source-code file, and it must precede all other declarations and statements in the file.
- Every package name should start with your Internet domain name in reverse order. After the domain name is reversed, you can choose any other names you want for your package.
- When compiling a class in a package, the javac command-line option -d specifies where to store the package and causes the compiler to create the package's directories if they do not exist.
- The package name is part of the fully qualified class name. This helps prevent name conflicts.
- A single-type-import declaration specifies one class to import. A type-import-on-demand declaration imports only the classes that the program uses from a particular package.
- The compiler uses a class loader to locate the classes it needs in the classpath. The classpath consists of a list of directories or archive files, each separated by a directory separator.
- The classpath for the compiler and JVM can be specified by providing the -classpath option to the javac or java command, or by setting the CLASSPATH environment variable. The classpath for the JVM can also be specified via the -cp command-line option. If classes must be loaded from the current directory, include a dot (.) in the classpath.
- If no access modifier is specified for a method or variable when it is declared in a class, the method or variable is considered to have package access.

Terminology

abstract data type (ADT)
access modifier
accessor method
attribute
behavior
class library
class loader
class scope
class variable
classpath
-classpath command line argument to javac
CLASSPATH environment variable
composition
constant variable
-d command line argument to javac
data abstraction
default constructor
directory separator
enum keyword
enum constant
EnumSet class
extensible language
extensions mechanism

finalize method
format method of String
garbage collector
gc method of System
has-a relationship
mark an object for garbage collection
memory leak
mutator method
name collision
name conflict
no-argument constructor
optional package
overloaded constructors
package access
package declaration
predicate method
principle of least privilege
private access modifier
protected access modifier
public access modifier
query method
range method of EnumSet
rapid application development (RAD)

resource leak   static import on demand
service of a class   termination housekeeping
simple name of a class, field or method   this keyword
single static import   type-import-on-demand declaration
single-type-import declaration   validity checking
static field (class variable)   values method of an enum
static import   variable is not modifiable

Self-Review Exercises

8.1   Fill in the blanks in each of the following statements:

a) When compiling a class in a package, the javac command-line option _____ specifies where to store the package and causes the compiler to create the package's directories if they do not exist.

b) String class static method _____ is similar to method System.out.printf, but returns a formatted String rather than displaying a String in a command window.

c) If a method contains a local variable with the same name as one of its class's fields, the local variable _____ the field in that method's scope.

d) The _____ method is called by the garbage collector just before it reclaims an object's memory.

e) A(n) _____ declaration specifies one class to import.

f) If a class declares constructors, the compiler will not create a(n) _____.

g) An object's _____ method is called implicitly when an object appears in code where a String is needed.

h) *Get* methods are commonly called _____ or _____.

i) A(n) _____ method tests whether a condition is true or false.

j) For every enum, the compiler generates a static method called _____ that returns an array of the enum's constants in the order in which they were declared.

k) Composition is sometimes referred to as a(n) _____ relationship.

l) A(n) _____ declaration contains a comma-separated list of constants.

m) A(n) _____ variable represents classwide information that is shared by all the objects of the class.

n) A(n) _____ declaration imports one static member.

o) The _____ states that code should be granted only the amount of privilege and access that the code needs to accomplish its designated task.

p) Keyword _____ specifies that a variable is not modifiable.

q) A(n) _____ consists of a data representation and the operations that can be performed on the data.

r) There can be only one _____ in a Java source-code file, and it must precede all other declarations and statements in the file.

s) A(n) _____ declaration imports only the classes that the program uses from a particular package.

t) The compiler uses a(n) _____ to locate the classes it needs in the classpath.

u) The classpath for the compiler and JVM can be specified with the _____ option to the javac or java command, or by setting the _____ environment variable.

v) *Set* methods are commonly called _____ because they typically change a value.

w) A(n) _____ imports all static members of a class.

x) The public methods of a class are also known as the class's _____ or _____.

y) System class static method _____ indicates that the garbage collector should make a best-effort attempt to reclaim objects that are eligible for garbage collection.

z) An object that contains _____ has data values that are always kept in range.

Answers to Self-Review Exercises

8.1   a) -d. b) `format`. c) shadows. d) `finalize`. e) single-type-import. f) default constructor. g) `toString`. h) accessor methods, query methods. i) predicate. j) `values`. k) *has-a*. l) enum. m) static. n) single `static` import. o) principle of least privilege. p) final. q) abstract data type (ADT). r) package declaration. s) type-import-on-demand. t) class loader. u) -`classpath`, CLASSPATH. v) mutator methods. w) `static` import on demand. x) `public` services, `public` interface. y) gc. z) consistent data.

Exercises

8.2   Explain the notion of package access in Java. Explain the negative aspects of package access.

8.3   What happens when a return type, even `void`, is specified for a constructor?

8.4   *(Rectangle Class)* Create a class `Rectangle`. The class has attributes `length` and `width`, each of which defaults to 1. It has methods that calculate the `perimeter` and the `area` of the rectangle. It has *set* and *get* methods for both `length` and `width`. The *set* methods should verify that `length` and `width` are each floating-point numbers larger than 0.0 and less than 20.0. Write a program to test class `Rectangle`.

8.5   *(Modifying the Internal Data Representation of a Class)* It would be perfectly reasonable for the `Time2` class of Fig. 8.5 to represent the time internally as the number of seconds since midnight rather than the three integer values `hour`, `minute` and `second`. Clients could use the same `public` methods and get the same results. Modify the `Time2` class of Fig. 8.5 to implement the `Time2` as the number of seconds since midnight and show that no change is visible to the clients of the class.

8.6   *(Savings Account Class)* Create class `SavingsAccount`. Use a `static` variable `annualInterestRate` to store the annual interest rate for all account holders. Each object of the class contains a `private` instance variable `savingsBalance` indicating the amount the saver currently has on deposit. Provide method `calculateMonthlyInterest` to calculate the monthly interest by multiplying the `savingsBalance` by `annualInterestRate` divided by 12—this interest should be added to `savingsBalance`. Provide a `static` method `modifyInterestRate` that sets the `annualInterestRate` to a new value. Write a program to test class `SavingsAccount`. Instantiate two `savingsAccount` objects, `saver1` and `saver2`, with balances of $2000.00 and $3000.00, respectively. Set `annualInterestRate` to 4%, then calculate the monthly interest and print the new balances for both savers. Then set the `annualInterestRate` to 5%, calculate the next month's interest and print the new balances for both savers.

8.7   *(Enhancing Class Time2)* Modify class `Time2` of Fig. 8.5 to include a `tick` method that increments the time stored in a `Time2` object by one second. Provide method `incrementMinute` to increment the minute and method `incrementHour` to increment the hour. The `Time2` object should always remain in a consistent state. Write a program that tests the `tick` method, the `incrementMinute` method and the `incrementHour` method to ensure that they work correctly. Be sure to test the following cases:

   a) incrementing into the next minute,
   b) incrementing into the next hour and
   c) incrementing into the next day (i.e., 11:59:59 PM to 12:00:00 AM).

8.8   *(Enhancing Class Date)* Modify class `Date` of Fig. 8.7 to perform error checking on the initializer values for instance variables `month`, `day` and `year` (currently it validates only the month and day). Provide a method `nextDay` to increment the day by one. The `Date` object should always remain in a consistent state. Write a program that tests the `nextDay` method in a loop that prints the date during each iteration of the loop to illustrate that the `nextDay` method works correctly. Test the following cases:

a) incrementing into the next month and
b) incrementing into the next year.

8.9   *(Returning Error Indicators from Methods)* Modify the *set* methods in class Time2 of Fig. 8.5 to return appropriate error values if an attempt is made to set one of the instance variables hour, minute or second of an object of class Time to an invalid value. [*Hint:* Use boolean return types on each method.] Write a program that tests these new *set* methods and outputs error messages when incorrect values are supplied.

8.10   Rewrite Fig. 8.14 to use a separate import declaration for each static member of class Math that is used in the example.

8.11   Write an enum type TrafficLight, whose constants (RED, GREEN, YELLOW) take one parameter—the duration of the light. Write a program to test the TrafficLight enum so that it displays the enum constants and their durations.

8.12   *(Complex Numbers)* Create a class called Complex for performing arithmetic with complex numbers. Complex numbers have the form

*realPart + imaginaryPart * i*

where *i* is

$$\sqrt{-1}$$

Write a program to test your class. Use floating-point variables to represent the private data of the class. Provide a constructor that enables an object of this class to be initialized when it is declared. Provide a no-argument constructor with default values in case no initializers are provided. Provide public methods that perform the following operations:
a) Add two Complex numbers: The real parts are added together and the imaginary parts are added together.
b) Subtract two Complex numbers: The real part of the right operand is subtracted from the real part of the left operand, and the imaginary part of the right operand is subtracted from the imaginary part of the left operand.
c) Print Complex numbers in the form (a, b), where a is the real part and b is the imaginary part.

8.13   *(Date and Time Class)* Create class DateAndTime that combines the modified Time2 class of Exercise 8.7 and the modified Date class of Exercise 8.8. Modify method incrementHour to call method nextDay if the time is incremented into the next day. Modify methods toStandardString and toUniversalString to output the date in addition to the time. Write a program to test the new class DateAndTime. Specifically, test incrementing the time to the next day.

8.14   *(Enhanced Rectangle Class)* Create a more sophisticated Rectangle class than the one you created in Exercise 8.4. This class stores only the Cartesian coordinates of the four corners of the rectangle. The constructor calls a *set* method that accepts four sets of coordinates and verifies that each of these is in the first quadrant with no single x- or y-coordinate larger than 20.0. The *set* method also verifies that the supplied coordinates specify a rectangle. Provide methods to calculate the length, width, perimeter and area. The length is the larger of the two dimensions. Include a predicate method isSquare which determines whether the rectangle is a square. Write a program to test class Rectangle.

8.15   *(Set of Integers)* Create class IntegerSet. Each IntegerSet object can hold integers in the range 0–100. The set is represented by an array of booleans. Array element a[i] is true if integer *i* is in the set. Array element a[j] is false if integer *j* is not in the set. The no-argument constructor initializes the Java array to the "empty set" (i.e., a set whose array representation contains all false values).

Provide the following methods: Method `union` creates a third set that is the set-theoretic union of two existing sets (i.e., an element of the third set's array is set to `true` if that element is `true` in either or both of the existing sets—otherwise, the element of the third set is set to `false`). Method `intersection` creates a third set which is the set-theoretic intersection of two existing sets (i.e., an element of the third set's array is set to `false` if that element is `false` in either or both of the existing sets—otherwise, the element of the third set is set to `true`). Method `insertElement` inserts a new integer *k* into a set (by setting a[k] to `true`). Method `deleteElement` deletes integer *m* (by setting a[m] to `false`). Method `toSetString` returns a string containing a set as a list of numbers separated by spaces. Include only those elements that are present in the set. Use --- to represent an empty set. Method `isEqualTo` determines whether two sets are equal. Write a program to test class `IntegerSet`. Instantiate several `IntegerSet` objects. Test that all your methods work properly.

8.16 *(Date Class)* Create class `Date` with the following capabilities:
  a) Output the date in multiple formats, such as

      MM/DD/YYYY
      June 14, 1992
      DDD YYYY

  b) Use overloaded constructors to create `Date` objects initialized with dates of the formats in part (a). In the first case the constructor should receive three integer values. In the second case it should receive a `String` and two integer values. In the third case it should receive two integer values, the first of which represents the day number in the year. [*Hint:* To convert the string representation of the month to a numeric value, compare strings using the `equals` method. For example, if s1 and s2 are strings, the method call s1.equals(s2) returns `true` if the strings are identical and otherwise returns `false`.]

8.17 *(Rational Numbers)* Create a class called `Rational` for performing arithmetic with fractions. Write a program to test your class. Use integer variables to represent the `private` instance variables of the class—the numerator and the denominator. Provide a constructor that enables an object of this class to be initialized when it is declared. The constructor should store the fraction in reduced form. The fraction

    2/4

is equivalent to 1/2 and would be stored in the object as 1 in the `numerator` and 2 in the `denominator`. Provide a no-argument constructor with default values in case no initializers are provided. Provide `public` methods that perform each of the following operations:
  a) Add two `Rational` numbers: The result of the addition should be stored in reduced form.
  b) Subtract two `Rational` numbers: The result of the subtraction should be stored in reduced form.
  c) Multiply two `Rational` numbers: The result of the multiplication should be stored in reduced form.
  d) Divide two `Rational` numbers: The result of the division should be stored in reduced form.
  e) Print `Rational` numbers in the form a/b, where a is the `numerator` and b is the denominator.
  f) Print `Rational` numbers in floating-point format. (Consider providing formatting capabilities that enable the user of the class to specify the number of digits of precision to the right of the decimal point.)

8.18 *(Huge Integer Class)* Create a class `HugeInteger` which uses a 40-element array of digits to store integers as large as 40 digits each. Provide methods `input`, `output`, `add` and `subtract`. For comparing `HugeInteger` objects, provide the following methods: `isEqualTo`, `isNotEqualTo`, `isGreaterThan`, `isLessThan`, `isGreaterThanOrEqualTo` and `isLessThanOrEqualTo`. Each of these is a predicate method that returns `true` if the relationship holds between the two `HugeInteger` objects and returns `false` if the relationship does not hold. Provide a predicate method `isZero`. If you feel ambitious, also provide methods `multiply`, `divide` and `remainder`. [*Note:* Primitive boolean values can be output as the word "true" or the word "false" with format specifier %b.]

8.19 *(Tic-Tac-Toe)* Create a class `TicTacToe` that will enable you to write a complete program to play the game of Tic-Tac-Toe. The class contains a private 3-by-3 two-dimensional array of integers. The constructor should initialize the empty board to all zeros. Allow two human players. Wherever the first player moves, place a 1 in the specified square, and place a 2 wherever the second player moves. Each move must be to an empty square. After each move, determine whether the game has been won and whether it is a draw. If you feel ambitious, modify your program so that the computer makes the moves for one of the players. Also, allow the player to specify whether he or she wants to go first or second. If you feel exceptionally ambitious, develop a program that will play three-dimensional Tic-Tac-Toe on a 4-by-4-by-4 board [*Note:* This is a challenging project that could take many weeks of effort!].

Object-Oriented Programming: Inheritance

OBJECTIVES

In this chapter you will learn:

- How inheritance promotes software reusability.
- The notions of superclasses and subclasses.
- To use keyword **extends** to create a class that inherits attributes and behaviors from another class.
- To use access modifier **protected** to give subclass methods access to superclass members.
- To access superclass members with **super**.
- How constructors are used in inheritance hierarchies.
- The methods of class **Object**, the direct or indirect superclass of all classes in Java.

9.1 Introduction

This chapter continues our discussion of object-oriented programming (OOP) by introducing one of its primary features—**inheritance**, which is a form of software reuse in which a new class is created by absorbing an existing class's members and embellishing them with new or modified capabilities. With inheritance, programmers save time during program development by reusing proven and debugged high-quality software. This also increases the likelihood that a system will be implemented effectively.

When creating a class, rather than declaring completely new members, the programmer can designate that the new class should inherit the members of an existing class. The existing class is called the **superclass**, and the new class is the **subclass**. (The C++ programming language refers to the superclass as the **base class** and the subclass as the **derived class**.) Each subclass can become the superclass for future subclasses.

A subclass normally adds its own fields and methods. Therefore, a subclass is more specific than its superclass and represents a more specialized group of objects. Typically, the subclass exhibits the behaviors of its superclass and additional behaviors that are specific to the subclass.

The **direct superclass** is the superclass from which the subclass explicitly inherits. An **indirect superclass** is any class above the direct superclass in the **class hierarchy**, which defines the inheritance relationships between classes. In Java, the class hierarchy begins with class Object (in package java.lang), which *every* class in Java directly or indirectly **extends** (or "inherits from"). Section 9.7 lists the methods of class Object, which every other class inherits. In the case of **single inheritance,** a class is derived from one direct superclass. Java, unlike C++, does not support multiple inheritance (which occurs when a class is derived from more than one direct superclass). In Chapter 10, Object-Oriented Programming: Polymorphism, we explain how Java programmers can use interfaces to realize many of the benefits of multiple inheritance while avoiding the associated problems.

Experience in building software systems indicates that significant amounts of code deal with closely-related special cases. When programmers are preoccupied with special cases, the details can obscure the big picture. With object-oriented programming, programmers focus on the commonalities among objects in the system rather than on the special cases.

We distinguish between the "is-a" relationship and the "has-a" relationship. "Is-a" represents inheritance. In an "is-a" relationship, an object of a subclass can also be treated as an object of its superclass. For example, a car *is a* vehicle. By contrast, "has-a" represents composition (see Chapter 8). In a "has-a" relationship, an object contains one or more object references as members. For example, a car *has a* steering wheel (and a car object has a reference to a steering wheel object).

New classes can inherit from classes in class libraries. Organizations develop their own class libraries and can take advantage of others available worldwide. Some day, most new software likely will be constructed from standardized reusable components, just as automobiles and most computer hardware are constructed today. This will facilitate the development of more powerful, abundant and economical software.

9.2 Superclasses and Subclasses

Often, an object of one class "is an" object of another class as well. For example, in geometry, a rectangle *is a* quadrilateral (as are squares, parallelograms and trapezoids). Thus, in Java, class Rectangle can be said to inherit from class Quadrilateral. In this context, class Quadrilateral is a superclass and class Rectangle is a subclass. A rectangle *is a* specific type of quadrilateral, but it is incorrect to claim that every quadrilateral *is a* rectangle—the quadrilateral could be a parallelogram or some other shape. Figure 9.1 lists several simple examples of superclasses and subclasses—note that superclasses tend to be "more general" and subclasses tend to be "more specific."

Because every subclass object "is an" object of its superclass, and one superclass can have many subclasses, the set of objects represented by a superclass is typically larger than the set of objects represented by any of its subclasses. For example, the superclass Vehicle represents all vehicles, including cars, trucks, boats, bicycles and so on. By contrast, subclass Car represents a smaller, more specific subset of vehicles.

Superclass	Subclasses
Student	GraduateStudent, UndergraduateStudent
Shape	Circle, Triangle, Rectangle
Loan	CarLoan, HomeImprovementLoan, MortgageLoan
Employee	Faculty, Staff
BankAccount	CheckingAccount, SavingsAccount

Fig. 9.1 | Inheritance examples.

Inheritance relationships form tree-like hierarchical structures. A superclass exists in a hierarchical relationship with its subclasses. When classes participate in inheritance relationships, they become "affiliated" with other classes. A class becomes either a superclass, supplying members to other classes, or a subclass, inheriting its members from other classes. In some cases, a class is both a superclass and a subclass.

Let us develop a sample class hierarchy (Fig. 9.2), also called an inheritance hierarchy. A university community has thousands of members, including employees, students and alumni. Employees are either faculty members or staff members. Faculty members are either administrators (such as deans and department chairpersons) or teachers. Note that the hierarchy could contain many other classes. For example, students can be graduate or undergraduate students. Undergraduate students can be freshmen, sophomores, juniors or seniors.

Each arrow in the hierarchy represents an "is-a" relationship. As we follow the arrows in this class hierarchy, we can state, for instance, that "an Employee *is a* CommunityMember" and "a Teacher *is a* Faculty member." CommunityMember is the direct superclass of Employee, Student and Alumnus, and is an indirect superclass of all the other classes in the diagram. Starting from the bottom of the diagram, the reader can follow the arrows and apply the "is-a" relationship up to the topmost superclass. For example, an Administrator *is a* Faculty member, *is an* Employee and *is a* CommunityMember.

Now consider the Shape inheritance hierarchy in Fig. 9.3. This hierarchy begins with superclass Shape, which is extended by subclasses TwoDimensionalShape and ThreeDimensionalShape—Shapes are either TwoDimensionalShapes or ThreeDimensionalShapes. The third level of this hierarchy contains some more specific types of TwoDimensionalShapes and ThreeDimensionalShapes. As in Fig. 9.2, we can follow the arrows from the bottom of the diagram to the topmost superclass in this class hierarchy to identify several "is-a" relationships. For instance, a Triangle *is a* TwoDimensionalShape and *is a* Shape, while a Sphere *is a* ThreeDimensionalShape and *is a* Shape. Note that this hierarchy could contain many other classes. For example, ellipses and trapezoids are TwoDimensionalShapes.

Not every class relationship is an inheritance relationship. In Chapter 8, we discussed the "has-a" relationship, in which classes have members that are references to objects of other classes. Such relationships create classes by composition of existing classes. For

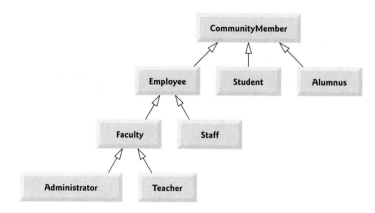

Fig. 9.2 | Inheritance hierarchy for university CommunityMembers.

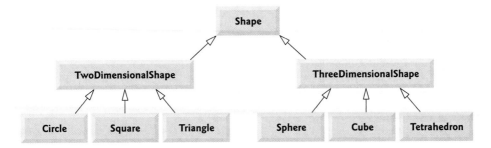

Fig. 9.3 | Inheritance hierarchy for Shapes.

example, given the classes Employee, BirthDate and TelephoneNumber, it is improper to say that an Employee *is a* BirthDate or that an Employee *is a* TelephoneNumber. However, an Employee *has a* BirthDate, and an Employee *has a* TelephoneNumber.

It is possible to treat superclass objects and subclass objects similarly—their commonalities are expressed in the members of the superclass. Objects of all classes that extend a common superclass can be treated as objects of that superclass (i.e., such objects have an "is-a" relationship with the superclass). However, superclass objects cannot be treated as objects of their subclasses. For example, all cars are vehicles, but not all vehicles are cars (the other vehicles could be trucks, planes or bicycles, for example). Later in this chapter and in Chapter 10, Object-Oriented Programming: Polymorphism, we consider many examples that take advantage of the "is-a" relationship.

One problem with inheritance is that a subclass can inherit methods that it does not need or should not have. Even when a superclass method is appropriate for a subclass, that subclass often needs a customized version of the method. In such cases, the subclass can override (redefine) the superclass method with an appropriate implementation, as we will see often in the chapter's code examples.

9.3 protected Members

Chapter 8 discussed access modifiers public and private. A class's public members are accessible wherever the program has a reference to an object of that class or one of its subclasses. A class's private members are accessible only from within the class itself. A superclass's private members are not inherited by its subclasses. In this section, we introduce access modifier **protected**. Using protected access offers an intermediate level of access between public and private. A superclass's protected members can be accessed by members of that superclass, by members of its subclasses and by members of other classes in the same package (i.e., protected members also have package access).

All public and protected superclass members retain their original access modifier when they become members of the subclass (i.e., public members of the superclass become public members of the subclass, and protected members of the superclass become protected members of the subclass).

Subclass methods can refer to public and protected members inherited from the superclass simply by using the member names. When a subclass method overrides a superclass method, the superclass method can be accessed from the subclass by preceding the superclass method name with keyword **super** and a dot (.) separator. We discuss accessing overridden members of the superclass in Section 9.4.

Software Engineering Observation 9.1

Methods of a subclass cannot directly access private *members of their superclass. A subclass can change the state of* private *superclass instance variables only through non-*private *methods provided in the superclass and inherited by the subclass.*

Software Engineering Observation 9.2

Declaring private *instance variables helps programmers test, debug and correctly modify systems. If a subclass could access its superclass's* private *instance variables, classes that inherit from that subclass could access the instance variables as well. This would propagate access to what should be* private *instance variables, and the benefits of information hiding would be lost.*

9.4 Relationship between Superclasses and Subclasses

In this section, we use an inheritance hierarchy containing types of employees in a company's payroll application to discuss the relationship between a superclass and its subclass. In this company, commission employees (who will be represented as objects of a superclass) are paid a percentage of their sales, while base-salaried commission employees (who will be represented as objects of a subclass) receive a base salary plus a percentage of their sales.

We divide our discussion of the relationship between commission employees and base-salaried commission employees into five examples. The first example declares class CommissionEmployee, which directly inherits from class Object and declares as private instance variables a first name, last name, social security number, commission rate and gross (i.e., total) sales amount.

The second example declares class BasePlusCommissionEmployee, which also directly inherits from class Object and declares as private instance variables a first name, last name, social security number, commission rate, gross sales amount and base salary. We create the latter class by writing every line of code the class requires—we will soon see that it is much more efficient to create this class by inheriting from class CommissionEmployee.

The third example declares a separate BasePlusCommissionEmployee2 class that extends class CommissionEmployee (i.e., a BasePlusCommissionEmployee2 *is a* CommissionEmployee who also has a base salary) and attempts to access class CommissionEmployee's private members—this results in compilation errors, because the subclass cannot access the superclass's private instance variables.

The fourth example shows that if CommissionEmployee's instance variables are declared as protected, a BasePlusCommissionEmployee3 class that extends class CommissionEmployee2 can access that data directly. For this purpose, we declare class CommissionEmployee2 with protected instance variables. Both of the BasePlusCommissionEmployee classes contain identical functionality, but we show how the class BasePlusCommissionEmployee3 is easier to create and manage.

After we discuss the convenience of using protected instance variables, we create the fifth example, which sets the CommissionEmployee instance variables back to private in class CommissionEmployee3 to enforce good software engineering. Then we show how a separate BasePlusCommissionEmployee4 class, which extends class CommissionEmployee3, can use CommissionEmployee3's public methods to manipulate CommissionEmployee3's private instance variables.

9.4.1 Creating and Using a CommissionEmployee Class

We begin by declaring class CommissionEmployee (Fig. 9.4). Line 4 begins the class declaration and indicates that class CommissionEmployee extends (i.e., inherits from) class Object (from package java.lang). Java programmers use inheritance to create classes from existing classes. In fact, every class in Java (except Object) extends an existing class. Because class CommissionEmployee extends class Object, class CommissionEmployee inherits the methods of class Object—class Object does not have any fields. In fact, every Java class directly or indirectly inherits Object's methods. If a class does not specify that it extends another class, the new class implicitly extends Object. For this reason, programmers typically do not include "extends Object" in their code—we do so in this example for demonstration purposes.

 Software Engineering Observation 9.3

The Java compiler sets the superclass of a class to Object when the class declaration does not explicitly extend a superclass.

```
1   // Fig. 9.4: CommissionEmployee.java
2   // CommissionEmployee class represents a commission employee.
3
4   public class CommissionEmployee extends Object
5   {
6      private String firstName;
7      private String lastName;
8      private String socialSecurityNumber;
9      private double grossSales; // gross weekly sales
10     private double commissionRate; // commission percentage
11
12     // five-argument constructor
13     public CommissionEmployee( String first, String last, String ssn,
14        double sales, double rate )
15     {
16        // implicit call to Object constructor occurs here
17        firstName = first;
18        lastName = last;
19        socialSecurityNumber = ssn;
20        setGrossSales( sales ); // validate and store gross sales
21        setCommissionRate( rate ); // validate and store commission rate
22     } // end five-argument CommissionEmployee constructor
23
24     // set first name
25     public void setFirstName( String first )
26     {
27        firstName = first;
28     } // end method setFirstName
29
30     // return first name
31     public String getFirstName()
32     {
```

Fig. 9.4 | CommissionEmployee class represents an employee paid a percentage of gross sales. (Part 1 of 3.)

```
33           return firstName;
34        } // end method getFirstName
35
36        // set last name
37        public void setLastName( String last )
38        {
39           lastName = last;
40        } // end method setLastName
41
42        // return last name
43        public String getLastName()
44        {
45           return lastName;
46        } // end method getLastName
47
48        // set social security number
49        public void setSocialSecurityNumber( String ssn )
50        {
51           socialSecurityNumber = ssn; // should validate
52        } // end method setSocialSecurityNumber
53
54        // return social security number
55        public String getSocialSecurityNumber()
56        {
57           return socialSecurityNumber;
58        } // end method getSocialSecurityNumber
59
60        // set gross sales amount
61        public void setGrossSales( double sales )
62        {
63           grossSales = ( sales < 0.0 ) ? 0.0 : sales;
64        } // end method setGrossSales
65
66        // return gross sales amount
67        public double getGrossSales()
68        {
69           return grossSales;
70        } // end method getGrossSales
71
72        // set commission rate
73        public void setCommissionRate( double rate )
74        {
75           commissionRate = ( rate > 0.0 && rate < 1.0 ) ? rate : 0.0;
76        } // end method setCommissionRate
77
78        // return commission rate
79        public double getCommissionRate()
80        {
81           return commissionRate;
82        } // end method getCommissionRate
83
```

Fig. 9.4 | CommissionEmployee class represents an employee paid a percentage of gross sales. (Part 2 of 3.)

```
84        // calculate earnings
85        public double earnings()
86        {
87           return commissionRate * grossSales;
88        } // end method earnings
89
90        // return String representation of CommissionEmployee object
91        public String toString()
92        {
93           return String.format( "%s: %s %s\n%s: %s\n%s: %.2f\n%s: %.2f",
94              "commission employee", firstName, lastName,
95              "social security number", socialSecurityNumber,
96              "gross sales", grossSales,
97              "commission rate", commissionRate );
98        } // end method toString
99     } // end class CommissionEmployee
```

Fig. 9.4 | `CommissionEmployee` class represents an employee paid a percentage of gross sales. (Part 3 of 3.)

The `public` services of class `CommissionEmployee` include a constructor (lines 13–22) and methods `earnings` (lines 85–88) and `toString` (lines 91–98). Lines 25–82 declare `public` *get* and *set* methods for manipulating the class's instance variables (declared in lines 6–10) `firstName`, `lastName`, `socialSecurityNumber`, `grossSales` and `commissionRate`. Class `CommissionEmployee` declares each of its instance variables as `private`, so objects of other classes cannot directly access these variables. Declaring instance variables as `private` and providing *get* and *set* methods to manipulate and validate the instance variables helps enforce good software engineering. Methods `setGrossSales` and `setCommissionRate`, for example, validate their arguments before assigning the values to instance variables `grossSales` and `commissionRate`, respectively.

Constructors are not inherited, so class `CommissionEmployee` does not inherit class `Object`'s constructor. However, class `CommissionEmployee`'s constructor calls class `Object`'s constructor implicitly. In fact, the first task of any subclass constructor is to call its direct superclass's constructor, either explicitly or implicitly (if no constructor call is specified), to ensure that the instance variables inherited from the superclass are initialized properly. The syntax for calling a superclass constructor explicitly is discussed in Section 9.4.3. If the code does not include an explicit call to the superclass constructor, Java implicitly calls the superclass's default or no-argument constructor. The comment in line 16 of Fig. 9.4 indicates where the implicit call to the superclass `Object`'s default constructor is made (the programmer does not write the code for this call). `Object`'s default (empty) constructor does nothing. Note that even if a class does not have constructors, the default constructor that the compiler implicitly declares for the class will call the superclass's default or no-argument constructor.

After the implicit call to `Object`'s constructor occurs, lines 17–21 of `CommissionEmployee`'s constructor assign values to the class's instance variables. Note that we do not validate the values of arguments `first`, `last` and `ssn` before assigning them to the corresponding instance variables. While validating data is good software engineering, including extensive validation in this class could add a potentially large amount of code that would obscure the focus of this example. We certainly could validate the first and last names—perhaps by ensuring that they are of a reasonable length. Similarly, a social security number could be validated to ensure that it contains nine digits, with or without dashes (e.g., 123-45-6789 or 123456789).

Method earnings (lines 85–88) calculates a CommissionEmployee's earnings. Line 87 multiplies the commissionRate by the grossSales and returns the result.

Method toString (lines 91–98) is special—it is one of the methods that every class inherits directly or indirectly from class Object, which is the root of the Java class hierarchy. Section 9.7 summarizes class Object's methods. Method toString returns a String representing an object. This method is called implicitly by a program whenever an object must be converted to a string representation, such as when an object is output by printf or String method format using the %s format specifier. Class Object's toString method returns a String that includes the name of the object's class. It is primarily a placeholder that can be overridden by a subclass to specify an appropriate string representation of the data in a subclass object. Method toString of class CommissionEmployee overrides (redefines) class Object's toString method. When invoked, CommissionEmployee's toString method uses String method format to return a String containing information about the CommissionEmployee. We use format specifier %.2f to format both the grossSales and the commissionRate with two digits of precision to the right of the decimal point. To override a superclass method, a subclass must declare a method with the same signature (method name, number of parameters and parameter types) as the superclass method—Object's toString method takes no parameters, so CommissionEmployee declares toString with no parameters.

Common Programming Error 9.1

It is a syntax error to override a method with a more restricted access modifier—a public method of the superclass cannot become a protected or private method in the subclass; a protected method of the superclass cannot become a private method in the subclass. Doing so would break the "is-a" relationship in which it is required that all subclass objects be able to respond to method calls that are made to public methods declared in the superclass. If a public method could be overridden as a protected or private method, the subclass objects would not be able to respond to the same method calls as superclass objects. Once a method is declared public in a superclass, the method remains public for all that class's direct and indirect subclasses.

Figure 9.5 tests class CommissionEmployee. Lines 9–10 instantiate a CommissionEmployee object and invoke CommissionEmployee's constructor (lines 13–22 of Fig. 9.4) to

```
1   // Fig. 9.5: CommissionEmployeeTest.java
2   // Testing class CommissionEmployee.
3
4   public class CommissionEmployeeTest
5   {
6      public static void main( String args[] )
7      {
8         // instantiate CommissionEmployee object
9         CommissionEmployee employee = new CommissionEmployee(
10           "Sue", "Jones", "222-22-2222", 10000, .06 );
11
```

Fig. 9.5 | CommissionEmployee class test program. (Part 1 of 2.)

```
12          // get commission employee data
13          System.out.println(
14             "Employee information obtained by get methods: \n" );
15          System.out.printf( "%s %s\n", "First name is",
16             employee.getFirstName() );
17          System.out.printf( "%s %s\n", "Last name is",
18             employee.getLastName() );
19          System.out.printf( "%s %s\n", "Social security number is",
20             employee.getSocialSecurityNumber() );
21          System.out.printf( "%s %.2f\n", "Gross sales is",
22             employee.getGrossSales() );
23          System.out.printf( "%s %.2f\n", "Commission rate is",
24             employee.getCommissionRate() );
25
26          employee.setGrossSales( 500 ); // set gross sales
27          employee.setCommissionRate( .1 ); // set commission rate
28
29          System.out.printf( "\n%s:\n\n%s\n",
30             "Updated employee information obtained by toString", employee );
31       } // end main
32    } // end class CommissionEmployeeTest
```

```
Employee information obtained by get methods:

First name is Sue
Last name is Jones
Social security number is 222-22-2222
Gross sales is 10000.00
Commission rate is 0.06

Updated employee information obtained by toString:

commission employee: Sue Jones
social security number: 222-22-2222
gross sales: 500.00
commission rate: 0.10
```

Fig. 9.5 | CommissionEmployee class test program. (Part 2 of 2.)

initialize it with "Sue" as the first name, "Jones" as the last name, "222-22-2222" as the social security number, 10000 as the gross sales amount and .06 as the commission rate. Lines 15–24 use CommissionEmployee's *get* methods to retrieve the object's instance variable values for output. Lines 26–27 invoke the object's methods setGrossSales and set-CommissionRate to change the values of instance variables grossSales and commissionRate. Lines 29–30 output the string representation of the updated CommissionEmployee. Note that when an object is output using the %s format specifier, the object's toString method is invoked implicitly to obtain the object's string representation.

9.4.2 Creating a BasePlusCommissionEmployee Class without Using Inheritance

We now discuss the second part of our introduction to inheritance by declaring and testing (a completely new and independent) class BasePlusCommissionEmployee (Fig. 9.6), which contains a first name, last name, social security number, gross sales amount, commission rate and base salary. Class BasePlusCommissionEmployee's public services include a BasePlusCommissionEmployee constructor (lines 15–25) and methods earnings

```
1    // Fig. 9.6: BasePlusCommissionEmployee.java
2    // BasePlusCommissionEmployee class represents an employee that receives
3    // a base salary in addition to commission.
4
5    public class BasePlusCommissionEmployee
6    {
7       private String firstName;
8       private String lastName;
9       private String socialSecurityNumber;
10      private double grossSales; // gross weekly sales
11      private double commissionRate; // commission percentage
12      private double baseSalary; // base salary per week
13
14      // six-argument constructor
15      public BasePlusCommissionEmployee( String first, String last,
16         String ssn, double sales, double rate, double salary )
17      {
18         // implicit call to Object constructor occurs here
19         firstName = first;
20         lastName = last;
21         socialSecurityNumber = ssn;
22         setGrossSales( sales ); // validate and store gross sales
23         setCommissionRate( rate ); // validate and store commission rate
24         setBaseSalary( salary ); // validate and store base salary
25      } // end six-argument BasePlusCommissionEmployee constructor
26
27      // set first name
28      public void setFirstName( String first )
29      {
30         firstName = first;
31      } // end method setFirstName
32
33      // return first name
34      public String getFirstName()
35      {
36         return firstName;
37      } // end method getFirstName
38
39      // set last name
40      public void setLastName( String last )
41      {
42         lastName = last;
43      } // end method setLastName
44
45      // return last name
46      public String getLastName()
47      {
```

Fig. 9.6 | BasePlusCommissionEmployee class represents an employee who receives a base salary in addition to a commission. (Part 1 of 3.)

```
48          return lastName;
49       } // end method getLastName
50
51       // set social security number
52       public void setSocialSecurityNumber( String ssn )
53       {
54          socialSecurityNumber = ssn; // should validate
55       } // end method setSocialSecurityNumber
56
57       // return social security number
58       public String getSocialSecurityNumber()
59       {
60          return socialSecurityNumber;
61       } // end method getSocialSecurityNumber
62
63       // set gross sales amount
64       public void setGrossSales( double sales )
65       {
66          grossSales = ( sales < 0.0 ) ? 0.0 : sales;
67       } // end method setGrossSales
68
69       // return gross sales amount
70       public double getGrossSales()
71       {
72          return grossSales;
73       } // end method getGrossSales
74
75       // set commission rate
76       public void setCommissionRate( double rate )
77       {
78          commissionRate = ( rate > 0.0 && rate < 1.0 ) ? rate : 0.0;
79       } // end method setCommissionRate
80
81       // return commission rate
82       public double getCommissionRate()
83       {
84          return commissionRate;
85       } // end method getCommissionRate
86
87       // set base salary
88       public void setBaseSalary( double salary )
89       {
90          baseSalary = ( salary < 0.0 ) ? 0.0 : salary;
91       } // end method setBaseSalary
92
93       // return base salary
94       public double getBaseSalary()
95       {
96          return baseSalary;
97       } // end method getBaseSalary
98
```

Fig. 9.6 | `BasePlusCommissionEmployee` class represents an employee who receives a base salary in addition to a commission. (Part 2 of 3.)

```
99    // calculate earnings
100   public double earnings()
101   {
102      return baseSalary + ( commissionRate * grossSales );
103   } // end method earnings
104
105   // return String representation of BasePlusCommissionEmployee
106   public String toString()
107   {
108      return String.format(
109         "%s: %s %s\n%s: %s\n%s: %.2f\n%s: %.2f\n%s: %.2f",
110         "base-salaried commission employee", firstName, lastName,
111         "social security number", socialSecurityNumber,
112         "gross sales", grossSales, "commission rate", commissionRate,
113         "base salary", baseSalary );
114   } // end method toString
115 } // end class BasePlusCommissionEmployee
```

Fig. 9.6 | BasePlusCommissionEmployee class represents an employee who receives a base salary in addition to a commission. (Part 3 of 3.)

(lines 100–103) and toString (lines 106–114). Lines 28–97 declare public *get* and *set* methods for the class's private instance variables (declared in lines 7–12) firstName, lastName, socialSecurityNumber, grossSales, commissionRate and baseSalary. These variables and methods encapsulate all the necessary features of a base-salaried commission employee. Note the similarity between this class and class CommissionEmployee (Fig. 9.4)—in this example, we will not yet exploit that similarity.

Note that class BasePlusCommissionEmployee does not specify "extends Object" on line 5, so the class implicitly extends Object. Also note that, like class CommissionEmployee's constructor (lines 13–22 of Fig. 9.4), class BasePlusCommissionEmployee's constructor invokes class Object's default constructor implicitly, as noted in the comment on line 18.

Class BasePlusCommissionEmployee's earnings method (lines 100–103) computes the earnings of a base-salaried commission employee. Line 102 returns the result of adding the employee's base salary to the product of the commission rate and the employee's gross sales.

Class BasePlusCommissionEmployee overrides Object method toString to return a String containing the BasePlusCommissionEmployee's information. Once again, we use format specifier %.2f to format the gross sales, commission rate and base salary with two digits of precision to the right of the decimal point (line 109).

Figure 9.7 tests class BasePlusCommissionEmployee. Lines 9–11 instantiate a BasePlusCommissionEmployee object and pass "Bob", "Lewis", "333-33-3333", 5000, .04 and 300 to the constructor as the first name, last name, social security number, gross sales, commission rate and base salary, respectively. Lines 16–27 use BasePlusCommissionEmployee's *get* methods to retrieve the values of the object's instance variables for output. Line 29 invokes the object's setBaseSalary method to change the base salary. Method setBaseSalary (Fig. 9.6, lines 88–91) ensures that instance variable baseSalary is not assigned a negative value, because an employee's base salary cannot be negative. Lines 31–33 of Fig. 9.7 invoke the object's toString method explicitly to get the object's string representation.

```
1   // Fig. 9.7: BasePlusCommissionEmployeeTest.java
2   // Testing class BasePlusCommissionEmployee.
3
4   public class BasePlusCommissionEmployeeTest
5   {
6      public static void main( String args[] )
7      {
8         // instantiate BasePlusCommissionEmployee object
9         BasePlusCommissionEmployee employee =
10           new BasePlusCommissionEmployee(
11           "Bob", "Lewis", "333-33-3333", 5000, .04, 300 );
12
13        // get base-salaried commission employee data
14        System.out.println(
15           "Employee information obtained by get methods: \n" );
16        System.out.printf( "%s %s\n", "First name is",
17           employee.getFirstName() );
18        System.out.printf( "%s %s\n", "Last name is",
19           employee.getLastName() );
20        System.out.printf( "%s %s\n", "Social security number is",
21           employee.getSocialSecurityNumber() );
22        System.out.printf( "%s %.2f\n", "Gross sales is",
23           employee.getGrossSales() );
24        System.out.printf( "%s %.2f\n", "Commission rate is",
25           employee.getCommissionRate() );
26        System.out.printf( "%s %.2f\n", "Base salary is",
27           employee.getBaseSalary() );
28
29        employee.setBaseSalary( 1000 ); // set base salary
30
31        System.out.printf( "\n%s:\n\n%s\n",
32           "Updated employee information obtained by toString",
33           employee.toString() );
34     } // end main
35  } // end class BasePlusCommissionEmployeeTest
```

```
Employee information obtained by get methods:

First name is Bob
Last name is Lewis
Social security number is 333-33-3333
Gross sales is 5000.00
Commission rate is 0.04
Base salary is 300.00

Updated employee information obtained by toString:

base-salaried commission employee: Bob Lewis
social security number: 333-33-3333
gross sales: 5000.00
commission rate: 0.04
base salary: 1000.00
```

Fig. 9.7 | BasePlusCommissionEmployee test program.

Note that much of the code for class BasePlusCommissionEmployee (Fig. 9.6) is similar, if not identical, to the code for class CommissionEmployee (Fig. 9.4). For example, in class BasePlusCommissionEmployee, private instance variables firstName and lastName and methods setFirstName, getFirstName, setLastName and getLastName are identical to those of class CommissionEmployee. Classes CommissionEmployee and BasePlusCommissionEmployee also both contain private instance variables socialSecurityNumber, commissionRate and grossSales, as well as *get* and *set* methods to manipulate these variables. In addition, the BasePlusCommissionEmployee constructor is almost identical to that of class CommissionEmployee, except that BasePlusCommissionEmployee's constructor also sets the baseSalary. The other additions to class BasePlusCommissionEmployee are private instance variable baseSalary and methods setBaseSalary and getBaseSalary. Class BasePlusCommissionEmployee's toString method is nearly identical to that of class CommissionEmployee except that BasePlusCommissionEmployee's toString also outputs the value of instance variable baseSalary with two digits of precision to the right of the decimal point.

We literally copied code from class CommissionEmployee and pasted it into class BasePlusCommissionEmployee, then modified class BasePlusCommissionEmployee to include a base salary and methods that manipulate the base salary. This "copy-and-paste" approach is often error prone and time consuming. Worse yet, it can spread many physical copies of the same code throughout a system, creating a code-maintenance nightmare. Is there a way to "absorb" the instance variables and methods of one class in a way that makes them part of other classes without duplicating code? In the next several examples, we answer this question, using a more elegant approach to building classes that emphasizes the benefits of inheritance.

Software Engineering Observation 9.4

Copying and pasting code from one class to another can spread errors across multiple source code files. To avoid duplicating code (and possibly errors), use inheritance, rather than the "copy-and-paste" approach, in situations where you want one class to "absorb" the instance variables and methods of another class.

Software Engineering Observation 9.5

With inheritance, the common instance variables and methods of all the classes in the hierarchy are declared in a superclass. When changes are required for these common features, software developers need only to make the changes in the superclass—subclasses then inherit the changes. Without inheritance, changes would need to be made to all the source code files that contain a copy of the code in question.

9.4.3 Creating a CommissionEmployee-BasePlusCommissionEmployee Inheritance Hierarchy

Now we declare class BasePlusCommissionEmployee2 (Fig. 9.8), which extends class CommissionEmployee (Fig. 9.4). A BasePlusCommissionEmployee2 object *is a* CommissionEmployee (because inheritance passes on the capabilities of class CommissionEmployee), but class BasePlusCommissionEmployee2 also has instance variable baseSalary (Fig. 9.8, line 6). Keyword extends in line 4 of the class declaration indicates inheritance. As a subclass, BasePlusCommissionEmployee2 inherits the public and protected instance variables and methods of class CommissionEmployee. The constructor of class CommissionEmployee is not inherited. Thus, the public services of BasePlusCommissionEmployee2 include its constructor (lines 9–16), public methods inherited from class CommissionEmployee, method set-BaseSalary (lines 19–22), method getBaseSalary (lines 25–28), method earnings (lines 31–35) and method toString (lines 38–47).

```java
1   // Fig. 9.8: BasePlusCommissionEmployee2.java
2   // BasePlusCommissionEmployee2 inherits from class CommissionEmployee.
3
4   public class BasePlusCommissionEmployee2 extends CommissionEmployee
5   {
6      private double baseSalary; // base salary per week
7
8      // six-argument constructor
9      public BasePlusCommissionEmployee2( String first, String last,
10        String ssn, double sales, double rate, double salary )
11     {
12        // explicit call to superclass CommissionEmployee constructor
13        super( first, last, ssn, sales, rate );
14
15        setBaseSalary( amount ); // validate and store base salary
16     } // end six-argument BasePlusCommissionEmployee2 constructor
17
18     // set base salary
19     public void setBaseSalary( double salary )
20     {
21        baseSalary = ( salary < 0.0 ) ? 0.0 : salary;
22     } // end method setBaseSalary
23
24     // return base salary
25     public double getBaseSalary()
26     {
27        return baseSalary;
28     } // end method getBaseSalary
29
30     // calculate earnings
31     public double earnings()
32     {
33        // not allowed: commissionRate and grossSales private in superclass
34        return baseSalary + ( commissionRate * grossSales );
35     } // end method earnings
36
37     // return String representation of BasePlusCommissionEmployee2
38     public String toString()
39     {
40        // not allowed: attempts to access private superclass members
41        return String.format(
42           "%s: %s %s\n%s: %s\n%s: %.2f\n%s: %.2f\n%s: %.2f",
43           "base-salaried commission employee", firstName, lastName,
44           "social security number", socialSecurityNumber,
45           "gross sales", grossSales, "commission rate", commissionRate,
46           "base salary", baseSalary );
47     } // end method toString
48  } // end class BasePlusCommissionEmployee2
```

Fig. 9.8 | private superclass members cannot be accessed in a subclass. (Part I of 2.)

```
BasePlusCommissionEmployee2.java:34: commissionRate has private access in Com-
missionEmployee
      return baseSalary + ( commissionRate * grossSales );
                            ^
BasePlusCommissionEmployee2.java:34: grossSales has private access in
CommissionEmployee
      return baseSalary + ( commissionRate * grossSales );
                                             ^
BasePlusCommissionEmployee2.java:43: firstName has private access in
CommissionEmployee
         "base-salaried commission employee", firstName, lastName,
                                               ^
BasePlusCommissionEmployee2.java:43: lastName has private access in
CommissionEmployee
         "base-salaried commission employee", firstName, lastName,
                                                          ^
BasePlusCommissionEmployee2.java:44: socialSecurityNumber has private access
in CommissionEmployee
         "social security number", socialSecurityNumber,
                                   ^
BasePlusCommissionEmployee2.java:45: grossSales has private access in
CommissionEmployee
         "gross sales", grossSales, "commission rate", commissionRate,
                        ^
BasePlusCommissionEmployee2.java:45: commissionRate has private access in Com-
missionEmployee
         "gross sales", grossSales, "commission rate", commissionRate,
                                                        ^
7 errors
```

Fig. 9.8 | private superclass members cannot be accessed in a subclass. (Part 2 of 2.)

Each subclass constructor must implicitly or explicitly call its superclass constructor to ensure that the instance variables inherited from the superclass are initialized properly. BasePlusCommissionEmployee2's six-argument constructor (lines 9–16) explicitly calls class CommissionEmployee's five-argument constructor to initialize the superclass portion of a BasePlusCommissionEmployee2 object (i.e., variables firstName, lastName, social-SecurityNumber, grossSales and commissionRate). Line 13 in BasePlusCommission-Employee2's six-argument constructor invokes the CommissionEmployee's five-argument constructor (declared at lines 13–22 of Fig. 9.4) by using the superclass constructor call syntax—keyword super, followed by a set of parentheses containing the superclass constructor arguments. The arguments first, last, ssn, sales and rate are used to initialize superclass members firstName, lastName, socialSecurityNumber, grossSales and commissionRate, respectively. If BasePlusCommissionEmployee2's constructor did not invoke CommissionEmployee's constructor explicitly, Java would attempt to invoke class CommissionEmployee's no-argument or default constructor—but the class does not have such a constructor, so the compiler would issue an error. The explicit superclass constructor call on line 13 must be the first statement in the subclass constructor's body. Also, when a superclass contains a no-argument constructor, you can use super() to call that constructor explicitly, but this is rarely done.

Common Programming Error 9.2

A compilation error occurs if a subclass constructor calls one of its superclass constructors with arguments that do not match exactly the number and types of parameters specified in one of the superclass constructor declarations.

The compiler generates errors for line 34 of Fig. 9.8 because superclass Commission-Employee's instance variables commissionRate and grossSales are private—subclass BasePlusCommissionEmployee2's methods are not allowed to access superclass CommissionEmployee's private instance variables. Note that we used red text in Fig. 9.8 to indicate erroneous code. The compiler issues additional errors at lines 43–45 of BasePlusCommissionEmployee2's toString method for the same reason. The errors in BasePlusCommissionEmployee2 could have been prevented by using the *get* methods inherited from class CommissionEmployee. For example, line 34 could have used getCommissionRate and getGrossSales to access CommissionEmployee's private instance variables commissionRate and grossSales, respectively. Lines 43–45 also could have used appropriate *get* methods to retrieve the values of the superclass's instance variables.

9.4.4 CommissionEmployee–BasePlusCommissionEmployee Inheritance Hierarchy Using protected Instance Variables

To enable class BasePlusCommissionEmployee to directly access superclass instance variables firstName, lastName, socialSecurityNumber, grossSales and commissionRate, we can declare those members as protected in the superclass. As we discussed in Section 9.3, a superclass's protected members *are* inherited by all subclasses of that superclass. Class CommissionEmployee2 (Fig. 9.9) is a modification of class CommissionEmployee (Fig. 9.4)

```
 1   // Fig. 9.9: CommissionEmployee2.java
 2   // CommissionEmployee2 class represents a commission employee.
 3
 4   public class CommissionEmployee2
 5   {
 6      protected String firstName;
 7      protected String lastName;
 8      protected String socialSecurityNumber;
 9      protected double grossSales; // gross weekly sales
10      protected double commissionRate; // commission percentage
11
12      // five-argument constructor
13      public CommissionEmployee2( String first, String last, String ssn,
14         double sales, double rate )
15      {
16         // implicit call to Object constructor occurs here
17         firstName = first;
18         lastName = last;
19         socialSecurityNumber = ssn;
20         setGrossSales( sales ); // validate and store gross sales
21         setCommissionRate( rate ); // validate and store commission rate
22      } // end five-argument CommissionEmployee2 constructor
23
```

Fig. 9.9 | CommissionEmployee2 with protected instance variables. (Part 1 of 3.)

```
24      // set first name
25      public void setFirstName( String first )
26      {
27         firstName = first;
28      } // end method setFirstName
29
30      // return first name
31      public String getFirstName()
32      {
33         return firstName;
34      } // end method getFirstName
35
36      // set last name
37      public void setLastName( String last )
38      {
39         lastName = last;
40      } // end method setLastName
41
42      // return last name
43      public String getLastName()
44      {
45         return lastName;
46      } // end method getLastName
47
48      // set social security number
49      public void setSocialSecurityNumber( String ssn )
50      {
51         socialSecurityNumber = ssn; // should validate
52      } // end method setSocialSecurityNumber
53
54      // return social security number
55      public String getSocialSecurityNumber()
56      {
57         return socialSecurityNumber;
58      } // end method getSocialSecurityNumber
59
60      // set gross sales amount
61      public void setGrossSales( double sales )
62      {
63         grossSales = ( sales < 0.0 ) ? 0.0 : sales;
64      } // end method setGrossSales
65
66      // return gross sales amount
67      public double getGrossSales()
68      {
69         return grossSales;
70      } // end method getGrossSales
71
72      // set commission rate
73      public void setCommissionRate( double rate )
74      {
75         commissionRate = ( rate > 0.0 && rate < 1.0 ) ? rate : 0.0;
76      } // end method setCommissionRate
```

Fig. 9.9 | CommissionEmployee2 with protected instance variables. (Part 2 of 3.)

```
77
78      // return commission rate
79      public double getCommissionRate()
80      {
81         return commissionRate;
82      } // end method getCommissionRate
83
84      // calculate earnings
85      public double earnings()
86      {
87         return commissionRate * grossSales;
88      } // end method earnings
89
90      // return String representation of CommissionEmployee2 object
91      public String toString()
92      {
93         return String.format( "%s: %s %s\n%s: %s\n%s: %.2f\n%s: %.2f",
94            "commission employee", firstName, lastName,
95            "social security number", socialSecurityNumber,
96            "gross sales", grossSales,
97            "commission rate", commissionRate );
98      } // end method toString
99   } // end class CommissionEmployee2
```

Fig. 9.9 | CommissionEmployee2 with protected instance variables. (Part 3 of 3.)

that declares instance variables firstName, lastName, socialSecurityNumber, grossSales and commissionRate as protected (Fig. 9.9, lines 6–10) rather than private. Other than the change in the class name (and thus the change in the constructor name) to CommissionEmployee2, the rest of the class declaration in Fig. 9.9 is identical to that of Fig. 9.4.

We could have declared the superclass CommissionEmployee2's instance variables firstName, lastName, socialSecurityNumber, grossSales and commissionRate as public to enable subclass BasePlusCommissionEmployee2 to access the superclass instance variables. However, declaring public instance variables is poor software engineering because it allows unrestricted access to the instance variables, greatly increasing the chance of errors. With protected instance variables, the subclass gets access to the instance variables, but classes that are not subclasses and classes that are not in the same package cannot access these variables directly. Recall that protected class members are also visible to other classes in the same package.

Class BasePlusCommissionEmployee3 (Fig. 9.10) is a modification of class BasePlusCommissionEmployee2 (Fig. 9.8) that extends CommissionEmployee2 (line 5) rather than class CommissionEmployee. Objects of class BasePlusCommissionEmployee3 inherit CommissionEmployee2's protected instance variables firstName, lastName, socialSecurityNumber, grossSales and commissionRate—all these variables are now protected members of BasePlusCommissionEmployee3. As a result, the compiler does not generate errors when compiling line 32 of method earnings and lines 40–42 of method toString. If another class extends BasePlusCommissionEmployee3, the new subclass also inherits the protected members.

```java
 1   // Fig. 9.10: BasePlusCommissionEmployee3.java
 2   // BasePlusCommissionEmployee3 inherits from CommissionEmployee2 and has
 3   // access to CommissionEmployee2's protected members.
 4
 5   public class BasePlusCommissionEmployee3 extends CommissionEmployee2
 6   {
 7      private double baseSalary; // base salary per week
 8
 9      // six-argument constructor
10      public BasePlusCommissionEmployee3( String first, String last,
11         String ssn, double sales, double rate, double salary )
12      {
13         super( first, last, ssn, sales, rate );
14         setBaseSalary( salary ); // validate and store base salary
15      } // end six-argument BasePlusCommissionEmployee3 constructor
16
17      // set base salary
18      public void setBaseSalary( double salary )
19      {
20         baseSalary = ( salary < 0.0 ) ? 0.0 : salary;
21      } // end method setBaseSalary
22
23      // return base salary
24      public double getBaseSalary()
25      {
26         return baseSalary;
27      } // end method getBaseSalary
28
29      // calculate earnings
30      public double earnings()
31      {
32         return baseSalary + ( commissionRate * grossSales );
33      } // end method earnings
34
35      // return String representation of BasePlusCommissionEmployee3
36      public String toString()
37      {
38         return String.format(
39            "%s: %s %s\n%s: %s\n%s: %.2f\n%s: %.2f\n%s: %.2f",
40            "base-salaried commission employee", firstName, lastName,
41            "social security number", socialSecurityNumber,
42            "gross sales", grossSales, "commission rate", commissionRate,
43            "base salary", baseSalary );
44      } // end method toString
45   } // end class BasePlusCommissionEmployee3
```

Fig. 9.10 | BasePlusCommissionEmployee3 inherits protected instance variables from
CommissionEmployee2.

Class BasePlusCommissionEmployee3 does not inherit class CommissionEmployee2's
constructor. However, class BasePlusCommissionEmployee3's six-argument constructor
(lines 10–15) calls class CommissionEmployee2's five-argument constructor explicitly.
BasePlusCommissionEmployee3's six-argument constructor must explicitly call the five-

argument constructor of class CommissionEmployee2, because CommissionEmployee2 does not provide a no-argument constructor that could be invoked implicitly.

Figure 9.11 uses a BasePlusCommissionEmployee3 object to perform the same tasks that Fig. 9.7 performed on a BasePlusCommissionEmployee object (Fig. 9.6). Note that the outputs of the two programs are identical. Although we declared class BasePlusCommissionEmployee without using inheritance and declared class BasePlusCommissionEmployee3 using inheritance, both classes provide the same functionality. The source code for class BasePlusCommissionEmployee3, which is 45 lines, is considerably shorter than that for class BasePlusCommissionEmployee, which is 115 lines, because class BasePlusCommissionEmployee3 inherits most of its functionality from CommissionEmployee2, whereas class BasePlusCommissionEmployee inherits only class Object's functionality. Also, there is now only one copy of the commission employee functionality

```java
1   // Fig. 9.11: BasePlusCommissionEmployeeTest3.java
2   // Testing class BasePlusCommissionEmployee3.
3
4   public class BasePlusCommissionEmployeeTest3
5   {
6      public static void main( String args[] )
7      {
8         // instantiate BasePlusCommissionEmployee3 object
9         BasePlusCommissionEmployee3 employee =
10           new BasePlusCommissionEmployee3(
11           "Bob", "Lewis", "333-33-3333", 5000, .04, 300 );
12
13        // get base-salaried commission employee data
14        System.out.println(
15           "Employee information obtained by get methods: \n" );
16        System.out.printf( "%s %s\n", "First name is",
17           employee.getFirstName() );
18        System.out.printf( "%s %s\n", "Last name is",
19           employee.getLastName() );
20        System.out.printf( "%s %s\n", "Social security number is",
21           employee.getSocialSecurityNumber() );
22        System.out.printf( "%s %.2f\n", "Gross sales is",
23           employee.getGrossSales() );
24        System.out.printf( "%s %.2f\n", "Commission rate is",
25           employee.getCommissionRate() );
26        System.out.printf( "%s %.2f\n", "Base salary is",
27           employee.getBaseSalary() );
28
29        employee.setBaseSalary( 1000 ); // set base salary
30
31        System.out.printf( "\n%s:\n\n%s\n",
32           "Updated employee information obtained by toString",
33           employee.toString() );
34     } // end main
35  } // end class BasePlusCommissionEmployeeTest3
```

Fig. 9.11 | protected superclass members inherited into subclass BasePlusCommissionEmployee3. (Part 1 of 2.)

```
Employee information obtained by get methods:

First name is Bob
Last name is Lewis
Social security number is 333-33-3333
Gross sales is 5000.00
Commission rate is 0.04
Base salary is 300.00

Updated employee information obtained by toString:

base-salaried commission employee: Bob Lewis
social security number: 333-33-3333
gross sales: 5000.00
commission rate: 0.04
base salary: 1000.00
```

Fig. 9.11 | protected superclass members inherited into subclass BasePlusCommissionEmployee3. (Part 2 of 2.)

declared in class CommissionEmployee2. This makes the code easier to maintain, modify and debug, because the code related to a commission employee exists only in class CommissionEmployee2.

In this example, we declared superclass instance variables as protected so that subclasses could inherit them. Inheriting protected instance variables slightly increases performance, because we can directly access the variables in the subclass without incurring the overhead of a *set* or *get* method call. In most cases, however, it is better to use private instance variables to encourage proper software engineering, and leave code optimization issues to the compiler. Your code will be easier to maintain, modify and debug.

Using protected instance variables creates several potential problems. First, the subclass object can set an inherited variable's value directly without using a *set* method. Therefore, a subclass object can assign an invalid value to the variable, thus leaving the object in an inconsistent state. For example, if we were to declare CommissionEmployee3's instance variable grossSales as protected, a subclass object (e.g., BasePlusCommissionEmployee) could then assign a negative value to grossSales. The second problem with using protected instance variables is that subclass methods are more likely to be written so that they depend on the superclass's data implementation. In practice, subclasses should depend only on the superclass services (i.e., non-private methods) and not on the superclass data implementation. With protected instance variables in the superclass, we may need to modify all the subclasses of the superclass if the superclass implementation changes. For example, if for some reason we were to change the names of instance variables firstName and lastName to first and last, then we would have to do so for all occurrences in which a subclass directly references superclass instance variables firstName and lastName. In such a case, the software is said to be fragile or brittle, because a small change in the superclass can "break" subclass implementation. The programmer should be able to change the superclass implementation while still providing the same services to the subclasses. (Of course, if the superclass services change, we must reimplement our subclasses.) A third problem is that a class's protected members are visible to all classes in the same package as the class containing the protected members—this is not always desirable.

Software Engineering Observation 9.6

Use the protected access modifier when a superclass should provide a method only to its subclasses and other classes in the same package, but not to other clients.

Software Engineering Observation 9.7

Declaring superclass instance variables private *(as opposed to* protected*) enables the superclass implementation of these instance variables to change without affecting subclass implementations.*

Error-Prevention Tip 9.1

When possible, do not include protected *instance variables in a superclass. Instead, include non-private methods that access* private *instance variables. This will ensure that objects of the class maintain consistent states.*

9.4.5 CommissionEmployee–BasePlusCommissionEmployee Inheritance Hierarchy Using private Instance Variables

We now reexamine our hierarchy once more, this time using the best software engineering practices. Class CommissionEmployee3 (Fig. 9.12) declares instance variables firstName, lastName, socialSecurityNumber, grossSales and commissionRate as private (lines 6–10)

```java
1   // Fig. 9.12: CommissionEmployee3.java
2   // CommissionEmployee3 class represents a commission employee.
3
4   public class CommissionEmployee3
5   {
6      private String firstName;
7      private String lastName;
8      private String socialSecurityNumber;
9      private double grossSales; // gross weekly sales
10     private double commissionRate; // commission percentage
11
12     // five-argument constructor
13     public CommissionEmployee3( String first, String last, String ssn,
14        double sales, double rate )
15     {
16        // implicit call to Object constructor occurs here
17        firstName = first;
18        lastName = last;
19        socialSecurityNumber = ssn;
20        setGrossSales( sales ); // validate and store gross sales
21        setCommissionRate( rate ); // validate and store commission rate
22     } // end five-argument CommissionEmployee3 constructor
23
24     // set first name
25     public void setFirstName( String first )
26     {
27        firstName = first;
28     } // end method setFirstName
29
```

Fig. 9.12 | CommissionEmployee3 class uses methods to manipulate its private instance variables. (Part 1 of 3.)

```
30      // return first name
31      public String getFirstName()
32      {
33         return firstName;
34      } // end method getFirstName
35
36      // set last name
37      public void setLastName( String last )
38      {
39         lastName = last;
40      } // end method setLastName
41
42      // return last name
43      public String getLastName()
44      {
45         return lastName;
46      } // end method getLastName
47
48      // set social security number
49      public void setSocialSecurityNumber( String ssn )
50      {
51         socialSecurityNumber = ssn; // should validate
52      } // end method setSocialSecurityNumber
53
54      // return social security number
55      public String getSocialSecurityNumber()
56      {
57         return socialSecurityNumber;
58      } // end method getSocialSecurityNumber
59
60      // set gross sales amount
61      public void setGrossSales( double sales )
62      {
63         grossSales = ( sales < 0.0 ) ? 0.0 : sales;
64      } // end method setGrossSales
65
66      // return gross sales amount
67      public double getGrossSales()
68      {
69         return grossSales;
70      } // end method getGrossSales
71
72      // set commission rate
73      public void setCommissionRate( double rate )
74      {
75         commissionRate = ( rate > 0.0 && rate < 1.0 ) ? rate : 0.0;
76      } // end method setCommissionRate
77
78      // return commission rate
79      public double getCommissionRate()
80      {
```

Fig. 9.12 | CommissionEmployee3 class uses methods to manipulate its private instance variables. (Part 2 of 3.)

```
81          return commissionRate;
82      } // end method getCommissionRate
83
84      // calculate earnings
85      public double earnings()
86      {
87          return getCommissionRate() * getGrossSales();
88      } // end method earnings
89
90      // return String representation of CommissionEmployee3 object
91      public String toString()
92      {
93          return String.format( "%s: %s %s\n%s: %s\n%s: %.2f\n%s: %.2f",
94              "commission employee", getFirstName(), getLastName(),
95              "social security number", getSocialSecurityNumber(),
96              "gross sales", getGrossSales(),
97              "commission rate", getCommissionRate() );
98      } // end method toString
99  } // end class CommissionEmployee3
```

Fig. 9.12 | `CommissionEmployee3` class uses methods to manipulate its `private` instance variables. (Part 3 of 3.)

and provides `public` methods `setFirstName`, `getFirstName`, `setLastName`, `getLastName`, `setSocialSecurityNumber`, `getSocialSecurityNumber`, `setGrossSales`, `getGrossSales`, `setCommissionRate`, `getCommissionRate`, `earnings` and `toString` for manipulating these values. Note that methods `earnings` (lines 85–88) and `toString` (lines 91–98) use the class's *get* methods to obtain the values of its instance variables. If we decide to change the instance variable names, the `earnings` and `toString` declarations will not require modification—only the bodies of the *get* and *set* methods that directly manipulate the instance variables will need to change. Note that these changes occur solely within the superclass—no changes to the subclass are needed. Localizing the effects of changes like this is a good software engineering practice. Subclass `BasePlusCommissionEmployee4` (Fig. 9.13) inherits `CommissionEmployee3`'s non-private methods and can access the `private` superclass members via those methods.

Class `BasePlusCommissionEmployee4` (Fig. 9.13) has several changes to its method implementations that distinguish it from class `BasePlusCommissionEmployee3` (Fig. 9.10). Methods `earnings` (Fig. 9.13, lines 31–34) and `toString` (lines 37–41) each invoke method `getBaseSalary` to obtain the base salary value, rather than accessing `baseSalary` directly. If we decide to rename instance variable `baseSalary`, only the bodies of method `setBaseSalary` and `getBaseSalary` will need to change.

Class `BasePlusCommissionEmployee4`'s earnings method (Fig. 9.13, lines 31–34) overrides class `CommissionEmployee3`'s earnings method (Fig. 9.12, lines 85–88) to calculate the earnings of a base-salaried commission employee. The new version obtains the portion of the employee's earnings based on commission alone by calling `CommissionEmployee3`'s earnings method with the expression `super.earnings()` (Fig. 9.13, line 33). `BasePlusCommissionEmployee4`'s earnings method then adds the base salary to this value to calculate the total earnings of the employee. Note the syntax used to invoke an overridden superclass method from a subclass—place the keyword super and a dot (.) separator before the superclass method name. This method invocation

```
1    // Fig. 9.13: BasePlusCommissionEmployee4.java
2    // BasePlusCommissionEmployee4 class inherits from CommissionEmployee3 and
3    // accesses CommissionEmployee3's private data via CommissionEmployee3's
4    // public methods.
5
6    public class BasePlusCommissionEmployee4 extends CommissionEmployee3
7    {
8       private double baseSalary; // base salary per week
9
10      // six-argument constructor
11      public BasePlusCommissionEmployee4( String first, String last,
12         String ssn, double sales, double rate, double salary )
13      {
14         super( first, last, ssn, sales, rate );
15         setBaseSalary( salary ); // validate and store base salary
16      } // end six-argument BasePlusCommissionEmployee4 constructor
17
18      // set base salary
19      public void setBaseSalary( double salary )
20      {
21         baseSalary = ( salary < 0.0 ) ? 0.0 : salary;
22      } // end method setBaseSalary
23
24      // return base salary
25      public double getBaseSalary()
26      {
27         return baseSalary;
28      } // end method getBaseSalary
29
30      // calculate earnings
31      public double earnings()
32      {
33         return getBaseSalary() + super.earnings();
34      } // end method earnings
35
36      // return String representation of BasePlusCommissionEmployee4
37      public String toString()
38      {
39         return String.format( "%s %s\n%s: %.2f", "base-salaried",
40            super.toString(), "base salary", getBaseSalary() );
41      } // end method toString
42   } // end class BasePlusCommissionEmployee4
```

Fig. 9.13 | BasePlusCommissionEmployee4 class extends CommissionEmployee3, which provides only private instance variables.

is a good software-engineering practice: Recall from Software Engineering Observation 8.5 that if a method performs all or some of the actions needed by another method, call that method rather than duplicate its code. By having BasePlusCommissionEmployee4's earnings method invoke CommissionEmployee3's earnings method to calculate part of a BasePlusCommissionEmployee4 object's earnings, we avoid duplicating the code and reduce code-maintenance problems.

Common Programming Error 9.3

When a superclass method is overridden in a subclass, the subclass version often calls the super-class version to do a portion of the work. Failure to prefix the superclass method name with the keyword super and a dot (.) separator when referencing the superclass's method causes the sub-class method to call itself, creating an error called infinite recursion. Recursion, used correctly, is a powerful capability discussed in upper-level computer science courses.

Similarly, BasePlusCommissionEmployee4's toString method (Fig. 9.13, lines 37–41) overrides class CommissionEmployee3's toString method (Fig. 9.12, lines 91–98) to return a string representation that is appropriate for a base-salaried commission employee. The new version creates part of a BasePlusCommissionEmployee4 object's string representation (i.e., the string "commission employee" and the values of class CommissionEmployee3's private instance variables) by calling CommissionEmployee3's toString method with the expression super.toString() (Fig. 9.13, line 40). BasePlusCommissionEmployee4's toString method then outputs the remainder of a BasePlusCommissionEmployee4 object's string representation (i.e., the value of class BasePlusCommissionEmployee4's base salary).

Figure 9.14 performs the same manipulations on a BasePlusCommissionEmployee4 object as did Fig. 9.7 and Fig. 9.11 on objects of classes BasePlusCommissionEmployee and BasePlusCommissionEmployee3, respectively. Although each "base-salaried commission employee" class behaves identically, class BasePlusCommissionEmployee4 is the best engineered. By using inheritance and by calling methods that hide the data and ensure consistency, we have efficiently and effectively constructed a well-engineered class.

```
1   // Fig. 9.14: BasePlusCommissionEmployeeTest4.java
2   // Testing class BasePlusCommissionEmployee4.
3
4   public class BasePlusCommissionEmployeeTest4
5   {
6      public static void main( String args[] )
7      {
8         // instantiate BasePlusCommissionEmployee4 object
9         BasePlusCommissionEmployee4 employee =
10           new BasePlusCommissionEmployee4(
11           "Bob", "Lewis", "333-33-3333", 5000, .04, 300 );
12
13        // get base-salaried commission employee data
14        System.out.println(
15           "Employee information obtained by get methods: \n" );
16        System.out.printf( "%s %s\n", "First name is",
17           employee.getFirstName() );
18        System.out.printf( "%s %s\n", "Last name is",
19           employee.getLastName() );
20        System.out.printf( "%s %s\n", "Social security number is",
21           employee.getSocialSecurityNumber() );
22        System.out.printf( "%s %.2f\n", "Gross sales is",
23           employee.getGrossSales() );
```

Fig. 9.14 | Superclass private instance variables are accessible to a subclass via public or protected methods inherited by the subclass. (Part 1 of 2.)

```
24          System.out.printf( "%s %.2f\n", "Commission rate is",
25             employee.getCommissionRate() );
26          System.out.printf( "%s %.2f\n", "Base salary is",
27             employee.getBaseSalary() );
28
29          employee.setBaseSalary( 1000 ); // set base salary
30
31          System.out.printf( "\n%s:\n\n%s\n",
32             "Updated employee information obtained by toString",
33             employee.toString() );
34      } // end main
35  } // end class BasePlusCommissionEmployeeTest4
```

```
Employee information obtained by get methods:

First name is Bob
Last name is Lewis
Social security number is 333-33-3333
Gross sales is 5000.00
Commission rate is 0.04
Base salary is 300.00

Updated employee information obtained by toString:

base-salaried commission employee: Bob Lewis
social security number: 333-33-3333
gross sales: 5000.00
commission rate: 0.04
base salary: 1000.00
```

Fig. 9.14 | Superclass `private` instance variables are accessible to a subclass via `public` or `protected` methods inherited by the subclass. (Part 2 of 2.)

In this section, you saw an evolutionary set of examples that was carefully designed to teach key capabilities for good software engineering with inheritance. You learned how to use the keyword `extends` to create a subclass using inheritance, how to use `protected` super-class members to enable a subclass to access inherited superclass instance variables and how to override superclass methods to provide versions that are more appropriate for subclass objects. In addition, you learned how to apply software-engineering techniques from Chapter 8 and this chapter to create classes that are easy to maintain, modify and debug.

9.5 Constructors in Subclasses

As we explained in the preceding section, instantiating a subclass object begins a chain of constructor calls in which the subclass constructor, before performing its own tasks, invokes its direct superclass's constructor either explicitly (via the `super` reference) or implicitly (calling the superclass's default constructor or no-argument constructor). Similarly, if the super-class is derived from another class (as is, of course, every class except `Object`), the superclass constructor invokes the constructor of the next class up in the hierarchy, and so on. The last constructor called in the chain is always the constructor for class `Object`. The original sub-class constructor's body finishes executing last. Each superclass's constructor manipulates the superclass instance variables that the subclass object inherits. For example, consider again the

CommissionEmployee3–BasePlusCommissionEmployee4 hierarchy from Fig. 9.12 and Fig. 9.13. When a program creates a BasePlusCommissionEmployee4 object, the BasePlus-CommissionEmployee4 constructor is called. That constructor calls CommissionEmployee3's constructor, which in turn calls Object's constructor. Class Object's constructor has an empty body, so it immediately returns control to CommissionEmployee3's constructor, which then initializes the private instance variables of CommissionEmployee3 that are part of the BasePlusCommissionEmployee4 object. When CommissionEmployee3's constructor completes execution, it returns control to BasePlusCommissionEmployee4's constructor, which initializes the BasePlusCommissionEmployee4 object's baseSalary.

Software Engineering Observation 9.8

When a program creates a subclass object, the subclass constructor immediately calls the superclass constructor (explicitly, via super, or implicitly). The superclass constructor's body executes to initialize the superclass's instance variables that are part of the subclass object, then the subclass constructor's body executes to initialize the subclass-only instance variables. Java ensures that even if a constructor does not assign a value to an instance variable, the variable is still initialized to its default value (e.g., 0 for primitive numeric types, false for booleans, null for references).

Our next example revisits the commission employee hierarchy by declaring a CommissionEmployee4 class (Fig. 9.15) and a BasePlusCommissionEmployee5 class (Fig. 9.16). Each class's constructor prints a message when invoked, enabling us to observe the order in which the constructors in the hierarchy execute.

```
1   // Fig. 9.15: CommissionEmployee4.java
2   // CommissionEmployee4 class represents a commission employee.
3
4   public class CommissionEmployee4
5   {
6      private String firstName;
7      private String lastName;
8      private String socialSecurityNumber;
9      private double grossSales; // gross weekly sales
10     private double commissionRate; // commission percentage
11
12     // five-argument constructor
13     public CommissionEmployee4( String first, String last, String ssn,
14        double sales, double rate )
15     {
16        // implicit call to Object constructor occurs here
17        firstName = first;
18        lastName = last;
19        socialSecurityNumber = ssn;
20        setGrossSales( sales ); // validate and store gross sales
21        setCommissionRate( rate ); // validate and store commission rate
22
23        System.out.printf(
24           "\nCommissionEmployee4 constructor:\n%s\n", this );
25     } // end five-argument CommissionEmployee4 constructor
26
```

Fig. 9.15 | CommissionEmployee4's constructor outputs text. (Part 1 of 3.)

```
27        // set first name
28        public void setFirstName( String first )
29        {
30           firstName = first;
31        } // end method setFirstName
32
33        // return first name
34        public String getFirstName()
35        {
36           return firstName;
37        } // end method getFirstName
38
39        // set last name
40        public void setLastName( String last )
41        {
42           lastName = last;
43        } // end method setLastName
44
45        // return last name
46        public String getLastName()
47        {
48           return lastName;
49        } // end method getLastName
50
51        // set social security number
52        public void setSocialSecurityNumber( String ssn )
53        {
54           socialSecurityNumber = ssn; // should validate
55        } // end method setSocialSecurityNumber
56
57        // return social security number
58        public String getSocialSecurityNumber()
59        {
60           return socialSecurityNumber;
61        } // end method getSocialSecurityNumber
62
63        // set gross sales amount
64        public void setGrossSales( double sales )
65        {
66           grossSales = ( sales < 0.0 ) ? 0.0 : sales;
67        } // end method setGrossSales
68
69        // return gross sales amount
70        public double getGrossSales()
71        {
72           return grossSales;
73        } // end method getGrossSales
74
75        // set commission rate
76        public void setCommissionRate( double rate )
77        {
78           commissionRate = ( rate > 0.0 && rate < 1.0 ) ? rate : 0.0;
79        } // end method setCommissionRate
```

Fig. 9.15 | CommissionEmployee4's constructor outputs text. (Part 2 of 3.)

```
80
81     // return commission rate
82     public double getCommissionRate()
83     {
84        return commissionRate;
85     } // end method getCommissionRate
86
87     // calculate earnings
88     public double earnings()
89     {
90        return getCommissionRate() * getGrossSales();
91     } // end method earnings
92
93     // return String representation of CommissionEmployee4 object
94     public String toString()
95     {
96        return String.format( "%s: %s %s\n%s: %s\n%s: %.2f\n%s: %.2f",
97           "commission employee", getFirstName(), getLastName(),
98           "social security number", getSocialSecurityNumber(),
99           "gross sales", getGrossSales(),
100          "commission rate", getCommissionRate() );
101    } // end method toString
102 } // end class CommissionEmployee4
```

Fig. 9.15 | `CommissionEmployee4`'s constructor outputs text. (Part 3 of 3.)

Class `CommissionEmployee4` (Fig. 9.15) contains the same features as the version of the class shown in Fig. 9.4. We modified the constructor (lines 13–25) to output text upon its invocation. Note that outputting `this` with the `%s` format specifier (lines 23–24) implicitly invokes the `toString` method of the object being constructed to obtain the object's string representation.

Class `BasePlusCommissionEmployee5` (Fig. 9.16) is almost identical to `BasePlus-CommissionEmployee4` (Fig. 9.13), except that `BasePlusCommissionEmployee5`'s constructor also outputs text when invoked. As in `CommissionEmployee4` (Fig. 9.15), we output `this` using the `%s` format specifier in line 16 to obtain the object's string representation.

```
1     // Fig. 9.16: BasePlusCommissionEmployee5.java
2     // BasePlusCommissionEmployee5 class declaration.
3
4     public class BasePlusCommissionEmployee5 extends CommissionEmployee4
5     {
6        private double baseSalary; // base salary per week
7
8        // six-argument constructor
9        public BasePlusCommissionEmployee5( String first, String last,
10          String ssn, double sales, double rate, double salary )
11       {
12          super( first, last, ssn, sales, rate );
13          setBaseSalary( salary ); // validate and store base salary
14
```

Fig. 9.16 | `BasePlusCommissionEmployee5`'s constructor outputs text. (Part 1 of 2.)

```
15        System.out.printf(
16           "\nBasePlusCommissionEmployee5 constructor:\n%s\n", this );
17     } // end six-argument BasePlusCommissionEmployee5 constructor
18
19     // set base salary
20     public void setBaseSalary( double salary )
21     {
22        baseSalary = ( salary < 0.0 ) ? 0.0 : salary;
23     } // end method setBaseSalary
24
25     // return base salary
26     public double getBaseSalary()
27     {
28        return baseSalary;
29     } // end method getBaseSalary
30
31     // calculate earnings
32     public double earnings()
33     {
34        return getBaseSalary() + super.earnings();
35     } // end method earnings
36
37     // return String representation of BasePlusCommissionEmployee5
38     public String toString()
39     {
40        return String.format( "%s %s\n%s: %.2f", "base-salaried",
41           super.toString(), "base salary", getBaseSalary() );
42     } // end method toString
43  } // end class BasePlusCommissionEmployee5
```

Fig. 9.16 | BasePlusCommissionEmployee5's constructor outputs text. (Part 1 of 2.)

Figure 9.17 demonstrates the order in which constructors are called for objects of classes that are part of an inheritance hierarchy. Method main begins by instantiating CommissionEmployee4 object employee1 (lines 8–9). Next, lines 12–14 instantiate

```
1   // Fig. 9.17: ConstructorTest.java
2   // Display order in which superclass and subclass constructors are called.
3
4   public class ConstructorTest
5   {
6      public static void main( String args[] )
7      {
8         CommissionEmployee4 employee1 = new CommissionEmployee4(
9            "Bob", "Lewis", "333-33-3333", 5000, .04 );
10
11        System.out.println();
12        BasePlusCommissionEmployee5 employee2 =
13           new BasePlusCommissionEmployee5(
14           "Lisa", "Jones", "555-55-5555", 2000, .06, 800 );
15
```

Fig. 9.17 | Constructor call order. (Part 1 of 2.)

```
16          System.out.println();
17          BasePlusCommissionEmployee5 employee3 =
18             new BasePlusCommissionEmployee5(
19                "Mark", "Sands", "888-88-8888", 8000, .15, 2000 );
20       } // end main
21    } // end class ConstructorTest
```

```
CommissionEmployee4 constructor:
commission employee: Bob Lewis
social security number: 333-33-3333
gross sales: 5000.00
commission rate: 0.04


CommissionEmployee4 constructor:
base-salaried commission employee: Lisa Jones
social security number: 555-55-5555
gross sales: 2000.00
commission rate: 0.06
base salary: 0.00

BasePlusCommissionEmployee5 constructor:
base-salaried commission employee: Lisa Jones
social security number: 555-55-5555
gross sales: 2000.00
commission rate: 0.06
base salary: 800.00


CommissionEmployee4 constructor:
base-salaried commission employee: Mark Sands
social security number: 888-88-8888
gross sales: 8000.00
commission rate: 0.15
base salary: 0.00

BasePlusCommissionEmployee5 constructor:
base-salaried commission employee: Mark Sands
social security number: 888-88-8888
gross sales: 8000.00
commission rate: 0.15
base salary: 2000.00
```

Fig. 9.17 | Constructor call order. (Part 2 of 2.)

BasePlusCommissionEmployee5 object employee2. This invokes the CommissionEmployee4 constructor, which prints output with the values passed from the BasePlusCommissionEmployee5 constructor, then performs the output specified in the BasePlusCommissionEmployee5 constructor. Lines 17–19 then instantiate BasePlusCommissionEmployee5 object employee3. Again, the CommissionEmployee4 and BasePlusCommissionEmployee5 constructors are both called. In each case, the body of the CommissionEmployee4 constructor executes before the body of the BasePlusCommissionEmployee5 constructor executes. Note that employee2 is constructed completely before construction of employee3 begins.

9.6 Software Engineering with Inheritance

This section discusses customizing existing software with inheritance. When a new class extends an existing class, the new class inherits the non-`private` members of the existing class. We can customize the new class to meet our needs by including additional members and by overriding superclass members. Doing this does not require the subclass programmer to change the superclass's source code. Java simply requires access to the superclass's `.class` file so it can compile and execute any program that uses or extends the superclass. This powerful capability is attractive to independent software vendors (ISVs), who can develop proprietary classes for sale or license and make them available to users in bytecode format. Users then can derive new classes from these library classes rapidly and without accessing the ISVs' proprietary source code.

Software Engineering Observation 9.9

Despite the fact that inheriting from a class does not require access to the class's source code, developers often insist on seeing the source code to understand how the class is implemented. Developers in industry want to ensure that they are extending a solid class—for example, a class that performs well and is implemented securely.

Sometimes, students have difficulty appreciating the scope of the problems faced by designers who work on large-scale software projects in industry. People experienced with such projects say that effective software reuse improves the software development process. Object-oriented programming facilitates software reuse, potentially shortening development time.

The availability of substantial and useful class libraries delivers the maximum benefits of software reuse through inheritance. Application designers build their applications with these libraries, and library designers are rewarded by having their libraries included with the applications. The standard Java class libraries that are shipped with J2SE 5.0 tend to be rather general purpose. Many special-purpose class libraries exist and more are being created.

Software Engineering Observation 9.10

At the design stage in an object-oriented system, the designer often finds that certain classes are closely related. The designer should "factor out" common instance variables and methods and place them in a superclass. Then the designer should use inheritance to develop subclasses, specializing them with capabilities beyond those inherited from the superclass.

Software Engineering Observation 9.11

Declaring a subclass does not affect its superclass's source code. Inheritance preserves the integrity of the superclass.

Software Engineering Observation 9.12

Just as designers of non-object-oriented systems should avoid method proliferation, designers of object-oriented systems should avoid class proliferation. Such proliferation creates management problems and can hinder software reusability, because in a huge class library it becomes difficult for a client to locate the most appropriate classes. The alternative is to create fewer classes that provide more substantial functionality, but such classes might prove cumbersome.

Performance Tip 9.1

If subclasses are larger than they need to be (i.e., contain too much functionality), memory and processing resources might be wasted. Extend the superclass that contains the functionality that is closest to what is needed.

Reading subclass declarations can be confusing, because inherited members are not declared explicitly in the subclasses, but are nevertheless present in them. A similar problem exists in documenting subclass members.

9.7 Object Class

As we discussed earlier in this chapter, all classes in Java inherit directly or indirectly from the Object class (package java.lang), so its 11 methods are inherited by all other classes. Figure 9.18 summarizes Object's methods.

Method	Description
clone	This **protected** method, which takes no arguments and returns an Object reference, makes a copy of the object on which it is called. When cloning is required for objects of a class, the class should override method clone as a **public** method and should implement interface Cloneable (package java.lang). The default implementation of this method performs a so-called shallow copy—instance variable values in one object are copied into another object of the same type. For reference types, only the references are copied. A typical overridden clone method's implementation would perform a deep copy that creates a new object for each reference type instance variable. There are many subtleties to overriding method clone. You can learn more about cloning in the following article: java.sun.com/developer/JDCTechTips/2001/tt0306.html
equals	This method compares two objects for equality and returns true if they are equal and false otherwise. The method takes any Object as an argument. When objects of a particular class must be compared for equality, the class should override method equals to compare the contents of the two objects. The method's implementation should meet the following requirements: • It should return false if the argument is null. • It should return true if an object is compared to itself, as in object1.equals(object1). • It should return true only if both object1.equals(object2) and object2.equals(object1) would return true. • For three objects, if object1.equals(object2) returns true and object2.equals(object3) returns true, then object1.equals(object3) should also return true. • If equals is called multiple times with the two objects and the objects do not change, the method should consistently return true if the objects are equal and false otherwise. A class that overrides equals should also override hashCode to ensure that equal objects have identical hashcodes. The default equals implementation uses operator == to determine whether two references *refer to the same object in memory*.

Fig. 9.18 | Object methods that are inherited directly or indirectly by all classes. (Part 1 of 2.)

Method	Description
finalize	This **protected** method (introduced in Section 8.10 and Section 8.11) is called by the garbage collector to perform termination housekeeping on an object just before the garbage collector reclaims the object's memory. It is not guaranteed that the garbage collector will reclaim an object, so it cannot be guaranteed that the object's `finalize` method will execute. The method must specify an empty parameter list and must return `void`. The default implementation of this method serves as a placeholder that does nothing.
getClass	Every object in Java knows its own type at execution time. Method `getClass` (used in Section 10.5) returns an object of class `Class` (package `java.lang`) that contains information about the object's type, such as its class name (returned by `Class` method `getName`). You can learn more about class `Class` in the online API documentation at `java.sun.com/j2se/5.0/docs/api/java/lang/Class.html`.
hashCode	A hashtable is a data structure that relates one object, called the key, to another object, called the value. When initially inserting a value into a hashtable, the key's `hashCode` method is called. The hashcode value returned is used by the hashtable to determine the location at which to insert the corresponding value. The key's hashcode is also used by the hashtable to locate the key's corresponding value.
notify, notifyAll, wait	Methods `notify`, `notifyAll` and the three overloaded versions of `wait` are related to multithreading. In J2SE 5.0, the multithreading model has changed substantially, but these features continue to be supported.
toString	This method (introduced in Section 9.4.1) returns a `String` representation of an object. The default implementation of this method returns the package name and class name of the object's class followed by a hexadecimal representation of the value returned by the object's `hashCode` method.

Fig. 9.18 | `Object` methods that are inherited directly or indirectly by all classes. (Part 2 of 2.)

We discuss several of `Object` methods throughout this book (as indicated in the table). You can learn more about `Object`'s methods in `Object`'s online API documentation and in *The Java Tutorial* at the following sites:

```
java.sun.com/j2se/5.0/docs/api/java/lang/Object.html
java.sun.com/docs/books/tutorial/java/javaOO/objectclass
```

Recall from Chapter 7 that arrays are objects. As a result, like all other objects, an array inherits the members of class `Object`. Note that arrays have an overridden `clone` method that copies the array. However, if the array stores references to objects, the objects are not copied. For more information about the relationship between arrays and class `Object`, please see *Java Language Specification, Chapter 10*, at

```
java.sun.com/docs/books/jls/second_edition/html/arrays.doc.html
```

9.8 (Optional) GUI and Graphics Case Study: Displaying Text and Images Using Labels

Programs often use labels when they need to display information or instructions to the user in a graphical user interface. Labels are a convenient way of keeping the user informed about the current state of a program. In Java, an object of class JLabel (from package javax.swing) can display a single line of text, an image or both. The example in Fig. 9.19 demonstrates several JLabel features.

Lines 3–6 import the classes we need to display JLabels. BorderLayout from package java.awt contains constants that specify where we can place GUI components in the JFrame. Class ImageIcon represents an image that can be displayed on a JLabel, and class JFrame represents the window that will contain all the labels.

Line 13 creates a JLabel that displays its constructor argument—the string "North". Line 16 declares local variable labelIcon and assigns it a new ImageIcon. The constructor for ImageIcon receives a String that specifies the path to the image. Since we only specify a file name, Java assumes that it is in the same directory as class LabelDemo. ImageIcon can load images in GIF, JPEG and PNG image formats. Line 19 declares and initializes local variable centerLabel with a JLabel that displays the labelIcon. Line 22 declares and initializes local variable southLabel with a JLabel similar to the one in line 19. However, line 25 calls method setText to change the text the label displays. Method setText can be called on any JLabel to change its text. This JLabel displays both the icon and the text.

Line 28 creates the JFrame that displays the JLabels, and line 30 indicates that the program should terminate when the JFrame is closed. We attach the labels to the JFrame in lines 34–36 by calling an overloaded version of method add that takes two parameters. The first parameter is the component we want to attach, and the second is the region in which it should be placed. Each JFrame has an associated layout that helps the JFrame position the GUI components that are attached to it. The default layout for a JFrame is known as a BorderLayout and has five regions—NORTH (top), SOUTH (bottom), EAST (right side), WEST (left side) and CENTER. Each of these is declared as a constant in class BorderLayout. When calling method add with one argument, the JFrame places the component in the CENTER automatically. If a position already contains a component, then the new component takes its place. Lines 38 and 39 set the size of the JFrame and make it visible on screen.

```java
1   // Fig 9.19: LabelDemo.java
2   // Demonstrates the use of labels.
3   import java.awt.BorderLayout;
4   import javax.swing.ImageIcon;
5   import javax.swing.JLabel;
6   import javax.swing.JFrame;
7
8   public class LabelDemo
9   {
10     public static void main( String args[] )
11     {
12        // Create a label with plain text
13        JLabel northLabel = new JLabel( "North" );
```

Fig. 9.19 | JLabel with text and with images. (Part 1 of 2.)

```
14
15          // create an icon from an image so we can put it on a JLabel
16          ImageIcon labelIcon = new ImageIcon( "GUItip.gif" );
17
18          // create a label with an Icon instead of text
19          JLabel centerLabel = new JLabel( labelIcon );
20
21          // create another label with an Icon
22          JLabel southLabel = new JLabel( labelIcon );
23
24          // set the label to display text (as well as an icon)
25          southLabel.setText( "South" );
26
27          // create a frame to hold the labels
28          JFrame application = new JFrame();
29
30          application.setDefaultCloseOperation( JFrame.EXIT_ON_CLOSE );
31
32          // add the labels to the frame; the second argument specifies
33          // where on the frame to add the label
34          application.add( northLabel, BorderLayout.NORTH );
35          application.add( centerLabel, BorderLayout.CENTER );
36          application.add( southLabel, BorderLayout.SOUTH );
37
38          application.setSize( 300, 300 ); // set the size of the frame
39          application.setVisible( true ); // show the frame
40       } // end main
41    } // end class LabelDemo
```

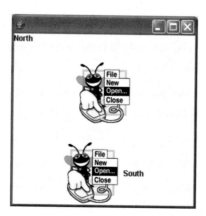

Fig. 9.19 | JLabel with text and with images. (Part 2 of 2.)

GUI and Graphics Case Study Exercise

9.1   Modify Exercise 8.1 to include a JLabel as a status bar that displays counts representing the number of each shape displayed. Class DrawPanel should declare a method that returns a String containing the status text. In main, first create the DrawPanel, then create the JLabel with the status text as an argument to the JLabel's constructor. Attach the JLabel to the SOUTH region of the JFrame, as shown in Fig. 9.20.

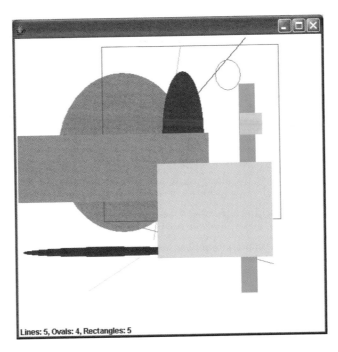

Fig. 9.20 | `JLabel` displaying shape statistics.

9.9 Wrap-Up

This chapter introduced inheritance—the ability to create classes by absorbing an existing class's members and embellishing them with new capabilities. You learned the notions of superclasses and subclasses and used keyword `extends` to create a subclass that inherits members from a superclass. The chapter introduced the access modifier `protected`; subclass methods can access `protected` superclass members. You learned how to access superclass members with `super`. You also saw how constructors are used in inheritance hierarchies. Finally, you learned about the methods of class `Object`, the direct or indirect superclass of all classes in Java.

In Chapter 10, Object-Oriented Programming: Polymorphism, we build on our discussion of inheritance by introducing polymorphism—an object-oriented concept that enables us to write programs that handle, in a more general manner, objects of a wide variety of classes related by inheritance. After studying Chapter 10, you will be familiar with classes, objects, encapsulation, inheritance and polymorphism—the most essential aspects of object-oriented programming.

Summary

- Software reuse reduces program-development time.
- The direct superclass of a subclass (specified by the keyword `extends` in the first line of a class declaration) is the superclass from which the subclass inherits. An indirect superclass of a subclass is two or more levels up the class hierarchy from that subclass.

- In single inheritance, a class is derived from one direct superclass. In multiple inheritance, a class is derived from more than one direct superclass. Java does not support multiple inheritance.
- A subclass is more specific than its superclass and represents a smaller group of objects.
- Every object of a subclass is also an object of that class's superclass. However, a superclass object is not an object of its class's subclasses.
- An "is-a" relationship represents inheritance. In an "is-a" relationship, an object of a subclass also can be treated as an object of its superclass.
- A "has-a" relationship represents composition. In a "has-a" relationship, a class object contains references to objects of other classes.
- A subclass cannot access or inherit the private members of its superclass—allowing this would violate the encapsulation of the superclass. A subclass can, however, inherit the non-private members of its superclass.
- A superclass method can be overridden in a subclass to declare an appropriate implementation for the subclass.
- Single-inheritance relationships form tree-like hierarchical structures—a superclass exists in a hierarchical relationship with its subclasses.
- A superclass's public members are accessible wherever the program has a reference to an object of that superclass or one of its subclasses.
- A superclass's private members are accessible only within the declaration of that superclass.
- A superclass's protected members have an intermediate level of protection between public and private access. They can be accessed by members of the superclass, by members of its subclasses and by members of other classes in the same package.
- The first task of any subclass constructor is to call its direct superclass's constructor, either explicitly or implicitly, to ensure that the instance variables inherited from the superclass are initialized properly.
- A subclass can explicitly invoke a constructor of its superclass by using the superclass constructor call syntax—keyword super, followed by a set of parentheses containing the superclass constructor arguments.
- When a subclass method overrides a superclass method, the superclass method can be accessed from the subclass if the superclass method name is preceded by the keyword super and a dot (.) separator.
- Declaring instance variables private, while providing non-private methods to manipulate and perform validation, helps enforce good software engineering.
- Method toString takes no arguments and returns a String. The Object class's toString method is normally overridden by a subclass.
- When an object is output using the %s format specifier, the object's toString method is called implicitly to obtain its string representation.

Terminology

base class
brittle software
class hierarchy
class library
clone method of class Object
composition

derived class
direct superclass
equals method of class Object
extends keyword
fragile software
getClass method of class Object

"has-a" relationship
hashCode method of class Object
hierarchical relationship
hierarchy diagram
indirect superclass
inheritance
inheritance hierarchy
inherited member
inherited method
invoke a superclass constructor
invoke a superclass method
"is-a" relationship
Object class
object of a subclass
object of a superclass
override (redefine) a superclass method

private superclass member
protected keyword
protected superclass member
public superclass member
single inheritance
software reusability
standardized reusable components
subclass
subclass constructor
super keyword
superclass
superclass constructor
superclass constructor call syntax
superclass no-argument constructor
toString method of class Object

Self-Review Exercises

9.1 Fill in the blanks in each of the following statements:

a) _____ is a form of software reusability in which new classes acquire the members of existing classes and embellish those classes with new capabilities.

b) A superclass's _____ members can be accessed in the superclass declaration and in subclass declarations.

c) In a(n) _____ relationship, an object of a subclass can also be treated as an object of its superclass.

d) In a(n) _____ relationship, a class object has references to objects of other classes as members.

e) In single inheritance, a class exists in a(n) _____ relationship with its subclasses.

f) A superclass's _____ members are accessible anywhere that the program has a reference to an object of that superclass or to an object of one of its subclasses.

g) When an object of a subclass is instantiated, a superclass _____ is called implicitly or explicitly.

h) Subclass constructors can call superclass constructors via the _____ keyword.

9.2 State whether each of the following is *true* or *false*. If a statement is *false*, explain why.

a) Superclass constructors are not inherited by subclasses.

b) A "has-a" relationship is implemented via inheritance.

c) A Car class has an "is-a" relationship with the SteeringWheel and Brakes classes.

d) Inheritance encourages the reuse of proven high-quality software.

e) When a subclass redefines a superclass method by using the same signature, the subclass is said to overload that superclass method.

Answers to Self-Review Exercises

9.1 a) Inheritance. b) public or protected. c) "is-a" or inheritance. d) "has-a" or composition. e) hierarchical. f) public. g) constructor. h) super.

9.2 a) True. b) False. A "has-a" relationship is implemented via composition. An "is-a" relationship is implemented via inheritance. c) False. This is an example of a "has-a" relationship. Class Car has an "is-a" relationship with class Vehicle. d) True. e) False. This is known as overriding, not overloading.

Exercises

9.3   Many programs written with inheritance could be written with composition instead, and vice versa. Rewrite class BasePlusCommissionEmployee4 (Fig. 9.13) of the CommissionEmployee3–BasePlusCommissionEmployee4 hierarchy to use composition rather than inheritance. After you do this, assess the relative merits of the two approaches for the CommissionEmployee3 and BasePlusCommissionEmployee4 problems, as well as for object-oriented programs in general. Which approach is more natural? Why?

9.4   Discuss the ways in which inheritance promotes software reuse, saves time during program development and helps prevent errors.

9.5   Draw an inheritance hierarchy for students at a university similar to the hierarchy shown in Fig. 9.2. Use Student as the superclass of the hierarchy, then extend Student with classes UndergraduateStudent and GraduateStudent. Continue to extend the hierarchy as deep (i.e., as many levels) as possible. For example, Freshman, Sophomore, Junior and Senior might extend UndergraduateStudent, and DoctoralStudent and MastersStudent might be subclasses of GraduateStudent. After drawing the hierarchy, discuss the relationships that exist between the classes. [*Note:* You do not need to write any code for this exercise.]

9.6   The world of shapes is much richer than the shapes included in the inheritance hierarchy of Fig. 9.3. Write down all the shapes you can think of—both two-dimensional and three-dimensional—and form them into a more complete Shape hierarchy with as many levels as possible. Your hierarchy should have class Shape at the top. Class TwoDimensionalShape and class ThreeDimensionalShape should extend Shape. Add additional subclasses, such as Quadrilateral and Sphere, at their correct locations in the hierarchy as necessary.

9.7   Some programmers prefer not to use protected access, because they believe it breaks the encapsulation of the superclass. Discuss the relative merits of using protected access vs. using private access in superclasses.

9.8   Write an inheritance hierarchy for classes Quadrilateral, Trapezoid, Parallelogram, Rectangle and Square. Use Quadrilateral as the superclass of the hierarchy. Make the hierarchy as deep (i.e., as many levels) as possible. Specify the instance variables and methods for each class. The private instance variables of Quadrilateral should be the *x-y* coordinate pairs for the four endpoints of the Quadrilateral. Write a program that instantiates objects of your classes and outputs each object's area (except Quadrilateral).

Object-Oriented Programming: Polymorphism

OBJECTIVES

In this chapter you will learn:

- The concept of polymorphism.
- To use overridden methods to effect polymorphism.
- To distinguish between abstract and concrete classes.
- To declare abstract methods to create abstract classes.
- How polymorphism makes systems extensible and maintainable.
- To determine an object's type at execution time.
- To declare and implement interfaces.

10.1 Introduction

We now continue our study of object-oriented programming by explaining and demonstrating polymorphism with inheritance hierarchies. Polymorphism enables us to "program in the general" rather than "program in the specific." In particular, polymorphism enables us to write programs that process objects that share the same superclass in a class hierarchy as if they are all objects of the superclass.

Consider the following example of polymorphism. Suppose we create a program that simulates the movement of several types of animals for a biological study. Classes `Fish`, `Frog` and `Bird` represent the three types of animals under investigation. Imagine that each of these classes extends superclass `Animal`, which contains a method `move` and maintains an animal's current location as *x-y* coordinates. Each subclass implements method `move`. Our program maintains an array of references to objects of the various `Animal` subclasses.

To simulate the animals' movements, the program sends each object the same message once per second—namely, move. However, each specific type of Animal responds to a move message in a unique way—a Fish might swim three feet, a Frog might jump five feet and a Bird might fly ten feet. The program issues the same message (i.e., move) to each animal object generically, but each object knows how to modify its *x-y* coordinates appropriately for its specific type of movement. Relying on each object to know how to "do the right thing" (i.e., do what is appropriate for that type of object) in response to the same method call is the key concept of polymorphism. The same message (in this case, move) sent to a variety of objects has "many forms" of results—hence the term polymorphism.

With polymorphism, we can design and implement systems that are easily extensible—new classes can be added with little or no modification to the general portions of the program, as long as the new classes are part of the inheritance hierarchy that the program processes generically. The only parts of a program that must be altered to accommodate new classes are those that require direct knowledge of the new classes that the programmer adds to the hierarchy. For example, if we extend class Animal to create class Tortoise (which might respond to a move message by crawling one inch), we need to write only the Tortoise class and the part of the simulation that instantiates a Tortoise object. The portions of the simulation that process each Animal generically can remain the same.

This chapter has several key parts. First, we discuss common examples of polymorphism. We then provide a live-code example demonstrating polymorphic behavior. As you will soon see, you will use superclass references to manipulate both superclass objects and subclass objects polymorphically.

We then present a case study that revisits the employee hierarchy of Section 9.4.5. We develop a simple payroll application that polymorphically calculates the weekly pay of several different types of employees using each employee's earnings method. Though the earnings of each type of employee are calculated in a specific way, polymorphism allows us to process the employees "in the general." In the case study, we enlarge the hierarchy to include two new classes—SalariedEmployee (for people paid a fixed weekly salary) and HourlyEmployee (for people paid an hourly salary and so-called time-and-a-half for overtime). We declare a common set of functionality for all the classes in the updated hierarchy in a so-called abstract class, Employee, from which classes SalariedEmployee, HourlyEmployee and CommissionEmployee inherit directly and class BasePlusCommissionEmployee4 inherits indirectly. As you will soon see, when we invoke each employee's earnings method off a superclass Employee reference, the correct earnings calculation is performed due to Java's polymorphic capabilities.

Occasionally, when performing polymorphic processing, we need to program "in the specific." Our Employee case study demonstrates that a program can determine the type of an object at execution time and act on that object accordingly. In the case study, we use these capabilities to determine whether a particular employee object *is a* BasePlusCommissionEmployee. If so, we increase that employee's base salary by 10%.

The chapter continues with an introduction to Java interfaces. An interface describes a set of methods that can be called on an object, but does not provide concrete implementations for the methods. Programmers can declare classes that implement (i.e., provide concrete implementations for the methods of) one or more interfaces. Each interface method must be declared in all the classes that implement the interface. Once a class implements an interface, all objects of that class have an *is-a* relationship with the interface type, and all objects of the class are guaranteed to provide the functionality described by the interface. This is true of all subclasses of that class as well.

Interfaces are particularly useful for assigning common functionality to possibly unrelated classes. This allows objects of unrelated classes to be processed polymorphically—objects of classes that implement the same interface can respond to the same method calls. To demonstrate creating and using interfaces, we modify our payroll application to create a general accounts payable application that can calculate payments due for company employees and invoice amounts to be billed for purchased goods. As you will see, interfaces enable polymorphic capabilities similar to those possible with inheritance.

10.2 Polymorphism Examples

We now consider several additional examples of polymorphism. If class `Rectangle` is derived from class `Quadrilateral`, then a `Rectangle` object is a more specific version of a `Quadrilateral` object. Any operation (e.g., calculating the perimeter or the area) that can be performed on a `Quadrilateral` object can also be performed on a `Rectangle` object. These operations can also be performed on other `Quadrilateral`s, such as `Square`s, `Parallelogram`s and `Trapezoid`s. The polymorphism occurs when a program invokes a method through a superclass variable—at execution time, the correct subclass version of the method is called, based on the type of the reference stored in the superclass variable. You will see a simple code example that illustrates this process in Section 10.3.

As another example, suppose we design a video game that manipulates objects of many different types, including objects of classes `Martian`, `Venusian`, `Plutonian`, `SpaceShip` and `LaserBeam`. Imagine that each class inherits from the common superclass called `SpaceObject`, which contains the `draw` method. Each subclass implements this method. A screen-manager program maintains a collection (e.g., a `SpaceObject` array) of references to objects of the various classes. To refresh the screen, the screen manager periodically sends each object the same message—namely, `draw`. However, each object responds in a unique way. For example, a `Martian` object might draw itself in red with the appropriate number of antennae. A `SpaceShip` object might draw itself as a bright silver flying saucer. A `LaserBeam` object might draw itself as a bright red beam across the screen. Again, the same message (in this case, `draw`) sent to a variety of objects has "many forms" of results.

A polymorphic screen manager might use polymorphism to facilitate adding new classes to a system with minimal modifications to the system's code. Suppose that we want to add `Mercurian` objects to our video game. To do so, we must build a class `Mercurian` that extends `SpaceObject` and provides its own `draw` method implementation. When objects of class `Mercurian` appear in the `SpaceObject` collection, the screen manager code invokes method `draw`, exactly as it does for every other object in the collection, regardless of its type. So the new `Mercurian` objects simply "plug right in" without any modification of the screen manager code by the programmer. Thus, without modifying the system (other than to build new classes and modify the code that creates new objects), programmers can use polymorphism to include additional types that were not envisioned when the system was created.

With polymorphism, the same method name and signature can be used to cause different actions to occur, depending on the type of object on which the method is invoked. This gives the programmer tremendous expressive capability.

Software Engineering Observation 10.1

Polymorphism enables programmers to deal in generalities and let the execution-time environment handle the specifics. Programmers can command objects to behave in manners appropriate to those objects, without knowing the types of the objects (as long as the objects belong to the same inheritance hierarchy).

Software Engineering Observation 10.2

Polymorphism promotes extensibility: Software that invokes polymorphic behavior is independent of the object types to which messages are sent. New object types that can respond to existing method calls can be incorporated into a system without requiring modification of the base system. Only client code that instantiates new objects must be modified to accommodate new types.

10.3 Demonstrating Polymorphic Behavior

Section 9.4 created a commission employee class hierarchy, in which class BasePlusCommissionEmployee inherited from class CommissionEmployee. The examples in that section manipulated CommissionEmployee and BasePlusCommissionEmployee objects by using references to them to invoke their methods. We aimed superclass references at superclass objects and subclass references at subclass objects. These assignments are natural and straightforward—superclass references are intended to refer to superclass objects, and subclass references are intended to refer to subclass objects. However, as you will soon see, other assignments are possible.

In the next example, we aim a superclass reference at a subclass object. We then show how invoking a method on a subclass object via a superclass reference invokes the subclass functionality—the type of the *actual referenced object*, not the type of the *reference*, determines which method is called. This example demonstrates the key concept that an object of a subclass can be treated as an object of its superclass. This enables various interesting manipulations. A program can create an array of superclass references that refer to objects of many subclass types. This is allowed because each subclass object *is an* object of its superclass. For instance, we can assign the reference of a BasePlusCommissionEmployee object to a superclass CommissionEmployee variable because a BasePlusCommissionEmployee *is a* CommissionEmployee—we can treat a BasePlusCommissionEmployee as a CommissionEmployee.

As you will learn later in the chapter, we cannot treat a superclass object as a subclass object because a superclass object is not an object of any of its subclasses. For example, we cannot assign the reference of a CommissionEmployee object to a subclass BasePlusCommissionEmployee variable because a CommissionEmployee is not a BasePlusCommissionEmployee—a CommissionEmployee does not have a baseSalary instance variable and does not have methods setBaseSalary and getBaseSalary. The *is-a* relationship applies only from a subclass to its direct (and indirect) superclasses, and not vice versa.

It turns out that the Java compiler does allow the assignment of a superclass reference to a subclass variable if we explicitly cast the superclass reference to the subclass type—a technique we discuss in greater detail in Section 10.5. Why would we ever want to perform such an assignment? A superclass reference can be used to invoke only the methods declared in the superclass—attempting to invoke subclass-only methods through a superclass reference results in compilation errors. If a program needs to perform a subclass-specific operation on a subclass object referenced by a superclass variable, the program must first cast the superclass reference to a subclass reference through a technique known as downcasting. This enables the program to invoke subclass methods that are not in the superclass. We will show you a concrete example of downcasting in Section 10.5.

The example in Fig. 10.1 demonstrates three ways to use superclass and subclass variables to store references to superclass and subclass objects. The first two are straightforward—as in Section 9.4, we assign a superclass reference to a superclass variable, and we assign a subclass reference to a subclass variable. Then we demonstrate the relationship between subclasses and superclasses (i.e., the *is-a* relationship) by assigning a subclass reference to a superclass variable. [*Note:* This program uses classes CommissionEmployee3 and BasePlusCommissionEmployee4 from Fig. 9.12 and Fig. 9.13, respectively.]

```java
1   // Fig. 10.1: PolymorphismTest.java
2   // Assigning superclass and subclass references to superclass and
3   // subclass variables.
4
5   public class PolymorphismTest
6   {
7      public static void main( String args[] )
8      {
9         // assign superclass reference to superclass variable
10        CommissionEmployee3 commissionEmployee = new CommissionEmployee3(
11           "Sue", "Jones", "222-22-2222", 10000, .06 );
12
13        // assign subclass reference to subclass variable
14        BasePlusCommissionEmployee4 basePlusCommissionEmployee =
15           new BasePlusCommissionEmployee4(
16           "Bob", "Lewis", "333-33-3333", 5000, .04, 300 );
17
18        // invoke toString on superclass object using superclass variable
19        System.out.printf( "%s %s:\n\n%s\n\n",
20           "Call CommissionEmployee3's toString with superclass reference ",
21           "to superclass object", commissionEmployee.toString() );
22
23        // invoke toString on subclass object using subclass variable
24        System.out.printf( "%s %s:\n\n%s\n\n",
25           "Call BasePlusCommissionEmployee4's toString with subclass",
26           "reference to subclass object",
27           basePlusCommissionEmployee.toString() );
28
29        // invoke toString on subclass object using superclass variable
30        CommissionEmployee3 commissionEmployee2 =
31           basePlusCommissionEmployee;
32        System.out.printf( "%s %s:\n\n%s\n",
33           "Call BasePlusCommissionEmployee4's toString with superclass",
34           "reference to subclass object", commissionEmployee2.toString() );
35     } // end main
36  } // end class PolymorphismTest
```

Fig. 10.1 | Assigning superclass and subclass references to superclass and subclass variables. (Part 1 of 2.)

```
Call CommissionEmployee3's toString with superclass reference to superclass
object:

commission employee: Sue Jones
social security number: 222-22-2222
gross sales: 10000.00
commission rate: 0.06

Call BasePlusCommissionEmployee4's toString with subclass reference to
subclass object:

base-salaried commission employee: Bob Lewis
social security number: 333-33-3333
gross sales: 5000.00
commission rate: 0.04
base salary: 300.00

Call BasePlusCommissionEmployee4's toString with superclass reference to
subclass object:

base-salaried commission employee: Bob Lewis
social security number: 333-33-3333
gross sales: 5000.00
commission rate: 0.04
base salary: 300.00
```

Fig. 10.1 | Assigning superclass and subclass references to superclass and subclass variables. (Part 2 of 2.)

In Fig. 10.1, lines 10–11 create a CommissionEmployee3 object and assign its reference to a CommissionEmployee3 variable. Lines 14–16 create a BasePlusCommissionEmployee4 object and assign its reference to a BasePlusCommissionEmployee4 variable. These assignments are natural—for example, a CommissionEmployee3 variable's primary purpose is to hold a reference to a CommissionEmployee3 object. Lines 19–21 use reference commissionEmployee to invoke toString explicitly. Because commissionEmployee refers to a CommissionEmployee3 object, superclass CommissionEmployee3's version of toString is called. Similarly, lines 24–27 use basePlusCommissionEmployee to invoke toString explicitly on the BasePlusCommissionEmployee4 object. This invokes subclass BasePlusCommissionEmployee4's version of toString.

Lines 30–31 then assign the reference to subclass object basePlusCommissionEmployee to a superclass CommissionEmployee3 variable, which lines 32–34 use to invoke method toString. A superclass variable that contains a reference to a subclass object and is used to call a method actually calls the subclass version of the method. Hence, commissionEmployee2.toString() in line 34 actually calls class BasePlusCommissionEmployee4's toString method. The Java compiler allows this "crossover" because an object of a subclass *is an* object of its superclass (but not vice versa). When the compiler encounters a method call made through a variable, the compiler determines if the method can be called by checking the variable's class type. If that class contains the proper method declaration (or inherits one), the compiler allows the call to be compiled. At execution time, the type of the object to which the variable refers determines the actual method to use.

10.4 Abstract Classes and Methods

When we think of a class type, we assume that programs will create objects of that type. In some cases, however, it is useful to declare classes for which the programmer never intends to instantiate objects. Such classes are called abstract classes. Because they are used only as super-classes in inheritance hierarchies, we refer to them as abstract superclasses. These classes cannot be used to instantiate objects, because, as we will soon see, abstract classes are incomplete. Subclasses must declare the "missing pieces." We demonstrate abstract classes in Section 10.5.

The purpose of an abstract class is primarily to provide an appropriate superclass from which other classes can inherit and thus share a common design. In the Shape hierarchy of Fig. 9.3, for example, subclasses inherit the notion of what it means to be a Shape—common attributes such as location, color and borderThickness, and behaviors such as draw, move, resize and changeColor. Classes that can be used to instantiate objects are called concrete classes. Such classes provide implementations of every method they declare (some of the implementations can be inherited). For example, we could derive concrete classes Circle, Square and Triangle from abstract superclass TwoDimensionalShape. Similarly, we could derive concrete classes Sphere, Cube and Tetrahedron from abstract superclass ThreeDimensionalShape. Abstract superclasses are too general to create real objects—they specify only what is common among subclasses. We need to be more specific before we can create objects. For example, if you send the draw message to abstract class TwoDimensionalShape, it knows that two-dimensional shapes should be drawable, but it does not know what specific shape to draw, so it cannot implement a real draw method. Concrete classes provide the specifics that make it reasonable to instantiate objects.

Not all inheritance hierarchies contain abstract classes. However, programmers often write client code that uses only abstract superclass types to reduce client code's dependencies on a range of specific subclass types. For example, a programmer can write a method with a parameter of an abstract superclass type. When called, such a method can be passed an object of any concrete class that directly or indirectly extends the superclass specified as the parameter's type.

Abstract classes sometimes constitute several levels of the hierarchy. For example, the Shape hierarchy of Fig. 9.3 begins with abstract class Shape. On the next level of the hierarchy are two more abstract classes, TwoDimensionalShape and ThreeDimensionalShape. The next level of the hierarchy declares concrete classes for TwoDimensionalShapes (Circle, Square and Triangle) and for ThreeDimensionalShapes (Sphere, Cube and Tetrahedron).

You make a class abstract by declaring it with keyword **abstract**. An abstract class normally contains one or more abstract methods. An abstract method is one with keyword abstract in its declaration, as in

```
public abstract void draw(); // abstract method
```

Abstract methods do not provide implementations. A class that contains any abstract methods must be declared as an abstract class even if that class contains concrete (non-abstract) methods. Each concrete subclass of an abstract superclass also must provide concrete implementations of the superclass's abstract methods. Constructors and **static** methods cannot be declared **abstract**. Constructors are not inherited, so an **abstract** constructor could never be implemented. Similarly, subclasses cannot override **static** methods, so an **abstract static** method could never be implemented.

Software Engineering Observation 10.3

An abstract class declares common attributes and behaviors of the various classes in a class hierarchy. An abstract class typically contains one or more abstract methods that subclasses must override if the subclasses are to be concrete. The instance variables and concrete methods of an abstract class are subject to the normal rules of inheritance.

Common Programming Error 10.1

Attempting to instantiate an object of an abstract class is a compilation error.

Common Programming Error 10.2

Failure to implement a superclass's abstract methods in a subclass is a compilation error unless the subclass is also declared `abstract`.

Although we cannot instantiate objects of abstract superclasses, you will soon see that we *can* use abstract superclasses to declare variables that can hold references to objects of any concrete class derived from those abstract classes. Programs typically use such variables to manipulate subclass objects polymorphically. We also can use abstract superclass names to invoke `static` methods declared in those abstract superclasses.

Consider another application of polymorphism. A drawing program needs to display many shapes, including new shape types that the programmer will add to the system after writing the drawing program. The drawing program might need to display shapes, such as `Circle`s, `Triangle`s, `Rectangle`s or others, that derive from abstract superclass `Shape`. The drawing program uses `Shape` variables to manage the objects that are displayed. To draw any object in this inheritance hierarchy, the drawing program uses a superclass `Shape` variable containing a reference to the subclass object to invoke the object's `draw` method. This method is declared `abstract` in superclass `Shape`, so each concrete subclass *must* implement method `draw` in a manner specific to that shape. Each object in the `Shape` inheritance hierarchy knows how to draw itself. The drawing program does not have to worry about the type of each object or whether the drawing program has ever encountered objects of that type.

Polymorphism is particularly effective for implementing so-called layered software systems. In operating systems, for example, each type of physical device could operate quite differently from the others. Even so, commands to read or write data from and to devices may have a certain uniformity. For each device, the operating system uses a piece of software called a device driver to control all communication between the system and the device. The write message sent to a device-driver object needs to be interpreted specifically in the context of that driver and how it manipulates devices of a specific type. However, the write call itself really is no different from the write to any other device in the system: Place some number of bytes from memory onto that device. An object-oriented operating system might use an abstract superclass to provide an "interface" appropriate for all device drivers. Then, through inheritance from that abstract superclass, subclasses are formed that all behave similarly. The device driver methods are declared as abstract methods in the abstract superclass. The implementations of these abstract methods are provided in the subclasses that correspond to the specific types of device drivers. New devices are always being developed, and often long after the operating system has been released. When you buy a new device, it comes with a device driver provided by the device vendor. The device is immediately operational after you connect it to your computer and install the driver. This is another elegant example of how polymorphism makes systems extensible.

It is common in object-oriented programming to declare an iterator class that can traverse all the objects in an array (Chapter 7). For example, a program can print an array of objects by creating an iterator object and using it to obtain the next array element each time the iterator is called. Iterators often are used in polymorphic programming to traverse an array that contains references to objects from various levels of a hierarchy. An array of objects of class TwoDimensionalShape, for example, could contain objects from subclasses Square, Circle, Triangle and so on. Calling method draw for each TwoDimensionalShape object off a TwoDimensionalShape variable would polymorphically draw each object correctly on the screen.

10.5 Case Study: Payroll System Using Polymorphism

This section reexamines the CommissionEmployee-BasePlusCommissionEmployee hierarchy that we explored throughout Section 9.4. Now we use an abstract method and polymorphism to perform payroll calculations based on the type of employee. We create an enhanced employee hierarchy to solve the following problem:

> *A company pays its employees on a weekly basis. The employees are of four types: Salaried employees are paid a fixed weekly salary regardless of the number of hours worked, hourly employees are paid by the hour and receive overtime pay for all hours worked in excess of 40 hours, commission employees are paid a percentage of their sales and salaried-commission employees receive a base salary plus a percentage of their sales. For the current pay period, the company has decided to reward salaried-commission employees by adding 10% to their base salaries. The company wants to implement a Java application that performs its payroll calculations polymorphically.*

We use abstract class Employee to represent the general concept of an employee. The classes that extend Employee are SalariedEmployee, CommissionEmployee and HourlyEmployee. Class BasePlusCommissionEmployee—which extends CommissionEmployee—represents the last employee type. The UML class diagram in Fig. 10.2 shows the inheritance hierarchy for our polymorphic employee-payroll application. Note that abstract class Employee is italicized, as per the convention of the UML.

Abstract superclass Employee declares the "interface" to the hierarchy—that is, the set of methods that a program can invoke on all Employee objects. We use the term "interface"

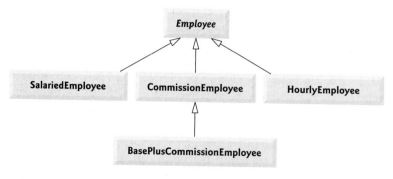

Fig. 10.2 | Employee hierarchy UML class diagram.

here in a general sense to refer to the various ways programs can communicate with objects of any Employee subclass. Be careful not to confuse the general notion of an "interface" to something with the formal notion of a Java interface, the subject of Section 10.7. Each employee, regardless of the way his or her earnings are calculated, has a first name, a last name and a social security number, so private instance variables firstName, lastName and socialSecurityNumber appear in abstract superclass Employee.

Software Engineering Observation 10.4

A subclass can inherit "interface" or "implementation" from a superclass. Hierarchies designed for implementation inheritance tend to have their functionality high in the hierarchy—each new subclass inherits one or more methods that were implemented in a superclass, and the subclass uses the superclass implementations. Hierarchies designed for interface inheritance tend to have their functionality lower in the hierarchy—a superclass specifies one or more abstract methods that must be declared for each concrete class in the hierarchy, and the individual subclasses override these methods to provide subclass-specific implementations.

The following sections implement the Employee class hierarchy. The first four sections each implement one of the concrete classes. The last section implements a test program that builds objects of all these classes and processes those objects polymorphically.

10.5.1 Creating Abstract Superclass Employee

Class Employee (Fig. 10.4) provides methods earnings and toString, in addition to the *get* and *set* methods that manipulate Employee's instance variables. An earnings method certainly applies generically to all employees. But each earnings calculation depends on the employee's class. So we declare earnings as abstract in superclass Employee because a default implementation does not make sense for that method—there is not enough information to determine what amount earnings should return. Each subclass overrides earnings with an appropriate implementation. To calculate an employee's earnings, the program assigns a reference to the employee's object to a superclass Employee variable, then invokes the earnings method on that variable. We maintain an array of Employee variables, each of which holds a reference to an Employee object (of course, there cannot be Employee objects because Employee is an abstract class—because of inheritance, however, all objects of all subclasses of Employee may nevertheless be thought of as Employee objects). The program iterates through the array and calls method earnings for each Employee object. Java processes these method calls polymorphically. Including earnings as an abstract method in Employee forces every direct subclass of Employee to override earnings in order to become a concrete class. This enables the designer of the class hierarchy to demand that each subclass provide an appropriate pay calculation.

Method toString in class Employee returns a String containing the first name, last name and social security number of the employee. As we will see, each subclass of Employee overrides method toString to create a string representation of an object of that class that contains the employee's type (e.g., "salaried employee:") followed by the rest of the employee's information.

The diagram in Fig. 10.3 shows each of the five classes in the hierarchy down the left side and methods earnings and toString across the top. For each class, the diagram shows the desired results of each method. [*Note:* We do not list superclass Employee's *get*

	earnings	toString
Employee	abstract	*firstName lastName* social security number: *SSN*
Salaried- Employee	weeklySalary	salaried employee: *firstName lastName* social security number: *SSN* weekly salary: *weeklysalary*

Hourly-
Employee
	If hours <= 40
	  wage * hours
	If hours > 40
	  40 * wage +
	  (hours - 40) *
	  wage * 1.5
		hourly employee: *firstName lastName*
		social security number: *SSN*
		hourly wage: *wage*; hours worked: *hours*

Commission- Employee	commissionRate * grossSales	commission employee: *firstName lastName* social security number: *SSN* gross sales: *grossSales*; commission rate: *commissionRate*
BasePlus- Commission- Employee	(commissionRate * grossSales) + baseSalary	base salaried commission employee: *firstName lastName* social security number: *SSN* gross sales: *grossSales*; commission rate: *commissionRate*; base salary: *baseSalary*

Fig. 10.3 | Polymorphic interface for the Employee hierarchy classes.

and *set* methods because they are not overridden in any of the subclasses—each of these methods is inherited and used "as is" by each of the subclasses.]

Let us consider class Employee's declaration (Fig. 10.4). The class includes a constructor that takes the first name, last name and social security number as arguments (lines 11–16); *get* methods that return the first name, last name and social security number (lines 25–28, 37–40 and 49–52, respectively); *set* methods that set the first name, last name and social security number (lines 19–22, 31–34 and 43–46, respectively); method toString (lines 55–59), which returns the string representation of Employee; and abstract method earnings (line 62), which will be implemented by subclasses. Note that the Employee constructor does not validate the social security number in this example. Normally, such validation should be provided.

Why did we decide to declare earnings as an abstract method? It simply does not make sense to provide an implementation of this method in class Employee. We cannot calculate the earnings for a general Employee—we first must know the specific Employee type to determine the appropriate earnings calculation. By declaring this method abstract, we indicate that each concrete subclass *must* provide an appropriate earnings implementation and that a program will be able to use superclass Employee variables to invoke method earnings polymorphically for any type of Employee.

```
 1   // Fig. 10.4: Employee.java
 2   // Employee abstract superclass.
 3
 4   public abstract class Employee
 5   {
 6      private String firstName;
 7      private String lastName;
 8      private String socialSecurityNumber;
 9
10      // three-argument constructor
11      public Employee( String first, String last, String ssn )
12      {
13         firstName = first;
14         lastName = last;
15         socialSecurityNumber = ssn;
16      } // end three-argument Employee constructor
17
18      // set first name
19      public void setFirstName( String first )
20      {
21         firstName = first;
22      } // end method setFirstName
23
24      // return first name
25      public String getFirstName()
26      {
27         return firstName;
28      } // end method getFirstName
29
30      // set last name
31      public void setLastName( String last )
32      {
33         lastName = last;
34      } // end method setLastName
35
36      // return last name
37      public String getLastName()
38      {
39         return lastName;
40      } // end method getLastName
41
42      // set social security number
43      public void setSocialSecurityNumber( String ssn )
44      {
45         socialSecurityNumber = ssn; // should validate
46      } // end method setSocialSecurityNumber
47
48      // return social security number
49      public String getSocialSecurityNumber()
50      {
51         return socialSecurityNumber;
52      } // end method getSocialSecurityNumber
```

Fig. 10.4 | Employee abstract superclass. (Part 1 of 2.)

```
53
54    // return String representation of Employee object
55    public String toString()
56    {
57       return String.format( "%s %s\nsocial security number: %s",
58          getFirstName(), getLastName(), getSocialSecurityNumber() );
59    } // end method toString
60
61    // abstract method overridden by subclasses
62    public abstract double earnings(); // no implementation here
63 } // end abstract class Employee
```

Fig. 10.4 | Employee abstract superclass. (Part 2 of 2.)

10.5.2 Creating Concrete Subclass SalariedEmployee

Class SalariedEmployee (Fig. 10.5) extends class Employee (line 4) and overrides earnings (lines 29–32), which makes SalariedEmployee a concrete class. The class includes a constructor (lines 9–14) that takes a first name, a last name, a social security number and a weekly salary as arguments; a *set* method to assign a new non-negative value to instance variable weeklySalary (lines 17–20); a *get* method to return weeklySalary's value (lines 23–26); a method earnings (lines 29–32) to calculate a SalariedEmployee's earnings; and a method toString (lines 35–39), which returns a String including the employee's type, namely, "salaried employee: " followed by employee-specific information produced by superclass Employee's toString method and SalariedEmployee's getWeeklySalary method. Class SalariedEmployee's constructor passes the first name, last name and social security number to the Employee constructor (line 12) to initialize the

```
1   // Fig. 10.5: SalariedEmployee.java
2   // SalariedEmployee class extends Employee.
3
4   public class SalariedEmployee extends Employee
5   {
6      private double weeklySalary;
7
8      // four-argument constructor
9      public SalariedEmployee( String first, String last, String ssn,
10        double salary )
11     {
12        super( first, last, ssn ); // pass to Employee constructor
13        setWeeklySalary( salary ); // validate and store salary
14     } // end four-argument SalariedEmployee constructor
15
16     // set salary
17     public void setWeeklySalary( double salary )
18     {
19        weeklySalary = salary < 0.0 ? 0.0 : salary;
20     } // end method setWeeklySalary
21
```

Fig. 10.5 | SalariedEmployee class derived from Employee. (Part 1 of 2.)

```
22        // return salary
23        public double getWeeklySalary()
24        {
25           return weeklySalary;
26        } // end method getWeeklySalary
27
28        // calculate earnings; override abstract method earnings in Employee
29        public double earnings()
30        {
31           return getWeeklySalary();
32        } // end method earnings
33
34        // return String representation of SalariedEmployee object
35        public String toString()
36        {
37           return String.format( "salaried employee: %s\n%s: $%,.2f",
38              super.toString(), "weekly salary", getWeeklySalary() );
39        } // end method toString
40     } // end class SalariedEmployee
```

Fig. 10.5 | SalariedEmployee class derived from Employee. (Part 2 of 2.)

private instance variables not inherited from the superclass. Method earnings overrides abstract method earnings in Employee to provide a concrete implementation that returns the SalariedEmployee's weekly salary. If we do not implement earnings, class SalariedEmployee must be declared abstract—otherwise, a compilation error occurs (and, of course, we want SalariedEmployee here to be a concrete class).

Method toString (lines 35–39) of class SalariedEmployee overrides Employee method toString. If class SalariedEmployee did not override toString, SalariedEmployee would have inherited the Employee version of toString. In that case, SalariedEmployee's toString method would simply return the employee's full name and social security number, which does not adequately represent a SalariedEmployee. To produce a complete string representation of a SalariedEmployee, the subclass's toString method returns "salaried employee: " followed by the superclass Employee-specific information (i.e., first name, last name and social security number) obtained by invoking the superclass's toString (line 38)—this is a nice example of code reuse. The string representation of a SalariedEmployee also contains the employee's weekly salary obtained by invoking the class's getWeeklySalary method.

10.5.3 Creating Concrete Subclass HourlyEmployee

Class HourlyEmployee (Fig. 10.6) also extends class Employee (line 4). The class includes a constructor (lines 10–16) that takes as arguments a first name, a last name, a social security number, an hourly wage and the number of hours worked. Lines 19–22 and 31–35 declare *set* methods that assign new values to instance variables wage and hours, respectively. Method setWage (lines 19–22) ensures that wage is non-negative, and method setHours (lines 31–35) ensures that hours is between 0 and 168 (the total number of hours in a week). Class HourlyEmployee also includes *get* methods (lines 25–28 and 38–41) to return the values of wage and hours, respectively; a method earnings (lines 44–50) to calculate an HourlyEmployee's earnings; and a method toString (lines 53–58), which returns the employee's type, namely, "hourly employee: " and employee-specific information. Note that the HourlyEmployee constructor, like the SalariedEmployee constructor, passes the first name, last name

```
 1   // Fig. 10.6: HourlyEmployee.java
 2   // HourlyEmployee class extends Employee.
 3
 4   public class HourlyEmployee extends Employee
 5   {
 6      private double wage; // wage per hour
 7      private double hours; // hours worked for week
 8
 9      // five-argument constructor
10      public HourlyEmployee( String first, String last, String ssn,
11         double hourlyWage, double hoursWorked )
12      {
13         super( first, last, ssn );
14         setWage( hourlyWage ); // validate hourly wage
15         setHours( hoursWorked ); // validate hours worked
16      } // end five-argument HourlyEmployee constructor
17
18      // set wage
19      public void setWage( double hourlyWage )
20      {
21         wage = ( hourlyWage < 0.0 ) ? 0.0 : hourlyWage;
22      } // end method setWage
23
24      // return wage
25      public double getWage()
26      {
27         return wage;
28      } // end method getWage
29
30      // set hours worked
31      public void setHours( double hoursWorked )
32      {
33         hours = ( ( hoursWorked >= 0.0 ) && ( hoursWorked <= 168.0 ) ) ?
34            hoursWorked : 0.0;
35      } // end method setHours
36
37      // return hours worked
38      public double getHours()
39      {
40         return hours;
41      } // end method getHours
42
43      // calculate earnings; override abstract method earnings in Employee
44      public double earnings()
45      {
46         if ( getHours() <= 40 ) // no overtime
47            return getWage() * getHours();
48         else
49            return 40 * getWage() + ( gethours() - 40 ) * getWage() * 1.5;
50      } // end method earnings
```

Fig. 10.6 | HourlyEmployee class derived from Employee. (Part 1 of 2.)

```
51
52     // return String representation of HourlyEmployee object
53     public String toString()
54     {
55        return String.format( "hourly employee: %s\n%s: $%,.2f; %s: %,.2f",
56           super.toString(), "hourly wage", getWage(),
57           "hours worked", getHours() );
58     } // end method toString
59  } // end class HourlyEmployee
```

Fig. 10.6 | HourlyEmployee class derived from Employee. (Part 2 of 2.)

and social security number to the superclass Employee constructor (line 13) to initialize the private instance variables. In addition, method toString calls superclass method toString (line 56) to obtain the Employee-specific information (i.e., first name, last name and social security number)—this is another nice example of code reuse.

10.5.4 Creating Concrete Subclass CommissionEmployee

Class CommissionEmployee (Fig. 10.7) extends class Employee (line 4). The class includes a constructor (lines 10–16) that takes a first name, a last name, a social security number, a sales amount and a commission rate; *set* methods (lines 19–22 and 31–34) to assign new values to instance variables commissionRate and grossSales, respectively; *get* methods (lines 25–28 and 37–40) that retrieve the values of these instance variables; method earnings (lines 43–46) to calculate a CommissionEmployee's earnings; and method toString

```
1   // Fig. 10.7: CommissionEmployee.java
2   // CommissionEmployee class extends Employee.
3
4   public class CommissionEmployee extends Employee
5   {
6      private double grossSales; // gross weekly sales
7      private double commissionRate; // commission percentage
8
9      // five-argument constructor
10     public CommissionEmployee( String first, String last, String ssn,
11        double sales, double rate )
12     {
13        super( first, last, ssn );
14        setGrossSales( sales );
15        setCommissionRate( rate );
16     } // end five-argument CommissionEmployee constructor
17
18     // set commission rate
19     public void setCommissionRate( double rate )
20     {
21        commissionRate = ( rate > 0.0 && rate < 1.0 ) ? rate : 0.0;
22     } // end method setCommissionRate
23
```

Fig. 10.7 | CommissionEmployee class derived from Employee. (Part 1 of 2.)

```
24      // return commission rate
25      public double getCommissionRate()
26      {
27         return commissionRate;
28      } // end method getCommissionRate
29
30      // set gross sales amount
31      public void setGrossSales( double sales )
32      {
33         grossSales = ( sales < 0.0 ) ? 0.0 : sales;
34      } // end method setGrossSales
35
36      // return gross sales amount
37      public double getGrossSales()
38      {
39         return grossSales;
40      } // end method getGrossSales
41
42      // calculate earnings; override abstract method earnings in Employee
43      public double earnings()
44      {
45         return getCommissionRate() * getGrossSales();
46      } // end method earnings
47
48      // return String representation of CommissionEmployee object
49      public String toString()
50      {
51         return String.format( "%s: %s\n%s: $%,.2f; %s: %.2f",
52            "commission employee", super.toString(),
53            "gross sales", getGrossSales(),
54            "commission rate", getCommissionRate() );
55      } // end method toString
56   } // end class CommissionEmployee
```

Fig. 10.7 | CommissionEmployee class derived from Employee. (Part 2 of 2.)

(lines 49–55), which returns the employee's type, namely, "commission employee: " and employee-specific information. The CommissionEmployee's constructor also passes the first name, last name and social security number to the Employee constructor (line 13) to initialize Employee's private instance variables. Method toString calls superclass method toString (line 52) to obtain the Employee-specific information (i.e., first name, last name and social security number).

10.5.5 Creating Indirect Concrete Subclass BasePlusCommissionEmployee

Class BasePlusCommissionEmployee (Fig. 10.8) extends class CommissionEmployee (line 4) and therefore is an indirect subclass of class Employee. Class BasePlusCommissionEmployee has a constructor (lines 9–14) that takes as arguments a first name, a last name, a social security number, a sales amount, a commission rate and a base salary. It then passes the first name, last name, social security number, sales amount and commission rate to the CommissionEmployee constructor (line 12) to initialize the inherited members. BasePlusCommis-

```
 1   // Fig. 10.8: BasePlusCommissionEmployee.java
 2   // BasePlusCommissionEmployee class extends CommissionEmployee.
 3
 4   public class BasePlusCommissionEmployee extends CommissionEmployee
 5   {
 6      private double baseSalary; // base salary per week
 7
 8      // six-argument constructor
 9      public BasePlusCommissionEmployee( String first, String last,
10         String ssn, double sales, double rate, double salary )
11      {
12         super( first, last, ssn, sales, rate );
13         setBaseSalary( salary ); // validate and store base salary
14      } // end six-argument BasePlusCommissionEmployee constructor
15
16      // set base salary
17      public void setBaseSalary( double salary )
18      {
19         baseSalary = ( salary < 0.0 ) ? 0.0 : salary; // non-negative
20      } // end method setBaseSalary
21
22      // return base salary
23      public double getBaseSalary()
24      {
25         return baseSalary;
26      } // end method getBaseSalary
27
28      // calculate earnings; override method earnings in CommissionEmployee
29      public double earnings()
30      {
31         return getBaseSalary() + super.earnings();
32      } // end method earnings
33
34      // return String representation of BasePlusCommissionEmployee object
35      public String toString()
36      {
37         return String.format( "%s %s; %s: $%,.2f",
38            "base-salaried", super.toString(),
39            "base salary", getBaseSalary() );
40      } // end method toString
41   } // end class BasePlusCommissionEmployee
```

Fig. 10.8 | BasePlusCommissionEmployee class derived from CommissionEmployee.

sionEmployee also contains a *set* method (lines 17–20) to assign a new value to instance variable baseSalary and a *get* method (lines 23–26) to return baseSalary's value. Method earnings (lines 29–32) calculates a BasePlusCommissionEmployee's earnings. Note that line 31 in method earnings calls superclass CommissionEmployee's earnings method to calculate the commission-based portion of the employee's earnings. This is a nice example of code reuse. BasePlusCommissionEmployee's toString method (lines 35–40) creates a string representation of a BasePlusCommissionEmployee that contains "base-salaried", followed by the String obtained by invoking superclass CommissionEmployee's toString method (another example of code reuse), then the base salary. The result is a String beginning with "base-salaried commission employee" followed by the rest of the BasePlus-CommissionEmployee's information. Recall that CommissionEmployee's toString obtains the employee's first name, last name and social security number by invoking the toString method of its superclass (i.e., Employee)—yet another example of code reuse. Note that BasePlusCommissionEmployee's toString initiates a chain of method calls that span all three levels of the Employee hierarchy.

10.5.6 Demonstrating Polymorphic Processing, Operator instanceof and Downcasting

To test our Employee hierarchy, the application in Fig. 10.9 creates an object of each of the four concrete classes SalariedEmployee, HourlyEmployee, CommissionEmployee and BasePlusCommissionEmployee. The program manipulates these objects, first via variables of each object's own type, then polymorphically, using an array of Employee variables. While processing the objects polymorphically, the program increases the base salary of each BasePlusCommissionEmployee by 10% (this, of course, requires determining the object's type at execution time). Finally, the program polymorphically determines and outputs the type of each object in the Employee array. Lines 9–18 create objects of each of the four concrete Employee subclasses. Lines 22–30 output the string representation and earnings of each of these objects. Note that each object's toString method is called implicitly by printf when the object is output as a String with the %s format specifier.

Line 33 declares employees and assigns it an array of four Employee variables. Line 36 assigns to element employees[0] the reference to a SalariedEmployee object. Line 37 assigns to element employees[1] the reference to an HourlyEmployee object. Line 38 assigns to element employees[2] the reference to a CommissionEmployee object. Line 39 assigns to element employee[3] the reference to a BasePlusCommissionEmployee object.

```
1   // Fig. 10.9: PayrollSystemTest.java
2   // Employee hierarchy test program.
3
4   public class PayrollSystemTest
5   {
6      public static void main( String args[] )
7      {
8         // create subclass objects
9         SalariedEmployee salariedEmployee =
10            new SalariedEmployee( "John", "Smith", "111-11-1111", 800.00 );
11        HourlyEmployee hourlyEmployee =
12            new HourlyEmployee( "Karen", "Price", "222-22-2222", 16.75, 40 );
13        CommissionEmployee commissionEmployee =
14            new CommissionEmployee(
15            "Sue", "Jones", "333-33-3333", 10000, .06 );
16        BasePlusCommissionEmployee basePlusCommissionEmployee =
17            new BasePlusCommissionEmployee(
18            "Bob", "Lewis", "444-44-4444", 5000, .04, 300 );
19
20        System.out.println( "Employees processed individually:\n" );
```

Fig. 10.9 | Employee class hierarchy test program. (Part 1 of 3.)

```
21
22        System.out.printf( "%s\n%s: $%,.2f\n\n",
23           salariedEmployee, "earned", salariedEmployee.earnings() );
24        System.out.printf( "%s\n%s: $%,.2f\n\n",
25           hourlyEmployee, "earned", hourlyEmployee.earnings() );
26        System.out.printf( "%s\n%s: $%,.2f\n\n",
27           commissionEmployee, "earned", commissionEmployee.earnings() );
28        System.out.printf( "%s\n%s: $%,.2f\n\n",
29           basePlusCommissionEmployee,
30           "earned", basePlusCommissionEmployee.earnings() );
31
32        // create four-element Employee array
33        Employee employees[] = new Employee[ 4 ];
34
35        // initialize array with Employees
36        employees[ 0 ] = salariedEmployee;
37        employees[ 1 ] = hourlyEmployee;
38        employees[ 2 ] = commissionEmployee;
39        employees[ 3 ] = basePlusCommissionEmployee;
40
41        System.out.println( "Employees processed polymorphically:\n" );
42
43        // generically process each element in array employees
44        for ( Employee currentEmployee : employees )
45        {
46           System.out.println( currentEmployee ); // invokes toString
47
48           // determine whether element is a BasePlusCommissionEmployee
49           if ( currentEmployee instanceof BasePlusCommissionEmployee )
50           {
51              // downcast Employee reference to
52              // BasePlusCommissionEmployee reference
53              BasePlusCommissionEmployee employee =
54                 ( BasePlusCommissionEmployee ) currentEmployee;
55
56              double oldBaseSalary = employee.getBaseSalary();
57              employee.setBaseSalary( 1.10 * oldBaseSalary );
58              System.out.printf(
59                 "new base salary with 10%% increase is: $%,.2f\n",
60                 employee.getBaseSalary() );
61           } // end if
62
63           System.out.printf(
64              "earned $%,.2f\n\n", currentEmployee.earnings() );
65        } // end for
66
67        // get type name of each object in employees array
68        for ( int j = 0; j < employees.length; j++ )
69           System.out.printf( "Employee %d is a %s\n", j,
70              employees[ j ].getClass().getName() );
71     } // end main
72  } // end class PayrollSystemTest
```

Fig. 10.9 | Employee class hierarchy test program. (Part 2 of 3.)

```
Employees processed individually:

salaried employee: John Smith
social security number: 111-11-1111
weekly salary: $800.00
earned: $800.00

hourly employee: Karen Price
social security number: 222-22-2222
hourly wage: $16.75; hours worked: 40.00
earned: $670.00

commission employee: Sue Jones
social security number: 333-33-3333
gross sales: $10,000.00; commission rate: 0.06
earned: $600.00

base-salaried commission employee: Bob Lewis
social security number: 444-44-4444
gross sales: $5,000.00; commission rate: 0.04; base salary: $300.00
earned: $500.00

Employees processed polymorphically:

salaried employee: John Smith
social security number: 111-11-1111
weekly salary: $800.00
earned $800.00

hourly employee: Karen Price
social security number: 222-22-2222
hourly wage: $16.75; hours worked: 40.00
earned $670.00

commission employee: Sue Jones
social security number: 333-33-3333
gross sales: $10,000.00; commission rate: 0.06
earned $600.00

base-salaried commission employee: Bob Lewis
social security number: 444-44-4444
gross sales: $5,000.00; commission rate: 0.04; base salary: $300.00
new base salary with 10% increase is: $330.00
earned $530.00

Employee 0 is a SalariedEmployee
Employee 1 is a HourlyEmployee
Employee 2 is a CommissionEmployee
Employee 3 is a BasePlusCommissionEmployee
```

Fig. 10.9 | Employee class hierarchy test program. (Part 3 of 3.)

Each assignment is allowed, because a SalariedEmployee *is an* Employee, an HourlyEmployee *is an* Employee, a CommissionEmployee *is an* Employee and a BasePlusCommissionEmployee *is an* Employee. Therefore, we can assign the references of SalariedEmployee,

HourlyEmployee, CommissionEmployee and BasePlusCommissionEmployee objects to superclass Employee variables, even though Employee is an abstract class.

Lines 44–65 iterate through array employees and invoke methods toString and earnings with Employee variable currentEmployee, which is assigned the reference to a different Employee in the array during each iteration. The output illustrates that the appropriate methods for each class are indeed invoked. All calls to method toString and earnings are resolved at execution time, based on the type of the object to which currentEmployee refers. This process is known as *dynamic binding* or *late binding*. For example, line 46 implicitly invokes method toString of the object to which currentEmployee refers. As a result of dynamic binding, Java decides which class's toString method to call at execution time rather than at compile time. Please note that only the methods of class Employee can be called via an Employee variable (and Employee, of course, includes the methods of class Object). (Section 9.7 discusses the set of methods that all classes inherit from class Object.) A superclass reference can be used to invoke only methods of the superclass.

We perform special processing on BasePlusCommissionEmployee objects—as we encounter these objects, we increase their base salary by 10%. When processing objects polymorphically, we typically do not need to worry about the "specifics," but to adjust the base salary, we do have to determine the specific type of Employee object at execution time. Line 49 uses the instanceof operator to determine whether a particular Employee object's type is BasePlusCommissionEmployee. The condition in line 49 is true if the object referenced by currentEmployee *is a* BasePlusCommissionEmployee. This would also be true for any object of a BasePlusCommissionEmployee subclass because of the *is-a* relationship a subclass has with its superclass. Lines 53–54 downcast currentEmployee from type Employee to type BasePlusCommissionEmployee—this cast is allowed only if the object has an *is-a* relationship with BasePlusCommissionEmployee. The condition at line 49 ensures that this is the case. This cast is required if we are to invoke subclass BasePlusCommissionEmployee methods getBaseSalary and setBaseSalary on the current Employee object—as you will see momentarily, attempting to invoke a subclass-only method directly on a superclass reference is a compilation error.

Common Programming Error 10.3

Assigning a superclass variable to a subclass variable (without an explicit cast) is a compilation error.

Software Engineering Observation 10.5

If at execution time the reference of a subclass object has been assigned to a variable of one of its direct or indirect superclasses, it is acceptable to cast the reference stored in that superclass variable back to a reference of the subclass type. Before performing such a cast, use the instanceof operator to ensure that the object is indeed an object of an appropriate subclass type.

Common Programming Error 10.4

When downcasting an object, a ClassCastException occurs, if at execution time the object does not have an is-a relationship with the type specified in the cast operator. An object can be cast only to its own type or to the type of one of its superclasses.

If the instanceof expression in line 49 is true, the if statement (lines 49–61) performs the special processing required for the BasePlusCommissionEmployee object. Using

BasePlusCommissionEmployee variable employee, lines 56 and 57 invoke subclass-only methods getBaseSalary and setBaseSalary to retrieve and update the employee's base salary with the 10% raise.

Lines 63–64 invoke method earnings on currentEmployee, which calls the appropriate subclass object's earnings method polymorphically. Note that obtaining the earnings of the SalariedEmployee, HourlyEmployee and CommissionEmployee polymorphically in lines 63–64 produces the same result as obtaining these employees' earnings individually in lines 22–27. However, the earnings amount obtained for the BasePlus-CommissionEmployee in lines 63–64 is higher than that obtained in lines 28–30, due to the 10% increase in its base salary.

Lines 68–70 display each employee's type as a string. Every object in Java knows its own class and can access this information through method getClass, which all classes inherit from class Object. Method getClass returns an object of type Class (package java.lang), which contains information about the object's type, including its class name. Line 70 invokes method getClass on the object to get its runtime class (i.e., a Class object that represents the object's type). Then method getName is invoked on the object returned by getClass to get the class's name.

In the previous example, we avoid several compilation errors by downcasting an Employee variable to a BasePlusCommissionEmployee variable in lines 53–54. If we remove the cast operator (BasePlusCommissionEmployee) from line 54 and attempt to assign Employee variable currentEmployee directly to BasePlusCommissionEmployee variable employee, we would receive an "incompatible types" compilation error. This error indicates that the attempt to assign the reference of superclass object commissionEmployee to subclass variable basePlusCommissionEmployee is not allowed. The compiler prevents this assignment because a CommissionEmployee is not a BasePlusCommissionEmployee—the *is-a* relationship applies only between the subclass and its superclasses, not vice versa.

Similarly, if lines 56, 57 and 60 used superclass variable currentEmployee, rather than subclass variable employee, to invoke subclass-only methods getBaseSalary and setBaseSalary, we would receive a "cannot find symbol" compilation error on each of these lines. Attempting to invoke subclass-only methods on a superclass reference is not allowed. While lines 56, 57 and 60 execute only if instanceof in line 49 returns true to indicate that currentEmployee has been assigned a reference to a BasePlusCommission-Employee object, we cannot attempt to invoke subclass BasePlusCommissionEmployee methods getBaseSalary and setBaseSalary on superclass Employee reference current-Employee. The compiler would generate errors on lines 56, 57 and 60, because getBaseSalary and setBaseSalary are not superclass methods and cannot be invoked on a superclass variable. Although the actual method that is called depends on the object's type at execution time, a variable can be used to invoke only those methods that are members of that variable's type, which the compiler verifies. Using a superclass Employee variable, we can invoke only methods found in class Employee—earnings, toString and Employee's *get* and *set* methods.

10.5.7 Summary of the Allowed Assignments Between Superclass and Subclass Variables

Now that you have seen a complete application that processes diverse subclass objects polymorphically, we summarize what you can and cannot do with superclass and subclass objects and variables. Although a subclass object also *is a* superclass object, the two objects are nevertheless different. As discussed previously, subclass objects can be treated as if they are superclass objects. However, the subclass can have additional subclass-only members. For this reason, assigning a superclass reference to a subclass variable is not allowed without an explicit cast—such an assignment would leave the subclass members undefined for the superclass object.

In the current section, in Section 10.3 and in Chapter 9, we have discussed four ways to assign superclass and subclass references to variables of superclass and subclass types:

1. Assigning a superclass reference to a superclass variable is straightforward.

2. Assigning a subclass reference to a subclass variable is straightforward.

3. Assigning a subclass reference to a superclass variable is safe, because the subclass object *is an* object of its superclass. However, this reference can be used to refer only to superclass members. If this code refers to subclass-only members through the superclass variable, the compiler reports errors.

4. Attempting to assign a superclass reference to a subclass variable is a compilation error. To avoid this error, the superclass reference must be cast to a subclass type explicitly. At execution time, if the object to which the reference refers is not a subclass object, an error will occur. The instanceof operator can be used to ensure that such a cast is performed only if the object is a subclass object.

10.6 final Methods and Classes

We saw in Section 6.10 that variables can be declared final to indicate that they cannot be modified after they are declared and that they must be initialized when they are declared—such variables represent constant values. It is also possible to declare methods and classes with the final modifier.

A method that is declared final in a superclass cannot be overridden in a subclass. Methods that are declared private are implicitly final, because it is impossible to override them in a subclass (though the subclass can declare a new method with the same signature as the private method in the superclass). Methods that are declared static are also implicitly final, because static methods cannot be overridden either. A final method's declaration can never change, so all subclasses use the same method implementation and calls to final methods are resolved at compile time—this is known as static binding. Since the compiler knows that final methods cannot be overridden, it can optimize programs by removing calls to final methods and replacing them with the expanded code of their declarations at each method call location—a technique known as inlining the code.

Performance Tip 10.1
The compiler can decide to inline a final method call and will do so for small, simple final methods. Inlining does not violate encapsulation or information hiding, but does improve performance because it eliminates the overhead of making a method call.

A class that is declared final cannot be a superclass (i.e., a class cannot extend a final class). All methods in a final class are implicitly final. Class String is an example of a final class. This class cannot be extended, so programs that use Strings can rely on the functionality of String objects as specified in the Java API. Making the class final also prevents programmers from creating subclasses that might bypass security restrictions. For more information on `final` classes and methods, visit `java.sun.com/docs/books/tutorial/java/java00/final.html`. This site contains additional insights into using `final` classes to improve the security of a system.

Common Programming Error 10.5

Attempting to declare a subclass of a `final` class is a compilation error.

Software Engineering Observation 10.6

In the Java API, the vast majority of classes are not declared `final`. This enables inheritance and polymorphism—the fundamental capabilities of object-oriented programming. However, in some cases, it is important to declare classes `final`—typically for security reasons.

10.7 Case Study: Creating and Using Interfaces

Our next example (Fig. 10.11–Fig. 10.13) reexamines the payroll system of Section 10.5. Suppose that the company involved wishes to perform several accounting operations in a single accounts payable application—in addition to calculating the earnings that must be paid to each employee, the company must also calculate the payment due on each of several invoices (i.e., bills for goods purchased). Though applied to unrelated things (i.e., employees and invoices), both operations have to do with obtaining some kind of payment amount. For an employee, the payment refers to the employee's earnings. For an invoice, the payment refers to the total cost of the goods listed on the invoice. Can we calculate such different things as the payments due for employees and invoices in a single application polymorphically? Does Java offer a capability that requires that unrelated classes implement a set of common methods (e.g., a method that calculates a payment amount)? Java interfaces offer exactly this capability.

Interfaces define and standardize the ways in which things such as people and systems can interact with one another. For example, the controls on a radio serve as an interface between radio users and a radio's internal components. The controls allow users to perform only a limited set of operations (e.g., changing the station, adjusting the volume, choosing between AM and FM), and different radios may implement the controls in different ways (e.g., using push buttons, dials, voice commands). The interface specifies *what* operations a radio must permit users to perform but does not specify *how* the operations are performed. Similarly, the interface between a driver and a car with a manual transmission includes the steering wheel, the gear shift, the clutch pedal, the gas pedal and the brake pedal. This same interface is found in nearly all manual transmission cars, enabling someone who knows how to drive one particular manual transmission car to drive just about any manual transmission car. The components of each individual car may look different, but the components' general purpose is the same—to allow people to drive the car.

Software objects also communicate via interfaces. A Java interface describes a set of methods that can be called on an object, to tell the object to perform some task or return some piece of information, for example. The next example introduces an interface named `Payable` to describe the functionality of any object that must be capable of being paid and thus must offer a method to determine the proper payment amount due. An interface declaration begins with the keyword `interface` and contains only constants and abstract methods. Unlike classes, all interface members must be `public`, and interfaces may not specify any implementation details, such as concrete method declarations and instance variables. So all methods declared in an interface are implicitly `public abstract` methods and all fields are implicitly `public`, `static` and `final`.

Good Programming Practice 10.1

According to Chapter 9 of the Java Language Specification, *it is proper style to declare an interface's methods without keywords* `public` *and* `abstract` *because they are redundant in interface method declarations. Similarly, constants should be declared without keywords* `public`, `static` *and* `final` *because they, too, are redundant.*

To use an interface, a concrete class must specify that it `implements` the interface and must declare each method in the interface with the signature specified in the interface declaration. A class that does not implement all the methods of the interface is an abstract class and must be declared `abstract`. Implementing an interface is like signing a contract with the compiler that states, "I will declare all the methods specified by the interface or I will declare my class `abstract`."

Common Programming Error 10.6

Failing to implement any method of an interface in a concrete class that `implements` *the interface results in a syntax error indicating that the class must be declared* `abstract`.

An interface is typically used when disparate (i.e., unrelated) classes need to share common methods and constants. This allows objects of unrelated classes to be processed polymorphically—objects of classes that implement the same interface can respond to the same method calls. Programmers can create an interface that describes the desired functionality, then implement this interface in any classes that require that functionality. For example, in the accounts payable application developed in this section, we implement interface `Payable` in any class that must be able to calculate a payment amount (e.g., `Employee`, `Invoice`).

An interface is often used in place of an `abstract` class when there is no default implementation to inherit—that is, no fields and no default method implementations. Like `public abstract` classes, interfaces are typically `public` types, so they are normally declared in files by themselves with the same name as the interface and the `.java` file-name extension.

10.7.1 Developing a `Payable` Hierarchy

To build an application that can determine payments for employees and invoices alike, we first create interface `Payable` (Fig. 10.11). Interface `Payable` contains method `getPaymentAmount` that returns a `double` amount that must be paid for an object of any class that implements the interface. Method `getPaymentAmount` is a general purpose version of method `earnings` of the `Employee` hierarchy—method `earnings` calculates a payment amount specifically for an `Employee`, while `getPaymentAmount` can be applied to a broad range of unrelated objects. After declaring interface `Payable`, we introduce class `Invoice` (Fig. 10.12), which implements interface `Payable`. We then modify class `Employee` such that it also implements interface `Payable`. Finally, we update `Employee` subclass `SalariedEmployee` to "fit" into the `Payable` hierarchy (i.e., rename `SalariedEmployee` method `earnings` as `getPaymentAmount`).

Good Programming Practice 10.2

When declaring a method in an interface, choose a method name that describes the method's purpose in a general manner, because the method may be implemented by a broad range of unrelated classes.

Classes `Invoice` and `Employee` both represent things for which the company must be able to calculate a payment amount. Both classes implement `Payable`, so a program can invoke method `getPaymentAmount` on `Invoice` objects and `Employee` objects alike. As we will soon see, this enables the polymorphic processing of `Invoices` and `Employees` required for our company's accounts payable application.

The UML class diagram in Fig. 10.10 shows the hierarchy used in our accounts payable application. The hierarchy begins with interface `Payable`. The UML distinguishes an interface from other classes by placing the word "interface" in guillemets (« and ») above the interface name. The UML expresses the relationship between a class and an interface through a relationship known as a realization. A class is said to "realize," or implement, the methods of an interface. A class diagram models a realization as a dashed arrow with a hollow arrowhead pointing from the implementing class to the interface. The diagram in Fig. 10.10 indicates that classes `Invoice` and `Employee` each realize (i.e., implement) interface `Payable`. Note that, as in the class diagram of Fig. 10.2, class `Employee` appears in italics, indicating that it is an abstract class. Concrete class `SalariedEmployee` extends `Employee` and inherits its superclass's realization relationship with interface `Payable`.

10.7.2 Declaring Interface `Payable`

The declaration of interface `Payable` begins in Fig. 10.11 at line 4. Interface `Payable` contains `public abstract` method `getPaymentAmount` (line 6). Note that the method is not explicitly declared `public` or `abstract`. Interface methods must be `public` and `abstract`, so they do not need to be declared as such. Interface `Payable` has only one method—interfaces can have any number of methods. (Java offers the notion of "tagging interfaces"—these actually have *no* methods. In fact, a tagging interface contains no constant values either—it simply contains an empty interface declaration.) In addition, method `getPaymentAmount` has no parameters, but interface methods can have parameters.

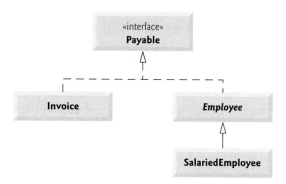

Fig. 10.10 | `Payable` interface hierarchy UML class diagram.

```
 1   // Fig. 10.11: Payable.java
 2   // Payable interface declaration.
 3
 4   public interface Payable
 5   {
 6      double getPaymentAmount(); // calculate payment; no implementation
 7   } // end interface Payable
```

Fig. 10.11 | Payable interface declaration.

10.7.3 Creating Class Invoice

We now create class Invoice (Fig. 10.12) to represent a simple invoice that contains billing information for only one kind of part. The class declares private instance variables partNumber, partDescription, quantity and pricePerItem (in lines 6–9) that indicate the part number, a description of the part, the quantity of the part ordered and the price per item. Class Invoice also contains a constructor (lines 12–19), *get* and *set* methods (lines 22–67) that manipulate the class's instance variables and a toString method (lines

```
 1   // Fig. 10.12: Invoice.java
 2   // Invoice class implements Payable.
 3
 4   public class Invoice implements Payable
 5   {
 6      private String partNumber;
 7      private String partDescription;
 8      private int quantity;
 9      private double pricePerItem;
10
11      // four-argument constructor
12      public Invoice( String part, String description, int count,
13         double price )
14      {
15         partNumber = part;
16         partDescription = description;
17         setQuantity( count ); // validate and store quantity
18         setPricePerItem( price ); // validate and store price per item
19      } // end four-argument Invoice constructor
20
21      // set part number
22      public void setPartNumber( String part )
23      {
24         partNumber = part;
25      } // end method setPartNumber
26
27      // get part number
28      public String getPartNumber()
29      {
30         return partNumber;
31      } // end method getPartNumber
```

Fig. 10.12 | Invoice class that implements Payable. (Part 1 of 2.)

```
32
33      // set description
34      public void setPartDescription( String description )
35      {
36         partDescription = description;
37      } // end method setPartDescription
38
39      // get description
40      public String getPartDescription()
41      {
42         return partDescription;
43      } // end method getPartDescription
44
45      // set quantity
46      public void setQuantity( int count )
47      {
48         quantity = ( count < 0 ) ? 0 : count; // quantity cannot be negative
49      } // end method setQuantity
50
51      // get quantity
52      public int getQuantity()
53      {
54         return quantity;
55      } // end method getQuantity
56
57      // set price per item
58      public void setPricePerItem( double price )
59      {
60         pricePerItem = ( price < 0.0 ) ? 0.0 : price; // validate price
61      } // end method setPricePerItem
62
63      // get price per item
64      public double getPricePerItem()
65      {
66         return pricePerItem;
67      } // end method getPricePerItem
68
69      // return String representation of Invoice object
70      public String toString()
71      {
72         return String.format( "%s: \n%s: %s (%s) \n%s: %d \n%s: $%,.2f",
73            "invoice", "part number", getPartNumber(), getPartDescription(),
74            "quantity", getQuantity(), "price per item", getPricePerItem() );
75      } // end method toString
76
77      // method required to carry out contract with interface Payable
78      public double getPaymentAmount()
79      {
80         return getQuantity() * getPricePerItem(); // calculate total cost
81      } // end method getPaymentAmount
82   } // end class Invoice
```

Fig. 10.12 | Invoice class that implements Payable. (Part 2 of 2.)

70–75) that returns a string representation of an `Invoice` object. Note that methods `set-Quantity` (lines 46–49) and `setPricePerItem` (lines 58–61) ensure that `quantity` and `pricePerItem` obtain only non-negative values.

Line 4 of Fig. 10.12 indicates that class `Invoice` implements interface `Payable`. Like all classes, class `Invoice` also implicitly extends `Object`. Java does not allow subclasses to inherit from more than one superclass, but it does allow a class to inherit from a superclass and implement more than one interface. In fact, a class can implement as many interfaces as it needs, in addition to extending another class. To implement more than one interface, use a comma-separated list of interface names after keyword `implements` in the class declaration, as in:

```
public class ClassName extends SuperclassName implements FirstInterface,
   SecondInterface, ...
```

All objects of a class that implement multiple interfaces have the *is-a* relationship with each implemented interface type.

Class `Invoice` implements the one method in interface `Payable`. Method `getPaymentAmount` is declared in lines 78–81. The method calculates the total payment required to pay the invoice. The method multiplies the values of `quantity` and `pricePerItem` (obtained through the appropriate *get* methods) and returns the result (line 80). This method satisfies the implementation requirement for this method in interface `Payable`—we have fulfilled the interface contract with the compiler.

10.7.4 Modifying Class `Employee` to Implement Interface `Payable`

We now modify class `Employee` such that it implements interface `Payable`. Figure 10.13 contains the modified `Employee` class. This class declaration is identical to that of Fig. 10.4 with only two exceptions. First, line 4 of Fig. 10.13 indicates that class `Employee` now implements interface `Payable`. Second, since `Employee` now implements interface `Payable`, we must rename `earnings` to `getPaymentAmount` throughout the `Employee` hierarchy. As with method `earnings` in the version of class `Employee` in Fig. 10.4, however, it does not

```
1   // Fig. 10.13: Employee.java
2   // Employee abstract superclass implements Payable.
3
4   public abstract class Employee implements Payable
5   {
6      private String firstName;
7      private String lastName;
8      private String socialSecurityNumber;
9
10     // three-argument constructor
11     public Employee( String first, String last, String ssn )
12     {
13        firstName = first;
14        lastName = last;
15        socialSecurityNumber = ssn;
16     } // end three-argument Employee constructor
17
```

Fig. 10.13 | `Employee` class that implements `Payable`. (Part 1 of 2.)

```
18      // set first name
19      public void setFirstName( String first )
20      {
21         firstName = first;
22      } // end method setFirstName
23
24      // return first name
25      public String getFirstName()
26      {
27         return firstName;
28      } // end method getFirstName
29
30      // set last name
31      public void setLastName( String last )
32      {
33         lastName = last;
34      } // end method setLastName
35
36      // return last name
37      public String getLastName()
38      {
39         return lastName;
40      } // end method getLastName
41
42      // set social security number
43      public void setSocialSecurityNumber( String ssn )
44      {
45         socialSecurityNumber = ssn; // should validate
46      } // end method setSocialSecurityNumber
47
48      // return social security number
49      public String getSocialSecurityNumber()
50      {
51         return socialSecurityNumber;
52      } // end method getSocialSecurityNumber
53
54      // return String representation of Employee object
55      public String toString()
56      {
57         return String.format( "%s %s\nsocial security number: %s",
58            getFirstName(), getLastName(), getSocialSecurityNumber() );
59      } // end method toString
60
61      // Note: We do not implement Payable method getPaymentAmount here so
62      // this class must be declared abstract to avoid a compilation error.
63   } // end abstract class Employee
```

Fig. 10.13 | Employee class that implements Payable. (Part 2 of 2.)

make sense to implement method getPaymentAmount in class Employee because we cannot calculate the earnings payment owed to a general Employee—first we must know the specific type of Employee. In Fig. 10.4, we declared method earnings as abstract for this reason, and as a result class Employee had to be declared abstract. This forced each Employee subclass to override earnings with a concrete implementation.

In Fig. 10.13, we handle this situation differently. Recall that when a class implements an interface, the class makes a contract with the compiler stating either that the class will implement each of the methods in the interface or that the class will be declared `abstract`. If the latter option is chosen, we do not need to declare the interface methods as `abstract` in the abstract class—they are already implicitly declared as such in the interface. Any concrete subclass of the abstract class must implement the interface methods to fulfill the superclass's contract with the compiler. If the subclass does not do so, it too must be declared `abstract`. As indicated by the comments in lines 61–62, class `Employee` of Fig. 10.13 does not implement method `getPaymentAmount`, so the class is declared `abstract`. Each direct `Employee` subclass inherits the superclass's contract to implement method `getPaymentAmount` and thus must implement this method to become a concrete class for which objects can be instantiated. A class that extends one of `Employee`'s concrete subclasses will inherit an implementation of `getPaymentAmount` and thus will also be a concrete class.

10.7.5 Modifying Class SalariedEmployee for Use in the Payable Hierarchy

Figure 10.14 contains a modified version of class `SalariedEmployee` that extends `Employee` and fulfills superclass `Employee`'s contract to implement method `getPaymentAmount` of interface `Payable`. This version of `SalariedEmployee` is identical to that of Fig. 10.5 with the exception that the version here implements method `getPaymentAmount` (lines 30–33) instead of method `earnings`. The two methods contain the same functionality but have different names. Recall that the `Payable` version of the method has a more general name to be applicable to possibly disparate classes. The remaining `Employee` subclasses (e.g., `HourlyEmployee`, `CommissionEmployee` and `BasePlusCommissionEmployee`) also must be modified to contain method `getPaymentAmount` in place of `earnings` to reflect the fact that `Employee` now implements `Payable`. We leave these modifications as an exercise and use only `SalariedEmployee` in our test program in this section.

When a class implements an interface, the same *is-a* relationship provided by inheritance applies. For example, class `Employee` implements `Payable`, so we can say that an `Employee` *is a* `Payable`. In fact, objects of any classes that extend `Employee` are also `Payable` objects. `SalariedEmployee` objects, for instance, are `Payable` objects. As with inheritance relationships, an object of a class that implements an interface may be thought of as an object of the interface class. Objects of any subclasses of the class that implements the interface can also be thought of as objects of the interface class. Thus, just as we can assign the reference of a `SalariedEmployee` object to a superclass `Employee` variable, we can assign the reference of a `SalariedEmployee` object to an interface `Payable` variable. `Invoice` implements `Payable`, so an `Invoice` object also *is a* `Payable` object, and we can assign the reference of an `Invoice` object to a `Payable` variable.

> ### Software Engineering Observation 10.7
> *Inheritance and interfaces are similar in their implementation of the "is-a" relationship. An object of a class that implements an interface may be thought of as an object of that interface type. An object of any subclasses of a class that implements an interface also can be thought of as an object of the interface type.*

```java
1   // Fig. 10.14: SalariedEmployee.java
2   // SalariedEmployee class extends Employee, which implements Payable.
3
4   public class SalariedEmployee extends Employee
5   {
6      private double weeklySalary;
7
8      // four-argument constructor
9      public SalariedEmployee( String first, String last, String ssn,
10        double salary )
11     {
12        super( first, last, ssn ); // pass to Employee constructor
13        setWeeklySalary( salary ); // validate and store salary
14     } // end four-argument SalariedEmployee constructor
15
16     // set salary
17     public void setWeeklySalary( double salary )
18     {
19        weeklySalary = salary < 0.0 ? 0.0 : salary;
20     } // end method setWeeklySalary
21
22     // return salary
23     public double getWeeklySalary()
24     {
25        return weeklySalary;
26     } // end method getWeeklySalary
27
28     // calculate earnings; implement interface Payable method that was
29     // abstract in superclass Employee
30     public double getPaymentAmount()
31     {
32        return getWeeklySalary();
33     } // end method getPaymentAmount
34
35     // return String representation of SalariedEmployee object
36     public String toString()
37     {
38        return String.format( "salaried employee: %s\n%s: $%,.2f",
39           super.toString(), "weekly salary", getWeeklySalary() );
40     } // end method toString
41  } // end class SalariedEmployee
```

Fig. 10.14 | SalariedEmployee class that implements interface Payable method
getPaymentAmount.

Software Engineering Observation 10.8

The "is-a" relationship that exists between superclasses and subclasses, and between interfaces and the classes that implement them, holds when passing an object to a method. When a method parameter receives a variable of a superclass or interface type, the method processes the object received as an argument polymorphically.

> ### Software Engineering Observation 10.9
>
> *Using a superclass reference, we can polymorphically invoke any method specified in the superclass declaration (and in class* Object*). Using an interface reference, we can polymorphically invoke any method specified in the interface declaration (and in class* Object*).*

10.7.6 Using Interface Payable to Process Invoices and Employees Polymorphically

PayableInterfaceTest (Fig. 10.15) illustrates that interface Payable can be used to process a set of Invoices and Employees polymorphically in a single application. Line 9 declares payableObjects and assigns it an array of four Payable variables. Lines 12–13 assign the references of Invoice objects to the first two elements of payableObjects. Lines 14–17 then assign the references of SalariedEmployee objects to the remaining two elements of payableObjects. These assignments are allowed because an Invoice *is a* Payable, a SalariedEmployee *is an* Employee and an Employee *is a* Payable. Lines 23–29 use the enhanced for statement to polymorphically process each Payable object in payableObjects, printing

```
1   // Fig. 10.15: PayableInterfaceTest.java
2   // Tests interface Payable.
3
4   public class PayableInterfaceTest
5   {
6      public static void main( String args[] )
7      {
8         // create four-element Payable array
9         Payable payableObjects[] = new Payable[ 4 ];
10
11        // populate array with objects that implement Payable
12        payableObjects[ 0 ] = new Invoice( "01234", "seat", 2, 375.00 );
13        payableObjects[ 1 ] = new Invoice( "56789", "tire", 4, 79.95 );
14        payableObjects[ 2 ] =
15           new SalariedEmployee( "John", "Smith", "111-11-1111", 800.00 );
16        payableObjects[ 3 ] =
17           new SalariedEmployee( "Lisa", "Barnes", "888-88-8888", 1200.00 );
18
19        System.out.println(
20           "Invoices and Employees processed polymorphically:\n" );
21
22        // generically process each element in array payableObjects
23        for ( Payable currentPayable : payableObjects )
24        {
25           // output currentPayable and its appropriate payment amount
26           System.out.printf( "%s \n%s: $%,.2f\n\n",
27              currentPayable.toString(),
28              "payment due", currentPayable.getPaymentAmount() );
29        } // end for
30     } // end main
31  } // end class PayableInterfaceTest
```

Fig. 10.15 | Payable interface test program processing Invoices and Employees polymorphically. (Part 1 of 2.)

```
Invoices and Employees processed polymorphically:

invoice:
part number: 01234 (seat)
quantity: 2
price per item: $375.00
payment due: $750.00

invoice:
part number: 56789 (tire)
quantity: 4
price per item: $79.95
payment due: $319.80

salaried employee: John Smith
social security number: 111-11-1111
weekly salary: $800.00
payment due: $800.00

salaried employee: Lisa Barnes
social security number: 888-88-8888
weekly salary: $1,200.00
payment due: $1,200.00
```

Fig. 10.15 | `Payable` interface test program processing `Invoices` and `Employees` polymorphically. (Part 2 of 2.)

the object as a `String`, along with the payment amount due. Note that line 27 invokes method `toString` off a `Payable` interface reference, even though `toString` is not declared in interface `Payable`—all references (including those of interface types) refer to objects that extend `Object` and therefore have a `toString` method. Line 28 invokes `Payable` method `getPaymentAmount` to obtain the payment amount for each object in `payableObjects`, regardless of the actual type of the object. The output reveals that the method calls in lines 27–28 invoke the appropriate class's implementation of methods `toString` and `getPaymentAmount`. For instance, when `currentEmployee` refers to an `Invoice` during the first iteration of the `for` loop, class `Invoice`'s `toString` and `getPaymentAmount` execute.

Software Engineering Observation 10.10

All methods of class `Object` can be called by using a reference of an interface type. A reference refers to an object, and all objects inherit the methods of class `Object`.

10.7.7 Declaring Constants with Interfaces

As we mentioned in Section 10.7, an interface can declare constants. The constants are implicitly `public`, `static` and `final`—again, these keywords are not required in the interface declaration. One popular use of an interface is to declare a set of constants that can be used in many class declarations. Consider interface `Constants`:

```
public interface Constants
{
   int ONE = 1;
   int TWO = 2;
   int THREE = 3;
}
```

A class can use these constants by importing the interface, then referring to each constant as Constants.ONE, Constants.TWO and Constants.THREE. Note that a class can refer to the imported constants with just their names (i.e., ONE, TWO and THREE) if it uses a static import declaration (presented in Section 8.12) to import the interface.

Software Engineering Observation 10.11

As of J2SE 5.0, it is considered a better programming practice to create sets of constants as enumerations with keyword enum. *See Section 6.10 for an introduction to* enum *and Section 8.9 for additional* enum *details.*

10.7.8 Common Interfaces of the Java API

In this section, we overview several common interfaces found in the Java API. The power and flexibility of interfaces is used frequently throughout the Java API. These interfaces are implemented and used in the same manner as the interfaces you create (e.g., interface Payable in Section 10.7.2). The Java API's interfaces enable you to extend many important aspects of Java with your own classes. Figure 10.16 presents a brief overview of a few of the more popular interfaces of the Java API.

Interface	Description
Comparable	As you learned in Chapter 2, Java contains several comparison operators (e.g., <, <=, >, >=, ==, !=) that allow you to compare primitive values. However, these operators cannot be used to compare the contents of objects. Interface Comparable is used to allow objects of a class that implements the interface to be compared to one another. The interface contains one method, compareTo, that compares the object that calls the method to the object passed as an argument to the method. Classes must implement compareTo such that it returns a value indicating whether the object on which it is invoked is less than (negative integer return value), equal to (0 return value) or greater than (positive integer return value) the object passed as an argument, using any criteria specified by the programmer. For example, if class Employee implements Comparable, its compareTo method could compare Employee objects by their earnings amounts. Interface Comparable is commonly used for ordering objects in a collection such as an array.
Serializable	A tagging interface used only to identify classes whose objects can be written to (i.e., serialized) or read from (i.e., deserialized) some type of storage (e.g., file on disk, database field) or transmitted across a network.
Runnable	Implemented by any class for which objects of that class should be able to execute in parallel using a technique called multithreading. The interface contains one method, run, which describes the behavior of an object when executed.

Fig. 10.16 | Common interfaces of the Java API. (Part 1 of 2.)

Interface	Description
GUI event-listener interfaces	You work with Graphical User Interfaces (GUIs) every day. For example, in your Web browser, you might type in a text field the address of a Web site to visit, or you might click a button to return to the previous site you visited. When you type a Web site address or click a button in the Web browser, the browser must respond to your interaction and perform the desired task for you. Your interaction is known as an event, and the code that the browser uses to respond to an event is known as an event handler. The event handlers are declared in classes that implement an appropriate event-listener interface. Each event listener interface specifies one or more methods that must be implemented to respond to user interactions.
SwingConstants	Contains a set of constants used in GUI programming to position GUI elements on the screen.

Fig. 10.16 | Common interfaces of the Java API. (Part 2 of 2.)

10.8 (Optional) GUI and Graphics Case Study: Drawing with Polymorphism

You may have noticed in the drawing program created in Exercise 8.1 (and modified in Exercise 9.1) that there are many similarities between the shape classes. Using inheritance, we can "factor out" the common features from all three classes and place them in a single shape superclass. We can then manipulate objects of all three shape types polymorphically using variables of the superclass type. Removing the redundancy in the code will result in a smaller, more flexible program that is easier to maintain.

GUI and Graphics Case Study Exercises

10.1   Modify the MyLine, MyOval and MyRectangle classes of Exercise 8.1 and Exercise 9.1 to create the class hierarchy in Fig. 10.17. Classes of the MyShape hierarchy should be "smart" shape classes that know how to draw themselves (if provided with a Graphics object that tells them where to draw). Once the program creates an object from this hierarchy, it can manipulate it polymorphically for the rest of its lifetime as a MyShape.

In your solution, class MyShape in Fig. 10.17 *must* be abstract. Since MyShape represents any shape in general, you cannot implement a draw method without knowing exactly what shape it is. The data representing the coordinates and color of the shapes in the hierarchy should be declared as private members of class MyShape. In addition to the common data, class MyShape should declare the following methods:

a) A no-argument constructor that sets all the coordinates of the shape to 0 and the color to Color.BLACK.

b) A constructor that initializes the coordinates and color to the values of the arguments supplied.

c) *Set* methods for the individual coordinates and color that allow the programmer to set any piece of data independently for a shape in the hierarchy.

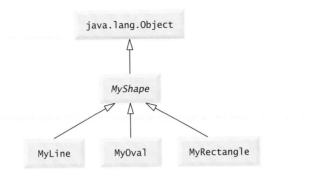

Fig. 10.17 | MyShape hierarchy.

d) *Get* methods for the individual coordinates and color that allow the programmer to retrieve any piece of data independently for a shape in the hierarchy.

e) The abstract method

```
public abstract void draw( Graphics g );
```

which will be called from the program's paintComponent method to draw a shape on the screen.

To ensure proper encapsulation, all data in class MyShape must be private. This requires declaring proper *set* and *get* methods to manipulate the data. Class MyLine should provide a no-argument constructor and a constructor with arguments for the coordinates and color. Classes MyOval and MyRect should provide a no-argument constructor and a constructor with arguments for the coordinates, color and determining whether the shape is filled. The no-argument constructor should, in addition to setting the default values, set the shape to be an unfilled shape.

You can draw lines, rectangles and ovals if you know two points in space. Lines require *x1, y1, x2* and *y2* coordinates. The drawLine method of the Graphics class will connect the two points supplied with a line. If you have the same four coordinate values (*x1, y1, x2* and *y2*) for ovals and rectangles, you can calculate the four arguments needed to draw them. Each requires an upper-left *x*-coordinate value (the smaller of the two *x*-coordinate values), an upper-left *y*-coordinate value (the smaller of the two *y* coordinate values), a *width* (the absolute value of the difference between the two *x*-coordinate values) and a *height* (the absolute value of the difference between the two *y*-coordinate values). Rectangles and ovals should also have a filled flag that determines whether to draw the shape as a filled shape.

There should be no MyLine, MyOval or MyRectangle variables in the program—only MyShape variables that contain references to MyLine, MyOval and MyRectangle objects. The program should generate random shapes and store them in an array of type MyShape. Method paintComponent should walk through the MyShape array and draw every shape (i.e., polymorphically calling every shape's draw method).

Allow the user to specify (via an input dialog) the number of shapes to generate. The program will then generate and display the shapes along with a status bar that informs the user how many of each shape were created.

10.2   *(Drawing Application Modification)* In Exercise 10.1, you created a MyShape hierarchy in which classes MyLine, MyOval and MyRectangle extend MyShape directly. If your hierarchy was properly designed, you should be able to see the similarities between the MyOval and MyRectangle classes. Redesign and reimplement the code for the MyOval and MyRectangle classes to "factor out" the common features into the abstract class MyBoundedShape to produce the hierarchy in Fig. 10.18.

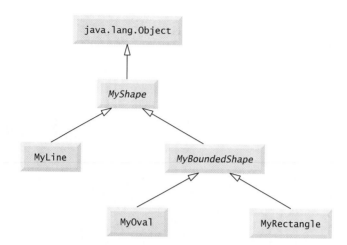

Fig. 10.18 | MyShape hierarchy with MyBoundedShape.

Class MyBoundedShape should declare two constructors that mimic the constructors of class MyShape, only with an added parameter to set whether the shape is filled. Class MyBoundedShape should also declare *get* and *set* methods for manipulating the filled flag and methods that calculate the upper-left *x*-coordinate, upper-left *y*-coordinate, width and height. Remember, the values needed to draw an oval or a rectangle can be calculated from two *(x, y)* coordinates. If designed properly, the new MyOval and MyRectangle classes should each have two constructors and a draw method.

10.9 Wrap-Up

This chapter introduced polymorphism—the ability to process objects that share the same superclass in a class hierarchy as if they are all objects of the superclass. The chapter discussed how polymorphism makes systems extensible and maintainable, then demonstrated how to use overridden methods to effect polymorphic behavior. We introduced abstract classes, which allow programmers to provide an appropriate superclass from which other classes can inherit. You learned that an abstract class can declare abstract methods that each subclass must implement to become a concrete class and that a program can use variables of an abstract class to invoke subclasses' implementations of abstract methods polymorphically. You also learned how to determine an object's type at execution time. Finally, the chapter discussed declaring and implementing an interface as another way to achieve polymorphic behavior.

You should now be familiar with classes, objects, encapsulation, inheritance, interfaces and polymorphism—the most essential aspects of object-oriented programming. Well, that's it for now. Congratulations on completing this introduction to Java programming. We wish you the best and hope that you will continue your study of Java. If you have any questions, please write to us at deitel@deitel.com and we will respond promptly. Ciao!

Summary

- With polymorphism, it is possible to design and implement systems that are more easily extensible. Programs can be written to process even objects of types that do not exist when the program is under development.

- There are many situations in which it is useful to declare abstract classes for which the programmer never intends to create objects. These are used only as superclasses, so we sometimes refer to them as abstract superclasses. You cannot instantiate objects of an abstract class.

- Classes from which objects can be created are called concrete classes.

- A class must be declared `abstract` if one or more of its methods are `abstract`. An abstract method is one with keyword `abstract` to the left of the return type in its declaration.

- If a class extends a class with an abstract method and does not provide a concrete implementation of that method, then that method remains abstract in the subclass. Consequently, the subclass is also an abstract class and must be declared `abstract`.

- Java enables polymorphism—the ability for objects of different classes related by inheritance or interface implementation to respond differently to the same method call.

- When a request is made through a superclass reference to a subclass object to use an `abstract` method, Java executes the implemented version of the method found in the subclass.

- Although we cannot instantiate objects of `abstract` classes, we can declare variables of abstract-class types. Such variables can be used to reference subclass objects.

- Due to dynamic binding (also called late binding), the specific type of a subclass object need not be known at compile time for a method call off a superclass variable to be compiled. At execution time, the correct subclass version of the method is called, based on the type of the reference stored in the superclass variable.

- Operator `instanceof` checks the type of the object to which its left operand refers and determines whether this type has an *is-a* relationship with the type specified as its right operand. If the two have an *is-a* relationship, the `instanceof` expression is `true`. If not, the `instanceof` expression is `false`.

- Every object in Java knows its own class and can access this information through method `getClass`, which all classes inherit from class `Object`. Method `getClass` returns an object of type `Class` (package `java.lang`), which contains information about the object's type that can be accessed using `Class`'s `public` methods. `Class` method `getName`, for example, returns the name of the class.

- An interface declaration begins with the keyword `interface` and contains a set of `public` abstract methods. Interfaces may also contain `public static final` fields.

- To use an interface, a class must specify that it `implements` the interface and must either declare every method in the interface with the signatures specified in the interface declaration or be declared `abstract`.

- An interface is typically used when disparate (i.e., unrelated) classes need to provide common functionality (i.e., methods) or use common constants.

- An interface is often used in place of an `abstract` class when there is no default implementation to inherit.

- When a class implements an interface, it establishes an *is-a* relationship with the interface type, as do all its subclasses.

- To implement more than one interface, simply provide a comma-separated list of interface names after keyword `implements` in the class declaration.

Terminology

abstract class	implementation inheritance
`abstract` keyword	`implements` keyword
abstract method	inlining code
abstract superclass	`instanceof` operator
`Class` class	interface declaration
concrete class	interface inheritance
constants declared in an interface	`interface` keyword
downcasting	iterator class
dynamic binding	late binding
`final` class	polymorphism
`final` method	static binding
`getClass` method of `Object`	subclass reference
`getName` method of `Class`	superclass reference
implement an interface	

Self-Review Exercises

10.1   Fill in the blanks in each of the following statements:
   a) Polymorphism helps eliminate _____ logic.
   b) If a class contains at least one abstract method, it is a(n) _____ class.
   c) Classes from which objects can be instantiated are called _____ classes.
   d) _____ involves using a superclass variable to invoke methods on superclass and subclass objects, enabling you to "program in the general."
   e) Methods that are not interface methods and that do not provide implementations must be declared using keyword _____.
   f) Casting a reference stored in a superclass variable to a subclass type is called _____.

10.2   State whether each of the statements that follows is *true* or *false*. If *false*, explain why.
   a) It is possible to treat superclass objects and subclass objects similarly.
   b) All methods in an `abstract` class must be declared as `abstract` methods.
   c) It is dangerous to try to invoke a subclass-only method through a subclass variable.
   d) If a superclass declares an `abstract` method, a subclass must implement that method.
   e) An object of a class that implements an interface may be thought of as an object of that interface type.

Answers to Self-Review Exercises

10.1   a) `switch`. b) abstract. c) concrete. d) Polymorphism. e) `abstract`. f) downcasting.

10.2   a) True. b) False. An abstract class can include methods with implementations and abstract methods. c) False. Trying to invoke a subclass-only method with a superclass variable is dangerous. d) False. Only a concrete subclass must implement the method. e) True.

Exercises

10.3   How does polymorphism enable you to program "in the general" rather than "in the specific"? Discuss the key advantages of programming "in the general."

10.4   A subclass can inherit "interface" or "implementation" from a superclass. How do inheritance hierarchies designed for inheriting interface differ from those designed for inheriting implementation?

10.5   What are abstract methods? Describe the circumstances in which an abstract method would be appropriate.

10.6   How does polymorphism promote extensibility?

10.7   Discuss four ways in which you can assign superclass and subclass references to variables of superclass and subclass types.

10.8   Compare and contrast abstract classes and interfaces. Why would you use an abstract class? Why would you use an interface?

10.9   *(Payroll System Modification)* Modify the payroll system of Fig. 10.4–Fig. 10.9 to include private instance variable birthDate in class Employee. Use class Date of Fig. 8.7 to represent an employee's birthday. Add *get* methods to class Date and replace method toDateString with method toString. Assume that payroll is processed once per month. Create an array of Employee variables to store references to the various employee objects. In a loop, calculate the payroll for each Employee (polymorphically), and add a $100.00 bonus to the person's payroll amount if the current month is the month in which the Employee's birthday occurs.

10.10   *(Shape Hierarchy)* Implement the Shape hierarchy shown in Fig. 9.3. Each TwoDimensionalShape should contain method getArea to calculate the area of the two-dimensional shape. Each ThreeDimensionalShape should have methods getArea and getVolume to calculate the surface area and volume, respectively, of the three-dimensional shape. Create a program that uses an array of Shape references to objects of each concrete class in the hierarchy. The program should print a text description of the object to which each array element refers. Also, in the loop that processes all the shapes in the array, determine whether each shape is a TwoDimensionalShape or a ThreeDimensionalShape. If a shape is a TwoDimensionalShape, display its area. If a shape is a ThreeDimensionalShape, display its area and volume.

10.11   *(Payroll System Modification)* Modify the payroll system of Fig. 10.4–Fig. 10.9 to include an additional Employee subclass PieceWorker that represents an employee whose pay is based on the number of pieces of merchandise produced. Class PieceWorker should contain private instance variables wage (to store the employee's wage per piece) and pieces (to store the number of pieces produced). Provide a concrete implementation of method earnings in class PieceWorker that calculates the employee's earnings by multiplying the number of pieces produced by the wage per piece. Create an array of Employee variables to store references to objects of each concrete class in the new Employee hierarchy. For each Employee, display its string representation and earnings.

10.12   *(Accounts Payable System Modification)* In this exercise, we modify the accounts payable application of Fig. 10.11–Fig. 10.15 to include the complete functionality of the payroll application of Fig. 10.4–Fig. 10.9. The application should still process two Invoice objects, but now should process one object of each of the four Employee subclasses. If the object currently being processed is a BasePlusCommissionEmployee, the application should increase the BasePlusCommissionEmployee's base salary by 10%. Finally, the application should output the payment amount for each object. Complete the following steps to create the new application:

    a)   Modify classes HourlyEmployee (Fig. 10.6) and CommissionEmployee (Fig. 10.7) to place them in the Payable hierarchy as subclasses of the version of Employee (Fig. 10.13) that implements Payable. [*Hint:* Change the name of method earnings to getPaymentAmount in each subclass so that the class satisfies its inherited contract with interface Payable.]

    b)   Modify class BasePlusCommissionEmployee (Fig. 10.8) such that it extends the version of class CommissionEmployee created in Part *a*.

    c)   Modify PayableInterfaceTest (Fig. 10.15) to polymorphically process two Invoices, one SalariedEmployee, one HourlyEmployee, one CommissionEmployee and one BasePlusCommissionEmployee. First output a string representation of each Payable object. Next, if an object is a BasePlusCommissionEmployee, increase its base salary by 10%. Finally, output the payment amount for each Payable object.

Operator Precedence Chart

A.1 Operator Precedence

Operators are shown in decreasing order of precedence from top to bottom (Fig. A.1).

Operator	Description	Associativity
++ --	unary postfix increment unary postfix decrement	right to left
++ -- + - ! ~ (*type*)	unary prefix increment unary prefix decrement unary plus unary minus unary logical negation unary bitwise complement unary cast	right to left
* / %	multiplication division remainder	left to right
+ -	addition or string concatenation subtraction	left to right
<< >> >>>	left shift signed right shift unsigned right shift	left to right

Fig. A.1 | Operator precedence chart. (Part 1 of 2.)

Operator	Description	Associativity

`<`
`<=`
`>`
`>=`
`instanceof`
	less than
	less than or equal to
	greater than
	greater than or equal to
	type comparison
		left to right

`==` `!=`	is equal to is not equal to	left to right
`&`	bitwise AND boolean logical AND	left to right
`^`	bitwise exclusive OR boolean logical exclusive OR	left to right
`|`	bitwise inclusive OR boolean logical inclusive OR	left to right
`&&`	conditional AND	left to right
`||`	conditional OR	left to right
`?:`	conditional	right to left

`=`
`+=`
`-=`
`*=`
`/=`
`%=`
`&=`
`^=`
`|=`
`<<=`
`>>=`
`>>>=`
	assignment
	addition assignment
	subtraction assignment
	multiplication assignment
	division assignment
	remainder assignment
	bitwise AND assignment
	bitwise exclusive OR assignment
	bitwise inclusive OR assignment
	bitwise left shift assignment
	bitwise signed-right-shift assignment
	bitwise unsigned-right-shift assignment
		right to left

Fig. A.1 | Operator precedence chart. (Part 2 of 2.)

B

ASCII Character Set

	0	1	2	3	4	5	6	7	8	9
0	nul	soh	stx	etx	eot	enq	ack	bel	bs	ht
1	nl	vt	ff	cr	so	si	dle	dc1	dc2	dc3
2	dc4	nak	syn	etb	can	em	sub	esc	fs	gs
3	rs	us	sp	!	"	#	$	%	&	'
4	(	)	*	+	,	-	.	/	0	1
5	2	3	4	5	6	7	8	9	:	;
6	<	=	>	?	@	A	B	C	D	E
7	F	G	H	I	J	K	L	M	N	O
8	P	Q	R	S	T	U	V	W	X	Y
9	Z	[	\	]	^	_	'	a	b	c
10	d	e	f	g	h	i	j	k	l	m
11	n	o	p	q	r	s	t	u	v	w
12	x	y	z	{	|	}	~	del		

Fig. B.1 | ASCII Character Set.

The digits at the left of the table are the left digits of the decimal equivalent (0–127) of the character code, and the digits at the top of the table are the right digits of the character code. For example, the character code for "F" is 70, and the character code for "&" is 38.

Most users of this book are interested in the ASCII character set used to represent English characters on many computers. The ASCII character set is a subset of the Unicode character set used by Java to represent characters from most of the world's languages. For more information on the Unicode character set, see Appendix F.

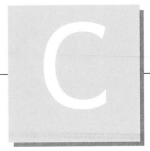

Keywords and Reserved Words

Java Keywords				
abstract	assert	boolean	break	byte
case	catch	char	class	continue
default	do	double	else	enum
extends	final	finally	float	for
if	implements	import	instanceof	int
interface	long	native	new	package
private	protected	public	return	short
static	strictfp	super	switch	synchronized
this	throw	throws	transient	try
void	volatile	while		

Keywords that are not currently used

const	goto

Fig. C.1 | Java keywords.

Java also contains the reserved words true and false, which are boolean literals, and null, which is the literal that represents a reference to nothing. Like keywords, these reserved words cannot be used as identifiers.

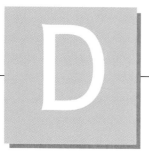

Primitive Types

Type	Size in bits	Values	Standard
boolean		true or false	
[*Note:* A **boolean**'s representation is specific to the Java Virtual Machine on each platform.]			
char	16	'\u0000' to '\uFFFF' (0 to 65535)	(ISO Unicode character set)
byte	8	-128 to $+127$ (-2^7 to $2^7 - 1$)	
short	16	$-32{,}768$ to $+32{,}767$ (-2^{15} to $2^{15} - 1$)	
int	32	$-2{,}147{,}483{,}648$ to $+2{,}147{,}483{,}647$ (-2^{31} to $2^{31} - 1$)	
long	64	$-9{,}223{,}372{,}036{,}854{,}775{,}808$ to $+9{,}223{,}372{,}036{,}854{,}775{,}807$ (-2^{63} to $2^{63} - 1$)	
float	32	*Negative range:* $-3.4028234663852886E+38$ to $-1.40129846432481707e-45$ *Positive range:* $1.40129846432481707e-45$ to $3.4028234663852886E+38$	(IEEE 754 floating point)
double	64	*Negative range:* $-1.7976931348623157E+308$ to $-4.94065645841246544e-324$ *Positive range:* $4.94065645841246544e-324$ to $1.7976931348623157E+308$	(IEEE 754 floating point)

Fig. D.1 | Java primitive types.

For more information on IEEE 754 visit grouper.ieee.org/groups/754/. For more information on Unicode, see Appendix F, Unicode®.

E

Number Systems

OBJECTIVES

In this appendix you will learn:

- To understand basic number systems concepts, such as base, positional value and symbol value.

- To understand how to work with numbers represented in the binary, octal and hexadecimal number systems.

- To abbreviate binary numbers as octal numbers or hexadecimal numbers.

- To convert octal numbers and hexadecimal numbers to binary numbers.

- To covnert back and forth between decimal numbers and their binary, octal and hexadecimal equivalents.

- To understand binary arithmetic and how negative binary numbers are represented using two's complement notation.

E.1 Introduction

In this appendix, we introduce the key number systems that Java programmers use, especially when they are working on software projects that require close interaction with machine-level hardware. Projects like this include operating systems, computer networking software, compilers, database systems and applications requiring high performance.

When we write an integer such as 227 or –63 in a Java program, the number is assumed to be in the decimal (base 10) number system. The digits in the decimal number system are 0, 1, 2, 3, 4, 5, 6, 7, 8 and 9. The lowest digit is 0 and the highest digit is 9—one less than the base of 10. Internally, computers use the binary (base 2) number system. The binary number system has only two digits, namely 0 and 1. Its lowest digit is 0 and its highest digit is 1—one less than the base of 2.

As we will see, binary numbers tend to be much longer than their decimal equivalents. Programmers who work in assembly languages and in high-level languages like Java that enable programmers to reach down to the machine level, find it cumbersome to work with binary numbers. So two other number systems—the octal number system (base 8) and the hexadecimal number system (base 16)—are popular primarily because they make it convenient to abbreviate binary numbers.

In the octal number system, the digits range from 0 to 7. Because both the binary number system and the octal number system have fewer digits than the decimal number system, their digits are the same as the corresponding digits in decimal.

The hexadecimal number system poses a problem because it requires 16 digits—a lowest digit of 0 and a highest digit with a value equivalent to decimal 15 (one less than the base of 16). By convention, we use the letters A through F to represent the hexadecimal digits corresponding to decimal values 10 through 15. Thus in hexadecimal we can have numbers like 876 consisting solely of decimal-like digits, numbers like 8A55F consisting of digits and letters and numbers like FFE consisting solely of letters. Occasionally, a hexadecimal number spells a common word such as FACE or FEED—this can appear strange to programmers accustomed to working with numbers. The digits of the binary, octal, decimal and hexadecimal number systems are summarized in Fig. E.1–Fig. E.2.

Each of these number systems uses positional notation—each position in which a digit is written has a different positional value. For example, in the decimal number 937 (the 9, the 3 and the 7 are referred to as symbol values), we say that the 7 is written in the ones position, the 3 is written in the tens position and the 9 is written in the hundreds position. Note that each of these positions is a power of the base (base 10) and that these powers begin at 0 and increase by 1 as we move left in the number (Fig. E.3).

Binary digit	Octal digit	Decimal digit	Hexadecimal digit
0	0	0	0
1	1	1	1
	2	2	2
	3	3	3
	4	4	4
	5	5	5
	6	6	6
	7	7	7
		8	8
		9	9
			A (decimal value of 10)
			B (decimal value of 11)
			C (decimal value of 12)
			D (decimal value of 13)
			E (decimal value of 14)
			F (decimal value of 15)

Fig. E.1 | Digits of the binary, octal, decimal and hexadecimal number systems.

Attribute	Binary	Octal	Decimal	Hexadecimal
Base	2	8	10	16
Lowest digit	0	0	0	0
Highest digit	1	7	9	F

Fig. E.2 | Comparing the binary, octal, decimal and hexadecimal number systems.

Positional values in the decimal number system			
Decimal digit	9	3	7
Position name	Hundreds	Tens	Ones
Positional value	100	10	1
Positional value as a power of the base (10)	10^2	10^1	10^0

Fig. E.3 | Positional values in the decimal number system.

For longer decimal numbers, the next positions to the left would be the thousands position (10 to the 3rd power), the ten-thousands position (10 to the 4th power), the hundred-thousands position (10 to the 5th power), the millions position (10 to the 6th power), the ten-millions position (10 to the 7th power) and so on.

In the binary number 101, the rightmost 1 is written in the ones position, the 0 is written in the twos position and the leftmost 1 is written in the fours position. Note that each position is a power of the base (base 2) and that these powers begin at 0 and increase by 1 as we move left in the number (Fig. E.4). So, $101 = 2^2 + 2^0 = 4 + 1 = 5$.

For longer binary numbers, the next positions to the left would be the eights position (2 to the 3rd power), the sixteens position (2 to the 4th power), the thirty-twos position (2 to the 5th power), the sixty-fours position (2 to the 6th power) and so on.

In the octal number 425, we say that the 5 is written in the ones position, the 2 is written in the eights position and the 4 is written in the sixty-fours position. Note that each of these positions is a power of the base (base 8) and that these powers begin at 0 and increase by 1 as we move left in the number (Fig. E.5).

For longer octal numbers, the next positions to the left would be the five-hundred-and-twelves position (8 to the 3rd power), the four-thousand-and-ninety-sixes position (8 to the 4th power), the thirty-two-thousand-seven-hundred-and-sixty-eights position (8 to the 5th power) and so on.

In the hexadecimal number 3DA, we say that the A is written in the ones position, the D is written in the sixteens position and the 3 is written in the two-hundred-and-fifty-sixes position. Note that each of these positions is a power of the base (base 16) and that these powers begin at 0 and increase by 1 as we move left in the number (Fig. E.6).

For longer hexadecimal numbers, the next positions to the left would be the four-thousand-and-ninety-sixes position (16 to the 3rd power), the sixty-five-thousand-five-hundred-and-thirty-sixes position (16 to the 4th power) and so on.

Positional values in the binary number system			
Binary digit	1	0	1
Position name	Fours	Twos	Ones
Positional value	4	2	1
Positional value as a power of the base (2)	2^2	2^1	2^0

Fig. E.4 | Positional values in the binary number system.

Positional values in the octal number system			
Decimal digit	4	2	5
Position name	Sixty-fours	Eights	Ones
Positional value	64	8	1
Positional value as a power of the base (8)	8^2	8^1	8^0

Fig. E.5 | Positional values in the octal number system.

Positional values in the hexadecimal number system			
Decimal digit	3	D	A
Position name	Two-hundred-and-fifty-sixes	Sixteens	Ones
Positional value	256	16	1
Positional value as a power of the base (16)	16^2	16^1	16^0

Fig. E.6 | Positional values in the hexadecimal number system.

E.2 Abbreviating Binary Numbers as Octal and Hexadecimal Numbers

The main use for octal and hexadecimal numbers in computing is for abbreviating lengthy binary representations. Figure E.7 highlights the fact that lengthy binary numbers can be expressed concisely in number systems with higher bases than the binary number system.

Decimal number	Binary representation	Octal representation	Hexadecimal representation
0	0	0	0
1	1	1	1
2	10	2	2
3	11	3	3
4	100	4	4
5	101	5	5
6	110	6	6
7	111	7	7
8	1000	10	8
9	1001	11	9
10	1010	12	A
11	1011	13	B
12	1100	14	C
13	1101	15	D
14	1110	16	E
15	1111	17	F
16	10000	20	10

Fig. E.7 | Decimal, binary, octal and hexadecimal equivalents.

A particularly important relationship that both the octal number system and the hexa-decimal number system have to the binary system is that the bases of octal and hexadec-imal (8 and 16 respectively) are powers of the base of the binary number system (base 2). Consider the following 12-digit binary number and its octal and hexadecimal equivalents. See if you can determine how this relationship makes it convenient to abbreviate binary numbers in octal or hexadecimal. The answer follows the numbers.

Binary number	Octal equivalent	Hexadecimal equivalent
100011010001	4321	8D1

To see how the binary number converts easily to octal, simply break the 12-digit binary number into groups of three consecutive bits each and write those groups over the corresponding digits of the octal number as follows:

100	011	010	001
4	3	2	1

Note that the octal digit you have written under each group of thee bits corresponds precisely to the octal equivalent of that 3-digit binary number, as shown in Fig. E.7.

The same kind of relationship can be observed in converting from binary to hexadec-imal. Break the 12-digit binary number into groups of four consecutive bits each and write those groups over the corresponding digits of the hexadecimal number as follows:

1000	1101	0001
8	D	1

Notice that the hexadecimal digit you wrote under each group of four bits corre-sponds precisely to the hexadecimal equivalent of that 4-digit binary number as shown in Fig. E.7.

E.3 Converting Octal and Hexadecimal Numbers to Binary Numbers

In the previous section, we saw how to convert binary numbers to their octal and hexadec-imal equivalents by forming groups of binary digits and simply rewriting them as their equivalent octal digit values or hexadecimal digit values. This process may be used in re-verse to produce the binary equivalent of a given octal or hexadecimal number.

For example, the octal number 653 is converted to binary simply by writing the 6 as its 3-digit binary equivalent 110, the 5 as its 3-digit binary equivalent 101 and the 3 as its 3-digit binary equivalent 011 to form the 9-digit binary number 110101011.

The hexadecimal number FAD5 is converted to binary simply by writing the F as its 4-digit binary equivalent 1111, the A as its 4-digit binary equivalent 1010, the D as its 4-digit binary equivalent 1101 and the 5 as its 4-digit binary equivalent 0101 to form the 16-digit 1111101011010101.

E.4 Converting from Binary, Octal or Hexadecimal to Decimal

We are accustomed to working in decimal, and therefore it is often convenient to convert a binary, octal, or hexadecimal number to decimal to get a sense of what the number is "really" worth. Our diagrams in Section E.1 express the positional values in decimal. To convert a number to decimal from another base, multiply the decimal equivalent of each digit by its positional value and sum these products. For example, the binary number 110101 is converted to decimal 53, as shown in Fig. E.8.

To convert octal 7614 to decimal 3980, we use the same technique, this time using appropriate octal positional values, as shown in Fig. E.9.

To convert hexadecimal AD3B to decimal 44347, we use the same technique, this time using appropriate hexadecimal positional values, as shown in Fig. E.10.

Converting a binary number to decimal					
Postional values:	32	16	8	4	2	1
Symbol values:	1	1	0	1	0	1
Products:	1*32=32	1*16=16	0*8=0	1*4=4	0*2=0	1*1=1
Sum:	= 32 + 16 + 0 + 4 + 0s + 1 = 53					

Fig. E.8 | Converting a binary number to decimal.

Converting an octal number to decimal			
Positional values:	512	64	8	1
Symbol values:	7	6	1	4
Products	7*512=3584	6*64=384	1*8=8	4*1=4
Sum:	= 3584 + 384 + 8 + 4 = 3980			

Fig. E.9 | Converting an octal number to decimal.

Converting a hexadecimal number to decimal			
Postional values:	4096	256	16	1
Symbol values:	A	D	3	B
Products	A*4096=40960	D*256=3328	3*16=48	B*1=11
Sum:	= 40960 + 3328 + 48 + 11 = 44347			

Fig. E.10 | Converting a hexadecimal number to decimal.

E.5 Converting from Decimal to Binary, Octal or Hexadecimal

The conversions in Section E.4 follow naturally from the positional notation conventions. Converting from decimal to binary, octal, or hexadecimal also follows these conventions.

Suppose we wish to convert decimal 57 to binary. We begin by writing the positional values of the columns right to left until we reach a column whose positional value is greater than the decimal number. We do not need that column, so we discard it. Thus, we first write:

Positional values: 64   32   16   8   4   2   1

Then we discard the column with positional value 64, leaving:

Positional values: 32   16   8   4   2   1

Next we work from the leftmost column to the right. We divide 32 into 57 and observe that there is one 32 in 57 with a remainder of 25, so we write 1 in the 32 column. We divide 16 into 25 and observe that there is one 16 in 25 with a remainder of 9 and write 1 in the 16 column. We divide 8 into 9 and observe that there is one 8 in 9 with a remainder of 1. The next two columns each produce quotients of 0 when their positional values are divided into 1, so we write 0s in the 4 and 2 columns. Finally, 1 into 1 is 1, so we write 1 in the 1 column. This yields:

Positional values: 32   16   8   4   2   1
Symbol values: 1   1   1   0   0   1

and thus decimal 57 is equivalent to binary 111001.

To convert decimal 103 to octal, we begin by writing the positional values of the columns until we reach a column whose positional value is greater than the decimal number. We do not need that column, so we discard it. Thus, we first write:

Positional values: 512   64   8   1

Then we discard the column with positional value 512, yielding:

Positional values: 64   8   1

Next we work from the leftmost column to the right. We divide 64 into 103 and observe that there is one 64 in 103 with a remainder of 39, so we write 1 in the 64 column. We divide 8 into 39 and observe that there are four 8s in 39 with a remainder of 7 and write 4 in the 8 column. Finally, we divide 1 into 7 and observe that there are seven 1s in 7 with no remainder, so we write 7 in the 1 column. This yields:

Positional values: 64   8   1
Symbol values: 1   4   7

and thus decimal 103 is equivalent to octal 147.

To convert decimal 375 to hexadecimal, we begin by writing the positional values of the columns until we reach a column whose positional value is greater than the decimal number. We do not need that column, so we discard it. Thus, we first write:

Positional values: 4096   256   16   1

Then we discard the column with positional value 4096, yielding:

Positional values: 256   16   1

Next we work from the leftmost column to the right. We divide 256 into 375 and observe that there is one 256 in 375 with a remainder of 119, so we write 1 in the 256 column. We divide 16 into 119 and observe that there are seven 16s in 119 with a remainder of 7 and write 7 in the 16 column. Finally, we divide 1 into 7 and observe that there are seven 1s in 7 with no remainder, so we write 7 in the 1 column. This yields:

Positional values: 256   16   1
Symbol values: 1   7   7

and thus decimal 375 is equivalent to hexadecimal 177.

E.6 Negative Binary Numbers: Two's Complement Notation

The discussion so far in this appendix has focused on positive numbers. In this section, we explain how computers represent negative numbers using *two's complement notation*. First we explain how the two's complement of a binary number is formed, then we show why it represents the negative value of the given binary number.

Consider a machine with 32-bit integers. Suppose

```
int value = 13;
```

The 32-bit representation of value is

00000000 00000000 00000000 00001101

To form the negative of value we first form its *one's complement* by applying Java's bitwise complement operator (~):

```
onesComplementOfValue = ~value;
```

Internally, ~value is now value with each of its bits reversed—ones become zeros and zeros become ones, as follows:

value:
00000000 00000000 00000000 00001101

~value (i.e., value's ones complement):
11111111 11111111 11111111 11110010

To form the two's complement of value, we simply add 1 to value's one's complement. Thus

Two's complement of value:
11111111 11111111 11111111 11110011

Now if this is in fact equal to –13, we should be able to add it to binary 13 and obtain a result of 0. Let us try this:

```
  00000000 00000000 00000000 00001101
 +11111111 11111111 11111111 11110011
 ------------------------------------
  00000000 00000000 00000000 00000000
```

The carry bit coming out of the leftmost column is discarded and we indeed get 0 as a result. If we add the one's complement of a number to the number, the result would be all 1s. The key to getting a result of all zeros is that the twos complement is one more than the one's complement. The addition of 1 causes each column to add to 0 with a carry of 1. The carry keeps moving leftward until it is discarded from the leftmost bit, and thus the resulting number is all zeros.

Computers actually perform a subtraction, such as

```
x = a - value;
```

by adding the two's complement of value to a, as follows:

```
x = a + (~value + 1);
```

Suppose a is 27 and value is 13 as before. If the two's complement of value is actually the negative of value, then adding the two's complement of value to a should produce the result 14. Let us try this:

```
a (i.e., 27)       00000000 00000000 00000000 00011011
+(~value + 1)     +11111111 11111111 11111111 11110011
                  -----------------------------------
                   00000000 00000000 00000000 00001110
```

which is indeed equal to 14.

Summary

- An integer such as 19 or 227 or –63 in a Java program is assumed to be in the decimal (base 10) number system. The digits in the decimal number system are 0, 1, 2, 3, 4, 5, 6, 7, 8 and 9. The lowest digit is 0 and the highest digit is 9—one less than the base of 10.

- Internally, computers use the binary (base 2) number system. The binary number system has only two digits, namely 0 and 1. Its lowest digit is 0 and its highest digit is 1—one less than the base of 2.

- The octal number system (base 8) and the hexadecimal number system (base 16) are popular primarily because they make it convenient to abbreviate binary numbers.

- The digits of the octal number system range from 0 to 7.

- The hexadecimal number system poses a problem because it requires 16 digits—a lowest digit of 0 and a highest digit with a value equivalent to decimal 15 (one less than the base of 16). By convention, we use the letters A through F to represent the hexadecimal digits corresponding to decimal values 10 through 15.

- Each number system uses positional notation—each position in which a digit is written has a different positional value.

- A particularly important relationship of both the octal number system and the hexadecimal number system to the binary system is that the bases of octal and hexadecimal (8 and 16 respectively) are powers of the base of the binary number system (base 2).

- To convert an octal to a binary number, replace each octal digit with its three-digit binary equivalent.

- To convert a hexadecimal number to a binary number, simply replace each hexadecimal digit with its four-digit binary equivalent.

- Because we are accustomed to working in decimal, it is convenient to convert a binary, octal or hexadecimal number to decimal to get a sense of the number's "real" worth.

- To convert a number to decimal from another base, multiply the decimal equivalent of each digit by its positional value and sum the products.

- Computers represent negative numbers using two's complement notation.

- To form the negative of a value in binary, first form its one's complement by applying Java's bitwise complement operator (~). This reverses the bits of the value. To form the two's complement of a value, simply add one to the value's one's complement.

Terminology

base	digit
base 2 number system	hexadecimal number system
base 8 number system	negative value
base 10 number system	octal number system
base 16 number system	one's complement notation
binary number system	positional notation
bitwise complement operator (~)	positional value
conversions	symbol value
decimal number system	two's complement notation

Self-Review Exercises

E.1   The bases of the decimal, binary, octal and hexadecimal number systems are _____, _____, _____ and _____ respectively.

E.2   In general, the decimal, octal and hexadecimal representations of a given binary number contain (more/fewer) digits than the binary number contains.

E.3   (*True/False*) A popular reason for using the decimal number system is that it forms a convenient notation for abbreviating binary numbers simply by substituting one decimal digit per group of four binary bits.

E.4   The (octal / hexadecimal / decimal) representation of a large binary value is the most concise (of the given alternatives).

E.5   (*True/False*) The highest digit in any base is one more than the base.

E.6   (*True/False*) The lowest digit in any base is one less than the base.

E.7   The positional value of the rightmost digit of any number in either binary, octal, decimal or hexadecimal is always _____.

E.8   The positional value of the digit to the left of the rightmost digit of any number in binary, octal, decimal or hexadecimal is always equal to _____.

E.9   Fill in the missing values in this chart of positional values for the rightmost four positions in each of the indicated number systems:

decimal	1000	100	10	1
hexadecimal	. . .	256	. . .	. . .
binary	. . .	. . .	. . .	. . .
octal	512	. . .	8	. . .

E.10   Convert binary 110101011000 to octal and to hexadecimal.

E.11   Convert hexadecimal FACE to binary.

E.12   Convert octal 7316 to binary.

E.13   Convert hexadecimal 4FEC to octal. (*Hint:* First convert 4FEC to binary, then convert that binary number to octal.)

E.14   Convert binary 1101110 to decimal.

E.15   Convert octal 317 to decimal.

E.16   Convert hexadecimal EFD4 to decimal.

E.17   Convert decimal 177 to binary, to octal and to hexadecimal.

E.18   Show the binary representation of decimal 417. Then show the one's complement of 417 and the two's complement of 417.

E.19   What is the result when a number and its two's complement are added to each other?

Answers to Self-Review Exercises

E.1   10, 2, 8, 16.

E.2   Fewer.

E.3   False. Hexadecimal does this.

E.4   Hexadecimal.

E.5   False. The highest digit in any base is one less than the base.

E.6   False. The lowest digit in any base is zero.

E.7   1 (the base raised to the zero power).

E.8   The base of the number system.

E.9   Fill in the missing values in this chart of positional values for the rightmost four positions in each of the indicated number systems:

```
decimal      1000    100    10    1
hexadecimal  4096    256    16    1
binary          8      4     2    1
octal         512     64     8    1
```

E.10   Octal 6530; Hexadecimal D58.

E.11   Binary 1111 1010 1100 1110.

E.12   Binary 111 011 001 110.

E.13   Binary 0 100 111 111 101 100; Octal 47754.

E.14   Decimal 2+4+8+32+64=110.

E.15   Decimal 7+1*8+3*64=7+8+192=207.

E.16   Decimal 4+13*16+15*256+14*4096=61396.

E.17   Decimal 177
       to binary:

```
256 128 64 32 16 8 4 2 1
128 64 32 16 8 4 2 1
(1*128)+(0*64)+(1*32)+(1*16)+(0*8)+(0*4)+(0*2)+(1*1)
10110001
```

to octal:

```
512 64 8 1
64 8 1
(2*64)+(6*8)+(1*1)
261
```

to hexadecimal:

```
256 16 1
16 1
(11*16)+(1*1)
(B*16)+(1*1)
B1
```

E.18   Binary:

```
512 256 128 64 32 16 8 4 2 1
256 128 64 32 16 8 4 2 1
(1*256)+(1*128)+(0*64)+(1*32)+(0*16)+(0*8)+(0*4)+(0*2)+(1*1)
110100001
```

One's complement: 001011110
Two's complement: 001011111
Check: Original binary number + its two's complement

```
110100001
001011111
---------
000000000
```

E.19   Zero.

Exercises

E.20   Some people argue that many of our calculations would be easier in the base 12 number system because 12 is divisible by so many more numbers than 10 (for base 10). What is the lowest digit in base 12? What would be the highest symbol for the digit in base 12? What are the positional values of the rightmost four positions of any number in the base 12 number system?

E.21   Complete the following chart of positional values for the rightmost four positions in each of the indicated number systems:

```
decimal      1000     100      10      1
base 6       ...      ...       6     ...
base 13      ...      169     ...     ...
base 3        27      ...     ...     ...
```

E.22   Convert binary 100101111010 to octal and to hexadecimal.

E.23   Convert hexadecimal 3A7D to binary.

E.24   Convert hexadecimal 765F to octal. (*Hint:* First convert 765F to binary, then convert that binary number to octal.)

E.25   Convert binary 1011110 to decimal.

E.26   Convert octal 426 to decimal.

E.27   Convert hexadecimal FFFF to decimal.

E.28   Convert decimal 299 to binary, to octal and to hexadecimal.

E.29   Show the binary representation of decimal 779. Then show the one's complement of 779 and the two's complement of 779.

E.30   Show the two's complement of integer value −1 on a machine with 32-bit integers.

Unicode®

F.1 Introduction

The use of inconsistent character encodings (i.e., numeric values associated with characters) when developing global software products causes serious problems because computers process information using numbers. For example, the character "a" is converted to a numeric value so that a computer can manipulate that piece of data. Many countries and corporations have developed encoding systems that are incompatible with the encoding systems of other countries and corporations. For example, the Microsoft Windows operating system assigns the value 0xC0 to the character "A with a grave accent," while the Apple Macintosh operating system assigns the same value to an upside-down question mark. This results in the misrepresentation and possible corruption of data.

In the absence of a universal character encoding standard, global software developers had to localize their products extensively before distribution. Localization includes the language translation and cultural adaptation of content. The process of localization usually includes significant modifications to the source code (e.g., the conversion of numeric values and the underlying assumptions made by programmers), which results in increased costs and delays in releasing the software. For example, an English-speaking programmer might design a global software product assuming that a single character can be represented by one byte. However, when those products are localized in Asian markets, the programmer's assumptions are no longer valid because there are many more Asian characters, and therefore most of it, if not all, of the code needs to be rewritten. Localization is necessary with each release of a version. By the time a software product is localized for a particular market, a newer version, which needs to be localized as well, can be ready for distribution. As a result, it is cumbersome and costly to produce and distribute global software products in a market where there is no universal character encoding standard.

In response to this situation, the Unicode Standard, an encoding standard that facilitates the production and distribution of software, was created. The Unicode Standard outlines a specification to produce consistent encoding of the world's characters and symbols. Software products which handle text encoded in the Unicode Standard need to be localized, but the localization process is simpler and more efficient because the numeric values need not be converted and the assumptions made by programmers about the character encoding are universal. The Unicode Standard is maintained by a non-profit organization called the Unicode Consortium, whose members include Apple, IBM, Microsoft, Oracle, Sun Microsystems, Sybase and many others.

When the Consortium envisioned and developed the Unicode Standard, it wanted an encoding system that was universal, efficient, uniform and unambiguous. A universal encoding system encompasses all commonly used characters. An efficient encoding system allows text files to be parsed quickly. A uniform encoding system assigns fixed values to all characters. An unambiguous encoding system represents a given character in a consistent manner. These four terms are referred to as the Unicode Standard design basis.

F.2 Unicode Transformation Formats

Although Unicode incorporates the limited ASCII character set (i.e., a collection of characters), it encompasses a more comprehensive character set. In ASCII each character is represented by a byte containing 0s and 1s. One byte is capable of storing the binary numbers from 0 to 255. Each character is assigned a number between 0 and 255, thus ASCII-based systems can support only 256 characters, a tiny fraction of the world's characters. Unicode extends the ASCII character set by encoding the vast majority of the world's characters. The Unicode Standard encodes characters in a uniform numerical space from 0 to 10FFFF hexadecimal. An implementation will express these numbers in one of several transformation formats, choosing the one that best fits the particular application at hand.

Three such formats are in use, called UTF-8, UTF-16 and UTF-32. UTF-8, a variable-width encoding form, requires one to four bytes to express each Unicode character. UTF-8 data consists of 8-bit bytes (sequences of one, two, three or four bytes depending on the character being encoded) and is well suited for ASCII-based systems when there is a predominance of one-byte characters (ASCII represents characters as one-byte). Currently, UTF-8 is widely implemented in UNIX systems and in databases.

The variable-width UTF-16 encoding form expresses Unicode characters in units of 16-bits (i.e., as two adjacent bytes, or a short integer in many machines). Most characters of Unicode are expressed in a single 16-bit unit. However, characters with values above FFFF hexadecimal are expressed with an ordered pair of 16-bit units called surrogates. Surrogates are 16-bit integers in the range D800 through DFFF, which are used solely for the purpose of "escaping" into higher numbered characters. Approximately one million characters can be expressed in this manner. Although a surrogate pair requires 32 bits to represent characters, it is space-efficient to use these 16-bit units. Surrogates are rare characters in current implementations. Many string-handling implementations are written in terms of UTF-16. [*Note:* Details and sample-code for UTF-16 handling are available on the Unicode Consortium Web site at `www.unicode.org`.]

Implementations that require significant use of rare characters or entire scripts encoded above FFFF hexadecimal, should use UTF-32, a 32-bit fixed-width encoding form that usually requires twice as much memory as UTF-16 encoded characters. The major advantage of the fixed-width UTF-32 encoding form is that it expresses all characters uniformly, so it is easy to handle in arrays.

There are few guidelines that state when to use a particular encoding form. The best encoding form to use depends on the computer system and business protocol, not on the data itself. Typically, the UTF-8 encoding form should be used where computer systems and business protocols require data to be handled in 8-bit units, particularly in legacy systems being upgraded, because it often simplifies changes to existing programs. For this reason, UTF-8 has become the encoding form of choice on the Internet. Likewise, UTF-16 is the encoding form of choice on Microsoft Windows applications. UTF-32 is likely to become more widely used in the future as more characters are encoded with values above FFFF hexadecimal. UTF-32 requires less sophisticated handling than UTF-16 in the presence of surrogate pairs. Figure F.1 shows the different ways in which the three encoding forms handle character encoding.

F.3 Characters and Glyphs

The Unicode Standard consists of characters—written components (i.e., alphabets, numbers, punctuation marks, accent marks, etc.) that can be represented by numeric values. An example of such a character is U+0041 LATIN CAPITAL LETTER A. In the first character representation, U+*yyyy* is a code value, in which U+ refers to Unicode code values, as opposed to other hexadecimal values. The *yyyy* represents a four-digit hexadecimal number of an encoded character. Code values are bit combinations that represent encoded characters. Characters are represented using glyphs—various shapes, fonts and sizes for displaying characters. There are no code values for glyphs in the Unicode Standard. Examples of glyphs are shown in Fig. F.2.

Character	UTF-8	UTF-16	UTF-32
LATIN CAPITAL LETTER A	0x41	0x0041	0x00000041
GREEK CAPITAL LETTER ALPHA	0xCD 0x91	0x0391	0x00000391
CJK UNIFIED IDEO-GRAPH-4E95	0xE4 0xBA 0x95	0x4E95	0x00004E95
OLD ITALIC LETTER A	0xF0 0x80 0x83 0x80	0xDC00 0xDF00	0x00010300

Fig. F.1 | Correlation between the three encoding forms.

Fig. F.2 | Various glyphs of the character A.

The Unicode Standard encompasses the alphabets, ideographs, syllabaries, punctuation marks, **diacritics**, mathematical operators and other features. that comprise the written languages and scripts of the world. A diacritic is a special mark added to a character to distinguish it from another letter or to indicate an accent (e.g., in Spanish, the tilde "~" above the character "n"). Currently, Unicode provides code values for 96,382 character representations, with more than 878,000 code values reserved for future expansion.

F.4 Advantages/Disadvantages of Unicode

The Unicode Standard has several significant advantages that promote its use. One is the impact it has on the performance of the international economy. Unicode standardizes the characters for the world's writing systems to a uniform model that promotes transferring and sharing data. Programs developed using such a schema maintain their accuracy because each character has a single definition (i.e., *a* is always U+0061, % is always U+0025). This enables corporations to manage the high demands of international markets by processing different writing systems at the same time. All characters can be managed in an identical manner, thus avoiding any confusion caused by different character-code architectures. Moreover, managing data in a consistent manner eliminates data corruption, because data can be sorted, searched and manipulated using a consistent process.

Another advantage of the Unicode Standard is portability (i.e., software that can execute on disparate computers or with disparate operating systems). Most operating systems, databases, programming languages (including Java and Microsoft's .NET languages) and Web browsers currently support, or are planning to support, Unicode.

A disadvantage of the Unicode Standard is the amount of memory required by UTF-16 and UTF-32. ASCII character sets are 8-bits in length, so they require less storage than the default 16-bit Unicode character set. The **double-byte character set** (DBCS) encodes Asian characters with one or two bytes per character. The **multibyte character set** (MBCS) encodes characters with a variable number of bytes per character. In such instances, the UTF-16 or UTF-32 encoding forms may be used with little hindrance on memory and performance.

Another disadvantage of Unicode is that although it includes more characters than any other character set in common use, it does not yet encode all of the world's written characters. Also, UTF-8 and UTF-16 are variable-width encoding forms, so characters occupy different amounts of memory.

F.5 Unicode Consortium's Web Site

If you would like to learn more about the Unicode Standard, visit www.unicode.org. This site provides a wealth of information about the Unicode Standard that is insightful to those new to Unicode. The home page is organized into **Announcements**, **New to Unicode**, **General Information**, **The Consortium**, **For Members Only**, **The Unicode Standard**, **Key Specifications**, **Technical Publications** and **Work in Progress**.

The **Announcement** section lists recent product updates, releases and public reviews. This section also lists new members of the Unicode Consortium.

The **New to Unicode** section consists of four subsections: **What is Unicode**, **How to Use this Site**, **FAQ** and **Glossary of Unicode Terms**. The first subsection provides a technical introduction to Unicode by describing design principles, character interpretations and assignments, text processing and Unicode conformance. This subsection is recommended reading for anyone new to Unicode. It also includes a list of related links that can provide the reader with additional information about Unicode. The **How to Use this Site** subsection contains information about using and navigating the site as well hyperlinks to additional resources. The **FAQ** subsection organizes frequently asked questions into several topics. Each topic has a brief explanation that specifies what kinds of questions and answers are provided. Readers unfamiliar with vocabulary terms used by the Unicode Consortium can navigate to the **Glossary of Unicode Terms** subsection, which lists the Unicode terms and their definitions in alphabetical order.

The **General Information** section contains six subsections: **Where is my Character, Display Problems, Useful Resources, Unicode Enabled Products, Mail Lists** and **Conferences**. The main areas covered in this section include a link to the Unicode code charts (a complete listing of code values) assembled by the Unicode Consortium as well as a detailed outline on how to locate an encoded character in the code chart. The section also contains advice on how to configure different operating systems and Web browsers so that the Unicode characters can be viewed properly. Moreover, from this section, the user can navigate to other sites that provide information on such topics as, fonts, linguistics and other standards, such as the **Armenian Standards Page** and the **Chinese GB 18030 Encoding Standard**.

The **Consortium** section consists of six subsections: **Who we are, Our Members, How to Join, Press Info, Policies & Positions** and **Contact Us**. This section provides a list of the current Unicode Consortium members as well as information on how to become a member. Privileges for each member type—full, associate, specialist, individual and liaison—and the fees assessed to each member are listed here.

The **For Members Only** section consists of two subsections: **Member Resources** and **Working Documents**. These subsections are password protected—only consortium members can access these links.

The **Unicode Standard** section consists of five subsections: **Start Here, Latest Version, Code Charts, Unicode Character Database** and **Unihan Database**. This section describes the updates applied to the latest version of the Unicode Standard as well as categorizing all the defined encoding. The user can learn how the latest version has been modified to encompass more features and capabilities. For example, one enhancement of Version 4.0 is that it contains additional encoded characters.

The **Key Specification** section consists of five subsections: **Unicode Collation (UCA), Bidirectional Algorithm (Bidi), Normalization (NFC, NFD, ...), Locale Data (CLDR)** and **Scripts Codes (ISO 15924)**. These subsections describe the key specifications and projects that are related to Unicode.

The **Technical Publication** section consists of four subsections: **Technical Reports & Standards, Technical Notes, Online Data Table** and **Updates & Errata**. The **Technical Reports & Standards** subsection contains reports and standards used to implement and develop Unicode standard. The **Technical Notes** subsection lists papers that Unicode users or implementors may be interested in. The **Online Data Table** subsection provides machine-readable tables that are required to implement the Unicode standard. The **Updates & Errata** subsection lists errata that are known to the current version and are to be fixed in the next version.

The **Work in Progress** section consists of six subsections: **Calendar of Meetings, Unicode Technical Committee, Meeting Minutes, Proposals for Public Review, Proposed Characters** and **Submitting Proposals**. This section presents the user with a catalog characters recently included in the Unicode Standard scheme as well as characters being considered for inclusion. A user who determines that a character has been overlooked can submit a written proposal for the inclusion of that character. The **Submitting Proposals** subsection contains strict guidelines that must be adhered to when submitting written proposals.

F.6 Using Unicode

Numerous programming languages (e.g., C, Java, JavaScript, Perl, Visual Basic) provide some level of support for the Unicode Standard. The application shown in Fig. F.3–Fig. F.4 prints the text "Welcome to Unicode!" in eight different languages: English, Russian, French, German, Japanese, Portuguese, Spanish and Traditional Chinese.

```
1   // Fig. F.3: UnicodeJFrame.java
2   // Demonstrating how to use Unicode in Java programs.
3   import java.awt.GridLayout;
4   import javax.swing.JFrame;
5   import javax.swing.JLabel;
6
7   public class UnicodeJFrame extends JFrame
8   {
9      // constructor creates JLabels to display Unicode
10     public UnicodeJFrame()
11     {
12        super( "Demonstrating Unicode" );
13
14        setLayout( new GridLayout( 8, 1 ) ); // set frame layout
15
16        // create JLabels using Unicode
17        JLabel englishJLabel = new JLabel( "\u0057\u0065\u006C\u0063" +
18           "\u006F\u006D\u0065\u0020\u0074\u006F\u0020Unicode\u0021" );
19        englishJLabel.setToolTipText( "This is English" );
20        add( englishJLabel );
21
22        JLabel chineseJLabel = new JLabel( "\u6B22\u8FCE\u4F7F\u7528" +
23           "\u0020\u0020Unicode\u0021" );
24        chineseJLabel.setToolTipText( "This is Traditional Chinese" );
25        add( chineseJLabel );
26
27        JLabel cyrillicJLabel = new JLabel( "\u0414\u043E\u0431\u0440" +
28           "\u043E\u0020\u043F\u043E\u0436\u0430\u043B\u043E\u0432" +
29           "\u0430\u0442\u044A\u0020\u0432\u0020Unicode\u0021" );
30        cyrillicJLabel.setToolTipText( "This is Russian" );
31        add( cyrillicJLabel );
32
33        JLabel frenchJLabel = new JLabel( "\u0042\u0069\u0065\u006E\u0076" +
34           "\u0065\u006E\u0075\u0065\u0020\u0061\u0075\u0020Unicode\u0021");
35        frenchJLabel.setToolTipText( "This is French" );
36        add( frenchJLabel );
37
38        JLabel germanJLabel = new JLabel( "\u0057\u0069\u006C\u006B\u006F" +
39           "\u006D\u006D\u0065\u006E\u0020\u007A\u0075\u0020Unicode\u0021");
40        germanJLabel.setToolTipText( "This is German" );
41        add( germanJLabel );
```

Fig. F.3 | Java application that uses Unicode encoding (Part 1 of 2.).

```
42
43          JLabel japaneseJLabel = new JLabel( "Unicode\u3078\u3087\u3045" +
44              "\u3053\u305D\u0021" );
45          japaneseJLabel.setToolTipText( "This is Japanese" );
46          add( japaneseJLabel );
47
48          JLabel portugueseJLabel = new JLabel( "\u0053\u00E9\u006A\u0061" +
49              "\u0020\u0042\u0065\u006D\u0076\u0069\u006E\u0064\u006F\u0020" +
50              "Unicode\u0021" );
51          portugueseJLabel.setToolTipText( "This is Portuguese" );
52          add( portugueseJLabel );
53
54          JLabel spanishJLabel = new JLabel( "\u0042\u0069\u0065\u006E" +
55              "\u0076\u0065\u006E\u0069\u0064\u0061\u0020\u0061\u0020" +
56              "Unicode\u0021" );
57          spanishJLabel.setToolTipText( "This is Spanish" );
58          add( spanishJLabel );
59      } // end UnicodeJFrame constructor
60   } // end class UnicodeJFrame
```

Fig. F.3 | Java application that uses Unicode encoding (Part 2 of 2.).

```
1    // Fig. F.4: Unicode.java
2    // Display Unicode.
3    import javax.swing.JFrame;
4
5    public class Unicode
6    {
7       public static void main( String args[] )
8       {
9          UnicodeJFrame unicodeJFrame = new UnicodeJFrame();
10         unicodeJFrame.setDefaultCloseOperation( JFrame.EXIT_ON_CLOSE );
11         unicodeJFrame.setSize( 350, 250 );
12         unicodeJFrame.setVisible( true );
13      } // end method main
14   } // end class Unicode
```

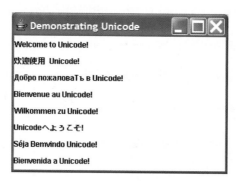

Fig. F.4 | Displaying Unicode.

Class `UnicodeJFrame` (Fig. F.3) uses escape sequences to represent characters. An escape sequence is in the form \u*yyyy*, where *yyyy* represents the four-digit hexadecimal code value. Lines 17–18 contain the series of escape sequences necessary to display "Welcome to Unicode!" in English. The first escape sequence (\u0057) equates to the character "W," the second escape sequence (\u0065) equates to the character "e," and so on. The \u0020 escape sequence (line 18) is the encoding for the space character. The \u0074 and \u006F escape sequences equate to the word "to." Note that "Unicode" is not encoded because it is a registered trademark and has no equivalent translation in most languages. Line 18 also contains the \u0021 escape sequence for the exclamation point (!).

Lines 22–56 contain the escape sequences for the other seven languages. The Unicode Consortium's Web site contains a link to code charts that lists the 16-bit Unicode code values. The English, French, German, Portuguese and Spanish characters are located in the **Basic Latin** block, the Japanese characters are located in the **Hiragana** block, the Russian characters are located in the **Cyrillic** block and the Traditional Chinese characters are located in the **CJK Unified Ideographs** block. The next section discusses these blocks.

F.7 Character Ranges

The Unicode Standard assigns code values, which range from 0000 (**Basic Latin**) to E007F (**Tags**), to the written characters of the world. Currently, there are code values for 96,382 characters. To simplify the search for a character and its associated code value, the Unicode Standard generally groups code values by script and function (i.e., Latin characters are grouped in a block, mathematical operators are grouped in another block, etc.). As a rule, a script is a single writing system that is used for multiple languages (e.g., the Latin script is used for English, French, Spanish, etc.). The **Code Charts** page on the Unicode Consortium Web site lists all the defined blocks and their respective code values. Figure F.5 lists some blocks (scripts) from the Web site and their range of code values.

Script	Range of code values
Arabic	U+0600–U+06FF
Basic Latin	U+0000–U+007F
Bengali (India)	U+0980–U+09FF
Cherokee (Native America)	U+13A0–U+13FF
CJK Unified Ideographs (East Asia)	U+4E00–U+9FFF
Cyrillic (Russia and Eastern Europe)	U+0400–U+04FF
Ethiopic	U+1200–U+137F
Greek	U+0370–U+03FF
Hangul Jamo (Korea)	U+1100–U+11FF
Hebrew	U+0590–U+05FF
Hiragana (Japan)	U+3040–U+309F
Khmer (Cambodia)	U+1780–U+17FF

Fig. F.5 | Some character ranges. (Part 1 of 2.)

Script	Range of code values
Lao (Laos)	U+0E80–U+0EFF
Mongolian	U+1800–U+18AF
Myanmar	U+1000–U+109F
Ogham (Ireland)	U+1680–U+169F
Runic (Germany and Scandinavia)	U+16A0–U+16FF
Sinhala (Sri Lanka)	U+0D80–U+0DFF
Telugu (India)	U+0C00–U+0C7F
Thai	U+0E00–U+0E7F

Fig. F.5 | Some character ranges. (Part 2 of 2.)

Summary

- Before Unicode, software developers were plagued by the use of inconsistent character encoding (i.e., numeric values for characters). Most countries and organizations had their own encoding systems, which were incompatible.

- Localization of global software requires significant modifications to the source code, which results in increased costs and delays in releasing the product.

- Localization is necessary with each release of a version. By the time a software product is localized for a particular market, a newer version, which needs to be localized as well, is ready for distribution. As a result, it is cumbersome and costly to produce and distribute global software products in a market where there is no universal character encoding standard.

- The Unicode Consortium developed the Unicode Standard in response to the serious problems created by multiple character encodings and the use of encodings.

- The Unicode Standard facilitates the production and distribution of localized software. It outlines a specification for the consistent encoding of the world's characters and symbols.

- Software products which handle text encoded in the Unicode Standard need to be localized, but the localization process is simpler and more efficient because the numeric values need not be converted.

- The Unicode Standard is designed to be universal, efficient, uniform and unambiguous.

- A universal encoding system encompasses all commonly used characters; an efficient encoding system parses text files easily; a uniform encoding system assigns fixed values to all characters; and a unambiguous encoding system represents the same character for any given value.

- Unicode extends the limited ASCII character set to include all the major characters of the world.

- Unicode makes use of three Unicode Transformation Formats (UTF): UTF-8, UTF-16 and UTF-32, each of which may be appropriate for use in different contexts.

- UTF-8 data consists of 8-bit bytes (sequences of one, two, three or four bytes depending on the character being encoded) and is well suited for ASCII-based systems when there is a predominance of one-byte characters (ASCII represents characters as one-byte).

- UTF-8 is a variable-width encoding form that is more compact for text involving mostly Latin characters and ASCII punctuation.

- UTF-16 is the default encoding form of the Unicode Standard. It is a variable-width encoding form that uses 16-bit code units instead of bytes. Most characters are represented by a single 16-bit unit, but some characters require surrogate pairs.

- UTF-32 is a 32-bit encoding form. The major advantage of the fixed-width encoding form is that it uniformly expresses all characters, so that they are easy to handle in arrays and other uses.

- Characters are represented using glyphs—shapes, fonts and sizes for displaying characters.

- Code values are bit combinations that represent encoded characters. The Unicode notation for a code value is U+*yyyy* in which U+ refers to the Unicode code values, as opposed to other hexadecimal values. The *yyyy* represents a four-digit hexadecimal number.

- Currently, the Unicode Standard provides code values for 96,382 character representations.

- An advantage of the Unicode Standard is its impact on the overall performance of the international economy. Applications that conform to an encoding standard can be processed easily by computers.

- Another advantage of the Unicode Standard is its portability. Applications written in Unicode can be easily transferred to different operating systems, databases and Web browsers. Most companies currently support, or are planning to support Unicode.

- Numerous programming languages provide some level of support for the Unicode Standard.

- In Java programs, the \u*yyyy* escape sequence represents a character, where *yyyy* is the four-digit hexadecimal code value. The \u0020 escape sequence is the universal encoding for the space character.

Terminology

\u*yyyy* escape sequence	script
block	surrogate
code value	unambiguous (Unicode design basis)
diacritic	Unicode Consortium
double-byte character set (DBCS)	Unicode design basis
efficient (Unicode design basis)	Unicode Standard
encode	Unicode Transformation Format (UTF)
glyph	uniform (Unicode design basis)
hexadecimal notation	universal (Unicode design basis)
localization	UTF-8
multibyte character set (MBCS)	UTF-16
portability	UTF-32

Self-Review Exercises

F.1   Fill in the blanks in each of the following.

    a) Global software developers had to _____ their products to a specific market before distribution.

    b) The Unicode Standard is a(n) _____ standard that facilitates the uniform production and distribution of software products.

    c) The four design basis that comprises the Unicode Standard are: _____, _____, _____ and _____.

    d) Characters are represented using _____.

    e) Software that can execute on different operating systems is said to be _____.

F.2   State whether each of the following is *true* or *false*. If *false*, explain why.

    a) The Unicode Standard encompasses all the world's characters.

b) A Unicode code value is represented as U+*yyyy*, where *yyyy* represents a number in binary notation.

c) A diacritic is a character with a special mark that emphasizes an accent.

d) Unicode is portable.

e) When designing Java programs, a Unicode escape sequence is denoted by /u*yyyy*.

Answers to Self-Review Exercises

F.1 a) localize. b) encoding. c) universal, efficient, uniform, unambiguous. d) glyphs. e) portable.

F.2 a) False. It encompasses the majority of the world's characters. b) False. The *yyyy* represents a hexadecimal number. c) False. A diacritic is a special mark added to a character to distinguish it from another letter or to indicate an accent. d) True. e) False. A Unicode escape sequence is denoted by \u*yyyy*.

Exercises

F.3 Navigate to the Unicode Consortium Web site (www.unicode.org) and write the hexadecimal code values for the following characters. In which block were they located?

a) Latin letter "Z."

b) Latin letter 'n' with the "tilde (~)."

c) Greek letter 'delta.'

d) Mathematical operator "less than or equal to."

e) Punctuation symbol "open quote (")."

F.4 Describe the Unicode Standard design basis.

F.5 Define the following terms:

a) code value.

b) surrogates.

c) Unicode Standard.

F.6 Define the following terms:

a) UTF-8.

b) UTF-16.

c) UTF-32.

F.7 Describe a scenario where it is optimal to store your data in UTF-16 format.

F.8 Using the Unicode Standard code values, write a Java program that prints your first and last name. The program should print your name in all uppercase letters and in all lowercase letters. If you know other languages, print your first and last name in those languages as well.

Using the Java API Documentation

G.1 Introduction

The Java class library contains thousands of predefined classes and interfaces that programmers can use to write their own applications. These classes are grouped into packages based on their functionality. For example, the classes and interfaces used for file processing are grouped into the java.io package, and the classes and interfaces for networking applications are grouped into the java.net package. The Java API documentation lists the public and protected members of each class and the public members of each interface in the Java class library. The documentation overviews all the classes and interfaces, summarizes their members (i.e., the fields, constructors and methods of classes, and the fields and methods of interfaces) and provides detailed descriptions of each member. Most Java programmers rely on this documentation when writing programs. Normally, programmers would search the API to find the following:

1. The package that contains a particular class or interface.

2. Relationships between a particular class or interface and other classes and interfaces.

3. Class or interface constants—normally declared as public static final fields.

4. Constructors to determine how an object of the class can be initialized.

5. The methods of a class to determine whether they are static or non-static, the number and types of the arguments you need to pass, the return types and any exceptions that might be thrown from the method.

In addition, programmers often rely on the documentation to discover classes and interfaces that they have not used before. For this reason, we demonstrate the documentation with classes you know and classes you may not have studied yet. We show how to use the documentation to locate the information you need to use a class or interface effectively.

[*Note:* Sun Microsystems has renamed the Java 2 Platform, Standard Edition version 1.5.0 to Java 2 Platform, Standard Edition version 5.0. However, they decided not to replace the occurrences of 1.5.0 with 5.0 in the documentation. Although the URLs that represent the documentation on Sun's Java Web site work with 5.0 in the URL, these URLs are redirected to ones that replace the 5.0 with 1.5.0. For this reason, all URLs in this appendix are listed with 1.5.0 in the URL.]

G.2 Navigating the Java API

The Java API documentation can be downloaded to your local hard disk or viewed on line. To download the Java API documentation, go to `java.sun.com/j2se/5.0/download.jsp` and locate the **DOWNLOAD** link in the **J2SE v 1.5.0 Documentation** section. You will be asked to accept a license agreement. To do this, click **Accept**, then click **Continue**. Click the **Java(TM) 2 SDK, Standard Edition Documentation 1.5.0, English** link to begin the download. After downloading the file, you can use a ZIP file-extraction program, such as Win-Zip (`www.winzip.com`), to extract the files. If you are using Windows, extract the contents to your `jdk1.5.0` directory or the directory where you installed Java. (See the *Before You Begin* section of this book for information on installing Java.) To view the API documentation on your local hard disk in Microsoft Windows, open `C:\Program Files\Java\jdk1.5.0\docs\api\index.html` page in your browser. To view the API documentation on line, go to `java.sun.com/j2se/1.5.0/docs/api/index.html` (Fig. G.1).

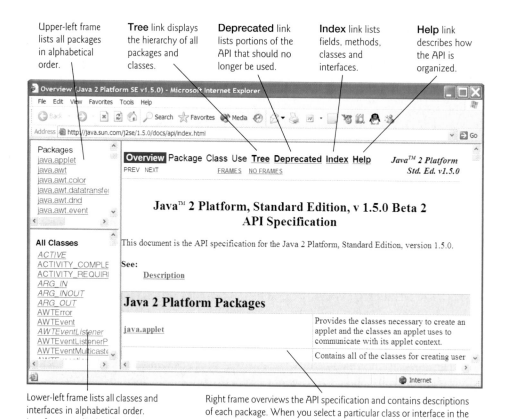

Fig. G.1 | Java API overview. (Courtesy of Sun Microsystems, Inc.)

Frames in the API Documentation's *index.html* Page

The API documentation is divided into three frames (see Fig. G.1). The upper-left frame lists all of the Java API's packages in alphabetical order. The lower-left frame initially lists the Java API's classes and interfaces in alphabetical order. Interface names are displayed in italic. When you click a specific package in the upper-left frame, the lower-left frame lists the classes and interfaces of the selected package. The right frame initially provides a brief description of each package of the Java API specification—read this overview to become familiar wth the general capabilities of the Java APIs. If you select a class or interface in the lower-left frame, the right frame displays information about that class or interface.

Important Links in the *index.html* Page

At the top of the right frame (Fig. G.1), there are four links—Tree, Deprecated, Index and Help. The Tree link displays the hierarchy of all packages, classes and interfaces in a tree structure. The Deprecated link displays interfaces, classes, exceptions, fields, constructors and methods that should no longer be used. The Index link displays classes, interfaces, fields, constructors and methods in alphabetical order. The Help link describes how the API documentation is organized. You should probably begin by reading the Help page.

Viewing the Index Page

If you do not know the name of the class you are looking for, but you do know the name of a method or field, you can use the documentation's index to locate the class. The Index link is located near the upper-right corner of the right frame. The index page (Fig. G.2)

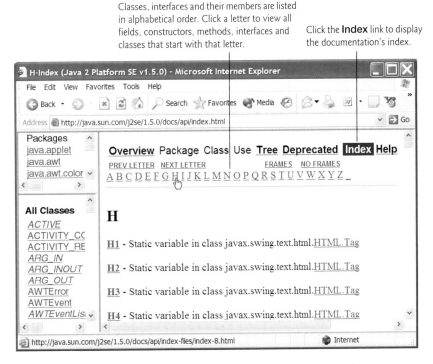

Classes, interfaces and their members are listed in alphabetical order. Click a letter to view all fields, constructors, methods, interfaces and classes that start with that letter.

Click the **Index** link to display the documentation's index.

Fig. G.2 | Viewing the **Index** page. (Courtesy of Sun Microsystems, Inc.)

displays fields, constructors, methods, interfaces and classes in alphabetical order. For example, if you are looking for `Scanner` method `hasNextInt`, but do not know the class name, you can click the **H** link to go to the alphabetical listing of all items in the Java API that begin with "h". Scroll to method `hasNextInt` (Fig. G.3). Once there, each method named `hasNextInt` is listed with the package name and class to which the method belongs. From there, you can click the class name to view the class's complete details, or you can click the method name to view the method's details.

Viewing a Specific Package

When you click the package name in the upper-left frame, all classes and interfaces from that package are displayed in the lower-left frame and are divided into five subsections— **Interfaces**, **Classes**, **Enums**, **Exceptions** and **Errors**—each listed alphabetically. For example, when you click `javax.swing` in the upper-left frame, the contents of package `javax.swing` are displayed in the lower-left frame (Fig. G.4). You can click the package name in the lower-left frame to get an overview of the package. If you think that a package contains several classes that could be useful in your application, the package overview can be especially helpful.

Viewing the Details of a Class

When you click a class name or interface name in the lower-left frame, the right frame displays the details of that class or interface. First you will see the class's package name followed by a hierarchy that shows the class's relationship to other classes. You will also see a list of the interfaces implemented by the class and the class's known subclasses. Figure G.5 shows the beginning of the documentation page for class `JButton` from the `javax.swing` package. The page first shows the package name in which the class appears. This is followed by the class hierarchy that leads to class `JButton`, the interfaces class `JButton` implements and the subclasses of class `JButton`. The bottom of the right frame shows the beginning of class `JButton`'s description. Note that when you look at the documentation

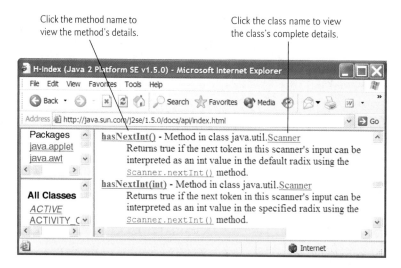

Fig. G.3 | Scroll to method `hasNextInt`. (Courtesy of Sun Microsystems, Inc.)

Click a package name in the upper-left frame to view all classes and interfaces defined in the package.

Click the package name in the lower-left frame to display a summary of that package in the right frame.

Contents of package `javax.swing` are displayed in the lower-left frame.

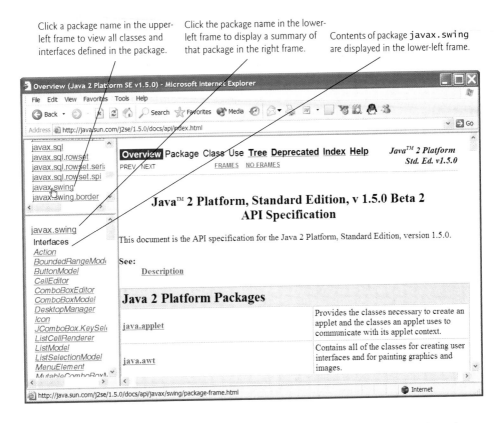

Fig. G.4 | Clicking a package name in the upper-left frame to view all classes and interfaces declared in this package. (Courtesy of Sun Microsystems, Inc.)

for an interface, the right frame does not display a hierarchy for that interface. Instead, the right frame lists the interface's superinterfaces, known subinterfaces and known implementing classes.

Summary Sections in a Class's Documentation Page

Other parts of each API page are listed below. Each part is presented only if the class contains or inherits the items specified. Class members shown in the summary sections are `public` unless they are explicitly marked as `protected`. A class's `private` members are not shown in the documentation, because they cannot be used directly in your programs.

1. The Nested Class Summary section summarizes the class's `public` and `protected` nested classes—i.e., classes that are defined inside the class. Unless explicitly specified, these classes are `public` and non-`static`.

2. The Field Summary section summarizes the class's `public` and `protected` fields. Unless explicitly specified, these fields are `public` and non-`static`. Figure G.6 shows the Field Summary section of class Color.

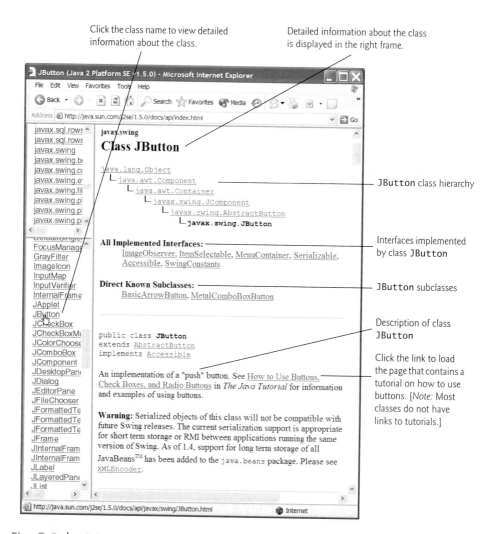

Fig. G.5 | Clicking a class name to view detailed information about the class. (Courtesy of Sun Microsystems, Inc.)

3. The Constructor Summary section summarizes the class's constructors. Constructors are not inherited, so this section appears in the documentation for a class only if the class declares one or more constructors. Figure G.7 shows the Constructor Summary section of class JButton.

4. The Method Summary section summarizes the class's public and protected methods. Unless explicitly specified, these methods are public and non-static. Figure G.8 shows the Method Summary section of class BufferedInputStream.

Note that the summary sections typically provide only a one-sentence description of a class member. Additional details are presented in the detail sections discussed next.

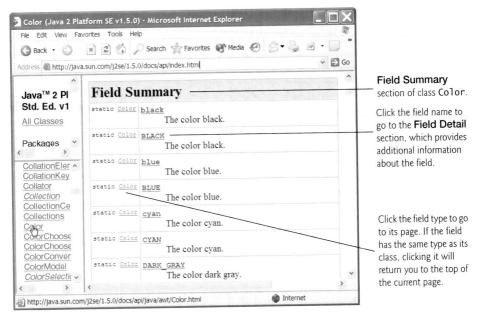

Field Summary section of class `Color`.

Click the field name to go to the **Field Detail** section, which provides additional information about the field.

Click the field type to go to its page. If the field has the same type as its class, clicking it will return you to the top of the current page.

Fig. G.6 | **Field Summary** section of class `Color`. (Courtesy of Sun Microsystems, Inc.)

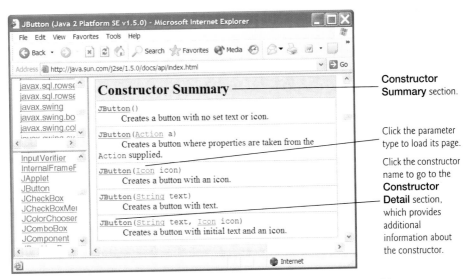

Constructor Summary section.

Click the parameter type to load its page.

Click the constructor name to go to the **Constructor Detail** section, which provides additional information about the constructor.

Fig. G.7 | **Constructor Summary** section of class `JButton`. (Courtesy of Sun Microsystems, Inc.)

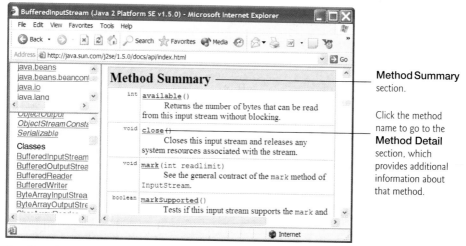

Fig. G.8 | **Method Summary** section of class `BufferedInputStream`. (Courtesy of Sun Microsystems, Inc.)

Detail Sections in a Class's Documentation Page

After the summary sections are detail sections that normally provide more discussion of particular class members. There is not a detail section for nested classes. When you click the link in the **Nested Class Summary** for a particular nested class, a documentation page describing that nested class is displayed. The detail sections are described below.

1. The Field Detail section provides the declaration of each field. It also discusses each field, including the field's modifiers and meaning. Figure G.9 shows the **Field Detail** section of class `Color`.

2. The Constructor Detail section provides the first line of each constructor's declaration and discusses the constructors. The discussion includes the modifiers of each constructor, a description of each constructor, each constructor's parameters and any exceptions thrown by each constructor. Figure G.10 shows the **Constructor Detail** section of class `JButton`.

3. The Method Detail section provides the first line of each method. The discussion of each method includes its modifiers, a more complete method description, the method's parameters, the method's return type and any exceptions thrown by the method. Figure G.11 shows the **Method Detail** section of class `BufferedInputStream`. The method details show you other methods that might be of interest (labeled as **See Also**). If the method overrides a method of the superclass, the name of the superclass method and the name of the superclass are provided so you can link to the method or superclass for more information.

As you look through the documentation, you will notice that there are often links to other fields, methods, nested-classes and top-level classes. These links enable you to jump from the class you are looking at to another relevant portion of the documentation.

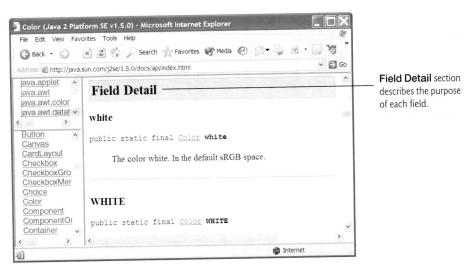

Field Detail section describes the purpose of each field.

Fig. G.9 | **Field Detail** section of class `Color`. (Courtesy of Sun Microsystems, Inc.)

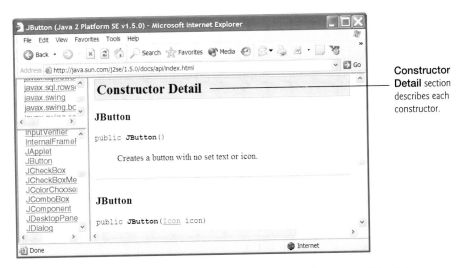

Constructor Detail section describes each constructor.

Fig. G.10 | **Constructor Detail** section of class `JButton`. (Courtesy of Sun Microsystems, Inc.)

Method **read** throws **IOException**. Click **IOException** to load the **IOException** class information page and learn more about the exception type (e.g., why such an exception might be thrown).

Method **read** overrides the **read** method in **FilterInputStream**. Click the name of the overridden method to view detailed information about the superclass's version of that method.

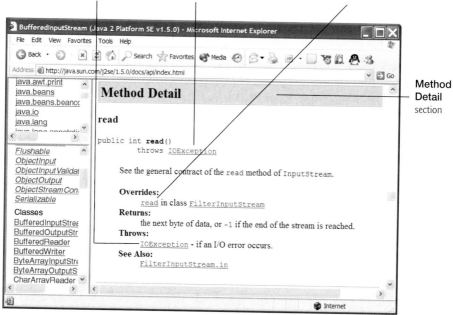

Method Detail section

Fig. G.11 | **Method Detail** section of class **BufferedInputStream**. (Courtesy of Sun Microsystems, Inc.)

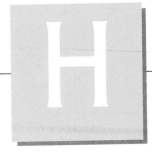

Creating Documentation with javadoc

H.1 Introduction

In this appendix, we provide an introduction to javadoc—a tool used to create HTML files that document Java code. This tool is used by Sun to create the Java API documentation (Fig. H.1). We discuss the special Java comments and tags required by javadoc to create documentation based on your source code and how to execute the javadoc tool. For detailed information on javadoc, visit the javadoc home page at

```
java.sun.com/j2se/javadoc/index.jsp
```

H.2 Documentation Comments

Before HTML files can be generated with the javadoc tool, programmers must insert special comments—called documentation comments—into their source files. Documentation comments are the only comments recognized by javadoc. Documentation comments begin with /** and end with */. Like the traditional comments, documentation comments can span multiple lines. An example of a simple documentation comment is

```
/** Sorts integer array using MySort algorithm */
```

Like other comments, documentation comments are not translated into bytecodes. Because javadoc is used to create HTML files, documentation comments can contain HTML tags. For example, the documentation comment

```
/** Sorts integer array using <B>MySort</B> algorithm */
```

contains the HTML bold tags <B> and </B>. In the generated HTML files, MySort will appear in bold. As we will see, javadoc tags can also be inserted into the documentation comments to help javadoc document your source code. These tags—which begin with an @ symbol—are not HTML tags.

H.3 Documenting Java Source Code

In this section, we document a modified version of the Time2 class from Fig. 8.5 using documentation comments. In the text that follows the example, we thoroughly discuss each of the javadoc tags used in the documentation comments. In the next section, we discuss how to use the javadoc tool to generate HTML documentation from this file.

Documentation comments are placed on the line before a class declaration, an interface declaration, a constructor, a method and a field (i.e., an instance variable or a reference). The first documentation comment (lines 5–9) introduces class Time. Line 6 is a description of class Time provided by the programmer. The description can contain as many lines as necessary to provide a description of the class to any programmer who may use it. Tags @see and @author are used to specify a See Also: note and an Author: note, respectively in the HTML documentation (Fig. H.2). The See Also: note specifies other related classes that may be of interest to a programmer using this class. The @author tag

```java
 1    // Fig. H.1: Time.java
 2    // Time class declaration with set and get methods.
 3    package com.deitel.jhtp6.appenH; // place Time in a package
 4
 5    /**
 6     * This class maintains the time in 24-hour format.
 7     * @see java.lang.Object
 8     * @author Deitel & Associates, Inc.
 9     */
10    public class Time
11    {
12       private int hour;   // 0 - 23
13       private int minute; // 0 - 59
14       private int second; // 0 - 59
15
16       /**
17        *  Time no-argument constructor initializes each instance variable
18        *  to zero. This ensures that Time objects start in a consistent
19        *  state. @throws Exception In the case of an invalid time
20        */
21       public Time() throws Exception
22       {
23          this( 0, 0, 0 ); // invoke Time constructor with three arguments
24       } // end no-argument Time constructor
25
26       /**
27        *  Time constructor
28        *  @param h the hour
29        *  @throws Exception In the case of an invalid time
30        */
31       public Time( int h ) throws Exception
32       {
33          this( h, 0, 0 ); // invoke Time constructor with three arguments
34       } // end one-argument Time constructor
35
```

Fig. H.1 | Java source code file containing documentation comments. (Part I of 4.)

```
36      /**
37       *   Time constructor
38       *   @param h the hour
39       *   @param m the minute
40       *   @throws Exception In the case of an invalid time
41       */
42      public Time( int h, int m ) throws Exception
43      {
44         this( h, m, 0 ); // invoke Time constructor with three arguments
45      } // end two-argument Time constructor
46
47      /**
48       *   Time constructor
49       *   @param h the hour
50       *   @param m the minute
51       *   @param s the second
52       *   @throws Exception In the case of an invalid time
53       */
54      public Time( int h, int m, int s ) throws Exception
55      {
56         setTime( h, m, s ); // invoke setTime to validate time
57      } // end three-argument Time constructor
58
59      /**
60       *   Time constructor
61       *   @param time A Time object with which to initialize
62       *   @throws Exception In the case of an invalid time
63       */
64      public Time( Time time ) throws Exception
65      {
66         // invoke Time constructor with three arguments
67         this( time.getHour(), time.getMinute(), time.getSecond() );
68      } // end Time constructor with Time argument
69
70      /**
71       *   Set a new time value using universal time. Perform
72       *   validity checks on the data. Set invalid values to zero.
73       *   @param h the hour
74       *   @param m the minute
75       *   @param s the second
76       *   @see com.deitel.jhtp6.appenH.Time#setHour
77       *   @see Time#setMinute
78       *   @see #setSecond
79       *   @throws Exception In the case of an invalid time
80       */
81      public void setTime( int h, int m, int s ) throws Exception
82      {
83         setHour( h );   // set the hour
84         setMinute( m ); // set the minute
85         setSecond( s ); // set the second
86      } // end method setTime
87
```

Fig. H.1 | Java source code file containing documentation comments. (Part 2 of 4.)

```
 88      /**
 89       *  Sets the hour.
 90       *  @param h the hour
 91       *  @throws Exception In the case of an invalid time
 92       */
 93      public void setHour( int h ) throws Exception
 94      {
 95         if ( h >= 0 && h < 24 )
 96            hour = h;
 97         else
 98            throw( new Exception() );
 99      } // end method setHour
100
101      /**
102       *  Sets the minute.
103       *  @param m the minute
104       *  @throws Exception In the case of an invalid time
105       */
106      public void setMinute( int m ) throws Exception
107      {
108         if ( m >= 0 && m < 60 )
109            minute = m;
110         else
111            throw( new Exception() );
112      } // end method setMinute
113
114      /**
115       *  Sets the second.
116       *  @param s the second.
117       *  @throws Exception In the case of an invalid time
118       */
119      public void setSecond( int s ) throws Exception
120      {
121         if ( s >= 0 && s < 60 )
122            second = s;
123         else
124            throw( new Exception() );
125      } // end method setSecond
126
127      /**
128       *  Gets the hour.
129       *  @return an <code>integer</code> specifying the hour.
130       */
131      public int getHour()
132      {
133         return hour;
134      } // end method getHour
135
136      /**
137       *  Gets the minute.
138       *  @return an <code>integer</code> specifying the minute.
139       */
```

Fig. H.1 | Java source code file containing documentation comments. (Part 3 of 4.)

```
140      public int getMinute()
141      {
142         return minute;
143      } // end method getMinute
144
145      /**
146       *  Gets the second.
147       *  @return an <code>integer</code> specifying the second.
148       */
149      public int getSecond()
150      {
151         return second;
152      } // end method getSecond
153
154      /**
155       *  Convert to String in universal-time format
156       *  @return a <code>String</code> representation
157       *  of the time in universal-time format
158       */
159      public String toUniversalString()
160      {
161         return String.format(
162            "%02d:%02d:%02d", getHour(), getMinute(), getSecond() );
163      } // end method toUniversalString
164
165      /**
166       *  Convert to String in standard-time format
167       *  @return a <code>String</code> representation
168       *  of the time in standard-time format
169       */
170      public String toStandardString()
171      {
172         return String.format( "%d:%02d:%02d %s",
173            ( ( getHour() == 0 || getHour() == 12 ) ? 12 : getHour() % 12 ),
174            getMinute(), getSecond(), ( getHour() < 12 ? "AM" : "PM" ) );
175      } // end method toStandardString
176   } // end class Time
```

Fig. H.1 | Java source code file containing documentation comments. (Part 4 of 4.)

specifies the author of the class. More than one @author tag can be used to document multiple authors. [*Note:* that the asterisks (*) on each line between /** and */ are not required. However, this is the recommended convention for aligning descriptions and javadoc tags. When parsing a documentation comment, javadoc discards all whitespace characters up to the first non-whitespace character in each line. If the first non-whitespace character encountered is an asterisk, it is also discarded.]

Note that this documentation comment immediately precedes the class declaration—any code placed between the documentation comment and the class declaration causes javadoc to ignore the documentation comment. This is also true of other code structures (e.g., constructors, methods, instance variables.).

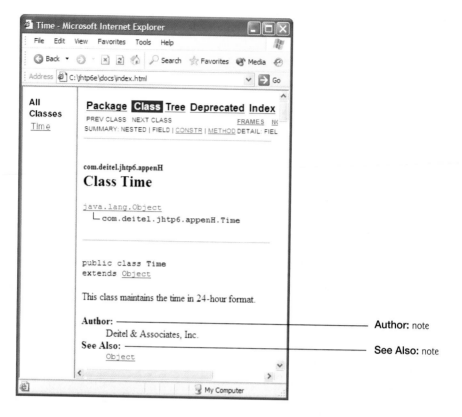

Fig. H.2 | **Author:** and **See Also:** notes generated by javadoc.

Common Programming Error H.1

Placing an import statement between the class comment and the class declaration is a logic error. This causes the class comment to be ignored by javadoc.

Software Engineering Observation H.1

Defining several fields in one comma-separated statement with a single comment above that statement will result in javadoc using that comment for all of the fields.

Software Engineering Observation H.2

To produce proper javadoc documentation, you must declare every instance variable on a separate line.

The documentation comment on lines 26–30 describes the Time constructor. Tag @param describes a parameter to the constructor. Parameters appear in the HTML document in a Parameters: note (Fig. H.3) that is followed by a list of all parameters specified with the @param tag. For this constructor, the parameter's name is h and its description is "the hour". Tag @param can be used only with methods and constructors.

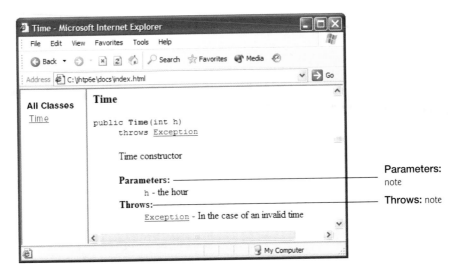

Fig. H.3 | **Parameters:** and **Throws:** note generated by `javadoc`.

The `@throws` tag specifies the exceptions thrown by this constructor. Like `@param` tags, `@throws` tags are only used with methods and constructors. One `@throws` should be supplied for each type of exception thrown by the method.

Documentation comments can contain multiple `@param` and `@see` tags. The documentation comment on lines 70–80 describes method `setTime`. The HTML generated for this method is shown in Fig. H.4. Three `@param` tags describe the method's parameters. This results in one **Parameters:** note which lists the three parameters. Methods `setHour`, `set-Minute` and `setSecond` are tagged with `@see` to create hyperlinks to their descriptions in the HTML document. A # character is used instead of a dot when tagging a method or a field. This creates a link to the field or method name that follows the # character. We demonstrate three different ways (i.e., the fully qualified name, the class name qualification and no qualification) to tag methods using `@see` on lines 76–78. Line 76 uses the fully qualified name to tag the `setHour` method. If the fully qualified name is not given (lines 77 and 78), `javadoc` looks for the specified method or field in the following order: current class, superclasses, package and imported files.

The only other tag used in this file is `@return`, which specifies a Returns: note in the HTML documentation (Fig. H.5). The comment on lines 127–130 documents method `getHour`. Tag `@return` describes a method's return type to help the programmer understand how to use the return value of the method. By `javadoc` convention, programmers typeset source code (i.e., keywords, identifiers and expressions) with the HTML tags `<code>` and `</code>`. Several other `javadoc` tags are briefly summarized in Fig. H.6.

Good Programming Practice H.1

Changing source code fonts in `javadoc` *tags helps code names stand out from the rest of the description.*

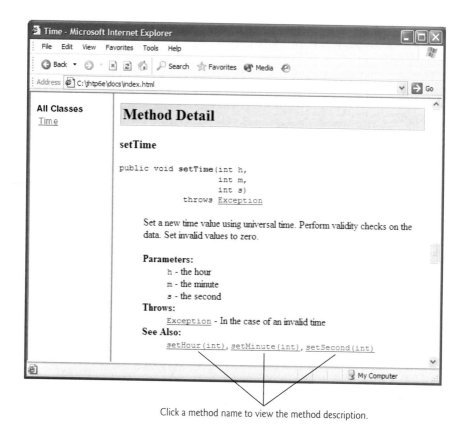

Click a method name to view the method description.

Fig. H.4 | HTML documentation for method setTime.

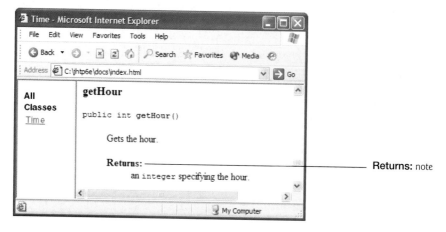

Fig. H.5 | HTML documentation for method getHour.

javadoc tag	Description
@deprecated	Adds a **Deprecated** note. These are notes to programmers indicating that they should not use the specified features of the class. **Deprecated** notes normally appear when a class has been enhanced with new and improved features, but older features are maintained for backwards compatibility.
{@link}	This allows the programmer to insert an explicit hyperlink to another HTML document.
@since	Adds a **Since:** note. These notes are used for new versions of a class to indicate when a feature was first introduced. For example, the Java API documentation uses this to indicate features that were introduced in Java 1.5.
@version	Adds a **Version** note. These notes help maintain version number of the software containing the class or method.

Fig. H.6 | Some common javadoc tags.

H.4 javadoc

In this section, we discuss how to execute the javadoc tool on a Java source file to create HTML documentation for the class in the file. Like other tools, javadoc is executed from the command line. The general form of the javadoc command is

javadoc *options packages sources @files*

where *options* is a list of command-line options, *packages* is a list of packages the user would like to document, *sources* is a list of java source files to document and *@files* is a list of text files containing the javadoc options, the names of packages and/or source files to send to the javadoc utility. [*Note:* All items are separated by spaces and *@files* is one word.] Figure H.7 shows a **Command Prompt** window containing the javadoc command we typed to generate the HTML documentation. For detailed information on the javadoc

Fig. H.7 | Using the javadoc tool.

command, visit the `javadoc` reference guide and examples at java.sun.com/j2se/5.0/ docs/tooldocs/windows/javadoc.html.

In Fig. H.7, the `-d` option specifies the directory (e.g., `C:\jhtp6\docs`) where the HTML files will be stored on disk. We use the `-link` option so that our documentation links to Sun's documentation (installed in the `C:\Program Files\java\jdk1.5.0\docs` directory). If the Sun documentation located in a different directory, specify that directory here; otherwise, you will receive an error from the `javadoc` tool. This creates a hyperlink between our documentation and Sun's documentation (see Fig. H.4, where Java class `Exception` from package `java.lang` is hyperlinked). Without the `-link` argument, `Exception` appears as text in the HTML document—not a hyperlink to the Java API documentation for class `Exception`. The `-author` option instructs `javadoc` to process the `@author` tag (it ignores this tag by default).

H.5 Files Produced by `javadoc`

In the last section, we executed the `javadoc` tool on the `Time.java` file. When `javadoc` executes, it displays the name of each HTML file it creates (see Fig. H.7). From the source file, `javadoc` created an HTML document for the class named `Time.html`. If the source file contains multiple classes or interfaces, a separate HTML document is created for each class. Because class `Time` belongs to a package, so the page will be created in the directory `C:\jhtp6\docs\com\deitel\jhtp3\appenH` (on Windows platforms). The `C:\jhtp6\docs` directory was specified with the `-d` command line option of `javadoc`, and the remaining directories were created based on the `package` statement.

Another file that `javadoc` creates is `index.html`. This is the starting HTML page in the documentation. To view the documentation you generate with `javadoc`, load `index.html` into your Web browser. In Fig. H.8, the right frame contains the page `index.html` and the left frame contains the page `allclasses-frame.html` which contains links to the source code's classes. [*Note:* Our example does not contain multiple packages, so there is no frame listing the packages. Normally this frame would appear above the left frame (containing "All Classes"), as in Fig. H.1]

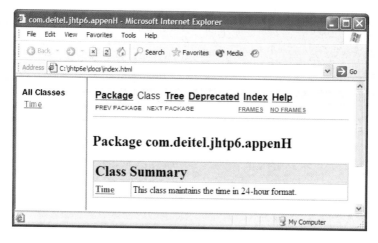

Fig. H.8 | Index page.

Figure H.9 shows class Time's index.html. Click **Time** in the left frame to load the Time class description. The navigation bar (at the top of the right frame) indicates which HTML page is currently loaded by highlighting the page's link (e.g., the **Class** link).

Clicking the **Tree** link (Fig. H.10) displays a class hierarchy for all the classes displayed in the left frame. In our example, we documented only class Time—which extends Object. Clicking the **Deprecated** link loads deprecated-list.html into the right frame. This page contains a list of all deprecated names. Because we did not use the @deprecated tag in this example, this page does not contain any information.

Fig. H.9 | **Class** page.

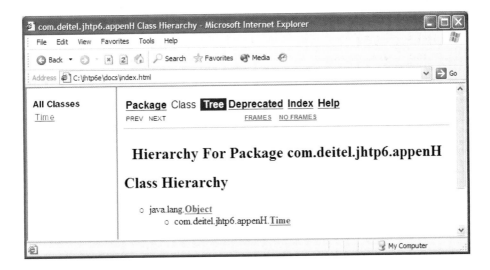

Fig. H.10 | **Tree** page.

Clicking the **Index** link loads the `index-all.html` page (Fig. H.11), which contains an alphabetical list of all classes, interfaces, methods and fields. Clicking the **Help** link loads `helpdoc.html` (Fig. H.12). This is a help file for navigating the documentation. A default help file is provided, but the programmer can specify other help files.

Among the other files generated by javadoc are `serialized-form.html` which documents `Serializable` and `Externalizable` classes and `package-list`, a text file rather than an HTML file, which lists package names and is not actually part of the documentation. The `package-list` file is used by the `-link` command-line argument to resolve the external cross references, i.e., allows other documentations to link to this documentation.

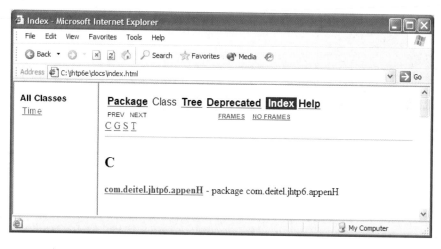

Fig. H.11 | Index page.

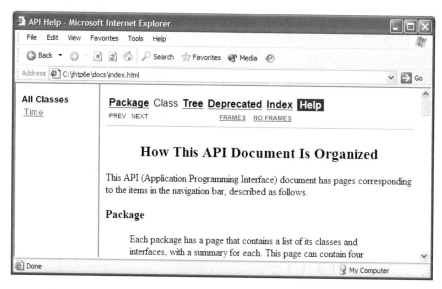

Fig. H.12 | Help page.

Labeled **break** and **continue** Statements

I.1 Introduction

In Chapter 5, we discussed Java's break and continue statements, which enable programmers to alter the flow of control in control statements. Java also provides the labeled break and continue statements for cases in which a programmer needs to conveniently alter the flow of control in nested control statements. This appendix demonstrates the labeled break and continue statements with examples using nested for statements.

I.2 Labeled **break** Statement

The break statement presented in Section 5.7 enables a program to break out of the while, for, do...while or switch in which the break statement appears. Sometimes these control statements are nested in other repetition statements. A program might need to exit the entire nested control statement in one operation, rather than wait for it to complete execution normally. To break out of such nested control statements, you can use the labeled break statement. This statement, when executed in a while, for, do...while or switch, causes immediate exit from that control statement and any number of enclosing statements. Program execution resumes with the first statement after the enclosing labeled statement. The statement that follows the label can be either a repetition statement or a block in which a repetition statement appears. Figure I.1 demonstrates the labeled break statement in a nested for statement.

The block (lines 7–26 in Fig. I.1) begins with a label (an identifier followed by a colon) at line 7; here we use the stop: label. The block is enclosed in braces (lines 8 and 26) and includes the nested for (lines 10–22) and the output statement at line 25. When the if at line 15 detects that row is equal to 5, the break statement at line 16 executes. This statement terminates both the for at lines 13–19 and its enclosing for at lines 10–22. Then the program proceeds immediately to the first statement after the labeled block—in this case, the end of main is reached and the program terminates. The outer for fully executes its body only four times. The output statement at line 25 never executes, because it is in the labeled block's body, and the outer for never completes.

```
 1   // Fig. K.1: BreakLabelTest.java
 2   // Labeled break statement exiting a nested for statement.
 3   public class BreakLabelTest
 4   {
 5      public static void main( String args[] )
 6      {
 7         stop: // labeled block
 8         {
 9            // count 10 rows
10            for ( int row = 1; row <= 10; row++ )
11            {
12               // count 5 columns
13               for ( int column = 1; column <= 5 ; column++ )
14               {
15                  if ( row == 5 ) // if row is 5,
16                     break stop;  // jump to end of stop block
17
18                  System.out.print( "* " );
19               } // end inner for
20
21               System.out.println(); // outputs a newline
22            } // end outer for
23
24            // following line is skipped
25            System.out.println( "\nLoops terminated normally" );
26         } // end labeled block
27      } // end main
28   } // end class BreakLabelTest
```

```
* * * * *
* * * * *
* * * * *
* * * * *
```

Fig. I.1 | Labeled **break** statement exiting a nested **for** statement.

Good Programming Practice I.1

Too many levels of nested control statements can make a program difficult to read. As a general rule, try to avoid using more than three levels of nesting.

I.3 Labeled continue Statement

The continue statement presented in Section 5.7 proceeds with the next iteration (repetition) of the immediately enclosing while, for or do…while. The labeled continue statement skips the remaining statements in that statement's body and any number of enclosing repetition statements and proceeds with the next iteration of the enclosing labeled repetition statement (i.e., a for, while or do…while preceded by a label). In labeled while and do…while statements, the program evaluates the loop-continuation test of the labeled loop immediately after the continue statement executes. In a labeled for, the increment expression is executed and the loop-continuation test is evaluated. Figure I.2 uses a labeled continue statement in a nested for to enable execution to continue with the next iteration of the outer for.

```
1    // Fig. K.2: ContinueLabelTest.java
2    // Labeled continue statement terminating a nested for statement.
3    public class ContinueLabelTest
4    {
5       public static void main( String args[] )
6       {
7          nextRow: // target label of continue statement
8
9             // count 5 rows
10            for ( int row = 1; row <= 5; row++ )
11            {
12               System.out.println(); // outputs a newline
13
14               // count 10 columns per row
15               for ( int column = 1; column <= 10; column++ )
16               {
17                  // if column greater than row, start next row
18                  if ( column > row )
19                     continue nextRow; // next iteration of labeled loop
20
21                  System.out.print( "* " );
22               } // end inner for
23            } // end outer for
24
25         System.out.println(); // outputs a newline
26      } // end main
27   } // end class ContinueLabelTest
```

```
*
* *
* * *
* * * *
* * * * *
```

Fig. I.2 | Labeled continue statement terminating a nested for statement.

The labeled for (lines 7–23) actually starts at the nextRow label. When the if at line 18 in the inner for (lines 15–22) detects that column is greater than row, the continue statement at line 19 executes, and program control continues with the increment of the control variable row of the outer for loop. Even though the inner for counts from 1 to 10, the number of * characters output on a row never exceeds the value of row, creating an interesting triangle pattern.

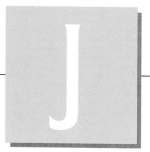

J

Using the Debugger

OBJECTIVES

In this appendix you will learn:

- To set breakpoints to debug applications.
- To use the **run** command to run an application through the debugger.
- To use the **stop** command to set a breakpoint.
- To use the **cont** command to continue execution.
- To use the **print** command to evaluate expressions.
- To use the **set** command to change variable values during program execution.
- To use the **step**, **step up** and **next** commands to control execution.
- To use the **watch** command to see how a field is modified during program execution.
- To use the **clear** command to list breakpoints or remove a breakpoint.

J.1 Introduction

In Chapter 2, you learned that there are two types of errors—syntax errors and logic errors—and you learned how to eliminate syntax errors from your code. Logic errors do not prevent the application from compiling successfully, but they do cause an application to produce erroneous results when it runs. The JDK 5.0 includes software called a debugger, which allows you to monitor the execution of your applications so you can locate and remove logic errors. The debugger will be one of your most important application development tools. Many IDEs provide their own debuggers similar to the one included in the JDK or provide a graphical user interface to the JDK's debugger.

This appendix demonstrates key features of the JDK's debugger using command-line applications that receive no input from the user. The same debugger features discussed here can be used to debug applications that take user input, but debugging such applications requires a slightly more complex setup. To focus on the debugger features, we have opted to demonstrate the debugger with simple command-line applications involving no user input. We provide instructions for debugging other types of applications at our Web site at `www.deitel.com/books/sjhtp6/index.html`. You can also find more information on the Java debugger at `java.sun.com/j2se/5.0/docs/tooldocs/windows/jdb.html`.

J.2 Breakpoints and the `run`, `stop`, `cont` and `print` Commands

We begin our study of the debugger by investigating breakpoints, which are markers that can be set at any executable line of code. When application execution reaches a breakpoint, execution pauses, allowing you to examine the values of variables to help determine whether logic errors exist. For example, you can examine the value of a variable that stores the result of a calculation to determine whether the calculation was performed correctly. Note that setting a breakpoint at a line of code that is not executable (such as a comment) causes the debugger to display an error message.

To illustrate the features of the debugger, we use application `AccountTest` (Fig. J.1), which creates and manipulates an object of class `Account` (Fig. 3.13). Execution of `AccountTest` begins in `main` (lines 7–24). Line 9 creates an `Account` object with an initial balance of $50.00. Recall that `Account`'s constructor accepts one argument, which specifies the `Account`'s initial `balance`. Lines 12–13 output the initial account balance using `Account` method `getBalance`. Line 15 declares and initializes a local variable `depositAmount`. Lines 17–19 then print `depositAmount` and add it to the `Account`'s `balance` using its credit method. Finally, lines 22–23 display the new balance. [*Note:* The examples directory for this appendix contains a copy of Account.java identical to that of Fig. 3.13.]

In the following steps, you will use breakpoints and various debugger commands to examine the value of the variable depositAmount declared in AccountTest (Fig. J.1).

1. *Opening the* Command Prompt *window and changing directories.* Open the Command Prompt window by selecting Start > Programs > Accessories > Command Prompt. Change to the directory containing the appendix's examples by typing cd C:\examples\debugger [*Note:* If your examples are in a different directory, use that directory here.]

2. *Compiling the application for debugging.* The Java debugger works only with .class files that were compiled with the -g compiler option, which generates information that is used by the debugger to help you debug your applications. Compile the application with the -g command-line option by typing javac -g AccountTest.java Account.java. Recall from Chapter 2 that this command compiles both AccountTest.java and Account.java. The command java -g *.java compiles all of the working directory's .java files for debugging.

```java
1   // Fig. J.1: AccountTest.java
2   // Create and manipulate an Account object.
3
4   public class AccountTest
5   {
6      // main method begins execution
7      public static void main( String args[] )
8      {
9         Account account = new Account( 50.00 ); // create Account object
10
11         // display initial balance of Account object
12         System.out.printf( "initial account balance: $%.2f\n",
13            account.getBalance() );
14
15         double depositAmount = 25.0; // deposit amount
16
17         System.out.printf( "\nadding %.2f to account balance\n\n",
18            depositAmount );
19         account.credit( depositAmount ); // add to account balance
20
21         // display new balance
22         System.out.printf( "new account balance: $%.2f\n",
23            account.getBalance() );
24      } // end main
25
26   } // end class AccountTest
```

```
initial account balance: $50.00

adding 25.00 to account balance

new account balance: $75.00
```

Fig. J.1 | AccountTest class creates and manipulates an Account object.

3. *Starting the debugger.* In the **Command Prompt**, type `jdb` (Fig. J.2). This command will start the Java debugger and enable you to use the debugger's features. [*Note:* We modified the colors of our **Command Prompt** window to allow us to highlight in yellow the user input required by each step.]

4. *Running an application in the debugger.* Run the `AccountTest` application through the debugger by typing `run AccountTest` (Fig. J.3). If you do not set any breakpoints before running your application in the debugger, the application will run just as it would using the `java` command.

5. *Restarting the debugger.* To make proper use of the debugger, you must set at least one breakpoint before running the application. Restart the debugger by typing `jdb`.

6. *Inserting breakpoints in Java.* You set a breakpoint at a specific line of code in your application. The line numbers used in these steps are from the source code in Fig. J.1. Set a breakpoint at line 12 in the source code by typing `stop at AccountTest:12` (Fig. J.4). The `stop command` inserts a breakpoint at the line number specified after the command. You can set as many breakpoints as necessary. Set another breakpoint at line 19 by typing `stop at AccountTest:19` (Fig. J.4). When the application runs, it suspends execution at any line that contains a breakpoint. The application is said to be in break mode when the debugger pauses the application's execution. Breakpoints can be set even after the debugging process has begun. Note that the debugger command `stop in`, followed by a class name, a period and a method name (e.g., `stop in Account.credit`) instructs the debugger to set a breakpoint at the first executable statement in the specified method. The debugger pauses execution when program control enters the method.

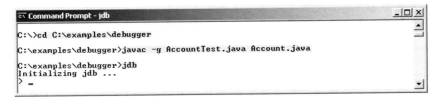

```
Command Prompt - jdb                                        _ |□| x|
C:\>cd C:\examples\debugger

C:\examples\debugger>javac -g AccountTest.java Account.java

C:\examples\debugger>jdb
Initializing jdb ...
> _
```

Fig. J.2 | Starting the Java debugger.

```
Command Prompt                                              _ |□| x|
C:\examples\debugger>jdb
Initializing jdb ...
> run AccountTest
run   AccountTest
Set uncaught java.lang.Throwable
Set deferred uncaught java.lang.Throwable
>
VM Started: initial account balance: $50.00

adding 25.00 to account balance

new account balance: $75.00

The application exited
```

Fig. J.3 | Running the `AccountTest` application through the debugger.

Fig. J.4 | Setting breakpoints at lines 12 and 19.

7. *Running the application and beginning the debugging process.* Type run AccountTest to execute your application and begin the debugging process (Fig. J.5). Note that the debugger prints text indicating that breakpoints were set at lines 12 and 19. The debugger calls each breakpoint a "deferred breakpoint" because each was set before the application began running in the debugger. The application pauses when execution reaches the breakpoint on line 12. At this point, the debugger notifies you that a breakpoint has been reached and it displays the source code at that line (12). That line of code is the next statement that will execute.

8. *Using the **cont** command to resume execution.* Type cont. The cont command causes the application to continue running until the next breakpoint is reached (line 19) at which point the debugger notifies you (Fig. J.6). Note that Account-Test's normal output appears between messages from the debugger.

9. *Examining a variable's value.* Type print depositAmount to display the current value stored in the depositAmount variable (Fig. J.7). The print command allows you to peek inside the computer at the value of one of your variables. This command will help you find and eliminate logic errors in your code. Notice that the value displayed is 25.0—the value assigned to depositAmount in line 15 of Fig. J.1.

10. *Continuing application execution.* Type cont to continue the application's execution. There are no more breakpoints, so the application is no longer in break mode. The application continues executing and eventually terminates (Fig. J.8). The debugger will stop when the application ends.

Breakpoint is reached

Next line of code to execute

Fig. J.5 | Restarting the AccountTest application.

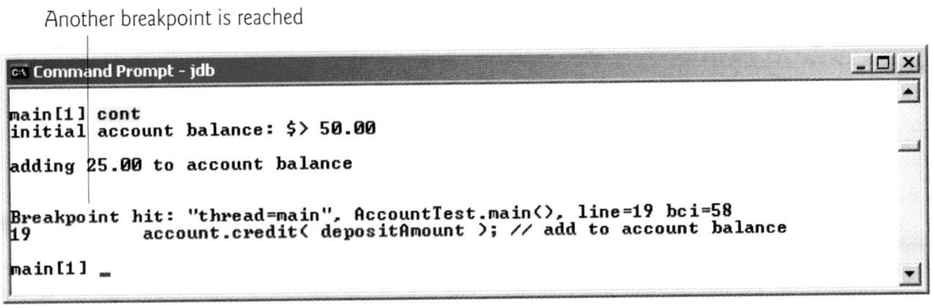

Another breakpoint is reached

```
Command Prompt - jdb                                                _ □ X
main[1] cont
initial account balance: $> 50.00

adding 25.00 to account balance

Breakpoint hit: "thread=main", AccountTest.main(), line=19 bci=58
19            account.credit( depositAmount ); // add to account balance

main[1] _
```

Fig. J.6 | Execution reaches the second breakpoint.

```
Command Prompt - jdb                                                _ □ X
main[1] print depositAmount
 depositAmount = 25.0
main[1] _
```

Fig. J.7 | Examining the value of variable deposit Amount.

```
Command Prompt                                                      _ □ X
 depositAmount = 25.0
main[1] cont
new account balance: $75.00
>
The application exited

C:\examples\debugger>_
```

Fig. J.8 | Continuing application execution and exiting the debugger.

In this section, you learned how to enable the debugger and set breakpoints so that you can examine variables with the print command while an application is running. You also learned how to use the cont command to continue execution after a breakpoint is reached.

J.3 The print and set Commands

In the preceding section, you learned how to use the debugger's print command to examine the value of a variable during program execution. In this section, you will learn how to use the print command to examine the value of more complex expressions. You will also learn the set command, which allows the programmer to assign new values to variables.

For this section, we assume that you have followed *Step 1* and *Step 2* in Section J.2 to open the **Command Prompt** window, change to the directory containing this appendix's examples (e.g., C:\examples\debugger) and compiled the AccountTest application (and class Account) for debugging.

1. *Starting debugging.* In the **Command Prompt**, type jdb to start the Java debugger.

2. *Inserting a breakpoint.* Set a breakpoint at line 19 in the source code by typing stop at AccountTest:19.

3. *Running the application and reaching a breakpoint.* Type run AccountTest to begin the debugging process (Fig. J.9). This will cause AccountTest's main to execute until the breakpoint at line 19 is reached. This suspends application execution and switches the application into break mode. At this point, the statements in lines 9–13 created an Account object and printed the initial balance of the Ac-

count obtained by calling its getBalance method. The statement in line 15 (Fig. J.1) declared and initialized local variable depositAmount to 25.0. The statement in line 19 is the next statement that will execute.

4. *Evaluating arithmetic and boolean expressions.* Recall from Section J.2 that once the application has entered break mode, you can explore the values of the application's variables using the debugger's print command. You can also use the print command to evaluate arithmetic and boolean expressions. In the **Command Prompt** window, type print depositAmount - 2.0. Notice that the print command returns the value 23.0 (Fig. J.10). However, this command does not actually change the value of depositAmount. In the **Command Prompt** window, type print depositAmount == 23.0. Expressions containing the == symbol are treated as boolean expressions. The value returned is false (Fig. J.10), because depositAmount does not currently contain the value 23.0—depositAmount is still 25.0.

5. *Modifying values.* The debugger allows you to change the values of variables during the application's execution. This can be valuable for experimenting with different values and for locating logic errors in applications. You can use the debugger's set command to change the value of a variable. Type set depositAmount = 75.0. The debugger changes the value of depositAmount and displays its new value (Fig. J.11).

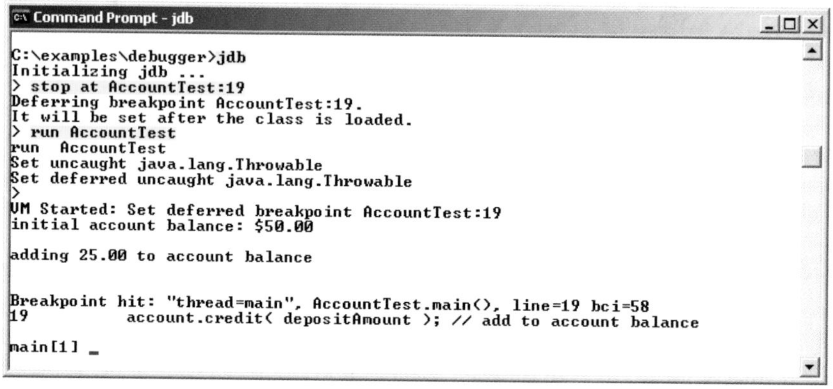

Fig. J.9 | Application execution suspended when debugger reaches the breakpoint at line 19.

Fig. J.10 | Examining the values of an arithmetic and boolean expression.

Fig. J.11 | Modifying values.

6. *Viewing the application result.* Type cont to continue application execution. Line 19 of AccountTest (Fig. J.1) executes, passing depositAmount to Account method credit. Method main then displays the new balance. Notice that the result is $125.00 (Fig. J.12). This shows that the previous step changed the value of depositAmount from its initial value (25.0) to 75.0.

In this section, you learned how to use the debugger's print command to evaluate arithmetic and boolean expressions. You also learned how to use the set command to modify the value of a variable during your application's execution.

J.4 Controlling Execution Using the step, step up and next Commands

Sometimes you will need to execute an application line by line to find and fix errors. Walking through a portion of your application this way can help you verify that a method's code executes correctly. In this section, you will learn how to use the debugger for this task. The commands you learn in this section allow you to execute a method line by line, execute all the statements of a method at once or execute only the remaining statements of a method (if you have already executed some statements within the method).

Once again, we assume you are working in the directory containing this appendix's examples and have compiled for debugging with the -g compiler option.

1. *Starting the debugger.* Start the debugger by typing jdb.

2. *Setting a breakpoint.* Type stop at AccountTest:19 to set a breakpoint at line 19.

3. *Running the application.* Run the application by typing run AccountTest. After the application displays its two output messages, the debugger indicates that the breakpoint has been reached and displays the code at line 19 (Fig. J.13). The debugger and application then pause and wait for the next command to be entered.

4. *Using the **step** command.* The step command executes the next statement in the application. If the next statement to execute is a method call, control transfers to the called method. The step command enables you to enter a method and study the individual statements of that method. For instance, you can use the print and set commands to view and modify the variables within the method. You will now use the step command to enter the credit method of class Account (Fig. 3.13) by typing step (Fig. J.14). The debugger indicates that the step has been completed and displays the next executable statement—in this case, line 21 of class Account (Fig. 3.13).

New account balance based on altered
value of variable depositAmount

Fig. J.12 | Output displayed after the debugging process.

```
C\ Command Prompt - jdb                                                    _ |□| x|
C:\examples\debugger>jdb
Initializing jdb ...
> stop at AccountTest:19
Deferring breakpoint AccountTest:19.
It will be set after the class is loaded.
> run AccountTest
run  AccountTest
Set uncaught java.lang.Throwable
Set deferred uncaught java.lang.Throwable
>
VM Started: Set deferred breakpoint AccountTest:19
initial account balance: $50.00

adding 25.00 to account balance


Breakpoint hit: "thread=main", AccountTest.main(), line=19 bci=58
19            account.credit( depositAmount ); // add to account balance

main[1] _
```

Fig. J.13 | Reaching the breakpoint in the AccountTest application.

```
C\ Command Prompt - jdb                                                    _ |□| x|
main[1] step
>
Step completed: "thread=main", Account.credit(), line=21 bci=0
21            balance = balance + amount; // add amount to balance

main[1] _
```

Fig. J.14 | Stepping into the credit method.

5. *Using the **step up** command.* After you have stepped into the credit method, type **step up**. This command executes the remaining statements in the method and returns control to the place where the method was called. The credit method contains only one statement to add the method's parameter amount to instance variable balance. The step up command executes this statement, then pauses before line 22 in AccountTest. Thus, the next action to occur will be to print the new account balance (Fig. J.15). In lengthy methods, you may want to look at a few key lines of code then continue debugging the caller's code. The step up command is useful for situations in which you do not want to continue stepping through the entire method line by line.

6. *Using the **cont** command to continue execution.* Enter the cont command (Fig. J.16) to continue execution. The statement at lines 22–23 executes, displaying the new balance, then the application and the debugger terminate.

7. *Restarting the debugger.* Restart the debugger by typing jdb.

8. *Setting a breakpoint.* Breakpoints persist only until the end of the debugging session in which they are set—once the debugger exits, all breakpoints are removed.

```
C\ Command Prompt - jdb                                                    _ |□| x|
main[1] step up
>
Step completed: "thread=main", AccountTest.main(), line=22 bci=63
22            System.out.printf( "new account balance: $%.2f\n",

main[1] _
```

Fig. J.15 | Stepping out of a method.

(In Section J.6, you'll learn how to manually clear a breakpoint before the end of the debugging session.) Thus, the breakpoint set for line 19 in *Step 2* no longer exists upon restarting the debugger in *Step 7*. To reset the breakpoint at line 19, once again type stop at AccountTest:19.

9. *Running the application.* Type run AccountTest to run the application. As in *Step 3*, AccountTest runs until the breakpoint at line 19 is reached, then the debugger pauses and waits for the next command (Fig. J.17).

10. *Using the* **next** *command.* Type next. This command behaves like the step command, except when the next statement to execute contains a method call. In that case, the called method executes in its entirety and the application advances to the next executable line after the method call (Fig. J.18). Recall from *Step 4* that the step command would enter the called method. In this example, the next command causes Account method credit to execute, then the debugger pauses at line 22 in AccountTest.

```
Command Prompt
main[1] cont
new account balance: $75.00
>
The application exited

C:\examples\debugger>_
```

Fig. J.16 / Continuing execution of the AccountTest application.

```
Command Prompt - jdb
C:\examples\debugger>jdb
Initializing jdb ...
> stop at AccountTest:19
Deferring breakpoint AccountTest:19.
It will be set after the class is loaded.
> run AccountTest
run  AccountTest
Set uncaught java.lang.Throwable
Set deferred uncaught java.lang.Throwable
>
VM Started: Set deferred breakpoint AccountTest:19
initial account balance: $50.00

adding 25.00 to account balance


Breakpoint hit: "thread=main", AccountTest.main(), line=19 bci=58
19            account.credit( depositAmount ); // add to account balance

main[1] _
```

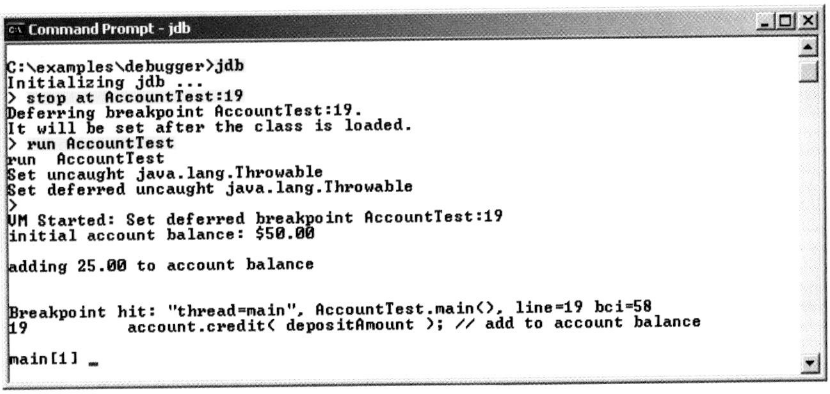

Fig. J.17 | Reaching the breakpoint in the AccountTest application.

```
Command Prompt - jdb
main[1] next
>
Step completed: "thread=main", AccountTest.main(), line=22 bci=63
22            System.out.printf( "new account balance: $%.2f\n",

main[1] _
```

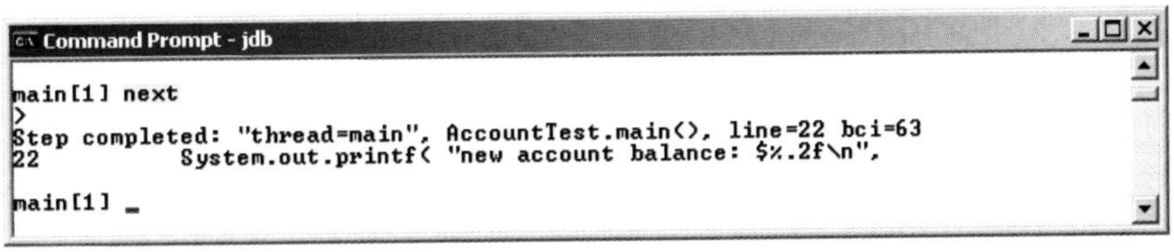

Fig. J.18 / Stepping over a method call.

11. *Using the* **exit** *command.* Use the exit command to end the debugging session (Fig. J.19). This command causes the AccountTest application to immediately terminate rather than execute the remaining statements in main. Note that when debugging some types of applications (e.g., GUI applications), the application continues to execute even after the debugging session ends.

In this section, you learned how to use the debugger's step and step up commands to debug methods called during your application's execution. You also saw how the next command can be used to step over a method call. You also learned that the exit command ends a debugging session.

J.5 The watch Command

In this section, we present the watch command, which tells the debugger to watch a field. When that field is about to change, the debugger will notify you. In this section, you will learn how to use the watch command to see how the Account object's field balance is modified during the execution of the AccountTest application.

As in the preceding two sections, we assume you have followed *Step 1* and *Step 2* in Section J.2 to open the **Command Prompt**, change to the correct examples directory and compile classes AccountTest and Account for debugging (i.e., with the -g compiler option).

1. *Starting the debugger.* Start the debugger by typing jdb.

2. *Watching a class's field.* Set a watch on Account's balance field by typing watch Account.balance (Fig. J.20). You can set a watch on any field during execution of the debugger. Whenever the value in a field is about to change, the debugger enters break mode and notifies you that the value will change. Watches can be placed only on fields, not on local variables.

3. *Running the application.* Run the application with the command run Account-Test. The debugger will now notify you that field balance's value will change (Fig. J.21). When the application begins, an instance of Account is created with an initial balance of $50.00 and a reference to the Account object is assigned to the local variable account (line 9, Fig. J.1). Recall from Fig. 3.13 that when the

Fig. J.19 / Exiting the debugger.

```
Command Prompt - jdb                                    _ □ ×
C:\examples\debugger>jdb
Initializing jdb ...
> watch Account.balance
Deferring watch modification of Account.balance.
It will be set after the class is loaded.
> _
```

Fig. J.20 | Setting a watch on Account's balance field.

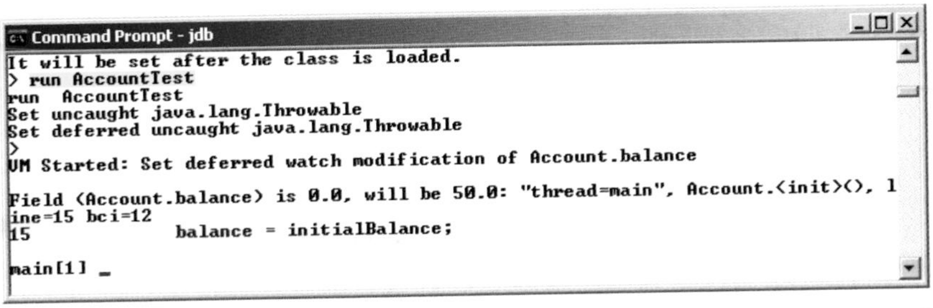

```
Command Prompt - jdb                                        _ | □ | x |
It will be set after the class is loaded.
> run AccountTest
run  AccountTest
Set uncaught java.lang.Throwable
Set deferred uncaught java.lang.Throwable
>
UM Started: Set deferred watch modification of Account.balance

Field (Account.balance) is 0.0, will be 50.0: "thread=main", Account.<init>(), l
ine=15 bci=12
15               balance = initialBalance;

main[1] _
```

Fig. J.21 | AccountTest application stops when account is created and its balance field will be modified.

constructor for this object runs, if parameter initialBalance is greater than 0.0, instance variable balance is assigned the value of parameter initialBalance. The debugger notifies you that the value of balance will be set to 50.0.

4. *Adding money to the account.* Type cont to continue executing the application. The application executes normally, before reaching the code on line 19 of Fig. J.1 that calls Account method credit to raise the Account object's balance by a specified amount. The debugger notifies you that instance variable balance will change (Fig. J.22). Note that although line 19 of class AccountTest calls method credit, it is line 21 in Account's method credit which actually changes the value of balance.

5. *Continuing execution.* Type cont—the application will finish executing because the application does not attempt any additional changes to balance (Fig. J.23).

6. *Restarting the debugger and resetting the watch on the variable.* Type jdb to restart the debugger. Once again, set a watch on Account instance variable balance by typing the watch Account.balance, then type run AccountTest to run the application (Fig. J.24).

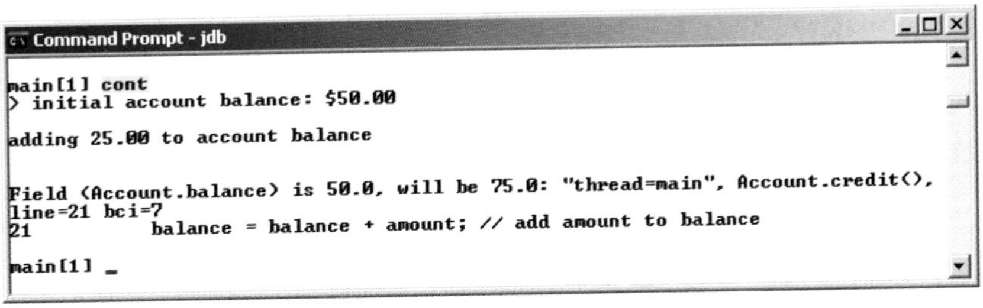

```
Command Prompt - jdb                                        _ | □ | x |
main[1] cont
> initial account balance: $50.00

adding 25.00 to account balance

Field (Account.balance) is 50.0, will be 75.0: "thread=main", Account.credit(),
line=21 bci=7
21               balance = balance + amount; // add amount to balance

main[1] _
```

Fig. J.22 | Changing the value of balance by calling Account method credit.

```
Command Prompt                                              _ | □ | x |
main[1] cont
new account balance: $75.00
>
The application exited

C:\examples\debugger>_
```

Fig. J.23 | Continuing execution of AccountTest.

Fig. J.24 | Restarting the debugger and resetting the watch on the variable `balance`.

7. ***Removing the watch on the field.*** Suppose you want to watch a field for only part of a program's execution. You can remove the debugger's watch on variable `balance` by typing `unwatch` `Account.balance` (Fig. J.25). Type `cont`—the application will finish executing without re-entering break mode.

8. ***Closing the*** **Command Prompt** ***window.*** Close the **Command Prompt** window by clicking its close button.

In this section, you learned how to use the `watch` command to enable the debugger to notify you of changes to the value of a field throughout the life of an application. You also learned how to use the `unwatch` command to remove a watch on a field before the end of the application.

J.6 The `clear` Command

In the preceding section, you learned to use the `unwatch` command to remove a watch on a field. The debugger also provides the `clear` command to remove a breakpoint from an application. You will often need to debug applications containing repetitive actions, such as a loop. You may want to examine the values of variables during several, but possibly not all, of the loop's iterations. If you set a breakpoint in the body of a loop, the debugger will pause before each execution of the line containing a breakpoint. After determining that the loop is working properly, you may want to remove the breakpoint and allow the remaining iterations to proceed normally. In this section, we use the compound interest application of Fig. 5.6 to demonstrate how the debugger behaves when you set a breakpoint in the body of a `for` statement and how to remove a breakpoint in the middle of a debugging session.

Fig. J.25 | Removing the watch on variable `balance`.

1. *Opening the* Command Prompt *window, changing directories and compiling the application for debugging.* Open the Command Prompt window, then change to the directory containing this appendix's examples. For your convenience, we have provided a copy of the `Interest.java` file in this directory. Compile the application for debugging by typing `javac -g Interest.java`.
2. *Starting the debugger and setting breakpoints.* Start the debugger by typing `jdb`. Set breakpoints at lines 13 and 22 of class `Interest` by typing `stop at Interest:13`, then `stop at Interest:22` (Fig. J.26).
3. *Running the application.* Run the application by typing `run Interest`. The application executes until reaching the breakpoint at line 13 (Fig. J.27).
4. *Continuing execution.* Type `cont` to continue—the application executes line 13, printing the column headings `"Year"` and `"Amount on deposit"`. Note that line 13 appears before the `for` statement at lines 16–23 in `Interest` (Fig. 5.6) and thus executes only once. Execution continues past line 13 until the breakpoint at line 22 is reached during the first iteration of the `for` statement (Fig. J.28).
5. *Examining variable values.* Type `print year` to examine the current value of variable `year` (i.e., the `for`'s control variable). Print the value of variable `amount`, also (Fig. J.29).
6. *Continuing execution.* Type `cont` to continue execution. Line 22 executes and prints the current values of `year` and `amount`. After the `for` enters its second iteration, the debugger notifies you that the breakpoint at line 22 was reached a second time. Note that the debugger pauses each time a line where a breakpoint has been set is about to execute—when the breakpoint appears in a loop, the debugger pauses during each iteration. Print the values of variables `year` and `amount` again to see how the values changed since the first iteration of the `for` (Fig. J.30).

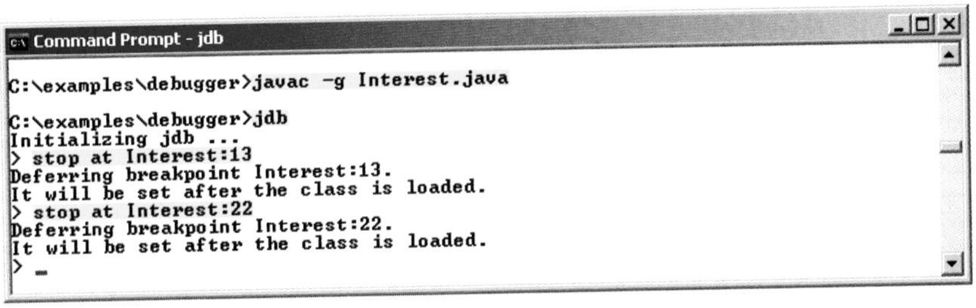

```
Command Prompt - jdb
C:\examples\debugger>javac -g Interest.java

C:\examples\debugger>jdb
Initializing jdb ...
> stop at Interest:13
Deferring breakpoint Interest:13.
It will be set after the class is loaded.
> stop at Interest:22
Deferring breakpoint Interest:22.
It will be set after the class is loaded.
> _
```

Fig. J.26 | Setting breakpoints in the `Interest` application.

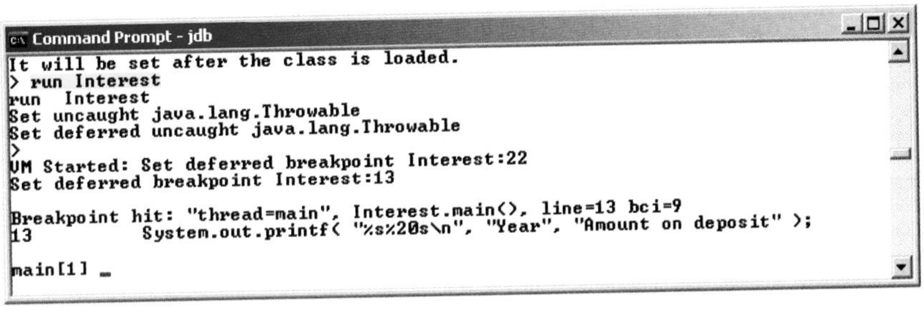

```
Command Prompt - jdb
It will be set after the class is loaded.
> run Interest
run  Interest
Set uncaught java.lang.Throwable
Set deferred uncaught java.lang.Throwable
>
VM Started: Set deferred breakpoint Interest:22
Set deferred breakpoint Interest:13

Breakpoint hit: "thread=main", Interest.main(), line=13 bci=9
13            System.out.printf( "%s%20s\n", "Year", "Amount on deposit" );

main[1] _
```

Fig. J.27 | Reaching the breakpoint at line 13 in the `Interest` application.

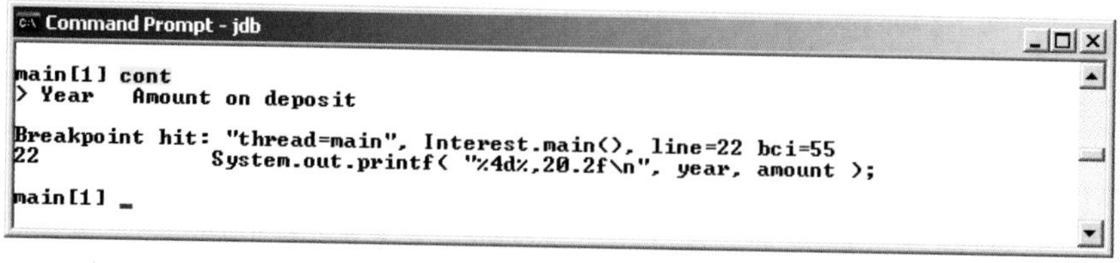

Fig. J.28 | Reaching the breakpoint at line 22 in the Interest application.

Fig. J.29 | Printing year and amount during the first iteration of Interest's for.

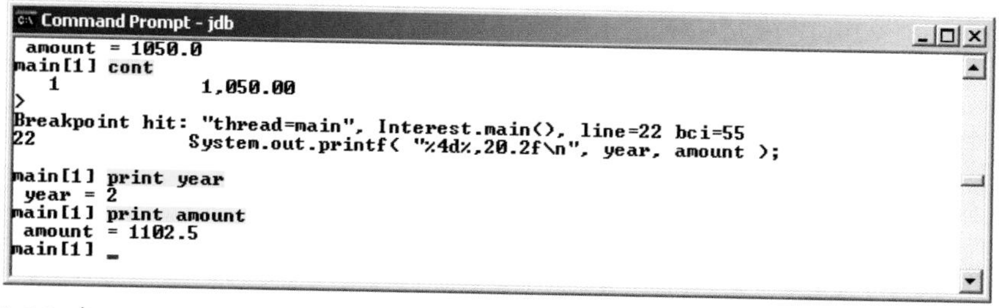

Fig. J.30 | Printing year and amount during the second iteration of Interest's for.

7. *Removing a breakpoint.* You can display a list of all the breakpoints in the application by typing clear (Fig. J.31). Suppose you are satisfied that the Interest application's for statement is working properly, so you want to remove the breakpoint at line 22 and allow the remaining iterations of the loop to proceed normally. You can remove the breakpoint at line 22 by typing clear Interest:22. Now type clear to list the remaining breakpoints in the application. The debugger should indicate that only the breakpoint at line 13 remains (Fig. J.31). Note that this breakpoint has already been reached and thus will no longer affect execution.

8. *Continuing execution after removing a breakpoint.* Type cont to continue execution. Recall that execution last paused before the printf statement in line 22. If the breakpoint at line 22 was removed successfully, continuing the application will produce the correct output for the current and remaining iterations of the for statement without the application halting (Fig. J.32).

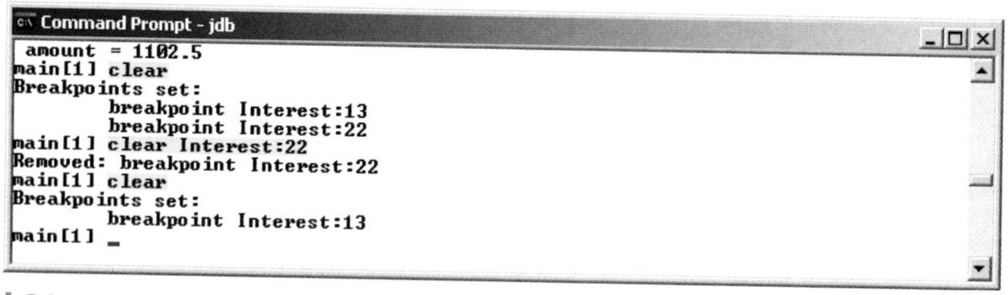

Fig. J.31 | Removing the breakpoint at line 22.

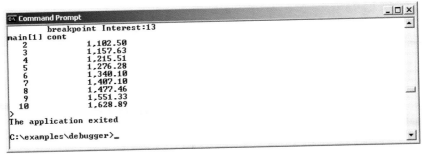

Application executes without a breakpoint at line 22 set.

In this section, you learned how to use the `clear` command to list all the breakpoints set for an application and remove a breakpoint.

J.7 Wrap-Up

In this appendix, you learned how to insert and remove breakpoints in the debugger. Breakpoints allow you to pause application execution so you can examine variable values with the debugger's `print` command. This capability will help you locate and fix logic errors in your applications. You saw how to use the `print` command to examine the value of an expression and how to use the `set` command to change the value of a variable. You also learned debugger commands (including the `step`, `step up` and `next` commands) that you can use to determine whether a method is executing correctly. You learned how to use the `watch` command to keep track of a field throughout the life of an application. Finally, you learned how to use the `clear` command to list all the breakpoints set for an application or remove individual breakpoints to continue execution without breakpoints.

Summary

- The debugger allows you to monitor the execution of an application so you can locate and remove logic errors.
- The -g compiler option compiles a class for debugging.
- The `jdb` command starts the debugger.
- The `run` command, followed by the class name of an application, runs that application through the debugger.
- The `stop` command, followed by the class name, a colon and a line number, sets a breakpoint at the specified line number.
- The `cont` command resumes execution after entering break mode.
- The `print` command, followed by the name of a variable, examines the contents of the specified variable.
- The `print` command can be used to examine an expression's value during the execution of an application.
- The `set` command modifies the value of a variable during the execution of an application.
- The `step` command executes the next statement in the application. If the next statement to execute is a method call, control is transferred to the called method.
- The `step up` command executes the statements in a method and returns control to the place where the method was called.

- The next command executes the next statement in the application. If the next statement to execute is a method call, the called method executes in its entirety (without transferring control and entering the method) and the application advances to the next executable line after the method call.
- The watch command tells the debugger to notify you if the specified field is modified.
- The unwatch command removes a watch on a field.
- The clear command, executed by itself, lists the breakpoints set for an application.
- The clear command, followed by a class name, a colon and a line number removes the specified breakpoint.

Terminology

break mode	print command
breakpoint	run command
clear command	set command
cont command	step command
debugger	step up command
exit command	stop command
-g compiler option	unwatch command
jdb command	watch command
next command	

Self-Review Exercises

J.1 Fill in the blanks in each of the following statements:
a) A breakpoint cannot be set at a(n) _____.
b) You can examine the value of an expression by using the debugger's _____ command.
c) You can modify the value of a variable by using the debugger's _____ command.
d) During debugging, the _____ command executes the remaining statements in the current method and returns program control to the place where the method was called.
e) The debugger's _____ command behaves like the step command when the next statement to execute does not contain a method call.
f) The watch debugger command allows you to view all changes to a(n) _____.

J.2 State whether each of the following is *true* or *false*. If *false*, explain why.
a) When application execution suspends at a breakpoint, the next statement to be executed is the statement after the breakpoint.
b) Watches can be removed using the debugger's clear command.
c) The -g compiler option must be used when compiling classes for debugging.
d) When a breakpoint appears in a loop, the debugger pauses only the first time that the breakpoint is encountered.

Answers to Self-Review Exercises

J.1 a) comment. b) print. c) set. d) step up. e) next. f) field.

J.2 a) False. When application execution suspends at a breakpoint, the next statement to be executed is the statement at the breakpoint. b) False. Watches can be removed using the debugger's unwatch command. c) True. d) False. When a breakpoint appears in a loop, the debugger pauses during each iteration.

Index

End User License Agreements

Prentice Hall License Agreement and Limited Warranty

READ THE FOLLOWING TERMS AND CONDITIONS CAREFULLY BEFORE OPENING THIS SOFTWARE PACKAGE. THIS LEGAL DOCUMENT IS AN AGREEMENT BETWEEN YOU AND PRENTICE-HALL, INC. (THE "COMPANY"). BY OPENING THIS SEALED SOFTWARE PACKAGE, YOU ARE AGREEING TO BE BOUND BY THESE TERMS AND CONDITIONS. IF YOU DO NOT AGREE WITH THESE TERMS AND CONDITIONS, DO NOT OPEN THE SOFTWARE PACKAGE. PROMPTLY RETURN THE UNOPENED SOFTWARE PACKAGE AND ALL ACCOMPANYING ITEMS TO THE PLACE YOU OBTAINED THEM FOR A FULL REFUND OF ANY SUMS YOU HAVE PAID.

1.GRANT OF LICENSE: In consideration of your purchase of this book, and your agreement to abide by the terms and conditions of this Agreement, the Company grants to you a nonexclusive right to use and display the copy of the enclosed software program (hereinafter the "SOFTWARE") on a single computer (i.e., with a single CPU) at a single location so long as you comply with the terms of this Agreement. The Company reserves all rights not expressly granted to you under this Agreement.

2.OWNERSHIP OF SOFTWARE: You own only the magnetic or physical media (the enclosed media) on which the SOFTWARE is recorded or fixed, but the Company and the software developers retain all the rights, title, and ownership to the SOFTWARE recorded on the original media copy(ies) and all subsequent copies of the SOFTWARE, regardless of the form or media on which the original or other copies may exist. This license is not a sale of the original SOFTWARE or any copy to you.

3.COPY RESTRICTIONS: This SOFTWARE and the accompanying printed materials and user manual (the "Documentation") are the subject of copyright. The individual programs on the media are copyrighted by the authors of each program. Some of the programs on the media include separate licensing agreements. If you intend to use one of these programs, you must read and follow its accompanying license agreement. You may not copy the Documentation or the SOFTWARE, except that you may make a single copy of the SOFTWARE for backup or archival purposes only. You may be held legally responsible for any copying or copyright infringement which is caused or encouraged by your failure to abide by the terms of this restriction.

4.USE RESTRICTIONS: You may not network the SOFTWARE or otherwise use it on more than one computer or computer terminal at the same time. You may physically transfer the SOFTWARE from one computer to another provided that the SOFTWARE is used on only one computer at a time. You may not distribute copies of the SOFTWARE or Documentation to others. You may not reverse engineer, disassemble, decompile, modify, adapt, translate, or create derivative works based on the SOFTWARE or the Documentation without the prior written consent of the Company.

5. TRANSFER RESTRICTIONS: The enclosed SOFTWARE is licensed only to you and may not be transferred to any one else without the prior written consent of the Company. Any unauthorized transfer of the SOFTWARE shall result in the immediate termination of this Agreement.

6. TERMINATION: This license is effective until terminated. This license will terminate automatically without notice from the Company and become null and void if you fail to comply with any provisions or limitations of this license. Upon termination, you shall destroy the Documentation and all copies of the SOFTWARE. All provisions of this Agreement as to warranties, limitation of liability, remedies or damages, and our ownership rights shall survive termination.

7. MISCELLANEOUS: This Agreement shall be construed in accordance with the laws of the United States of America and the State of New York and shall benefit the Company, its affiliates, and assignees.

8.LIMITED WARRANTY AND DISCLAIMER OF WARRANTY: The Company warrants that the SOFTWARE, when properly used in accordance with the Documentation, will operate in substantial conformity with the description of the SOFTWARE set forth in the Documentation. The Company does not warrant that the SOFTWARE will meet your requirements or that the operation of the SOFTWARE will be uninterrupted or error-free. The Company warrants that the media on which the SOFTWARE is delivered shall be free from defects in materials and workmanship under normal use for a period of thirty (30) days from the date of your purchase. Your only remedy and the Company's only obligation under these limited warranties is, at the Company's option, return of the warranted item for a refund of any amounts paid by you or replacement of the item. Any replacement of SOFTWARE or media under the warranties shall not extend the original warranty period. The limited warranty set forth above shall not apply to any SOFTWARE which the Company determines in good faith has been subject to misuse, neglect, improper installation, repair, alteration, or damage by you. EXCEPT FOR THE EXPRESSED WARRANTIES SET FORTH ABOVE, THE COMPANY DISCLAIMS ALL WARRANTIES, EXPRESS OR IMPLIED, INCLUDING WITHOUT LIMITATION, THE IMPLIED WARRANTIES OF MERCHANTABILITY AND FITNESS FOR A PARTICULAR PURPOSE. EXCEPT FOR THE EXPRESS WARRANTY SET FORTH ABOVE, THE COMPANY DOES NOT WARRANT, GUARANTEE, OR MAKE ANY REPRESENTATION REGARDING THE USE OR THE RESULTS OF THE USE OF THE SOFTWARE IN TERMS OF ITS CORRECTNESS, ACCURACY, RELIABILITY, CURRENTNESS, OR OTHERWISE.

IN NO EVENT, SHALL THE COMPANY OR ITS EMPLOYEES, AGENTS, SUPPLIERS, OR CONTRACTORS BE LIABLE FOR ANY INCIDENTAL, INDIRECT, SPECIAL, OR CONSEQUENTIAL DAMAGES ARISING OUT OF OR IN CONNECTION WITH THE LICENSE GRANTED UNDER THIS AGREEMENT, OR FOR LOSS OF USE, LOSS OF DATA, LOSS OF INCOME OR PROFIT, OR OTHER LOSSES, SUSTAINED AS A RESULT OF INJURY TO ANY PERSON, OR LOSS OF OR DAMAGE TO PROPERTY, OR CLAIMS OF THIRD PARTIES, EVEN IF THE COMPANY OR AN AUTHORIZED REPRESENTATIVE OF THE COMPANY HAS BEEN ADVISED OF THE POSSIBILITY OF SUCH DAMAGES. IN NO EVENT SHALL LIABILITY OF THE COMPANY FOR DAMAGES WITH

RESPECT TO THE SOFTWARE EXCEED THE AMOUNTS ACTUALLY PAID BY YOU, IF ANY, FOR THE SOFTWARE.

SOME JURISDICTIONS DO NOT ALLOW THE LIMITATION OF IMPLIED WARRANTIES OR LIABILITY FOR INCIDENTAL, INDIRECT, SPECIAL, OR CONSEQUENTIAL DAMAGES, SO THE ABOVE LIMITATIONS MAY NOT ALWAYS APPLY. THE WARRANTIES IN THIS AGREEMENT GIVE YOU SPECIFIC LEGAL RIGHTS AND YOU MAY ALSO HAVE OTHER RIGHTS WHICH VARY IN ACCORDANCE WITH LOCAL LAW.

ACKNOWLEDGMENT

YOU ACKNOWLEDGE THAT YOU HAVE READ THIS AGREEMENT, UNDERSTAND IT, AND AGREE TO BE BOUND BY ITS TERMS AND CONDITIONS. YOU ALSO AGREE THAT THIS AGREEMENT IS THE COMPLETE AND EXCLUSIVE STATEMENT OF THE AGREEMENT BETWEEN YOU AND THE COMPANY AND SUPERSEDES ALL PROPOSALS OR PRIOR AGREEMENTS, ORAL, OR WRITTEN, AND ANY OTHER COMMUNICATIONS BETWEEN YOU AND THE COMPANY OR ANY REPRESENTATIVE OF THE COMPANY RELATING TO THE SUBJECT MATTER OF THIS AGREEMENT.

Should you have any questions concerning this Agreement or if you wish to contact the Company for any reason, please contact in writing at the address below.

Robin Short
Prentice Hall PTR
One Lake Street
Upper Saddle River, New Jersey 07458

JCreator™ License Agreement

END-USER LICENSE AGREEMENT FOR JCREATOR NOTICE TO ALL USERS:CAREFULLY READ THE FOLLOWING LEGAL AGREEMENT, FOR THE LICENSE OF SPECIFIED SOFTWARE BY XINOX SOFTWARE. BY INSTALLING THE SOFTWARE, YOU (EITHER AN INDIVIDUAL OR A SINGLE ENTITY) CONSENT TO BE BOUND BY AND BECOME A PARTY TO THIS AGREEMENT. IF YOU DO NOT AGREE TO ALL OF THE TERMS OF THIS AGREEMENT, CLICK THE BUTTON THAT INDICATES THAT YOU DO NOT ACCEPT THE TERMS OF THIS AGREEMENT AND DO NOT INSTALL THE SOFTWARE.

1. DEFINITIONS

(a) "the Software" means the JCreator software program supplied by Xinox Software herewith, which may also include documentation, associated media, printed materials, and online and electronic documentation.

(b) "User" means an individual end-user of the Software, being either faculty, staff, or an enrolled student in the case of a university or full-time staff in the case of a public institution or industrial firm.

(c) "Licensee" is a User who has paid the license fee in full and who has been registered with Xinox Software.

(d) "Xinox Software" or "Company" means Xinox Software and its suppliers and licensors, if any.

(e) "Evaluation Period" means a version of the Software, so identified, to be used to review and evaluate the Software, only. See section 4.1 for more details.

(f) "Private/Academic Version" means a version of the Software, so identified, for private(home) use or use by students and faculty of educational institutions, only. Private/Academic Versions may not be used for, or distributed to any party for, any commercial purpose. See section 4.2 for more details.

2. GENERAL

This End-User License Agreement ("EULA") is a legal agreement between you and Xinox Software for the Xinox Software products identified above, which may include computer software and associated media, electronic documentation and printed materials ("The Software"). By installing, copying, distributing or otherwise using The Software you agree to be bound by the terms of this EULA. If you do not agree to the terms of this EULA, you must not install, use or distribute The Software, and you must destroy all copies of The Software that you have. The Software is protected by copyright laws and international copyright treaties, as well as other intellectual property laws and treaties. The Software is licensed, not sold and always remains the property of Xinox Software.

Xinox Software will supply the Licensee with a single copy of the Software and Documents in electronic format, using a distribution mechanism decided on by Xinox Software. Xinox Software also will additionally supply the Licensee with a serial number and registration key. The Licensee agrees to restrict distribution of the registration key only to staff members with a need to know for purposes of configuring the Software or recording registration information for the usual business records of the Licensee, and will make all reasonable efforts to prevent duplication and any form of publication of the registration material.

If you have not paid the registration fee for the Software, you are hereby granted an evaluation license to use the Software as described in section 4.1.

3. LICENSE GRANT

Subject to the payment of the applicable license fees, and subject to the terms and conditions of this Agreement, Xinox Software hereby grants to you a non-exclusive, non-transferable right to use the Software and the accompanying documentation (the "Documentation"). Except as set forth below, you may only install one copy of the Software on one computer, workstation or other electronic device for which the Software was designed (each, a "Client Device"). If the Software is licensed as a suite or bundle with more than one specified Software product, this license applies to all such specified Software products, subject to any restrictions or usage terms specified on the applicable price list or product packaging that apply to any of such Software products individually.

(a) Use. The Software is licensed as a single product; more than one user may not use it on more than one Client Device or at a time, except as set forth in this Section 3. The Software is "in use" on a Client Device when it is loaded into the temporary memory (i.e., random-access memory or RAM) or installed into the permanent memory (e.g., hard disk, CD-ROM, or other storage device) of that Client Device. This license authorizes you to make one copy of the Software solely for backup or archival purposes, provided that the copy you make contains all of the Software's proprietary notices.

(b) Multiple Client Devices. A licensed user is also granted a license to install the Software on more than one Client Device, for the sole use of that user.

(c) Server-Mode. You may use the Software on a Client Device as a server ("Server") within a multi-user or networked environment, on a single physical site, ("Server-Mode") only if such use is permitted in the applicable price list or product packaging for the Software. A separate license is required for each Client Device or "seat" that may connect to the Server at any time, regardless of whether such licensed Client Devices or seats are concurrently connected to, accessing or using the Software. Use of software or hardware that reduces the number of Client Devices or seats directly accessing or utilizing the Software (e.g., "multiplexing" or "pooling" software or hardware) does not reduce the number of licenses required (i.e., the required number of licenses would equal the number of distinct inputs to the multiplexing or pooling software or hardware "front end"). If the number of Client Devices or seats that can connect to the Software can exceed the number of licenses you have obtained, and then you must have a reasonable mechanism in place to ensure that your use of the Software does not exceed the use limits specified for the licenses you have obtained. This license authorizes you to make or download one copy of the Documentation for each Client Device or seat that is licensed, provided that each such copy contains all of the Documentation's proprietary notices.

(d) Volume Licenses. If the Software is licensed with volume license terms specified in the applicable price list or product packaging for the Software, you may make, use and install as many additional copies of the Software on the number of Client Devices as the volume license authorizes. You must have a reasonable mechanism in place to ensure that the number of Client Devices on which the Software has been installed does not exceed the number of licenses you have obtained. This license authorizes you to make or download one copy of the Documentation for each additional copy authorized by the volume license, provided that each such copy contains all of the Documentation's proprietary notices.

(e) Site Licenses. If the Software is licensed with site license terms, you may make, use and install unlimited copies of the Software within the organization site. This excludes Client Devices outside the organization, such as the home-computers of the students and staff members. This license authorizes you to make or download one copy of the Documentation for each copy authorized by the site license, provided that each such copy contains all of the Documentation's proprietary notices.

4. LICENSE RESTRICTIONS

(a) Sublicense, sell, assign, transfer, pledge, distribute, rent or remove any proprietary notices on the Software except as expressly permitted in this Agreement.

(b) Use, copy, adapt, disassemble, decompile, reverse engineer or modify the Software, in whole or in part, except as expressly permitted in this Agreement.

(c) Take any action designed to unlock or bypass any Company-implemented restrictions on usage, access to, or number of installations of the Software; or.

(d) Use the Software if you fail to pay any license fee due and the Company notifies you that your license is terminated.

(e) Disclose to third parties, or publish your registration details via electronic or other means.

IF YOU DO ANY OF THE FOREGOING, YOUR RIGHTS UNDER THIS LICENSE WILL AUTOMATICALLY TERMINATE. SUCH TERMINATION SHALL BE IN ADDITION TO AND NOT IN LIEU OF ANY CRIMINAL, CIVIL OR OTHER REMEDIES AVAILABLE TO XINOX SOFTWARE.

4.1 RESTRICTED USE DURING EVALUATION PERIOD

You have a nonexclusive, nontransferable license to load and execute the unregistered copy of the Software for a period of thirty (30) days. (the "Evaluation Period"). The unregistered copy of the Software may be used for evaluation and testing purposes only and not for general commercial use. Customer must pay a license fee for the Software to obtain the right to use the Software for general commercial use and(or) for unlimited period. The unregistered copy of Software contains a feature that will automatically disable the Software in thirty (30) days. If you agree to this License Agreement and pay the license fee, Xinox Software will deactivate this feature. Xinox Software will have no liability to you if the Software is disabled by this feature. You may not disable, destroy, or remove this feature of the Software, and any attempt to do so will terminate your license and rights under this Agreement.

4.2 RESTRICTED USE PRIVATE/ACADEMIC LICENSE

Subject to the terms of this EULA, use the Software for non-commercial purposes only including conducting academic research or providing educational services. You certify that use is directly related to teaching, private non-commercial development or that use is strictly for non-commercial research by students or and faculty members, where the results of such research or development are not intended primarily for the benefit of a third party. (The private/academic version contains the same methodology as the Professional Edition; the only difference is the license.)

5. UPDATES

You are entitled to download revisions and upgrades (maintenance releases) to the Software as and when Xinox Software publishes it via its web site or through other online services. Xinox Software may charge an upgrade fee for new releases which contain significant enhancements.

6. DISTRIBUTION

You are hereby licensed to make as many copies of the installation package for The Software as you wish; give exact copies of the original installation package for The Software to anyone; and distribute the original installation package for The Software in its unmodified form via electronic or other means. The Software must be clearly identified as a freeware or shareware version where described. You are specifically prohibited from charging, or requesting donations, for any such copies, however made; and from distributing The Software including documentation with other products (commercial or otherwise) without prior written permission from Xinox Software. You are also prohibited from distributing components of The Software other than the complete original installation package.

7. OWNERSHIP

The foregoing license gives you limited license to use the Software. Xinox Software and its suppliers retain all right, title and interest, including all copyrights, in and to the Software and all copies thereof. All rights not specifically granted in this EULA, including Federal and International Copyrights, are reserved by Xinox Software and its suppliers. All title, including but not limited to copyrights, in and to The Software and any copies thereof are owned by Xinox Software. All title and intellectual property rights in and to the content which may be accessed through use of The Software is the property of the respective content owner and may be protected by applicable copyright or other intellectual property laws and treaties. This EULA grants you no rights to use such content. All rights not expressly granted are reserved by Xinox Software.

8. WARRANTY AND DISCLAIMER

LIMITED WARRANTY TO THE MAXIMUM EXTENT PERMITTED BY APPLI-
CABLE LAW, XINOX SOFTWARE DISCLAIMS ALL WARRANTIES AND CON-
DITIONS, EITHER EXPRESS OR IMPLIED, INCLUDING, BUT NOT LIMITED
TO, IMPLIED WARRANTIES OF MERCHANTABILITY, FITNESS FOR A PAR-
TICULAR PURPOSE, TITLE, AND NON-INFRINGEMENT, WITH REGARD
TO THE SOFTWARE, AND THE PROVISION OF OR FAILURE TO PROVIDE
SUPPORT SERVICES.XINOX SOFTWARE DOES NOT WARRANT THAT THE
SOFTWARE WILL MEET YOUR REQUIREMENTS OR THAT THE OPERA-
TION OF THE SOFTWARE WILL BE UNINTERRUPTED OR ERROR
FREE.THE ENTIRE RISK AS TO SATISFACTORY QUALITY, PERFORMANCE,
ACCURACY, AND EFFORT IS WITH YOU, THE USER.

9. LIMITATION OF LIABILITY

LIMITATIONS OF REMEDIES AND LIABILITY TO THE MAXIMUM EXTENT
PERMITTED BY APPLICABLE LAW, IN NO EVENT SHALL XINOX SOFTWARE
BE LIABLE FOR ANY SPECIAL, INCIDENTAL, INDIRECT, CONSEQUENTIAL
OR OTHER DAMAGES WHATSOEVER (INCLUDING, WITHOUT LIMITA-
TION, DAMAGES FOR LOSS OF PROFITS, BUSINESS INTERRUPTION, LOSS
OF INFORMATION, OR ANY OTHER PECUNIARY LOSS) ARISING OUT OF
THE USE OF OR INABILITY TO USE THE SOFTWARE PRODUCT OR THE
PROVISION OF OR FAILURE TO PROVIDE SUPPORT SERVICES, EVEN IF XI-
NOX SOFTWARE HAS BEEN ADVISED OF THE POSSIBILITY OF SUCH DAM-
AGES. SOME STATES AND JURISDICTIONS DO NOT ALLOW THE
EXCLUSION OR LIMITATION OF LIABILITY, THE ABOVE LIMITATION MAY
NOT APPLY TO YOU.

10. HIGH RISK ACTIVITIES

The Software is not fault-tolerant and is not designed, manufactured or intended for use
or resale as on-line control equipment in hazardous environments requiring fail-safe performance, such as in the operation of nuclear facilities, aircraft navigation or communication systems, air traffic control, direct life support machines, or weapons systems, in which
the failure of the Software could lead directly to death, personal injury, or severe physical
or environmental damage ("High Risk Activities"). Accordingly, Xinox Software and its
suppliers and licensors specifically disclaim any express or implied warranty of fitness for
High Risk Activities. You agree that Xinox Software and its suppliers and licensors will not
be liable for any claims or damages arising from the use of the Software in such applications.

11. TERMINATION

Without prejudice to any other rights, Xinox Software may terminate this EULA if you
fail to comply with the terms and conditions of this EULA. In such event, you must destroy all copies of The Software.

12. MISCELLANEOUS

This license is governed by Dutch Law and is subject to exclusive jurisdiction of the Dutch
courts. This license constitutes the complete and exclusive statement of our agreement
with you and supercedes all proposals, representations, understandings and prior agreements whether oral or written and all communications with you relating thereto.

jEdit License Agreement

jEdit is released under the terms of the GNU General Public License, and developed by Slava Pestov and others.

GNU GENERAL PUBLIC LICENSE

Version 2, June 1991

Copyright (C) 1989, 1991 Free Software Foundation, Inc.

59 Temple Place - Suite 330, Boston, MA 02111-1307, USA

Everyone is permitted to copy and distribute verbatim copies

of this license document, but changing it is not allowed.

Preamble

The licenses for most software are designed to take away your freedom to share and change it. By contrast, the GNU General Public License is intended to guarantee your freedom to share and change free software--to make sure the software is free for all its users. This General Public License applies to most of the Free Software Foundation's software and to any other program whose authors commit to using it. (Some other Free Software Foundation software is covered by the GNU Library General Public License instead.) You can apply it to your programs, too.

When we speak of free software, we are referring to freedom, not price. Our General Public Licenses are designed to make sure that you have the freedom to distribute copies of free software (and charge for this service if you wish), that you receive source code or can get it if you want it, that you can change the software or use pieces of it in new free programs; and that you know you can do these things.

To protect your rights, we need to make restrictions that forbid anyone to deny you these rights or to ask you to surrender the rights. These restrictions translate to certain responsibilities for you if you distribute copies of the software, or if you modify it.

For example, if you distribute copies of such a program, whether gratis or for a fee, you must give the recipients all the rights that you have. You must make sure that they, too, receive or can get the source code. And you must show them these terms so they know their rights.

We protect your rights with two steps: (1) copyright the software, and (2) offer you this license which gives you legal permission to copy, distribute and/or modify the software.

Also, for each author's protection and ours, we want to make certain that everyone understands that there is no warranty for this free software. If the software is modified by someone else and passed on, we want its recipients to know that what they have is not the original, so that any problems introduced by others will not reflect on the original authors' reputations.

Finally, any free program is threatened constantly by software patents. We wish to avoid the danger that redistributors of a free program will individually obtain patent licenses, in effect making the program proprietary. To prevent this, we have made it clear that any patent must be licensed for everyone's free use or not licensed at all.

The precise terms and conditions for copying, distribution and modification follow.

TERMS AND CONDITIONS FOR COPYING, DISTRIBUTION AND MODIFICATION

0. This License applies to any program or other work which contains a notice placed by the copyright holder saying it may be distributed under the terms of this General Public License. The "Program", below, refers to any such program or work, and a "work based on the Program" means either the Program or any derivative work under copyright law: that is to say, a work containing the Program or a portion of it, either verbatim or with modifications and/or translated into another language. (Hereinafter, translation is included without limitation in the term "modification".) Each licensee is addressed as "you".

Activities other than copying, distribution and modification are not covered by this License; they are outside its scope. The act of running the Program is not restricted, and the output from the Program is covered only if its contents constitute a work based on the Program (independent of having been made by running the Program). Whether that is true depends on what the Program does.

1. You may copy and distribute verbatim copies of the Program's source code as you receive it, in any medium, provided that you conspicuously and appropriately publish on each copy an appropriate copyright notice and disclaimer of warranty; keep intact all the notices that refer to this License and to the absence of any warranty; and give any other recipients of the Program a copy of this License along with the Program.

You may charge a fee for the physical act of transferring a copy, and you may at your option offer warranty protection in exchange for a fee.

2. You may modify your copy or copies of the Program or any portion of it, thus forming a work based on the Program, and copy and distribute such modifications or work under the terms of Section 1 above, provided that you also meet all of these conditions:

a) You must cause the modified files to carry prominent notices stating that you changed the files and the date of any change.

b) You must cause any work that you distribute or publish, that in whole or in part contains or is derived from the Program or any part thereof, to be licensed as a whole at no charge to all third parties under the terms of this License.

c) If the modified program normally reads commands interactively when run, you must cause it, when started running for such interactive use in the most ordinary way, to print or display an announcement including an appropriate copyright notice and a notice that there is no warranty (or else, saying that you provide a warranty) and that users may redistribute the program under these conditions, and telling the user how to view a copy of this License. (Exception: if the Program itself is interactive but does not normally print such an announcement, your work based on the Program is not required to print an announcement.)

These requirements apply to the modified work as a whole. If identifiable sections of that work are not derived from the Program, and can be reasonably considered independent and separate works in themselves, then this License, and its terms, do not apply to those sections when you distribute them as separate works. But when you distribute the same sections as part of a whole which is a work based on the Program, the distribution of the whole must be on the terms of this License, whose permissions for other licensees extend to the entire whole, and thus to each and every part regardless of who wrote it.

Thus, it is not the intent of this section to claim rights or contest your rights to work written entirely by you; rather, the intent is to exercise the right to control the distribution of derivative or collective works based on the Program.

In addition, mere aggregation of another work not based on the Program with the Program (or with a work based on the Program) on a volume of a storage or distribution medium does not bring the other work under the scope of this License.

3. You may copy and distribute the Program (or a work based on it, under Section 2) in object code or executable form under the terms of Sections 1 and 2 above provided that you also do one of the following:

a) Accompany it with the complete corresponding machine-readable source code, which must be distributed under the terms of Sections 1 and 2 above on a medium customarily used for software interchange; or,

b) Accompany it with a written offer, valid for at least three years, to give any third party, for a charge no more than your cost of physically performing source distribution, a complete machine-readable copy of the corresponding source code, to be distributed under the terms of Sections 1 and 2 above on a medium customarily used for software interchange; or,

c) Accompany it with the information you received as to the offer to distribute corresponding source code. (This alternative is allowed only for noncommercial distribution and only if you received the program in object code or executable form with such an offer, in accord with Subsection b above.)

The source code for a work means the preferred form of the work for making modifications to it. For an executable work, complete source code means all the source code for all modules it contains, plus any associated interface definition files, plus the scripts used to control compilation and installation of the executable. However, as a special exception, the source code distributed need not include anything that is normally distributed (in either source or binary form) with the major components (compiler, kernel, and so on) of the operating system on which the executable runs, unless that component itself accompanies the executable.

If distribution of executable or object code is made by offering access to copy from a designated place, then offering equivalent access to copy the source code from the same place counts as distribution of the source code, even though third parties are not compelled to copy the source along with the object code.

4. You may not copy, modify, sublicense, or distribute the Program except as expressly provided under this License. Any attempt otherwise to copy, modify, sublicense or distribute the Program is void, and will automatically terminate your rights under this License. However, parties who have received copies, or rights, from you under this License will not have their licenses terminated so long as such parties remain in full compliance.

5. You are not required to accept this License, since you have not signed it. However, nothing else grants you permission to modify or distribute the Program or its derivative works. These actions are prohibited by law if you do not accept this License. Therefore, by modifying or distributing the Program (or any work based on the Program), you indicate your acceptance of this License to do so, and all its terms and conditions for copying, distributing or modifying the Program or works based on it.

6. Each time you redistribute the Program (or any work based on the Program), the recipient automatically receives a license from the original licensor to copy, distribute or modify

the Program subject to these terms and conditions. You may not impose any further restrictions on the recipients' exercise of the rights granted herein. You are not responsible
for enforcing compliance by third parties to this License.

7. If, as a consequence of a court judgment or allegation of patent infringement or for any
other reason (not limited to patent issues), conditions are imposed on you (whether by
court order, agreement or otherwise) that contradict the conditions of this License, they
do not excuse you from the conditions of this License. If you cannot distribute so as to
satisfy simultaneously your obligations under this License and any other pertinent obligations, then as a consequence you may not distribute the Program at all. For example, if a
patent license would not permit royalty-free redistribution of the Program by all those
who receive copies directly or indirectly through you, then the only way you could satisfy
both it and this License would be to refrain entirely from distribution of the Program.

If any portion of this section is held invalid or unenforceable under any particular cir-
cumstance, the balance of the section is intended to apply and the section as a whole is
intended to apply in other circumstances.

It is not the purpose of this section to induce you to infringe any patents or other
property right claims or to contest validity of any such claims; this section has the sole purpose of protecting the integrity of the free software distribution system, which is implemented by public license practices. Many people have made generous contributions to the
wide range of software distributed through that system in reliance on consistent application of that system; it is up to the author/donor to decide if he or she is willing to distribute
software through any other system and a licensee cannot impose that choice.

This section is intended to make thoroughly clear what is believed to be a consequence
of the rest of this License.

8. If the distribution and/or use of the Program is restricted in certain countries either by
patents or by copyrighted interfaces, the original copyright holder who places the Program
under this License may add an explicit geographical distribution limitation excluding
those countries, so that distribution is permitted only in or among countries not thus ex-
cluded. In such case, this License incorporates the limitation as if written in the body of
this License.

9. The Free Software Foundation may publish revised and/or new versions of the General
Public License from time to time. Such new versions will be similar in spirit to the present
version, but may differ in detail to address new problems or concerns.

Each version is given a distinguishing version number. If the Program specifies a version number of this License which applies to it and "any later version", you have the
option of following the terms and conditions either of that version or of any later version
published by the Free Software Foundation. If the Program does not specify a version
number of this License, you may choose any version ever published by the Free Software
Foundation.

10. If you wish to incorporate parts of the Program into other free programs whose distribution conditions are different, write to the author to ask for permission. For software
which is copyrighted by the Free Software Foundation, write to the Free Software Foundation; we sometimes make exceptions for this. Our decision will be guided by the two
goals of preserving the free status of all derivatives of our free software and of promoting
the sharing and reuse of software generally.

NO WARRANTY

11. BECAUSE THE PROGRAM IS LICENSED FREE OF CHARGE, THERE IS NO WARRANTY FOR THE PROGRAM, TO THE EXTENT PERMITTED BY APPLICABLE LAW. EXCEPT WHEN OTHERWISE STATED IN WRITING THE COPYRIGHT HOLDERS AND/OR OTHER PARTIES PROVIDE THE PROGRAM "AS IS" WITHOUT WARRANTY OF ANY KIND, EITHER EXPRESSED OR IMPLIED, INCLUDING, BUT NOT LIMITED TO, THE IMPLIED WARRANTIES OF MERCHANTABILITY AND FITNESS FOR A PARTICULAR PURPOSE. THE ENTIRE RISK AS TO THE QUALITY AND PERFORMANCE OF THE PROGRAM IS WITH YOU. SHOULD THE PROGRAM PROVE DEFECTIVE, YOU ASSUME THE COST OF ALL NECESSARY SERVICING, REPAIR OR CORRECTION.

12. IN NO EVENT UNLESS REQUIRED BY APPLICABLE LAW OR AGREED TO IN WRITING WILL ANY COPYRIGHT HOLDER, OR ANY OTHER PARTY WHO MAY MODIFY AND/OR REDISTRIBUTE THE PROGRAM AS PERMITTED ABOVE, BE LIABLE TO YOU FOR DAMAGES, INCLUDING ANY GENERAL, SPECIAL, INCIDENTAL OR CONSEQUENTIAL DAMAGES ARISING OUT OF THE USE OR INABILITY TO USE THE PROGRAM (INCLUDING BUT NOT LIMITED TO LOSS OF DATA OR DATA BEING RENDERED INACCURATE OR LOSSES SUSTAINED BY YOU OR THIRD PARTIES OR A FAILURE OF THE PROGRAM TO OPERATE WITH ANY OTHER PROGRAMS), EVEN IF SUCH HOLDER OR OTHER PARTY HAS BEEN ADVISED OF THE POSSIBILITY OF SUCH DAMAGES.

END OF TERMS AND CONDITIONS

How to Apply These Terms to Your New Programs

If you develop a new program, and you want it to be of the greatest possible use to the public, the best way to achieve this is to make it free software which everyone can redistribute and change under these terms.

To do so, attach the following notices to the program. It is safest to attach them to the start of each source file to most effectively convey the exclusion of warranty; and each file should have at least the "copyright" line and a pointer to where the full notice is found.

one line to give the program's name and an idea of what it does.
Copyright (C) yyyy name of author

This program is free software; you can redistribute it and/or
modify it under the terms of the GNU General Public License
as published by the Free Software Foundation; either version 2
of the License, or (at your option) any later version.

This program is distributed in the hope that it will be useful,
but WITHOUT ANY WARRANTY; without even the implied warranty of
MERCHANTABILITY or FITNESS FOR A PARTICULAR PURPOSE.
See the GNU General Public License for more details.

You should have received a copy of the GNU General Public License
along with this program; if not, write to the Free Software
Foundation, Inc., 59 Temple Place - Suite 330, Boston, MA 02111-1307, USA.

Also add information on how to contact you by electronic and paper mail.

If the program is interactive, make it output a short notice like this when it starts in an interactive mode:

Gnomovision version 69, Copyright (C) year name of author
Gnomovision comes with ABSOLUTELY NO WARRANTY; for details
type `show w'. This is free software, and you are welcome
to redistribute it under certain conditions; type `show c'
for details.

The hypothetical commands `show w' and `show c' should show the appropriate parts of the General Public License. Of course, the commands you use may be called something other than `show w' and `show c'; they could even be mouse-clicks or menu items--whatever suits your program.

You should also get your employer (if you work as a programmer) or your school, if any, to sign a "copyright disclaimer" for the program, if necessary. Here is a sample; alter the names:

Yoyodyne, Inc., hereby disclaims all copyright
interest in the program `Gnomovision'
(which makes passes at compilers) written
by James Hacker.

signature of Ty Coon, 1 April 1989
Ty Coon, President of Vice

This General Public License does not permit incorporating your program into proprietary programs. If your program is a subroutine library, you may consider it more useful to permit linking proprietary applications with the library. If this is what you want to do, use the GNU Library General Public License instead of this License.

jGRASP™ License Agreement

Software License for jGRASP Version 1.7.0
Copyright 1999-2004 Auburn University

Section 1. License Grant.

Auburn University grants to you a non-exclusive and non-transferable license to use jGRASP and the associated documentation provided in jgrasp/help, collectively "jGRASP". jGRASP may be installed for use on a single computer or on a local area network. The "wedge" source code provided in the jgrasp/src directory is free of license restrictions. It may be used or modified for any purpose. jGRASP is a Trademark of Auburn University.

Section 2. Restrictions

Distribution of jGRASP is not permitted without written permission (see Supplements), except that it may be distributed internally within a single organization. Distribution of components of jGRASP separately from the whole is not permitted, except that the complete associated documentation provided in jgrasp/help may be distributed separately. Reverse engineering of jGRASP is not permitted. Any use of image files, icons, or executable components of jGRASP separately from the whole is prohibited.

Section 3. Disclaimer of Warranty

jGRASP is licensed "as is". There are no express or implied warranties, including, but not limited to, the implied warranties of merchantability and fitness for a particular purpose. Auburn University makes no warranty with respect to the accuracy or completeness of information obtained through the use of this program. Auburn University does not warrant that jGRASP will meet all of your requirements or that its operation will be uninterrupted or error free or that any defect within jGRASP will be corrected. No oral or written information, representation, or advice given by Auburn University or an authorized representative of Auburn University shall create a warranty. Auburn University and its agents shall in no event be held liable to the user for any damages, including direct, indirect, incidental, or consequential damages, lost profits, lost savings, or other such damages arising out of the installation, use, improper use, or inability to use jGRASP, even if Auburn University has been advised of the possibility of such damages, or any claim by any other person or entity related thereto.

Supplements

Distribution for Educational Purposes - Publishers may distribute the jGRASP software and the jGRASP Handbook (Tutorials and Reference) on CDs that accompany their textbooks provided that (1) the title "jGRASP(TM) 1.7.0 copyright 1999-2004 Auburn University" is included on each CD label, (2) descriptions of the CD indicate that jGRASP is included on the CD, and (3) a list of the textbooks that include jGRASP is provided to Auburn University (crossATengDOTauburnDOTedu). Permission to distribute jGRASP for educational purposes covers all CDs created prior to December 31, 2004 for inclusion in textbooks. While it is anticipated that distribution of jGRASP for educational purposes will remain royalty free, this supplement of the jGRASP license will be re-evaluated on an annual basis.

For additional information, contact James H. Cross II, Computer Science and Software Engineering, 107 Dunstan Hall, Auburn University, AL 36849 (334-844-6315, crossATengDOTauburnDOTedu).

NetBeans™ License Agreement

Netbeans IDE and Netbeans Platform are based on software from netbeans.org, developed under Sun Public License (SPL). For more information visit www.netbeans.org.

SUN PUBLIC LICENSE
SUN PUBLIC LICENSE Version 1.0

1.0.1. "Commercial Use" means distribution or otherwise making the Covered Code available to a third party.

1.1. "Contributor" means each entity that creates or contributes to the creation of Modifications.

1.2. "Contributor Version" means the combination of the Original Code, prior Modifications used by a Contributor, and the Modifications made by that particular Contributor.

1.3. "Covered Code" means the Original Code or Modifications or the combination of the Original Code and Modifications, in each case including portions thereof and corresponding documentation released with the source code.

1.4. "Electronic Distribution Mechanism" means a mechanism generally accepted in the software development community for the electronic transfer of data.

1.5. "Executable" means Covered Code in any form other than Source Code.

1.6. "Initial Developer" means the individual or entity identified as the Initial Developer in the Source Code notice required by Exhibit A.

1.7. "Larger Work" means a work which combines Covered Code or portions thereof with code not governed by the terms of this License.

1.8. "License" means this document.

1.8.1. "Licensable" means having the right to grant, to the maximum extent possible, whether at the time of the initial grant or subsequently acquired, any and all of the rights conveyed herein.

1.9. "Modifications" means any addition to or deletion from the substance or structure of either the Original Code or any previous Modifications. When Covered Code is released as a series of files, a Modification is:

A. Any addition to or deletion from the contents of a file containing Original Code or previous Modifications.

B. Any new file that contains any part of the Original Code or previous Modifications.

1.10. "Original Code" means Source Code of computer software code which is described in the Source Code notice required by Exhibit A as Original Code, and which, at the time of its release under this License is not already Covered Code governed by this License.

1.10.1. "Patent Claims" means any patent claim(s), now owned or hereafter acquired, including without limitation, method, process, and apparatus claims, in any patent Licensable by grantor.

1.11. "Source Code" means the preferred form of the Covered Code for making modifications to it, including all modules it contains, plus any associated documentation, interface definition files, scripts used to control compilation and installation of an Executable, or source code differential comparisons against either the Original Code or another well known, available Covered Code of the Contributor's choice. The Source Code can be in a compressed or archival form, provided the appropriate decompression or de-archiving software is widely available for no charge.

1.12. "You" (or "Your") means an individual or a legal entity exercising rights under, and complying with all of the terms of, this License or a future version of this License issued under Section 6.1. For legal entities, "You" includes any entity which controls, is controlled by, or is under common control with You. For purposes of this definition, "control" means (a) the power, direct or indirect, to cause the direction or management of such entity, whether by contract or otherwise, or (b) ownership of more than fifty percent (50%) of the outstanding shares or beneficial ownership of such entity.

2. Source Code License.

2.1 The Initial Developer Grant.

The Initial Developer hereby grants You a world-wide, royalty-free, non-exclusive license, subject to third party intellectual property claims:

(a) under intellectual property rights (other than patent or trademark) Licensable by Initial Developer to use, reproduce, modify, display, perform, sublicense and distribute the Original Code (or portions thereof) with or without Modifications, and/or as part of a Larger Work; and

(b) under Patent Claims infringed by the making, using or selling of Original Code, to make, have made, use, practice, sell, and offer for sale, and/or otherwise dispose of the Original Code (or portions thereof).

(c) the licenses granted in this Section 2.1(a) and (b) are effective on the date Initial Developer first distributes Original Code under the terms of this License.

(d) Notwithstanding Section 2.1(b) above, no patent license is granted: 1) for code that You delete from the Original Code; 2) separate from the Original Code; or 3) for infringements caused by: i) the modification of the Original Code or ii) the combination of the Original Code with other software or devices.

2.2. Contributor Grant.

Subject to third party intellectual property claims, each Contributor hereby grants You a world-wide, royalty-free, non-exclusive license

(a) under intellectual property rights (other than patent or trademark) Licensable by Contributor, to use, reproduce, modify, display, perform, sublicense and distribute the Modifications created by such Contributor (or portions thereof) either on an unmodified basis, with other Modifications, as Covered Code and/or as part of a Larger Work; and

(b) under Patent Claims infringed by the making, using, or selling of Modifications made by that Contributor either alone and/or in combination with its Contributor Version (or portions of such combination), to make, use, sell, offer for sale, have made, and/or otherwise dispose of: 1) Modifications made by that Contributor (or portions thereof); and 2) the combination of Modifications made by that Contributor with its Contributor Version (or portions of such combination).

(c) the licenses granted in Sections 2.2(a) and 2.2(b) are effective on the date Contributor first makes Commercial Use of the Covered Code.

(d) notwithstanding Section 2.2(b) above, no patent license is granted: 1) for any code that Contributor has deleted from the Contributor Version; 2) separate from the Contributor Version; 3) for infringements caused by: i) third party modifications of Contributor Version or ii) the combination of Modifications made by that Contributor with other software (except as part of the Contributor Version) or other devices; or 4) under Patent Claims infringed by Covered Code in the absence of Modifications made by that Contributor.

3. Distribution Obligations.

3.1. Application of License.

The Modifications which You create or to which You contribute are governed by the terms of this License, including without limitation Section 2.2. The Source Code version of Covered Code may be distributed only under the terms of this License or a future version of this License released under Section 6.1, and You must include a copy of this License with every copy of the Source Code You distribute. You may not offer or impose any terms on any Source Code version that alters or restricts the applicable version of this

License or the recipients' rights hereunder. However, You may include an additional document offering the additional rights described in Section 3.5.

3.2. Availability of Source Code.

Any Modification which You create or to which You contribute must be made available in Source Code form under the terms of this License either on the same media as an Executable version or via an accepted Electronic Distribution Mechanism to anyone to whom you made an Executable version available; and if made available via Electronic Distribution Mechanism, must remain available for at least twelve (12) months after the date it initially became available, or at least six (6) months after a subsequent version of that particular Modification has been made available to such recipients. You are responsible for ensuring that the Source Code version remains available even if the Electronic Distribution Mechanism is maintained by a third party.

3.3. Description of Modifications.

You must cause all Covered Code to which You contribute to contain a file documenting the changes You made to create that Covered Code and the date of any change. You must include a prominent statement that the Modification is derived, directly or indirectly, from Original Code provided by the Initial Developer and including the name of the Initial Developer in (a) the Source Code, and (b) in any notice in an Executable version or related documentation in which You describe the origin or ownership of the Covered Code.

3.4. Intellectual Property Matters.

(a) Third Party Claims.

If Contributor has knowledge that a license under a third party's intellectual property rights is required to exercise the rights granted by such Contributor under Sections 2.1 or 2.2, Contributor must include a text file with the Source Code distribution titled "LEGAL" which describes the claim and the party making the claim in sufficient detail that a recipient will know whom to contact. If Contributor obtains such knowledge after the Modification is made available as described in Section 3.2, Contributor shall promptly modify the LEGAL file in all copies Contributor makes available thereafter and shall take other steps (such as notifying appropriate mailing lists or newsgroups) reasonably calculated to inform those who received the Covered Code that new knowledge has been obtained.

(b) Contributor APIs.

If Contributor's Modifications include an application programming interface ("API") and Contributor has knowledge of patent licenses which are reasonably necessary to implement that API, Contributor must also include this information in the LEGAL file.

(c) Representations.

Contributor represents that, except as disclosed pursuant to Section 3.4(a) above, Contributor believes that Contributor's Modifications are Contributor's original creation(s) and/or Contributor has sufficient rights to grant the rights conveyed by this License.

3.5. Required Notices.

You must duplicate the notice in Exhibit A in each file of the Source Code. If it is not possible to put such notice in a particular Source Code file due to its structure, then You must include such notice in a location (such as a relevant directory) where a user would be likely to look for such a notice. If You created one or more Modification(s) You may add your name as a Contributor to the notice described in Exhibit A. You must also duplicate this License in any documentation for the Source Code where You describe recipients' rights or ownership rights relating to Covered Code. You may choose to offer, and to charge a fee for, warranty, support, indemnity or liability obligations to one or more recipients of Covered Code. However, You may do so only on Your own behalf, and not on behalf of the Initial Developer or any Contributor. You must make it absolutely clear than any such warranty, support, indemnity or liability obligation is offered by You alone, and You hereby agree to indemnify the Initial Developer and every Contributor for any liability incurred by the Initial Developer or such Contributor as a result of warranty, support, indemnity or liability terms You offer.

3.6. Distribution of Executable Versions.

You may distribute Covered Code in Executable form only if therequirements of Section 3.1-3.5 have been met for that Covered Code,and if You include a notice stating that the Source Code version ofthe Covered Code is available under the terms of this License,including a description of how and where You have fulfilled theobligations of Section 3.2. The notice must be conspicuously includedin any notice in an Executable version, related documentation orcollateral in which You describe recipients' rights relating to theCovered Code. You may distribute the Executable version of CoveredCode or ownership rights under a license of Your choice, which maycontain terms different from this License, provided that You are incompliance with the terms of this License and that the license for theExecutable version does not attempt to limit or alter the recipient'srights in the Source Code version from the rights set forth in thisLicense. If You distribute the Executable version under a differentlicense You must make it absolutely clear that any terms which differfrom this License are offered by You alone, not by the InitialDeveloper or any Contributor. You hereby agree to indemnify theInitial Developer and every Contributor for any liability incurred bythe Initial Developer or such Contributor as a result of any suchterms You offer.

3.7. Larger Works.

You may create a Larger Work by combining Covered Code with other codenot governed by the terms of this License and distribute the LargerWork as a single product. In such a case, You must make sure therequirements of this License are fulfilled for the Covered Code.

4. Inability to Comply Due to Statute or Regulation.

If it is impossible for You to comply with any of the terms of thisLicense with respect to some or all of the Covered Code due tostatute, judicial order, or regulation then You must: (a) comply withthe terms of this License to the maximum extent possible; and (b)describe the limitations and the code they affect. Such descriptionmust be included in the LEGAL file described in Section 3.4 and mustbe included with all distributions of the Source Code. Except to theextent prohibited by statute or regulation, such description must besufficiently detailed for a recipient of ordinary skill to be able tounderstand it.

5. Application of this License.

This License applies to code to which the Initial Developer has attached the notice in Exhibit A and to related Covered Code.

6. Versions of the License.

6.1. New Versions.

Sun Microsystems, Inc. ("Sun") may publish revised and/or new versionsof the License from time to time. Each version will be given adistinguishing version number.

6.2. Effect of New Versions.

Once Covered Code has been published under a particular version of theLicense, You may always continue to use it under the terms of thatversion. You may also choose to use such Covered Code under the termsof any subsequent version of the License published by Sun. No oneother than Sun has the right to modify the terms applicable to CoveredCode created under this License.

6.3. Derivative Works.

If You create or use a modified version of this License (which you mayonly do in order to apply it to code which is not already Covered Codegoverned by this License), You must: (a) rename Your license so thatthe phrases "Sun," "Sun Public License," or "SPL" or any confusinglysimilar phrase do not appear in your license (except to note that yourlicense differs from this License) and (b) otherwise make it clearthat Your version of the license contains terms which differ from theSun Public License. (Filling in the name of the Initial Developer,Original Code or Contributor in the notice described in Exhibit Ashall not of themselves be deemed to be modifications of thisLicense.)

7. DISCLAIMER OF WARRANTY.

COVERED CODE IS PROVIDED UNDER THIS LICENSE ON AN "AS IS" BASIS,WITHOUT WARRANTY OF ANY KIND, EITHER EXPRESSED OR IMPLIED, INCLUDING,WITHOUT LIMITATION, WARRANTIES THAT THE COVERED CODE IS FREE OFDEFECTS, MERCHANTABLE, FIT FOR A PARTICULAR PURPOSE OR NON-INFRINGING.THE ENTIRE RISK AS TO THE QUALITY AND PERFORMANCE OF THE COVERED CODEIS WITH YOU. SHOULD ANY COVERED CODE PROVE DEFECTIVE IN ANY RESPECT,YOU (NOT THE INITIAL DEVELOPER OR ANY OTHER CONTRIBUTOR) ASSUME THECOST OF ANY NECESSARY SERVICING, REPAIR OR CORRECTION. THIS DISCLAIMEROF WARRANTY CONSTITUTES AN ESSENTIAL PART OF THIS LICENSE. NO USE OFANY COVERED CODE IS AUTHORIZED HEREUNDER EXCEPT UNDER THIS DISCLAIMER.

8. TERMINATION.

8.1. This License and the rights granted hereunder will terminateautomatically if You fail to comply with terms herein and fail to curesuch breach within 30 days of becoming aware of the breach. Allsublicenses to the Covered Code which are properly granted shallsurvive any termination of this License. Provisions which, by theirnature, must remain in effect beyond the termination of this Licenseshall survive.

8.2. If You initiate litigation by asserting a patent infringementclaim (excluding declaratory judgment actions) against Initial Developeror a Contributor (the Initial Developer or Contributor against whomYou file such action is referred to as "Participant") alleging that:

(a) such Participant's Contributor Version directly or indirectlyinfringes any patent, then any and all rights granted by suchParticipant to You under Sections 2.1 and/or 2.2 of this Licenseshall, upon 60 days notice from Participant terminate prospectively,unless if within 60 days after receipt of notice You either: (i)agree in writing to pay Participant a mutually agreeable reasonableroyalty for Your past and future use of Modifications made by suchParticipant, or (ii) withdraw Your litigation claim with respect tothe Contributor

Version against such Participant. If within 60 daysof notice, a reasonable royalty and payment arrangement are notmutually agreed upon in writing by the parties or the litigation claimis not withdrawn, the rights granted by Participant to You underSections 2.1 and/or 2.2 automatically terminate at the expiration ofthe 60 day notice period specified above.

(b) any software, hardware, or device, other than such Participant'sContributor Version, directly or indirectly infringes any patent, thenany rights granted to You by such Participant under Sections 2.1(b)and 2.2(b) are revoked effective as of the date You first made, used,sold, distributed, or had made, Modifications made by thatParticipant.

8.3. If You assert a patent infringement claim against Participantalleging that such Participant's Contributor Version directly orindirectly infringes any patent where such claim is resolved (such asby license or settlement) prior to the initiation of patentinfringement litigation, then the reasonable value of the licensesgranted by such Participant under Sections 2.1 or 2.2 shall be takeninto account in determining the amount or value of any payment orlicense.

8.4. In the event of termination under Sections 8.1 or 8.2 above, allend user license agreements (excluding distributors and resellers)which have been validly granted by You or any distributor hereunderprior to termination shall survive termination.

9. LIMITATION OF LIABILITY.

UNDER NO CIRCUMSTANCES AND UNDER NO LEGAL THEORY, WHETHER TORT(INCLUDING NEGLIGENCE), CONTRACT, OR OTHERWISE, SHALL YOU, THE INITIALDEVELOPER, ANY OTHER CONTRIBUTOR, OR ANY DISTRIBUTOR OF COVERED CODE,OR ANY SUPPLIER OF ANY OF SUCH PARTIES, BE LIABLE TO ANY PERSON FORANY INDIRECT, SPECIAL, INCIDENTAL, OR CONSEQUENTIAL DAMAGES OF ANYCHARACTER INCLUDING, WITHOUT LIMITATION, DAMAGES FOR LOSS OF GOODWILL,WORK STOPPAGE, COMPUTER FAILURE OR MALFUNCTION, OR ANY AND ALL OTHERCOMMERCIAL DAMAGES OR LOSSES, EVEN IF SUCH PARTY SHALL HAVE BEENINFORMED OF THE POSSIBILITY OF SUCH DAMAGES. THIS LIMITATION OFLIABILITY SHALL NOT APPLY TO LIABILITY FOR DEATH OR PERSONAL INJURYRESULTING FROM SUCH PARTY'S NEGLIGENCE TO THE EXTENT APPLICABLE LAWPROHIBITS SUCH LIMITATION. SOME JURISDICTIONS DO NOT ALLOW THEEXCLUSION OR LIMITATION OF INCIDENTAL OR CONSEQUENTIAL DAMAGES, SOTHIS EXCLUSION AND LIMITATION MAY NOT APPLY TO YOU.

10. U.S. GOVERNMENT END USERS.

The Covered Code is a "commercial item," as that term is defined in 48C.F.R. 2.101 (Oct. 1995), consisting of "commercial computer software"and "commercial computer software documentation," as such terms areused in 48 C.F.R. 12.212 (Sept. 1995). Consistent with 48 C.F.R.12.212 and 48 C.F.R. 227.7202-1 through 227.7202-4 (June 1995), allU.S. Government End Users acquire Covered Code with only those rightsset forth herein.

11. MISCELLANEOUS.

This License represents the complete agreement concerning subjectmatter hereof. If any provision of this License is held to beunenforceable, such provision shall be reformed only to the extentnecessary to make it enforceable. This License shall be governed byCalifornia law provisions (except to the extent applicable law, ifany, provides otherwise), excluding its conflict-of-law provisions.With respect to disputes in which at least one party is a citizen of,or an entity chartered or registered to do business in the UnitedStates of America, any litigation relating to this License shall besubject to the jurisdiction of the Federal Courts of the NorthernDistrict of California, with venue lying in Santa Clara County,California, with the losing party responsible for costs, includingwithout limitation, court costs and reasonable attorneys' fees andexpenses. The application of the United Nations Convention onContracts for the International Sale of Goods is expressly excluded.Any law or regulation which provides that the language of a contractshall be construed against the drafter shall not apply to thisLicense.

12. RESPONSIBILITY FOR CLAIMS.

As between Initial Developer and the Contributors, each party isresponsible for claims and damages arising, directly or indirectly,out of its utilization of rights under this License and You agree towork with Initial Developer and Contributors to distribute suchresponsibility on an equitable basis. Nothing herein is intended orshall be deemed to constitute any admission of liability.

13. MULTIPLE-LICENSED CODE.

Initial Developer may designate portions of the Covered Code as"Multiple-Licensed". "Multiple-Licensed" means that the InitialDeveloper permits you to utilize portions of the Covered Code underYour choice of the alternative licenses, if any, specified by theInitial Developer in the file described in Exhibit A.

Exhibit A -Sun Public License Notice.

The contents of this file are subject to the Sun Public LicenseVersion 1.0 (the "License"); you may not use this file except incompliance with the License. A copy of the License is available athttp://www.sun.com/

The Original Code is _____. The Initial Developer of theOriginal Code is _____. Portions created by _____ are Copyright(C)_____. All Rights Reserved.

Contributor(s): _____.

Alternatively, the contents of this file may be used under the termsof the _____ license (the "[___] License"), in which case theprovisions of [_____] License are applicable instead of those above.If you wish to allow use of your version of this file only under the terms of the [_____] License and not to allow others to use yourversion of this file under the SPL, indicate your decision by deletingthe provisions above and replace them with the notice and otherprovisions required by the [___] License. If you do not delete theprovisions above, a recipient may use your version of this file undereither the SPL or the [___] License."

[NOTE: The text of this Exhibit A may differ slightly from the text ofthe notices in the Source Code files of the Original Code. You shoulduse the text of this Exhibit A rather than the text found in theOriginal Code Source Code for Your Modifications.]

The DEITEL® Suite of Products...

HOW TO PROGRAM BOOKS

C++ How to Program Fourth Edition

BOOK / CD-ROM

©2003, 1400 pp., paper
(0-13-038474-7)

Designed for beginning through intermediate courses, this comprehensive, practical introduction to C++ includes hundreds of hands-on exercises, and uses 267 *LIVE-CODE* programs to demonstrate C++'s powerful capabilities. This edition includes a new chapter—Web Programming with CGI—that provides everything readers need to begin developing their own Web-based applications that will run on the Internet! The book provides a carefully designed sequence of examples that introduces inheritance and polymorphism and helps students understand the motivation and implementation of these key object-oriented programming concepts. In addition, the OOD/UML case study has been upgraded to UML 1.4 and all flowcharts and inheritance diagrams in the text have been converted to UML diagrams. The book presents an early introduction to strings and arrays as objects using standard C++ classes **string** and **vector**. The book also covers key concepts and techniques standard C++ developers need to master, including control statements, functions, arrays, pointers and strings, classes and data abstraction, operator overloading, inheritance, virtual functions, polymorphism, I/O, templates, exception handling, file processing, data structures and more.

📖 **Also available:** *C++ in the Lab, Fourth Edition,* a lab manual designed to accompany this book. Use ISBN 0-13-038478-X to order. A Student Solutions Manual is available for use with this text. Use ISBN 0-13-142578-1 to order.

Java™ How to Program Sixth Edition

BOOK / CD-ROM

©2005, 1500 pp., paper
(0-13-148398-6)

The complete authoritative DEITEL® *LIVE-CODE* introduction to programming with the new Java™ 2 Platform Standard Edition 5.0! New early classes and early objects approach. *Java How to Program, Sixth Edition* is up-to-date with J2SE™ 5.0 and includes comprehensive coverage of the fundamentals of object-oriented programming in Java; a new interior design including new colors, new fonts, new design elements and more; and a new optional automated teller machine (ATM) case study that teaches the fundamentals of software engineering and object oriented design with the UML in Chapters 1-8 and 10. Additional integrated case studies appear throughout the text, including GUI and graphics (Chapters 3-12), the **Time** class (Chapter 8), the **Employee** class (Chapters 9 and 10) and the **GradeBook** class in Chapters 3-8. New J2SE 5.0 topics covered included input/output, enhanced **for** loop, autoboxing, generics, new collections APIs and more.

📖 **Also available:** *Java in the Lab, Sixth Edition,* a lab manual designed to accompany this book. Use ISBN 0-13-149497-X. A Student Solutions Manual is available for this text. Use ISBN 0-13-149500-3 to order.

Small Java™ How to Program, Sixth Edition

BOOK / CD-ROM

©2005, 700 pp., paper
(0-13-148660-8)

Based on chapters 1-10 of *Java™ How to Program, Sixth Edition, Small Java* is up-to-date with J2SE™ 5.0, features a new early classes and early objects approach and comprehensive coverage of the fundamentals of object-oriented programming in Java. Key topics include applications, variables, data types, control statements, methods, arrays, object-based programming, inheritance and polymorphism.

📖 **Also available:** A *Student Solutions Manual* for use with this book. Use ISBN 0-13-148661-6 to order.

Sign up now for the FREE *DEITEL® Buzz Online* newsletter at:
w w w . d e i t e l . c o m / n e w s l e t t e r / s u b s c r i b e . h t m l

C How to Program
Fourth Edition

BOOK / CD-ROM

©2004, 1255 pp., paper
(0-13-142644-3)

C How to Program, Fourth Edition—the world's best-selling C text—is designed for introductory through intermediate courses as well as programming languages survey courses. This comprehensive text is aimed at readers with little or no programming experience through intermediate audiences. Highly practical in approach, it introduces fundamental notions of structured programming and software engineering and gets up to speed quickly.

📖 **A Student Solutions Manual is also available is for use with this text. Use ISBN 0-13-145245-2 to order.**

Getting Started with Microsoft® Visual C++™ 6 with an Introduction to MFC

BOOK / CD-ROM

©2000, 163 pp., paper
(0-13-016147-0)

Visual C++ .NET®
How To Program

BOOK / CD-ROM

©2004, 1400 pp., paper
(0-13-437377-4)

Written by the authors of the world's best-selling introductory/intermediate C and C++ textbooks, this comprehensive book thoroughly examines Visual C++® .NET. *Visual C++® .NET How to Program* begins with a strong foundation in the introductory and intermediate programming principles students will need in industry, including fundamental topics such as arrays, functions and control statements. Readers learn the concepts of object-oriented programming. The text then explores such essential topics as networking, databases, XML and multimedia. Graphical user interfaces are also extensively covered, giving students the tools to build compelling and fully interactive programs using the "drag-and-drop" techniques provided by Visual Studio .NET 2003.

Advanced Java™ 2 Platform How to Program

BOOK / CD-ROM

©2002, 1811 pp., paper
(0-13-089560-1)

Expanding on the world's best-selling Java textbook—*Java™ How to Program*—*Advanced Java™ 2 Platform How To Program* presents advanced Java topics for developing sophisticated, user-friendly GUIs; significant, scalable enterprise applications; wireless applications and distributed systems. Primarily based on Java 2 Enterprise Edition (J2EE), this textbook integrates technologies such as XML, JavaBeans, security, JDBC™, JavaServer Pages (JSP™), servlets, Remote Method Invocation (RMI), Enterprise JavaBeans™ (EJB), design patterns, Swing, J2ME™, Java 2D and 3D, XML, design patterns, CORBA, Jini™, JavaSpaces™, Jiro™, Java Management Extensions (JMX) and Peer-to-Peer networking with an introduction to JXTA.

C# How to Program

BOOK / CD-ROM

©2002, 1568 pp., paper
(0-13-062221-4)

C# How to Program provides a comprehensive introduction to Microsoft's C# object-oriented language. C# enables students to create powerful Web applications and components—ranging from XML-based Web services on Microsoft's .NET platform to middle-tier business objects and system-level applications. *C# How to Program* begins with a strong foundation in the introductory- and intermediate-programming principles students will need in industry. It then explores such essential topics as object-oriented programming and exception handling. Graphical user interfaces are extensively covered, giving readers the tools to build compelling and fully interactive programs. Internet technologies such as XML, ADO .NET and Web services are covered as well as topics including regular expressions, multithreading, networking, databases, files and data structures.

Visual Basic® .NET How to Program Second Edition

BOOK / CD-ROM

©2002, 1400 pp., paper
(0-13-029363-6)

Learn Visual Basic .NET programming from the ground up! This book provides a comprehensive introduction to Visual Basic .NET—featuring extensive updates and increased functionality. *Visual Basic .NET How to Program, Second Edition* covers introductory programming techniques as well as more advanced topics, featuring enhanced treatment of developing Web-based applications. Other topics discussed include XML and wireless applications, databases, SQL and ADO .NET, Web forms, Web services and ASP .NET.

Internet & World Wide Web How to Program Third Edition

BOOK / CD-ROM

©2004, 1250 pp., paper
(0-13-145091-3)

This book introduces students with little or no programming experience to the exciting world of Web-based applications. This text provides in-depth coverage of introductory programming principles, various markup languages (XHTML, Dynamic HTML and XML), several scripting languages (JavaScript, JScript .NET, ColdFusion, Flash ActionScript, Perl, PHP, VBScript and Python), Web servers (IIS and Apache) and relational databases (MySQL)—all the skills and tools needed to create dynamic Web-based applications. The text contains a comprehensive introduction to ASP .NET and the Microsoft .NET Framework. A case study illustrating how to build an online message board using ASP .NET and XML is also included. New in this edition are chapters on Macromedia ColdFusion, Macromedia Dreamweaver and a much enhanced treatment of Flash, including a case study on building a video game in Flash. After mastering the material in this book, students will be well prepared to build real-world, industrial-strength, Web-based applications.

Wireless Internet & Mobile Business How to Program

©2002, 1292 pp., paper
(0-13-062226-5)

This book offers a thorough treatment of both the management and technical aspects of this growing area, including coverage of current practices and future trends. The first half explores the business issues surrounding wireless technology and mobile business. The book then turns to programming for the wireless Internet, exploring topics such as WAP (including 2.0), WML, WMLScript, XML, XHTML™, wireless Java programming (J2ME™) and more. Other topics covered include career resources, wireless marketing, accessibility, Palm™, PocketPC, Windows CE, i-mode, Bluetooth, MIDP, MIDlets, ASP, Microsoft .NET Mobile Framework, BREW™, multimedia, Flash™ and VBScript.

Python How to Program

BOOK / CD-ROM

©2002, 1376 pp., paper
(0-13-092361-3)

This exciting textbook provides a comprehensive introduction to Python—a powerful object-oriented programming language with clear syntax and the ability to bring together various technologies quickly and easily. This book covers introductory-programming techniques and more advanced topics such as graphical user interfaces, databases, wireless Internet programming, networking, security, process management, multithreading, XHTML, CSS, PSP and multimedia. Readers will learn principles that are applicable to both systems development and Web programming.

e-Business & e-Commerce for Managers

©2001, 794 pp., cloth
(0-13-032364-0)

This comprehensive overview of building and managing e-businesses explores topics such as the decision to bring a business online, choosing a business model, accepting payments, marketing strategies and security, as well as many other important issues (such as career resources). The book features Web resources and online demonstrations that supplement the text and direct readers to additional materials. The book also includes an appendix that develops a complete Web-based shopping-cart application using HTML, JavaScript, VBScript, Active Server Pages, ADO, SQL, HTTP, XML and XSL. Plus, company-specific sections provide "real-world" examples of the concepts presented in the book.

XML How to Program

BOOK / CD-ROM

©2001, 934 pp., paper (0-13-028417-3)

This book is a comprehensive guide to programming in XML. It teaches how to use XML to create customized tags and includes chapters that address markup languages for science and technology, multimedia, commerce and many other fields. Concise introductions to Java, JavaServer Pages, VBScript, Active Server Pages and Perl/CGI provide readers with the essentials of these programming languages and server-side development technologies to enable them to work effectively with XML. The book also covers topics such as XSL, DOM™, SAX, a real-world e-commerce case study and a complete chapter on Web accessibility that addresses Voice XML. Other topics covered include XHTML, CSS, DTD, schema, parsers, XPath, XLink, namespaces, XBase, XInclude, XPointer, XSLT, XSL Formatting Objects, JavaServer Pages, XForms, topic maps, X3D, MathML, OpenMath, CML, BML, CDF, RDF, SVG, Cocoon, WML, XBRL and BizTalk™ and SOAP™ Web resources.

Perl How to Program

BOOK / CD-ROM

©2001, 1057 pp., paper (0-13-028418-1)

This comprehensive guide to Perl programming emphasizes the use of the Common Gateway Interface (CGI) with Perl to create powerful, dynamic multi-tier Web-based client/server applications. The book begins with a clear and careful introduction to programming concepts at a level suitable for beginners, and proceeds through advanced topics such as references and complex data structures. Key Perl topics such as regular expressions and string manipulation are covered in detail. The authors address important and topical issues such as object-oriented programming, the Perl database interface (DBI), graphics and security. Also included is a treatment of XML, a bonus chapter introducing the Python programming language, supplemental material on career resources and a complete chapter on Web accessibility.

e-Business & e-Commerce How to Program

BOOK / CD-ROM

©2001, 1254 pp., paper (0-13-028419-X)

This book explores programming technologies for developing Web-based e-business and e-commerce solutions, and covers e-business and e-commerce models and business issues. Readers learn a full range of options, from "build-your-own" to turnkey solutions. The book examines scores of the top e-businesses (examples include Amazon, eBay, Priceline, Travelocity, etc.), explaining the technical details of building successful e-business and e-commerce sites and their underlying business premises. Learn how to implement the dominant e-commerce models—shopping carts, auctions, name-your-own-price, comparison shopping and bots/intelligent agents—by using markup languages (HTML, Dynamic HTML and XML), scripting languages (JavaScript, VBScript and Perl), server-side technologies (Active Server Pages and Perl/CGI) and database (SQL and ADO), security and online payment technologies.

Visual Basic® 6 How to Program

BOOK / CD-ROM

©1999, 1015 pp., paper (0-13-456955-5)

The DEITEL® DEVELOPER SERIES!

Deitel & Associates is recognized worldwide for its best-selling *How to Program Series* of books for college and university students and its signature *LIVE-CODE Approach* to teaching programming languages. Now, for the first time, Deitel & Associates brings its proven teaching methods to a series of books specifically designed for professionals.

THREE TYPES
OF BOOKS
FOR THREE
DISTINCT
AUDIENCES

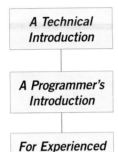

A Technical Introduction books provide programmers, technical managers, project managers and other technical professionals with introductions to broad new technology areas.

A Programmer's Introduction books offer focused treatments of programming fundamentals for practicing programmers. These books are also appropriate for novices.

For Experienced Programmers books are for experienced programmers who want a detailed treatment of a programming language or technology. These books contain condensed introductions to programming language fundamentals and provide extensive intermediate level coverage of high-end topics.

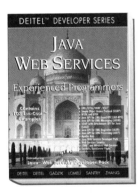

Java™ Web Services for Experienced Programmers

©2003, 700 pp., paper (0-13-046134-2)

Java™ Web Services for Experienced Programmers covers industry standards including XML, SOAP, WSDL and UDDI. Learn how to build and integrate Web services using the Java API for XML RPC, the Java API for XML Messaging, Apache Axis and the Java Web Services Developer Pack. Develop and deploy Web services on several major Web services platforms. Register and discover Web services through public registries and the Java API for XML Registries. Build Web services clients for several platforms, including J2ME. Significant Web services case studies also are included.

Web Services: A Technical Introduction

©2003, 400 pp., paper (0-13-046135-0)

Web Services: A Technical Introduction familiarizes programmers, technical managers and project managers with key Web services concepts, including what Web services are and why they are revolutionary. The book covers the business case for Web services—the underlying technologies, ways in which Web services can provide competitive advantages and opportunities for Web services-related lines of business. Readers learn the latest Web-services standards, including XML, SOAP, WSDL and UDDI; learn about Web services implementations in .NET and Java; benefit from an extensive comparison of Web services products and vendors; and read about Web services security options. Although this is not a programming book, the appendices show .NET and Java code examples to demonstrate the structure of Web services applications and documents. In addition, the book includes numerous case studies describing ways in which organizations are implementing Web services to increase efficiency, simplify business processes, create new revenue streams and interact better with partners and customers.

OneKey IS ALL YOU NEED

Convenience. Simplicity. Success.
Powered by CourseCompass, Blackboard and WebCT.

OneKey is Prentice Hall's exclusive new resource for instructors and students. OneKey gives you access to the best online teaching and learning tools—all available 24 hours a day, 7 days a week. OneKey means all your resources are in one place for maximum convenience, simplicity and success.

Convenience—Prepare more effectively, present more dramatically and assess more easily. All our best online resources have been combined into one easy-to-use site. Also, an abundance of searchable presentation material together with practice activities and test questions—all organized by chapter or topic—make course preparation easy.

Simplicity—With OneKey there is no longer any need for instructors or students to go to multiple Web sites to find the resources they need. All of our best resources can be accessed with one simple login.

Success—Thousands of test questions—in multiple formats—let instructors create and assign tests for automatic grading. More review and assessment tools let students practice, explore on their own or create study programs to fit their own personal learning style. OneKey is all you and your students need to succeed.

Additional features of CourseCompass, Blackboard and WebCT

Intuitive Browser-Based Interface

Your students will love our browser-based interface, designed to be user-friendly and easily accessible.

Our use of full-text searching and hyperlinking makes it easy to navigate.

Further Enhancements to the DEITEL® Signature LIVE-CODE Approach

Coming in Spring 2005! New full-feature OneKey course for Java How to Program, 6/e.

Hours of detailed, expert audio descriptions of thousands of lines of code help reinforce concepts. OneKey includes an innovative learning environment for your introductory programming students called CodeKey. CodeKey allows your students to run and modify the programming projects at the end of each chapter, and provides them with meaningful feedback about the structure and function of their programs. Additionally, you can use CodeKey for submission of programming projects for course credit within the OneKey environment.

Sign up now for the FREE *DEITEL® Buzz Online* newsletter at:
www.deitel.com/newsletter/subscribe.html

Deitel Course Management content available in CD-ROM based Complete Training Courses

An Abundance of Self-Assessment Material

Practice exams offer students hundreds of test questions with immediate feedback in addition to those found in the main text. Hundreds of self-review questions are drawn from the text, all with answers. Hundreds of programming exercises are drawn from the text, half with answers. (The main text does not contain answers to these exercises.)

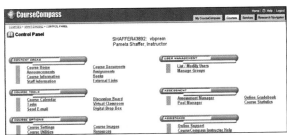

These Course Management Systems offer you:

- **Features to create and customize an online course** such as areas to post course information (e.g., contact information, policies, syllabi, announcements, assignments, grades, performance evaluations and progress tracking), class and student management tools, a gradebook, reporting tools, page tracking, a calendar and assignments.

- **Testing programs** allowing for you to create online quizzes and tests from questions directly linked to the text, and automatically grade and track results.

- **Design tools** and pre-set designs that help you create a custom look and feel for your course.

- **Support materials** that are available in print and online.

Also Available:

CD-ROM based Complete Training Courses

Many *How to Program* texts can be ordered as *Complete Training Course* packages, each containing the main text and the corresponding *Cyber Classroom*—an interactive, multimedia, tutorial version of the book. The *Complete Training Courses* are a great value, giving students additional hands-on experience and study aids for a minimal additional cost.

Each* *Complete Training Course* is compatible with Windows 95, Windows 98, Windows NT, Windows 2000, Windows ME and Windows XP and includes the following features:

- Intuitive browser-based interface designed to be easy and accessible for anyone who's ever used a Web browser.
- Each *Cyber Classroom* contains the full text, illustrations and program listings of its corresponding *How to Program* book.
- Hours of detailed, expert audio descriptions of thousands of lines of code help reinforce concepts.
- An abundance of self-assessment material, including practice exams, hundreds of programming exercises and self-review questions and answers.
- In most *Complete Training Courses*, students can load programs into specific compilers or software (usually on the book's accompanying CD), allowing them to modify and execute the programs with ease.

* The *Complete Visual Basic® 6 Training Course, Student Edition* is not compatible with Windows 2000 or Windows XP. The *Complete C# Training Course, Student Edition, The Complete Visual Basic® .NET Training Course, Student Edition* and *The Complete Python Training Course, Student Edition* are not compatible with Windows 95.

e-LEARNING • from Deitel & Associates, Inc.

Cyber Classrooms, Web-Based Training and Course Management Systems

DEITEL is committed to continuous research and development in e-Learning.

We are enhancing the *Multimedia Cyber Classroom* products to include more audio, pre- and post-assessment questions and Web-based labs with solutions for the benefit of professors and students alike. In addition, our *Multimedia Cyber Classroom* products, currently available in CD-ROM format, are being ported to Pearson's Premium CourseCompass course-management system—*a powerful e-platform for teaching and learning.* Many DEITEL® materials are available in WebCT, Blackboard and CourseCompass formats for colleges, and will soon be available for various corporate learning management systems. For more information on course management systems, please visit us on the Web at www·prenhall·com/cms.

PEARSON CHOICES

For Instructors and Students on DEITEL® Publications!

Today's students have increasing demands on their time and money, and they need to be resourceful about how, when and where they study. Pearson Education has responded to that need by creating PearsonChoices, which allows faculty and students to choose from a variety of formats and prices.

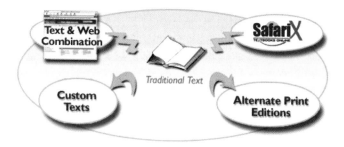

Visit www.pearsonchoices.com for more information!

We are pleased to announce PearsonChoices this fall for our brand new DEITEL publication:

- **Small Java, How to Program, Sixth Edition**—our alternative print edition to *Java How to Program, Sixth Edition* at a competitive price! *Small Java* brings the solid and proven pedagogy of our fully updated *Java How to Program 6/E* to a new, smaller text that is purely focused on CS1 courses and priced lower than our full and comprehensive *Java How to Program* and other competing texts in the CS1 market at just $52.50 net.

DEITEL Course Management content available in CD-ROM based Complete Training Courses

An Abundance of Self-Assessment Material

Practice exams offer students hundreds of test questions with immediate feedback in addition to those found in the main text. Hundreds of self-review questions are drawn from the text, all with answers. Hundreds of programming exercises are drawn from the text, half with answers. (The main text does not contain answers to these exercises.)

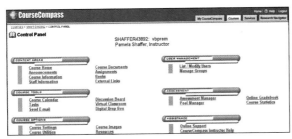

These Course Management Systems offer you:

- **Features to create and customize an online course** such as areas to post course information (e.g., contact information, policies, syllabi, announcements, assignments, grades, performance evaluations and progress tracking), class and student management tools, a gradebook, reporting tools, page tracking, a calendar and assignments.

- **Testing programs** allowing for you to create online quizzes and tests from questions directly linked to the text, and automatically grade and track results.

- **Design tools** and pre-set designs that help you create a custom look and feel for your course.

- **Support materials** that are available in print and online.

Also Available:

CD-ROM based Complete Training Courses

Many *How to Program* texts can be ordered as *Complete Training Course* packages, each containing the main text and the corresponding *Cyber Classroom*—an interactive, multimedia, tutorial version of the book. The *Complete Training Courses* are a great value, giving students additional hands-on experience and study aids for a minimal additional cost.

Each* *Complete Training Course* is compatible with Windows 95, Windows 98, Windows NT, Windows 2000, Windows ME and Windows XP and includes the following features:

- Intuitive browser-based interface designed to be easy and accessible for anyone who's ever used a Web browser.
- Each *Cyber Classroom* contains the full text, illustrations and program listings of its corresponding *How to Program* book.
- Hours of detailed, expert audio descriptions of thousands of lines of code help reinforce concepts.
- An abundance of self-assessment material, including practice exams, hundreds of programming exercises and self-review questions and answers.
- In most *Complete Training Courses*, students can load programs into specific compilers or software (usually on the book's accompanying CD), allowing them to modify and execute the programs with ease.

* The *Complete Visual Basic® 6 Training Course, Student Edition* is not compatible with Windows 2000 or Windows XP. The *Complete C# Training Course, Student Edition*, *The Complete Visual Basic® .NET Training Course, Student Edition* and *The Complete Python Training Course, Student Edition* are not compatible with Windows 95.

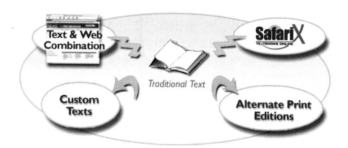

Our official e-mail newsletter, the DEITEL® BUZZ ONLINE, is now sent to over 37,000 opt-in subscribers per month. This free publication is designed to keep you updated on our publishing program, instructor-led corporate training courses, the latest industry topics and trends and more.

Each issue of our newsletter includes:

- Information on current and upcoming products that are of interest to professionals, students and instructors.

- Sample chapters from our current and forthcoming publications.

- Updates on what's happening at Deitel plus updates information on our publishing plans for 2005 and beyond.

- Information on our Dive Into™ Series corporate training courses delivered at organizations worldwide.

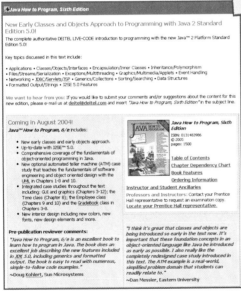

- Crossword puzzle using terms and definitions taken directly from our publications.

- Detailed ordering information for instructors, professors, students and professionals, along with additional book resources and downloads.

- Available in both full-color HTML or plain-text formats depending on client viewing preferences and e-mail capabilities.

Turn the page to find out more about Deitel & Associates!

To sign up for the DEITEL® BUZZ ONLINE newsletter, visit
www.deitel.com/newsletter/subscribe.html.

Deitel & Associates, Inc. provides intensive, lecture-and-laboratory courses to organizations worldwide. The programming courses use our signature *LIVE-CODE Approach*, presenting complete working programs.

Deitel & Associates, Inc. has trained over one million students and professionals worldwide through Dive Into Series™ corporate training courses, public seminars, university teaching, *How to Program Series* textbooks, *DEITEL® Developer Series* books, *Simply Series* textbooks, *Cyber Classroom Series* multimedia packages, *Complete Training Course Series* textbook and multimedia packages, broadcast-satellite courses and Web-based training.

Educational Consulting

Deitel & Associates, Inc. offers complete educational consulting services for corporate training programs and professional schools including:

- Curriculum design and development
- Preparation of Instructor Guides
- Customized courses and course materials
- Design and implementation of professional training certificate programs
- Instructor certification
- Train-the-trainers programs
- Delivery of software-related corporate training programs

Visit our Web site for more information on our Dive Into™ Series corporate training curriculum and to purchase our training products.

www.deitel.com/training

Would you like to review upcoming publications?

If you are a professor or senior industry professional interested in being a reviewer of our forthcoming publications, please contact us by email at **deitel@deitel.com**. Insert "Content Reviewer" in the subject heading.

Are you interested in a career in computer education, publishing and training?

We offer a limited number of full-time positions available for college graduates in computer science, information systems, information technology and management information systems. Please check our Web site for the latest job postings or contact us by email at **deitel@deitel. com**. Insert "Full-time Job" in the subject heading.

Are you a Boston-area college student looking for an internship?

We have a limited number of competitive summer positions and 20-hr./week school-year opportunities for computer science, IT/IS and MIS majors. Students work at our worldwide headquarters west of Boston. We also offer full-time internships for students taking a semester off from school. This is an excellent opportunity for students looking to gain industry experience and earn money to pay for school. Please contact us by email at **deitel@deitel.com**. Insert "Internship" in the subject heading.

Would you like to explore contract training opportunities with us?

Deitel & Associates, Inc. is looking for contract instructors to teach software-related topics at our clients' sites in the United States and worldwide. Applicants should be experienced professional trainers or college professors. For more information, please visit **www.deitel.com** and send your resume to Abbey Deitel at **abbey.deitel@deitel.com**.

Are you a training company in need of quality course materials?

Corporate training companies worldwide use our *How to Program Series* textbooks, *Complete Training Course Series* book and multimedia packages, *Simply Series* textbooks and our *DEITEL® Developer Series* books in their classes. We have extensive ancillary instructor materials for many of our products. For more details, please visit **www.deitel.com** or contact us by email at **deitel@deitel.com**.

License Agreement and Limited Warranty

Using the CD-ROM

The interface to the contents of this CD is designed to start automatically through the **AUTORUN.EXE** file. If a startup screen does not pop up automatically when you insert the CD into your computer, double click on the welcome.htm file to launch the Student CD or refer to the file **readme.txt** on the CD.

Contents of the CD-ROM

- Java™ 2 Platform Development Kit, Standard Edition Version 5.0
- BlueJ Version 1.3.5
- JCreator™ LE Version 3.10 (Windows Only)
- jEdit Version 4.1
- jGRASP Version 1.7.0
- NetBeans™ IDE Version 3.6
- Live code examples from the book *Small Java™ How to Program, 6th Edition*
- Web Resources -- Links to internet sites mentioned in the book *Small Java™ How to Program, 6th Edition*

Software and Hardware System Requirements

- 500 MHz (minimum) Pentium III or faster processor
- Microsoft® Windows® XP (with Service Pack 2), Windows XP Home, Windows 2000 Professional (with Service Pack 4), Windows 98 (1st and 2nd Editions), Windows ME, Windows Server 2003, or
- One of the following Linux distributions: Red Hat 9.0, SuSE 8.2, or TurboLinux 8.0
- 256 MB of RAM (minimum), 512 MB of RAM (recommended)
- CD-ROM drive
- Internet connection
- Web browser, Adobe® Acrobat® Reader® and a Zip decompression utility